M000275809

WRITING

INVITATION

AND

RESPONSE

WRITING

INVITATION

AND

RESPONSE

VINCENT RYAN RUGGIERO
Professor Emeritus *State University of New York at Delhi*

PATRICIA MORGAN
Louisiana State University

Harcourt Brace Jovanovich College Publishers

*Fort Worth   Philadelphia   San Diego   New York   Orlando   Austin   San Antonio
Toronto   Montreal   London   Sydney   Tokyo*

Editor-in-Chief	*Ted Buchholz*
Acquisitions Editor	*Michael Rosenberg*
Developmental Editor	*Cathlynn Richard*
Project Editor	*Nancy Lombardi*
Cover Design	*Nick Welch*
Senior Production Manager	*Ken Dunaway*
Text Design	*Circa 86*

Copyright © 1993 by Holt, Rinehart and Winston, Inc.

All rights reserved. No part of this publication may be reproduced or transmitted in any form or by any means, electronic or mechanical, including photocopy, recording or any information storage and retrieval system, without permission in writing from the publisher.

Requests for permission to make copies of any part of the work should be mailed to:
Permissions Department, Harcourt Brace Jovanovich, Publishers, 8th Floor, Orlando, Florida 32887.

Address for Editorial Correspondence:
Harcourt Brace Jovanovich, Inc., 301 Commerce Street, Suite 3700, Fort Worth, TX 76102.

Address for Orders:
Harcourt Brace Jovanovich, Inc., 6277 Sea Harbor Drive, Orlando, FL 32887
1-800-782-4479, or 1-800-433-0001 (in Florida)

Acknowledgements are on pages 000–000 which constitute a continuation of the copyright page.

Library of Congress Catalog Card Number: 92-70919

ISBN: 0-03-023089-6

Printed in the United States of America

2 3 4 5 6 7 8 9 0 1   039   9 8 7 6 5 4 3 2 1

TO THE STUDENT

Have you ever asked an instructor, "What do I do next?" and been given specific instructions that didn't work? Have you ever been told rather vaguely, "Well, that depends"? If either response has left you frustrated and still wondering what to do, you will appreciate the structure of this book. The answers to your questions will not be specific instructions that force you to work the way someone else expects. Neither will they be so vague that you still don't know what to do next. Instead, you will be given a framework in which to write, a framework that is flexible enough to lead you to your own best working habits, yet orderly enough to give direction to your work.

A basic metaphor of this book is that writing is a response to an invitation. The process of writing is actually a fluid, varied series of activities that is directed by you and your own answers to key questions. Ask yourself, "Do I want to write this down?" If the invitation is a class assignment, the answer, of course, is "yes." But realistically, you know that there are other times when you think of writing—a letter, a journal entry—and decide to answer the invitation with a "no."

When your answer is no, you go no further in the writing process; when it is yes, you gather material and ask yourself another question: "Do I have enough material to draft?" If not, you continue to gather material; if you do, you go on to draft your response. Further questions will help you decide if your draft is complete, organized, and logical; you will also decide if your draft is polished and ready for an audience. In each case, a no answer sends you back for further work—work that *you* have identified as necessary.

This pattern of asking **yourself** key questions about your writing is repeated throughout this text. This pattern teaches you the questions, not the answers. After all, the answers will change as you work. Sometimes the yes answers will come quickly and easily; sometimes, you will have to repeat activities that help you gather, organize, or revise material. Learning to ask the right questions is essential to providing productive answers; learning to answer the questions for yourself will make you independent of your instructor and confident of your own abilities.

Some chapters describe the kinds of invitations you might receive and the kinds of responses that are expected. Other chapters talk specifically about activities that shape your written response, activities that help you to explore a topic, gather material, organize a draft, recognize an audience, and polish your work. Much of the book is designed as a reference work—if you need help collecting material, turn to Chapter 6; if you need help using dialogue, turn to Chapter 13; if you need information about documentation of essay exams or literary analysis, there are specific chapters to answer your questions. In the classroom, your instructor will choose the material for study; outside of the classroom, you should find the catalogue in Part 3 useful for quick reference whenever you must respond in writing.

TO THE INSTRUCTOR

As writing instructors, we often wonder how to reach our students, both the competent writers who need to be challenged and the fearful writers who need to be reassured. They look to us for direction, and we respond by telling them to write. Often we begin by offering analogies to the writing process, comparisons to familiar, harmless processes that our students do not fear.

One of the simplest diagrams of writing is a pattern of invitation and response. Something prompts us; we respond by writing. The world is full of such invitations—to vent our anger, to evaluate a performance, to explain our actions, to express our gratitude. Many times we simply ignore them.

Yet there are other times when the invitation cannot be refused. Perhaps the prompt is so compelling that we must put our thoughts on paper; perhaps the invitation comes from an instructor or a supervisor and cannot be ignored. Voluntary or involuntary, our writing can be described as a response to an invitation.

However, this simple model of invitation and response will not suffice for the writing classroom. We want our students to see the activites that flow from that invitation to the written response, so we search for models of the writing process, a search that often ends in frustration.

Realistically, as writers, we know that "the" writing process is actually a collection of processes as varied as the writers and the contexts in which they write. Balanced against this knowledge are the needs of student writers who ask repeatedly, "How do I start?" "What do I do next?" Their questions urge us to present writing as an orderly process, moving inevitably from step to step toward a finished product, even though we know that a step-by-step model is only a partial reflection of the ways in which we write.

Our presentation of "writing process" is further complicated because, just as surely as we know that writing is *not* a series of neat steps, we also know that it *can* be exactly that. For every image we have of writing as a random collection of inspired, awkward, creative leaps, there is a memory of writing that actually flowed quickly and smoothly toward a finished product.

The challenge, then, is developing a model that allows for tremendous variation, for times when writing moves from prompt to paper with virtually no hesitation, and for others when we struggle with content, organization, and even with audience. In addition, it should be a model to which our students can relate, one that intrigues them as well as informs them.

One such model can be borrowed from a field that is an integral part of the late-twentieth century—computer science. Computer science is actually one of the most logical places to find a model of the writing process. Computers are giant mechanical brains, and computer scientists spend their days teaching these machines to think. A good bit of programming work is a representation of problem-solving, and in the efforts to capture the **thinking** process on paper, we can find a model to help us capture the **writing** process. More than one rhetorician has seen writing as "thinking on paper"; what more logical connection could exist than the one between teaching machines to problem-solve and teaching students to write?

We needn't study computer languages to borrow from the field. Programmers often begin with a **flow chart.** The flow chart illustrates the sequence of activities that lead from problem to solution. Three elements make up the chart: information (or input), operations, and evaluations (see Diagram A). Information is fed into the model. Operations are performed using that information; then an evaluation is performed to decide whether the operations are complete. In the simplest analogy to writing, a writer collects information, performs operations on it (selects, organizes, edits), then evaluates the work to decide if it is complete.

Is such a model a simple, step-by-step representation of the writing process? It can be. For those times when writing flows easily, the chart moves quickly through the operations and the evaluations, showing a straight flow from invitation or prompt to written response (see Diagram B on page viii).

Diagram A

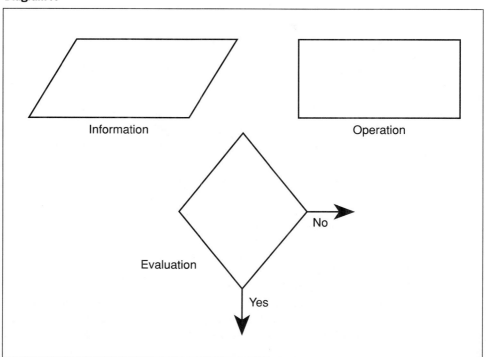

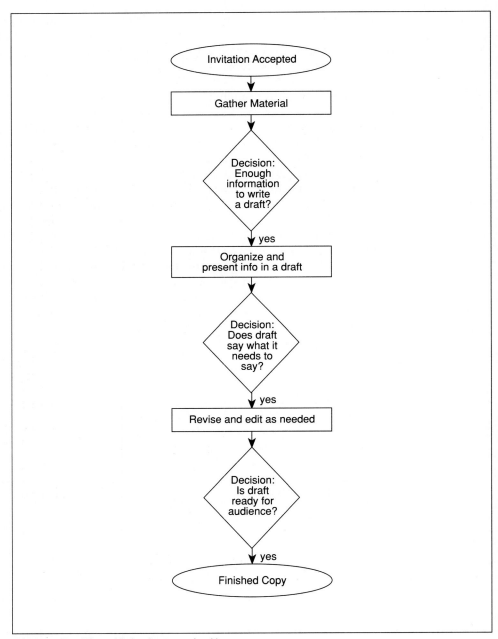

Diagram B   When All the Answers Are Yes

On the other hand, a computer flow chart also allows tremendous variation. For example, the evaluation forces the writer to make a decision: Is my work at this point complete? If the answer is yes, the writer can move quickly to the next phase of the process. However, when the answer is no, the writer is sent back to work on specific areas (see Diagram C).

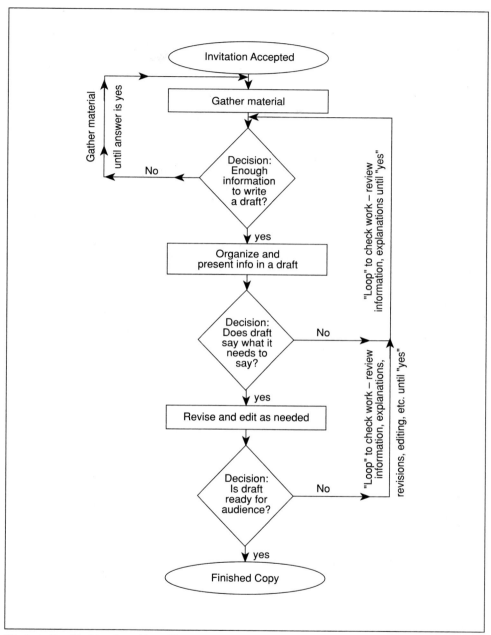

Diagram C   Working from No to Yes

To diagram writing on a computer flow chart, we must first identify the decisions that we expect student writers to make as they work. This text describes the initial decision to write and three decisions made during the process itself. Each decision either sends the writer back to do more work or directs the writer to another area.

To begin this process, the writer first decides to accept the invitation to write and begins to gather material. As the writer works, the next decision to be made is, Do I have enough material to start a draft? A no answer sends the writer back to explore the topic further; a yes sends the writer on to draft. The third decision is, Does my draft say what it needs to say, clearly and completely? A no answer sends the writer back—to find more material if necessary, to look again at organization, at logic, at presentation—a yes sends the writer on to revise and edit. Finally, the writer asks, Is this draft ready for its audience? A no sends the writer back to work; a yes sends the draft on to its readers.

Not only is the flow chart model flexible enough to accurately represent variations in the writing process, it also empowers student writers. Instead of receiving specific directions from an instructor, students are encouraged to ask and answer questions that evaluate their own writing.

These questions can be taught; they recur in any writing context. Specific questions encourage students to review their work in progress continuously, and their own evaluations (directed by the questions) tell them what needs to be done next.

Is such a model too complicated for our students? For the most part, students are intrigued by it. They know something of computers and see the parallels, or they know nothing about computers yet see the logic. Certainly the model is more complicated than neat steps or patterns of circles. Yet writing is both more complex than simple models allow and less complex than elaborate constructs would have us believe. A process modelled on a computer flow chart allows for infinite variation—the kind of variation inevitable in the writing process.

CONTENTS IN BRIEF

Contents

COMPLETE READINGS:

PART ONE

Overview of the Writer at Work

The Writer Thinking

This chapter examines a common misconception about writing, then explains that good writing is a product of both creative and critical thinking. It also identifies the "voices" that guide a writer (the creative voice, the critical voice, and the editorial voice) and it suggests ways to use the three effectively.

THE WRITER AS WORKER

Many struggling writers look at published work and imagine that successful authors are producing page after flawless page with little effort. It seems their art bursts forth effortlessly from their gifted minds.

More than likely, you have shared in that perception. Because you do not see an author's early notes and drafts in progress, the finished book creates the impression that professionals write with ease. Had you been allowed to see writers at work, you would have found that the difficulties you experience with your writing—the struggle to organize fragments of thought, to express your ideas precisely, to write vivid and graceful prose—are all challenges which exist for professional writers as well.

Humorist James Thurber once explained to an interviewer that for him the act of writing was essentially rewriting. "It's part of a constant attempt on my part," he said, "to make the finished version smooth, to make it seem effortless." The hard work of composing is a reality that has largely been obscured. Thus the novice writer too often expects to produce without effort. Brenda Ueland, a long-time teacher of writing and author of *If You Want to Write,* wrote:

> Of course, in fairness, I must remind you of this: that we writers are the most lily-livered of all craftsmen. We expect more, for the most peewee efforts, than any other people.
>
> A gifted young woman writes a poem. It is rejected. She does not write another perhaps for two years, perhaps all her life. Think of the patience and love that a tap-dancer or vaudeville actor puts into his work.
>
> (1938, p. 9)

The notion that good writing stems from effort and practice should be encouraging. Becoming an effective writer primarily requires a willingness to work. If you have that, be confident that you can become a competent writer.

In short, being a writer is something you do, not something you are. By examining the attitudes and actions of skilled writers, you can improve your own work and develop confidence in your abilities.

THE WRITER AS THINKER

Creative thinking encourages you to see new possibilities and new connections while critical thinking guides you to sort and evaluate options. Rarely does one approach exist in isolation; instead, we collect and evaluate and then explore new directions suggested by evaluations.

Written responses are the particular focus of this book, but the kinds of thinking we describe here are not limited to writing. In fact, if you perceive writing as a means of thinking on paper, you will see it as part of life and not merely part of your academic world.

More often than not, writing is a reflection of your thinking. And, as you have doubtless observed, you don't always think the same way or for the same reasons. The chart below illustrates how daily decisions inspire creative plans that are shaped by critical thinking:

Situation: The cafeteria is closed on weekends, so I must make other plans for food. But my budget is limited.

Creative Prompts	Critical Considerations
Where can I eat with little money to spend?	What have I heard about the place? Is the food good? Is the location safe?
What kind of food do I want?	Who told me about it?
What restaurants are near campus?	Do I trust the source?
How can I find extra cash?	What are the advantages of this part-time job?

Skilled writers hear a kind of dialogue between creative suggestions and critical examinations. All of us think creatively and critically, but to improve our thinking (and our writing), we need to understand the two approaches and learn to focus our thinking as the situation demands. In practice, of course, the two approaches are not neatly divided, but for discussion let's look at the nature and function of creative and critical thinking separately.

Creative Thinking

You may believe that certain writers produce creative responses because of what they, the writers, are. But the truth is, every writer can offer a significant, one-of-a-kind reaction to any given subject. What we learn from good writers is that their writing is creative because they work harder to translate their own feelings and experiences into words that we recognize as distinctly theirs. And when we identify the strategies these writers use to encourage creative ideas, we can use them to improve our own writing.

One of the ways to foster creative ideas is to consciously adopt a special kind of thinking—creative thinking. It is open, uninhibited, and daring. And that is the secret to its effectiveness.

Confident writers know how to encourage creative thinking. They listen to their creative inner voices. Exploring the possibilities of a topic, the creative voice says, "Let's try these two ideas together," or "Let's follow this thread for awhile." Creative thinking may seem almost childlike; at its best, it is playful and undaunted by "adult" realities, unfettered by concerns of practicality or precedent.

A scene from a recent television show illustrates playful, productive creative thinking. Two advertising executives are looking for an idea for an ad campaign. They toss ideas back and forth, many of them silly and some deliberately so. One idea suggests another, and a tape recorder keeps track. No idea, even the most ridiculous, is eliminated. Later, the two executives go through the tape and find several workable approaches to their project.

That scene should encourage us to allow the playfulness that can lead to new perceptions and to keep the cold voice of reality from dousing the enthusiastic voice of creativity. The creative voice often speaks to itself without immediate concern for correctness or even clarity. Yet we often find it difficult to turn off our well-schooled concerns about logic or grammar or spelling.

Are we suggesting that all concerns for correctness and clarity be abandoned? We are not. Correctness and clarity are vital to good writing and must be emphasized at the appropriate time. But creative thinking is a distinct attitude that can be confused, even stifled, if we do not let it run free for a while. The material gathered by creative exploration will be developed into finished copy for an audience, but it must first be collected.

We are also not suggesting that you begin to write by pushing one button marked "creative thinking—on" and that you push another marked "creative thinking—off" when you work on final drafts. Realistically, creative and critical thinking work together to produce a dialogue. Whether you hear it or not, the creative voice is always whispering. Even as you check spelling, the voice is suggesting other words and other bits of detail. Many writers insist on typing every draft of their work themselves because changes are constantly coming to mind. What those writers can do (and what you can learn to do) is to *hear* the creative voice. You can learn to listen for it as you begin to gather ideas about a subject, as you look for connections between those ideas, even as you revise and edit your logic and style and spelling. Learning to listen to your creative voice will help you to produce writing that is original and creative.

An idea or a composition is properly called creative if it is unique; in other words, if something about it sets it apart from the common reactions of others. The two student writings that follow illustrate creative approaches.

SAMPLE ONE

In response to an essay describing various pressures of college life, several students described the pressures in their own lives. Most of the papers were predictable discussions of money shortages and grade requirements. One student, though, took a more creative approach to the topic and wrote about the pressures of his own situation:

As a student returning to college after serving in the Army, I find myself faced with pressures that my fellow students just don't understand. They talk about not having enough money to party this weekend while I think about my wife working to support our family while I get a degree. They talk about grades good enough for law school while I think about her face if I play around and don't earn a full semester's worth of credit. They talk about enough time for fraternity activities while I juggle a part-time job, a full load of classes, a marriage, and a four-year-old daughter. My wife and I realize why time and money are so short now, but how does a four-year-old understand that her daddy just doesn't have time to play? Walking to the mailbox can be an adventure when Mandy stops to discover flowers and doodle bugs and caterpillars; how can I explain to her that I have to hurry up to study for a calculus test? How can I explain to myself that our future will make up for that hurt look on her face? And how can I learn to live with this kind of pressure long enough to earn a college degree?

SAMPLE TWO

After reading an essay about death and dying, one student wrote about American attitudes toward death, arguing that dying at home should be a choice supported by the family. She cited experts and statistics on cost, then she added:

> When my great-grandmother was dying, she was put in a hospital so that she could be "comfortable." Now I wonder how comfortable she was. I remember sitting in her green, sterile hospital room with the single flower arrangement in the window, thinking that she loved pink. I remembered the little pink flowers in her wallpaper and the shades of pink in the quilt she had made. I remembered the view from her bedroom window of the apple trees on the hill, and I wondered how we could say she was more comfortable away from all of that.

Neither of these subjects is original or startling, yet the papers are perceptive, moving, **creative** responses to assignments. What these two excerpts show is a willingness to explore personal feelings and experiences in writing. These two students used incidents from their own lives to write creative papers in their own unique voices.

> Everybody is original, if he tells the truth, if he speaks from himself. But it must be from his *true* self and not from the self he thinks he *should* be. . . . self-trust is one of the very most important things in writing.
>
> (Brenda Ueland)

Trusting yourself and your voice means more than writing revealing personal narratives. It also means trusting your reactions and perceptions as you examine issues, and refusing to accept ideas simply because other people believe in them strongly. Trusting yourself frees you to explore subjects creatively, to transcend the boundaries defined by what has already been said and written. Such creativity in thinking will inevitably be reflected in your writing.

Remember, creativity can be developed. Anyone who wants to can learn the techniques and strategies that encourage creative responses, the same techniques and strategies that guide other effective writers. These techniques and strategies will be detailed in the chapters that follow. But you can anticipate them by applying the following guidelines in your early composition efforts:

1. **Press yourself to go deeper than the first layer of thought about your topics.** Early ideas tend to be common ideas. They are the ideas that everyone else will probably think of, too. By making yourself produce fifty or a hundred ideas, you increase your chances of producing some original ones and of seeing new connections. Look again at the excerpt on pressures. The writer thought of money and grades as pressure points, but he went beyond his first impulse to find something of his own to write about.

2. **Focus on specifics.** General statements are seldom very creative. If you are recounting a personal experience, include concrete details. If you are informing your readers about an interesting or famous person, place, or thing, show your readers what you see. The excerpt above about the writer's great-grandmother gains much of its power from the specific contrast between the sterile hospital and the bedroom at home. The writer allowed us to share her visions; she did not leave us to guess what she meant.

3. **Trust yourself and your own voice.** Do not discard ideas that are not reinforced by other voices. You are not bound to follow only where others have gone. The student who used her great-grandmother's experience to support a call for new attitudes toward death and dying did not hesitate because her audience had not had the same experience; you too should trust that your experiences are a valid form of evidence.

Y O U R   T U R N

Papers about people often turn into routine descriptions that almost anyone who knows those persons could write. Try the suggestions above to see if you can find a unique approach to a paper about you and your parents:

Make a long list:
What is your first response to the assignment, "Write about the differences between you and one of your parents"? Make a quick list of the most obvious differences. Now ask yourself, "What on this list is known by other people?" Try to find the things that only you—from your unique perspective—could say about the subject. Make the list longer—think of areas like taste in friends or definitions of fun activities. Think about serious things like religious philosophies and attitudes toward social problems.

Keep the list open so that you can add to it as you think of more areas. Circle back over the list and check off things that feel promising. Write down every idea—don't omit anything, regardless of how trivial or silly you might think it to be.

Think in specifics:

As you look at an item on your list, think of a way to show the point to someone else—can you remember something that happened when you or the parent showed a definite opinion? Can you show us one or both of you in action—saying something, doing something, or arguing with each other?

Trust yourself:

If you think that an incident reveals selfishness or hostility, don't hesitate to say so. You may see a person from a different angle— and that insight can become the significant focus of your paper.

If you think of more items for the list, keep adding. Later, you can make some decisions about the best points for a paper.

Save your notes. In fact, if you set aside an envelope or a folder for the short notes and exercises you do in class, you will have a good source for paper topics when the teacher doesn't give you a specific assignment.

Critical Thinking

Creative thinking can lead to unusual insights and ingenious solutions, but you should not regard it as infallible. Much of what it produces is at the very least flawed and at the very worst, worthless. This may surprise you, but it should not discourage you. The writer who expects every idea to be valuable is as foolish and as frustrated as the coach who expects the team to score on every play.

If you want your writing to be reasonable, you cannot merely assume that your ideas are sound. You must prove to yourself that they are. That means examining and evaluating all the ideas you have produced, being alert to every shallow, narrow-minded, or illogical interpretation or conclusion. To do this you must employ another kind of thinking: **critical thinking.**

Critical thinking is an active mental process in which you scrutinize your ideas (or other people's ideas), probe their stated and implied meaning, and decide whether that meaning is defensible. Such thinking depends on three characteristics:

1. A questioning attitude toward all interpretations and conclusions
2. Skill in separating fact from opinion and taste from judgment
3. Sensitivity to the connections between ideas

To sharpen your own critical thinking, apply these characteristics to the following observations:

1. In the first game of the season, our starting quarterback did not score a single touchdown. He is obviously not as good a quarterback as he was last year.
2. I heard that one of my teachers was charged with drunken driving. I knew she wasn't much of a teacher.
3. *Aliens* is just another science fiction extravaganza. It won't be worth any more than any of those silly movies about space creatures.

Analysis:

Note that critical thinking requires a questioning attitude. None of the three statements should be accepted at face value; each demands further examination, further clarification, further proof. For example, if the quarterback performed well throughout last year, surely one bad game, particularly the first game, doesn't prove that his career is over. Also, must a quarterback score touchdowns himself to have a good game? Perhaps he did other things well. Consider the second comment. Was the source reliable? Was the charge substantiated? Is the situation related to teaching ability? And the condemnation of *Aliens* is equally unconvincing. Can you fairly dismiss a movie because you don't like others of its type?

Incidentally, when you have examined the statements above and explore the situations, you may find that the remarks were justified. The quarterback might be ineffective, the teacher incompetent, and the movie worthless, but your judgment should be reserved until additional information is obtained and analysis is complete.

As you can see, critical thinking is an essential part of good writing—and good thinking. With a critical mindset, you examine ideas and ask questions about content. As a critical thinker, you discard, group, sort, and classify ideas. Critical thinking also tests logic and practicality. It is the voice that says "Yes, but. . . ," the voice that wants to know how something works and how it fits together, the voice that asks, "Is this information relevant?" "Are these observations important?" "Are these conclusions logical?" And it is the cold voice of reality that says, "Clever and cute are not sufficient."

The critical voice does three important things for a writer:

1. It evaluates the ideas generated and collected during the writer's exploration of a topic. It questions logic and relevance and accuracy; it tests ideas and discards the commonplace, the absurd and the

invalid. The critical voice separates facts from opinions and tastes from judgments.

2. It selects and organizes ideas. The critical voice recognizes connections between ideas and identifies logical patterns of contrast or chronology or cause. It reveals the frameworks beneath masses of ideas, and thus guides the writer's selection of form and strategy.

3. It can assume the role of a designated audience and point out repetitions or superfluous explanation; as an audience, it can also ask for more definitions or clearer descriptions. Thus critical examination can become the impetus for the revision of current ideas and the generation of more ideas.

Y O U R   T U R N

1. Assigned to write a letter of complaint, a student submitted the following:

Dear University Traffic Board,
    The prohibition against left turns by northbound vehicles at the intersection of Highland Road and Stadium Drive is an unnecessary nuisance. Left turns are permitted at every other intersection at Highland Road, so the traffic flow at that intersection cannot be any different. The road is wide enough to create a turning lane, so no expensive construction will be necessary. I got a ticket for turning left there last week, and the delay caused me to miss an important exam. Students have enough problems with traffic delays on this campus, and allowing left turns will give us an easier route to class. In addition, university police will not have to monitor that intersection anymore. For all of these reasons, I ask you to change the traffic regulations at this intersection.

Sincerely,
Stephen Tuttle

Evaluate Tuttle's claims. Are the connections between his statements logical? Sufficient? Do you accept his proposal? Why or why not?

2. Bring in several letters to the editor from your local paper or from the campus newspaper. Examine the claims the writers are making. Separate fact from opinion and look for support. [Facts may be unappealing but can be verified; in contrast, conflicting opinions can be held by reasonable people. Thus facts need less substanti-

ation than opinions which must be well supported.] Test the logical connections between the statements. Remember that you are not trying to destroy the claims, only to test their logic and clarity. Try to find both weak and strong letters.

Two Voices: Monologues or Dialogue?

Talking about creative thinking and critical thinking in two separate sections may give the impression that you work with only half of your mind at a time. That impression can be misleading. Your brain is capable of many levels and kinds of activities at one time, so it is likely that you will often think both creatively and critically simultaneously. If you are aware that there are two voices, and if you listen carefully for each voice, you can begin to use the input from each more effectively, both in your daily decision making and in your writing.

Understanding the different mental approaches to writing is easier if you put writing activities into a framework. One way to think of writing is to see it as a response to an invitation. Something invites or encourages you to write, and you respond to the invitation—or perhaps you do not. In an essay class, it might be an assignment that requires a response. But there are many other situations that invite written response. Sometimes you will write directly to an audience—a report for a committee or a letter to a friend. At other times, you write for yourself—journal entries or short notes. You may be writing in response to a direct request (like that class assignment), or you may feel a need to work some ideas or feelings out on paper. Whatever the occasion, the pattern of invitation (or stimulus) and response is easily identified.

The invitation to write prompts the creative voice to explore a topic. The uninhibited, unquestioned exploration will produce the raw materials of your project.

When you have a body of material to examine, you then apply the precepts of critical thinking. Your critical evaluation of the writing may encourage the creative voice to make more suggestions. The resulting dialogue may sound something like this:

Creative Voice: A main cause of stress in my academic life is lack of money.

Critical Voice: I like that observation. Are there other causes of stress?

Creative Voice: Well, fear of parental disapproval—or disappointment. And I'm often afraid in class that I'll say the wrong thing and embarrass myself.

Creative Voice: I think many divorces are caused by feminist ideas.

Critical Voice: Can you prove that connection?

Creative Voice: Well, many men expect wives to play traditional roles. If new roles are developed without the husbands' consent, the men might feel threatened, even betrayed. Some men cannot adapt to change. In addition, women who have played traditional roles become aware of other options; they may feel frustrated, even caged. The tensions that result can certainly lead to strain in relationships, perhaps even to divorce.

It would be too simple to say that the critical voice asks questions and the creative voice answers them. Both voices ask (and answer) questions. However, different strategies are involved. The creative voice is interested in *producing* ideas; the critical voices in *evaluating* ideas.

In short, the two voices in your head often engage in a productive dialogue. At every point in the writing process, from the earliest responses that begin to gather material to the final polishing of the manuscript, you can hear this dialogue at work. The creative voice will continue to whisper, "Why not try this?" and "Can we look at it this way?" while the critical voice will continue to ask, "How will it work?" and "Is this the best choice?"

The Editorial Voice

As the material takes shape, your primary focus shifts from ideas and content to text and a third voice enters the conversation. This voice is the **editorial voice,** in some ways the strongest of the three. *The editorial voice is concerned with correctness and clarity: it is the proofreader that checks spelling and grammar and punctuation; it is the checker that "listens" to sentences to detect structures that may be incorrect as well as graceless.* This voice is often the strongest because it is the one most often exercised in the classroom. It has been inspired by the conventions of grammar and mechanics you have studied since first grade.

Because it is so well-trained, the editorial voice often intimidates the other two; it drowns them out, stifling creativity and suspending critical evaluation of content. When you check the spelling of a word, you are no longer questioning its appropriateness; when you correct the grammatical structure of a sentence, you are unlikely to see its content as superfluous or irrelevant. The editorial voice is also very possessive—once you have responded to its prompting, you will find it very difficult to eliminate the sentence or the passage you have just "fixed."

Don't think that the concerns of the editorial voice are petty concerns that should be ignored in favor of "larger" matters like ideas. Writing is the all-important vehicle that conveys those ideas to the audience, and the editorial input serves two very important needs:

1. First, imprecise sentences often send imprecise messages. One writer devoted five hundred words to a defense of pit bulls, insisting that the dogs are not naturally "viscous" [having a sticky, fluid consistency] but can be made so. The readers inevitably wondered how—and why—owners would create viscous dogs. Even seemingly minor errors can distract the reader who speculates on possible shades of meaning or on hilarious pictures you've unintentionally painted.

2. Second, sending unfinished work to an audience—any audience—is a clear message that the project and the audience are not worth your time and effort. The writer who submitted a critique of the politics of Ronald Raegun [sic] and George Busch [sic] didn't know or care enough about the subject to spell the names correctly. Why should an audience give such work any consideration at all?

The editorial voice, then, is a necessary part of the process. It will ensure that you neither confuse nor insult your audience. Remember, too, that it is an extremely powerful voice whose input must be heeded—at the appropriate time. After you are satisfied that the ideas are developed, the explanations complete, the examples relevant and sufficient, then you can call on the editorial red pen to check over your manuscript. (Even in proofreading final drafts, though, be alert for whispers of dialogue that suggest new approaches or demand further explorations.)

YOUR TURN

Read the following passage carefully, noting the ambiguity and confusion allowed by a careless editor. Strengthen the problem areas, using your own best guess about the writer's meaning.

Sometimes we all have problems. Things we can't face without help. I just had a situation like that. Things were bad, my parents were fighting, I couldn't talk to anyone. Then it happened. My friend was really they're for me. He showed me that I could count on him when no one else was a round. We shared alot, feelings and thoughts and emotions and I don't think I will ever forget what he did for me. I wont to be their for my friends like he was for me. Than I know I will be a true friend.

Listening to the Voices

Eudora Welty, a Pulitzer Prize-winning fiction writer, begins her description of One Writer's Beginnings with a section called "Listening." She writes,

Ever since I was first read to, then started reading to myself, there has never been a line read that I didn't hear. As my eyes followed the sentence, a voice was saying it silently to me. . . . I have supposed, but never found out, that this is the case with all readers—to read as listeners—and with all writers, to write as listeners. . . . The sound of what falls on the page begins the process of testing it for truth, for me.

My own words, when I am at work on a story, I hear too as they go, in the same voice that I hear when I read in books. When I write and the sound of it comes back to my ears, then I act to make my changes. I have always trusted this voice.

As you write, you will hear, as Welty describes, distinct voices. You will hear the creative voice that helps to generate and explore a body of raw material, and you will hear the critical voice that helps to evaluate and organize your ideas. The editing voice will emerge as you produce written copy, a voice that helps polish your writing until it is clear and correct. If you are listening, you will hear all these voices when you write.

Since all three voices offer important advice to a writer, you should educate the voices and encourage them. Remembering that only rarely do they work together at full power (those too-infrequent times when writing is almost effortless and endlessly productive), you must also learn to control the voices, to call on each at appropriate times and to silence the competing voices until you are ready to hear them.

Personifying the voices can help you to understand and control them. Give the voices bodies, give them faces. Give each voice a tone, a distinct sound—the creative voice might be a child's voice, the critical voice might be the voice of your too-practical best friend, the editing voice of your perfectionist grandmother. If you can give the voices form and substance, you will be better able to call on each and control the unruly ones. Practice with each kind of thinking, hearing the voice you have assigned, until you know the tones and can identify the speaker.

If you have trouble turning off the editor (which seems to be the most persistent and domineering of the three), assign the sound of its voice a place, but an insignificant one. For example, make the voice a distant sound on a distant radio station, or make it the voice of a person in another room down a hall. When you visualize such distinct settings, you can control the participants—turn down the radio or close the door in your scene. With some practice, you can relegate the most insistent voice to a controlled space and call it back up when you are ready to hear .its comments.

Prewriting activities (discussed in some detail in Part Three) are often designed to help you control the input from the voices. Structured activities may have "gimmicks" that focus the attention of the inhibiting voices on some external (a clock or a cube, for example) while the creative voice is urged to produce quantities of material. Picture the creative voice as a child who has managed to slip away from controls and constraints to run free. When you accept that it is good and necessary to turn off the controls for a time, you will find your own most effective ways to free the creative voice within.

YOUR TURN

1. Given an assignment to write about a dramatic incident that had affected the writer's attitude about himself or his activities, one student produced the following first-effort pre-writing:

   There was a terrible accident near my house last weekend. Four teenagers were killed. The pickup truck they were riding in overturned and the four of them were flipped out of the truck bed. They landed on the side of the road near a neighborhood park where a kids' softball game was in progress and two died instantly. Two doctors in the game crowd kept the other two breathing, but they died at the hospital later that night. The road was wet and the driver was racing a friend in another truck. He ran off the road and hit something. The truck flipped. The driver was not hurt. He is now in jail. All of the teenagers had been drinking. The kids in my neighborhood went to the accident site. They are still talking about the bodies. One little girl is having nightmares. She says she can see a bloody hand lying on her pillow.

   As a piece of pre-writing, this passage is filled with possibilities. As a base, the writer has a dramatic incident and its effect on the children who saw it. But which story does the writer really want to tell? There are some vivid details (and certainly there are other dramatic details which could be added), but the writer has not yet decided what to write about. Looking at the passage, though, it is easy to see possible directions. More thinking and writing about each will be necessary before the writer begins a draft.

   Try your own hand at developing this topic. Decide which story you want to tell, and explore the possibilities of that one. You will need to draw on your own experiences to fill in the many gaps, so feel free to add further details or comments—was the accident unavoidable? Should the driver be in jail? OR: should the neighborhood children have been allowed to see the wreck? Were they really perverse because they wanted to? In other words, take the report of an incident and write about it from your own perspective. Bring to your work what only you can bring—have you had a similar experience? Do you have strong feelings about the deaths or the charges or the children's behavior?

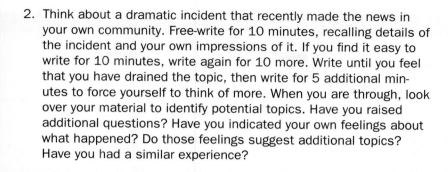

2. Think about a dramatic incident that recently made the news in your own community. Free-write for 10 minutes, recalling details of the incident and your own impressions of it. If you find it easy to write for 10 minutes, write again for 10 more. Write until you feel that you have drained the topic, then write for 5 additional minutes to force yourself to think of more. When you are through, look over your material to identify potential topics. Have you raised additional questions? Have you indicated your own feelings about what happened? Do those feelings suggest additional topics? Have you had a similar experience?

SUMMARY

Becoming a confident and effective writer calls for an examination of your own thinking, both what you think about writing and how you think when you write. Recognize the work that goes into all writing, especially into the polished writing you usually read in books and magazines. Become familiar with the kinds of thinking that you do, and see the role each "voice" plays in your considerations of ideas. Ultimately, your ability to recognize, to understand, and to control the creative, critical and editorial voices will improve your writing and your thinking.

CHAPTER TWO

The Writer Writing

This chapter examines the nature of composition and the composition process. The description shows a multi-leveled process, with the first level exploring ideas and the last polishing written text. The writer does not work in neat, self-contained steps but follows a recursive motion that works fluidly among the levels.

THINKING AND WRITING

As a writer (and as a thinking resident of earth), you adapt your thinking to the particular needs of a situation. Sometimes you think creatively, imagining possible responses and speculating outcomes. Sometimes you think critically, weighing and questioning your ideas and the ideas of others. You think creatively as you write, exploring a subject and looking for fresh ideas, and you think critically as you test your material for logic and clarity and as you examine it for errors in spelling and mechanics.

This chapter will show you writing as a process, from first invitation to completed response. The levels described here will be discussed in greater detail in later chapters, but this overview will give you a sense of direction—a sense of how the different activities of writing produce a composition.

COMPOSITION: A RESPONSE

Many writers think of composition only as a finished product with a title, introduction, body, and conclusion. But the very word "composition" implies much more. Consider the root "compose" which means to select, shape, and arrange. Composers take raw material and work it as sculptors do stone or potters clay, turning random thoughts into focused thoughts, rough sentences into polished sentences, disorganized paragraphs into organized paragraphs. Remember, too, that composing requires both construction and discovery. Your creative voice continues to supply raw materials even as your critical voice evaluates your work. The continuing dialogue between your creative and critical voices will help you to explore ideas and to recognize subtle connections. Often, you will fully understand your material only after you have written about it.

A composition is a written response to an invitation or stimulus. In the academic world, that invitation is usually an assignment of some kind. But as you learn and practice writing skills, remember that every area of your life contains invitations to write. Situations that move you to write loving tributes, angry letters, thoughtful evaluations, or cautious advice are all invitations.

Responses to an invitation to write may include awareness of a relationship between you, your audience, and your ideas. This awareness can influence your writing from the very beginning.

> Ask yourself:
> Who will read this work?
> What do I hope to accomplish?
>
> Then decide:
> How will I approach the topic?
> What ideas will I include in the composition?
> Which will be the controlling idea (thesis)?
> What form will the composition take?
> What does my audience know already?
> How much more information will my audience need?

THE NATURE OF THE WRITING PROCESS

The process of writing may give the impression that writing is one neat series of steps. In reality, process should emphasize that writing is something that you do, not something that you produce. The activities that produce a written response are varied, allowing you and every other writer to develop individual working styles. As you develop your own style, you can study what other writers do and you can recognize that writers seek to accomplish similar objectives: to understand material and to communicate ideas to an audience.

This book describes levels of activities, characterized by attitudes and activities and goals. On the first level, the writer explores the topic and gathers information; on the second, the writer develops connections between ideas and audience and puts together a working draft; on the third, the writer reviews and polishes the draft.

Sometimes writing progresses smoothly from first thought to finished product. More often, though, the motion of writing resembles bobbing up and down between the three levels. Imagine a scuba diver exploring a stretch of unfamiliar water. She first swims near the surface, looking forward, down, and around as she tries to get a sense of where she is and what the territory is like. In a similar manner, your creative approach to a topic often begins with a sweeping scan of the territory as you look around for ideas and angles. Picture the scuba diver as she sees something intriguing. She dives to another level, checking out the possibilities and gathering potentially valuable material. You might make a similar "descent" to another level as you think of specific words or phrases that might be used in a final draft, or as your critical voice notes connections between your ideas. Then, like the diver, you might return to that earlier level where you continue to survey the broad topic before you, looking for some entry into a specific area to explore. You are like that diver as you think about the topic, creatively exploring and critically evaluating, free to move back and forth between levels of activity.

As you can see, a step-by-step guide to writing might seem reassuring to you, but it is not realistic. In fact, it is quite likely that your "writing process" will change each time you respond to an invitation to write.

Y O U R T U R N

As you read the description of writing that follows, explore a general subject area to see if your personal approach to writing matches the pattern here. Your teacher may assign a subject here, or you can select one. Since you are a student, the academic environment offers you limitless opportunities for observation and experience. Just for practice, decide on an area like "Dorm Life" or "Challenges Facing Non-Typical Students" or "The Confusion of Registration." Remember that you are like the scuba diver facing a vast body of interesting but undefined material. Your topic will take shape or even change directions as you begin to explore the available material. So, recognizing that your first topic is likely to need more definition as you proceed, write it down and refer to it as you read through the sections below.

❏ The First Decision: To Accept the Invitation to Write

In class, the "invitation" to write usually comes from the teacher in the form of an assignment, but life is full of such invitations. You are moved by a performance and want to explain why it has reached you; you are angered by an unjust situation and want others to share your indignation; you are aware of a problem and have thought of a solution that should be known. You accept the invitation when you decide to communicate your ideas to an audience in writing.

Exploring Your Ideas

As you prepare to write, you gather a body of knowledge. You examine your knowledge and your feelings about the topic; you may do some research about the subject; you may try some pre-writing or exploratory exercises (covered in more detail in Part Three). Your goal is to see as many possibilities and approaches as you can, making no demands of logic or appropriateness on your ideas. Think of the scuba diver moving easily through the first level, with no commitments to a specific direction.

You might probe your subject at random when you first begin, but as you begin to see your own feelings and observations, you will begin to think of an audience for your ideas and the probing becomes more directed. When you are ready to put ideas together in a draft, you will be ready to look for connections.

| **The Writer at Work** | Assigned to write a personal narrative about the first day of school, Anna Daniels soon realized that the topic was bigger than it first appeared—as a 30-year-old mother of two, she had experienced a number of opening days, both her own and her children's. Her quick list of vivid memories looked like this: |

The silly orange knapsack Barry loved
Barry disappeared after school
Shopping for school supplies
Margaret's bus did not stop in our neighborhood
I got lost on campus
First day of work—agony at the pre-school
Trying to dress for the occasion
Parking problems

Anna found that one memory triggered another, and that her creative voice continued to supply ideas even when she was not actively writing. From trying to find something to write, Anna's problem quickly changed to selecting from a long list of possibilities. She also recognized that some of her thoughts were vivid specific details, and she began to group the items on her list and to underline details she could use later.

As she worked, Anna realized that the most vivid moments on her list involved her children's experiences. She thought that most of her classmates would write about their own experiences, but she decided to write about memories that still made her feel panic and relief, her children's misadventures on the bus. She also decided to address her sister, whose oldest child was about to start school. So, she began a more directed exploration of the topic, looking carefully at the incidents involving first-day busing mistakes. More ideas came to mind as Anna pictured her sister reading the essay and tried to supply vivid details that would entertain her sister without making the essay too long.

Comment: Anna's early exploration of her topic is much like the scuba diver's early survey; she looks around to see what is available before she makes any decisions, and she begins to see connections and possibilities even before she selects an idea to develop.

Anna also follows the guidelines offered in Chapter 1 to encourage creative thinking: she puts down as many ideas as she can without dismissing any; she records specific details; she trusts her own instincts about topic.

Note

Anna Daniels' final draft appears on pp. 35–36.

YOUR   TURN

Begin to scan your topic for possibilities. Can you see any vivid scenes yet? Any colorful characters? Any incidents you remember clearly? Can you define some possibilities here? What is your response to your subject so far? Are you amused? Concerned? Angry? Do you like or dislike your subject so far? Do you have in mind someone who would read your essay with interest? Do you want the reader to feel a certain way about your subject? about you?

Seeing Connections

Don't worry yet about the form of the paper—if you know the purpose of the essay, many times the form will be obvious when you begin to write. If no such pattern seems obvious, you can make decisions about form later. In any case, focusing too early on the form of the paper might block you from seeing other good approaches to the content.

Even though you have gathered a body of knowledge about a subject and made some preliminary decisions about what you want the essay to do, you should continue to explore your ideas. As you begin to see possible audiences and purposes, your probing becomes more directed. Think again of the scuba diver as she begins to see points of interest in her underground world and begins to make decisions about where she will spend her time. She might choose to save the cave for another dive and focus instead on the reef, or she might choose to explore a specific part of a shipwreck. These decisions are not irreversible; if the reef proves dull or the cabin area inaccessible, the diver (like you) is free to change directions.

The Writer at Work

Anna Daniels decided that she would try to show her sister how scary it is to send a child off into the school world, but with a light touch. She didn't want to make the essay sound like a horror story. The vivid images she had conjured up while the children were missing were truly horrifying and fortunately not prophetic; Anna decided not to tell her sister all of the grim possibilities she had imagined. After all, she reasoned, her sister could think up her own nightmares.

Comment: Anna's analysis of her topic continues to supply more details, even as she sees connections between incidents. She also recognizes that some of her decisions can be put off until after she has a rough draft. And, her decision to show a mother's fears with a light touch influenced her selection of details.

Y O U R   T U R N

What reaction do you wish to get from your audience? Try a few direct statements here: "I want my reader to feel how confusing and frustrating registration is" or "I want my reader to laugh at the weird characters in my dorm."

These early sentences will give some direction to your material. If your roommate is dull or normal, a description of her won't be included in a paper on strange characters. If you found the lines at the payment center to be orderly and efficient, you won't talk about them in your essay on registration confusions.

Some writers like to ask themselves specific questions to direct their information gathering; others like to make lists or draw diagrams. (Chapter 6 catalogues different methods of exploring topics.) Whatever your own approach, keep a pen handy to record your ideas.

In this early planning stage, be alert to logical connections between your ideas:

- Some ideas are similar; perhaps they could be compared or even classified into like categories.
- Some are in sharp contrast, even total opposition.
- Some ideas occur in a sequence of time.
- Others line up in logical patterns such as most important to trivial.
- Some ideas suggest causes or effects.
- Some ideas are connected to each other spatially: near-to-far, top-to-bottom, left-to-right.

(Additional information on common patterns can be found in Chapter 12.)

Some initial connections should not dictate the shape of your final essay, but do note on paper possible relationships between ideas. You are free to play with ideas here. The direction is not so well-defined that it cannot be easily changed if something more promising occurs to you.

The Writer at Work

Anna Daniels saw two patterns in her essay almost immediately. The details of the incidents lined up chronologically, but she could also see that the two children's adventures had a similar center. Still, she wasn't sure that she would write about both children's experiences; she decided to collect her ideas in prose to see how long the essay was going to be.

Comment: Anna's body of material continued to grow, but she did not cut off her explorations of the topic. Instead, she decided to see how much material she really had before she made any firm decisions.

Y O U R   T U R N

Are there patterns developing in your topic? Do you see ideas that relate to each other? Are there incidents that caused other incidents to happen? Are there similarities, i.e., several people who share the same weird sleeping habits? What logical patterns do you see?

Discovery activities like gathering and planning and evaluating ideas often go on throughout your writing. If you think of yourself as an explorer, you will see that all journeys do not end with great discoveries. You may try out an idea and discover that you don't know enough about it to write—or that you are simply repeating what has been said by many before you. Do not hesitate to scrap the expedition and begin again. But save your notes—another direction might occur to you later.

❏ The Second Decision: To Draft a Response

When you decide that you have enough raw material to begin drafting, your work shifts from exploration to explanation as you draft a prose response, making more specific choices about subject and audience.

Drafting for Yourself

Being aware of your audience when you initially decide to write can shape your written response. However, your first writings are often for yourself as you collect and sort your own knowledge and ideas. If you begin by worrying about the reactions of a specific audience, you may stifle your own responses. To encourage your own observations, consider delaying a detailed analysis of your audience until you have made some decisions about your thesis or controlling idea and your purpose. The audience, of course, is there; however, recognize that you need to identify your own feelings before you tailor your material to a specific audience. As you draft for yourself, then, do two things:

Put Ideas into Prose

The only "requirement" is that you put your material into sentences. Be sure that you have included everything you wanted to say. Don't worry if the draft seems long or disorganized; it is not the final copy.

Identify Your Controlling Idea (Thesis)

- What do you want to describe? To explain? To argue?
- What ideas do you want to include?
- Why do you want to use those ideas?
- Identifying your controlling idea is a conscious act. However, your personal computer (the one between your ears) has been sifting and narrowing, and you might be surprised to discover how much shape and direction your paper already has.

Y O U R **T U R N**

- Collect your notes into draft form. Do not put any constraints on this draft; at this point, you want only to put your ideas on paper.
- Look over your notes now and mark any promising ideas. A check in the margin will suffice. If you like color, try a bright highlighting pen to mark your favorites.
- Put your focus into words in a single sentence. Use a complete sentence and give both your subject and the point you want to make about it (not, "Problems in the grading system at my university" but "The P.E. Department has no definite guidelines for conditioning classes, so students in some sections do more work and receive lower grades than students in other sections of the same course.").
- If your first writings include several possible ideas, evaluate the material you have and your own feelings about what you want to say. When you have made a choice, save your other notes for later writings.

**The Writer
at Work**

Anna Daniels' first draft of her narrative was a lengthy description of two incidents: her son's first ride home on the school bus when he got off at the wrong stop, and her daughter's first ride home when the bus driver failed to stop in her neighborhood. Reading over the draft, Anna decided to keep both incidents because they reinforced an idea she felt was a key worry of parents: children cannot be prepared for or protected from everything that the world will throw at them. She decided to present that idea as the thesis of her paper, using the two incidents as support.

Drafting for Your Audience

When your ideas are gathered and sorted to your own satisfaction, you can shape writing to best suit your audience and purpose. The general subject of your writing is often determined by the invitation to write. But what you choose to say about the subject, the audience to whom you will say it, and the impact you wish to have on your readers, are more complex concerns.

Sometimes you will have something to say and will have to decide who should hear it; for example, if you want to persuade an audience to take specific action (to fix a parking lot, for example), you will direct your presentation to someone with the necessary authority.

Sometimes you begin with a topic and choose an audience to hear your views (for example, a Letter to the Editor), and then you decide on the purpose and the specific contents of your letter.

Or, you might be assigned to write to a specific audience about a specific subject, and you must decide whether you want to persuade, to inform, or to involve that audience imaginatively.

As you write, give yourself conscious direction:

- Identify your purpose
- Define a specific audience
- Adopt the audience's perspective
- Ask a friend for some feedback

Identify Your Purpose

Define what you hope to accomplish with this writing. Some goals are personal, so allow for the possibility that your final audience might be yourself. For illustration, consider the invitations below. Speculate about the subjects, audiences, and purposes of these contexts:

- You are assigned to investigate the rent increases ordered for Married Student Housing; your audience is the readership of the university newspaper. What are some of the possible purposes of your writing? How will your purpose and your awareness of audience affect the content of your work? If you find scandals and abuses of power, who else might need a report on the problem? If you address university officials, does your purpose change?

- You are assigned to write a light, humorous essay for class to demonstrate the use of irony. Your audience is your classmates; your purpose is to amuse. How are subject and content affected by the terms of the assignment?
- You decide to write a reassuring letter to a nervous relative or friend, explaining that life in the fast lane of the university has not altered your value system. Consider directing different letters to at least two very different people. How does your content change, even though your purpose and your general subject remain the same?

The Writer at Work

Anna reviewed her material and the tentative decisions she had made. She liked her controlling idea about parents' inability to shelter their children, but she decided that her material was dramatic enough to make her point without being gruesome or melodramatic, so she decided against adding material about missing children or drug abuse. She also decided to keep her material light, even humorous, reasoning that mothers already shared her fears and that there was enough tension in the topic itself.

Y O U R   T U R N

What impact do you want to have on your readers?

- Do you want to involve their imaginations, inviting them to share vicariously in your pleasure at a peaceful scene or your terror during a horrifying enounter?
- Do you want to inform them about a subject to increase their understanding?
- Do you want to convince them of something, to have them reconsider their attitudes or to take some specific action?

Define a Specific Audience

Visualize your readers. Be realistic about their interests; very few topics are *really* written for a "general audience of educated readers." In most cases, the audience has some predisposition to read your work.

For example, what audience wants to read about grading inconsistencies in the P.E. Department? The general public won't be nearly as interested as the students who suspected they were not treated fairly. Perhaps the department ought to hear from a concerned student. Perhaps the university administration should be made aware of the situation.

When you can picture a specific audience, you will make better decisions about what to say to that audience and how to say it. So, before you begin to shape your draft, know what you want to say and to whom you wish to say it.

The Writer at Work

Anna had thought of her sister as an audience from the very beginning, partially because her sister's oldest child would soon be starting school and partially because her sister was convinced that she could indeed protect her children from all unpleasant experiences by telling them what to do in advance. Anna did not want to sound preachy, so she decided to make herself and her own reactions the focus of her essay.

Adopt the Audience's Perspective

See your draft through the eyes of your audience. What would they already know? What would they care about this topic? Do they have any concerns that you hadn't thought about? For example, does the administration have a serious budgetary problem that will keep it from making any changes? Make a list of the new ideas that you uncover from this different perspective.

YOUR TURN

Think of possible audiences for the topics you've been tinkering with. Does another student need to hear that registration was confusing? Maybe a friend who did not go to college would appreciate the scene.

How much would that audience know about your subject? If you're planning a picture of registration chaos, can your audience picture the scene easily, or must you give them specific layouts? Try out several audiences and decide whether the various audiences need different information.

With your audience clearly in mind, revise your draft so that it is directed to your readers. If necessary, write a completely new draft. Reread your work to make sure that your language and examples are appropriate and clear for this audience.

Ask a Friend for Some Feedback

One of the hardest shifts for a writer is to see the paper through the eyes of the audience. To see if your ideas are as clear to an audience as they are to you, ask a friend to play the role of your intended audience. (For help in getting effective feedback from peer evaluations, review the material in Chapter 14.)

The Writer at Work

Anna's essay was directed to her sister. Her directions to the friend who reviewed it were to think about what it was like to have young children. She also pointed out to the reader that her sister would know about the two children in the essay, so details about their appearance or age would be excessive.

Note

A final version of Anna's essay appears at the end of this chapter.

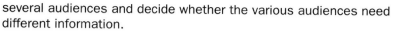

Y O U R   T U R N

Explain to a friend the specific audience you picture for this paper, and ask the friend to read the paper from that perspective. Be sure to explain that you don't expect proofreading, just a second opinion on the audience's probable understanding.

❑ The Third Decision: To Review the Work in Progress

As your draft moves closer to completion, you will need to both revise it and edit it. The distinction between the two is based on the focus of your attention. When you are working with content, making sure it is logical and clear and complete and relevant, you are revising. When you focus on questions of correctness, on matters such as grammar and spelling and punctuation, you are editing.

An attitude that can really cripple your writing is the belief that once a draft is on paper, no new ideas should be added. At whatever level you are working, including the editor's check of spelling and punctuation, be open to new connections and examples.

Revising the Content

If you are not happy with the content, you can always consciously shift back to another level and review earlier notes. As an explorer, you are always free to abandon a direction that is not productive or to return to an interesting site for further work.

Y O U R **T U R N**

Review your draft and your notes. Is the focus consistent? Is the content appropriate for your purpose and your audience? Are the points logical? The explanations complete? The examples specific and illuminating?

(Only when you are satisfied that your discussion is complete should you be concerned about proofreading.)

Editing Your Text

If you have been wondering when all the years you spent studying the fine points of grammar and mechanics would be useful, that time is now. With confidence that you have a thorough and logical discussion, call on the editorial voice to look for misspelled words, awkward sentences, excess commas, and misplaced modifiers. As we noted in Chapter 1, the editorial voice is extremely possessive, so wait until content is complete before editing.

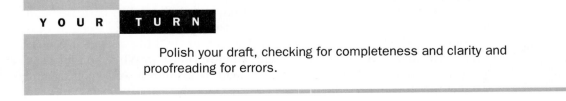

Y O U R **T U R N**

Polish your draft, checking for completeness and clarity and proofreading for errors.

❑ **The Final Decision: To Send the Draft to Its Audience**

Some writers never feel that their work is finished. They correct and expand and reorganize every time they read through a draft. Other writers want to be rid of a work as soon as the first draft is complete. You must find a reasonable middle ground. Look over the draft carefully. Is it ready for its audience? If you have doubts, ask again:

- Is information adequate?
- Are explanations complete?
- Are connections logical?
- Are style, grammar, and mechanics accurate?
- Does this draft need more work?

Be sure of your answers before you consider your response complete. Any hesitation should send you back to review your work, but a "yes" to these questions will complete your writing, so look carefully before you respond.

Learning by Doing

At this point you have only a general outline of what you will be studying in your writing course. Subsequent chapters will fill in that outline and deepen your understanding of the writing process. Yet you will begin writing at once, and you may feel you are being asked to do something before you have learned how to do it. You are free to read any section of this book if you want more detailed information about a skill or a strategy. Unfortunately, though, you can't learn to write by reading about it.

Writing is a skill, and skills are learned by doing. When you were younger, you undoubtedly played basketball before you mastered all the skills of the game. Even if you spent some time every day working on the individual skills like dribbling, shooting, and playing defense, you also spent time putting all the skills together in a game. Writing is also more than working on skills: it is blending those skills as the situation demands. If you never play a game, you won't know how to fit the skills together. That is why you will be expected to complete written responses as you learn about the various principles and techniques of composition.

Y O U R   T U R N

An Invitation

You should have a broad picture of the writing process as a series of levels, much like the depths of an undersea territory to be explored. Selecting one of the topics listed below (or one of your

own), try a "diving expedition" that leads you deeper into the topic but allows you to move freely between the surface and the depths:

violence	recreation	roommates
movies	professors	phobias
cannibalism	nature	censorship

(Additional invitations appear with readings at the end of this section.)

Put Everything in Writing

Make a habit of writing as you think. You may be in the habit of doing preliminary work in your head. However, we suggest that you put everything down on paper, no matter how fragmented or tentative the ideas seem.

Consider:

- You might scribble an idea in passing that later proves very useful—one you might have forgotten without written notes.
- Writing down an idea may help you think of others that are related to it.
- An almost magical relationship exists between writing often and writing easily. If you can make the translation of ideas to paper a habit, longer pieces will flow more easily after a while.

Find your own best style of note-taking.   These notes are strictly for you. If single words or phrases bring images to mind, then don't feel compelled to write complete passages. But don't be afraid to let your pen go if you have a vivid idea and want to get it on paper. This early stage should be as free as possible—don't worry about spelling or grammar or logic; just write.

❏ The First Decision: To Accept the Invitation to Write

You have received an "invitation" to write. When you decide to accept it, begin by:

Exploring Your Ideas

Ask yourself:
  What do I know about this topic?
  Have I had any personal experiences with any aspect of it?
  Has anyone I know had such experiences?
  Are there any people associated with this topic? Think of names; think
    of people in action; think of job categories.

Reminder
Write down all your early responses, even if you discard them almost immediately as possibilities for this paper.

Seeing Connections

Ask yourself:
What can I compare my ideas with?
Are any of my ideas similar to others in this material?
Do my ideas contrast sharply with any ideas of other people?
Are any of my ideas in sharp contrast to each other?
Are there any logical connections like causes or effects?
Are there any steps in chronological sequence?

If you see some connections, note them in the margins. Also, check to see if the connections are complete. For example, if there are two steps in a sequence, are there others? If there are three points of comparison, are there any more?

❏ **The Second Decision: To Draft a Response**

When you have sufficient raw materials to draft, collect your ideas in prose and direct them to an audience.

Drafting for Yourself

Put Ideas into Prose:
When you have gathered a body of material, write a long, loose draft that shows your knowledge and feelings about this topic.

Identify a Controlling Idea:
Are there ideas that keep emerging in the rough draft?
What is the most important thing about this topic?
What do I most want to say?

Drafting for Your Audience

Look closely at your invitation to write. The situation or assignment might already contain a specific audience and purpose for your response. If not, you must identify your audience and purpose.

Define a Specific Audience:
Who would be interested in this information?
Who would be affected by this information?
Who could use this information?
Who could take action about this situation?

Identify a Purpose:
Do I want to make my readers feel something in particular, like anger or shock or amusement?

Do I want my audience to do something?
Do I want my audience to learn something?
Do I want my audience to change their minds about something?

Adopt the Audience's Perspective:
What do my readers know about this topic?
What do I need to explain more carefully?
What do they feel about this topic? Are they against me?
How much explanation will I need to convince them that I'm right?

Now write a draft that is directed more carefully to your audience. Think about what they know and what they need to know.

Ask a Friend for Some Feedback. When you have a draft that you feel is complete and is directed toward your audience, ask a classmate to read it. Be sure to tell your reader what role to play—should the reader pretend to be a student at another college? your mother? Ask the reader to react as that audience would and to help you find areas that might need further explanation.

❏   **The Third Decision: To Review the Draft**

When your prose draft has been directed to an audience, review your work to make sure that content and text are complete and accurate.

Revising the Content

Write down a sentence that expresses the idea you want to convey to your audience. Give both your subject area and an idea about it. For example, "The grading system is unfair," *not* "This is about the grading system."

Ask yourself questions about the content:
Have I covered all the main points?
Have I offered examples?
Have I defined unfamiliar terms?
Are my opinions explained and supported?
Are my connections logical?

Editing Your Text

Go through the text with the editor's red pencil and check for correctness. You will need to make your own checklist for the editing phase, listing commonly misspelled words, punctuation problems, grammatical uncertainties. For example, you might keep a list of errors marked on old papers to identify previous problem areas. Does parallel structure confuse you? Semicolon usage puzzle you? Mark the items you want to double check before you turn in a draft to be graded.

❏ **The Final Decision: To Send the Draft to Its Audience**

Read over your work, reviewing its content and presentation. Your decision here can end the process, so look carefully for areas needing further work.

Note

When the invitation to write is a classroom assignment, be sure to check with your instructor for specific requirements for each assignment, both for content and form.

If your written response does not satisfy a length requirement, survey the topic again to see if you have omitted major points. If the paper remains too short, you have two acceptable options: you can recognize it as finished and accept whatever penalty might be assessed (usually less than the penalty for padded fluff), or you can recognize the limitations of the topic and re-define it to include more material.

LEAVING THE NEST

Anna Daniels' Final Draft:

There are few events in a child's life that are more anticipated than the first day of school. Whether we send our children to private or to public schools, putting them on a big yellow bus and sending them across town or across the street is still a trying moment for us parents. There are all the mixed feelings about watching them grow up and knowing that we are growing older. And there are also some fears mixed into the occasion. As the bus drives off, our children leave the shelter of our arms and enter a world that is capable of swallowing them up, no matter how hard we try to prevent it.

When Barry started school, I was sure that I had covered all the bases. We went to school early in the week and walked around, finding the classroom and the lunchroom and the bathroom. He had his new orange knapsack that was guaranteed to make him visible even in a dense fog, and he had new red tennis shoes that would make him jump higher and run faster than even his dog. I took pictures of him waiting at the end of the driveway for the bus, and I made sure that I was home early to meet him when he came home. Only he didn't come home.

The bus stopped and children poured off of it; Barry did not appear. I called school and was assured that many kindergarteners fall asleep on the bus, but when his bus returned to the schoolyard, he was not on it. The bus driver remembered the orange knapsack; she was sure that he had been on the bus and just as sure that he had gotten off somewhere along the route.

No mother has to be told what went through my head in the next few minutes. I was looking up the number for the police station when I heard a car in the driveway and Barry came tumbling into the kitchen, looking more aggravated than frightened. He had gone home with a friend, and the mother, knowing what was in my mind, had brought him home when she came in from work. Did his mother know he was there? she had asked. "No," he said, "but it's OK. I know where I am." How can we balance our own fears with the confident, secure world picture of a five-year-old?

Margaret's adventure was shorter, but it was more traumatic for her. Her father and I were standing in the front yard as the bus roared by; her brother waved to her as it rounded the corner; she waved to us rather frantically as the bus roared by again on its way out of the neighborhood. Three phone calls and thirty minutes later, a shattered little girl stepped numbly off the bus and ran into the house in tears. The bus driver was new; she had made a mistake. But what did that matter to the little girl crying inside? And what else could I have done to make sure that her day had a happier ending?

Both incidents made me realize, in different ways, that there are roads out there that I cannot travel with my children. I cannot anticipate every turn, and I cannot fill in every pothole. For someone who reads the newspapers and watches television, that is a frightening realization.

SUMMARY

The process of taking an idea (assigned or inspired) and turning it into a composition is not a series of neat steps that move from one to the next without a backward glance. Instead, the process more resembles a series of levels. This overview has traced the process from the first level of exploring your ideas and your knowledge about a subject, through the second level of compiling drafts for yourself and for a defined audience, to the third level of revision and editing. It is designed to give you an awareness of the whole process as you work on specific areas in the next chapters.

Additional Readings for Part One

"Take This Fish and Look at It"

Samuel H. Scudder

Samuel H. Scudder (1837–1911) was an American scientist who special-ized in the study of butterflies, grasshoppers, and crickets. The narrative that follows describes one of his encounters with the methods of Louis Agassiz.

Becoming an Active Reader:

1. The title offers rather simple advice to a serious student of science. How long do you think it should take for the student to see what needs to be seen?
2. Looking at the fish seems to be a first step. What else would you expect Scudder to do as he studies the fish?

1   It was more than fifteen years ago that I entered the laboratory of Professor Agassiz, and told him I had enrolled my name in the Scientific School as a student of natural history. He asked me a few questions about my object in coming, my antecedents generally, the mode in which I afterwards proposed to use the knowledge I might acquire, and, finally, whether I wished to study any special branch. To the latter I replied that, while I wished to be well grounded in all departments of zoology, I purposed to devote myself specially to insects.

2   "When do you wish to begin?" he asked.

3   "Now," I replied.

4   This seemed to please him, and with an energetic "Very well!" he reached from a shelf a huge jar of specimens in yellow alcohol. "Take this fish," he said, "and look at it; we call it a haemulon; by and by I will ask what you have seen."

5   With that he left me, but in a moment returned with explicit instructions as to the care of the object entrusted to me.

6   "No man is fit to be a naturalist," said he, "who does not know how to take care of specimens."

7   I was to keep the fish before me in a tin tray, and occasionally moisten the surface with alcohol from the jar, always taking care to replace the stopper tightly. Those were not the days of ground-glass stoppers and elegantly shaped exhibition jars; all the old students will recall the huge neckless glass bottles with their leaky, wax-besmeared corks, half eaten by insects, and begrimed with cellar dust. Entomology was a cleaner science than ichthyology, but the example of the Professor, who had unhesitatingly plunged to the bottom of the jar to produce the fish, was infectious; and though this alcohol had a "very ancient and fishlike smell," I really dared not show any aversion within these sacred precincts, and treated the alcohol as though it were pure water. Still I was conscious of a passing feeling of disappointment, for gazing at a fish did not commend itself to an ardent entomologist. My friends at home, too, were annoyed when they discovered that no amount of eau-de-Cologne would drown the perfume which haunted me like a shadow.

8   In ten minutes I had seen all that could be seen in that fish, and started in search of the Professor—who had, however, left the Museum; and when I returned, after lingering over some of the odd animals stored in the upper apartment, my specimen was dry all over. I dashed the fluid over the fish as if to resuscitate the beast from a fainting fit, and looked with anxiety for a return of the normal sloppy appearance. This little excitement over, nothing was to be done but to return to a steadfast gaze at my mute companion. Half an hour passed—an hour—another hour; the fish began to look loathsome. I turned it over and around; looked it in the face—ghastly; from behind, beneath, above, sideways, at a three-quarters' view—just as ghastly. I was in despair; at an early hour I concluded that lunch was necessary; so, with infinite relief, the fish was carefully replaced in the jar, and for an hour I was free.

9   On my return, I learned that Professor Agassiz had been at the Museum, but had gone, and would not return for several hours. My fellow-students were too busy to be disturbed by continued conversation. Slowly I drew forth that hideous fish, and with a feeling of desperation again looked at it. I might not use a magnifying-glass; instruments of all kinds were interdicted. My two hands, my two eyes, and the fish: it seemed a most limited field. I pushed my finger down its throat to feel how sharp the teeth were. I began to count the scales in the different rows, until I was convinced that was nonsense. At last a happy thought stuck me—I would draw the fish; and now with surprise I began to discover new features in the creature. Just then the Professor returned.

10   "That is right," said he; "a pencil is one of the best of eyes. I am glad to notice, too, that you keep your specimen wet, and your bottle corked."

11   With these encouraging words, he added:

12   "Well, what is it like?"

13   He listened attentively to my brief rehearsal of the structure of parts whose names were still unknown to me: the fringed gill-arches and movable operculum; the pores of the head, fleshy lips and lidless eyes; the lateral line, the spinous fins and forked tail; the compressed and arched body. When I finished, he waited as if expecting more, and then, with an air of disappointment:

14   "You have not looked very carefully; why," he continued more earnestly, "you haven't even seen one of the most conspicuous features of the animal, which is plainly before your eyes as the fish itself; look again, look again!" and he left me to my misery.

15   I was piqued; I was mortified. Still more of that wretched fish! But now I set myself to my task with a will, and discovered one new thing after another, until I saw how just the Professor's criticism had been. The afternoon passed quickly; and when, towards its close, the Professor inquired:

16   "Do you see it yet?"

17   "No," I replied, "I am certain I do not, but I see how little I saw before."

18   "That is next best," said he, earnestly, "but I won't hear you now; put away your fish and go home; perhaps you will be ready with a better answer in the morning. I will examine you before you look at the fish."

19   This was disconcerting. Not only must I think of my fish all night, studying, without the object before me, what this unknown but most visible feature might be; but also, without reviewing my discoveries, I must give an exact account of them the next day. I had a bad memory; so I walked home by Charles River in a distracted state, with my two perplexities.

20   The cordial greeting from the Professor the next morning was reassuring; here was a man who seemed to be quite as anxious as I that I should see for myself what he saw.

21   "Do you perhaps mean," I asked, "that the fish has symmetrical sides with paired organs?"

22   His thoroughly pleased "Of course! Of course!" repaid the wakeful hours of the previous night. After he had discoursed most happily and enthusiastically—as he always did—upon the importance of this point, I ventured to ask what I should do next.

23   "Oh, look at your fish!" he said, and left me again to my own devices. In a little more than an hour he returned, and heard my new catalogue.

24   "That is good, that is good!" he repeated; "but that is not all; go on"; and so for three long days he placed that fish before my eyes, forbidding me to look at anything else, or to use any artificial aid. "Look, look, look," was his repeated injunction.

25   This was the best entomological lesson I ever had—a lesson whose influence has extended to the details of every subsequent study; a legacy the Professor had left to me, as he has left it to so many others, of inestimable value, which we could not buy, with which we cannot part.

26   A year afterward, some of us were amusing ourselves with chalking out-landish beasts on the Museum blackboard. We drew prancing starfishes; frogs in mortal combat; hydra-headed worms; stately craw-fishes, standing on their tails, bearing aloft umbrellas; and grotesque fishes with gaping mouths and staring eyes. The Professor came in short-ly after, and was as amused as any at our experiments. He looked at the fishes.

27   "Haemulons, every one of them," he said; "Mr. ——— drew them."

28   True; and to this day, if I attempt a fish, I can draw nothing but haemulons.

29   The fourth day, a second fish of the same group was placed beside the first, and I was bidden to point out the resemblances and differences between the two; another and another followed, until the entire family lay before me, and a whole legion of jars covered the table and surround-ing shelves; the odor had become a pleasant perfume; and even now, the sight of an old, six-inch, worm-eaten cork brings fragrant memories.

30   The whole group of haemulons was thus brought in review; and, whether engaged upon the dissection of the internal organs, the prepara-tion and examination of the bony framework, or the description of the various parts, Agassiz's training in the method of observing facts and their orderly arrangement was ever accompanied by the urgent exhorta-tion not to be content with them.

31   "Facts are stupid things," he would say, "until brought into connection with some general law."

32   At the end of eight months, it was almost with reluctance that I left these friends and turned to insects; but what I had gained by this outside experience has been of greater value than years of later investigation in my favorite groups.

Thinking about a Subject and Writing for Yourself:

Prompts for Journal Writing and Class Discussion

1. Scudder is given a task to accomplish. Is his initial approach to the task creative? How does Agassiz force him to change his approach?

2. What is the relationship between Scudder and Agassiz when the narrative begins? How does Scudder feel about working with Agas-siz when the narrative begins? How do his feelings change as the experience progresses? How does he feel about the experience as he looks back on it more than fifteen years later?

3. What does Agassiz hope to teach Scudder about observation? How is his lesson similar to the ideas about creative thinking presented in this chapter? What kinds of thinking is Scudder expected to do? Which paragraphs illustrate those kinds of thinking?

4. In paragraph 8, Scudder writes, "In ten minutes I had seen all that could be seen in the fish. . . ." Had he? Have you ever felt that you had explored a topic thoroughly only to return to it later and find much more?

5. Scudder narrates an incident that he has come to see as significant to his education. He writes, ". . . what I had gained by this outside experience has been of greater value than years of later investigation. . . ." As you look back over your life, identify an experience that you now realize taught you something of lasting value. You need not have recognized the lesson immediately, but it must be something that you now see as significant to your development as a student or as a person.

   Assume that your presentation will appear (anonymously if you so request) in a collection of similar essays published by the Student Government Association for distribution to incoming freshmen next year.

6. Scudder writes, "For three long days he placed that fish before my eyes, forbidding me to look at anything else, . . ." and he admits that from such scrutiny, discovery followed new discovery. Parallel Scudder's experience with your own discovery of the true nature of someone you once knew only casually but now regard as a close friend. Begin with your initial observations and progress to your current perceptions. Be sure to give specific details of your discoveries. Your account should be directed to a third friend who has just dismissed a person based on a first lukewarm impression.

"In Praise of 9 to 5"

Ansen Dibell

Wordperfect Magazine May 1989

When you think about writing as a process, you might think of it as one process done much the same way by any number of writers. But Ansen Dibell (the writing name of Nan Dibble), who is both an editor at Writer's Digest Books and a writer of both science fiction and non-fiction, will show you another perspective. As you read her essay, notice what she has to say about her own process of writing.

Becoming an Active Reader:

1. What does the phrase "9-to-5" suggest to you? Do you have a positive or a negative reaction to it?

2. Dibell begins her essay by saying, "Like most writers, I used to think that . . . I'd quit my regular job and write full time." You are a

writer, too. Do you find it easier to write when you have nothing else on your mind? Can you imagine being a writer full-time? What would a "full-time" writing schedule be like?

3. Dibell says that if she had the entire day to write, she would waste much of it. Have you ever had a huge span of time to complete a project but found yourself doing it at the last minute anyway? Do you think that everyone works the same way? Is Dibell making a statement about all writers who write full-time?

1   Like most writers, I used to think that if only I could make one big sale, I'd quit my regular job and write full time.

2   I've changed my mind about that dream.

3   Aside from the precarious finances of the freelance life, there are drawbacks to hanging around at home.

4   You see things that need doing: dishes or clothes to wash, trash to take out, the garage to dejunk. There are soaps and game shows to watch.

5   Your family and neighbors don't help. To them, working means going to an office. If you're home all day, you're obviously available for babysitting, chauffeuring kids to the dentist, and going door to door to collect for assorted charities. If you say no, you're met with puzzled expressions and hurt feelings. Explain that you're writing and you'll get the skeptical eyebrow lift you'd get if, staring into space, you explained that you're *thinking*.

6   Your own psychology can turn against you, too. Because a lot of the time, you *won't* be writing. And you'll feel guilty about it.

7   Fitzgerald said writing was like swimming under water, and it does feel like that: holding your breath and yanking yourself blindly forward as hard as you can, as long as you can, until you blurrily surface to find it's 4 a.m. I tend to think of writing as being like taking SAT test for hours and hours, sometimes days, at a stretch. That much intensity and concentration, that kind of absolute focus.

8   Nobody can maintain that kind of sustained mental and emotional effort 9-to-5, every day, week in and week out. At least I can't.

9   It's probably different for writers who are sprinters, who tend to do short pieces—short stories, articles, poetry. A short piece can be done in a single, white-hot burst and then revised and polished at leisure. For sprinters, the perennial advice to write every day, on a steady schedule, may actually work.

10   But we marathoners, who write books, tend to need correspondingly long rhythms of work and rest. Each weekend, I can generally turn out a chapter of whatever book I'm working on: between 6,000 and 10,000 words. But toward Sunday night, I'm starting to slow and stumble. By then, I'm rolling purely on built-up momentum: knowing where I'm going because I've been aiming myself, and the writing, steadily since the beginning of that session. Any tired horse knows how to go home. And so the chapter gets done, for minor tinkering and revision on weekday evenings.

11   I've come to realize that if I had the whole of every day at my disposal, I wouldn't be writing. I'd either, waste time, read, play video games, watch old tapes, and go collecting door to door for Save the Seals. What's worse, I'd feel bad about it. I'd feel I *should* be writing: after all, that's what I'm home to do, isn't it? I'd start feeling guilty about *not* writing, and that would leech away the energy and concentration I need *for* writing. I'd end up doing *less,* and with more difficulty, than I do in my concentrated weekend sessions.

12   What seems to work for me is a 1 to 3 ratio: If I write for two solid days, over a weekend, I need between five and six days to gear up for the next prolonged session. That is, by happy coincidence, a standard work week.

13   What's hard isn't enforcing time to write. What's hard is enforcing a total rhythm between writing and rest: writing and *getting ready to write.* What's hard is recognizing that *not writing* is also a necessary part of writing, and that there's no use feeling guilty about it. Forced effort and guilt only make the good writing harder when it comes.

14   So I've put away the dream of full-time freelancing and come to a fresh appreciation of the fact that I go to the office every day at 7:30, and leave at 4. I appreciate the chats with co-workers around me and with the writers I deal with (I'm an editor). I find that I write better and faster for working hard on other things during the week, then switching that energy over to writing on the weekends. Because, by then, I'm ready. I've missed writing, and I've used the intervening time to think my way ahead in the story or book. I'm ready to get started when I sit down at the keyboard, Saturday mornings. Ready? I can't wait!

Thinking about a Subject and Writing for Yourself:

Prompts for Journal Writing and Class Discussion

1. What full-time job does Dibell hold? Where does Dibell do her writing? What disadvantages does she see for writers who work at home?

2. As you read Dibell's essay, think about what you know about the writing process. How does Dibell's work pattern fit the general description in Chapter 2? How does her work pattern vary from the process described in this text? Do you think that most writers fit the process described very closely?

3. Dibell compares sprinters and marathoners in her essay. Explain the connection between writing and running that Dibell presents. Does the analogy make sense to you? Can you think of other ways that runners and writers might be similar?

4. Dibell uses several other figurative images to describe writing and writers. Make a list of them as you read.

5. Most writers maintain that their biggest enemy is lack of time. Does Dibell agree with them?

6. What does Dibell mean when she says that ". . . not writing is also a necessary part of writing, . . ."?

7. When an essay begins with a statement of some idea from the past, it is safe to assume that the essay itself will present a new idea or a new understanding. As you read, notice the references to the old idea (or, "that dream"). How does Dibell use her beginning to make an ending? What does she say to make the beginning and the ending work like bookends to define the middle?

8. What was the last thing you wrote? Even if it was a list rather than a prose passage, why did you write it? After you have identified the invitation to write, think of what you did between the time you decided to write and the time you were finished. Did you think about your subject much before you started writing? Did you scratch things out or start over? Did you write more than one draft? Did you expect anyone else to read it? How do you usually write? Is it the same every time? Do you sometimes find it harder to write than other times?

9. Dibell is a professional writer; that is, she gets paid for what she writes. In her essay, she explains what she has discovered about her own process of writing, contrasting her discovery with her earlier view. In a similar way, Scudder explains discoveries about ways of looking that contradict earlier perceptions. Look carefully at the two essays to see the pattern of "Once I thought . . . but now I know." Think about your own voyages of discovery. What understanding do you now have about yourself or about the world or the people in it? How does your present comprehension differ from an earlier view?

10. Dibell calls herself a "marathoner" and contrasts her own work habits with other writers that she calls "sprinters." Think about your way of doing something. It may not be a unique approach that no one else shares, but think about other styles. Contrast your way of doing something with another approach. Are there any similarities? What are the biggest differences between the two styles? If there are more than two styles, pick two that you think are radically different from each other.

PART TWO

Invitations to Write

Imagine that you drive into your campus parking lot early one Monday morning and bounce through a succession of crater-like potholes. You grit your teeth as you jounce toward a parking spot, clouds of dark thoughts gathering in your head. "Somebody ought to hear about this miserable parking lot," you mutter.

In your stormy mutterings lie the basic elements of writing. You have a subject—the miserable condition of the parking lot. You have something to say about it—the damage to your car, the responsibility of the university, the expense of realignment, your sore neck. And you have an audience in mind—the "somebody" who ought to hear your story.

But before you start to write, there is another element to identify: the purpose of your writing. What is it that you want your writing to do? How do you want it to affect your audience? Do you want your writing to amuse your audience? To anger them or to make them nod their heads in understanding? Are you writing a friend to entertain with the story of your great expedition through the dangerous land of the potholes? Are you writing to the administration to spur repairs? Are you writing to maintenance to notify them of the condition of the lot? The identification of purpose, like the identification of audience, can influence both the content and form of your writing.

At the same time, purpose and audience are so closely related that it is often difficult to tell which is decided first. If you have a burning desire to see that repairs are made, you know your purpose and must then decide on an appropriate audience. But sometimes you think first of the audience—"I'll have to tell Jackie about this"—and then determine purpose when you decide to make your story an amusing narrative or a pitiful appeal for money. Deciding on purpose may even alter your decision about audience: realizing that you will need money to realign your car, you decide that Jackie is not the best one to hear your story and you write to your tender-hearted aunt instead.

Your purpose is sometimes clear from the first moment you decide to write, but you should always think about it before you begin. Your decision can influence your choice of audience and your choice of material for that audience. It will also affect the development of your paper, determining the kind and amount of support each of your ideas will require.

In fact, determination of purpose has such an impact on your writing that it is one of the most logical bases for classification of writing. Regardless of the subject or the audience, writing that aims to improve the readers' understanding of a subject is informative and writing that seeks to convince the readers to reconsider their views is persuasive. A third category of writing seeks to involve the emotions of the readers, to have them share the writer's feelings about an admired person or a special retreat or a traumatic incident. In each of these categories—to inform, to convince, and to involve—the purpose of your writing will influence your choice of material and your presentation of it.

Defining purpose is part of recognizing the rhetorical context of your writing. When you jostled through the parking lot potholes, planning an angry letter to campus maintenance, your awareness of subject and audience and purpose created a rhetorical context. In other words, you saw a framework in which you wrote not only about *something but* to *someone. Whenever you identify the contexts of your writing, you become clearer about whom you will address, and you define the effect you hope to have on that audience.*

In this part, you will find a variety of rhetorical contexts. While your instructor provides the stimulus for your academic writing, you should begin to see that writing does not automatically end when your grades are averaged. You will find samples of writing done by other students, by professional writers, and by non-academic, non-professional writers who found themselves in situations that invited written responses. As you look at these samples, notice that writers in varied situations use similar activities or processes to collect material, draft responses, and review their work. The advice in this book will certainly help you respond to classroom assignments, but you can expect that it will help you to respond to situations outside of the classroom as well.

Writing to Inform the Audience

Informative writing is intended to improve understanding of a topic rather than to change opinions or evoke emotional responses. While it may concern controversial subjects, informative writing presents issues with objectivity. This chapter demonstrates the process and products of effective informative writing. It contains sample readings, writing prompts, and suggestions for preparing written responses.

When you write to inform, you present factual data in an objective way, aiming to improve readers' understanding of the topic rather than to convince them of something or to involve them vicariously in an experience. Informative writing has many applications, including business reports, encyclopedia articles, textbooks, and many trade books. News articles in newspapers and many articles in magazines are also written to inform. You might give information about such varied topics as a person's biography, an explanation of how to do something, the points of interest in a particular city or state, or new developments in science, law, or technology.

In short, you write to inform whenever your purpose is to explain the unfamiliar or to report what has happened. If there is little chance that your audience will question or challenge your material, you are probably writing to inform.

CHARACTERISTICS OF INFORMATIVE WRITING

Informative writing cannot be readily distinguished from other writing by examining form. A narrative of Custer's Last Stand, for example, might help the reader understand the strategic errors made before and during the battle. And, a narrative that focused on one man's errors might be used to convince readers that he should be blamed for the disaster. Narrative topics in the same subject area could invite the reader to respond emotionally, to understand the feelings of the men involved. It is not form, then, that signals purpose.

Informative writing has one essential difference from writing that convinces: informative writing does not take sides. Unlike persuasive writing that presents a judgment about an issue, informative writing remains objective about its material. In fact, if you have such strong views that you cannot write about a subject without taking a stand, then you should recognize that your purpose is to convince rather than to inform.

You can, of course, write informatively about even the most controversial subject. To remain objective, however, you must genuinely be more concerned about presenting facts than about advancing a particular viewpoint.

As you read the following discussion of a controversial proposal, notice that the writer has taken neither side but has attempted to present each of the two views as reasonable and educated:

> One proposal to slow the spread of AIDS among IV drug users is to distribute clean needles free of charge. Proponents of the plan argue that the spread of disease is a medical, not a moral issue, and that clean needles will protect not only the drug users but those with whom they come in contact. Opponents insist that providing drug paraphernalia condones drug use. They also argue that addicts will simply share the clean needles and that the plan will thus have no significant impact on the problem.

SITUATIONS THAT PROMPT INFORMATIVE WRITING

Informative writing is a mainstay of academic writing. When you are asked to prepare reports on backgrounds of subjects, current events, or current thinking on a topic, your instructor expects you to expand your own understanding of the subject as you collect and present information to an audience. Analysis and evaluation call for your own judgments, but much of what you write for the classroom is intended to inform.

Beyond the classroom, information about activities or programs or policies appears in public and private writing such as brochures, newsletters, memos, and personal letters. Job-related writing may seek to convince others that your ideas are sound, but it just as often presents information to co-workers and clients. Like the writer whose profile follows, you may be surprised at the amount of writing you do on the job.

Writing beyond the Classroom

When Georgia Ford left Concord College with an honors degree in mathematics, she encountered a job market that was flooded with applicants for every position. She expected that her math skills and her high GPA would open doors for her, but to her surprise, the edge that earned her a position as a group underwriter for Life of Virginia was a well-written letter of application. She remembers, "The company was delighted to have someone who already knew how to write." The experience planted a seed for Ford, who had not anticipated that she would do much writing after college. Today she is the owner of Georgia H. Ford & Assoc. New York Life Agency, a chartered life underwriter and financial consultant. And she credits her success to her ability to organize and present ideas clearly to her clients.

Writing on the job has become routine for Ford, but it is a part of her work that she takes very seriously. Much of her work is done under a deadline, so she does not linger. Instead, she organizes quickly and efficiently, using a word processor to help her revise longer pieces but doing much of the planning for shorter works in her head. "I tend to think in sequences," she says, "in terms of what points need emphasis or what steps need to be taken—1-2-3." The ability to outline mentally began with her mathematics training and, she says, a solid English course she took in high school. Her writing reflects that habit of mind; the framework is visible whether she is issuing in-house instructions for her staff or summarizing information for clients.

Her strategy, she points out, changes with her audience. For example, she provides detailed lists of specific tasks for in-house instruction, not gambling that someone else will fill in any gaps. In contrast, she compresses complex financial and tax information into summaries of critical data, knowing that most clients will not wade through pages of complicated details. "They rely on me to simplify the issues," Ford says, adding that her ability to do so accurately and clearly has been a big plus in her career.

Writing under a deadline necessarily compresses the process of writing. Ford draws her material from her own experience and training, adding research from the company's extensive library when necessary. She organizes quickly, either in her head or on her word processor (she adds that keyboard skills are a virtual necessity in today's hi-tech business world), and drafts material in list form. Clients, she says, appreciate the clarity of a list, and staff can easily check off listed tasks as each is completed.

A primary objective of client-directed writing is to get the attention of the reader. Research has proven, Ford says, that she has seventeen seconds to get the full attention of her audience, and that she will not have that attention for long. Concise, orderly presentations are a must. On some of her presentation work she consults with her partner, and the two discuss phrasing or information that will make the presentation clearer to the client. As professionals, she and her partner are primarily concerned with quality service for clients; ego games of who says what or whose ideas are best are simply a waste of their valuable time.

After her work is drafted and reviewed, Ford insists on doing her own editing. She has confidence in her own knowledge of material and of grammar and mechanics, and is consequently unwilling to let someone else affect the presentation of her ideas. She stresses that the impression a written communication makes is critical to business—her credibility, her expertise, her attention to detail are all evident in the writing she shares with clients and staff. Some samples of Ford's writing appear in this chapter. (All names and addresses have been changed to protect the professional relationship with clients.)

Initiating Contact with a Potential Client. (Note the reminder that the client has met Ford, the references to mutual acquaintances, and the generally positive tone. Note, too, that the tone is formal without being stilted, and the writer presents herself as a fellow business person who understands the attitude and the busy schedule of the contact.)

June 25, 1990

Mr. John Doe

Fine's Restaurant

123 Anystreet

Baton Rouge, LA 70817

Dear Mr. Doe:

Thank you and your staff for a most enjoyable lunch. I was introduced to you by my guest, Jane Smith. It was my first time to eat at Fine's, although I have heard wonderful comments from other friends, including John Jones (who would rather eat at Fine's than anywhere in Louisiana!). Your reputation is well-deserved.

As a professional in my field, I would appreciate an opportunity to meet with you briefly to share some business ideas, and to show you how I work for my clients. This would in no way be a "sales" interview. Rather it would be a time to discuss how we could be of assistance to one another, and to see if I could be of any service, either now or in the future.

My business, as I suspect yours is, is one of service, professionally given and of high quality. I work for long-term relationships that are mutually beneficial.

Later this week, I will call you to see if we can meet at your convenience. I will certainly be respectful of your time, and would appreciate the courtesy of fifteen or twenty minutes.

Sincerely,

Georgia H. Ford, CLU

Chartered Financial Consultant

A Follow-up Letter After a Meeting with a Potential Client. (Note the slightly more casual tone of this letter; the business relationship between the writer and the audience is more clearly defined. Note, too, the brief paragraphs that convey precise information about deadlines and about follow-up activities.):

July 19, 1990

Mr. Allen Smith

A-B-C Supplies

345 Anystreet

Baton Rouge, LA 70817

Dear Mr. Smith:

I just wanted to send you a small reminder that the quotes we have for your group major medical plan are valid for only 2 more weeks (August 1 effective date).

I will call you in a few days to see if we need to get new quotes for a September 1 effective date.

If, however, you have reached a decision on which plan you prefer, we will be happy to come out and enroll the group for an August 1 effective date.

I look forward to speaking with you soon. Let me know if I can provide you with any additional information.

Sincerely,

Georgia H. Ford, CLU

Chartered Financial Consultant

Excerpts from a Memorandum to Key Clients. These are designed to open a dialogue about changes in investments as a response to changes in tax laws (Such memorandums, Ford notes, are sent with disclaimers emphasizing that further consultation and explanation from tax experts is necessary. Note the relatively technical nature of the information, suggesting that it is directed to clients with particular backgounds or interests. Note, too, the use of comparative structure.):

POSSIBLE TAX LAW CHANGES UNDER CONSIDERATION: [excerpt]

1. Congress is considering changing the current law regarding the Unlimited Marital Deduction under estate tax law. Consider reducing it to allow the greater of one-half or $500,000 to be passed to your spouse.

2. Under very serious consideration is to limit the amount allowed as gifts to a lifetime total of $30,000. Current law permits gifts of $10,000 per year free of tax.

3. Current law allows a deduction of $600,000 of your estate to pass outside of your spouse, free of estate taxes. Possible change is to reduce that to $255,000.

In-house Communication. (Note the assumption that the staff is familiar with the terms and tasks so that the list is a reminder rather than a detailed instruction card.)

Sample 1:

July 5, 1990

Met with John and Jane Doe to discuss investment options for their SEP plan. They decided that the Govt. Plus Fund would be best for the

employees, including Jane. John is very interested in a SPDA for his
money, since he has over $10,000 in his account.

We need to:

1. Get a SPDA illustration for John. Use $12,000. Until Bob Jones
    completes the document, and runs the percentages, we won't know
    the exact amount.

2. Check with Bob to see when the document will be completed.

3. Get all paperwork completed on our part. We need Mackay Shields
    forms for each employee who will be under the plan. We set up an
    IRA for each one. Pull the necessary forms, and highlight where
    they need to be signed.

4. What is the set-up fee for each IRA? Can John write a separate
    check for that? Can it be deducted from the total contribution
    instead? If John writes a check separately, is that fee deductible?
    Can we use the business address to have all the statements mailed
    to John's company? Do we need to give each person a prospectus?
    Probably yes.

Sample 2:

July 16, 1990

Met with Mr. & Mrs. Doe and need to do the following:

1. Call their son James and let him know that his parents want the
    new contract delivered to him for safekeeping. I want it mailed by
    Airborne Express, or a form of mail that is registered so that we
    know it has been received, to either his office or home, whichever
    he prefers.

2. Before sending policy, make a complete (total) copy and send to Mr.
    Doe with a very nice letter—our thanks for his confidence, etc.—and
    that we have followed his instructions about mailing the contract to

his son. Also note that we will contact him a month in advance of the annual premium's due date next spring.

3. Put into the computer calendar in March to contact Mr. Doe about each child's portion of the premium due. Ask him how he wants us to proceed on collecting the premiums.

4. Change address of record to the son James' home address.

Additional Readings That Inform

Intriguing places, unusual discoveries, skills to be taught, new products on the market, and problems of the day all invite informative writing. The sampling of essays below illustrates some of the ways writers offer information to their readers.

America's Amazing Treasure Chest
Randy Fitzgerald

Randy Fitzgerald's essay about the Library of Congress is both informative and astonishing, a lively description of a genuine treasure chest.

Becoming an Active Reader

1. Before you begin this article, what do you know about the Library of Congress? What do you think it contains?

2. What expectations does the title phrase "treasure chest" create for you?

3. Notice that the author begins with three diverse incidents. What do these three incidents have in common?

1 • When U.S. troops landed in Grenada in 1983, dozens of reporters tried unsuccessfully to place operator-assisted calls to the island. One enterprising newsman got through, however. He called the Library of Congress and was given several key phone numbers from the Grenada telephone directory. With that information, he was able to place calls and obtain dramatic firsthand reports.

2 • In 1987, when actor Sam Waterston was preparing to play Abraham Lincoln in a TV mini-series, he wanted an authentic accent. At the Library of Congress he listened to rare recordings of regional dialects like those of Lincoln's boyhood.

3 • A New Yorker, planning to build a classic timber-frame sea-captain's house on an island off the coast of Maine, obtained plans of a similar

18th-century structure from the print and photo archives of the Library of Congress.

4   Called a time capsule of human knowledge, a storehouse of our national memory, the Library of Congress is all this and more. Located across the street from the U.S. Congress, this largest library in the world contains some 535 miles of shelves holding over 85 million items, just 20 million of which are books. There are more maps, globes, newsreels, recordings, sheet music, government documents and personal papers than anyplace else on earth. The library also boasts the oldest motion picture, the earliest example of printing and the smallest book every published.

5   Each day over 31,000 new books, periodicals and recordings pour into the library's mailroom. More contributions arrive from scholars, philanthropists, missionaries and other Americans who have something of interest to share.

6   A few years ago, a visitor mentioned to a reference librarian that he was the grandson of John Thompson Ford, owner of Ford's Theatre in Washington, D.C., where Abraham Lincoln was shot. The man possessed a collection of theater souvenirs from that period, and the librarian casually suggested he donate the materials to ensure their preservation. What John Ford Sollers, Sr., turned over in 1987 was a gold mine of playbills, scripts, scrapbooks, photos and letters—some relating to Lincoln's assassination. These joined the library's collection of items Lincoln had with him the night he was fatally shot, including two pairs of gold-rimmed glasses, a pocketknife and a billfold containing a $5 Confederate bill.

7   The Library of Congress embraces the entire globe. Three-quarters of its books are in one of 470 foreign languages. It has the largest Arab library in the world. There are more Tibetan holdings here than in Tibet and more pictures of pre-revolutionary Russia than in the Soviet Union itself.

8   You need no special credentials to use the library. Its 23 reading rooms are open to anyone with an avid curiosity. At any given moment, you might find an author doing research for a historical novel, a conductor poring over an original composition by Beethoven, a movie costume designer looking at photos of 19th-century fashions, an Indian family resurrecting tribal folklore or a grandmother charting her family history.

9   When the U.S. Congress moved from Philadelphia to Washington in 1800, $5000 worth of books were purchased to serve the needs of the legislators. But in 1814 British troops set fire to the Capitol building, and the entire library went up in flames. Former President Thomas Jefferson then sold his library of 6487 books as a replacement. The ten wagonloads constituted the largest and most sophisticated collection in the nation, covering every imaginable subject. In 1851 another fire broke out in the Capitol, destroying two-thirds of the library holding—including most of the Jefferson collection.

10   In 1870 Congress passed a law requiring anyone claiming a copyright on a book, chart, map, photograph, print, engraving or musical

composition to send two copies to the library. Soon it was inundated with material. Congress voted to build a separate structure to house the overflow. Opened in 1897, the granite building, an example of Italian Renaissance architecture, was a work of art. Some 50 artists created paintings and statues for the interior.

11   By 1935 that building, too, had filled with treasures. An even larger one was built across the street, and by 1965 that also was overflowing. Warehouses were leased outside Washington to store new items until construction of the James Madison Memorial Building was completed in 1980. This third building in the complex is not only larger than the first two structures combined, but also the biggest single library building in the world.

12   Of the library's nearly 5000 employees, about 900 work directly for the House and Senate as part of the Congressional Research Service—the largest applied-research staff in the world. Last year it answered more than 400,000 inquiries from members of Congress and their staffs. Other library employees distribute recordings, tapes and literature in Braille to over 700,000 of the nation's blind and physically handicapped each year.

13   The collection itself is so vast that you can find artifacts of information on almost every imaginable subject. The library's rare-book division, for example, boasts the most valuable printed volume of all, a Gutenberg Bible from 1455. The first book ever produced with movable type, it's one of only three perfect vellum copies in existence. There's a second-century papyrus fragment of Homer's *Iliad,* as well as the 1640 Massachusetts *Bay Psalm Book,* the earliest surviving book printed in North America.

14   There are also over 1500 miniature volumes, all less than four inches in height, dating from the 15th century to the present. Oddest of all is the smallest book ever printed, *Old King Cole,* from Scotland. Tinier than an ant, the book can be read only through a microscope or with a powerful magnifying glass.

15   You just need a good pair of eyes, though, to pore through the 11,000 collections of personal papers of men and women who have shaped American history. Jefferson's first draft of the Declaration of Independence is there, with handwritten notations by Ben Franklin and John Adams. The Orville and Wilbur Wright collection features the historic photo of their first powered flight near Kitty Hawk, N.C., in 1903, along with the triumphant telegram they sent their father.

16   The library also has four million maps inside two acres of storage cabinets. You can find maps of the moon, the sea beds and most cities of the world. Historic maps include a sailor's chart of the Mediterranean area drawn on sheepskin between 1320 and 1350, a 1482 edition of Ptolemy's atlas depicting the ends of the earth and maps from the 17th century showing California to be a giant island.

17   Other files hold some nine million photographs and negatives, 110,000 woodcuts, engravings and lithographs and 75,000 posters. The Master

Photographer Collection boasts originals from the inception of photography in the 1840s, including portraits of Presidents John Quincy Adams, James K. Polk and Andrew Jackson.

18   In the recordings division, you can listen to actress Sarah Bernhardt performing at the turn of the century, the voice of Kaiser Wilhelm II of Germany in 1904 or an 1898 speech by Buffalo Bill Cody. There are over 1.3 million musical and spoken-word recordings in all, ranging from 19th-century popular songs to tapes of early American radio broadcasts, such as Orson Welles's classic "War of the Worlds." Here, too, are vaudeville sketches, political speeches, literary readings, ethnic humor, as well as several thousand taped interviews of American GIs in the Pacific during World War II.

19   As part of its documentation of traditional folklife, the library maintains over 300,000 recorded songs, instrumentals and spoken tales from all over the world. Many are priceless. Among the cylinder recordings are the dances and chants of most American Indian tribes. "We see ourselves as protectors of folk arts that otherwise would be lost forever," explains Alan Jabbour, director of the American Folklife Center at the library. "The regional artistry of a Kentucky fiddler is like the creation of a species—if you lose that, the whole world is the poorer for it."

20   The staff of every great library fears destruction like the fire that ravaged the ancient library of Alexandria in 47 B.C. But these days the greatest danger comes from another kind of destroyer, one that smolders over many years. Books and documents printed since the mid-19th century used an acid-based paper-making process that gradually self-destructs, usually within 25 to 100 years. Up to 70,000 of the volumes in the Library of Congress become brittle or crumble to dust each year. Ironically, ancient manuscripts and books printed more than 150 years ago contain no acid and are not affected.

21   Over the past decade, however, library scientists have developed a de-acidification process that neutralizes the acids in the pages. Once this process becomes fully operational in 1991, it will resolve a pressing problem for the Library of Congress that also haunts every other library, archive and courthouse in the world.

22   To preserve other parts of our national heritage, newspapers are microfilmed immediately on receipt, motion pictures are stored in refrigerated vaults, manuscripts are fumigated to kill mold and insects, and maps are enclosed in polyester envelopes. Eventually, books may be preserved simply by scanning and storing each page digitally on optical discs, each of which has the capability of storing up to 10,000 pages indefinitely. This would help alleviate a monumental problem of the next century—storage space.

23   James H. Billington, who as Librarian of Congress directs this vast institution, sees it as a great resource for dealing with illiteracy and improving educational standards. He says, "It is also the individual's link with the memory, mind and imagination of all the rest of humanity."

Thinking about a Subject and Writing for Yourself:

Prompts for Journal Writing and Class Discussion

1. Fitzgerald's essay presents an astonishing amount and variety of detail. What strategies are used to present statistics, anecdotes, and historical background? Look over the catalogue in Chapter 15 to help you label the various methods.

2. What parts of the material are organized by classification? What other organizational patterns can be found in the essay?

3. Much of the information provided is surprising. What did you find the most incredible? Why do you think the author has included so much that is unusual and extraordinary?

4. From the description, what would you like to see or hear if you visit the Library of Congress? Why?

Strangers Can Enrich Your Life

Ardis Whitman

Ardis Whitman explains that strangers are just friends we haven't met and gives instructions for starting conversations. In addition to giving instructions, though, Whitman also works to persuade the readers that approaching strangers is a positive experience.

Becoming an Active Reader

1. Whitman's essay explains how to meet strangers, but before the process is presented, the essay first argues that strangers can enrich our lives. What is your feeling about meeting strangers? Do you feel ready to accept Whitman's ideas?

2. The title of the essay shows the author's enthusiasm about meeting strangers. What does this attitude suggest about the author? What kind of person do you think would enjoy meeting strangers? As you read, decide whether Whitman is the kind of person you expected.

1   It was a warm day in Nova Scotia, but I shivered as I stood on the station platform. The train was bringing a distinguished writer. As an editor of my college newspaper, I had been dispatched to greet him.

2   Eventually, the great man arrived, and after a tongue-tide moment I managed to say, "I write too."

3   He kindly replied, "Then we'll have a lot to talk about." But I was stricken mute, believing I had said the wrong thing.

4   It happens to all of us, this fear of strangers—at parties where we can't think of anything witty or important to say; in job interviews where we struggle to impress; anywhere, in fact, that we encounter interesting-looking people, but are too unsure of ourselves to start a conversation.

5   Yet, knowing how to meet people with ease enables us to widen the circle of our acquaintance—and enrich the fabric of our lives. During the years I traveled the world as a journalist, my conversations with strangers were among the most memorable events of my life—a constant opening of gift boxes, with no idea of what was inside. Indeed, the charm of the stranger lies precisely in the fact that we don't know him.

6   There was the nun from New Orleans who seemed gentle and uninvolved with the harsh world. But I soon found out that her job was putting tough young criminals back on their feet after prison. There was the prim, elderly woman encountered on a Canadian train who told me that she was traveling to a village on the Arctic Circle because she'd heard she could see polar bears walking in the streets there!

7   I've rarely talked to a stranger who did not contribute to my store of knowledge.

8   A gardener I met in a park told me more about how things grow than I had ever learned before—or since. A taxi driver in Egypt's Valley of the Kings invited me to tea in his family's earthen-floor home and helped me learn about a way of life very different from my own. In Oslo, Norway, a man who had been a Resistance fighter in World War II took me to a lonely plateau where the wind from the sea sighed in the grasses. There he told me of the hostages who were executed on that spot by the Nazis in retaliation for successful attacks by the Resistance.

9   The person we never met before can even teach us something about ourselves. For we may say things to a stranger that we've always wanted to say, but never dared mention to family or friends, and thus see ourselves through new eyes.

10   With luck, a chance meeting with a stranger can also result in a lifetime friendship. Recently I re-read a letter from someone I had known for 30 years. Our relationship began on a bench in Pennsylvania Station in New York City, while we waited for a train. Come to think of it, weren't nearly all our friends once strangers? As a sign in a park I've visited says: "There are no strangers in the world; only friends waiting to be met."

11   So how can we learn to make the most of an encounter with a stranger? Although there is no magic formula, there are certain approaches that may open the door:

12   *1. Comment honestly on how you are feeling.* At a dinner party, for example, you may be thinking, *I'm too shy for gatherings like this.* Or conversely, *A lot of people find parties like these a bore, but I love them.*

13   Whatever it is, say it to the first person who seems ready to listen. You may find your sentiments echoed exactly. In any case, it's far better to

say frankly "I am shy" or "I'm a stranger here" than to come off seeming stiff and unfriendly. The best conversationalist is the one who has the wit and courage to be honest. And—as a bonus—if we speak honestly about ourselves, the other person will feel free to say what he is thinking.

14   Once I talked to a psychologist who had written a brilliant book. I usually found such interviews comfortable and rewarding, so it was a shock to realize that I was so terrified I could hardly begin. Finally I said, "I don't understand it, but I am afraid of you." He found the statement intriguing, and conversation came naturally after that.

15   *2. Talk about the surroundings.* If you have an active curiosity, you will see something to remark on. One time, a stranger looked about appraisingly and broke the ice with me, saying, "What a comment on the human race a cocktail party is!" Now there was a lively beginning for a conversation.

16   I remember a very reserved woman I sat beside for several hours on a train. No amount of effort on my part produced anything interesting until about a half-hour before we were due to separate. We were passing an inlet of the ocean when we both caught sight of a house that sat all by itself on a distant promontory. She watched it until it had vanished. Then she said suddenly, "When I was little, I lived in a lighthouse in a lonely place like that," and went on to bring alive both the desolation and the beauty of such a life.

17   *3. Say something about your companion.* I once heard a woman say to an obvious stranger, "You have a lovely, lovely face." Perhaps most of us wouldn't have the courage for that, but we can say something like: "I saw you across the room when you came in and I thought . . . ." Or, "You are reading my favorite book."

18   *4. Ask questions.* Many unforgettable conversations start with a query. I often ask people, "What is a day in your working life like?" Usually they'll respond enthusiastically.

19   *5. Listen to the answers.* Half of a good conversation is in the listening, and there can be no real dialogue without it. But it, too, is an art.

20   Look at your new acquaintance intently as she talks. Respond in a way that will encourage her to continue. Listening then becomes not passive but active, an explorer's journey. The purpose of good conversation—as opposed to small talk—is simply this: to discover and understand each other.

21   So what can you in turn bring to a conversation? Remember this: people are as curious about you as you are about them, and you can add to their lives as they add to yours. A one-way talk involving only the other person is no better than one involving only you.

22   The trouble is that very few people realize what they have to give. Sometimes they think of themselves as shy or dull and they tell me,

"Nothing much has happened to me." They are almost always wrong. The truth is that most people are interesting.

23   In her book *Speech Can Change Your Life,* Dorothy Sarnoff wrote: "There really is something wonderful about every imperfect, mixed-up, uncertain human being." So when I talk with you, I have before me a marvelous puzzle. What kind of person are you? What sort of story do you have to tell?

24   Too many of us try to say what is expected of us and worry because we see ourselves as different from others. But it's just at the point of that difference that all the drama lies; and when we honestly disclose ourselves to each other with no other purpose than to understand and be understood, a moving encounter is in progress.

25   We need the stimulus of the stranger, the person who is not like us, who for a little while is a mystery to us. Besides, an encounter with the stranger never leaves you as it finds you. At its best, it is a meeting of hearts and minds, a meeting that will always thereafter be part of the substance of your life.

26   Moreover, encounters with strangers may allow us to make a small contribution to our world, for they can persuade us not to think of our fellow humans, however different they seem at first, as alien but rather as caring, suffering, exploring, enjoying people—just like ourselves.

27   There is no shortage of people in the world. So open your heart and enjoy. Reach out—and meet someone.

Thinking about a Subject and Writing for Yourself:

Prompts for Journal Writing and Class Discussion

1. Whitman offers many personal experiences to show that the suggestions work. What picture do you get of Whitman's persona as we read? Do you believe that you, too, will get the same results?

2. Are Whitman's guidelines meant to be used in sequence? Why or why not?

3. What parts of the essay are ordered by classification? What parts by cause-effect? Do you see other logical patterns in the essay?

4. What do Whitman's personal anecdotes reveal about people in general? What do they reveal about Whitman?

5. Have you ever wanted to start a conversation with a stranger? Have you ever taken such a chance? If not, what stopped you? If so, what happened?

6. Is Whitman's advice realistic in today's world? Under what circumstances would you hesitate to follow this advice? Under what circumstances would you feel safe enough to consider doing so?

A Letter's Better
Letitia Baldridge

Like the Whitman essay, Letitia Baldridge's instructions on letter writing first show readers that the activities presented will enrich their lives.

Becoming an Active Reader

1. Are you a letter-writer? Do you write often? Under what circumstances?

2. Baldridge's title is a bit ambiguous. "Better than what?" you should ask. Do you agree that letters are better?

3. Look at the opening paragraph. What do you learn about Baldridge? Why do you think she has given you this information in the first paragraph? What is your feeling toward her now that you have this information?

1   During the years I worked in the White House and served as an adviser to four First Ladies, I was continually impressed by these busy women's grace and promptness in writing thank-you letters. Jacqueline Kennedy, for example, always sent charming, witty notes the day after flowers arrived.

2   Other forms of modern communication—telephone, CB radio, computer—are faster, but none has the warmth, personal appeal and longevity of a letter. The problem, of course, is that the right words are sometimes difficult to summon in times of stress—such as when you are grieving over a friend's loss or you want to apologize. And even a simple thank-you note may be skipped because you are afraid of sounding stilted, unnatural or phony.

3   Don't let such concerns stop you. When you are motivated by kindness and consideration, it is hard to go wrong. The thought is what matters. With knowledge of a few basic rules—and a little practice—almost anyone can become a great letter writer.

When to Write

4   There are many good reasons for corresponding other than just keeping in touch with a loved one. Thank-yous—for presents, favors, dinners, weekends—are an obvious must for ordinary people as well as First Ladies. The putting of pen to paper (or fingers to type-writer) should also be automatic response upon hearing important news of a relative, friend or business associate. This could be a happy event (a marriage, new baby, job promotion) or a sad one (a death, illness or divorce). It could even be one of those bittersweet milestones in between, such as a retirement or a move. Writing can also be a tool of diplomacy; it is often the easiest means of apologizing or taking the first step to make up after a quarrel.

5   A good letter states its purpose in the first paragraph. Try to start with a word other than "I" and to put any bad news near the beginning. It's best to close with something friendly and cheerful. Always try to end on an "up" note.

Replying to an Invitation

6   A formal invitation requires a written reply, but so many people are derelict in this duty that many invitations now include as RSVP card with a self-addressed, stamped envelope. All you have to do is check if off and mail it back. Personally I find this appalling. I prefer the formal reply that begins: *Mr. and Mrs. Andrew Cummings accept with pleasure the kind invitation of* . . . and is set up like a wedding invitation.

7   When you must decline an invitation, I think it is especially important to write a letter of explanation. Checking off a "Regrets" box on a reply card is just too cold. Such a letter might go something like this:

8   *You cannot imagine how sad we are to have to miss the big day, but we've already made travel plans that cannot be changed. I'm sure Cynthia will be the most beautiful bride in the world. We will be with you in spirit, and look forward to seeing the pictures and hearing all about it when we get home. In the meantime, please give Cynthia and Jim our best wishes.*

9   If your excuse is something your hostess might consider unimportant or easily changed—a tennis date, say—it's better to cite no reason at all. Just emphasize your regret at being unable to attend such a special occasion.

Expressing Your Appreciation

10   The thank-you note is not just a formality, it's a positive act of friendship. Every gift—Christmas, birthday, graduation, housewarming—deserves one. The considerate recipient writes promptly—within a week, if possible.

11   The bride who receives a great many presents is allowed three months to acknowledge them. Delaying longer than six months is considered bad manners. She might try writing a few notes every day so she doesn't get so tired that she resorts to boring, trite letters. She can also share the task. Here, for example, is a nice note from a groom:

12   *Sally and I really like your casserole. It's good-looking and it certainly "goes from oven to table" in our household. We have even become competitive as to who can come up with the most exotic recipe to prepare in it. Since we seem to use it almost every night, you obviously hit the spot.*

13   *As soon as we get the apartment in order, we'd like you to visit.*

14   Most gifts do get acknowledged eventually. It's the thank-you letter for a party or a meal that's the most neglected form of etiquette today. A phone call is not enough. It may come at an inconvenient time, making it a nuisance rather than a pleasure. When you write a note, on the other hand, the recipient can reread it and show it to others.

15   Give the matter some thought. *We had a very good time last night.
Thank you so much for having us* . . . won't do. You need to recall details
and some flavor of the evening. Sample:

16   *We had a terrific time at your house last night. Bill and I agree that we
have never tasted a roast lamb like that one. And your table was so pretty!*

17   *It was a cozy group, and we loved meeting your friends, the Jenkinses.
They're really a lot of fun. Thanks from us both for a perfect evening.*

18   If the food was terrible or the guest of honor impossible, you need not
lie. Just write a short note expressing how much you enjoyed seeing your
friend.

Celebrating Happy News

19   A note to someone close to you should be warm and friendly. To an
individual you know less well—an older person perhaps, or a superior at
work—the tone can be more formal.

20   To a good friend, who has just given birth, for example, you might
write:

21   *I am dancing with joy for you. A beautiful, healthy baby girl! I hope
she'll play tennis like her father and have a combination of both your
brains.*

22   Years later a letter to the same pal might go like this: *There it was,
jumping out of the morning paper at us, the announcement that Elizabeth
had won a full college scholarship. You both must be so proud.*

23   On the other hand, a letter to the chairman of your company or
your church pastor would be written in a more restrained manner. For
example:

24   *I can imagine how proud you must be of the newest addition to your
family. We have all heard that George is a beautiful little boy. I hope
your wife is feeling well and that both she and the baby are home now.
Everyone here joins me in sending all three of you our warmest congratulations.*

Commiserating over Bad News

25   You should write immediately when someone close to you has had a
sad experience. A friend of mine, whose son was jailed on a drug charge,
received a letter from a neighbor. It had such a profoundly salutory effect
on her and her husband that she allowed me to use it, with the names
changed.

26   *. . . We just heard about Freddie's arrest. Bill and I are standing at the
ready to do ANYTHING to help you and Herb. Allow us to act. We love
that boy. We can research the very best lawyer for you* . . . We'll run your
errands, do your cooking . . . *You will make us feel better by letting us
help. . . .*

27   There are, of course, times when it's better to pretend not to have
heard bad news. If your friend's husband was picked up on a morals
charge, but the scandal never made the newspaper, it's best to ignore it

—unless *she* brings it up. In that case, listen sympathetically, then reaffirm your feelings in writing.

28   When a friend's baby is born deformed or retarded, it cannot be kept a secret. Your letter should be short and compassionate.

29   *The news about the baby breaks my heart, but knowing you both, I'm sure you'll shoulder the problems with energy and dignity—and that the baby will bring you great happiness. Hank and I are thinking of you and hoping you will let us help in some way.*

30   For someone who's ill or injured, remember that a printed greeting card is not enough. A note should be written on the card itself, or a letter tucked inside. First offer sympathy and then try to make the person laugh. Relate the latest office or neighborhood gossip. Tell the newest joke or the corniest one you ever heard. If someone close to you is bedbound, try to write every few days—even if it's only a few sentences.

31   The same degree of loving care should be expended on the friend who's lost a job. Being fired is an isolating, depressing, even shocking experience. It's important to get off a quick note, pointing out the person's assets and issuing an invitation to lunch or dinner "so we can put our heads together and come up with some really creative thinking." Such letters of friendship are never forgotten.

Expressing Condolences

32   The sympathy letter is, of course, the toughest of them all. It should be written the minute you learn about a death, even if that's months later. The bereaved family expects to hear from you if you are a relative, a good friend or someone who used to be. A note—even one from a casual acquaintence—is always appreciated. If in doubt, write it.

33   Try to accomplish several things in a letter of condolence:

34
- Express your understanding of the family's grief, even if the deceased was elderly and suffered a great deal in the end. For example: *It's hard to believe he is gone. He meant so much to us. The pain of losing him must be terrible for you.*

35
- Relate some personal memories. Tell an anecdote that the family might not know about. *I will never forget the time she sent me a note when I was in the hospital. 'All I can afford is one flower,' she wrote. Accompanying her letter was a pink crepe-paper carnation with a three-foot stem. The blossom had the circumference of large umbrella and cheered up the entire hospital.*

36
- If the family does not know you, begin by explaining your relationship to the deceased: *We used to play tennis together after work once a week* or *I sat next to her in the church choir.*

37
- Ask if you can be of assistance.

38
- If the deceased was a religious person and you are too, your words can be of special comfort. *I am praying for him, and you are in m~ prayers too, because these are such dark days.*

39   • When you lose someone very close to you, let your emotions show in your letter: *I can't bear to think she will no longer be at the other end of the telephone. She was my friend, my adviser, my comforter. I grieve for you, for all of her family, but I grieve for myself too. She meant so very much to me.*

40   A beautifully expressed letter of condolence is indeed never easy to write, but it is appreciated above all others.

Appearance Counts

41   We send ourselves with our letters, and we should take pride in their appearance. Formal letters have traditionally been handwritten in black ink on white or ecru paper, but colored stationery is acceptable for most purposes today. (Ink should still be black, navy or brown, however.) If your handwriting is as illegible as mine, you will be forgiven for typing your letters. Either way, they should be centered neatly on the page with healthy margins.

42   Don't fret about spelling, punctuation or grammar; a dictionary can help you avoid obvious errors. The important thing is to get the letter finished and mailed. I happen to write the way I talk, but many people prefer a more formal mode of expression. The key thing is to sound natural— and that means writing in your own style.

Be Sure before You Write

43   To follow my own advice and end on an "up" note, I offer a small, rueful warning. Before you send off a letter in response to a piece of news, check its accuracy. I know whereof I speak, having caused embarrassment to myself and others by reacting to rumors that proved to be false. Once I wrote a woman friend about her divorce when she was still very much married—and happily so. I also wrote a lengthy sympathy letter to the family of another friend who, despite what I'd heard, was alive and well. "Goodness!" she told me later, laughing, "I had no idea I possessed all the virtues you described in your letter to my parents. You had better treat me with respect!"

44   Naturally I had to try to undo my gaffes by writing additional letters of apology.

Thinking about a Subject and Writing for Yourself:

Prompts for Journal Writing and Class Discussion

1. Baldridge offers some general guidelines about letter-writing for any occasion. Summarize her advice.
2. What logical patterns organize this essay? Are the bold-faced subheadings in the essay a good clue to its organization patterns? Why or why not?

3. Baldridge gives five occasions which merit written response. Following her recommendations and her models, write a letter for each occasion. You may write in response to actual or to imagined events.

4. After writing, comment on her directions. Did they make your task easier and your letters more effective than usual? Do you have more confidence in your ability to write personal letters?

5. What letters have you received in the last few years? Do any of them stand out as special? Why? Do you have a friend who is an effective letter writer? If so, what makes his/her letters better than others?

Kid's Program a Delight to Use
Michael Himowitz

Michael Himowitz writes a newspaper column, Himowitz on Computers, *that is "user-friendly." In other words, you do not have to be a computer genius to understand his discussions.*

Becoming an Active Reader

1. How much do you know about computers? Do you "feel" anything toward computers? What kinds of feelings might various audiences have toward computers?

2. The title of the article identifies its subject as a "kid's program." Do you think Himowitz targets children as his audience? Where was this essay first published?

1   Ever since my son became old enough to recognize the letters on the keyboard, he has been interested in using his computer for word processing.

2   He has an ulterior motive; penmanship is not one of his strong points. I was worried about that and deliberately held off using the computer for word processing, figuring it would be better if he mastered the mechanics of handwriting first.

3   But eventually his teacher encouraged me, and I set about trying to find word processing software suitable for a 9-year-old.

4   That is not as easy as it sounds. Most word processing programs are fairly complex. The 80-character screen displays are too confusing for younger children, and the setup required to make the software do "interesting" things that creative children enjoy is too complicated.

5   Last week I stumbled on The Children's Writing & Publishing Center from The Learning Company, a delightful program that makes writing easy and fun.

6   In fact, The Children's Writing & Publishing Center goes a step further, adding graphics and desktop publishing features that turn the software into a creative tool for youngsters.

7   The version I bought, for the Apple IIe, came on three disks. One contains the program, one contains the graphics and the third is for storage of documents.

8   The 100-page manual is clearly written and well-suited for children. However, at the outset it recommends that parents work with their youngsters to familiarize them with the program. It is good advice.

9   When you run the program, you get a colorful graphics menu with three choices: start a report, start a newsletter or retrieve a document from disk.

10   The "report" and "newsletter" are the two formats the program supports. The report prints everything in one column across an entire page. The newsletter breaks the page into two columns.

11   Once you have selected your format, you create a heading for it. The heading is a large banner printed at the top of the page. It can have both graphics and text.

12   The graphics are selected from a disk with 97 different pictures, including people, animals, trucks, planes, birds, holiday symbols, sports figures, monsters, maps and other illustrations. The program will also load graphics created by the popular Print Shop and Print Master programs.

13   With the cursor keys or a mouse, you can place the graphic at the right or left side of the banner. Then it is time to type the text. A simple menu choice lets you select eight different type styles and sizes. With a single keystroke, you can center the text or set it flush with the right or left margins.

14   Then it is time to work on the body of the document. The commands are the same. You can type text or select a graphic at any time. When you place a picture, the type automatically flows around it. If you place your pictures on a page first, you can type in text later, and the words will automatically wrap around the graphics.

15   The type is big and easy to read—a must for youngsters. At any time, you can get a quick look at the layout of your entire document in thumbnail form, which shows the placement of text and graphics on every page.

16   That is really all there is to it. No worries about page length, margins or tab settings. The program takes care of it. With a little help from mom or dad, a child should be able to pick up everything he needs to know in an hour.

17   On-screen help is clear and plentiful. In fact, help screens automatically pop up as you move from one step to the next, a feature you can turn off once you are familiar with the program.

18   The Writing and Publishing Center supports a wide variety of printers. Just choose yours from a menu (that is probably a job for Mom or Dad).

19   If you have a color printer, the program will print its own graphics in color, although graphics created by other programs are printed in black-and-white.

20   The program worked flawlessly with our Star NX-100 Rainbow, an inexpensive color printer that has given us much pleasure (the Star emulates Epson's color machines).

21   No one will mistake the output for a high-end desktop publishing system, but it is clear, legible and, thanks to the graphics, entertaining. For home or school use, it is great.

22   The program retails for $49.95. For information, contact The Learning Company, 6493 Kasier Drive, Fremont, California 94555.

Thinking about a Subject and Writing for Yourself:

Prompts for Journal Writing and Class Discussion

1. Himowitz creates a non-threatening persona in the first paragraphs. Two questions: *how* does he make his persona seem ordinary and accessible, and *why* does he make a point of talking about a technical subject in everyday language? What does his persona tell you about his understanding of his audience?

2. For all his casual tone, Himowitz does use computer terminology. Find some examples of such diction. Does he define all terms? Why or why not? What does his diction tell you about his audience?

3. Summarize the criteria that Himowitz uses to evaluate this software. Are his criteria controversial? Do you think that most of his readers will agree with his ideas of what is important?

4. What information about the software does Himowitz's evaluation supply? Do you have enough information to make a decision about buying it?

5. Does Himowitz offer a clear opinion of the software?

Cities Find Pit Bull Laws Hard to Enact, Enforce
Fred Bayles

Fred Bayles writes about a controversial issue, the efforts of cities to ban pit bulls from their limits.

Becoming an Active Reader

1. Pit bull owners defend their dogs but others see the dogs as vicious and unpredictable. What is your attitude toward pit bulls?

2. Does your city have an ordinance restricting pit bulls or other so-called "vicious" breeds? What do you think about such laws?

1   LYNN, Mass.—Michael Barry has spent a year researching canine blood lines. Not a dog breeder but a city attorney, Barry is seeking a way to keep pit bulls out of Lynn.

2   "The question has taken up our time, but we're glad we've done it," said Barry, who has already faced one court test of a city ordinance that puts special constraints on pit bull owners. "The number of incidents with pit bulls has gone down dramatically."

3   Spurred by attacks on humans by such dogs, cities and towns across the country are looking for a legal response, ranging from outright bans on the breed to ordinances carrying heavy fines for irresponsible owners.

4   The Humane Society of the United States estimates some 40 communities have passed laws or are considering legislation.

5   But passing and enforcing such laws is difficult. Laws aimed at one breed nearly always bring well-organized challenges from owners' groups and kennel clubs.

6   "Lots of communities are panicking and passing laws that turn out to be unconstitutional," said Madeline Bernstein, a vice president and attorney with the American Society for the Prevention of Cruelty to Animals. "You have to respect the rights of legitimate owners and you have to remember the dog has rights, too."

7   The debate centers around pit bulls, an umbrella term for dogs of several breeds including the Staffordshire Bull Terrier, the American Staffordshire Terrier, the American Pit Butt Terrier and, sometimes, the Bull Terrier, known as companion to both Gen. George Patton Jr. and villain Bill Sikes in the movie musical "Oliver," and more recently, as Spuds MacKenzie, the "party dog" in TV beer commercials.

8   The animals weigh 40 to 60 pounds and have powerful chest, neck and jaw muscles.

9   Devoted owners say the dogs are smart and affectionate. They point to such American icons as Buster Brown's dog, Tige; Pete, the dog in the Our Gang comedies; and the RCA Victor dog as examples of the breeds' finer qualities.

10   But the breeds have a sinister reputation. Bred over centuries for dog fighting, a vicious, now illegal blood sport, pit bulls are tenacious, aggressive animals.

11   They are considered dangerous because of their tendency to lock onto a victim with their powerful jaws. Donald Clifford, a veterinarian and director of laboratory animal medicine at the Medical College of Ohio in Toledo, said his study of the animals makes him believe their "gameness" sets them apart from other breeds.

12   "Other dogs will eventually quit an attack, whereas pit bulls continue to fight," he said. "You read how once they lock onto a little kid, it's goodbye little kid. They don't injure you a little bit. They continue to drill in."

13   Moreover, problems associated with pit bulls are exacerbated by some of their owners, according to Michael Ushijima, general counsel for the 200,000-member American Dog Owners Association. Many owners, including drug dealers, are attracted to the breed by its reputation of toughness and train the dogs to be vicious.

14   "The problem is not with American Pit Bull Terriers, it's with jerks and idiots who own them," Ushijima said. "If they eliminated this breed, the jerks would turn to another one."

15   Some 25,000 pit bull dogs are registered with various kennel clubs. But Kate Rindy, a Humane Society researcher, estimates that up to half a million dogs have some pit bull ancestry.

16   According the Humane Society, five deaths have been attributed to pit bulls in 1987. Last year, seven of 13 such deaths were blamed on pit bulls.

17   The more recent cases include:

18

- A 67-year-old man in Kettering, Ohio, mauled by two pit bulls while visiting another home.

19   • A 16-month-old girl killed by a family pet in Jones, Oklahoma.

20   • The on-camera attack of a Los Angeles animal control officer investigat-

21   ing an earlier attack by a pit bull. The officer's hand was crushed.

- $2^1/_2$-year-old Santa Clara, California, boy fatally savaged by a neighbor's dog. The child was killed when he wandered into a yard where the dog was guarding his master's marijuana patch.

22   The laws passed in response to such attacks have met with varying levels of acceptance.

23   In Lynn, where Barry said four or five attacked had been recorded in the past two years, an attack on a mailman prompted a temporary mail boycott of the street where the dog lived. City officials then refused to register any more pit bulls.

24   "The intent was that if any new pit bulls were brought in, they would be banned from the city," said Barry.

25   But a court challenge by several groups, including the dog owners association, succeeded in removing the ban. Pit bull owners now must keep their dogs in secured areas and take them off the property only to visit a vet. That section of the the ordinance is also under appeal.

26   Dog owners have also challenged a law in Cincinnati that bans sale or possession of pit bulls within the city limits. Assistant City Solicitor Bob Johnstone said the law was working.

27   "Four or five dogs were turned over to the city and destroyed," he said, "We haven't had an incident in quite a while."

28   In Chester, Pa., a year-old law that requires owners to carry hefty liability policies and pay $500 annual fees to license their pit bulls was recently upheld in U.S. District Court.

29   But dog advocates say any law that tries to target one breed of dog will eventually fall to court appeals.

30   "They are being thrown out because of vagueness," said Roy Carlberg, executive secretary of the American Kennel Club. "A majority of the dogs in this country are of the non-descript variety. How could someone be expected to discern whether a dog manifests characteristics of a certain breed?"

31   The ASPCA, the AKC and other dog owner groups endorse laws aimed at all vicious dogs and irresponsible owners. The Los Angeles City Council last week passed an ordinance giving animal officers the power to immediately impound any dog that bites a person and destroy the animal if it is deemed dangerous.

32   Washington state has a law carrying a manslaughter sentence for the owner of any dog that severely injures or causes a human death.

33   Ushijima said such so-called vicious dog ordinances were fairer and easier to enforce.

34   "One of the major problems with a law that singles out one breed is identifying the dog," he said. "We know what Lassie looks like, but that doesn't mean all collies look like that. There is no scientific test to determine what breed an individual dog is."

Thinking about a Subject and Writing for Yourself:

Prompts for Journal Writing and Class Discussion

1. What controversies does Bayles report about the breed itself?
2. What problems does Bayles identify with the laws against pit bulls?
3. Can you identify Bayles' attitude toward pit bulls? toward the laws? Explain your answer, giving details from his writing.
4. What effect does the list of attacks have on your reaction to the problem? Does it belong in an objective report? Why or why not?
5. After reading this article, how would you summarize the issues involved in restricting pit bulls?

SUMMARY

As this chapter illustrates, writing that informs is part of academic and professional writing as well as personal writing. Any number of strategies and patterns can be used to present your material; the distinguishing feature of informative writing is its neutral tone. When you write to provide information for an audience, remember to present your material without bias.

Y O U R   T U R N

Invitations to Write to Inform

Your world is filled with invitations to produce informative writing. Academic contexts repeatedly demand such work; in addition, both on the job and in your everyday life you will find yourself explaining and reporting again and again. You will want your audiences to understand the procedures that must be followed, the sources that should be contacted, or the locations of equipment and information. You will need to explain what has been done, to evaluate changes and traditions, or to report on ideas and proceedings. Written instructions about feeding the dog and watering the plant are informative writings; so, too, are reports of committee activities and lists of community resources. Situations that invite, even demand, informative written responses are virtually endless.

Sometimes your readers will want information about existing programs or problems. You might be expected to explain the background of an event or a place, to explain the resources available in your community, or to explain a situation without taking a side. These kinds of explanations often involve research followed by a report on what you have discovered. Here are some samples:

1. You are part of a committee to welcome newcomers to your campus or community. One of your projects is a booklet that describes available resources. You are expected to choose an area and develop a thorough, organized survey of the programs and resources available to residents. Some suggestions include campus and community resources for:

   • handicapped students;
   • health care;
   • inexpensive, nourishing food;
   • health problems, including substance abuse and mental health problems;
   • health and fitness, focusing on open-to-the public options and/or private facilities;
   • inexpensive entertainment;
   • historic sites or other tourist attractions;
   • the arts.

2. You have noticed that the air quality in your community has been rated as "poor" for most of the past month, and you decide to find out about the problem. A small local group of conservation activists learns of your efforts and asks you for a report of the problem. The group does not need an opinion from you; it will use your information to make a decision about a possible group response to the problem. Some research will probably be required.

   Variation: Report to the conservation group about any environmental problems in your area, from litter to toxic waste.

3. You have watched, listened, and read as two groups have debated the existence of a Constitutional right to burn the American flag. You can see that the two sides are emotionally involved and you believe that neither side is really listening to the other. So, you

write a letter to the editor of your local paper that summarizes what you believe to be the major issues expressed by each side. You do not express your own opinion; your letter intends to reduce the rhetoric and name-calling to a rational of the two major positions.

Many reports on resources, backgrounds, or issues do not expect you to judge or to recommend, but there will be times when you are asked to evaluate your subject. Your evaluation might assign ratings to a list of restaurants, or you might be asked to recommend a summer camp or a veterinarian or a teacher. In such cases, your report should include both information and judgment. Here are some samples:

4. Your knowledge of stereo equipment (or some other mystical technology like computer hardware or culinary appliances or power tools) has made you a legend among your peers. In fact, you have been invited to write a weekly column describing and evaluating both the newest entries in the field and the classic models still on the market. For your opening column, you decide to explain the basic equipment necessary for even the rankest novice. Explain a moderately priced initial set-up, planning as much as possible to avoid immediate obsolescence and to allow for future expansion. You anticipate that your column is not for the general reader, but you do want to be understood by a beginner seeking information.

5. As your high school class prepares for its fifth reunion, you are asked to recommend a place for the day's events. The Activities Committee has planned a day of picnics, volleyball games, softball, and similar outdoor activities. You know that some of your classmates are married and have small children, and that most will come with companions. The estimated attendance, total, is approximately 180 people. Recommend to the committee a facility that will accommodate the reunion plans. Include information about fees or restrictions. Be sure to explain the criteria used in selecting this site.

   Variation: Recommend a facility for a different purpose. For example, recommend an auditorium for your child's dance recital, or a hotel for a convention, or a recreational facility for a family vacation, or a site for a movie location shoot.

6. Your child has been part of the school district's gifted and talented resource program for three years. A friend whose child has been labelled "gifted" is moving into the area soon and asks you to explain the program and rate its effectiveness. After checking with the local school district to make sure that your facts are straight, you send her your descriptive evaluation of the program.

Variation: Any program can be the subject of such a report. Consider these possibilities: a local effort to feed the homeless, a community arts program, a city recreation program, an annual campus festival, a statewide competition, a racquetball regional championship, a feeder program for high school varsity athletics, a beauty pageant, a diet program.

Knowing how things work might cast you in the role of expert. When you are called upon to explain how the company operates or what steps should be followed, your information about processes and procedures should be clear and organized. Here are some samples:

7. After you have been employed at a particular place for four years, you are promoted to training supervisor. Your first assignment is to write a handout for new employees that explains daily workplace procedures, including uniform or dress code, behavior toward customers and toward other employees, and any other areas you feel are important. The turnover rate in this job is high, and the average new employee is a high school student beginning a first job, earning minimum hourly wages. No intelligence requirements must be met for the job, but you do not want to insult your audience with overly-simple directions.

   Variation: You may choose to explain a specific procedure to a traineee.

8. Your experience in the family business (or your experience in a previous job) has given you inside information about some process that is mysterious to the average citizen. People who know your job experience often ask you how such things are done; in fact, a friend who lives in another area has asked you to explain in detail. You respond enthusiastically with a letter that explains the trade secrets. Possible topics include the raising of future fast-food fried chickens, the manufacture of paper clips, the production of billboards, the process of embalming, the disposal of toxic waste, the procedures for offering and accepting bribes, or the operation of a police vehicle.

9. As an older student on campus, you have found that much of what you feared about returning to school was only a figment of an anxious imagination. Write to a friend who is afraid to return to school, demystifying one process that really terrified you when you first thought of coming back to school. Was it the initial inquiry at the registrar's office? Computerized registration? The first day of classes? Assume that your friend's fears are a mirror of your own, and help him to understand the procedure.

SUGGESTED APPROACHES TO YOUR RESPONSE

A key difference separates informative writing from other kinds of writing: your objective approach to the material. Regardless of the controversial nature of your subject, if your purpose is to increase understanding rather than to convince readers to accept your ideas, your persona must remain unbiased. Therefore, as you gather, draft, and revise your material, keep your approach impartial.

❏ **The First Decision: To Accept the Invitation to Write**

When you decide to accept the invitation to write, you begin your response by gathering material. You may find that you know a great deal about the topic and that your major efforts will be directed to organizing and polishing your draft. But you may also discover that you need more information to offer a thorough report or analysis to your readers. The following diagram (Figure 3–1) illustrates **some** of the resources available to you:

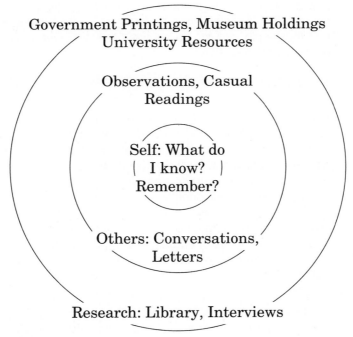

Government Printings, Museum Holdings
University Resources

Observations, Casual
Readings

Self: What do
I know?
Remember?

Others: Conversations,
Letters

Research: Library, Interviews

Figure 3-1

Two Reminders:

   Written notes are more reliable than mental ones.
   Using clusters and cubes will help you recall material and see connections between ideas.

> **Cross-Reference:** Check the catalogue of pre-writing strategies in Chapter 6 for more information about the following:
>
> - Cubing
> - Clustering
> - Forcing Assoications
> - Probing for Patterns
>
> Gathering futher information by research: Check Chapter 19 for information about field research and about library investigations.

When you have collected a body of material, your critical voice should review it, identifying connections between ideas and noting recurring ideas to help you define your thesis.

Reminder:

The thesis will sometimes be easier to define after you have compiled material into a rough draft. Do not be anxious if it is not evident when you review your notes.

> **Cross-Reference:** Chapters 8 and 20 will review attitudes and strategies for critical review of material and identification for controlling idea.

❏ The Second Decision: To Draft a Response

Trying to make one draft accomplish several goals can be a major obstacle to confident drafting. If you accept from the beginning that you will probably need more than one draft, you can remove much of the pressure on yourself and draft to achieve one goal at a time. All of the following are reasonable goals for your drafts:

1. **The earliest drafts need only to put material in prose.** Review your material and do some tentative groupings of ideas, then write out those ideas in complete sentences. Do not be overly concerned about organization; many writers find it easier to organize material after they can see it on paper.

2. **Drafts will help you to identify both thin and well-developed areas.** Once material is compiled into prose, you can readily see which points need more discussion. Recognize strengths, too, by marking points that seem clear and well-supported.

3. **Drafts will help you to recognize logical connections.** Your material often suggests its own organizational patterns. Compar-

isons, chronologies, and classifications show themselves as you put material into prose.

4. **Drafts will help you to define your thesis.** If you have not yet selected a thesis, looking at a rough draft can reveal recurring ideas and points that seem to cluster in support of main points.

Cross-Reference: Chapter 19 catalogues various organization patterns; Chapter 13 encourages you to review the logic of the connections you have identified.

Like organization, **method of presentation** is often determined by the amount and kind of material you want to include. For example:

Material	Method of Presentation
Instruction/ process:	Steps
Mass of material:	List or classification
Trend or development:	Tracing/chronology
Characterization:	Direct quotation/dialogue

Reminder:

"America's Amazing Treasure Chest" (p. 56) illustrates varied methods of presentation. Some passages list, some trace, others explain processes.

Cross-Reference: For a review of **methods of presentation,** look at the catalogue in Chapter 11; in particular, see:

- Listing
- Defining Literally
- Tracing
- Presenting a Process
- Using Analogies
- Citing Examples
- Quoting
- Paraphrasing
- Explaining

❑ **The Third Decision: To Review the Work in Progress**

Connecting Audience, Content, and Purpose

Your first drafts organize and develop ideas. As you work, think about the audience and the reaction you would like to evoke. What could you say to achieve that response? How should you sound so that you and your ideas will be respected? Your audience, your purpose, and the content and organization of your draft, should be logically connected.

Knowledge:

- Are you introducing something new or explaining something familiar in more detail?
- What specific knowledge is needed to understand this report or explanation?
- What experience has your audience had with this topic?
- Is your audience likely to be confused by this material?
- Are you using any technical or obscure vocabulary?

Attitudes:

- Does this topic inspire strong feelings that might get in the way of rational discussion?
- If so, does your audience have a definite emotional stance to be considered? Might they already feel frightened or angry or sympathetic when this topic is mentioned?
- Would your audience find expert testimony convincing? Have you cited your sources?

Expectations:

- Would your audience be reassured by a familiar tone and casual diction? Or would they feel patronized?
- Is your most effective persona an authority? A fellow citizen also learning? A voice sympathetic to their confusion? A reassuring, parent type?

Reminder:

It is better to repeat than to leave out essential material.

Cross-Reference: If you need more information on analyzing your audience, review Chapter 14.

Reminder:

When your reader-directed draft is complete, ask a friend to read your work and report on his or her reactions.

Polishing the Draft

One of your biggest decisions is what information to include in your draft. The background and the expectations of your audience should guide your selection, so review the contents with the occasion and the readers clearly in mind.

Review the contents:

- Is there adequate explanation and definition?
- Does all material support a central idea?
- Is there interesting but secondary information to edit out?
- Are the logical patterns (chronologies, comparisons, classifications) in the material used to organize it?

Cross-Reference: Chapter 9 reviews organizational patterns. Look over the material, then see which patterns already exist in your draft.

A carefully-structured framework (the title, introduction, transitions, and conclusion) will support your material and clarify the presentation of your ideas.

The title:

- Creates expectations
- Intrigues
- Informs

The introduction:

- Indicates subject
- Arouses interest
- Reveals persona

Transitions:

- Demonstrate connections
- Signal changes

The conclusion:

- Re-states
- Re-affirms
- Provokes action or thought
- Completes

Cross-Reference: Chapter 15 presents additional matterial on titles, introductions and conclusions.

When the framework is solid, direct your editorial voice to examine smaller elements like paragraphs, sentence structures and diction. Review your earlier writing to identify trouble spots, and give those areas particular attention. Some additional considerations are suggested below.

> **Cross-Reference:** Chapters 16 and 17 present additional material on paragraphs, sentence structures, and diction problems.

Improving Paragraphs:

- Basic patterns
- Coherence

Improving Sentences:

- Coordination and subordination
- Parallel structure

Improving Diction:

- Sexism
- Wordiness

Final Considerations

As you review your writing, check:

- **The rhetorical situation**   Has your writing responded directly and appropriately to the invitation? Have you addressed a specific audience, in a tone and style suitable to the occasion?
- **The logical connections between ideas**   Is your reasoning clear and logical? Have you explained the relationships between ideas? Have you left the readers to figure out their own conclusions?
- **The methods of presentation**   Is your material presented in fitting ways? Are lists complete and accurate? Are chronologies suited to the material?
- **The accuracy of the text**   Have you double-checked for your own most common grammatical or mechanical errors? Have you proofread carefully for text errors in spelling and punctuation and miscopied or omitted words?

CALIFORNIA
BOUND

A Student Writes to Inform Her Readers

Sally McClendan

Sally McClendan's best friend was contemplating a major change in her career plans, and wrote to Sally asking for some objective advice. Sally's letter not only compared her friend's possible future careers, but she also suggested some immediate considerations.

Planning her reply, Sally began by making a list of areas that she thought Rita should consider. She charted all of the information Rita had sent her about both LSU and the nursing school. Then she talked with a friend who is a nurse and checked the local newspapers to find out more about nurses' training and job opportunies.

Sally's response to Rita evolved through several drafts, three of which are printed here:

Sally's First Draft

Sally wrote the first letter very quickly, but decided not to send it when she realized how much it pressured Rita to decide in favor of LSU. She reworked it to make it less assertive and more informative in tone. Her notes to herself are included here.

Dear Rita,

I was surprised to hear that your plan to major in computer science at LSU has suddenly come unstuck. You have always been such a whiz in math and science, especially physics. How amazing that your mother's friends in Los Angeles, who haven't written you in years, should suddenly take such a strong interest in your career plans! (*I sound really skeptical*) They must have been really impressed when you visited them this past summer. I must admit, however, that I was even more astonished to hear that you are even considering becoming a nurse. I remember that when we were in biology together in high school, you always made someone else cut up our animals. You couldn't even stand to look at them, much less touch them. I cannot imagine your being able to take an anatomy class, let alone help a doctor sew up an accident victim! (*a little strong here—I sound like a parent!*) But I haven't seen you in a couple of years, so maybe your ideas have changed a lot. You really seem to have gotten interested in the health care field, since it was your original plan to get a master's degree in nuclear medicine.

It was really nice of your mom's friends to use their influence to get you accepted into the new class at the nursing school near them. It was also considerate of them to find you a room on the bus line so transportation would be fairly easy. How much do you think your room, board, and transportation will cost? I hear that living in Los Angeles is quite expensive. (*I'm pre-judging here—I should urge Rita to check things out carefully and decide for herself.*) Didn't you tell me that your aunt in Baton Rouge who lives right on the LSU free bus line had offered to let you stay with her? Have your friends in California found you a job that will pay as well as the student job you will have at LSU? I know that tuition at LSU is twice as high as the nursing school tuition, but what would your total expenses at each school be? Answering that question is really going to take some figuring.

Certainly there are a lot of advantages to being able to finish school in two-and-a-half years and have a secure job market available instead of waiting four-and-a-half years to start work. Of course, nowadays, R.N.s are hired as floor nurses and don't have the opportunities for advancement that B.S. nurses have. So you would have to go back to school someday if you wanted to specialize or get any promotions. On the other hand, I understand that physicists in cancer treatment centers start off at $50,000 to $60,000 a year and that they never have any problem finding jobs either. (*I'm giving judgments again.*) So, you could earn as much in your first two years as a medical physicist as you could in four or five years as an R.N.

I know that you're hoping to get married some day and have a family. I think you're wise to plan a career that you can keep on with after you get married or go back to when your children are in school. It seems to me that both of these professions would let you do that. Nurses are always in demand, and it seems that almost every town with more than 20,000 people has a radiation treatment center. As for meeting the right guy, I can't decide whether that would be easier at a large state university or in a huge city. (*This is getting awfully personal—I'll have to think about leaving it out.*) I think that you'll find him no matter where you go to school. Certainly the possibility of finding "Mr. Right" shouldn't be a major factor in making your decision about school.

You're really fortunate to have two good-sounding opportunities for school. I know it's tough to make a decision in such a short time, but I think you can do it wisely. I'm looking forward to hearing from you soon and finding out whether or not you're California bound!

Sally's Second and Third Drafts

The second draft is less persuasive in tone, but Sally decided that she really had not included enough information. She checked her notes to find the details you will see added to the third draft. She also decided to ask Rita some questions that would help to fill in the gaps in her comparison/contrast chart.

Dear Rita,

I was surprised to hear that your plan to major in computer science at LSU has suddenly come unstuck. You have always been a whiz in math and science, especially physics, and I admit that I was astonished to hear that you are even considering becoming a nurse. I remember that when we were in biology together in high school, you always made me cut up your animals. You couldn't even stand to look at them, much less touch them. I cannot imagine you in an anatomy class, let alone helping a doctor sew up an accident victim! But I haven't seen you in a couple of years, so it's likely that you have changed a great deal. Your last letter sounded very enthusiastic about hands-on health care and nursing, even more excited than you were last spring about your plans to get a master's degree in nuclear medicine.

Before I offer that sounding board you asked for, let me be sure that I understand the situation. Your mother's friends are encouraging you to attend school in Los Angeles, and they have found a room on the bus line so that your transportation will be simple, even without a car. Your other option is to go ahead with your plan to attend LSU and stay with your aunt who lives near the LSU bus line.

One of my first reactions is that the living expenses will be different. The tuition figures you sent me show that LSU will cost you roughly twice what the nursing school will charge, but be sure to look at total living expenses when you figure cost. (I need some specific figures here) Your aunt's offer is generous, of course, leaving you with virtually no room or board charges other than your own soft drinks or snacks. When you figure the $450 monthly rent, does that include utilities? Will you be on a meal plan at school? Will you be able to store food and prepare it in your room? Be realistic about food costs for both places. Answering the questions about living expenses will really take some figuring. (*More ideas needed here—transportation, maybe?*)

Are you sure that your parents will back your decision if you go to California? It's a lot farther from home than Baton Rouge is, and I remember that your father was really protective of you. Can you count on them for emotional and financial support? I'm glad that you have thought about a student job at the nursing school. Is it a sure thing? Does it pay as well as the job you've been promised at LSU? Your balance sheet of income and outgo will probably be your biggest chore. (*There are other things to consider besides money—am I helping Rita see the big picture?*)

Certainly there are some real advantages to being able to finish school in two-and-a-half years and have a secure job market available instead of having to wait four-and-a-half years to start work. Nowadays R.N.s are hired as floor nurses and don't have the opportunities for advancement that nurses with college degrees have. (*I really don't know much about this—but I know where to get some actual salaries.*) So you can expect to go back to school someday if you want to specialize or get any promotions. On the other hand, physicists in cancer treatment centers start off at $50,000 to $60,000 a year and there is no shortage of such jobs either. If salary and lifestyle are important to you, consider that you can earn as much in two years as a medical physicist as you could in four or five as an R.N.

I hope that these thoughts will help you to see more sides of your decision. As for your other questions, I honestly can't help you with the personal parts. I can't even comment on your ideas about social life and careers and families; you will really have to work those details out for yourself. (*I feel much better about this answer.*)

You're fortunate to have two good-sounding opportunities for school. I know it's tough to make a decision in such a short time, but I think you can do it wisely. I'm looking forward to hearing from you soon and finding out whether or not you're California bound!

Love always,

Sally

Dear Rita,

I was surprised to hear that your plan to major in computer science at LSU has suddenly come unstuck. You have always been such a whiz in math and science, especially physics, that I was astonished to hear that you are even considering becoming a nurse. I remember that when we were in high school biology together, you always made me cut up your animals. You couldn't even stand to look at them, much less touch them. I cannot imagine you in an anatomy class, let alone helping a doctor sew up an accident victim! But I haven't seen you in a couple of years, so it's likely that you have changed some. You must really be interested in health-care, since your most recent plan was to get an M.S. in nuclear medicine as soon as you finished your computer science degree.

Before I offer that sounding board you asked for, let me make sure that I understand the situation. Your mom's best friend and her husband, a doctor, are encouraging you to enter the nursing program at the community college near where they live in Los Angeles. They have found a room on the city bus line so that your transportation would be fairly easy, even without a car. Your other option is to go ahead with your plan to attend LSU and stay with your aunt in Baton Rouge who lives near the LSU bus line. Your parents have said that they will back your decision to go to California even though it's much farther from Hattiesburg than Baton Rouge is. It's great that you can count on them for emotional (and some financial) support no matter where you go. I know that since your dad has had to retire, you're going to need to pay most of your expenses.

One of my first reactions is that the costs will be different. The catalog you sent me shows that LSU will cost about $2,800 a semester for tuition, fees and books while the charges at the comunity college in Los Angeles are only $2,900 a year. But you also need to look at living expenses when you estimate costs. Your aunt's offer is generous, of course, leaving you with virtually no room or board charges other than your own soft drinks or snacks. How much have you budgeted for those, including eating some of your lunches at school? I think you need to figure at least $150 per month. Does the $450 monthly rent you mentioned for the room in L.A. include utilities? Does the nursing school have a meal plan? Will you be able to use your landlord's kitchen or store food and prepare it in your room? Be realistic about food costs in both places. Don't forget to consider the cost of commuting in L.A. Do students ride public transportation free as they do in Baton Rouge? Answering the questions about living expenses will really take some figuring.

I'm glad that Dr. and Mrs. Corona have offered to help you find work as a sitter at the hospital. $8.00 an hour sounds good for night and weekend work. Is it a sure thing? How many hours a week will you be able to work? Will you have enough time and energy left for studying? You said the student job at LSU will pay $5.00 an hour, twenty hours a week, or about $400 a month. Working out your balance sheet of income and outgo will proabably be your biggest chore.

There are many advantages to being able to finish school in two-and-a-half years and have a secure job market available instead of having to wait four-and-a-half years to start work. Even though the starting salary for both college graduate nurses and R.N.s is about $21,000 a year, R.N.s are hired as floor nurses and don't have the opportunities for advancement that nurses with college degrees have. So you can expect to go back to school someday if you want to specialize or get any promotions or substantial raises. On the other hand, physicists in cancer treatment centers start off at $50,000 to $60,000 a year and there is no shortage of such jobs either. If salary and lifestyle are important to you, consider that you can earn as much in two years as a medical physicist as you could in four or five as an R.N.

I hope that these thoughts will help you to see more sides of your decision. As for your other questions, I honestly can't help you with the personal parts. I can't even comment on your ideas about social life and careers and families; you will really have to work those details out for yourself.

You're fortunate to have two good-sounding opportunities for school. I know it's tough to make a decision in such a short time, but I trust you can do it wisely. I'm looking forward to hearing from you soon and finding out whether or not you're California bound!

Love always,

Sally

Writing to Convince Your Readers

Writing to convince your readers demands careful attention to audience and to persona. This chapter reviews those demands and examines the techniques of effective persuasion. Samples include unpublished work from students and the general public as well as a variety of published arguments. Suggested approaches to written argument are cross-referenced to relevant material in other chapters.

The image of "argument" has become rather tarnished: it is often seen as a loud, tense affair, less than half a step removed from a fight. Lessons in argument, you might think, are best learned in actual combat. But such arguments are not the subject of this chapter. Here, argument means a clash of reasoned judgments, a testing ground for logical ideas, not a display of sarcasm and hostility.

A distinction is often made between persuasion and argument, a distinction that associates persuasion with emotional appeals and argument with rational appeals. In practice, though, very little of our writing (or our thinking) is so neatly divided. Instead, most of our persuasive writing incorporates both logical and emotional appeals. Thus it is more realistic to spend time recognizing and controlling these two appeals than it is to try to isolate elements of each. In this discussion, the terms *argument* and *persuasion* are virtually interchangeable.

Written arguments are usually addressed to an audience that does not accept the views expressed. Their attitude toward the assertions may be total disagreement, or it may be neutral. (An audience that already endorses the views is rarely addressed.) In either case, your task is to convince these readers that your views are reasonable and deserve consideration. Do not expect to convert each reader totally to your cause, but you can anticipate that many will nod their heads and say, "You've got a point there." Convincing your readers to open their minds and really listen to your ideas may not seem dramatic, but do not be misled—it is no easy job.

How, then, do you write to a skeptical, even hostile, audience? The comforting fact is that you write much the same way you write other papers. You will find that the rhetorical situation creates a relationship between thesis, audience, and persona, and that the relationship largely determines your content and your presentation. The activities that produce effective writing—the strategies for gathering, reviewing, drafting, revising, and editing—remain very much the same when you write to convince.

CHARACTERISTICS OF WRITING THAT CONVINCES

There are, of course, some additional considerations in persuasive writing. Good arguments emerge from careful selection of subject, clear expression of thesis, adequate support of asserconcerns:d detailed attention to audience. When you write to convince, you should address these concerns:

1. **Choose your conflicts wisely.** It is possible to fight about anything, but argument is a reasonable exercise and must find its topics in arguable matters. Matters of fact, for instance, can be easily checked and cannot be resolved by debate. In addition, matters of taste result in useless arguments. Your logic cannot convince someone else to like or dislike the taste of certain food or the characteristics of certain movies or the sound of particular music. What people accept based on internal criteria is largely beyond the reach of logic and reason.

   For the same reasons, matters of faith also make poor arguments. Religious beliefs are often based on acceptance of ideas without logical proof. Thus all of your logic and rational analysis may not reach the internalized, deeply held beliefs of another.

   You should draw your arguments from matters of public controversy, from the problems and proposals that affect you and your readers. It is true that you can "argue" with yourself, but you will most likely write to convince someone else of the reasonableness of your ideas.

2. **Develop an arguable thesis.** As you saw in Chapter 3, it is possible to write an even-handed description of a controversy—but such writing intends to inform, not to convince. For argument, you must take a clear stand that has definite reasonable opposition. When you identify a thesis, ask yourself, "Are there reasonable people who disagree with this?"

   Beware of heated pseudo-arguments that stem from controversial topics but do not have reasonable opposition. For example, if you "argue" that child abuse is a terrible act of violence, is there a reasonable person who opposes your view? Be sure that your thesis is focused on an area of genuine disagreement, on a proposed law, for example, or on the role of the teacher who suspects abuse.

3. **Go beyond explanation to prove your assertions.** Since your audience is at the very least skeptical, you must work to demonstrate

the reasonableness of your stand. As you gather material for this essay, remember that descriptions will make your points clear, but evidence—statistics, observations, expert testimony—will be needed to convince your readers.

4. **Understand that your audience is essential to your purpose.** While you should not change your opinions to please an audience, knowing their attitudes should direct your organization of points and selection of evidence. It will also help you to define an appropriate persona.

One additional note: **Persuasive writing of necessity presents opinion.** There is nothing taboo about offering an opinion; in fact, persuasive writing is rather useless unless it contributes a point of view about the dispute. There is need for only so many summaries of the issues in the handling of school children with AIDS, so you should not hesitate to offer your logical and practical solution to the problem. Opinions are without value only if they are left unsupported. The danger is **not** in writing about your opinions; the danger is in failing to do so. Persuasive writing that straddles the fence or avoids judgment is doomed to be ineffective.

The excerpt that follows takes a clear stand in opposition to a current policy:

> The voting age should be returned to 21. When it was lowered to 18, a basic argument was that 18-year-olds could be drafted and, if 18 is old enough to fight, it is also old enough to vote. That argument has been proved consistently false. The qualities of a good fighter include a willingness to follow orders without questioning, hardly a good mindset for a thinking voter.

A final consideration as you look over your material and identify your purpose: if you are confused or uncertain about which side of an issue is the best one, then you should consider writing an informative composition rather than a persuasive one.

EVALUATING ARGUMENTS

One way to see how arguments work is to examine attempts at persuasion and note how they succeed or fail. Using what you know about the characteristics of argument, look closely at the two samples below. But first, consider the background:

A columnist for a campus newspaper wrote an article that was critical of fraternities. In brief, he complained that on more than one occasion, men whom he had considered friends had snubbed him when they were with their fraternity brothers. The same thing happened to other people as well. Something seems to happen to men when they join a fraternity, he reasoned; they become clannish and snobbish. He concluded that the actions of fraternity men give little evidence of concern for brotherhood, because brotherhood means more than "secret handshakes, Greek letters, mumbo-jumbo, 'Rah! Rah!'-songs, and fancy jackets with emblems"; it means accepting all men as brothers.

The columnist's criticism, predictably, caused a furor on campus, especially among fraternity men. A number of people wrote letters to the editor. Here are excerpts from two such letters. Read each one carefully, and consider how persuasive it would be for the columnist and those who agree with him.

Dear Editor:

I cannot let Jim Pepper's attack on fraternities go unanswered. It is true that fraternity men take separate tables when they are together. They are proud to be frat men—and for the best of reasons. They have achieved brotherhood in the truest sense of the word. Living in a college dormitory does not permit a person to develop brotherhood. In fact, it exposes him to pettiness, selfishness, irresponsibility, lack of dedication, and a thousand other human frailties. Living in a fraternity means rising above these frailties. When a young man joins a fraternity, he becomes a truly dedicated person. He is willing to put aside former ways and former relationships, because he has found something higher and nobler. . . .

It is true that fraternity men are connected with wild parties and drinking. This is because they place high value on good living. Warmth and good cheer are an expression of the joy that comes from brotherly association. Wild parties and drinking are a basic part of growing up. (Besides, a fellow has to have some stories to tell his children.)

I realize that it is impossible for an "independent" to understand fraternity life, for it can only be understood from the inside. Whether that lack of understanding is joined with envy and resentment or just honest wondering, it never results in valid criticism. Ideally, an outsider will simply admit that there are some profound and mysterious situations in life that are closed to him. Such situations his mind can't penetrate, no matter how powerful it may be. And one of them is the brotherhood of fraternity men.

Sincerely,

Benjamin Woodstone

Dear Editor:

I am writing in response to Jim Pepper's article on fraternities. I am a fraternity member myself, and can verify that much of what Mr. Pepper says is true. The charge that fraternities tend to make men clannish and snobbish can be documented on this campus at any time of the day — in the library, the snack bar, the athletic fields, the classrooms. Something does seem to happen to many men when they join fraternities. They do often ignore their former friends. It is understandable and right that such behavior makes nonfraternity observers angry and resentful. For that matter, it doesn't please everyone in fraternities. . . .

Mr. Pepper's comments about brotherhood cut deep. The temptation is strong for a fraternity man to deny them and attack him for making them . . . . But the fact is, what he says is true. And many of us in fraternities tend to forget it.

If I feel this way, why don't I quit my fraternity? The question is sure to arise. Well, I won't quit. I believe with Jim Pepper that there should be the larger type of brotherhood in the world. I believe that fraternities often unknowingly work against it. But I do believe they can work toward it. We can't behave right toward the world until we learn to behave right toward those around us, the little worlds of our everyday associations. A fraternity with the right emphases can develop the idea of brotherhood and prepare its members to be brothers to all men. Because it is a close-knit association, it can do so better than dorm life can. There are, I think, more than a few fraternity members who are trying to make it do so.

Sincerely,

John Taylor

There are differences between these two letters. The first shows little understanding of the columnist's position, suggesting instead that he was not entitled even to judge from his own experience because fraternity life is too "profound and mysterious" to be judged from the outside. Ironically, this comment (and others) displays the same quality of snobbishness the columnist was attacking. Further, the first letter offers a very unbalanced, biased case—to the point of absurdity. It even characterizes wild parties and drinking as almost noble activities. (The writer would have done better not to mention them at all.) And the author clearly never bothered to wonder what his readers' reactions would be. Or perhaps he didn't care. For though his formal intention seems to have been to persuade others, his approach shows he was really only stroking his ego.

The second letter is very different. It shows openness of mind and willingness to acknowledge the truth, even when it is unpleasant. It makes generous concessions and demonstrates great sensitivity to the readers and awareness of their probable reactions. Look again at the question that begins the last paragraph. It is precisely the question that would occur to most readers at that point, and it demonstrates the writer's awareness of audience. Yet despite all the concessions and the cordial manner, this letter is by no means weak. Where it expresses a point that opposes the columnist's position, it does so directly and forcefully and reasonably.

The two letters demonstrate the importance of persona as an element of persuasion. Your "voice" can affect the readers' impression of your ideas; if you come across as unpleasant or unreliable, your efforts to convince the readers may well be in vain. But if you appear to be knowledgeable and reasonable, your readers are more likely to consider your ideas. Take a lesson from the two writers above, and be sure that your persona meets these criteria:

1. **Do you show respect for your readers?** Check your diction to be sure that you have not labelled those who oppose you as fools or idiots. But also check that you have not patronized or dismissed the concerns of your audience, making them feel in any way belittled or unimportant. Asking a friend to review your work with this question in mind can be useful.

2. **Do you show that you understand the opposition?** Regardless of your opinion, you are expected to be accurate as you discuss the issues. If you make mistakes about other proposals, your own credibility is weakened. In addition, if you exercise your wit by sarcastic comments and name-calling, your readers might conclude that such tactics are a substitute for genuine understanding.

3. **Do you anticipate your readers' reactions?** If you have analyzed your audience, you should know their main objections and concerns. Anticipating their reactions means answering questions they are likely to ask and reassuring them that their voices have been heard.

4. **Do you present a balanced case?** You may be tempted to unload your frustrations by blasting away at the opposition; you may get a feeling of power by belittling those who disagree with you. But be warned. Such tactics may give you great emotional release and may indeed be satisfying. And if satisfaction is your purpose in writing, then you'll have written successfully. But if your purpose in writing is to persuade someone to hear you and to adopt your views, you'll have failed dismally.

   Resist the temptation to attack character flaws and concentrate instead on logic and evidence. Keep a sense of perspective about issues. Omit none of the important points, no matter how delicate the issues being raised, but do not include a lot of unnecessary secondary points

5. **Is your image moderate and reasonable?** Two techniques that build a reasonable image for you are understatement and concession. Use understatement to express points the readers might be especially sensitive about. Understatement has two benefits: it softens the effect of your criticism or disagreement, and it suggests that you have a sense of restraint, one of the marks of a good mind. Another tactic is to concede whenever the opposing side of the argument has a point, and to do so generously. You will look more reasonable. Be cautious, though, about giving too much emphasis to strong opposing arguments.

The image of your persona is an important element of persuasion. Even if you write in third person, your voice can make an impression on the readers. You may try to neutralize that impression, making sure that your persona at least does not have negative impact. In some arguments, though, you will work to create an accessible, acceptable persona that encourages readers to listen with an open mind. In a Rogerian approach to argument, for example, your persona seeks to establish common ground with the audience, implying that you and your readers are on the same side and share the same concerns. With that identification, you can then argue that both of you pursue the same goal and that your proposal will help you both achieve it. Look at this short sample of a Rogerian approach:

All of us want a healthy environment for our children. All of us want them to grow up with clean air to breathe, with clean water to drink, with nourishing food produced in uncontaminated soil. And all of us may have to make some sacrifices to have such an environment.

To this point, who can argue with the writer? Who would not sacrifice to achieve such a world—for the children? From this stance, the argument can go on to propose changes. And, the establishment of middle ground, of common goals, creates an environment that encourages open-mindedness and compromise. Whatever the form or the approach of your argument, such an environment will help you to convince your readers of the reasonableness of your views.

SITUATIONS THAT PROMPT WRITING TO CONVINCE

When you feel strongly that your ideas are reasonable and logical, your purpose is to persuade your audience to give your ideas the attention they deserve. Sometimes you want the readers to accept your position in lieu of their own. Sometimes you want your readers to change their attitudes or to act on your suggestion. Your evaluation of a restaurant or a movie or a compact disc player may be the issue; you may want your audience to vote down a proposal or accept an increase in tuition. The desired response might be concrete, measurable action, or it might be subtle changes in philosophy—but the purpose remains to convince your audience that your idea is logical and reasonable. Like the writers in the example that follows, you might want your readers to hire you for a major project.

Writing beyond the Classroom

When Rosanna Marino finished a general studies degree, she had only vague plans about working. She spent ten years working for the State Consumer Protection Office, but lost that job when budget cuts eliminated the position. While she was unemployed, a friend encouraged her to work at McDonald's—he had the contract to maintain the landscaping, and needed help with the planting.

Then the friend, William Rountree, was asked by Exxon to submit a plan for a greenbelt near the company's Baton Rouge plant. The area near the plant was suffering from urban blight, and Exxon saw a chance to buy out discouraged homeowners and to develop a park-like space to provide a buffer between the plant and the surrounding neighborhood. If Rountree's plan was accepted, his company would have both a lucrative contract and an opportunity to improve an industrial environment. So he and Marino worked up a proposal.

Marino acknowledges that neither of them had ever written a proposal quite like this one before. While Rountree had the technical expertise, she was more comfortable with writing, so the two collaborated. Marino also notes that each of them has a different approach to projects—Rountree works up methodical lists and outlines, while she wants to write everything down and then revise extensively. Both admit that producing the document was an exercise in patience and compromise, yet both also agree the proposal is much stronger because of their different strengths.

Their first decision was to produce a prospectus that would describe the problem and point out the advantages of the greenbelt itself. It would also explain what needed to be done first and estimate the time and costs of the initial surveys. Rountree knew that Exxon's engineers would have first approval on the plan, so the proposal was geared to a technical audience. In addition, the writers recognized that they were selling a plan to Exxon but that they were also selling themselves indirectly. While only Rountree had been asked for an initial proposal, he knew that if his projections were unacceptable, someone else would have the next opportunity.

Getting started was the hardest part. Neither of the two had had much experience with such proposals, and Exxon was not particularly helpful about its plans or its expectations. They began by talking about the project—what it should accomplish, who would read the proposal, what it should include, who would make the decision. Their initial dialogue identified areas of concern, and Rountree began to research similar projects to get an idea of timetables and costs. Both of them studied maps of the area and visited the site to begin an inventory of work to be done. Marino turned to books about writing—an old college English handbook and some books about technical writing that contained information on writing proposals. She found much advice in the books, but notes that the multitude of suggestions left her feeling overwhelmed. As the collection of raw material grew, though, the two writers began to make decisions about content and format and Marino compiled a handwritten, very rough draft.

Looking at the draft quickly showed areas needing further work. As Rountree did more research, Marino began to organize material and think about the readers. They read sections aloud, talking about awkward parts and marking sections that needed more explanation. When the initial draft was thoroughly annotated, Marino typed a second copy and the writers began to review it again. They consulted their original lists of points to cover, making sure that all essentials had been included. They also made sure that the language was appropriate for an audience of engineers. Marino acknowledges that Rountree's expertise was more useful in that goal; she insisted that words be chosen with attention to precise definition and nuance—a dictionary she has had for years proved to be the most helpful tool.

The writers continue to see awkward sentences and paragraphs that need expansion; both agree that the proposal could have used more revision, but the project came with a deadline. After a week of intense work, then, the following proposal was submitted to Exxon:

PROPOSAL TO EXXON CHEMICAL PLANT ON SCENIC HIGHWAY GREENBELT DEVELOPMENT FROM WILLIAM K. ROUNTREE, ASLA THROUGH BATON ROUGE GREEN

Exxon is responding to the overall need in the Baton Rouge community to reclaim blighted areas. Adjacent to the Exxon Chemical Plant, along Scenic Highway, such an area has progressively deteriorated. With the advent of decling property values in the adjacent area, the neighborhood has begun a spiral of decay. For those remaining homeowners, the reality has been entrappment in an environment rife with crime, drugs, and despair. Rapid expansion and failure to plan for temporary contractor parking have led to the piecemeal acquisition by Exxon of property along Scenic Highway. Few improvements of aesthetic value have been made to the acquired property. Abandoned and decaying buildings also have contributed to the blight.

Exxon, in its commitment to the enhancement of the Baton Rouge community, recognizing the problem and rather than ignoring it, has decided to act on it. A visually enhanced corridor along Scenic Highway has been proposed. Exxon has undertaken the initial development of the greenbelt, beginning with the property directly across from Exxon Chemical Plant.

Acquisition of property in the blighted district has multi-fold benefits. First, it provides homeowners with fair market values for homes previously considered unsellable. This, in turn, stimulates the Baton Rouge low-income housing real estate market. Second, removal of the acquired buildings should decrease crime in the immediate area by depriving criminals of havens. Furthermore, controlled redevelopment of the area will entail removal of declining plant material, recontouring of existing grades, and additional plantings to create a park-like environment.

Ecological improvements will be realized from the greening of the area. Reorganization of the parking lots will result in reduction of the visual detriment which parking lots invariably create.

An undertaking of this magnitude requires long-term planning and budgeting. A comprehensive masterplan will provide visual conceptualization of the project and ensure controlled development and budgeting.

Due to the manner of acquisition of properties, a series of plans will be necessary. The overall project area at this point is defined by Evangeline Street, Scenic Highway, Monte Sano Bayou, and Knox Canal. While the initial plan will encompass the entire area, concentration of design will be limited to the section bounded by Evangeline Street, Scenic Highway, Hollywood Avenue, and Alamonster Street. The back area will be conceptually represented but will be open for future program elements. Exxon's desire to create a park-like atmosphere lends itself well to visual continuity of the development in stages due to the nature of the park-like design. The clean, pastoral format of grassy areas, shrubbery, and large tree plantings, while preserving quality, existing specimens on site, is easily repeatable in stages.

The master plan itself will be a color rendering, 30 inches by 42 inches, at 1 inch equals 100 foot scale. Accompanying the masterplan will be a detail plan that depicts the area bounded by Evangeline, Scenic, Beech, and Alamonster. This will be a 30 inch by 42 inch color rendering at 1 inch equals 30 foot scale.

Essential to the development of such a plan are extensive site inventory, research, and analysis. Site inventory will encompass development of site base maps through the use of aerial photographs, plot plans, and site survey. Inventory of existing plant material, structures, roadways, and utilities will be recorded onto base maps. Research and analysis will entail compilation and synthesis of program elements, existing conditions, site inventory, and research information into a working plan. The next phase, the design for the project area, will then be developed. The graphic presentation stage will compile the work as a whole into a visual, finished product. Achievement of the graphic presentation will be accomplished through pen-and-ink drawings from which prints will be made. Application of Prismacolor and marker will be used to accentuate the drawings.

A project of this scope requires an orderly work schedule. A reasonable estimate of time allotted for each phase follows.

PHASE	NUMBER OF HOURS LANDSCAPE ARCHITECT/STAFF
Development of Base Maps, Site inventory and Research	96/72
Analysis and Research	48/24
Design of Masterplan	40/20
Design of Detail Plan	32/12
Graphic Presentation	25
Construction Cost Estimates	25
TOTAL NUMBER OF HOURS	266/128

EXPENSES	COSTS
Landscape Architect:	
266 Hours at $40/Hour	$10,768.00
Staff:	
128 Hours at $12/Hour	1,536.00
Printing Costs	400.00
General Overhead (Travel)	200.00
TOTAL ESTIMATED COSTS	$12,904.00

Revision will be billed at $40/Hour plus incurred expenses.

WILLIAM K. ROUNTREE, ASLA

June 25, 1990

For comparison, one of the earlier drafts is printed below. Notice the editorial changes in sentence structure, verb tense, and diction as the writers polished their work.

PROPOSAL TO EXXON CHEMICAL PLANT
(FROM WILLIAM K. ROUNTREE, *ASLA*)
(THROUGH BATON ROUGE GREEN)
ON SCENIC HIGHWAY GRENBELT DEVELOPMENT

Exxon is responding to the overall need in the Baton Rouge community to reclaim blighted areas. Adjacent to the Exxon Chemical Plant, along Scenic Highway, *such* an area has progressiv/ely deteriorated. With the advent of declining property values in the *is* adjacent area, the neighborhood *has* began a spiral of decay. For those remaining homeowners, the reality *has been* was entrappment in an environment rife with crime, drugs, and despair. Rapid expansion and failure to plan for temporary contractor parking *have* led to the piecemeal acquisition by Exxon of property adjacent to *along* Scenic Highway. Few improvements of aesthetic value *have been* were made to the *acquired* property. Abandoned and decaying buildings *also have* contributed to the blight.

Exxon, *in its* committed *ment* to the enhancement of the Baton Rouge community, *has* recognized *ed* the problem *of deterioration in the neighborhood* and, rather than ignoring it, decided to act on it. A visually enhanced corridor along Scenic Highway has been proposed. Exxon has undertaken the initial development of the geen belt, beginning with the property directly across from the Exxon Cehmical *Plant*.

Acquisition of property in the blighted district has multi-fold benefits. *A fair market value for homes* First, it provides the outlet for homeowners *who* previously unable to *make find buyers for* sell their homes, *W*which, in turn, stimulates the Baton Rouge real estate low-income housing market. Secondly, removal of the acquired buildings should decrease crime in the immediate area by depriving criminals of havens. Furthermore, controlled redevelopment of the area *will* would entail removal of declining plant material, recontouring of existing grades, and additional planting to develop a park-like environment. Ecological improvements *will* would be realized from the greening of the area. Reorganization of the parking lots *will* would result in reduction of the visual detriment which parking lots invariably create.

First, it provides homeowners with fair market values for homes that were previously considered unsellable: unsellable.

An undertaking of this magnitude requires long-term planning and budgeting. A comprehensive masterplan would provide visual conceptualization of the project and ensure controlled development *and budgeting.*

Due to the manner of acquisition of properties, a series of plans will be necessary. The overall project area at this point, is defined by Evangeline, Scenic, Monte Sano Bayou and Know Canal. While the initial plan will encompass the entire area, concentration of design will be limited to the section bounded by Evangeline, Scenic, Hollywood and Alamonster. The back area will be conceptually represented but will be open for future program elements. Exxon's desire to create a park-like atmosphere lends itself well to visual continuity of the development in stages due to the nature of the park-like design. The clean, pastoral format of grassy areas, *shrubbery* and large tree plantings which retain the *while reserving* quality specimen *existing* on site, and some shrubs. is easily repeatable is stages.

The master plan itself will be a color rendering, 30 inches by 42 inches, at 1 inch equals 100 foot scale. Accompanying the master plan will be a detail plan that depicts the area bounded by Evangeline, Scenic, Beech and Alamonster. This will be a 30 inch by 42 inch color rendering at 30 foot scale. *1 inch equals* Essential to the development of such a plan are extensive site inventory, research and analysis.

New paragraph?

Site inventory will encompass development of site base maps though the use of aerial photographs, plot plans, and site survey. Inventory of existing plant material, structures, roadways, and utilities will be recorded onto the base maps. Research and analysis will entail compilation and synthesis of program elements, existing conditions, site inventory, and research information into a working plan. In the next phase, the design for the project area will be developed. *will* The graphic presentation stage is the *compile* compilation of the work as a whole into a visual, finished product. Achievement of the product is accomplished through *graphic presentation will be* a series of steps involving pen and ink drawings from which prints are made and application of prisma color and marker to accentuate the drawings. *will be* *will be used*

Additional Readings That Convince

The sample readings in this section come from a variety of print sources, and they illustrate distinct approaches to argument. As you read, recognize that some of the essays identify problems, others propose solutions, and still others challenge the proposals, the arguments and even the attitudes they see around them.

New Phone Service Threatens Privacy
Gary T. Marx

Gary Marx, a professor of sociology at MIT, is author of "Undercover: Police Surveillance in America." Marx begins by describing a new and "wonderful" service soon to be offered by the phone company. But it is soon apparent that he does not applaud the "advance."

Becoming an Active Reader:

1. What do you know about "call-identification"? Does it sound like a good idea? What would be some of the advantages of knowing who is calling you?
2. Have you ever wanted to know the identity of a caller? Have you ever made a call and wanted to remain anonymous? Explain.
3. What do you know about Gary Marx? Do you listen with more respect to Marx because of his position?

1   The people who brought us call-forwarding and call-waiting have done it again—this time in the form of call-identification. Telephone customers in many parts of the country who are willing to spend an extra $6 a month will soon be able to know the number from which an incoming call was dialed before they pick up their phone. The service requires purchasing a video display device that keeps a record of the time and phone number of incoming calls.

2   The system offers many advantages. It can deter (or determine the origin of) crank calls and false alarms. It will provide the location of persons who request emergency help. It can mean faster consumer services (a sales representative can have your record displayed even as the phone is being answered). Burglars who telephone to be sure that no one is home may be identified by the phone number they unwittingly leave. Call-identification permits screening calls (you don't answer if it is a tiresome relative).

3   People calling know your number; isn't it only fair that you should know theirs?

4   Not necessary. There may be times when an imbalance in the relationship is desirable. Anonymity has positive as well as negative consequences. Persons with unlisted phone numbers may involuntarily have to disclose them. Calls to law enforcement and counseling hot lines may decline because of the suspicion that anonymity is no longer guaranteed.

5   Those calling for information about goods and services may receive an avalanche of unwanted phone and mail solicitations, particularly if their names are distributed by a mass-marketing company.

6   The new visibility encroaches on white lies, spontaneity and quiet personal detective work. Our sense of autonomy and self are enmeshed in a complex web of privacy, secrecy, diplomacy and fabrication. Anything that curtails social maneuverability and alters those delicate relationships, whatever its other benefits, is likely to be morally ambiguous.

7   The increased ease of verifying location might be thought to make people more honest, but this is balanced by the fact that a record will be left of the act of verification. Thus, if you invite friends to a party and they say they can't come because of an obligation at home, you may be less likely to call to check if they were telling the truth since there will be a record that you called. Knowing that, they may be more likely to lie.

8   Supervision in the home will become more intensive and democratic. Spouses, parents and children will find it easier to check up on each other. The spouse who is visiting a friend can no longer call home and say that he or she is working late; the teenager prohibited from associating with a certain person will find it more difficult to take calls from that person, while pretending to be talking to someone else. Gone is the freedom to hang up if a person we do not want to talk to answers, or if we develop second thoughts about making the call.

9   The consequences of the service will depend partly on how it is offered. Callers could be told that the line they have reached has call-identification and be given the option of hanging up before their number is shown. Or callers could be told that they can block call-identification by entering several digits. Or callers could be denied any controls and their number displayed without their knowledge or consent. The latter will be the case for callers in New York and New England served by Nynex. The interests of the receiver are put above those of the caller. In the system proposed by Pacific Telesis for its West Coast customers, callers will be able to block the display of their number.

10   The West Coast offering is far superior. It preserves the caller's privacy, but not at a cost of being unable to make the phone call. Those receiving the call would be given some information that the party calling did not want his or her number shown. Crank callers could still be identified through another new phone company service—call-tracing.

11   In their marketing research the phone companies found that West Coast customers were much more concerned with privacy protection than were East Coast customers. But when matters of principle are at stake, marketing research ought not to prevail. There are important questions of informed consent and privacy here. As phone company customers, we are both callers and receivers and the interests of both ought to be served.

12   Call-identification is a small eddy in a torrent of new information-gathering technologies that are turning us into a transparent or surveillance society. Liberty to do good or evil partly resides in the cracks of inefficient technology. As those are patched, our vigilance must increase.

Thinking about a Subject and Writing for Yourself:

Prompts for Journal Writing and Class Discussion

1. Do you agree with Marx that there are "important questions here," or do you think he is over-reacting?

2. Marx must speculate about effects because the system is not yet available. Does the hypothetical nature of his situations make them less convincing?

3. Given that Marx's examples are hypothetical, are they realistic and probable? Do you find his reasoning convincing?

4. Marx compares the new system with the West Coast version and finds the latter "far superior." What do you think?

5. What do you think about Marx's report that West Coast customers were more concerned with their privacy than East Coast customers? Can you speculate about reasons why that might be so?

6. Marx does not use "I" in his essay, but he does occasionally use "you" and "we" or "our." What effect does the first person plural have on the audience? Do you think Marx made a deliberate choice, or is the pronoun shift a mistake?

Television Insults Men, Too
Bernard R. Goldberg

Bernard Goldberg writes about a familiar subject—the stereotyping of a class of people—but he argues that this time the victims are men.

Becoming an Active Reader:

1. Does Goldberg's title arouse any response in you? Why do you think he includes the word "too"?

2. Do you think that women have legitimate complaints about stereotyping? Before you read this article, do you think that men also have a problem?

1   It was front-page news and it made the TV networks. A mother from Michigan single-handedly persuades some of America's biggest advertisers to review or cancel their sponsorship of Fox Television's "Married . . . with Children" because, as she put it, the show blatantly exploits women and the family.

2   The program is about a blue-collar family in which the husband is a chauvinist pig and his wife is—excuse the expression—a bimbo.

3   These are the late 1980s, and making fun of a whole class of people— on TV on less, in front of millions of people—is frowned upon. Unless, of course, they are men. Then it's okay.

4   Take "Roseanne," the hit show about another blue-collar family. In this one, the wife calls her husband and kids names. Roseanne Barr, the star of the show, has made a career saying such cute things as, "You may marry the man of your dreams, ladies, but 15 years later you are married to a reclining chair that burps." Or to her TV-show son: "You're not stupid. You're just clumsy like your daddy." No one, to my knowledge, is pulling commercials from "Roseanne."

5   It has become part of the accepted orthodoxy—of many feminists and a lot of the media anyway—that only women have the right to complain. Men do not. Which helps to explain why there have been so many commercials ridiculing men—and getting away with it.

6   • A breakfast-cereal commercial shows a husband and wife playing tennis. She is perky and he is jerky.

7   She doesn't miss a shot. He lets the ball hit him in the head. She is a regular Martina Navratilova of the suburbs and he is virtually dead (because he wasn't smart enough to eat the right cereal).

8   • A razor commercial shows a woman in an evening gown smacking a man in a tuxedo across the face, suggesting, I suppose, that the male face takes enough punishment to deserve a nice, smooth shave. If he hit her (an absolutely inconceivable notion, if a sponsor is trying to sell a woman something) he would be a batterer.

9   • An airline commercial shows two reporters from competing newspapers. She's strong and smart. He's a nerd. He says: "I read your story this morning; you scooped me again." She replies: "I didn't know you could read."

10   In 1987, Fred Hayward, the founder of an organization called Men's Rights (MR, Inc.)—yes, there is a men's rights movement—studied hundreds of TV and print ads and concluded: "If there's a sleazy character in an ad, 100 percent of them are male. If there's an incompetent character, 100 percent of them are male."

11   Garrett Epps, a journalist who has written on these matters, told me: "The female executive who is driven, who is strong, who lives for her work, is a very positive symbol in our culture now. The male who has the same traits is a disaster: he's cold, he's unfeeling, he's hurtful."

12   Barbara Lippert, an advertising critic for *Adweek,* says advertisers are afraid to fool around with women's roles. They know, as she puts it, they'll "set off the feminist emergency-broadcast system" if they do. So, she concludes, men are fair game.

13   The crusading mother from Michigan hit on a legitimate issue. No more cheap shots, she seems to have said. And the advertisers listened. No more cheap shots is what a lot of men are saying also. Too bad nobody is listening to *them.*

Thinking about a Subject and Writing for Yourself:

Prompts for Journal Writing and Class Discussion

1. Goldberg waits until the end of the third paragraph to indicate his specific topic. As you read about the Michigan woman's crusade, did you sympathize with her ideas, or did you think she was over-reacting? Do you feel the same way about Goldberg's assertions, or does your view change when he reveals the target of the discrimination he sees?

2. Watch television for a week, being alert to the kind of stereotyping Goldberg describes. Does your observation support his assertions?

3. Goldberg suggests that women's complaints are heeded. Does your own observation support the idea that female stereotyping is being reduced?

4. Goldberg discusses TV images; are stereotypes evident in other media?

5. What impression do you get of Goldberg's persona? Is he unsympathetic to women's claims? Why or why not? How does his attitude toward women's claims affect your attitude toward him?

The Luck Illusion
Caryl Rivers

Caryl Rivers identifies a problem that, she argues, is part of women's cultural conditioning.

Becoming an Active Reader:

1. Have you ever responded to a compliment by giving credit to "luck"? Did you honestly feel that you were just lucky?

2. How do you think people should respond to congratulations or compliments or awards?

1   Somewhere there's an ex-Little League infielder who thinks I am completely unhinged. I don't blame her. She played on my son's team and was one of the best they had. While most of the boys could be counted on to hit slow dribblers, our pony-tailed infielder smacked a solid double or triple every time she came to bat. Unlike the boys, however, she never talked about her feats.

2   Whenever a boy managed to beat out a bunt, his postgame description made it sound like a Reggie Jackson clout. But when our girl hit a triple and drove in the winning run one day, she responded to her teammates' congratulations with: "I was just lucky!"

3   That's when I lost control. "Lucky!" I shouted, leaping up from the grass. "You are *not* lucky!" I screeched. "You are *good!*"

4   I jumped at the poor kid because the phrase she had just uttered—"I was just lucky"—is a pet peeve of mine. Both men and women use it, but research shows that women *mean* it much more often. They fall prey to what might be called "The Luck Illusion." It can have a profound and damaging effect on a woman's life—leading to depression, low self-esteem and a feeling that she's "out of control."

5   Behavioral scientists know that it's not only what we *do* that's important, but also how we explain our behavior to ourselves. Of particular interest is the way we interpret our successes.

6   Jennifer, for example, lives near an industrial dump site that has the townspeople worried. Jennifer was asked to put together a PTA seminar. She studied up on toxic waste, invited speakers, chaired the meeting and wrote the resolution sent to the state legislature. When she was congratulated for doing a bang-up job, she said, "Well, I was lucky to have the superintendent helping me."

7   Then there's Lisa, a bright, capable woman who decided to go back to school after a number of years at home. She was accepted into a good program with very stiff requirements. Her explanation: "I guess they needed women."

8   Jennifer and Lisa are not just modest; they have fallen for The Luck Illusion. They see success—positive results they worked hard to achieve—as beyond their control. They believe they did well only because they had help—or were in the right place at the right time. Luck may have played a part, but ability and hard work were clearly the decisive factors. Why don't Jennifer and Lisa recognize that?

9   When you think a good performance is due to luck—or anything other than your own ability—you can't build on your accomplishments. After all, skill and talent won't disappear—but luck can. So one of the results of falling for The Luck Illusion is that you underrate your ability.

10   Believing you're not as good as you really are makes it impossible to live up to your potential. In one study, 7,700 college seniors were asked if they thought they could do postgraduate work. The men with C plus averages said yes; the women with B plus averages thought it would be too tough! The men weren't bothered by their lack of academic achievement, but the women were afraid to risk a higher challenge.

11   This reluctance to take risks is all too common in women. It hampers their effectiveness in everything from making friends to investing money. It's especially damaging in the job market, where many women aim too low. When one company advertised for a woman to take on a demanding position that paid $25,000, there were few responses. But when the salary was dropped to $18,000, applications poured in. Fear of risk can keep a woman stuck on the lower rungs of the career ladder.

12   The flip side of The Luck Illusion is that women clutch their failures, always blaming an inherent flaw rather than bad luck or poor timing.

Karen, a competent athlete, joined the town softball team. In her first game she went to bat three times without getting a hit. She happened to be coming down with the flu that day, but no matter; she concluded she wasn't good enough and quit the team. Men are less likely to let one poor performance deter them.

13   Making light of successes and focusing on failures also makes women feel they are not in control of their lives. In studies at the Wellesley College Center for Research on Women, psychologists Grace Baruch and Rosalind Barnett found that those who felt in control of their lives were not depressed or anxious—and vice versa.

14   If you think Lady Luck is determining your destiny, it's hard to make realistic plans for the future. And nothing is more likely to produce anxiety than drifting aimlessly through life. Whenever you feel you're not entitled to claim your achievements, your self-esteem is bound to suffer. You can't take pride in being lucky, but solid accomplishments *can*—and do—build good feelings about yourself.

15   Fortunately, The Luck Illusion isn't terminal. It can even be cured. One way is to ask for the candid opinion of someone who really knows your abilities. One woman—afraid of being fired when a staff cutback was announced—asked her boss about her chances. To her astonishment, she learned that she was regarded as one of the most valuable employees in the whole company.

16   Once you are aware of the trap that snares so many women—underrating personal abilities—you should be able to steer clear of it. The Luck Illusion might finally go the way of whopping cough and bubonic plague. Then, when someone congratulates you for a job well done, you can say, "Thank you. I guess I was just—good!"

Thinking about a Subject and Writing for Yourself:

Prompts for Journal Writing and Class Discussion

1. Rivers argues that the attitude she describes is widespread. Have you ever observed any such tendencies? Do you think that she is right about it being a woman's attitude? What does your experience tell you?

2. Rivers says that the survey of college seniors about postgraduate work showed that women were "afraid to risk a higher challenge." Is her interpretation logical? Is it the only possible explanation?

3. What are some of the effects of The Luck Illusion on women's lives? Are Rivers' examples and speculations convincing? Are her generalizations about men and women adequately supported by her examples?

4. Rivers' only clue to her own persona is the opening anecdote. How, then, does she work to make her presentation credible? What kinds of evidence does she use?

5. If you do not agree with Rivers' assertions, where do you find her arguments weak? What would it take to make them more convincing for you?

6. Rivers' essay begins with an anecdote about children. At what point do you realize that she is not talking about a children's problem?

7. After the opening anecdote, Rivers' essay largely uses "you." Why do you think she chose second-person? What does that choice reveal about her intended audience?

Looking Behind the Proposition 48 Image
Allen L. Sack

Allen Sack was a member of the championship Notre Dame football team in 1966. He is currently professor of sociology at the University of New Haven.

Becoming an Active Reader:

1. What do you learn about Sack before you read the essay? Does his background make you more open to his comments?

2. What does the title suggest to you? Is looking behind the image likely to support or to challenge the image?

1   The practice of setting lower admissions standards for athletes than for other students has become commonplace. As a result, athletes with extremely limited verbal and mathematical skills have become a standard feature at almost all Division I schools. Under the best of circumstances, marginal students such as these would have difficulty with college-level work. When they are also expected to meet the high-pressure demands of college sport, it is not surprising that they often fail to make satisfactory academic progress. The low graduation rates of Division I athletes have become a national scandal.

2   Given the public perception that there has been a total breakdown of academic standards for athletes, it is understandable that the National Collegiate Athletic Association's new eligibility requirements, known as Proposition 48, has been received by many with considerable enthusiasm. Most media references to the new rules credit the N.C.A.A. with "setting tough new academic standards" or with "restoring academic integrity" in college sport. The general impression is that a bold new initiative has been taken to insure that college athletes can compete in the classroom as well as on the playing field.

3   Unfortunately, a close look at Proposition 48 reveals that it is more of an exercise in skillful public relations than a serious effort to institute academic reform. The gist of this legislation is that athletes at Division I schools must meet certain minimum academic standards in order to be eligible for freshman sports. To be eligible, athletes must have a 2.0 aver-

age in a core curriculum of high school courses and scores of at least 700 on the Scholastic Aptitude Test (S.A.T.) or 15 on the American College Testing Program's examination (A.C.T.).

4   The most serious loophole in Proposition 48, and what renders it virtually worthless as a mechanism for raising academic standards, is that it is merely concerned with freshman eligibility. What many people fail to realize is that under this new rule, schools can continue to admit athletes who fail to meet the N.C.A.A.'s freshman eligibility requirements and can grant them scholarships. All the Proposition 48 says is that these athletes will not be eligible for freshman sports. After sitting out a year, athletes who were not eligible as freshmen are free to enter the high-pressure world of commercial college sport.

5   I cannot for the life of me see how Proposition 48 raises academic standards or constitutes a bold new initiative. All it really does it bar extremely marginal students, many of whom do not belong in college in the first place, from playing freshman sports. When I played football at Notre Dame in the mid-1960's, freshmen, including National Merit Scholars, were not eligible for varsity sports. In this respect, Proposition 48 fails to come up to standards that existed two decades ago.

6   If the N.C.A.A. and its member institutions had really been committed to substantive reforms, they could, at the very least, have made {a combined score of 700 on the S.A.T. exam (or the equivalent A.C.T. score) a minimum eligibility requirement for participation in Division I sports, regardless of year in college. This would, in effect, bar students who cannot meet the N.C.A.A. minimum from ever participating in big-time college sports. Such a rule would not interfere with an individual school's admission policies, but merely extend the N.C.A.A.'s freshman eligibility requirements to the sophomore, junior and senior years. The University of Georgia has already adopted this policy. The N.C.A.A. could easily do likewise.

7   I obviously disagree with those who say that admissions exams like the S.A.T. are meaningless. It is true that they do not measure innate intelligence. But they do give a rough idea of what kind of educational background a student has had. A combined score of below 700 on the S.A.T.s, for instance, suggests that a student has either attended inferior schools or comes from a neighborhood or family that lacks the material and cultural resources to emphasize the development of skills needed for success in college. Such a student may also have spent more time and energy on sports than on school work while in primary or secondary school.

8   Remedial programs can help these poorly prepared students to make up for valuable time lost in lower grades. However, it takes more than two semesters of not playing college sports to make up for 17 years of rotten schools, nonsupportive educational environments, and other disadvantages caused by discrimination, poverty, unemployment, and centuries of educational neglect. Our nation's universities have a moral obligation to recruit and to provide financial aid for academically motivated students from educationally disadvantaged backgrounds. This

includes students who perform poorly on admissions tests. But it is educationally insane for such students to be allowed to enter the high-pressure world of big-time college sports.

9 Even athletes who score 700 and above and are highly motivated will need all the help they can get to juggle the contradictory demands of sports and school work. No single reform would do more to give athletes the education they were promised in return for athletic services than providing a fifth year of scholarship aid beyond four years of athletic eligibility. The N.C.A.A. currently requires athletes to complete 12 credits of course work a semester in order to maintain satisfactory academic progress. This is probably as many courses as an athlete can handle and still meet the demands of sports. The problem is that an athlete who meets the N.C.A.A.'s satisfactory progress guidelines over a four-year period will end up with only 96 credits, far short of the approximately 120 needed to graduate.

10 N.C.A.A. legislation guaranteeing a fifth year of scholarship aid to athletes who have competed for their schools for four years would meet this problem head on. Such a proposal would make it unnecessary to debate the issue of freshman eligibility. Athletes could sit out their freshman year, if this seemed academically advisable. Or they could finish school in four years, or they could complete their educations after their athletic responsibilities were ended. Many schools already provide athletes with a fifth year of aid. This simple reform, coupled with the extension of the freshman eligibility requirement to the sophomore, junior and senior years, would demonstrate a genuine commitment to academic reform. Such reforms would also send shock waves down into the high schools and junior high schools.

11 If colleges simply stopped recruiting athletes whose verbal and mathematical abilities are extremely limited, the message would be clear. Kids who presently spend all of their time bouncing basketballs and dreaming of athletic stardom would have to confront the reality that exceptional athletic ability will not guarantee college admission. Proposition 48 sends out no such message. This fall, hundreds of star athletes who failed to meet the N.C.A.A.'s new requirements were admitted to Division I schools, and almost all of them received athletics scholarships. After sitting out a year, these athletes will represent their schools in sports and demonstrate to American's young people that colleges will never turn away a talented athlete, even if he or she can barely read and write. This, unfortunately, is the message of Proposition 48.

12 It should be noted, in closing, that if universities really wanted to restore academic integrity in their athletic programs, they would simply enforce the admissions requirements they already have on the books. This would mean that athletes would have to meet the same standards as other students. As a result, schools with highly competitive admissions standards would no longer be able to recruit talented "blue-chip" athletes

who are only marginal students. And this would severely disrupt the competitive balance within the college sports industry. Academically competitive schools like Notre Dame and Michigan would no longer be athletic powers, and less selective state universities would corner the market on "blue-chip" athletes, as well as on national championships. Over all, the quality of play would suffer and commercial college sport, as we know it, would probably not survive.

13   Given this reality, it is not reasonable to expect those who control college sport to make academic integrity a top priority. As long as universities function as centers for mass commercial entertainment, athletic ability will continue to take precedence over academic standard. Nonetheless, I am not convinced that the survival of college sport as a business necessitates the almost total abandonment of standards that is given legitimacy by a rule like Proposition 48. What is desperately needed in American education today is a return to higher standards. Young people need to be prodded and goaded to higher levels of achievement. Extending the N.C.A.A.'s new freshman eligibility rules to sophomore, junior, and senior years would be a modest step in the right direction. Giving athletes five years to finish their degrees would be a giant step.

Thinking about a Subject and Writing for Yourself:

Prompts for Journal Writing and Class Discussion

1. How much do you know about Proposition 48? If your knowledge was skimpy, does the article provide enough information to satisfy you?

2. Does Sack believe that there is any problem with the current relationship between college athletics and academics? Does Sack think that Proposition 48 is an effective measure?

3. How does Sack incorporate his own athletic background into the essay? What effect does his reference to his own playing days have on you?

4. Does Sack want to bar poorly prepared students from college? What does he want to do with them? Should they be recruited to play college ball? Why or why not?

5. Summarize Sack's proposals. Do you think they would make the difference he suggests? Why do you think the N.C.A.A. changed the earlier rules to allow freshman to play varsity ball?

Rules for Athletes Are Elitist
Gary R. Roberts

Gary Roberts is a professor of law at Tulane University in New Orleans. He does not challenge a specific piece of writing or defend a specific proposal, but argues instead that a prevailing attitude should be examined.

Becoming an Active Reader:

1. What does Roberts' position at Tulane lead you to expect in a discussion of athletes and academics? Does the title support your expectations?

1   The continuing efforts to impose unrealistic academic standards on college athletes deserve only scorn. They are premised on an elitist notion that a university's mission excludes all but purely cerebral endeavors. They are a vestige of bygone days when universities were seen as ivory towers isolated and protected from the ugly influences and values of the working classes. It's time to discard these notions.

2   Regardless of an athlete's academic aptitude or motivation, if he wants a chance to play professional basketball or football, he must go to college. Virtually every young man out of high school needs additional physical development and training before he can hope to play at the professional level. The only preprofessional programs are at colleges.

3   Those who defend the National Collegiate Athletic Association's rules advance three arguments: colleges should not be the farm system for professional teams; the mission of a university is perverted when dumb athletes enroll; luring young athletes when they have no reasonable chance of graduating is exploitative, immoral, and harmful to the athlete. Not one of these has any merit.

4   The argument that the professional football and basketball leagues should set up minor leagues is both irrelevant and wrong: irrelevant, because cost restraints prevent them from doing so, and wrong, because the current system was not created by the professional leagues. Major intercollegiate sports are driven by legitimate market forces, which schools cannot and should not ignore.

5   Nor does allowing poor students to play collegiate athletics pervert the university and its mission. Today the mission of many universities, by the schools' own choice, includes providing athletic training to young athletes and athletic entertainment to the public. The athletic mission is not perverse or inherently inconsistent with a primary scholarly one.

6   Universities, for instance, have historically admitted students who do not meet normal academic criteria but who possess unique nonacademic talents—artists, musicians, actors. The university is not scolded for undermining its mission by admitting them. It reflects prejudice to readily accept artists but not sweaty athletes.

7   Furthermore, underachieving students are admitted at every university for other reasons, such as because a parent is a professor, major donor, or alumnus. This is not perverse if it is not excessive, and the quality of education and research is not diminished by enrolling a few mediocre students.

8   Finally, there is the exploitation argument. I have often heard universities criticized for admitting athletes who had little chance to graduate,

as if graduating were a universal prerequisite for a better life. In fact, whether a school exploits an athlete hinges not on his graduating but on whether he materially benefits from the college experience. Rarely does a scholarship athlete leave college worse off than when he entered.

9   Certainly, a young man who goes on to a lucrative professional career is not exploited. But even most who do not become professional athletes gain much in college to improve their lives, whether or not they graduate. Almost every athlete will be better prepared for adult life because of athletic skills he developed, things he learned in classes and experiences he encountered outside of his often disadvantaged home environment.

10   Athletes should be encouraged and assisted academically, worked into the mainstream of campus life and required to be students. The N.C.A.A. should require that colleges meet their ethical obligation to offer athletes an opportunity to improve and mature as people. Schools should provide adequate counseling and tutoring, make athletes attend and participate in class, make meaningful courses available for each athlete at his intellectual level, abolish dorms for athletes that shelter them from the rest of the university, and do everything reasonable to bring athletes into the mainstream of campus life.

11   But it is unconscionable to deny a young man the chance at a lucrative career and the public the opportunity to see him perform, solely because he does not meet intellectual standards unrelated to his athletic career.

Thinking about a Subject and Writing for Yourself:

Prompts for Journal Writing and Class Discussion

1. Roberts' persona is implied by the introduction. Explain how it is reinforced by his writing style and diction. Why do you think he maintains a formal, academic persona as he argues for admitting athletes with marginal academic abilities?

2. What does Roberts present as the arguments of his opposition? Do you think his summary is fair? Does it include the major arguments?

3. Roberts systematically responds to the arguments he has identified. Do you find his response adequate? How does he support his assertions? Are his comparisons logical? His evidence sufficient?

4. Roberts' essay makes careful use of paragraphs and transitions to mark his ideas. Do you find his discussion easy to follow? Does his formal diction make the essay hard to read? Why or why not?

5. What does Roberts see as the advantages of college life? Is his attitude more like Thakur's or like Sack's?

6. How does Roberts identify his opposition? Why do you think he is not more specific?

We Are God in Here: Amnesty International Letter
John G. Healey

John G. Healey's letter was part of a mailout to encourage membership in Amnesty International.

Becoming an Active Reader:

1. What do you know about Amnesty International? Its goals? Its targets? Its methods?
2. Is there a place for emotional appeal in legitimate arguments? What kinds of causes could or should use emotional appeals?

Dear Friend,

1. Though frightening and shocking to even contemplate . . . right now, today, the horrors of torture and political detention are every day incidents in fully one-third of the world's governments.

2. Torture is terrible and disgusting. It mocks the most sacred and most universal human value—the sanctity of human life. It is physical and mental degradation, assault, burning of flesh with cigarettes, electric shock, living a year or more blindfolded in total darkness, being stretched and broken on the rack, having the unspeakable become a living nightmare.

3. Believe me, I do not recount these facts to be morbid or to provide excessive shock value.

4. We at *Amnesty International* have learned that the truth must be told so that the world's peoples can respond with the moral outrage required to stop the hideous crime against humanity that torture is.

5. My plea to you is that you join me and more than half a million compassionate fellow human beings worldwide in Amnesty International. I urge you to add your name to the roster of members of the only organization of its kind in history to have won the *Nobel Prize for Peace.*

6. It is the mission of Amnesty International to abolish torture. We work impartially on behalf of victims of human rights violations. The great majority of cases we undertake involve what we call "prisoners of conscience"—men and women who are imprisoned anywhere for their beliefs, color, sex, ethnic origin, language, or religion, provided they have neither used nor advocated violence.

7. We work to end their torture. We work to secure for them fair and prompt trials. We work to prevent their execution. We work to secure their freedom. And a critical tool in Amnesty's fight against torture is our *Urgent Action Network.*

8   This extraordinary international Network is a highly organized system of concerned people who agree to be on call to send immediate Urgent Action letters on behalf of tortured prisoners of conscience.

9   When Amnesty receives reliable information about a detainee needing immediate aid, we activate our Network at virtually a moment's notice. Our researchers verify facts about the case. The facts are fed into our massive telecommunications network. And volunteers respond with telegrams and letters—all within a matter of hours.

10   About 50,000 people belong to the Urgent Action Network worldwide; 5,000 of them are Americans. And our Network works. Our surveys show that 40 to 45 percent of prisoners are either released or treated better when the Network is mobilized on their behalf.

11   I'm convinced our Network is so extraordinarily effective because it's ordinary people, more than governments, who have the power to stop torture. The thousands of responses that governments receive from caring people around the world give notice to prison and government officials that their actions have been exposed. Even the most tyrannical governments don't want to appear repressive before their own citizens or before other countries. Their bankers have to negotiate with representatives of other countries, and their ships have to dock in foreign ports.

12   So our Urgent Action Network effectively strips away the masks of decency through which governments rationalize their human rights violations, forcing them to address questions arising from their abuses. Eventually, governments must ask themselves, "Is this particular prisoner worth all this negative publicity?" "Is keeping this individual in jail or torturing this person worth all the trouble it's causing?" "Can we afford further damage to our internal and international image?"

13   We at Amnesty International *know* governments ask these questions, because they do in fact release prisoners of conscience whom we have adopted and fought for and because former prisoners have contacted us to thank us . . .

14   A released prisoner from Malaysia wrote about the letters he received while in prison: "It is hard to describe the feelings in my heart . . . these (letters) I regarded as *precious jewels.*"

15   A freed Paraguayan prisoner aided by Amnesty wrote: "On Christmas Eve the door to my cell opened and the guard tossed in a crumpled piece of paper. It said, 'Take heart. *The world knows you're alive.* We're with you.' That letter saved my life."

16   But our Urgent Action Network is only one part of our wide-ranging efforts to abolish torture.

17   Amnesty International also brings pressure to bear against offending governments through our consultative status with the United Nations and the Council of Europe, and through cooperative relations with governmental bodies in Africa and Latin America.

18   Within the United States, we are expanding our network of legal, medical, and political experts. In fact, we already have 1,500 lawyers from 25 states on our Legal Support Network and over 1,200 health professionals who participate in actions to release prisoners of conscience.

19   Also, in hearings before Congress and in private meetings with lawmakers, Amnesty representatives urge U.S. officials to carefully consider human rights data when making foreign policy. We even press our officials to pay personal visits to prisoners of conscience.

20   On another front, Amnesty will be working more closely with target groups—such as business, labor, politicians—meeting with them and sharing ways they can work with us to help stop the torture of innocent people.

21   And over the coming months and years, we intend to intensify our pressure upon governments to adopt *specific measures* for eliminating the practice of torture.

22   We at Amnesty do not believe—as some do—that torture is a regrettable, but incurable, disease. Slavery was once viewed in a similar light; it is now all but extinguished throughout the world. The same fate *is* possible for torture.

23   Perhaps the words of one small child whom Amnesty helped speak most eloquently for the worth of our work.

24   Alfonso Hernandez, a small E1 Salvadorian boy, was kept hidden indoors for over two years by his grandparents to avoid death squads while his mother was illegally imprisoned and tortured.

25   Little Alfonso is so happy to be free, he now says he *"wants to kiss everybody"* he meets.

26   Your name has been suggested as one who might wish to support Amnesty's vital efforts to free the "Alfonsos"—and prisoners of conscience—around the world whose lives are living nightmares.

27   So I sincerely hope you'll take this opportunity to join Amnesty International.

28   Torture *can* be stopped. Prisoners *can* be freed. Lives *can* be saved through direct action by Amnesty International.

29   But . . . our life-saving work can *only* continue to function if caring, unselfish people who abhor the practice of torture are willing to play just a small—yet important—role in stopping it.

30   Our need for your support is so terribly urgent because, even as I write this letter to you, someplace in the world—in Communist countries, in Western societies, in the Third World—innocent victims of government abuse are imprisoned, suffering unspeakable physical and mental agonies.

31   In Vietnam . . . a prominent poet, Hoang Cam, is in prison for attempting to deliver a collection of unpublished poems to the United States. In Pakistan, Ghanshyam Parkash, a medical student active in the Democratic Students Federation, was sentenced to seven years imprisonment

for possessing pamphlets deemed "objectionable." In Peru, Mauro Aristides Ochoa Ochoa, a 29-year-old peasant community advisor, is being tried on charges of terrorism. Lawyers say that a confession extracted under torture is the only evidence against him.

32   It is up to us—you and me—to free these prisoners of conscience and thousands like them around the world.

33   And that's why I urge you to take a moment right now, while you have my letter in front of you, to complete the enclosed membership form and return it to me with your tax-deductible membership check for $25—or more if you can possibly manage.

34   As soon as I hear from you, I'll see that you begin receiving our newspaper, *Amesty Action,* which will keep you up-to-date on every facet of Amnesty's work.

35   "The letters kept coming," "precious jewels," "the world knows you're alive," "kiss everybody." These words echo the hope and love people in need share with people who care.

36   We are these people, and they are us. So please, join Amnesty International today. We need you. Mail your enclosed membership form today. Thank you.

Sincerely yours,

John G. Healey
Executive Director

37   P.S. Here's what one prisoner told us after he was freed:

"When the first 200 letters (from Amnesty) came, the guard gave me back my clothes. Then the next 200 letters came and the prison director came to see me. *The letters kept coming.* The President called the prison and told them to let me go."

Thinking about a Subject and Writing for Yourself:

Prompts for Journal Writing and Class Discussion

1. Why do you think that there is a paragraph offered before the letter opens? What is the effect of the heading and opening incident?

2. The letter begins with shocking and horrible information, but the third paragraph reassures the readers that the main intention is not to shock. What effect does that explanation have on you? Are you any less shocked? Why do you think that paragraph is included?

3. Where does the letter reveal its purpose? How is the statement of purpose emphasized in the format of the letter?

4. Healey's persona is only a part of the image that is created for the readers. How is the organization itself characterized? What is the effect of using both "I" and "we"? What other diction choices create connotative associations for the readers?

5. What kinds of evidence does Healey present? What assertion is he supporting?

6. The letter uses both logical and emotional appeals. Identify some of each. Which appeals are dominant here? Why do you think that such a strategy is used?

7. Analyze the strategy of the closing of the letter, including the final paragraphs of the main text and the postscript.

SUMMARY

Writing to convince may be the most common kind of writing you do. You may identify problems, propose solutions, challenge the ideas of others, or appeal for specific action. Whatever form it takes, though, writing to convince demands careful attention to the audience—its interests, concerns, and fears. Effective argument is a blend of appropriate persona, selected points, sufficient evidence, and thoughtful organization.

Y O U R T U R N

Invitations to Write to Convince

Identifying a Problem: Before a problem can be solved, it must be identified. In these topics, you are not asked for solutions. You are asked only to argue the existence and/or the severity of a problem.

1. As the newest employee in a fast food restaurant, you are studying the training manual and working hard to learn your job. You need the money and this job not only pays well, it is near your home and the hours suit your schedule. But you have noticed a problem. Other employees take shortcuts in preparing food and in cleaning equipment, and you believe that some of these shortcuts are creating real health hazards for customers. You are reluctant to say anything to anyone at first, but the problem seems to be increasing as you continue to observe it. There is an employee suggestion box, and there is also a manager who has assured you that you can come to her with any problems. When you can stand it no longer, you put your fears in writing, arguing that there is a problem and that it is indeed serious.

2. The label "date rape" has been used to describe a sexual attack on a woman by a friend or a date. You attend a campus-sponsored forum and hear some students argue that there is no such thing, that so-called date rape is no more than a spiteful woman trying to make trouble for a man. You also hear stories ranging from persistent, unwelcome advances to vicious attacks. You have had no experience with the questions and have heard such a variety of stories that you decide to investigate the problem further, doing some reading and asking friends about their own experiences and ideas. In a very short time you have formed an opinion about the existence of the problem, and you write to the school newspaper, arguing that date rape is (is not) a serious problem.

3. There has been much discussion about laws that seem designed to protect citizens from themselves—for example, laws requiring use of seat belts and children's car seats and motorcycle helmets. Do you think that there is a problem with these laws? Would you like to see them changed? Or, do you think that there is a problem serious enough to warrant their existence? Your own state legislature plans to debate these laws in the next session. Write a letter to the local newspaper or to your district representative arguing that there is a problem, either with the laws themselves or with the public's attitude. Make your persona clear—are you writing as a concerned parent? As a taxpayer? As a conscientious motorcyclist?

Proposing a Solution: Some problems are unquestionably serious, but there is little agreement on solutions or even attitudes about those problems. For these topics, you will not need to prove that there is a problem. You can mention the size and scope of the problem, but your primary focus is on responses to the problem.

4. News reports have made it clear that drug use is a major problem in competitive athletics. You know some of the varsity athletes on your campus, and they are defensive about accusations and unhappy about suggestions that they are using any kind of banned substances. They are also angry that they are assumed guilty; they want their word to mean something. You think about the problems and the attitudes, and you work out a proposal that addresses the drug problem at the college level. You send these suggestions on to your school's athletic director, stressing that you are concerned not only about the individuals involved but also about the reputation of the program itself.

5. You have listened to friends and family discuss political campaigns and candidates for the last few years, and you are

unhappy with the attitude toward elections. Many of your friends seem to be basing their votes on absurd criteria; others are convinced that their votes are insignificant; others see no difference between candidates and refuse to participate. You can see that such attitudes lead to low voter turnout, and you have a proposal to encourage more active, informed participation. Send a copy of your proposal to the local newspaper or to some other party that might be directly involved (for example, if your plan requires action by the city council, then send it to a council member).

6. You know that there is an increase in the number of plagiarism cases brought before the Dean of Students, and that a similar increase is reported across the country. You review your own experiences and what others have told you, and you think about more effective ways of handling students accused of plagiarism. Send your guidelines to the Dean of Students, explaining your reasons for this more lenient (more severe) approach to the problem.

Challenging the ideas and writings of others: Many arguments are reactions to the written or spoken ideas of others. The topics below invite you to explain your disagreement with current policy, current thinking, or current writing.

7. Stereotypes may illustrate the attitudes of a culture, but widespread acceptance of these images does not make them accurate. At a recent family reunion, you listened to a cousin expound on the nature of *all* recipients of social welfare programs, and you have been simmering over his illogical descriptions. So you decide to write to him, telling him that you were surprised to hear his opinions and explaining to him why you think he is wrong. You are angry but determined to appear more reasonable than he did; you also realize that he is "family," but that you have never been particularly close. (Variation: select another stereotype that offends you and challenge the "reasoning" behind it. Possibilities: the incompetent woman driver, the dumb athlete, the beauty pageant bubblehead)

8. Something you read has disturbed you to the point that you are ready to write a response. You do not have an audience in mind; your first target, you realize, is yourself: you want to explain your disagreement with this writing as completely and thoroughly as you can. If the original text was part of a class assignment, you may want to present your response in class; if it appeared in the newspaper, you may send it as a letter to the editor. Possible texts for your refutation:

a. Review the readings in this chapter for stands on controversial issues that you cannot accept. Explain your disagreement with the ideas in the text.

b. Review editorials and letters to the editor in newspapers and magazines. The ones with which you most strongly disagree make the best subjects for refutation.

In any case, remember that you must do more than say "I don't think so." You are expected to explain and support your own ideas. You also want to appear *at least* as reasonable as the writer of the original, perhaps more so.

An appeal for specific action: Handouts and letters often encourage readers to take immediate and specific action. Writers of such material know that emotion is effective in getting immediate response.

9. You have been working with a community project and have been impressed by the work it does. However, the project will soon end if more volunteers are not forthcoming. You know many people who could find the time for this project, so you decide to appeal to them for help. Whom would you address? What would you say to move them? Suggested projects: shelter for the homeless, community food bank, disaster relief, Big Brothers and Sisters, preschool enrichment.

10. Your roommate has announced plans to run for a school office. You agree to work with the campaign, and you are asked to use your considerable writing talent to create handouts that give information and encourage voter response. You are free to decide on the manner of distribution (mail, door-to-door, table outside the student union, etc.), and you plan to tailor the heading and contents to the audience. If graphics are to be included, you may sketch or describe what you would like and another artist will complete the picture. What would you write? To whom would you write it?

SUGGESTED APPROACHES TO YOUR RESPONSE

The relationship between your audience and your material cannot be overemphasized when you write to convince your readers. From your earliest explorations of your subject to the final review of your draft, keep in mind that your ideas will be tested by your readers. Their skepticism, their fears, their questions, and their expectations should guide your decisions about content and organization and persona. However, the audience should not influence your thesis. Your basic feelings about the subject must be respected and reflected in your thesis.

❏ The First Decision: To Accept the Invitation to Write

When you begin to gather material for an argument, your initial task is to inventory your knowledge and opinions of your intended subject. Remember that points need more than explanation; a skeptical audience will expect evidence to *prove* that your assertions are reasonable. So, as you gather points, look for various kinds of evidence to support them.

Kinds of Evidence

1. *Confirmed Details or Statistics:*

   How many drug-related deaths were there in the United States last year?

   What percentage of our taxes is spent on defense?

   What is the present rate of illiteracy in New York state?

   The answers to these questions, which can be found in any library, are examples of confirmed details or statistics. Most audiences readily accept this kind of evidence because it is least subject to error or bias.

2. *Personal Experience and Observation:*

   What has happened to you?

   What have you seen happening to others?

   Personal experience is the one kind of evidence about which you can speak with authority regardless of your credentials. As first-hand testimony, it has special force with your readers—if it is accurate and relevant.

3. *Authority:*

   Who are the experts in this area?

   What do the experts say?

   Do they agree?

   Experts are in command of a subject and, while not infallible, they are less likely to err than amateurs. Moreover, their errors tend to occur in a framework of valid ideas. Thus expert testimony and judgments are usually convincing to most audiences.

To strengthen such testimony, give information on background or credentials. Check with your professors and librarians to verify reputation. The source, too, adds credibility; a scholarly text is authoritative while *National Enquirer* is not. And bibliographies can show how often and how recently the expert has published.

4. *Other People's Experience and Observation:*

What have you heard from other people?

What have you heard or read in the media?

A major concern is the reliability of the source. Be warned that such information is second-hand and subject to error. Try to verify it from as many sources as possible.

Two reminders:

Keep your mind open. As you learn about your subject, your attitudes might change. Forming strong opinions early could hinder free exploration.

Working on paper has numerous advantages over working in your head, so record even your earliest lists.

Cross-Reference: Any of the exploring strategies outlined in Chapter 3 can be used for exploring controversial issues, but these are particularly useful:

- Listing
- Imaginary Dialogue
- Probing for Patterns

As you work, encourage a dialogue between creative and critical voices that evaluates material to recognize strong points and strengthen weak ones.

Reminder:

Strengths and weaknesses are relative to your audience—what will readers find convincing?

The audience:
- Should be considered early and often
- Should influence the points you develop
- Should influence the amount and kind of evidence

Cross-Reference: Critical thinking skills (Chapter 7) will encourage the creative/critical dialogue to evaluate material.

For more information about analyzing audience, review Chapter 12. For more detail about the audience and opposition of arguments, see Chapter 4.

- Evaluating Evidence
- Analyzing the Opposition
- Accommodating the Audience

For additional information on gathering evidence, Chapter 14 suggests research strategies for library and field work. For help in screening your evidence, review Chapter 19:

- Evaluating Evidence

❏   The Second Decision: To Draft the Response

As you draft your response, your readers are a major influence on your material—both the points you select and the organization of those points. However, do not demand of your draft that it be complete on the first try. Instead, expect to review and draft repeatedly. Keep these guidelines in mind:

1. **Your first draft aims only to put ideas on paper.** It commits you to nothing. Do not put great pressure on yourself to organize at the same time that you are struggling to express your ideas.

2. **Review your draft to identify your thesis.** Recognize points that support your main idea and make sure that they are backed by evidence.

3. **Identifying supporting points and gathering evidence will result in a mass of material to be organized.** The kind of material and the kind of audience will both affect the organization of your paper. Look for existing patterns or connections like cause-effect and comparison. Also, use your knowledge of your audience to identify and emphasize crucial points and to place the thesis effectively.

Two reminders:

Are you refuting ideas?

Are you using deductive and/or inductive reasoning?

> **Cross-Reference:** As you draft, consult the catalogue in Chapter 9 for discussions of logical patterns, including the patterns of argument. Chapter 10 will also be helpful as you evaluate the logic of the connections between your ideas.

A good argument draws supporting evidence from outside sources as well as personal experience. While methods like definition and analogy and even process analysis are useful in argument, presenting evidence from sources may require summary, paraphrase, and direct and indirect quotation.

Note, too, that analysis of your evidence is as important as its relevance and accuracy. If you simply report on the research, the readers may draw their own conclusions—and those conclusions may not match yours. In other words, it is not enough to **report** that the population of New Mexico is increasing; you must also **interpret** that report to argue that tax incentives (or illegal alien policies or religious beliefs) are the cause.

Reminder:

Documentation of sources is not only ethical; it is also effective in building your credibility.

Review Chapter 19 for guidelines to documenting material from sources.

> **Cross-Reference:** Chapter 12 catalogues strategies useful for presenting evidence to your readers, and it also reviews the tactics for such processes as evaluating, challenging, and connecting information. As you draft, review these strategies.
>
> For presenting material:
>
> - Summarizing
> - Paraphrasing
> - Quoting
>
> For interpreting material:
>
> - Explaining
> - Evaluating
> - Challenging
> - Speculating
> - Connecting

❏ **The Third Decision: To Review the Work in Progress**

Connecting Audience, Content, and Purpose

The relationship between your audience, your persona, your supporting points, and your organization is essential to effective argument. Use these questions to analyze the background and expectations of your readers:

Knowledge:
- Do your readers understand all of the issues?
- Have they considered all of the available data?
- Have they understood all of the fine print?
- Is there anything you can explain or clarify that might have an effect on their opinions?
- Where are they most likely to misunderstand your argument?
- How can you reduce misunderstandings?

Opinions:
- On which points do you and your readers agree?
- Which are their weakest points of disagreement? That is, which can you attack most thoroughly?
- Which are their strongest points of disagreement?
- To which of your points will they most strongly react?
- What objections will they raise?
- How can you best construct your points to avoid or to answer their objections?

Expectations:
- Have you used any words that might offend them unnecessarily and undermine persuasion?
- If so, what words might you substitute without altering meaning?
- Are they likely to conclude that you understand their position and have dealt with it fairly? If not, what might you add to the presentation to get a more favorable reaction?

Reminder:

Your audience should influence the contents and organization of your draft, but it must not influence your opinions.

Polishing the Draft

A complete draft is not a finished draft. When you have organized your material into blocks of prose, look again at the content of the draft and the image of your persona. Then consider the framework (title, introduction, transitions, and conclusion), the paragraphs, sentences and word choices.

The contents should demonstrate:

- Logical presentation of information
- Thorough analysis of material
- Explicit connections between evidence and assertions
- Appropriate awareness of audience concerns
- Documentation of sources

The persona should be:

- Strong yet inoffensive
- Confident without arrogance
- Credible to the audience

Two Reminders:

Your material should be organized and your persona developed with consideration of your audience.

Ask a friend to react to your argument. Listen carefully to the comments.

Cross-Reference: Review the material on logic and fallacies in Chapter 10.

A solid framework (title, introduction, transitions, and conclusion) will present the material clearly and help your readers follow your arguments.

The title:
- Hints at the subject
- Arouses curiosity

The introduction:
- Identifies the topic
- Avoids offense
- Intrigues the reader

Transitions:
- Demonstrate connections
- Signal changes

The conclusion:
- Signals a clear end
- Affirms the stand
- Calls for action
- Leaves a strong impression

A final review of text (paragraphing, sentence structures, and diction) can add to the effectiveness of your argument.

> **Cross-Reference:** If you feel that your creative energies are running low, review Chapter 15 for some ideas on introductions, conclusions, and titles.

Paragraphing:

- Orders the assertions and the evidence
- Separates and emphasizes points

Sentence structure:

- Controls pace
- Emphasizes points
- Leads readers toward conclusion

Diction:

- Indicates persona
- Creates mood
- Evokes emotional response
- Influences readers

Reminder:

Casual diction may present you as a nonthreatening presence, but it can slip into carelessness.

Formal diction may sound scholarly and authoritative, but it can create pompous, jargonistic prose.

> **Cross-Reference:** As you edit text, look carefully at paragraphs, sentences, and word choices. The catalogues listed below can help:
>
> Improving Paragraphs
>
> - Natural Junctures
> - Opinions/Cases in Point
> - Perspective/Reasons
>
> Improving Sentences
>
> - Variations of Order
>
> Improving Diction
>
> - Level
> - Pretentiousness
> - Jargon
> - Exactness
> - Wordiness

Final Considerations

As you review your writing, check:

- **The rhetorical situation**
  Has your writing satisfied the expectations created by the context? Are your subject and your thesis appropriate to the situation? Is your audience likely to accept your persona and your material as reasonable?
- **The logical connections between ideas**
  Are your causes reasonable? Your classifications consistent? Your comparisons valid?
- **The methods of presentation**
  Are they suited to the nature of your material?
- **The accuracy of the text**
  Have you proofread for your own most common errors as well as other problems with grammar, spelling, and mechanics? Have you proofread for new errors created by typographical mistakes or by careless copying?

A Student Writes to Convince His Readers

Alex deWilde is planning a career in political science, and he tries hard to keep up with international affairs. He sees himself as a future policy maker and is not afraid to take unpopular stands on difficult issues.

His problem-solution paper is, he admits, ambitious. But he points out that defining a position is a necessary start to any foreign policy.

Alex's first response to the assignment was done rather quickly. He had strong feelings about his subject and expressed his opinion that the U.S. should intervene in foreign countries. His initial feelings about his draft were positive. He thought his ideas were clear and logical, and he expected his peer reviewer to agree with him.

But Alex was surprised, even a little offended, when the reviewer asked for evidence. Deciding that the reviewer was simply too uninformed to see his logic, Alex decided to present a more detailed argument to prove that his policy was logical and necessary.

As he examined recent history, though, he began to question his original assertions. He could not find the clear support he had assumed was available; instead, the lesson of history seemed to contradict his original position. Alex took his ideas to his political science instructor, and after they had discussed the examples, Alex decided to alter his stand.

As you can see from the two drafts given here, the final version reverses Alex's original position.

Where Do We Draw the Line?

Comments from peer evaluations:

Students in Tienanmen Square, children in Ethiopia, teenagers in the Middle East, villagers in Nicaragua--all of them are victims of violent political oppression, or so we believe. What can we do about them? How can we intervene? In fact, <u>should</u> we intervene? Americans, I believe, are haunted by the notion, popularized in post-Holocaust literature, that the Allies could have prevented the murder of 6,000,000 Jews by actively and publicly involving themselves in what official Nazi German policy called "internal" affairs.

Should we ever interfere? Do we ever?

Whether or not such intervention would have succeeded is, tragically, impossible to know. The question remains, "To what, if any, extent is it proper for one government or its citizens to attempt to influence the actions and policies of another?" As Americans, we are frequently caught between our belief in self-determination and our sense of the value of individual human lives. We are shocked by what we perceive to be some foreign governments' denial of the rights of their citizens, yet we insist that each country should have the right to establish its own form of government. So, what should we do? Should we refuse to buy goods from South Africa until the government gives full franchise to its black citizens? Should we continue to send food to Ethiopia when we know that the Ethiopian government is denying food supplies sent for famine relief to those who are in rebellion against it? Should we stop selling grain to China until it

do we "all" agree with your ideas here? Prove it.

What about Iran? the Phillipines? Did we interfere?

frees all the students who have been arrested this summer
and restores their rights as citizens? Should we try to
establish a public policy regarding international human
rights issues?

*Name some.
Are all
democracies
free
countries?*

Yes, we should establish such a policy. We should refuse
to spend any public money, ~~including~~ *or such items as* subsidized grain sales,
arms and technology sales, and so on, that will *in effect* support
repressive regimes. On the other hand, we should give
humanitarian aid only (food, clothing, and medical supplies)
to groups which are seeking to advance human rights causes
around the world. By these two actions, the United States *even if they do not have support of their now government.*
would make it clear that we support the rights of individuals
around the world to freedom and self-determination. If

*What
countries
are you
thinking
of here?*

American businesses learned that our government would not
protect their profit margins at the expense of human rights,
then they would no longer have vested interests in encouraging military expansion and economic exploitation of minori-
ties.

Although this proposal does not solve all of the international humanitarian/human rights issues, its adoption would
be a beginning. Once such a policy is consistently followed,
then other policies regarding military and direct financial aid
can be established.

*Alex — What has the U.S. done in the past?
Have our actions helped?
Do we always identify "good guys"
and "bad guys"?*

Alex's Final Draft

Where Do We Draw the Line

"Again I looked and saw all the oppression

that was taking place under the sun:

I saw the tears of the oppressed —

and they have no comforter;

power was on the side of their oppressors —

and they have no comforter."

Ecclesiastes 4:1

We Americans watch television and see students in Tienanmen Square, children in Ethiopia, teenagers in the Middle East, villagers in Nicaragua —all victims of violent political oppression, or so we believe. We wonder how we can "comfort" the oppressed. As a nation we are a compassionate people, responding quickly to news of natural disasters around the world. Experienced in organizing and delivering aid for victims of earthquakes, floods and hurricanes, we are so generous that oftentimes word must go out to stop sending food and clothes because distribution centers are overwhelmed with supplies. Our actions as private citizens are matched by government response in the form of direct financial aid and technical expertise. However, deciding how to respond to "unnatural" disasters is more difficult. We are concerned about both the propriety and effectiveness of intervention in the internal affairs of other countries.

The most important question is whether or not it is proper for one government or its citizens to attempt to influence the actions and policies of another. As Americans, we are frequently caught between our belief in self-determination and our sense of the value of individual human lives. We are shocked by what we perceive to be some foreign governments' denial of the rights of their citizens, yet we insist that each country should have the right to establish its own form of government. In the twentieth century, we have qualified our insistence on self-determination by supporting developing democracies and assuming that budding totalitarian regimes should be discouraged. Implementation of this policy has made it apparent that "democracy" is difficult to define and that governmental leaders are not necessarily consistent once they gain control. Both Ferdinand Marcos of the Philippines and Shah Reza Pahlevi in Iran presented themselves to the American government as enlightened leaders in order to gain our support, and both became extremely repressive. Given the demonstrated inability of our government to predict the outcome of supporting individuals seeking to reform their governments, it seems clear that living up to our belief in the rights of both individuals and governments to self-determination might best be done through a policy of non-intervention.

Not only does history seem to show the impropriety of intervention, it does not offer us any clear proof that either military or economic participation in the actions of other countries is effective. Many Americans, I think, are haunted by the notion, reiterated most recently in the popular television productions of Wouk's *The Winds of War* and *War and Remembrance,* that the Allies might have prevented the murder of 6,000,000 Jews by actively and publicly involving themselves in what official Nazi German policy called "internal" affairs. Whether or not early, massive intervention would have succeeded is, tragically, impossible to know. On the contrary, we are confronted, by recollections of the Vietnam era, with the fact that our military involvement on behalf of one party in a divided country will not necessarily succeed. Economic sanctions are not always successful, either. Cuba has managed to survive for thirty years without trading with the United States. Decreasing our participation in the economy of South Africa has not yet brought about the collapse of the apartheid government. Years of sending both military and humanitarian support to the Contras have not enabled them to overthrow the Marxist government in Nicaragua. Neither does withdrawal of support from a repressive regime uniformly lead to improvement in the circumstances of the citizens of a country. For example, Aquino's accession to power in the Philippines led to the collapse of the Marcos bureaucracy which, in turn, led to an almost complete inability of the government to maintain vital services ranging from systematic garbage pickup to health and welfare delivery. So political oppression was replaced by governmental chaos, and, according to a friend of mine who travels through the Philippines frequently, the people were much worse off. On the other hand, quiet military support of the rebels in Afghanistan may have affected the decision of the Soviet Union to withdraw its troops from that country. It is too soon to tell what will happen to the government of Afghanistan now.

Thus, the preponderance of evidence seems to show that active intervention is neither proper nor effective. It is so difficult to predict the long-range effects of our commitment to one or another faction within another country that we should avoid doing so. This does not rule out attempts to deliver strictly humanitarian aid such as food and medical supplies to war-torn and famine-ridden countries like Ethiopia and Nicaragua. However, it does dictate that we should use extreme caution when deciding to adopt economic sanctions or deliver military aid to any other country. We should be motivated primarily by concern that our intervention not actually worsen the condition of those we are seeking to aid. We should be careful to determine that we are, in fact, bringing comfort to the oppressed.

Writing to Involve the Audience

When you write to involve, your goal is to reach readers emotionally, recreating experience so that they share it vicariously. This chapter describes the characteristics of such writing and provides varied sample essays. Situations that invite written response are followed by suggested approaches with careful cross-referencing to the catalogue in Part Three.

When you recreate an amusing experience, you want your audience to share your amusement. When you write about a person whom you admire, you want your audience to share your admiration. When you describe an eerie cave, you want your audience to share your fearful discomfort. In all of these writings, your general goal is to recreate your subject in the imagination of your readers so that they can feel what you want them to feel. The purpose of your writing is not to give information or to change attitudes; instead, it is to involve the readers' emotions as you recreate an actual person or scene or incident. (This focus on actual experience distinguishes such writing from fiction, which also seeks to involve the audience's imagination and emotion.)

The techniques most often used to involve the readers vicariously are narrating and describing, but narrating and describing are not purposes in themselves. To illuminate the distinction, consider that a narrative of a surgical procedure might be intended to inform the audience of the new techniques used. Such a narrative aims to improve understanding. In contrast, writing to involve recreates the experience in considerable detail and with considerable dramatic intensity to make the readers feel that they are experiencing the situation themselves, with all the emotional reactions of the person or persons to whom it happened.

CHARACTERISTICS OF WRITING THAT INVOLVES

Even a brief piece of writing can involve the audience by recreating a scene with dramatic intensity:

> I had managed to forget my fear—until I heard a low moan from behind the door to the dentist's office. Then I grew tense. My

stomach ached. I felt very cold, yet perspiration was running down my forehead. "Make an excuse to the receptionist," I thought. "Just get out." I wanted to run, but some battered sense of duty held me. For the next twenty minutes I sat fixed to my chair, heart pounding, legs trembling.

(student writer)

This writer urges the audience to sit with him, providing details that are familiar yet intense so that the experience is shared rather than reported.

Your writing can take many forms when you seek to involve your readers' emotions. However, effective writing often shows these characteristics:

1. It usually focuses on a **single incident or scene.** Including several focal points in a short piece may reduce dramatic intensity.

2. The subject is vivid enough to make you, the **writer,** feel again the tranquility or the pain. Such vivid recollections have the potential to affect the readers, too.

3. The subject is an **actual event or scene.** It recreates vivid experiences from your own memory bank.

SITUATIONS THAT PROMPT WRITING THAT INVOLVES

It is probably easiest for you to see the rhetorical context of the classroom assignment. But writing to involve is common outside of the academic environment. Newspaper and magazine articles invite readers to share a nostalgic moment, and correspondence to friends and family is likely to recreate incidents or recall experiences, involving the emotions of the audience. Or, like the writer in the following example, you may be asked to explain why someone you love has been important to you.

Writing beyond the Classroom

In 1981, Joseph Robert Barry was presented with the Sertoma Man of the Year Award. His son Robert nominated him for the award and, in presenting it, invited the audience to see his father as he did.

Dr. Robert Barry is an educated man who worked with the Experimental Agricultural Research Center of a major university. The piece about his father was, he says, a difficult one to write. He started several weeks before the awards presentation, beginning with some oral discussions with his family. His mother in particular was an important source of information. At first, Dr. Barry collected material without making any attempt to evaluate or to exclude any recollections. Sometimes, he says, he would make a few notes about details that he thought were especially revealing.

After a week or so of collecting his materials and making random notes, he began to list his observations with more care. The occasion demanded a review of his father's civic accomplishments, but Dr. Barry also wanted to show the personal side of the man. He began to draw from incidents revealing the character traits that he saw in his father's words and actions, and he began to think of other incidents that illustrated similar traits. Soon, he recalls, he had far too much material for the brief presentation.

His next step was to mark the traits he wanted to describe to the audience. Then he selected some incidents and some comments others had made about his father and the impact he had had on their lives. He tried several organization patterns, finally deciding that he would give the expected information about his father's contributions to the community first. He knew that his father was a very private man, and he did not want to embarrass him, so Dr. Barry planned only a brief summary of personal details.

With an organization plan in mind, he drafted a text that was still too long for his purposes. But he continued to read it aloud to his family and to himself, re-organizing parts and getting audience feedback about the effectiveness of his material. As usual, he says, his wife Karleen was "his best critic." In reviewing his draft, he decided to close with his own testimony to his father's life. Given the occasion and his father's feelings, though, he made sure it was restrained and dignified.

When he was satisfied with the content of his material, he prepared a final copy and asked his wife to help him proofread for mistakes. The night of the dinner, Dr. Barry presented the award to his father and offered this picture to the audience:

Service to Mankind Award — 1981
Sunset Area Sertoma Club
Recipient: J. R. Barry, Sr.

J. R. "Robbie" Barry has been a successful farmer and an outstanding civic leader in the Grand Coteau-Sunset area of Louisiana for over 60 years. Robbie, as he is lovingly called in this community, is known as a model citizen. He is an honest, hard-working farmer and civic leader who has contributed significantly to the development of agriculture at both the community and the state levels. He was a pioneer grower and shipper of sweet potatoes (yams) in Louisiana and was instrumental in organizing the Louisiana Sweet Potato Association. He served as the first Association president and for several terms thereafter. He also served on the

Louisiana State Market Commission and on the Louisiana Farm Council where he donated much time and effort toward the betterment of Louisiana agriculture.

During his farming career he frequently cooperated with the Louisiana State University researchers by providing land, labor, and equipment to aid in research designed to benefit the sweet potato industry. During the period from 1930 through 1970, the sweet potato industry was the mainstay of the local economy, and Robbie played a substantial part in the development of this industry. In 1952 he was recognized by the yam industry, being selected as the sixth Louisiana Yambilee King.

He was again recognized in 1978 when he received the Distinguished Service Award presented by the Louisiana Sweet Potato Association for his outstanding contribution to the industry. He also worked closely with the U.S. Soil Conservation Service terracing and drainage projects. His farm was the first in the community to be terraced to prevent soil erosion, and it has served as a model for many area farmers over the years.

Robbie was also active in many local civic organizations and served as president of the Sunset Young Men's Business Club for several terms. He is a veteran of World War I and has been a member of the American Legion for over 50 years.

But such a list of achievements does not explain Robbie Barry's relationship with his fellow man. He has been more than a good farmer and a good father. He has been a good neighbor. When someone is sick, it is Robbie who can be counted on to see that medical help is given, even if it means a late night ride to the emergency room thirty-five miles away. No one with an honest need has ever left his door without help.

He is a man of honor who keeps his side of every bargain. I have heard him stand on the front porch on a dusty afternoon, bargaining with God for rain. When it did rain, he always put the promised extra money in the collection plate. No one, not even his wife Odilia, could convince him that he owed nothing because it would have rained anyway.

Robbie Barry is married to the former Odilia Brinkhaus who has been a life-long partner and motivator in his achievements. Together they live on the Barry farm near Grand Coteau. They have two children and seventeen grandchildren. At age 87, Robbie takes pride in his vegetable gardening hobby, and he enjoys growing and sharing fresh vegetables with his many friends and neighbors.

Perhaps contributions to agriculture and to the community by this life-long team, Robbie and Odilia Barry, are not their greatest gifts to mankind. Their friends and family know that they have taken care of their family, worked their land, and helped their neighbors. Their example over the years as good, honest, hard-working, concerned citizens who helped many others during depression and war years and made the American way of life work could be their greatest gift to Americans of the present and of the future.

Additional Readings That Involve

The subject of an essay that intends to involve its readers is virtually unlimited. Personal reminiscences, nostalgic descriptions, dramatic moments, colorful characters—all of these are excellent subjects for essays that recreate experience for readers to share vicariously.

The Making of a Father
Anna Quindlen

Special occasions like award presentations, birthdays, and retirement parties often inspire tributes to people who have influenced our lives. Anna Quindlen, former columnist at The New York Times, *wrote this tribute to her husband for Father's Day.*

Becoming an Active Reader

1. What do you think a father should be like? Is your image of a father traditional?

2. How would you describe your own dad? Yourself or your spouse as a parent?

3. Quindlen says that her oldest child described his father as "silly." Before you read the essay, what is your reaction to that description?

1   It is bathtime, and I am in the bedroom laying out the pajamas when I hear whispering from the hallway. In a moment I am surrounded by boys. They are inflicting upon me something they call, with great glee, "the knuckle machine," a cross between an attack and tickle. They come at me from different angles while the baby lies on the bed, wide-eyed, perhaps wondering whether she will be next. One gets me on the left, one on the right, another in a low blow just beneath the navel. One is 3, another 5. The third attacker, and the most practiced, is 36 years old, my husband, everyone else's dad. It is worth noting that he is the one who invented the knuckle machine.

2   I didn't figure on marrying a father. Now that women are marrying later, when they are less foolish and more forward-thinking, some of my friends in that category tell me that when they meet a man they find themselves looking for someone who is good father material. They are looking for someone who is dependable, responsible, kind, perhaps a bit serious—in short, the Walter Cronkite type.

3   But when I met the boy who grew into the man who became my husband, we were both 18, and the things that dazzled me about him were not at all what we think of as fatherly things. I loved the way he danced, how his jeans hung on his hips, a certain scorn he affected for things establishmentarian, his sense of humor and of the ridiculous.

4   Above all, I suspect, I was entranced by the fact that he seemed forever young, Peter Pan in wire-rimmed glasses and T-shirts. I thought then that he would always somehow be that way, and I was right. What I did not suspect was that he would someday be the father of three children, and that he would be so natural in the role.

5   He did not suspect it either. Although he had always wanted children, it was not until I was wearing maternity clothes that he realized, panicked, that he was going to turn into a dad. He was convinced that he would have to become a man who wore pajamas and slippers, who never swore, who was avuncular and wise and a bit remote, a cross between Fred MacMurray and Ward Cleaver. He was not up to that challenge.

6   People our own age tried to convince him that he had an outdated idea of what constituted father readiness. He had to be warm, tender and a whiz with a diaper, a guy who slipped into a Snugli and strode off to see the pediatrician—no problem Alan Alda by way of Dr. Spock. It was hard to say which stereotype was more daunting.

7   And birth is just the beginning of the dichotomy between now and then, between the old imagined dad and the new. Once upon a time fathers offered a model of supremacy without vulnerability. Today they must conform to some new, crazy-quilt standard of maleness that supposes they will be warmer and tenderer than even their mothers may have been. A generation ago the most absent father could fall back on pride in his role as breadwinner. Now many men contribute half a loaf in this brave new world in which so many women work. The bottom line is that men who are going to be good at raising children have to find their

own way, cut from the cloth of their own personality, not the expectations framed by sitcoms and commercials.

8   For the men of our generation have been raised between a rock and a hard place, and neither spot seems to have much to do with being human or fallible. The vast changes in father image are clear from the moment their wives become pregnant and current mores expect them to attend Lamaze class and speak knowledgeably of Braxton-Hicks contractions and breech deliveries. The stereotype the men of my generation grew up with, the one of the expectant father pacing the waiting room while his wife labors out of sight, has had to be chucked wholesale. Even Prince Charles has been expected to time the contractions, wipe his wife's brow and cut the cord. On the one hand, a friend told me she would never feel the same about her husband if he was not in the labor room with her. On the other, my own father has five children and has never seen a baby born except on public television.

9   I shouldn't just say the men were raised on the expectations. I had them, too. When I was young I found my father a disappointment because he wasn't a bit like God the Father, bearded and regal on his cloud throne, or Beaver's father, who had a den and a serious way of talking to you about what counted. My father was quite young and irreverent and was more interested in sharing a good joke with me than his notions of honor or fair play. (If this description sounds very much like my husband—well, that's no accident. And Sigmund Freud was no fool.) It took me many years to stop yearning for the standard-issue father, and many years after that to realize that such a father would have bored me blind. My father sometimes infuriated me, but he never bored me, and in that I consider myself very lucky.

10   I suspect that my husband will never bore his children either, and so, in that sense, I suppose I unwittingly chose a good father when I chose a good husband. There's no doubt that the man still has a lot of the boy left in him. I can tell, because I can somehow never imagine Walter Cronkite sticking his face between the banisters and shouting, "UGA BUGA! UGA BUGA!" at his sons on the way up to their bedroom. Or sitting on the living room floor with them playing Dizzy Dizzy Dinosaur.

11   When I watch him watching Road Runner and Wile E. Coyote with the other two boys of the house, I am surprised to realize how well this sort of behavior qualifies him for one of life's most important positions. The children, perhaps instinctively, have always known this. They recognize in him a kindred spirit, someone who knows the ropes but has taken his knocks in learning them, someone whose sense of adventure has been tempered, but never muted, by self-knowledge. Someone who, like them, thinks that jumping off the diving board while making funny faces is just about the most entertaining thing to do in the universe.

12   Sometimes, when my husband shares his big leather lounge chair with one of his children during a basketball game or the evening news, I can see that they see him as a bulwark, an authority, a sort of deity. And a

big kid. The kind of father who is strong enough to inform, secure enough to say, "I don't know," warm enough to kiss and cuddle, and wild enough to invent the knuckle machine.

13   My husband deserves a day in his honor every June. I remember how shocked he was, and how shocked I was too on that first Father's Day after our older son was born, when we realized that a celebration was in order. I remember, too, how last year the boys wanted to buy him a toy, not a tie, as a gift, and how the firstborn, when asked by his teacher for one word to describe his father, came up with "silly." That may sound as though the man's children take him lightly, but that's not true. They just know him as he is, and they love him that way too.

Thinking about a Subject and Writing for Yourself:

Prompts for Journal Writing or Class Discussion

1. As you read, note your reactions to Quindlen's descriptions of her husband.

   • What is he doing when she first describes him? How do you feel about his behavior?
   • How does she describe him at 18? How did she feel about him then?
   • How does she feel about his behavior at the time of her essay?

2. What impression do you get of Quindlen herself? What do you learn about her and her background and feelings? How do you feel about her?

3. How does Quindlen contrast the traditional expectations of the father image with the new role for "men of our generation"? According to Quindlen, is it only men who are raised on these expectations? Explain.

4. How does Quindlen compare her husband as father to her own father? How would those two men compare to a strong male figure in your own background?

5. What does Quindlen feel that her husband brings to his role as father?

6. Do you think that the Quindlen children have a healthy relationship with their father? Give a brief description of the image you would like your children to have of you as a parent.

Once More to the Lake
E. B. White

E. B. White's classic description of a summer trip to a lake remembered from childhood vacations is on one level a description of the trip. On another level, he uses the occasion to comment on man's understanding of time passing in his life.

Becoming an Active Reader:

1. Recall a place that you visited when you were young. How clearly can you remember it?

2. Have you ever returned to a place from your past? What was your return like? Had the place changed?

3. Have you ever wanted to bring someone from your present to a place from your past? Have you ever done it? What was the experience like?

August 1941

1 One summer, along about 1904, my father rented a camp on a lake in Maine and took us all there for the month of August. We all got ringworm from some kittens and had to rub Pond's Extract on our arms and legs night and morning, and my father rolled over in a canoe with all his clothes on; but outside of that the vacation was a success and from then on none of us ever thought there was any place in the world like that lake in Maine. We returned summer after summer—always on August 1 for one month. I have since become a salt-water man, but sometimes in summer there are days when the restlessness of the tides and the fearful cold of the sea water and the incessant wind that blows across the afternoon and into the evening make me wish for the placidity of a lake in the woods. A few weeks ago this feeling got so strong I bought myself a couple of bass hooks and a spinner and returned to the lake where we used to go, for a week's fishing and to revisit old haunts.

2 I took along my son, who had never had any fresh water up his nose and who had seen lily pads only from train windows. On the journey over to the lake I began to wonder what it would be like. I wondered how time would have marred this unique, this holy spot—the coves and streams, the hills that the sun set behind, the camps and the paths behind the camps. I was sure that the tarred road would have found it out, and I wondered in what other ways it would be desolated. It is strange how much you can remember about places like that once you allow your mind to return into the grooves that lead back. You remember one thing, and that suddenly reminds you of another thing. I guess I remembered clearest of all the early mornings, when the lake was cool and motionless, remembered how the bedroom smelled of the lumber it was made of and of the wet woods whose scent entered through the screen. The partitions in the camp were thin and did not extend clear to the top of the rooms, and as I was always the first up I would dress softly so as not to wake the others, and sneak out into the sweet outdoors and start out in the canoe, keeping close along the shore in the long shadows of the pines. I remembered being very careful never to rub my paddle against the gunwale for fear of disturbing the stillness of the cathedral.

3   The lake had never been what you would call a wild lake. There were cottages sprinkled around the shores, and it was in farming country although the shores of the lake were quite heavily wooded. Some of the cottages were owned by nearby farmers, and you would lice at the shore and eat your meals at the farmhouse. That's what our family did. But although it wasn't wild, it was a fairly large and undisturbed lake and there were places in it that, to a child at least, seemed infinitely remote and primeval.

4   I was right about the tar: it led to within half a mile of the shore. But when I got back there, with my boy, and we settled into a camp near a farmhouse and into the kind of summertime I had known, I could tell that it was going to be pretty much the same as it had been before—I knew it, lying in bed the first morning smelling the bedroom and hearing the boy sneak quietly out and go off along the shore in a boat. I began to sustain the illusion that he was I, and therefore, by simple transposition, that I was my father. This sensation persisted, kept cropping up all the time we were there. It was not an entirely new feeling, but in this setting it grew much stronger. I seemed to be living a dual existence. I would be in the middle of some simple act, I would be picking up a bait box or laying down a table fork, or I would be saying something and suddenly it would be not I but my father who was saying the words or making the gesture. It gave me a creepy sensation.

5   We went fishing the first morning. I felt the same damp moss covering the worms in the bait can, and saw the dragonfly alight on the tip of my rod as it hovered a few inches from the surface of the water. It was the arrival of this fly that convinced me beyond any doubt that everything was as it always had been, that the years were a mirage and that there had been no years. The small waves were the same, chucking the rowboat under the chin as we fished at anchor, and the boat was the same boat, the same color green and the ribs broken in the same places, and under the floorboards the same fresh water leavings and débris—the dead helgramite, the wisps of moss, the rusty discarded fishhook, the dried blood from yesterday's catch. We stared silently at the tips of our rods, at the dragonflies that came and went. I lowered the tip of mine into the water, tentatively, pensively dislodging the fly, which darted two feet away, poised, darted two feet back, and came to rest again a little farther up the rod. There had been no years between the ducking of this dragonfly and the other one—the one that was part of memory. I looked at the boy, who was silently watching his fly, and it was my hands that held his rod, my eyes watching. I felt dizzy and didn't know which rod I was at the end of.

6   We caught two bass, hauling them in briskly as though they were mackerel, pulling them over the side of the boat in a businesslike manner without any landing net, and stunning them with a blow on the back of the head. When we got back for a swim before lunch, the lake was exactly where we had left it, the same number of inches from the dock, and there was only the merest suggestion of a breeze. This seemed an utterly

enchanted sea, this lake you could leave to its own devices for a few hours and come back to, and find that it had not stirred, this constant and trustworthy body of water. In the shallows, the dark, water-soaked sticks and twigs, smooth and old, were undulating in clusters on the bottom against the clean ribbed sand, and the track of the mussel was plain. A school of minnows swam by, each minnow with its small individual shadow, doubling the attendance, so clear and sharp in the sunlight. Some of the other campers were in swimming, along the shore, one of them with a cake of soap, and the water felt thin and clear and unsubstantial. Over the years there had been this person with the cake of soap, this cultist, and here he was. There had been no years.

7   Up to the farmhouse to dinner through the teeming dusty field, the road under our sneakers was only a two-track road. The middle track was missing, the one with the marks of the hooves and the splotches of dried, flaky manure. There had always been three tracks to choose from in choosing which track to walk in; now the choice was narrowed down to two. For a moment I missed terribly the middle alternative. But the way led past the tennis court, and something about the way it lay there in the sun reassured me; the tape had loosened along the backline, the alleys were green with plantains and other weeds, and the net (installed in June and removed in September) sagged in the dry noon, and the whole place steamed with midday heat and hunger and emptiness. There was a choice of pie of dessert, and one was blueberry and one was apple, and the waitresses were the same country girls, there having been no passage of time, only the illusion of it as in a dropped curtain— the waitresses were still fifteen; their hair had been washed, that was the only difference— they had been to the movies and seen the pretty girls with the clean hair.

8   Summertime, oh, summertime, pattern of life indelible with fade-proof lake, the wood unshatterable, the pasture with the sweetfern and the juniper forever and ever, summer without end; this was the background, and the life along the shore was the design, the cottages with their innocent and tranquil design, their tiny docks with the flagpole and the American flag floating against the white clouds in the blue sky, the little paths over the roots of the trees leading from camp to camp and the paths leading back to the outhouses and the can of lime for sprinkling, and at the souvenir counters at the store the miniature birch-bark canoes and the postcards that showed things looking a little better than they looked. This was the American family at play, escaping the city heat, wondering whether the newcomers in the camp at the head of the cove were "common" or "nice," wondering whether it was true that the people who drove up for Sunday dinner at the farmhouse were turned away because there wasn't enough chicken.

9   It seemed to me, as I kept remembering all this, that those times and those summers had been infinitely precious and worth saving. There had been jollity and peace and goodness. The arriving (at the beginning of August) had been so big a business in itself, at the railway station the

farm wagon drawn up, the first smell of the pine-laden air, the first glimpse of the smiling farmer, and the great importance of the trunks and your father's enormous authority in such matters, and the feel of the wagon under you for the long ten-mile haul, and at the top of the last long hill catching the first view of the lake after eleven months of not seeing this cherished body of water. The shouts and cries of the other campers when they saw you, and the trunks to be unpacked, to give up their rich burden. (Arriving was less exciting nowadays, when you sneaked up in your car and parked it under a tree near the camp and took out the bags and in five minutes it was all over, no fuss, no loud wonderful fuss about trunks.)

10   Peace and goodness and jollity. The only thing that was wrong now, really, was the sound of the place, an unfamiliar nervous sound of the outboard motors. This was the note that jarred, the one thing that would sometimes break the illusion and set the years moving. In those other summertimes all motors were inboard; and when they were at a little distance, the noise they made was a sedative, an ingredient of summer sleep. They were one-cylinder and two-cylinder engines, and some were make-and-break and some were jump-spark, but they all made a sleepy sound across the lake. The one-lungers throbbed and fluttered, and the twin-cylinder ones purred and purred, and that was a quiet sound, too. But now the campers all had outboards. In the daytime, in the hot mornings, these motors made a petulant, irritable sound; at night in the still evening wha petulant, irritable sound; at night in the still evening when the afterglow lit the water, they whined about one's ears like mosquitoes. My boy loved our rented outboard, and his great desire was to achieve single-handed mastery over it, and authority, and he soon learned the trick of choking it a little (but not too much), and the adjustment of the needle valve. Watching him I would remember the things you could do with the old one-cylinder engine with the heavy flywheel, how you could have it eating out of your hand if you got really close to it spiritually. Motorboats in those days didn't have clutches, and you would make a landing by shutting off the motor at the proper time and coasting in with a dead rudder. But there was a way of reversing them, if you learned the trick, by cutting the switch and putting it on again exactly on the final dying revolution of the flywheel, so that it would kick back against compression and begin reversing. Approaching a dock in a strong following breeze, it was difficult to slow up sufficiently by the ordinary coasting method, and if a boy felt he had complete mastery over his motor, he was tempted to keep it running beyond its time and then reverse it a few feet from the dock. It took a cool nerve, because if you threw the switch a twentieth of a second too soon you would catch the flywheel when it still had speed enough to go up past center, and the boat would leap ahead, charging bull-fashion at the dock.

11   We had a good week at the camp. The bass were biting well and the sun shone endlessly, day after day. We would be tired at night and lie down in the accumulated heat of the little bedrooms after the long hot

day and the breeze would stir almost imperceptibly outside and the smell of the swamp drift in through the rusty screens. Sleep would come easily and in the morning the red squirrel would be on the roof, tapping out his gay routine. I kept remembering everything, lying in bed in the mornings—the small steamboat that had a long rounded stern like the lip of a Ubangi, and how quietly she ran on the moon-light sails, when the older boys played their mandolins and the girls sang and we ate doughnuts dipped in sugar, and how sweet the music was on the water in the shining night, and what it had felt like to think about girls then. After breakfast we would go up to the store and the things were in the same place— the minnows in a bottle, the plugs and spinners disarranged and pawed over by the youngsters from the boys' camp, the Fig Newtons and the Beeman's gum. Outside, the road was tarred and cars stood in front of the store. Inside, all was just as it had always been, except there was more Coca-Cola and not so much Moxie and root beer and birch beer and sarsaparilla. We would walk out with the bottle of pop apiece and sometimes the pop would backfire up our noses and hurt. We explored the streams, quietly, where the turtles slid off the sunny logs and dug their way into the soft bottom; and we lay on the town wharf and fed worms to the tame bass. Everywhere we went I had trouble making out which was I, the one walking at my side, the one walking in my pants.

12   One afternoon while we were at that lake a thunderstorm came up. It was like the revival of an old melodrama that I had seen long ago with childish awe, The second-act climax of the drama of the electrical disturbance over a lake in America had not changed in any important respect. This was the big scene, still the big scene. The whole thing was so familiar, the first feeling of oppression and heat and a general air around camp of not wanting to go very far away. In midafternoon (it was all the same) a curious darkening of the sky, and a lull in everything that had made life tick; and then the way the boats suddenly swung the other way at their moorings with the coming of a breeze out of the new quarter, and the premonitory rumble. Then the kettle drum, then the snare, then the bass drum and cymbals, then crackling light against the dark, and the gods grinning and licking their chops in the hills. Afterward the calm, the rain steadily rustling in the calm lake, the return of light and hope and spirits, and the campers running out in joy and relief to go swimming in the rain, their bright cries perpetuating the deathless joke about how they were getting simply drenched, and the children screaming with delight at the new sensation of bathing in the rain, and the joke about getting drenched linking the generations in a strong indestructible chain. And the comedian who waded in carrying an umbrella.

13   When the others went swimming my son said he was going in, too. He pulled his dripping trunks from the line where they had hung all through the shower and wrung them out. Languidly, and with no thought of going in, I watched him, his hard little body, skinny and bare, saw him wince slightly as he pulled up around his vitals the small, soggy, icy garment. As he buckled the swollen belt, suddenly my groin felt the chill of death.

Thinking about a Subject and Writing for Yourself:

Prompts for Journal Writing or Class Discussion

1. How did White find out about this particular lake? What feeling made him return to the lake?

2. Notice the careful details White includes to be sure that you can see the scene with him. What images does he use to help you see and smell and hear the place? Is it a place you would want to be?

3. What impression do you get of White himself? How do you feel about his persona in this essay?

4. White includes his son in the trip and in the essay. Identify the references to his son. Are there many? Had he omitted all references to his son, how would the essay be different?

5. At times White identifies with his son. At what points does he see himself in the boy's actions? At what points does he see the boy as his son? How does the presence of the boy help him to see that time is passing? Why do you think White does not give the boy's name?

6. White is comparing what he sees to what he remembers. What changes does White find in the lake area? What changes does he find in himself? Why does he feel, at the end of the essay, "the chill of death"? Why is it significant that he feels it in his groin?

7. What scene stands out most vividly in your mind? What details in that particular description show you vivid pictures?

8. Think about a childhood experience (or cherished place) you have introduced to someone else. Describe your reactions and observations as well as the reactions of the other person. Like White, you should end your description with a comment on your overall impression of this introduction.

Blackballed
Beverly Lowry

Beverly Lowry's description of her college sorority experiences appeared in Southern Magazine, but her enduring pain from the rejection is not a regional phenomenon. Neither is her experience that remembering an event resulted in "a flash of certain truth" that "cracked the past wide open."

Becoming an Active Reader:

1. What does the term "blackballed" mean?

2. Have you ever wanted to be included in a group that did not want you? How long ago? Can you remember your feelings?

3. Have you ever been part of a group that excluded someone else from membership, formally or informally? What were your reasons? How did you feel at the time? Do you feel now that you were right?

1   I was running when I figured out who had done it. The day before, I'd been swapping stories with a writing class I was teaching in Houston. We'd been talking about rejection letters—a student had written a short story in that form—and how from the lushly apologetic opening sentence, if not from the salutation itself, you can tell how the rest of the letter is going to go. The story I told was "Panhellenic Regrets."

2   The kids all laughed. "You were a frat rat!" one of them exclaimed.

3   "It was a long time ago," I told them. "And here's the deal: They broke my heart."

4   Running down Mandell Street, I wondered who it was I thought "they" were. Then, passing Hawthorne, I figured it out. All these years I'd thought it was the girls. Out of the blue, a flash of certain truth came home to me and cracked the past wide open.

5   Interesting about stories. I've told "Panhellenic Regrets" more than a few times. People always listen hard and respond with feeling. One reason is sympathy, as the story keys into listeners' memories of how their own adolescent hearts were broken, one way or the other. Another is bafflement. People want to know why I still get so wrought up about being left out of—of all things—a *sorority*. Many offer up the notion that I should feel proud to have been the sort of person a sorority would not want to have as its sister.

6   Well, yes. I know what they mean. But if being cut is never easy—and it's not—then being blackballed because of who you irreversibly are, with nothing to do to amend your fortune except having been born a different person, plugs the flesh to the bone.

7   I went to the University of Mississippi in 1956. Ole Miss was not my first choice, but, given family circumstances and certain personal disinclinations, it was the choice I was stuck with. As I left home that September, my expectations were high: After all, I had been a model high school honor student. My reputation led me to believe I'd do well. My father said I'd be a big fish in a little pond. Indeed.

8   The summer before, I'd worked 40 to 45 hours a week as a lifeguard at a country club swimming pool. As a result, my skin was so dark that on my legs white women's stockings looked like nurses' hose, so I wore stockings meant for black women instead. They were only part of the, to me, snazzy wardrobe I had bought with my dollar-an-hour lifeguarding money. I'd also gotten a fuzzy yellow blanket for my dormitory bed and a clever little off-white plastic clock radio. My hair was bleached blond by the sun.

9   Was I going out for sorority rush? At Ole Miss in 1956 any girl who wanted to be some kind of a well-liked girl—and I did, I did—went out for sorority rush. The desires of a girl who wanted to be a *special* some-kind-

of-a-girl were even more specific. That girl yearned to pledge not just any sorority but the star number-one group, that sisterhood of beauty queens and Miss Americas, Chi Omega. Or—we called it fondly, by its nick-name—Chi O.

10 Of course we—they, the sorority girls—were children, 18, 19 years old. What did we know? But sorority girls did not seem like children to me. They were so serene. And they had such power! By some unknown osmot-ic process—as mysterious, no doubt, to them as to us—each sorority had acquired a personality. Kappas had a reputation for glamor, Phi Mus were smart, DGs athletic, KDs raucous, Tri-Delts slim and energetic (they also had a grand, new addition to their house). But all of this was small-potatoes niggling. Chi O was the Queen Mother, the gold medal, the Nobel Prize of sororities. At that time and in that place, Chi O was the veritable Kentucky Derby of Greek sisterhoods, and I wanted in. How could I not? Membership meant security, a home. Once in, I would be socially accepted, a sure thing. I would have the ability to affect a casual, knowing attitude. (I think it was the casual attitude I craved most, that sense of being so much a part of the Right Group that I never had to worry anymore about whether I belonged, or whether I had done the right thing, or whether my fuzzy yellow blanket was the *right* kind of fuzzy blanket. Which of course it was not. The better girls' blankets were not fuzzy. Or even yellow.)

11 During the first days of freshman orientation I made a number of friends. Like me, my new pals were going out for rush. Some were lega-cies—their mothers or sisters had been sorority members. Others spoke of recommendations—called "recs"—written for them by sorority alumnae. One girl said Chi O required two recs before they would even consider a girl; another said that was only hearsay. I knew a number of women who'd been Chi O's; I assumed they'd have written recs for me, but I had not gone out campaigning. Counting on my reputation and marketable assets—sororities were required to keep their grade point average high—I didn't worry much.

12 The first round of rush parties took place on a Sunday afternoon. After the traditional Panhellenic Tea, all seven sororities held open house. The open house party was for show only, a cattle call gathering that any girl going out for rush was free to attend. We were ushered into each sorority house graciously and with many smiles. Great stuff, but we knew the score. Next up was the slash. (Did I think I'd make the first-round cut? No question about it. My longing was too great, I thought, too be denied.)

13 The next day a card was delivered, informing us to which of the sec-ond-round parties we had been invited. We could reply in the affirmative to only five. (I kept a scrapbook in which I pasted party favors and paper napkins imprinted with Greek letters. My handwritten comments are girlishly hyperbolic: "Rush!!! Hada WONderful time!" I dotted my i's with big circles, all the rage that year.) Nervous but optimistic, I pulled out the

card. Two sororities had invited me to their second party, my two bottom choices, the very two I'd have cut, given the chance. One was widely known as the "dog" sorority.

14   I looked at myself in the mirror. Was it my sun-bleached hair? My too-tan legs? I was overweight, but that wasn't it. There were fat Chi O's, if only a few. Family background? Unquestionably that was important. So was beauty. Beauty gave some girls a free ride. A beautiful girl—especially a dark-eyed beauty with dark hair and red lips, one who stood a good chance of being elected Beauty or Homecoming Queen—could slide into the sorority of her choice even if she'd been born in the red light district of Midnight, Mississippi, and didn't have a rec to her name.

15   Rather than be rushed by a sorority I didn't want to join, I dropped out. I called my parents. In a rage, my mother swore by the end of the first semester to have gathered up Chi O recommendations from every town in Mississippi. My mother never went to college, never wanted to. From her first day in first grade, she'd told me, all she ever wanted from school was out. I am sure my mother had no use for sororities. She just wanted me to be happy. In the scrapbook, next to the party favors, I have recorded this appraisal of my first experience with sorority rush: "A week of happiness, disappointment, smiles and tears. Of 'So glad to meet yous' and 'It was a wonderful party.'"

16   By the end of the first semester, my reputation among college officials and hometown boosters was strong. With a 4.6 grade point average, I was on the dean's list, had been asked to become a University Scholar, and was one of only 16 freshman girls invited to join a national scholastic society. I was on the student council, had been in a play, had joined the yearbook staff, and was active in a church club. I had gained 10 pounds. My summer tan had faded. In an effort to look neater and more cautiously in control, I'd cut my hair. A picture printed in my hometown and other Mississippi newspapers with a story about the honors I'd obtained shows a round-faced girl in pearls and understated white blouse, a fringe of bangs dancing across her high, wide forehead. The picture and the stories are in my scrapbook. My comment: "ME!!"

17   In January, I went out for mid-year rush, a much abbreviated version of the one in the fall. (In the scrapbook: "RUSH Again!") By then I had two roommates, both Chi O pledges. All my friends were Chi Os. True to her vow, my mother had called women all over the state, women she barely knew, asking them to write recommendations for me. Naturally they all said yes.

18   Mid-year rush was limited to two parties. Except for the two sororities I had cut in the fall, I was widely courted. Tri-Delts sang "We want you for a sister" to the tune of "I'll String Along with You." KDs begged me to "be a KD Cutie." Kappas gave me a cardboard key. At the Chi O party I giggled with my roommates and friends. Not just Tri-Delts but everybody, it seemed, wanted me for their sister!

19   The last party was as serious as testimony night in a tent revival. Tears sparkled from members' eyes as one by one they described the warmth, the joys, the soul-throbbing *meaningfulness* of sisterhood. Afterward, rushees were directed to go to a large auditorium. There, with many empty seats between us, we pondered our preference cards, knowing that, at that same moment, sororities were meeting to decide which of us they would invite into membership.

20   I sat with my preference card. There were three slots to be filled. I could write down Chi O, Chi O, Chi O, or put it first and list two others in order of preference. I wanted nothing less than to be Chi O, but I hesitated. *Caution,* I warned myself. *Take care.* Too fearful to go for broke, I listed my top three choices.

21   Invitations were hand-delivered the next morning. It was Sunday. The dorm was all but empty. My roommates had gone to the sorority house to welcome their new sisters. I remember the room as being dark and cold. It probably wasn't. I pretended to study. The knock came. A member of the Panhellenic Council handed me a white envelope with my name on it.

22   I pulled out the card. I read only the first two words: "Panhellenic regrets. . . ."

23   It was just a sorority—I *know*—but I wanted it so badly. My longing for Sure-Thing status and my dream of attaining it had made me wildly hopeful, embarrassingly vulnerable. I felt stupid. At least I'd kept my mouth shut about the preference card. Nobody had to know I'd been turned down not by one, but by three sororities.

24   While I gathered up the courage to call my mother, the phone rang. The dean of women identified herself. A late bid had been offered, which I was free to accept or turn down. A sorority—my third choice—wanted me to be a member. Would I like to accept the bid? Without hesitation, I said yes. I did not think I could stand another semester of spending Wednesday nights in the dormitory with girls I hardly knew while all my friends went off to meetings. The dean of women said I could go on down to my new sorority house; a formal bid would be issued later.

25   The president of my sorority later told me they had not offered me a bid the first time around because they all assumed I'd go Chi O. Good thing they had room for me, she said, because they truly did want me for a sister. In my scrapbook are notes from her and other members. All the notes say the same things. *We love you. Love you. Love you.* I taped a long-stemmed white rose next to the notes with this comment, "I am a *pledge!*"

26   My sorority was known as a party-girl group. Fun-loving girls, they liked to drive to the county line to drink beer and have a good time. My sisters were kind to me. I cannot fault them in any way, except for a fact neither they nor I could do anything about: I did not fit in. They were not my friends. I did not know them or they me. Alone in the dormitory while others were at football games, I stole brownies from cake tins sent by other girls' mothers. If I had known how to be a good-time girl,

drinking from flasks at football games, I would have been one. I hadn't a clue.

27   My reputation led my sisters to believe I'd be a good leader. After I'd been a full member for one semester, they elected me president. I'd barely learned the secret handshake by then, but nobody else wanted the job. My father said now I was a bigger fish in an even smaller pond. I had gained another 10 pounds.

28   As president, I was given the biggest room in the sorority house. No one chose to room with me, and I can't say that I blame them. I stocked my corner of the communal refrigerator with white bread and mayonnaise. I ate ice cream. After a time—feeling that my sisters should be my friends—I grew distant from my real friends and former roommates. Finally, during the summer after my sophomore year, in the middle of my presidency, I left Ole Miss and went to Memphis State, where I dropped out of not only sorority life, but of the game itself—that mad rush for glory and prizes at which I'd been so successful. I became a drama student, an actress in black tights, a bohemian of sorts. When I was offered membership in a scholarship society at Memphis State, I turned it down. I stopped pasting souvenirs in my scrapbook. I no longer dotted my i's with big circles.

29   It came to me on the streets of Houston, out of the blue. There was nothing my mother or I could have done to help satisfy my girlish longings. I was blackballed, and a Chi O alum did it. The vision was clear and, because of its clarity, I knew it to be true. It happened; she did it. I have no doubts.

30   The message of the blackball was that no matter how I tried or how many honors I collected, I would never be a Chi O kind of girl; I did not come from a Chi O kind of family or carry myself in a Chi O kind of way. The blackballer was in a good position to know. A mentor of sorts, a woman I admired, she knew me well. She knew that Chi O blood did not run in my veins. In her own mind, she'd probably convinced herself she was only thinking of me.

31   The truth may be otherwise, but I can't afford to think so. In "Starwood," a short story by Helen Norris which I admire a great deal, a man's wife disappears, seemingly into thin air. The man looks and looks for his wife, with no success. Finally his sister— whose son has been declared missing in action in World War II— tells her brother that he must stop looking for his wife. He must figure out for himself what has happened, and believe it. He must not tell anyone. If he tells, do-gooders may come along and correct his version of the truth. They might tell him a story he cannot bear to hear.

32   Am I grateful to the blackballer? In a way. Being a flop as a social butterfly has had its assets. But when I think of the fat girl in pearls stealing brownies—never. Remembering her, I feel unrepentantly unforgiving. I will have to wait and see if this flash of new information helps begin to heal the bitterness I still feel.

Thinking about a Subject and Writing for Yourself:

Prompts for Journal Writing or Class Discussion

1. What is the author's image of the sorority girls she first encounters at Ole Miss? Have you ever looked at a group from the outside and had a similar feeling about the members?

2. What is the author's attitude about her chances when she first begins the process known as "rush"? How do you feel about her as she describes herself? How does her attitude affect her reaction to the sororities' decisions?

3. How do you respond when the author reads the words, "Panhellenic regrets . . ."? Were you surprised? Why or why not?

4. What is the point of Lowry's mention of the Norris story? What has she chosen to believe? What do you think she does not want to hear?

5. Who blackballed Lowry? How does Lowry feel about the woman's actions? How do you feel?

6. Lowry writes, "Being a flop as a social butterfly has had its assets." What do you think she means?

7. Lowry suggests that one reason people "listen hard and respond with feeling" to her story is that it recalls their own memories of heartbreak. Did you remember a similar incident? Is this story only about sororities and rush?

8. Under what circumstances does Lowry retell her story? Had she ever told the story before? When does she experience the "flash of certain truth"? How would you explain the difference in the timing?

When Only the Phantom's Left
Ellen Goodman

Ellen Goodman's memory of her dog stops short of being maudlin, but it is not unemotional. Yet she insists that her Samantha was not unusual. Does Sam's very ordinariness make her more likely to reach out to the readers' emotions?

Becoming an Active Reader:

1. Think of any pets you have had. Are any of them special in your memory? Would other people think of them as special?

1   The rug has gone to the cleaners. The bowls have gone through the dishwasher. The leash has been put away. The leftover food has gone to a neighbor's dog.

2   Still the house if full of Samantha's shadows and sounds. I hear her tags jingling from the hall. My husband opens the front door carefully, as

if she were still sleeping near it. I catch myself putting a cereal bowl down on the floor. We both instinctively think about letting her out, letting her in.

3   Thus, we say to each, is what people must mean when they talk about a phantom limb. It takes time to get used to what isn't there. What isn't here anymore is Sam.

4   Sam was no wonder dog. She had no tricks to speak of, unless you count her agility at emptying wastebaskets. She was no candidate for David Letterman unless he is fascinated by dogs that eat apple cores. She did what most of her kind do today. She kept a family company while the kids were growing up. It was her job.

5   If Disney made films about the lives of ordinary canines, I could contribute a few on the Urban Adventure of Sam. The time she jumped out of my sister's second story window. The time she was mugged by a more aggressive street dog. The time she was hit by a car. The time she gave birth on the staircase. The time she found her way home across three miles of traffic. The time (times) she wound up in the pound.

6   Now it seems like such a cliche: The kids leave, the dog dies. Puff the Magic Dragon and 16 years have passed.

7   Old age came in its time and we saw it in her pace. She simply slowed down. For years Sam would show her impatience with the two-footed species by racing circles around me. Then one year I became impatient at her pace. The next year, she gave up distance running all together. Then she gave up the stairs.

8   Gradually there were more days when we caught her falling or leaning against the wall, when she didn't hear us or see us, when she seemed confused and crippled. There were days when we began to think about what the vet had called so discreetly, "other choices." Of which there was only one.

9   Maybe in the rural societies they take these things more easily. By these things I mean life and death. The power to choose life or death.

10   Maybe it's the times. Today we confront the questions of mercy killing with a battery of ethicists and double-handed questions. On the one hand this, on the other that. Maybe the same human questions have infiltrated our treatment of animals.

11   In any case, as Sam noticeably failed, I talked about this with everyone I knew. What are the parameters? How do you know when there is too much misery? Or pain for that matter? Were we selfishly keeping her alive because we couldn't bear to be accomplices in her death? Was it wrong to make a life and death decisions based on crippling? On incontinence? On confusion? How do you assess your responsibility to a creature in your care?

12   Many had been through this before, but they offered no certain advice, not even the friend who insisted that I was being excessive in my anxiety. He said to me wryly, "Hey we're talking about a dog. We're not talking about a parent."

13   But I know no one who found this an easy exercise of their power, their ownership. There are very few guidelines about love and death.

14   In the end, Sam saved us from uncertainty. It was her last gift. On Friday afternoon, she fell down and couldn't get up. We wrapped her in a blanket and drove her to the animal hospital, where the vet told us what we knew: She was dying. We came home without her.

15   For all the talk, all the vain considering of "choices," the moral decisions came upon us suddenly, in crisis. I suppose that is always true. Suddenly we have to choose between life and death: a few more days of life and instant death. Choose now. This decision was at least clear.

16   The vet, a kind young woman, tried to ease my way as she eased Sam's. But cradling Sam for the seconds it took for the injection, the seconds it took to stop breathing, I felt, literally in my hands, how faint the line is that we draw between life and death.

17   Now, maybe, when the rug comes back I won't think of it as hers. Time goes by. But today the house still seems to echo with her tinkling name tags.

Thinking about a Subject and Writing for Yourself:

Prompts for Journal Writing or Class Discussion

1. Goodman says that she understands what people mean when they talk about a "phantom limb." Do you? Explain what you think she means. Have you ever experienced this phenomenon in any way?

2. Explain Goodman's allusions to David Letterman, to Disney, and to Puff the Magic Dragon. Do these allusions suggest anything about her audience? Do these allusions seriously limit her audience?

3. There is no physical description of Sam. Why do you think Goodman has omitted such details? If you pictured a dog in her place, where did your physical image come from?

4. Goodman suggests that the decision to put Sam down was, at the end, "clear." Why has it been so muddy before? Have you ever made such a decision? What factors should influence it?

5. Some people, Goodman says, did not understand her agonizing over "a dog." How do you feel? Does Goodman have your sympathy or your impatience?

6. What transitional paragraph moves the discussion from Sam as an active part of family life to Sam as an aging pet?

7. When are you first told that Samantha is gone? That she is dead? Are you surprised? What clues in diction and in detail have suggested her death before it is explicitly mentioned? Is Goodman easing the emotional impact or intensifying it with these details?

8. What details does Goodman use to connect the beginning and the end of the essay?

Graduation Day
Renee Hawkley

Renee Hawkley writes about an experience common to all parents, the so-called "emptying of the nest."

Becoming an Active Reader:

1. What were your feelings about your own graduation day? Did you move out of your childhood home when you graduated from high school? What were the circumstances?

2. How do you think your parents felt when you graduated and/or left home? If you have children, what are your own feelings about that occasion?

3. When was the last time you cleaned out a room, your own or someone else's? Did you find any "life forms . . . developing under the bed" or any other surprises?

1 I never thought it would come to this. Our oldest son is graduating from high school. The 18-year-old whirlwind is about to relocate.

2 One day soon, I will enter his "untouchable" room. I expect to find out once and for all what causes that persistent smell—an intriguing aroma best described as something between sweaty socks and peanut-butter cups. I will find the pair of matching sheets that never end up on his bed together. I will put the matching pillow case on the pillow and align the lengthwise part of the bedspread with the lengthwise part of the bed.

3 I will go through the stuffed bottom drawer of the chest and count the candy bar wrappers. I will marvel that its owner has never had a cavity. I will vacuum corners and louvered doors to see if wood is still located beneath the dust. I will see if life forms are developing under the bed.

4 Then I'll organize the stamp collection for storage. I will bag up five pairs of holey sneakers for the garbage can. And then I'll close the door, fully expecting to open it later to the organized sight I left behind.

5 It will be the dawn of a new day for me.

6 He won't be spending 45 minutes morning and night running the hot water out of the shower. He won't be pulling my car out of the driveway just as I am about to use it.

7 He won't be phoning to see if tonight's curfew is the same as last week's. We won't be hearing "Huh?" instead of "What?" anymore. The kitchen-cupboard doors will stay closed. "Is there anything good to eat?" will be heard less. I won't holler "Turn it down!" so often.

8 No more complaints that I didn't get the shirts out of the dryer soon enough. No more friends who favor me with a "Hi" only after the refrigerator, cupboards and freezer have been stripped of dip, chip and pizza.

9 No more hassle over haircuts. No more late-night waiting and worrying.

10   And no more looking up into those ocean-blue eyes that used to belong to a boy.

11   Maybe if I practice smiling enough, I will be convincing on graduation day. I don't want to spoil what he has pegged as the happiest day of his life.

12   It will be one of the saddest of mine.

Thinking about a Subject and Writing for Yourself:

Prompts for Journal Writing or Class Discussion

1. How does Hawkley characterize her son and his room? As she describes what she expects to find in his room, do you begin to picture it? Is her picture exaggerated?

2. How does Hawkley initially seem to characterize the "new day"? Does it sound good to you? Where does Hawkley first shift her attitude to suggest that the "new day" might not be appealing?

3. What does Hawkley show you about herself as a mother? Do you like her?

4. Hawkley writes about a time of transition in her life. When are such moments of transition likely to occur? Can you identify some of these passages in your own life?

5. Hawkley says that her son has graduation day "pegged as the happiest day of his life." Do you think he is experiencing any mixed emotions about the coming changes? Explain.

WRITING TO INVOLVE WHEN THE SUBJECT IS CONTROVERSIAL

When you write about controversial subjects, it is almost inevitable that your essay will encourage readers to accept your interpretations and perceptions. A description of a homeless child may indeed move a reader to change an attitude or even to donate time and money to a homeless shelter. But all writing, to some degree, asks the reader to accept the writer's vision of life. If you reach your readers emotionally, they may in fact be moved to action. Nonetheless, you can still write with the primary intent of involving the readers emotionally.

A Family's Legacy, *touches on a potential controversy, organ donation. Linda Rivers' account of her own family's decision does not argue the issues; it recreates an experience for the readers. The readers may infer that organ donation is a positive experience for donor and recipient, but Rivers does not explore the pros and cons of donation. Her focus is on her feelings; her invitation, to share her mix of pain and pride.*

A Family Legacy
Linda Rivers

1   I'll never forget that warm summer day in 1965 when my mother suddenly died of an unexplained illness at the age of 36. Later that afternoon, a police officer stopped by to ask my father's permission for the hospital to use Mother's aorta valve and the corneas from her eyes. I was absolutely stunned. *The doctors want to dissect Mom and give her away to other people!* I thought as I ran into the house in tears.

2   At 14, I just could not understand why anyone would take apart a person I loved. To top it off, my father told him, "Yes."

3   "How can you let them do that to her!" I screamed at him. "My mom came into this world in one piece and that is how she should go out."

4   "Linda," he said quietly, putting his arms around me, "the greatest gift you can give is a part of yourself. Your mother and I decided long ago that if we can make a difference in just one person's life after we die, our death will have meaning." He went on to explain they had both decided to be organ donors.

5   The lesson my father taught me that day became one of the most important in my life.

6   Years passed. I married and had a family of my own. In 1980, my father became seriously ill with emphysema and moved in with us. For the next six years, we spent many hours talking about life and death.

7   He cheerfully told me that when he died, he wanted to donate whatever was in good condition, especially his eyes. "Sight is one of the greatest gifts a person can give," he said, noting how wonderful it would be if a child could be helped to see and draw horses the way my daughter Wendy did.

8   She had been drawing horses all her life, winning award after award. "Just imagine how proud another parent would feel if her daughter could draw like Wendy," Dad said. "Think how proud you would feel knowing that my eyes were making it possible."

9   I told Wendy what her Grandpa had said, and with tears in her eyes, she gave him a big hug. She was only 14 years old—the same age at which I was introduced to the donor program. What a difference!

10   My father died April 11, 1986, and we donated his eyes as he had wanted. Three days later, Wendy said, "Mom, I'm so proud of what you did for Granpa."

11   "That makes you proud?" I asked.

12   "You bet! Have you ever thought what is would be like not to see? When I die, I want my eyes donated just like Grandpa."

13   At that moment I realized that my father gave much more than his eyes. What he left behind sparkled in my daughter's eyes—pride.

14   What I couldn't know that day, as I held Wendy in my arms, was that only two weeks later I would once again be signing papers for the donor program.

15   My lovely, talented Wendy was killed when a truck hit her and the horse she was riding along the roadside. As I signed the papers, her words echoed over and over: *Have you ever thought what it would be like not to see?*

16   Three weeks after Wendy's death, we received a letter from the Oregon Lions Eye Bank:

17
> Dear Mr. and Mrs. Rivers,
>
> We want you to know that the corneal transplantation was successful, and now two people who were blind have regained their sight. They represent a living memorial to your daughter—a person who cared enough about life to share its beauties.

18   If somewhere across these states, a recipient discovers a new love for horses and sits down to sketch one, I think I know who the donor was. A blond-haired, blue-eyed girl will still be drawing.

SUMMARY

Writing that recreates memories of events, scenes, and people invites readers to share those memories. Involving the readers means presenting vivid images with description, dialogue, or narration—but those strategies alone are not sufficient. Your sincere "voice" as you present material that lives in your memory will involve the reader in your writing.

Y O U R   T U R N

❏ Invitations to Write to Involve

As the varied readings in this chapter have shown you, people, places, and events are all good subjects for writing that involves its readers emotionally. Your own writing may be prompted by classroom assignments or it may be a response to contexts in your world like those that produced the essays in this chapter.

Writing about people you know or have known may take several forms. Perhaps you will be asked to write a nomination or a tribute; perhaps you will want to recall someone who influenced you greatly. Here are some possibilities:

1. Someone who worked with you when you were younger is being honored for outstanding service to youth. You have been asked to write a testimonial recognizing that person's influence on you. Your audience will gather to honor the person, and you may

assume that most of them are familiar with the honoree's life. Your task is to involve your audience in your reminiscence, recreating the feelings you have for that person and inviting the audience to share your memory. Consider writing about a former teacher or coach, a scout leader, a church-connected youth group leader, or a former supervisor. As you write, be sure to give specific examples and to avoid cliches like "she was always there for me."

2. A person very near to you has died, and at the memorial service you are dismayed when a stranger conducts the service without recognizing the special qualities of the deceased. You decide to collect your own thoughts about that person into an organized written tribute. You plan to share your writing with close friends and family, sending them copies of your remembrance. And, you want to include details about eccentricities, even faults, to avoid making the tribute too perfect and too unrealistic.

Places that have meaning for you might also be subjects for your writings. That meaning may or may not be pleasant; your recollections should help the reader understand and share your feelings.

3. Each summer while your great-grandmother was alive, your family gathered at her home to celebrate holidays like Memorial Day and the Fourth of July. Her place was torn down recently to make way for a new highway. Now, your own children want to know about your childhood and you decide to write about that place. Since it is gone, you will probably want some description, but be sure to explain to your children why the place is a special part of your memories.

4. Your high school is about to disappear under the city's new consolidation plan. The alumni association plans a special gathering of graduates to honor the place, and, as part of that gathering, the association plans to publish a collection of essays from former students. You know that you and most of your friends really hated the place, and you decide to submit an essay explaining your honest feelings about the ugly old building and the inadequate facilities. You doubt that it will be published in the booklet, but you truly believe that most of the recent graduates share your feelings.

Events can also be material for recollection and sharing. A specific incident, or a long-term encounter can have profound influence on the decisions we make and the people we become. You might be asked to share some of the influences on your life. Here are some samples:

5. For five years, you attended a summer scout camp several hundred miles from your home. You remember those days as some of

the most challenging and rewarding of your life, and the friends you made at the camp are still among your best. Now you hear that the camp will be closed soon unless enrollment increases within the next few months. You are asked to write to scout councils in your area to explain what it meant to you to go to a camp in another state.

6. An exercise in a peer counseling workshop has asked you to examine influences on your development as a person. Looking back over the last few years, you recognize key events that have had a strong influence on you. Some events taught you lessons about yourself or others; some forced you in directions that you would not otherwise have chosen. You find it difficult to share such personal analysis with an audience, so you decide that before the next workshop session you will write about one particular incident to show how it has affected you. You decide that your discussion should also describe the way you were before the incident and the way that you are now. You know that other people will read the essay, but you also want to be as honest about the experience as you can be.

7. A national campus magazine is sponsoring an essay contest to find the most embarrassing moments of college life. You can immediately think of several times when you wanted to rewind the clock and start a scene over, so you plan to win the contest. The prize, after all, is an expense-paid trip for four, anywhere in the United States, for the week of spring break. You decide that such a prize is worth soul-baring honesty. So you recount the most embarrassing (publishable) moment of your college life, one that is burned vividly in your mind, complete with dialogue.

Written recollections about people, places, or events invite readers to share your feelings. The recollections can also urge your readers to see your perspective and to understand your views. Here is a sample:

8. Your return to college after some years working and raising a family has not been met with overwhelming approval. One friend, in particular, has ridiculed your decision.

Variation: Your best friend has chosen not to go to college, but has instead gone to work for a major family-owned company at a good salary. He or she has often pressured you to forget school and to start a career immediately.

As a result, you are feeling a little defensive about your college experiences. Still, you want to share your new environment with your friend, so you write to tell her or him about some particular place or activity on campus that you are really enjoying. Remember that your friend has never seen or experienced anything similar. Also, you want your friend to accept, even respect, your decision.

9. Your views about a controversial topic have been greatly influenced by something you have done or seen. Now, a friend is urging you to change your stand. Describe your experience to that friend, trying to make him or her share your feelings.

Examples:

- You are a strong supporter of volunteer work with young children because you have experienced the thrill of helping a child learn a basic skill.
- You are a strong supporter of mandatory helmets for motorcyclists because your best friend was severely injured in a crash.

SUGGESTED APPROACHES TO YOUR RESPONSE

To involve an audience, you recreate incidents, scenes, or people. Before you draft, it is essential that you recreate your subject for yourself. Does it stir your feelings? Can you recall the smell, the touch or the sound of the moment? If your own memories are vague, do not expect your readers to see the moment any more clearly. Choose wisely and recall vividly when your purpose is to stir the emotions and imaginations of your readers.

❏ The First Decision: Accept the Invitation to Write

In "Once More to the Lake," E. B. White wrote, "It is strange how much you can remember . . . once you allow your mind to return into the grooves that lead back. You remember one thing, and that suddenly reminds you of another thing." When you write a personal reminiscence about a person or a place or an incident, you gather information by looking for those "grooves that lead back." The starting point may be in your own memory, or in a certain smell or sound, or in a conversation with a friend. When you find the groove, you will be amazed at how easily and how clearly you remember.

Two Reminders:

Your subject must engage your own imagination before you can recreate it for your readers.

If you keep written notes, you are less likely to forget details and more likely to see connections between ideas.

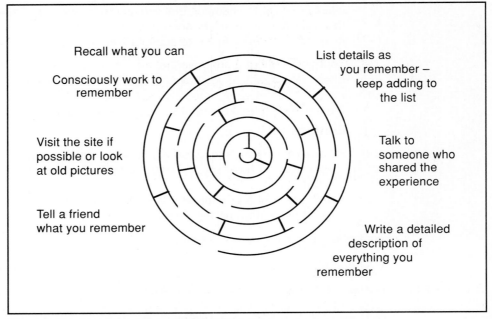

Figure 5-1 Looking for "grooves that lead back"

Cross-Reference: Part Three Chapter 6 catalogues pre-writing strategies to explore subjects for personal reminiscences. For further detail, see:

- Explaining
- Listing
- Freewriting
- Imaginary Dialogue

When you have collected material, encourage the critical voice to review your ideas, consciously seeking vivid details and recognizing connections. Evaluating the material before you begin to draft can also point to the controlling idea of your writing.

To identify main ideas, ask yourself:

- What do I most want to say?
- Do I return to moments or feelings?
- Does material repeatedly address similar points or images?

Do not think that you must know exactly what you are going to say before you begin to write. Drafting helps you to explore material and to identify your own feelings about your subject.

Reminder:

Put no pressure on early drafts. Aim for prose passages that expand your notes.

> **Cross-Reference:** As you collect material, evaluate it continuously. Chapter 7 discusses critical reviews of ideas.
>
> Identifying main ideas as detailed in Chapter 8.

❑ The Second Decision: To Draft a Response

Compiling material into prose, identifying what yu most want to say, organizing it and making it clear to your readers are all reasonable goals for your drafts. As you work, stay aware of what you are trying to accomplish. These guidelines can help:

1. **Early drafts can be written for yourself.** Quite the critical voice while you get your ideas on paper. Be free to ramble and to explore. As new ideas or memories occur, include them, too. Sometimes your direction and purpose are clear, and you begin immediately to write for an audience. But don't feel that you must do so. Early drafts are often personal, written for yourself to find what you most want to say. You can adapt your material for your readers in later drafts.

2. **Expect to write more than one draft.** As you work, invite the critical voice to evaluate material. Look for vivid details, logical connections between ideas, and patterns that are emerging in your draft. Tinker with your material and your organization until you feel comfortable with it.

Two Reminders:

Recreating incidents is not limited to strict chronology.

Descriptive detail should be arranged so that readers see what you see with your mind's eye.

> **Cross-Reference:** The catalogue of drafting strategies in Part Three, Chapter 9 explains patterns that organize your response. As your critical voice evaluates material, check these sections for more information:
>
> Organizing Information
> - Spatial Order
> - Ordering by Importance
> - Chronological Order
> - Comparison/Contrast

Methods of presentation should *show* your material to your readers. Telling them how to react is not as effective as giving specific, concrete details of actions, dialogue, and appearance to make your material vivid. Try contrasting your subject to something similar or dissimilar to help your readers see what you see. And remember that figurative definition often conveys the essence of the experience more vividly than paragraphs of description.

Reminder:

Letting your audience "hear" the person's voice in dialogue can create vivid, memorable pictures.

Cross-Reference: As you review content, look carefully at the following:

Recreating Experience (p. 347)
- Describing
- Narrating
- Using Dialogue
- Figurative Definition
- Combining Strategies

❑ **The Third Decision: To Review the Work in Progress**

Connecting Audience, Content and Purpose

What reaction do you want from your audience? You are recreating a memory for your readers—do you want them to laugh? to recoil in horror? to sympathize? Understanding your specific goal is as important as understanding your readers. Identifying both will help you to select material and present it effectively.

Listen to the dialogue between the creative and critical voices as you picture your readers and their reactions to your words:

Knowledge:
- Is your audience familiar with the setting of this account?
- Is a detailed explanation of the scene needed?
- What terms need definition?
- Are there similar scenes or incidents that could be used for comparison?
- How much does your audience know (or need to know) about backgrounds of this subject?

Attitudes:

- Does this audience have strong feelings or opinions about any part of this subject?
- Will the audience be offended by any of the descriptions or incidents?
- Will the audience be offended by informal diction or slang?

Expectations:

- What persona will be effective here? Do you want to be comic? Sympathetic? A fellow traveller who has shared this road?

Cross-Reference: For a more detailed discussion of audience analysis, see Chapter 14.

Reminder:

Stepping away from your own writing to review it can be difficult. Tell a friend what audience you have in mind and ask the friend to read from that perspective.

Cross-Reference: Review the material on drafting for an audience (p. 361) and effective peer evaluations (p. 375).

The content of your draft must satisfy you—that is, it must say what you honestly wanted to say about the subject. But you are also reaching out to an audience. Read over the draft, thinking about your audience reacting to your material.

Reviewing content:

- Have I said what I wanted to say?
- Do all the details contribute to my intended effect?
- Are non-essential details eliminated?
- Are sequences of events clear?

Reminder:

One vivid incident, presented in detail, is usually more effective than a list of everything that happened.

Polishing the Draft

Completing a draft can be such a relief that you want to call it finished and walk away. Before you send it on to your readers, though, look closely at the framework (title, introduction, and conclusion), paragraphing, sentences, and diction. A solid framework (title, introduction, transitions, and conclusion) will influence the readers' first response to your work and help you to sustain the effect you wish to have on them.

The title:
- Hints at the subject
- Arouses curiosity

The introduction:
- Intrigues the reader
- Sets the mood

Transitions:
- Demonstrate connections
- Guide readers to changes in action or locale

The conclusion:
- Signals a clear end
- Reinforces the effect

Cross-Reference: For detailed information, review Chapter 15, on introductions, conclusions and titles.

Paragraphs reflect organization by grouping ideas. Both paragraphs and sentences also influence pace, guiding the reader quickly or slowly through material, gathering details for emphasis, separating information for impact. Diction too creates impact. There are subtle and not-so-subtle differences in meaning that you should consider as you review your work.

Cross-Reference: For discussion of effective paragraphs, sentences and word choices, see these entries:

Improving Paragraphs (p. 391)
- Natural Junctures
- Length
- Generalizations and Specific Details

Improving Sentences (p. 408)
- Simple Sentences/Expanding Sentences
- Active and Passive Voice

Improving Diction (p. 428)
- Exactness
- Level
- Concreteness
- Clarity
- Tone
- Liveliness

Final Considerations

As you review your writing, check:

- **The rhetorical situation**
  Has your writing responded directly and appropriately to the invitation? Have you addressed a specific audience, in a tone and style suitable to the occasion?

- **The logical connections between ideas**
  Is your reasoning clear and logical? Have you explained the relationships between ideas? Have you left the readers to figure out their own conclusions?

- **The methods of presentation**
  Is your material presented in fitting ways? Are lists complete and accurate? Are chronologies suited to the material?

- **The accuracy of the text**
  Have you double-checked for your own most common grammatical or mechanical errors? Have you proofread carefully for text errors in spelling and punctuation and miscopied or omitted words? If someone else types your final draft, be sure to proofread it carefully for errors— you will be held responsible, not your typist.

A Student Writes to Involve Her Readers

As a returning student, Elinor Dawes was afraid that she would have nothing to write about in composition class. She was sure that she would be older than any of her classmates, possibly even her instructors, and she could not imagine that they would want to hear what she had to say. But when her composition instructor asked for a discussion of an event that had made an impact on the writer, Elinor knew that she had her subject. The death of Elinor Dawes' father-in-law had made her re-think her own feelings about death. In her own feelings, she found echoes of the ways all human beings respond to death.

One of her decisions was to include the sudden death of a friend in a car crash. She reasoned that not all of her readers would have elderly parents or in-laws, but that many would have had friends or classmates die in accidents.

Her essay involves her readers partially because its subject is an experience that all humans to some degree fear, the loss of a loved one. But in the universal experience, she also offers glimpses of herself, showing a mature and thoughtful persona who is able to link incidents into meaningful patterns.

Death Is Always Sudden

I can't say that I was particularly surprised when the phone rang about 4:30 that morning. But when I answered it and Mike said, "Honey, Dad's gone," the breath left my body as though I had been punched hard in the stomach. Somehow or other, I had thought that the months of my father-in-law's illness were preparing us for this moment. I had believed we would be glad that he wasn't in agony. I had supposed we, too, would feel released.

As we had stood witness to the onslaught of cancer, had read books by Kübler-Ross and others, had prayed for controllable pain levels, and had talked with and comforted and cared for this very private man whose being was under siege, I had assumed that we were grieving, that we were practicing for the real leave-taking. I had, in attempts to console myself, said, "At least we have time to say good-by. At least this is not like waking up to find someone you had lunch with only yesterday gone without a word. At least we can say to ourselves that we have done and said all that we wanted to do and say."

I was wrong.

This death was no less unexpected than that of my friend from college days who had waved farewell from his VW van and headed for San Francisco only to die in a fiery crash near Lake Charles three hours later. It was just as shocking as the news that my husband's favorite professor had put a shotgun in his mouth and pulled the trigger. I was as ready for this announcement as I had been the year before for the doctor's telling my best friend, as we sat in the hall of the hospital emergency treatment area, that the team had tried to install a pace-maker in her husband's chest but it hadn't worked and he was dead.

Death is always sudden.

I realize now that when an octogenarian goes to sleep and doesn't wake up she has not "gone peacefully to rest." I know that when a deformed baby dies, the death is not "a blessing in disguise." I am certain that even those who have spent years tenderly caring for and talking with those they love are haunted by the memory of something left undone, some important message undelivered.

Now I know that it doesn't make any difference how old a person is. It's immaterial how long or how intensely someone has suffered. No matter how many times the doctor has said, "It'll be any day now" or "He can't possibly last the night," the act of dying startles us onlookers.

The Writer's Response

Part Three is a reference section. Arranged to echo the areas of activity outlined in Chapter 2 and repeated throughout the text, it catalogues strategies and techniques used to respond to various invitations to write.

The first decision, to accept the invitation to write, encourages the writer to gather information and ideas on a subject, to evaluate the soundness of that material, and to select a controlling idea or thesis that will shape the written response. The second decision, to draft the response, directs the writer to give shape to the material, to identify and to evaluate the connections between ideas and between audience and material. The third decision, the decision to review what has been written, recognizes that the material is complete and directs the writer's attention to the form of the text.

A key to this part of the text is a flexible attitude. Sometimes you know your subject well and gathering information is effortless and quick. At other times, you might try several pre-writing strategies before you are satisfied with your raw materials. Some responses seem to literally shape themselves into comparisons or classifications, and sometimes the relationship between audience and material is self-evident. At other times, you must struggle with every sentence.

Part Three can help you through those times in at least two ways. First, when you are working on a specific written response, it will suggest new approaches and illustrate various techniques to generate and organize material, regardless of the purpose of your writing. Second, it offers practice sessions on specific skills so that you can, if you wish, flex your writing muscles on short pieces. Such practice will improve your confidence when you are expected to respond in writing; like the freethrow shooter who has made a thousand shots in practice, you will feel progressively more comfortable expressing your ideas on paper.

You are not expected to work from the first page of the section to the last; instead, you are encouraged to look over the techniques presented in each level of activity. Expect that some will be more useful to you than others, so try a variety until you find your own favorites.

❏ The First Decision: To Accept the Invitation to Write

You leave a movie and want to warn your friends to save their money. Or, you see an old photograph and wish that you had time to write to a friend from years ago. Or, you read that budget cuts will affect the public broadcasting station in your state and decide to tell your state representative that such programming is important. Perhaps you write those letters; perhaps you don't.

In everyday life, there are many situations that invite you to respond, but not all of those invitations are accepted. When you do decide to put your ideas on paper, you begin a series of activities that will end only when you are satisfied that your response is complete. That first decision, to accept the invitation, is made for you in academic contexts. The English essay, the sociology report and the lab experiment must all end up on paper so that your work can be evaluated by your instructors. Whether the written response is assigned or chosen, though, it is produced by a series of activities loosely called the process of writing. In this first section of The Writer's Response, you will find strategies used by many writers to find a subject and to generate ideas. You will also be advised to apply critical thinking skills to evaluate your material, and you will be encouraged to identify a thesis (controlling idea) to give direction to your work. At this level, drafts are tools for exploring ideas and collecting material into prose; do not pressure yourself to produce a polished written response.

Prewriting Strategies: Exploring a Subject and Generating Ideas

This chapter describes how writers select and explore subjects effectively. It also details techniques to produce more ideas and more creative ideas. The final section shows how a rough draft is used to explore a topic.

INVITATION AND RESPONSE

In the first section of this book, we talked about writing as a response—a creative response—to an invitation. There are many such invitations (or stimuli) in life: you receive a letter and write one in answer; you encounter a nasty sales clerk and file a written complaint; you receive a gift and respond with warmth and gratitude.

In such situations, many of your choices are made for you. You already have a specific, focused topic and you know the audience for your response. You also have a clear idea of why you are writing to that audience and how you would like for them to respond. As a result, your writing efforts will be devoted to gathering ideas and shaping your response.

In an academic setting, most assignments follow naturally from your studies. The instructor may give you a specific topic or leave you free to choose your own, but your final decisions about subject are made as you examine the assignment for direction.

Because we recognize that class assignments usually leave you with the most choices (and often the most anxiety), this book often uses the production of an assigned essay as a model for the writing process. Remember, though, that the process is not substantially different whenever you are invited to respond in writing.

A NOTE ABOUT WRITER'S BLOCK

Regardless of the invitation to write, most written responses share a common objective: to reach an audience effectively. You might be surprised to know that writers at all levels feel pressured by that need. When you need a response from your audience (a replacement of a faulty stereo, or the cancellation of an incorrect bill, or a good grade), the pressure may strangle your creative voice, leaving you uninspired, even cold with dread.

If you're like most people, you've suffered on more than one occasion from the "I'm afraid I've got nothing to say" syndrome. Such frustration is not limited to student writers. Professionals, too, encounter it. It even has a name—writer's block. Fortunately, it is curable. The strategies presented below are used by writers of all levels to identify subjects and generate ideas.

Finding a Subject

You are looking only for a starting point here. Think of the scuba diver from Chapter 2 and imagine that you are slipping into the water for the first time. What instructions have you received? Are you diving into totally unknown waters or have you been given a general idea of what to look for?

Cross-Reference: If you have been given some specifics about a subject, you can skip the rest of this section and move to p. 187, Generating Ideas.

Begin by considering your reason for writing. If you are writing because of an assignment, has the instructor given any specifics that must be satisfied? Consider that an assignment to write a paper on any interesting character is certainly less specific than one that requests a profile of an American military figure. Even more specific would be a request to profile an American naval officer stationed in the Pacific during World War II.

For many writers, the most challenging assignments are those that begin, "Write about someone who is important" or "Write about something that happened." The writer is then like a diver, feeling abandoned in a vast ocean, uncertain of any direction to travel or base from which to work. Let's consider a strategy here for charting those unknown waters.

Your first objective is to find a subject that you care about. If you choose a subject that bores you, your effort to interest your readers will be an uphill struggle.

Similarly, you should estimate your knowledge of the subject realistically. Do you know enough about the subject to have an informed opinion? Have you had any personal experience with some phase of it? You needn't be an expert; if the subject really interests you, a little research will fill in gaps and establish your credibility. Be warned, though: if you attempt to bluster your way through, your discussion is likely to sound trite, shallow, or opinionated.

There is no foolproof test to determine sufficient knowledge. You might write perceptively about the subject of divorce without knowing a single divorced person. A little reading or television viewing, followed by some reflection on the subject, particularly on the various effects of divorce on all the people involved (including children), can be enough to produce insights. On the other hand, you may have witnessed divorce numerous times in your own family, have been strongly affected by it yourself, and yet be unable to write effectively about it because you have never really stopped to think about it or because you are too emotionally involved.

All things being equal, the best subjects for you to write about are the ones that you have had some experience with and that you are willing and able to examine and interpret.

Exploring Subject Possibilities

You may think there is no subject you know well enough to write about, but such thoughts are wrong. You've had countless contacts with people and places and things; you've enjoyed (and in some cases not enjoyed) hundreds of thousands of experiences, and you've drawn and revised innumerable conclusions about those experiences. Only you can recreate those experiences and conclusions on paper.

Even an experience shared by hundreds of people is perceived by each in a different way. When you graduated from high school, for example, the ceremony was perceived with as many feelings as there were people on stage and in the audience. Only you can tell what you were feeling.

The truth of the matter is, if you were to remember and record all of your individual perceptions clearly and begin to write them down, you would have enough material for a lifetime of writing—and you would not even have tapped your potential for new thoughts, new conclusions.

What you need most, therefore, is a quick way to review the range of topic possibilities—to jog your memory, trigger associations, and reveal areas of interest and knowledge to choose from. If you have been left absolute freedom to choose a topic, here are some tactics to help you get started:

1. Review your special areas of experience and competency: your hobbies, jobs you've had, your relationships with your parents and brothers and sisters, singing or playing an instrument, driving or fixing cars, leisure activities. Do not overlook the obvious. Have your readers had similar experiences? If not, you can introduce the audience to something new. If so, the readers will relate to your presentation.

2. Consider interesting places you've visited, extraordinary people you've met, unusual situations you've been in, and memorable experiences you've had.

3. Consider emotions you've felt and the occasions they call to mind.

Jumpstarters:

hatred	aggravation	depression
pity	satisfaction	worry
fear	jealousy	greed
grief	resentment	anger
love	remorse	shame
passion	sorrow	pride
disgust	compassion	frustration

4. Review good and bad qualities that people display, and let these qualities suggest particular experiences, feelings, and ideas. Consider these qualities and their opposites to jumpstart your thinking:

humility	kindness	helpfulness
friendship	courtesy	fairness
concern	courage	innocence
thrift	selflessness	gratitude
tact	respect	wisdom
mercy	honesty	responsibility
charity	patience	sincerity
sympathy	generosity	enthusiasm

5. Consider interesting quotations and the thoughts they bring to mind. Don't try to guess what the author meant; instead, analyze your own responses. For example:

   a. If you bungle raising your children, I don't think whatever else you do well matters very much. (Jacqueline Kennedy Onassis)

   b. Nothing is illegal if one hundred businessmen decide to do it. (Andrew Young)

   c. Choice has always been a privilege for those who could afford to pay for it. (Ellen Frankfort)

   d. The image of woman as we know it is an image created by men and fashioned to suit their needs. (Kate Millet)

   e. Sports do not build character. They reveal it. (Heywood Hale Broun)

   f. I despair of teaching the ordinary parent how to handle his child. . . . I would prefer to turn child-rearing over to specialists. (B. F. Skinner)

g. There would be no powerful will bending hers in that blind persistence with which men and women believe they have a right to impose a private will upon a fellow creature. A kind intention or a cruel intention made the act seem no less a crime. . . . (Kate Chopin, "The Story of an Hour")

h. Everyone is his own enemy. (St. Bernard)

i. Whoever lies for you will lie against you. (Bosnian proverb)

j. That man is richest whose pleasures are the cheapest. (Henry David Thoreau)

k. The Christian ideal has not been tried and found wanting. It has been found difficult and left untried. (G. K. Chesterton)

l. Travel makes a wise man better but a fool worse. (Thomas Fuller)

m. To be successful, a woman has to be much better at her job than a man. (Golda Meir)

n. The unexamined life is not worth living. (Socrates)

o. The cruelest lies are often told in silence. (Robert Louis Stevenson)

p. How glorious it is—and how painful—to be an exception. (Alfred de Musset)

q. The emotional, sexual, and psychological stereotyping of females begins when the doctor says: "It's a girl." (Shirley Chisholm)

r. Conscience is, in most men, an anticipation of the opinion of others. (Sir Henry Taylor)

s. Anger makes a dull man witty, but keeps him poor. (Elizabeth I)

t. If there has been a decline of decency in the modern world and a revolt against law and fair dealing, it is precisely because of the decline in the belief in each man as something precious. (James Reston)

u. We believe whatever we want to believe. (Demosthenes)

v. Laws are good or bad, less by themselves than by the manner in which they are applied. (Anatole France)

w. One is always changed into the image of what one admires. (Paul Sabatier)

x. I am afraid most parents don't know what they want and don't mean what they say because they have no convictions. (Erich Fromm)

y. Friendship is always a . . . responsibility, never an opportunity. (Kahlil Gibran)

z. How awful to reflect that what people say of us is true. (L. P. Smith)

aa. In quarreling the truth is always lost. (Publilius Syras)

bb. The greatest mistake you can make in life is to be continually fearing you will make one. (E. Hubbard)

cc. The girl who can't dance says the band can't play. (Yiddish proverb) dd. People hate those who make them feel their own inferiority. (Phillip Dormer Stanhope, Earl of Chesterfield)

ee. The moment we understand and feel sorry for the next man and forgive him, we wash ourselves, and it is a cleaner world. (Albert Schweitzer)

ff. Those who cannot remember the past are condemned to repeat it. (George Santayana)

gg. A man's worst difficulties begin when he is able to do as he likes. (T. H. Huxley)

hh. There is nothing noble in being superior to some other man. The true nobility is in being superior to your former self. (Hindu proverb)

6. Consult a list of general subjects to stimulate your thinking. Here is a brief list:

America	marriage	religion
self-interest	dieting	astrology
pranks	careers	insanity
habits	violence	cigarettes
bigotry	inventions	television
pretending	suicide	pornography
food	alcohol	censorship
ESP	jogging	prejudice
sports	pollution	self-defense
death	intuition	dormitories
cars	childhood	borrowing
war	roommates	swearing
movies	cheating	evil
sex	manners	trash
fashion	hypocrisy	illiteracy
recreation	high school	athletics
punctuality	money	rudeness
the seasons	dreams	virginity
morality	art	gambling
nature	nudity	marijuana
snobbery	beauty	toys
English class	dating	privacy
poetry	poverty	sleep
imagination	health	humor
confusion	phobias	sanitation
saving face	travel	theater
mercy killing	paranoia	MTV
dancing	homosexuality	pets
crime	advertising	filth
security	prostitution	aggression

competition	music	anxiety
depression	flying saucers	communism
professors	cannibalism	the human body

Y O U R   T U R N

Take a sheet of paper and go through the six ways of finding a subject detailed above. List all the subjects about which you have any knowledge or concern. Don't skimp on this list—aim for at least twenty-five subjects.

GATHERING RAW MATERIALS: GENERATING IDEAS

At this point in your "diving expedition," you have identified areas for further exploration. Your next decision (one which can be easily changed at any time you find the exploration unproductive) is to choose an area to examine in more depth.

Your objective here is to collect on paper information and ideas about your tentative subject. You are not ready to make decisions about the composition, nor about audience or form or purpose. Instead, you will concentrate on assembling a mass of raw materials. You are not expected to do extensive formal research on this topic; instead, you will examine your own experiences and observations to determine what you already know about the subject. Most of the material in your essays will come from your existing knowledge and analysis of that knowledge; information to fill any gaps can be researched later.

This section will examine helpful techniques for collecting and generating ideas. First, however, let's note the important principles that underlie all such techniques:

1. **Thinking on paper is more effective than thinking only in your head.** Many studies have documented that the act of writing down one idea often triggers a whole series of ideas. That doesn't mean you should ignore the ideas that pop up while you're jogging or driving or even sitting in another class (many writers carry a small notebook or tape recorder to record the ideas that occur in unlikely places); it does mean that you should also set aside time to put those ideas (and the ones that inevitably follow) down on paper. (A fringe benefit is that such unpressured writing practice will

eventually make the act of transferring ideas to paper an easy and natural one.)

2. **All ideas should be accepted initially without judgment.** Recall the discussion about the three voices which prompt you as you write. While the critical voice which evaluates ideas and the editorial voice which insists on correctness will have their turn, that time has not come. The creative voice must be encouraged now, that too often timid voice that hesitates to offer suggestions. One of the chief objectives of these techniques is to encourage that voice and to control the input from the other two.

3. **Initially, quantity takes priority over quality.** Studies have demonstrated that the original idea, the penetrating insight, the creative breakthrough is more apt to come when you make an extended effort to produce a number of ideas than when you settle for the first few that come to mind. Such studies reveal that the early ideas are often not particularly good. They tend to be more predictable, more common, less original. But if you let them, they can stimulate the production of the later, better ideas. It is almost as if the mind requires a warming-up exercise before performing at its best. Picture that timid creative voice, offering up safe and conventional ideas until it gains some confidence that it will be listened to. Don't pressure that voice; accept with equal enthusiasm all of the ideas that come and have confidence that the creative voice will grow bolder and stronger.

In sum:

1. Think on paper
2. Accept all ideas without criticism
3. Push yourself to produce quantity

Now let's turn to some techniques for generating ideas. As you become more comfortable as a writer, you may find other "triggers" that work better for you. To get you started, though, try some or all of these:

- Explaining
- Listing
- Freewriting
- Forcing associations
- Cubing
- Imaginary dialogue
- Clustering
- Probing for patterns

These techniques are not only useful for exploring a subject and generating ideas, but also for fostering creativity. Try some of the activities that follow each description whenever you have a few spare minutes. If the activities seem childish or silly, remember that you are trying to stimulate the playful tendencies of the creative voice.

Explaining

Explain a topic by working from the outside. Examine the topic, then explain to someone else what you think the topic means—what the assignment calls for, what subject is indicated, what you think you could do with it. Your comments move from surface impressions of the topic (the outside) toward more detailed insights (the inside). You also move from open discussion (the outside) to further thoughts about the issues that stimulate more private exploration, much of it on paper (the inside).

When talking about your first impressions of the topic, you might record your comments. But you might also sit and talk with someone who is willing to listen without making many comments. You are talking to yourself, in a way, but talking out loud to an audience will force you to carry a thought to its conclusion. Your comments should be filled with phrases like, "I think the instructor wants . . ." and "Maybe I could show . . ." and "I wonder if I ought to talk about Y before I talk about Z."

The wondering, the speculation, the uncertainty may make you reluctant to present your ideas to another person. If you are really uncomfortable doing so, talk to yourself first. Push yourself to complete thoughts: "What would happen if I tried that?" and "Maybe it could work if I. . . ." Don't dismiss anything yet, even if it seems complicated or foolish.

When you overcome the reluctance to share such unformed ideas, you may find that having an audience, even a relatively silent one, challenges you to put the ideas together and to state them clearly. As you talk, you may come up with vivid bits of description and precise examples that will indeed appear in your final copy, but don't worry too much about the quality of every word out of your mouth.

Find someone who will not criticize or direct your thinking, preferably someone who knows little about the subject. That kind of audience can test the thoroughness of your explanation by signalling areas that are not clear. You will be forced to explain and define and provide examples even at this early stage. Good choices for the audience include classmates who might expect you to listen to their explanations next, or a good friend who is willing to listen carefully and ask questions only to clarify. Beware of the listener who wants to correct your mistakes or interrupt to present his or her own ideas; you need to work in a nonjudgmental atmosphere.

After discussion, make notes about your commentary. The most vivid ideas and the ones that seemed to work the best will be remembered, but write down in any form (words, phrases, abbreviations and so forth) as much as you can so that you can recall your ideas as you continue to explore and write.

YOUR TURN

Explaining

Choose a topic from the list below and explain it, first to yourself and then to a friend. Your explanation has no specific requirements; you want only to see the topic from the outside, working your way in to specifics as you talk.

1. For whom do teenagers dress? To please themselves or to please someone else?
2. What changes will college make in your independence? Increase or decrease?
3. Are social conditions in this country improving or deteriorating?
4. What are the dangers surrounding you as you go through your daily life? Are you constantly aware of them? Do you protect yourself consciously?

Listing

One of the simplest methods (yet one of the most effective) for generating ideas is **listing.** This familiar yet challenging approach to exploring your knowledge of a subject works in several ways:

1. **Listing is basically nonthreatening.** No demands of correctness or completeness or clarity are placed on your writing, so the creative voice is given a clear field in which to operate. The only disturbance is likely to come from the critical voice as it evaluates the items on the list, but you can short circuit the critic by imposing a quota of items, say twenty-five or thirty, so that the critical voice is occupied with counting.

2. **Listing stimulates you to work beyond the obvious.** The first items on the list are likely to be the conventional approaches or ideas that occur to any reasonable person, but the need to fill out a list will push you to think of more. It is the second level of effort that usually produces the unusual, the perceptive, the creative ideas.

3. **Listing is a paradox; it is a conventional and traditional structure that encourages, even demands creative thinking.** It insists that we go beyond our first thoughts and encourages us to think of details. If your subject is "The Human Body," you can produce a longer list with such details as "toenails, bunions, arches, Achilles tendon" than you can with "feet."

To begin:

1. **Decide what you will list.** One list might be names of people associated with the subject; another might be places in the library where further material can be found. You can list reasons for an occurrence, or ways in which two things are alike or unlike. If you were to explore the topic "habits" by listing, your work might look like the list below.

2. **Define boundaries for your listing.** You might aim for a specific number of items or you might challenge yourself to see how many items you can produce in five or ten minutes. Several such efforts may be more productive and more manageable than one gargantuan effort. An additional benefit is that such boundaries will focus the attention of the critical voice on numbers and minutes and allow the creative voice to gather momentum.

Sample List

Habits

good habits
bad habits
old habits
ones I still have

good habits
   brush teeth
   exercise
   eat right

bad habits
   nail biting
   telling secrets
   sarcasm

telling secrets
ruins surprises
   Jim's party
   the award to Uncle Steve
sometimes hurts friends
   Jane's feelings about Ben
   Ann's shoplifting experience

Comment: The list begins with absolutely ordinary entries, not likely to become topics for papers. But as the student forces more entries, the topics become more detailed.

Y O U R   T U R N

Listing

    Listing has only one rule: Nothing is too bizarre or impractical to put on the list.

1. List different forms of transportation used to get from your home to the campus.
2. List edible things that could be put on a piece of bread.
3. List things which have at least one wheel.
4. List people you would like to spend an afternoon with.
5. List things on campus about which you would warn a friend.
6. List uses for a paper clip.

Freewriting

Freewriting is useful in two very different situations. One occurs when you want to write about your topic but the blank page creates a mental block for you. The other occurs when you know you have a great deal to say but the sheer number of your ideas leaves you undecided where to begin recording.

    Your aim in freewriting is simply to fill a page (or two or three pages) with writing. Your best ally here is the creative voice, unhampered by the questions of the critical voice or the quibbles of the editor. In freewriting, you are completely unconcerned about the usefulness of your words, or their organization, or even their coherence. Since no one but you will see the writing, there is no need to make it meet any standard—and that includes the standards of spelling, grammar, and usage.

    Freewriting has only one guideline: Don't stop writing. Pausing to ponder a thought or to decide what to say next is acceptable in other idea-producing strategies and in later stages of the composition process but unacceptable in freewriting because pausing aggravates the problem you are trying to solve. So don't let your pencil or typewriter be idle for a moment.

    When you first begin to freewrite, set a timer for a specified amount of time. Then you know before you start that your agonizing effort has a limit on it. Try a few sessions at five minutes each. Try a ten-minute session. Each writer has a private clock, a point at which the effort to produce outweighs the results. Find your span and push yourself a little beyond. If, for example, you find that ten minutes is an effort but not an unbearable one, set the timer for twelve.

If a dry period occurs, write through it. Make yourself continue, even if you are writing no more than the same word over and over. Merely writing "courage" over and over, and keeping your mind open to associations, may eventually stimulate you to write, "Aunt Sarah's final illness," and from there it's a short step to wondering (and writing), "Was she really courageous or was she just foolish?" "What distinguishes the hero from the foolhardy person?" "Can you be afraid and still be courageous?" "Maybe the hero is more afraid, not less, but just handles fear differently."

If you are meticulous about your work and feel guilty about producing a messy page, remember that you are working to discover ideas at this stage, not to communicate them. Although neatness is a virtue in final drafts intended for other people's eyes, it is a vice here if it slows you down or distracts you. When the ideas begin to flow, you may not be able to write fast enough to get them down. So sacrifice neatness and forget about grammar and usage, paragraphing and organization. Write in fragments and your own personal shorthand. As long as you can decipher your notes later, they're neat enough.

Let's say that you chose the topic "The Human Body" to write about. The sample below illustrates how your freewriting might look.

Later, when you've filled one or more pages with freewriting, you can call on the other voices to sort out what you've written and decide what you wish to include in your composition. Your work may be even less presentable than this, but that is nothing to worry about. Your freewriting will have called on the creative voice to produce ideas, and that is all this technique needs to do.

Sample Freewriting

The Human Body

Not my favorite topic. Reminds me of high school biology class. I'm not comfortable with my own body. I don't like its shape and size. All kinds of shapes and sizes around. Amazing variation. Yet they all seem to work. Astonishing how much the outside changes, inside is basically alike.

Sometimes the body fails. What happens then? Transplants are an amazing idea to me. Would I want somebody else's body parts inside of mine? I guess if I would die I wouldn't worry. Would I want to give my own body parts to someone else? Not while I'm alive!! I don't know, I might, if it would really save someone I loved. But when I'm dead, they can have anything they want. As long as I'm really dead. I wonder how they make sure.

Comment: Freewriting sometimes leads in surprising directions. After working on this passage, the student saw a possible topic in organ donation and decided to answer the questions that occurred to him.

Y O U R **T U R N**

Freewriting

When you're not working on an essay, try freewriting as a way to practice putting ideas on paper. Set a timer for ten or fifteen minutes and write on the following subjects **(Remember: do not stop writing)**:

1. A book you have recently finished
2. Trees
3. Dormitory or apartment life
4. Your dream meal
5. Your dream trip
6. An embarrassing, triumphant or, frustrating moment
7. A historic event that changed the lives of thousands
8. Any scientific breakthrough

If you are working on a specific topic already, try freewriting to explore it.

Forcing Associations

Forcing associations can accomplish two aims: *discovering* various aspects and dimensions of your topic to include in your composition, and *identifying* the associations that the broad topic and its specific subheadings have for you. The critical voice and the editorial voice can stop you cold if you listen to their laughter or their critiques. Make a conscious effort to welcome and encourage all associations, however bizarre or irrelevant they at first appear. See Figure 6.1 for a sample forced association.

To use this approach, you need only ask the following questions about your topic and answer each as thoroughly as you can. (Occasionally one or more of these questions will be inapplicable to your topic. However, most of them will apply to any topic you choose.).

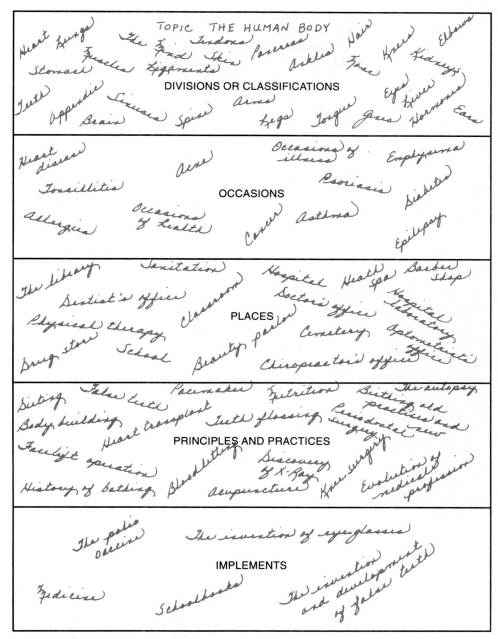

Figure 6.1 Sample Forced Association

What are the divisions or classifications of the topic? (What subtopics does it cover?)

What special occasions in the history of the topic are of major importance or unusual interest?

What important places are associated with the topic?

What special principles and practices are associated with the topic?

What implements are associated with the topic?

What individuals, organizations, or agencies have contributed to the development of the topic?

What significant personal experiences have you or people you know had with this topic?

Do you have a strong opinion about some part of your answer to one of the questions above? If so, what is that opinion?

Y O U R   T U R N

Forced Associations

Apply the questions just listed to the following subjects. Neatness is not expected, but written responses are. (Remember: do not evaluate or eliminate any responses at this point; record all ideas.)

1. Automobiles
2. Rock concerts
3. Designer clothes
4. Politics
5. Your family
6. Habits

Cubing

Cubing is very similar to forcing associations (described above). Imagine that you have before you a cube. Label each of its six sides with an area to explore or with a question to answer. (Some writers like to have an actual cube before them; you will have to decide if the physical prop makes the technique more effective for you.) To begin cubing, choose one side and answer the question as fully as you can. Set a timer, if you'd like, and freewrite about the designated area for a specific amount of time. When your timer rings, or when you have decided that this side of the cube is no longer producing ideas, turn the cube to another side and begin again.

Like forcing associations, cubing points you in a number of directions and urges you to explore varied possibilities. The primary difference is that cubing provides a graphic image that orders your work. Try both approaches to find out which one works more effectively for you.

The prompts you assign to each side of the cube will vary with the type of subject to be explored. For example, a cube to explore a place might contain physical prompts like "sounds" or "smells," while a cube to explore an event might ask, "Who was there?" or "How did I feel?" or "Why did it happen?" Your own thoughts about a subject should guide your selection of prompts; don't be limited by samples or suggestions.

Sample Cubing Exercise

Topic: A Learning Experience

Cubing Approaches:

- Physical setting
- Background information
- Major characters
- My expectations
- The actual event
- Lessons learned

Physical Setting:
city park lagoon area—paddleboat rental shop—summer afternoon— hot, humid—lots of bugs—crowded area

Background Info:
long awaited outing—always looked so romantic and peaceful—wife was dragged along—not a physically active person

Major Characters:
myself, my wife, couple in the other boat, the hungry goose, the sarcastic teenagers

My Expectations:
romantic experience—paddling along peaceful lagoon area—cooler on the water—stop under shady tree with my sweetheart—impress her with my boat-handling ability

Comment: The cube encouraged this writer to call up details of the day that he thought he had forgotten. He decided that his own expectations had been somewhat influenced by movies and television, and that he was still trying to force the day's experience into some kind of script. The contrast between his idealistic expectations and the realities of the experience became a framework for his paper.

Y O U R   T U R N

Cubing

Visualize a cube and assign each of its sides a question or a prompt of some kind. If you cannot think of six prompts, then use four or five, but respond thoughtfully to each side of the cube. Record all of your ideas; you can evaluate and select later.

Sample prompts:

appearance
temperament
results
earliest memory
emotional responses

people involved
achievements
background
favorite activity

Use cubing to explore the following subjects:

1. A person about whom you have strong feelings

2. A tragedy involving you or your friends

3. The most disgusting sight you ever saw

4. Your opinion about a social problem: poverty, the homeless, school dropouts

If you are working on an essay, try cubing to explore various sides of the topic.

Imaginary Dialogue

The **imaginary dialogue** approach enables you to see a subject through someone else's eyes. Naturally, it is impossible to enter other people's perspectives totally. But you can approximate their views. Even the least perceptive person is aware of how others may react in some situations. How many times have you said, " I know what my mother is going to do when she finds out about this"? Obviously you were familiar enough with her past reactions to predict with some accuracy how she would react in a similar situation. It's the same with other people and other situations.

With a little effort and imagination, you could probably predict how a teacher from high school or a friend from your hometown would react to something you've seen or experienced in college. And by making an even greater effort, you could predict (granted, a little more tentatively) how a store owner who had been robbed half a dozen times would feel about lenient judges and parole boards. Or how a woman whose husband had been killed in Vietnam would feel about draft evaders.

In addition to generating ideas, this technique can raise aspects of a topic you might not otherwise have considered. It can also challenge you to respond more precisely and more completely than you would otherwise have done.

A word of caution here: There is a strong tendency to let the critical voice interrupt and comment on the accuracy of your dialogue. Hold out, though, and continue to record all fragments of conversation regardless of nagging doubts. Don't let the dialogue become a debate with your critical voice. Keep a clear image of the two participants in the dialogue and listen for their voices; ignore any other asides or interruptions.

Here's how to use this approach: Think of someone you know who has a firm viewpoint on the topic, preferably someone you've discussed it with before. Imagine yourself discussing the topic with that person now. Take the notes you produced through freewriting and forcing associations and look at each of your points as that person would view it. Jot down next to each point the response that person would make to it. Then write down your reaction to the response. Let's say the topic you're exploring is peer pressure to smoke cigarettes. You might imagine yourself discussing the matter with one of your childhood friends who exerted the most pressure on you and others. Figure 6.2 (on page 200) shows how part of your idea sheet might look.

Y O U R **T U R N**

Imaginary Dialogues

Remember as you do these exercises that imaginary dialogues should encourage you to recall and collect what you know about a subject by seeing it from another perspective.

1. Select a character from a book or movie or television show, a character whom you think you understand. Script an interview with that character, asking questions about a subject appropriate to his or her interests. For example, you might ask Batman about crime, Cliff Huxtable about parenting, Barbara Walters about talking to celebrities, Jane Fonda about exercise classes. If you are working on a paper, think of a person to interview about your subject area.

2. Pick a controversial issue and imagine holding a conversation with someone you know fairly well. Develop a specific dialogue; "you say/they say/you say." For example, carry on an imaginary dialogue with your father about AIDS. Try the same topic on someone more or less conservative—your high school counselor, your best friend from high school, your pastor. Encourage a diversity of responses.

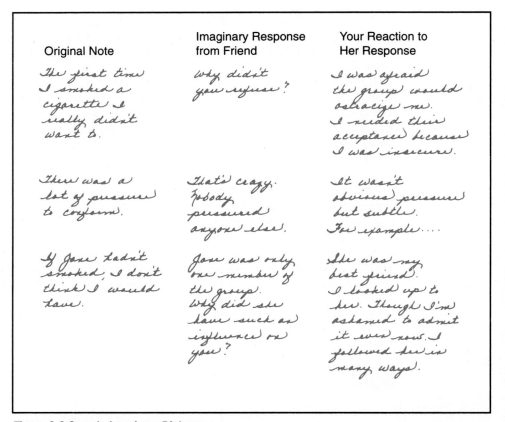

Figure 6.2 Sample Imaginary Dialogue

Clustering

Clustering is a way of examining a topic by looking for connected ideas. Because it is done without attention to specific form, clustering leaves your mind free to wander over the topic, moving in a particular direction for as long as you wish, then moving easily to another direction. Clustering also is a graph of ideas and their possible connections, so if you work easily from diagrams and charts, you may find clustering particularly useful.

When you explore your subject by clustering, begin by giving yourself some working space. Use a chalkboard if you have one, or find a large piece of blank paper. If you are working with your regular notebook, try turning it sideways to give yourself more room to add clusters. The first writing on the page (approximately in the center of your space) should be a brief indication of your subject; for example, you might write

"Registration" or "My Sister's Bad Habits" or "Traffic Problems." Then, draw a short line from the middle of the phrase upward and write down something associated with the topic. The subjects just cited might make you think of such entries as "long lines" or "hiding food" or "speeding." Move to the right of the first line and draw a second line, and write down something else about the subject ("money," "tells lies," or "construction"). Do not worry if the second item has no apparent connection to the first; it needs only to relate to the subject on the center of the page. Continue to work around the centered words, adding lines and entries until you have circled the subject.

Next, scan your entries so far. Do any of them seem related? Circle any that seem to be connected. If you seem to have ten or fifteen totally differ- ent entries, then you have a veritable treasure chest of material to draw from. Connections will emerge as you continue to work.

Choose a promising entry and draw a line radiating outward from that entry. What does it make you think of? Draw a second line, stemming from the same entry. What else does it make you think of? Enter as many items as you can, drawing lines from the entry that inspired the thought. (See Figure 6.3) Any time you seem to run out of ideas, switch to another entry on the cluster and see if you can branch out again.

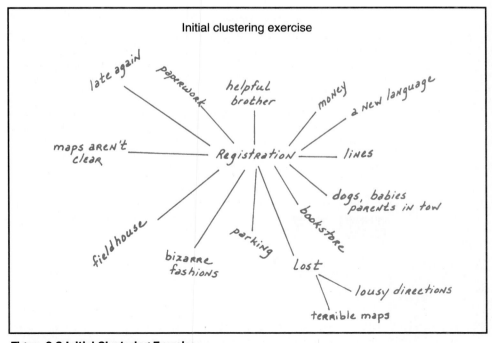

Figure 6.3 Initial Clustering Exercise

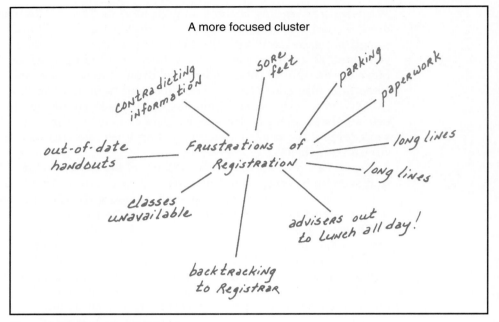

Figure 6.4 A More Focused Cluster

Pause occasionally to see if there are patterns emerging. If you see that some ideas lead to nothing and others lead to seemingly endless ideas, don't hesitate to scratch out or to highlight. If you see similar ideas emerging, circle them. If one group of items seems particularly productive, you may wish to start a new cluster. The student who begins a cluster with "Registration" may find that the entry "Frustrating" quickly inspires other entries. A new sheet with the subject "The Frustrations of Registration" will narrow the writer's focus and still offer a wealth of material. (See Figure 6.4)

Y O U R   T U R N

Clustering Practice
(Do not attempt to edit ideas yet; include everything that comes to mind):

1. Turn your paper sideways and write a concrete noun in the center of the page. Practice clustering by radiating lines from that word, entering ideas at the end of each line. Try a second layer

of entries, then a third. If some lines become unproductive, concentrate on those that spark further associations.

Try these words:

dolls
schoolyards
automobiles
money
books
games

Notice that most of these words are extremely general. To write creatively about any of them, you will need to find a specific angle that reflects your own experience. Remember the advice in Chapter 1 about thinking creatively—force yourself to go beyond the immediate reactions and force yourself to think in specifics.

2. Clustering also works with less concrete starting points. Writing down a feeling or an occasion or another abstract concept will also give your cluster a beginning. Try clustering with some of the following subjects:

an embarrassing moment
the thrill of victory
turning points
contentment
adulthood
innocence
frustration
what I learned from (person, event, time span)

As you use clustering to explore your subject, you may find it more effective to pursue one line of thought at a time. Or, you may decide to work on several lines at once. Your own work habits will determine the best way for you to cluster. Don't feel bound to one pattern of exploration; instead, let the creative voice play freely with ideas.

Probing for Patterns

Logical patterns dominate our lives. Consider that when you first noticed that your cries were answered by your parents, you became aware of cause and effect, and that you have been listing in order of importance since that first Christmas wish list began "What I want most of all is. . . ."

Those same logical patterns can help you explore your topic. Do not *select* a pattern here; if you commit yourself to one approach, you might miss out on other more rewarding analyses. Instead, consider the topic and briefly describe a possible paper that would fit each pattern. For example, if your topic is college registration, you might describe a **chronological ordering** of the steps in the registration process. You might also analyze the **causes** of confusion, or the **effects** of a poor schedule. You might **classify** the types of problems encountered or explain the **most important** considerations in filling out a schedule. (Logical patterns are discussed in more detail in Chapter 9.) A sample probe follows.

Of course, not every topic can be discussed from every logical perspective. However, by seeing your topic as it might be presented in several different patterns, you will encourage your creative voice to see new sides of the topic. And, you might surprise yourself with a stunningly original insight.

Looking for Possible Patterns in Material

Topic: Registration—New Telephone System

Chronological Order
Early preparation—going over the catalogue requirements and the course offerings, making out a tentative schedule, setting up a list of second choices—waiting for my assigned time—optimism when I first dialed— the busy signal—try again—the busy signal—the frustration mounts— the busy signal continues—most of the afternoon spent trying to connect with the computer—the sections I wanted were closed—frantic readjustments— finally got enough classes to be full-time

Comparison-Contrast
Registration last year before the phone system—frustrating, but at least I was moving and talking to people who told me "No Way"—the busy signal is worse
But—I had to keep going back to the departments to see if anyone had dropped a class—the computer could check immediately; no 12-hour lag— at least I knew my schedule when I finally got off the phone
More comparisons could be made here—friends' reactions, costs, time involved, efficiency, distribution of class loads

Cause-Effect
Why was the new system started? I don't really care
What was the verdict on this semester's registration?
Maybe—lots of comment in the school newspaper, from the administration and from the students—was it a success?

Classification
I don't see enough detail here to classify.

Comment: The student looked for patterns in the material he had already collected; he found that some patterns suggested new ideas, and that he could find more material that compared the two systems.

YOUR **TURN**

Probing for Patterns

Turn a sheet of paper sideways, and divide it into six columns. Describe your topic as briefly as possible, using the description as the heading for the sheet. Head each column with a pattern: Chronology, Spatial, Importance, Cause-Effect, Comparison-Contrast, Classification (these patterns are discussed in more detail in Chapter 12). Then, jot down as many ideas as you can under each heading. Don't leave any blank spaces and don't discard any ideas as too silly—encourage the creative voice to produce quantity.

Try the probe with these topics:

Traffic in this area
University football teams
A memorable celebration
A political figure (any level)
A colorful relative

Reminder

You are not selecting a pattern for your writing; you are simply probing for useful associations. If this exercise gives you a framework for a draft, then use it—but do not feel that you have made any commitments to a particular pattern.

As you use these techniques for generating ideas, remember that ideas will not come to you only when you are making a formal effort to produce them. Many good ideas occur at odd moments and in strange places—in church, in a bus, in a bathtub. Many an artist or inventor has awakened with the solution to a problem that seemed unsolvable the night before. But such ideas are elusive; they will not linger. As noted, thinking on paper has multiple benefits; make an effort to record those fleeting bits of inspiration as soon as possible.

ENCOURAGING CREATIVE THINKING

These techniques are intended to generate ideas about your subject. Ideally, you will generate some ideas that are creative and insightful, ideas that will make your writing unique and significant. But such ideas, by definition, will not be the easy, obvious ones that anyone could produce.

Look again at the section in Chapter 1 on creative thinking and apply the guidelines offered to your own work :

1. As you look over the notes that explaining, listing, freewriting, probing for patterns, clustering, forcing associations, cubing, and dialogues have produced, press yourself to go a little deeper. Ask, "What else do I know?" "What else fits in this pattern?"

2. Then, press yourself for specific details, for actual people and costumes and scenery. If your notes on a character say, "sense of humor," press for an example of that humor in action; if your notes on a scene say "homelike atmosphere," press for a vivid image of furniture and wall covering and curtains.

3. Trust your ability to respond meaningfully. Do not try to imagine what others are expecting you to say. Write down what you think about a subject.

Creativity comes from what people do, not what they are. So take advantage of every technique and trick to foster the creative voice within.

GATHERING FURTHER INFORMATION

The techniques presented above are primarily concerned with exploring your knowledge and ideas. Sometimes, though, what you already think or know is not enough. Recognizing the limits of your own knowledge need not cause you to abandon a project. If you feel that your material is too sketchy and if you have the time to gather more information, your initial explorations can direct your research. You may think of research as something limited to work assigned as "research papers." But research can improve the quality of your papers (and of your thinking) because you are opening your mind to new information and new ideas. When you decide to supplement your current knowledge, you probably think first of the library. It is a good starting point and, for some topics, the library will contain all of the information you need. But there are other ways to gather information for a paper. Whether you are working on an extensive research project or looking for just a little more information, consider the following methods of gathering information:

Researching Written Materials

The Library

The most comprehensive source of written work is undoubtedly the library. Whether you need a little more information or extensive research, you most often start at the library. You can expect to find not only books on your subject but also magazine and journal articles and newspaper coverage both in print and on microfilm. You should be familiar with the resources of your particular library, including both the campus and the community libraries. An extensive discussion of library resources and research strategies appears in Chapter 19, "Writing the Research Paper."

In addition to the materials in the library, most newspapers keep back files (often called the "morgue") that are available to the public. If you are writing about a campus issue, check with your campus newspaper about dated and cross-referenced back issues. Remember, too, that most libraries keep such files of local papers and of major papers like the *New York Times.* Find the issues for several weeks following an incident and check editorials and letters to the editor to get contemporary reactions to the topic.

Research in the Field

Chapter 19 ("Writing the Research Paper") details various methods of field research, including personal observation, surveys and polls, and interviews. Such strategies for gathering information are useful in any project when the information you recall seems inadequate. "Field research" may sound complicated and time-consuming, but it need not be extensive to be useful.

EXPLORING YOUR SUBJECT BY DRAFTING

When you have explored your subject on paper, using one or more of these pre-writing techniques, your next objective is to put your raw materials into prose form. You can call this production a rough draft if you'd like, but realize at this stage the draft is intended only for your eyes. Such a limited audience should relieve much of the pressure associated with writing assignments—no one will red-pencil your spelling and no one will care if you repeat yourself. Remember that the purpose of this piece of writing remains exploration of the subject, so list and expand new approaches as they occur to you.

Producing a Draft for Yourself

Begin this initial draft by surveying your raw materials. As you read through lists and verbal sketches, develop a system for marking bits that you like—fresh ideas or vivid descriptions or apt comparisons. You might like to work with a colorful highlighting pen, or you might draw bold stars in the margins. As you survey your early gatherings, make a list of the ideas and approaches you find. Don't think of anything so formal as an outline; just list in whatever form (phrases, sentences) is comfortable for you. List the items as you find them, and tell the critical voice it can do some sorting later.

With a list in front of you, scan for ideas that seem to belong together—two that are similar; one that results from another; several that fall into a chronological sequence. If you see no connections at this time, don't worry. Further discussion will usually reveal the relationships between your ideas.

Now, pick an idea that appeals to you and explain it on paper. Remember that you are not writing for an audience that needs catchy introductions or careful handling; this discussion is aimed at an audience of one and needs only to be put on paper. Of course, if you have an idea for a skillful beginning, you can try it out here. In fact, try out anything you'd like. You do not need to make choices about material here; ramble on and discuss everything that occurs to you. If you repeat yourself, so much the better—you'll have two passages to choose from when you begin to revise.

A reasonable objective for this first draft is to make it as long as possible. If the assignment called for a 500-word essay, you might find it reassuring that you can produce 800 words in a first effort. Include every example that comes to mind and don't be afraid to add, "Another point that should have been discussed earlier is. . . ." You have no formal outline or commitment to discuss ideas in any particular order.

If you are having trouble beginning, set a timer for twenty minutes and write, "I don't know where to start this discussion, but one thing I want to say is. . . ." Pick the first item on your list, or pick the one you like best, but force yourself to write for twenty minutes, however awkward your writing feels. Then reset the timer and write for twenty more. Don't stop until you have at least mentioned every item on your list. If you are using a word processor of any kind, this is a good time to print out your draft. Count the pages. Estimate the number of words produced. Then take a break. (Notice that we have confidence in your work habits. We believe that you didn't wait until two hours before the paper was due to start writing.) Even if you don't realize it, your hardest physical effort is behind you.

Y O U R   T U R N

Exploring by Drafting

If you are currently working on an assignment, explore the subject first using some of the other methods explained in this chapter.

[OR: Take one of the subjects you explored with another method of prewriting.]

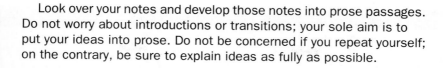

Look over your notes and develop those notes into prose passages. Do not worry about introductions or transitions; your sole aim is to put your ideas into prose. Do not be concerned if you repeat yourself; on the contrary, be sure to explain ideas as fully as possible.

SUMMARY

The purpose of all the activities here, from simple listing to self-directed drafting, is exploration of a subject. Your goal here is to assemble what you know and what you think about a subject; you have not yet made any irreversible decisions about content, audience, or form.

CHAPTER SEVEN

Applying Critical Thinking Skills

This chapter stresses the importance of testing ideas early and often. It reviews the characteristics of critical thinking—a questioning attitude, the separation of fact from opinion and taste from judgment, and sensitivity to the connections between ideas. It then describes how to apply those characteristics when you evaluate your writing and your judgments.

EVALUATING EARLY DRAFTS

When you use the technique described in Chapter 6 of exploring a subject by drafting, you produce a draft that aims only to put your ideas into prose. Since you are the audience for that draft, you are probably the one who will review what you've written. Even if you ask a friend to read over it, remember that your objectives for this draft were simple and be sure that the critical voice (yours or someone else's) agrees to evaluate according to those standards. It is easy to check for spelling; in fact, your word processor may be able to do that for you. But spelling errors are not the target of this evaluation.

What are you looking for in this draft? Remember that you are still in the exploration phase of your writing process, so a reasonable procedure is to mark the ideas you've discussed. (Highlighting pens or stars or squiggly lines will do just fine.) If you see passages that discuss the same or similar ideas, move them next to each other. That is simple enough with a word processor, but a pair of scissors and a roll of tape will also serve.

The next step is a bit more complex. It asks you to step outside your role as writer of the text (most writers are very sensitive about just-produced copy, so try not to feel defensive if anyone questions your explanations or reasoning). You will need to apply critical thinking skills as you evaluate your draft, so let's look again at the characteristics of such a mindset.

SHIFTING TO CRITICAL THINKING

As Chapter 1 explained, critical thinking is an active mental process in which you scrutinize your ideas (or other people's ideas), probe their stated and implied meaning, and decide whether that meaning is defensible. Such thinking depends on three characteristics:

- A questioning attitude toward all interpretations and conclusions
- Skill in separating fact from opinion and taste from judgment
- Sensitivity to the connections between ideas

Adopt a Questioning Attitude

When your approach to your writing shifts from enthusiastic acceptance to critical appraisal, the most important part of the shift is the adoption of a questioning attitude. Unlike the unqualified acceptance required of the creative stance, a questioning attitude depends on the expectation of error. It begins with the realization that humans are imperfect and that anything of human invention or design (including statements of belief) can be flawed.

To be a good critical thinker, you must learn to ask questions about every significant idea you encounter or produce. You should be especially inquisitive about ideas you feel strongly about or are familiar to you because people around you accept them. In short, suspend your allegiances long enough to examine them closely.

As you look at your draft, mark the ideas with which you are most comfortable and the ideas you have heard from friends and family. Those familiar ideas are often accepted without much evaluation, and you want to look at them carefully now.

Separate Fact from Opinion

One of the most important determinations made during a critical appraisal is the separation of fact from opinion. Facts are ideas that have been shown beyond a reasonable doubt to be so. They are commonly found in encyclopedias, dictionaries, biographical reference books, and almanacs. Opinions are ideas that lack the certainty of facts; they are ideas that knowledgeable people still disagree about. If your subject area is currently researched, you should be aware of copyright dates. Scientific discoveries have changed many "facts," so be sure that your data is current.

Another area needing careful evaluation is the ideas you share with friends and family. If you and most of your peers accept an idea, that idea is comfortable because it is unchallenged. If you look carefully at such comfortable ideas, you might be surprised to see that many of them are opinions, not facts. Reasonable writing labels facts and opinions properly, so look more closely at the nature of opinion.

The word opinion often causes a great deal of confusion because it covers everything from expressions of taste to expressions of judgment. Tastes are personal preferences, based on internal evidence that is not affected by reason. A preference for chocolate or for mystery novels is not suitable matter for debate. In contrast, judgments are conclusions reached by consideration of impersonal evidence and are therefore open to debate.

Thus when someone says, "It's my opinion that . . . ," he can mean "I prefer to believe . . ." (taste) or "I haven't really thought about the matter, but I have a feeling that . . ." (impulse or conditioned reflex) or "I have researched the matter and after careful deliberation have concluded that . . ." (judgment). The problem is that these meanings are not interchangeable, so look carefully at the basis for opinions before you begin a discussion.

Also, resist the intellectual shortcut that no discussion is necessary because one opinion is as good as another. To insist that all opinions are equal is to surrender all attempts at critical thinking and to accept all observations, however ignorant or dangerous. If all opinions are truly equal, the ancient idea that the earth is the center of our solar system is as right as the modern idea that the sun is; such meaningless relativism would suggest that Hitler was right to invade other countries, draw the world into war, and exterminate over nine million human beings.

To be a good critical thinker, you must not confuse matters of taste and matters of judgment. When you are writing about matters of judgment, remember that uninformed and unsupported opinions carry no weight.

Y O U R T U R N

Take a close look at your draft. Label your statements as fact or opinion, then consider the basis for your opinions. Are you ready to explain why you believe as you do? Do you need to offer examples or statistics to show that your opinion is indeed based on external evidence?

Examine Logical Connections between Ideas

Look carefully at the statements below. Each conclusion proceeds from the statements before it, but you can readily see that there is some flaw in the reasoning:

1. Fish live in water.
   Whales live in water.
   Therefore, whales are fish.

(Does the first statement assert that *only* fish live in water?)

2. Low grades are a sign a teacher doesn't like a student.
   Mr. Snipswitch gave me a low grade on my composition.
   Therefore, Mr. Snipswitch doesn't like me.

(Can low grades be a sign of anything else?
Does *every* low grade indicate a personality conflict? Perhaps the composition was poor.)

3. Students who study hard make good grades.
   John makes good grades.
   Therefore, John must study hard.

(Is it *only* those who study hard who make good grades? Perhaps John is gifted; perhaps he cheats.)

The three-part structure above, called a syllogism, is a diagram of the reasoning behind these conclusions. In such a diagram, you can pinpoint the half-truths and the unjustified assumptions that make the conclusions worthless. Unfortunately, in most cases the judgments you scrutinize will not be expressed in such neat logical outlines. Instead of appearing as two premises and a conclusion, they will be expressed as a single, seemingly self-evident idea. For example, you may say," Mr. Snipswitch gave me a low grade on my composition because he doesn't like me." The error of that idea, however, is precisely the same. It is merely more hidden and therefore more difficult to see. (Of course, it is possible that Mr. Snipswitch did grade the student harshly because of personal feelings, but more evidence would be needed.)

Naturally you don't have time to break down every complex idea into its components and scrutinize them. But you can try to be sensitive to the stated and implied connections between your ideas.

Y O U R T U R N

When you evaluate logical thinking, there are some labels applied to common errors. Chapter 10 reviews the terminology used to identify logical fallacies, but it is also possible to describe the logical problems here without precise labels.

1. Examine the following letter to the editor, looking closely at the reasoning behind the writer's statements:

   Your editorial said Mayor Slither's handling of the street-paving contract bids should be investigated. That suggestion is outrageous. The mayor is one of the most hard-working officials who has ever held office in this city. He has never taken a vacation and in spite of his busy schedule has always found time to assist in fund-raising drives and to mediate community disputes.

2. Each of the following brief excerpts from letters to the editor and editorials contains at least one shallow, narrow-minded, or illogical idea. Read each selection carefully and determine what

is wrong with it. Be sure to approach your evaluation with a questioning attitude; with alertness to the distinctions between fact and opinion, taste and judgment; and with sensitivity to the connections between ideas.

a. Marriage in today's world is risky business. Divorce is at an all-time high. Since divorce is costly to the state and to the individuals involved, some laws should be enacted to lower the rate. For starters, no one under the age of twenty-five should be allowed to marry.

b. The average person who wants to see a movie this weekend will find nothing fit to watch. R- and X-rated movies dominate the screens. The only decent movies available are the Disney classics on videocassettes. This country's fascination with sex and violence is a clear sign of moral ruin.

c. Women in the service are clearly a detriment to this country's security. As mothers, they are often absent from their posts and prone to medical problems. Their physical weakness makes them unfit to perform most of the work necessary to keep this nation strong. Since our founding fathers saw no need to put guns in the hands of women, I see no point in changing a system that has proven to be the most effective in the world. At no time in history have there been strong fighting forces with women anywhere near the front lines.

Now that you've practiced your critical thinking skills on someone else's reasoning, take a close look at your own draft. Consider the reasoning behind your own statements, paying close attention to those you labelled opinions. If you find illogical reasoning, can you strengthen your explanation with better analysis? If not, you may need to define a more defensible position.

RAISING IMPORTANT QUESTIONS

Developing the three characteristics just discussed will enhance your critical thinking. But you can do more than that. You can raise specific questions about the ideas you intend to use in your composition. The following questions are especially helpful because they address the most common problems that occur in writing.

Which of My Ideas Are Judgments?

Don't be afraid to use opinion—if the opinion is a judgment and not a matter of taste. Judgments are essential if you are going to do more than simply list facts. Judgments are your contribution to the topic, your way of dealing with facts—sorting them out, combining them, learning from them, and putting them to use.

Of course, since judgments are a form of opinion, they are subject to errors in thinking that do not occur with facts. Identifying your judgments will help you focus on the places where errors are most likely to occur and where you will need to defend your statements to your reader.

Y O U R   T U R N

If it were always easy to distinguish among facts, expressions of taste, and judgments, then you could simply look at your notes and decide which are which. Unfortunately, they sometimes look alike. Let's examine a variety of ideas and see how they are best classified:

I hate Professor Mentor's class. He is an unbelievably boring lecturer. Any normal person falls asleep the moment Mentor opens his mouth.

Henry David Thoreau was born in 1817 and died in 1862. He was a naturalist and author. Two of his best known works are *A Week on the Concord and Merrimack Rivers* and *Walden*.

Henry David Thoreau's best work is *Walden*.

Walden is one of the most interesting books I have ever read.

Afghanistan occupies an area of 25l,773 square miles. Its population according to a l98l estimate by the International Demographic Data Center, is 15,400,000. Its capital is Kabul and its monetary unit, the afghani.

Russia's invasion of Afghanistan in 1979 was an act of aggression.

Be especially careful of judgments that are shared by many of your friends and family. The more widely accepted your judgments are, the more they are likely to seem indisputable. If you fail to recognize opinions, you may also fail to evaluate them critically. Take nothing for granted. Any idea that can be disputed by honest and intelligent people is best considered a judgment that needs defending, not a fact, no matter how strongly you feel about it.

To What Extent Are My Judgments Influenced by Preconceived Notions?

Preconceived notions are firm convictions about people, places, and things that we form before we encounter them. Most of us succumb to at least a few such notions. They save mental effort and spare us the confusion of dealing with complex decisions. But they could also be harmful if they prevent us from seeing reality.

Y O U R   T U R N

Some preconceived notions persist in human thought. Examine your thinking in each of the areas below, refusing to accept opinions as fact and demanding that critical thinking standards be applied:

1. One preconceived idea is that people of the same race, religion, ethnic group, or social class have the same traits. Supply examples of stereotypes based on such arbitrary criteria as race, sex, creed, nationalities, and age. Is there any logical support for these stereotypes?

2. A common idea is that familiar ideas are more valuable than unfamiliar ideas. There is something secure in familiar ideas, yet every creative breakthrough, every discovery, every invention, every fresh insight is by definition new and unfamiliar. Identify instances where new ideas are rejected in favor of "the way it has always been done." Think of inefficient procedures at work or at any level of government that were continued because of a reluctance to change. Read "The Lottery" by Shirley Jackson and consider how "the old ways" are destructive.

3. A third preconceived notion is that whatever the majority accepts must be acceptable. Don't think that you have to reject *everything* the majority accepts; any kind of preconceived response eliminates critical thinking. To accept the majority view because you believe it is the best view is sensible; to accept it simply because it is the majority view is an insult to your intelligence. After all, men of good faith and intellect once asserted that the world was flat. Can you think of more recent majority opinions that have been proven wrong?

4. It is also a mistake to endorse the notion that people in authority must be right. We have long rejected the defense of the man who "was only following orders," and you should check your own opinions to make sure that you have not let someone else do your thinking for you. Can you provide recent examples of

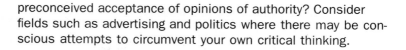

preconceived acceptance of opinions of authority? Consider fields such as advertising and politics where there may be conscious attempts to circumvent your own critical thinking.

To What Extent Is My Reasoning Self-Serving?

Most people want to be open-minded and objective about issues. But intending to be so is easier than being so. Consider the story of a boy who went fishing with three friends. At first, they all agreed that the catch would be split four ways. Then, one boy began reeling in more fish than the others, and his attitude began to change. By the end of the day, when his catch was far greater than theirs, he had become violently opposed to splitting at all. He couldn't understand why a good fisherman should be penalized for the incompetence and bad luck of others. As his perspective changed, so did his judgment.

Like the boy in the story, most of us tend to judge issues and ideas narrowly, in a way that serves our own interests. Where more than one view of an issue is possible, we tend to embrace the one that is closest to our view, selecting those facts that support our view and ignoring those that challenge it. Sometimes we become defensive, frantically seeking excuses for ourselves and our views.

These tendencies are part of the human condition. As James Harvey Robinson accurately observed, "Most of our so-called reasoning consists in finding arguments for going on believing as we already do." To be a critical thinker, you must realize your tendency to be self-serving in your thinking. You must work to make your ideas fit the facts rather than selecting the facts to support your ideas.

Have I Judged too Hastily?

A judgment arrived at quickly is not necessarily an inferior judgment. The judgment that flashes to mind may prove to be the most sensible. Yet the odds are against its being so, especially when you are dealing with a complex issue.

You can be reasonably sure your judgments are not made too hastily if two conditions are met:

- First, you have obtained a fair sampling of the facts and interpreted them carefully.
- Second, you have examined the arguments on both sides of the issue and honestly considered a number of possible judgments before settling on one.

Have I Assumed too Much?

To assume is to take something for granted without even consciously thinking about it. When you attend a class each day, you seldom wonder whether your instructor will be there, unless he or she has missed a number of classes in the past. You merely assume that the instructor will be there.

But to assume that middle-aged people do not understand the problems of young people, or that the rating of a movie is an index of its quality, or that a person who attends church is more honest than one who doesn't, is unwarranted. What makes each of these assumptions unwarranted is that in each case the reverse is as likely to be true. There is no special probability supporting the assumed idea.

To avoid assuming too much, examine your judgments and ask what assumptions they reveal. Then decide if those assumptions are warranted by the facts or by past experience.

Have I Overlooked Important Distinctions?

Whenever you fail to make distinctions, you confuse things that should not be confused. For example, when you look unfavorably on the ideas of people you dislike and favorably on the ideas of people you like, you are confusing the idea with the person. Similarly, when you evaluate the soundness of an idea by speculating about the motives of the person who expresses it, you are confusing what is said with why it is said.

At a town meeting, for instance, a person may propose that land owned by the town be leased or sold to a developer for a new shopping center. Now, he may stand to gain personally from such a development. But the possibility that he is making the proposal entirely for personal reasons does not make it a bad proposal. Critical thinking demands that you separate the idea from the person and his motives, and consider the idea on its own merits.

Are My Judgments Reasonable?

The most reasonable judgment is the one that fits the facts better than all other possible judgments. To be sure your judgments are reasonable, make them meet the exacting standards given here:

1. When the facts will not support any firm or final judgment, make your judgment appropriately tentative. Many writers do almost the opposite. The slimmer their evidence, the more forceful and final their judgments. They actually believe that extravagance of expression will hide the weakness of their position. It may from the undiscerning reader, but not from anyone else.

2. If you cannot speak with certainty, then don't. Make it clear that you are merely speculating, stating what seems to be so, or indicating what is probable. No sensible reader will think less of you for saying "This evidence suggests," instead of "This evidence proves," or "I find this persuasive," instead of "This is the only answer that makes any sense." You may think this means you should "ride the fence" on issues. It does not. Riding the fence is refusing to take a stand that the facts permit you to take. That is very different from recognizing when the facts will not permit a conclusive stand.

3. When the facts will not support a generalized judgment, particularize your judgment. If you have a 1985 Ford Mustang and are pleased with its performance, you might easily think and write, "Ford Mustangs are the best small cars on the market today," when your facts cover only a single Ford Mustang. You are justified in extending a judgment about a small number of things to all members of that class only when you have good reason to believe that the small sample you are familiar with—people or anything else—is typical of all others. Otherwise, make your judgment no more general than your facts will support.

4. When the issue is complex, be sure your judgment does not oversimplify. Whenever those who know a great deal about a complex subject speak to (or write for) those who know little or nothing about it, they must reduce the subject to a less complicated form. There is nothing wrong with simplification so long as it does not twist and distort the reality it describes. Oversimplification is an obstacle to effective thinking because it presents partial truths as truths. (What is partly true, of course, is also partly false.) Thus it makes your thinking and writing shallow and often inaccurate.

   For example, to say that divorce is a social evil or divorce is a social good, and leave it at that, is to oversimplify. The truth about divorce is that it is not merely a social evil or a social good; it is a complex phenomenon that cannot be neatly pigeon-holed.

   The most common cause of oversimplification is the tendency to see everything as black or white, to demand a world of absolutes. Thus communism must be all bad and capitalism all good (or vice versa), and humans must be either heroes or villains.

   To avoid oversimplifying, consider the possibility that the best judgment is neither an absolute "Yes" nor an absolute "No," but rather a balanced answer that rejects extremes and matches the complex nature of the issue.

5. Even when the facts support a firm judgment, use moderation and understatement. There is nothing really wrong about writing in superlatives when the facts warrant doing so. Yet the frequent use of superlatives can become a handicap. Once you say something is

the "most significant" or the "greatest," what can you call something else that is even more significant or greater?

But there is an even better reason to avoid superlatives. The opposite tendency in expression, understatement, shows the sense of restraint and caution that has traditionally been associated with good thinking. It takes discipline to write, "We mustn't underestimate the dangers of inflation," when you really want to say, "Sound the alarm—inflation is killing us!" And it is precisely that discipline that will make your judgments impressive to the critical reader.

IS THERE A RIGHT TIME TO ASK QUESTIONS?

Knowing how to ask the right questions is a powerful tool for evaluating your ideas. It is even more important to know how to answer honestly and, where appropriate, to modify your ideas to eliminate any shallowness, narrow-mindedness, or illogical thinking.

Note that asking critical questions is not something you do at one designated time and then abandon. Ideally, it is an ongoing activity that helps you evaluate your thinking and your writing at every stage of the process. Used in the early drafting stage, asking questions and weeding out unreasonable or indefensible assertions will give you confidence in the logic of your later work. But do not forget to use the tool in the later stages of your writing. Illogical ideas surface because they are often appealing and comfortable, so be prepared to evaluate your thinking and your writing on a recurring basis.

YOUR TURN

The critical thinking skills outlined in this chapter may not be automatic, but they can be developed and sharpened with practice. Read each of the following statements carefully to decide whether you agree or disagree with it. If you agree with a statement, let it stand as your own. If you disagree, modify it to reflect your position. (You may change it as drastically as you wish.) Then select the four statements you feel most strongly about and ask yourself whether what you have written is fact, opinion, taste, or judgment.

1. Homosexuals should not be granted equal rights because homosexuality is abnormal and represents a danger to society.

2. Most of us are brought up to be concerned for our neighbors and to help those in need. But that idea makes poor people dependent and indulges laziness. A better idea is to let everyone look out for himself. Then if people are poor, they have only themselves to blame.

3. If we were really serious about solving the crime problem in this country, we'd get rid of laws that tie the hands of the police. The police should be allowed any means they wish to deal with suspects. They are close to the problem of crime and know what must be done.

4. Prostitution should be legalized. People should be able to use their bodies as they wish as long as they don't injure anyone else.

5. When parents teach a child their religious and political views and their values, they take away the child's individuality.

6. It is hypocritical for states to have laws against drunken driving and continue to license bars that can be reached only by car. Liquor licenses should be granted only to those bars that are within village or city limits (and presumably within walking distance of patrons' homes).

7. Doctors, lawyers, and dentists should be prohibited from advertising their services in newspapers and magazines and on radio and television. Such advertising is unprofessional.

8. Anyone who fails to achieve a twelfth-grade level of reading and writing proficiency should be denied a high school diploma.

9. Girls should not be allowed to play on boys' varsity teams because they are not equal to boys athletically and they cannot handle the strenuous training required to be a varsity athlete.

SUMMARY

The key to reasonable writing is early and frequent evaluation of ideas. As soon as you have compiled your thoughts in prose form, you should focus your critical thinking skills on the draft to appraise your ideas before going further in the writing process.

YOUR TURN

Select one of the following topics as the basis for discussion. Explore the topic thoroughly, using any or all of the techniques described in Chapter 6. When you have compiled your ideas, examine them carefully. Ask yourself:

- Which of my ideas are judgments?
- To what extent are my judgments influenced by preconceived notions?

- To what extent is my reasoning self- serving?
- Have I judged too hastily?
- Have I assumed too much?
- Have I overlooked important distinctions?
- Are my judgments reasonable?

1. Should suicide be condemned as immoral?

2. Should parents be granted the right to decide whether their retarded child should be sterilized?

3. Should teachers be held legally liable (for malpractice) if their students do not learn?

4. Should a person who has lived with someone for several years but never married be granted alimony when the relationship ends?

5. Should parents be allowed to keep their children out of school if they believe they can educate them better at home?

6. Are pornographic books and movies harmful?

7. Should the drinking age in your state be raised, lowered, or left as it is?

8. Should Congress pass a gun-control law restricting the right to own handguns, or rifles and shotguns, or both?

9. Should it be required that the theory of creation (that God created the world and everything in it) be taught in biology classrooms along with the theory of evolution?

10. Should college students be allowed to miss classes without penalty as long as they are responsible for all work covered?

CHAPTER EIGHT

Identifying a Thesis

At this stage in your writing process, you should find the answer to a crucial question: "What do I want to say about this subject?" This chapter will present important considerations in defining and articulating the controlling idea of your work.

THE RHETORICAL SITUATION

Your nine-year-old daughter has been very excited about trying out for her school baseball team. Today, though, she comes home upset because the coach refused to let her practice. His action is in clear violation of school policy, and you are not going to let his decision go unchallenged. After a few heated phone calls, you decide to put your protest in writing. The invitation to write has been heard, and the response begins to take shape.

Sometimes that shape emerges quickly—for example, you know the school board has the power to overrule the coach's decision, and you know what you want to say about the unfairness and illegality of his actions. You also have a clear objective in mind: Immediate action should be taken to reverse the decision. You have a vision of yourself as writer presenting specific ideas to a definite audience, and you can see that audience reacting to the force of your words. What you have defined so clearly is a triangle called the rhetorical situation—the relationship between you, your ideas, and your audience.

Such a clear and immediate perception of the rhetorical situation does not occur every time you write. In fact, more often the writing process begins as an unfocused blur. The stimulus—an aggravation, an observation, an assignment—identifies only a general subject; you explore the subject and evaluate your ideas, and in this early stage you identify feelings that most need expression or areas that most need explanation. Out of this early stage of exploration and discovery, you identify your controlling idea, also called your thesis.

THE THESIS (CONTROLLING IDEA)

A **controlling idea** or **thesis** is the idea central to the meaning you want to convey, the essential message. Sometimes you will begin with a distinct controlling idea; more often, you will have to separate it from the welter of data and ideas that surface when you decide to respond to a stimulus.

If your daughter is excluded from tryouts for the school baseball team, for example, you may immediately focus on the idea that the tryouts should be open to all. But you may also think of other areas of school policy that are similarly ignored. You might think of the discipline problems or the dress code or you might think of how little your tuition seems to buy, or you might think that curriculum changes are overdue, or you might think that school parties are a waste of time or that playground equipment is outdated and dangerous. There is an abundance of choice here; certainly a paper that tried to include all of these thoughts would be unfocused, even confusing. There is not even one idea that is more important than any other. Instead, you must make some decisions about what you want to say in this paper—in short, you must select a thesis from among the possibilities.

Selecting a Thesis

As you survey the ideas you've compiled so far, a controlling idea *might* leap immediately to the front. If your focus remains buried, asking yourself some simple questions will help to uncover it:

What Do I Really Want to Say?

First explorations probably include ideas that you had heard expressed by friends or family or even instructors. When you select your thesis, though, be sure that it expresses your own views. Otherwise, you may fall into the trap of saying what you think you are expected to say.

Consider this topic: "The Value of the Honor Society in My High School." You may want to say that in your high school the honor society was a joke, that really deserving students were often passed over while less worthy students who "played the game" or came from important families were selected. However, you may decide that the teacher expects you to write that the National Honor Society had a positive influence on students, encouraging them to pursue excellence not only in school but in later life as well. And so you may suppress your own ideas.

Such decisions compromise your integrity and inevitably produce conventional papers without much character, creativity, or value. Protecting and presenting your own ideas involves risk, yet such risk-taking makes writing a fulfilling activity. Parroting the ideas of others may be safe, but it is inevitably dull.

How Much Time and Space Do I Have?

Most rhetorical situations impose limits on the controlling idea. If your audience will give you only a minute of its time, you will need to focus quickly on one point. If you are writing a lengthy article for a magazine devoted to in-depth analysis, you will be expected to explore not only your proposal but also the pros and cons of the opposition. In short, the boundaries of the situation will determine what you can discuss as well as what you can't.

As you define your thesis, then, you must consider the expectations of the situation. Are you writing a memo? A letter? A journal article? In most academic assignments, your instructor will define expectations. Your task is to broaden or narrow the focus of your writing to fit. If the instructor requests 500–800 words, you cannot realistically expect to explain the history of the Republican Party, but you can expect to discuss the political background of one minor candidate. A thorough discussion of a smaller topic is almost always superior to a superficial scan of a big one.

Neither should you try to pad a discussion to satisfy length requirements. If you can describe your first experience in a canoe in 300 words, stretching it out to 600 words will not improve it. In such a case, redefining the controlling idea to include more material (perhaps your additional frustrating struggles with unfamiliar fishing equipment) is a better tactic.

What Ideas Have Already Been Covered?

One more paper that offers a recitation of the obvious is unnecessary. Most people have already been told that there is too much violence on television and that professional athletes are overpaid. Unless you have a new perspective on an old issue, you will do your readers and yourself a favor by not making such opinions the controlling idea of a composition. You can, of course, challenge such ideas or use them to develop other points, but do not belabor a familiar point or you risk boring your readers.

If your subject is one that has been much discussed, identify what needs to be said about an issue or find a perspective that has been neglected. For example, you can find many writers who identify a problem, deplore it, and attack the conditions and people responsible for it. Far fewer writers offer ways to overcome the problem. Thus one more paper on the problems of the homeless or the devastating impact of AIDS might get little attention, while a thoughtful proposal to relieve such suffering would be worth reading carefully.

It is also possible to take a common idea and give it an uncommon treatment. Consider that familiar ideas are often accepted primarily because they are familiar. You might want to challenge such comfortable assumptions by arguing, for example, that there is actually very little violence on television or that some violence on TV is a healthy outlet for aggression. Or you might argue that superstars who are thought to be overpaid are in fact paid only a small portion of the money their popularity generates, so they are really paid no more than they are worth. The basic topic—TV violence or overpaid athletes—would remain the same. But the thesis would be unexpected.

Expressing the Thesis

In much of your writing, the thesis is explicitly stated. Less often, it is left for the reader to infer. But whether or not you put the controlling idea into words for your audience, put it into words for yourself. Like an anchor, a *written* thesis will keep your writing from drifting away from what you want to say.

Since the thesis has such control over the content of your work, express it with care. The thesis statement that comes out on paper should be the same one you had in your mind.

The Form of the Thesis Statement

Your thesis should be expressed as a complete sentence with a subject and a predicate, each of which is expressed precisely. The subject identifies the specific area of your topic to be discussed, and the predicate is what you say about the subject of your sentence. For example, in the sentence "Few nations have learned to find peaceful ways to settle their differences," the subject is "few nations" and the predicate is everything else. Any imprecision in the expression of the controlling idea may result in failure to say what you want to say.

This first written statement serves as a visual anchor for your discussion. Do not worry about subtlety or grace; make it a bold, direct statement that expresses clearly what you want this writing to say.

Reminder

As you work on your thesis statement, keep these guidelines in mind:

Make the Subject Specific

A specific subject keeps your paper tightly anchored. If you want to write about discrimination against women in sports, identify that precise subject in your controlling idea. If you write "Discrimination against women is wrong," you have left room for your writing to drift to other waters.

Make the Predicate Precise

Select a predicate that is direct and specific, using careful diction and precise tense. Compare the sentence "The mayor of Plainview lied about his opponent during the campaign" to "The mayor of Plainview made incorrect statements about his opponent during the campaign." The first sentence says the mayor knowingly misrepresented the facts. The second sentence merely says that the mayor, perhaps innocently, was wrong.

Tense choices also indicate significant differences in meaning. Saying that a town *has* numerous recreational activities for teenagers is not the same as saying that a town *had* numerous recreational activities for teenagers. The latter implies it no longer has such activities.

✳ Include All Necessary Qualifications

Qualifications of time, place, degree of certainty, and condition should be explicitly stated.

→ **Qualifications of Time:** Does it really happen all the time (or never)? Or is it usually, often, sometimes, occasionally, infrequently, or only on the third Tuesday of each month?

Compare:
Congress controlled the President's budgetary proposals.

During Reagan's administration, Congress sometimes controlled the President's budgetary proposals.

Twice in the last ten years, Congress controlled the President's budgetary proposals.

→ **Qualifications of Place:** Is it really everywhere (or nowhere)? Or is it in most places, many places, some places, a few places, or only in Dubuque?

Compare:
Skateboarding traffic has become a major concern.

In the downtown area, skateboarding traffic has become a major concern.

Four major malls and two governmental office parks have reported problems with skateboarding traffic.

→ **Qualifications of Certainty:** Is what you are saving absolutely certain? Or is it probable or only possible?

Compare:
Without budgetary cuts, new taxes are inevitable.

Without budgetary cuts, new taxes become probable.

Without budgetary cuts, further options, including new taxes, must be explored.

→ **Qualifications of Condition:** Does it happen in all circumstances (or no circumstances)? Or is it in most cases, many cases, some cases, a few cases, or only when it has rained for seven days immediately after a full moon in early summer?

Compare:
The new grocery store is unable to keep its shelves properly stocked.

During its grand opening sale, the new grocery store could not keep its shelves properly stocked.

Make the Statement Detailed but Flexible

Realistically, expect the thesis to change as you work on a draft. Be exhilarated by such growth and remember that the act of writing is an act of discovery. In fact, producing an initial thesis statement that is ready to be chiselled in marble is neither possible nor desirable.

So that the thesis can give direction to your exploration, express it as completely as possible. That is, if you are already speculating about causes, let the controlling idea show that direction: "Discrimination against women in sports exists because of cultural conditioning and because of fear." Or, you might see taking shape a discussion of cross-over effects and you write, "Discrimination against women in sports eventually teaches females that competition is unfeminine, so it effectively hampers their efforts to succeed in the business world."

In short, a detailed expression of the controlling idea makes it not only an anchor but also a visual reminder to you of the direction of your discussion.

As these guidelines suggest, the best thesis statements don't usually appear spontaneously. Instead, you construct them by making a preliminary statement and then refining that statement. You work to make the subject specific and the predicate precise, and you include details about probable areas of discussion. The following revisions illustrate the process:

Preliminary Controlling Idea Statement:
My roommate gets drunk all the time.

Revised:
Whether my roommate is going to a movie with his friends or to a dance with his girlfriend, he will ruin the evening by getting drunk and embarrassing everyone around him.

Preliminary:
Our college basketball team will probably get an N.C.A.A. bid.

Revised:
Our college basketball team is virtually assured of an N.C.A.A. bid if several key players remain eligible and uninjured and if we defeat our archrival, Southwestern Tech.

Preliminary:
The poor are going to revolt against the rich.

Revised:
In countries where the rich minority openly exploit the poor majority, conditions are ripe for revolution; and though American military aid may postpone the overthrow of governments, it will not prevent it.

Preliminary:
Ethnic jokes may seem harmless, but they are actually harmful.

Revised:
Though many people consider ethnic jokes to be harmless, they are actually quite harmful. They not only cause people embarrassment but also perpetuate stereotyping and scapegoating, thereby denying many people a basic right—the right to be regarded as individuals.

Y O U R   T U R N

1. Each of the following thesis idea statements is less than effective. Following the guidelines given in the chapter, revise each statement to make it effective. Feel free to speculate about possible subjects and predicates, adding ideas or changing the focus of the statements as you wish:

   a. Many male supervisors use their positions to harass female subordinates sexually.

   b. Some actors fit their roles so well we cannot separate the character from the man.

   c. People who marry to escape boredom are running a great risk.

   d. It's not up to the professor alone to make the class interesting. Students share the responsibility.

   e. Getting along with one's in-laws is an art.

   f. Most TV commercials are boring.

   g. I never anticipated the confusion of my first registration day at college.

   h. Growing up in a large family is better than growing up in a small family.

   i. Every student should be made to take a foreign language in high school.

2. Assume that you have selected one of the following topics and have produced one of the lists of ideas shown below. From this brief survey, see if you can find relationships between ideas and identify areas of interest. Speculate about controlling ideas that could be developed on this subject. Express those ideas in statements that are specific and detailed about both subject and predicate.

   a. My friend waxed cars.
   My sister worked at Burger King.
   I worked as an aide at a hospital.
   A job teaches you how to deal with people.

It can help clarify career plans (one way is by deflating unrealistic notions).

It helps parents financially by letting a teenager pay for his or her own clothing, books, movies, and so on.

It builds a sense of confidence and self-worth.

It teaches a teen to budget time.

My job in the hospital made me more aware of how fragile (and precious) life is.

I became a more careful driver by seeing what takes place in emergency rooms after auto accidents.

It's difficult today for kids to get jobs.

A job teaches a teen to deal with a routine without losing creativity or enthusiasm.

It makes a teenager grow up faster.

Several of my friends applied at lots of places but didn't find work.

Sometimes kids "turn off" employers by their appearance or attitude.

Parents should encourage their kids to get part-time and summer jobs as soon as the kids are old enough.

b. A criminal's chances of getting off easily (sometimes completely free) are usually very good.

Our legal system today is more concerned for criminals' rights than victims' rights.

Some say the solution is to let policemen use any means at their disposal to deal with suspects.

I believe the solution to the problem lies with legislators, lawyers, and judges meeting their responsibilities to society more fully. Policemen are the closest ones to the problem of crime, I realize.

Policemen should not be allowed to act as judge and jury.

A suspect is just that—one suspected of a crime—not one convicted of a crime.

When police have too much freedom, our liberty is in danger.

Sometimes the police are too close to crime to be objective.

If a policeman has to use strong measures to protect his own life or the lives of innocent bystanders, then he should be free to use those measures.

The temptation to kick, punch, and even shoot suspects is at times very strong, particularly suspects in certain crimes, such as physical assaults on the elderly and child molestation.

Racial and ethnic prejudice can too easily influence one's judgment of who is a suspect. Personal animosities can hide as justice.

Even criminals must be granted some rights—such as the

right to personal safety during and after arrest, the right to legal counsel, and the right to a fair trial.

Defense lawyers should be less concerned with finding loopholes for their clients and more concerned with seeing justice done and keeping society safe from criminals.

A good example of the law being too concerned with criminals' rights is the case where a conviction for a violent crime is overturned by a court because a freely offered confession did not meet some minute legal standard. Before handing down decisions, judges should weigh the effects of those decisions on the community.

Penalties should be stiffened by the legislature, particularly penalties for second offenders.

SUMMARY

Identifying your thesis is essential to clear writing. How you honestly feel about your subject is one indicator of thesis; what you have to offer that has not already been said is another. Remember that your thesis may be altered as you draft, but do your best to identify the particular aspect of the subject that you plan to discuss.

❐ The Second Decision: To Draft the Response

You begin to process of responding in writing by collecting material through recollection and research. As you evaluate your idea, you also make decisions about what you really want your paper to say. You often have some idea of how it should be said and who should read it. At this point, you are ready to shape your ideas by drafting. Think of "draft" as an action, to a thing; you do produce a "draft," but you often "draft" more than one.

There are times, of course when your first draft is clear and complete and needs little additional work. But there are other times when organizing information and directing it to an audience comes slowly. Whatever the path of your work, this section can improve your drafting by explaining the decisions which direct your written response. Your rought draft will take shape as you look for logical connections between your ideas and arrange those ideas into patterns. You will also be encouraged to review the logic of your thinking and the methods used to present material.

Identifying Patterns

Recognizing the logical order in which material is presented is more than a rhetorical exercise. It can help you spot missing pieces of a pattern and thus help to generate further discussion. It can also help you note diversions that may need redirection or elimination.

ARRANGEMENTS OF IDEAS

Patterns are the logical arrangements of your ideas. It is possible to begin exploring your subject with a specific pattern in mind; for example, if your history professor calls for an analysis of the causes of a particular event, you direct even your earliest exploration to filling in a cause-effect framework. However, even if you do not begin with a pattern in mind, by the time you have compiled material in a rough draft, patterns have emerged and evolved without your conscious direction. You might find yourself comparing two possible causes, or you might find yourself classifying the causes you have identified. Even in the most random explorations, patterns emerge.

Such "spontaneous" ordering is not really surprising; after all, you have been recognizing order and structure in your world since your first cries were answered and you discovered cause and effect. Preschoolers are taught to sort things by shape or by color, and young children quickly learn that people are both alike and different.

Understanding that much of what you know is connected in some way to something else is the key. These connections are reflected in patterns of organization that occur naturally and need only to be recognized; as a result, you will find it easier to recognize the logical patterns than to attempt to artificially impose them.

Problems with Patterns

Starting with a pattern in mind may seem like the simplest approach. After all, most writing situations do indicate some pattern for the response. And, a consideration of possible patterns of organization might even suggest an unusual approach (see "Probing for Patterns" in Chapter

6). But be warned: while awareness of logical pattern can direct exploration, it can also stifle creative responses and blind you to productive and original approaches. For example, if you decide that you will compare the personalities of two political figures, you might squelch any impulse to look at one candidate in depth and you might sacrifice a chance to analyze the causes of the candidate's conservative stand. An inflexible decision about the kind of paper you will write can result in predictable, even boring discussions.

Another good reason to delay identification of patterns is that most pieces of writing use more than one pattern. If you decide early to write a classification paper, you might cut off any other pattern of discussion. That might be a mistake. A thorough discussion rarely adheres rigidly to a single pattern. An analysis of the **causes** for a fashion trend, for example, may also trace the evolution of the fad using **chronological order** and it may also **compare** the rise of this trend to a similar one. In short, it is more important to present a thorough discussion of the topic, using whatever patterns and techniques are necessary, than it is to follow one particular pattern throughout the text.

Advantages of Patterns

If you define patterns too strictly, you can effectively kill the creativity and originality in your work. Why, then, should you consider patterns at all?

There are two good reasons to be aware of these patterns. First, a working knowledge of the patterns of organization will help you make your discussions thorough. Second, understanding the basic pattern will help you recognize and control your variations of it. Let's look closely at these two considerations:

> Testing for Completeness—If you recognize that your ideas are part of a pattern, and if you know the general "shape" of the pattern, you can then recognize missing pieces. If you recognize that your discussion is organized largely by types, you can then ask your creative voice some specific questions like "Are there any more types to be included?" and "What other examples can I include?" Similarly, you can specifically explore for other causes or additional points of comparison or additional events in the chronology.

> Testing for Control—When you have identified the pattern that emerges, you can easily spot the variations on that pattern. Patterns are not rigid frames that tolerate no variations; rather, you can control your deviations. Knowing the dominant pattern of your work can direct you to questions like these: "If events are out of sequence, is the shift intentional?" "Does this flashback intensify a contrast? Or suggest a cause? Or is it a weak point that can be strengthened?"

"Do I want to compare two reasons, or should I create a catalogue of possible causes?"

PATTERNS OF IDEAS

Some patterns are relatively concrete and simple to follow; others involve more complex decisions about logical relationships. Some of the most common patterns are described here.

Spatial Order

When you arrange the details in spatial order, you move across a scene from left to right or top to bottom or near to far. Describing a scene for a reader virtually demands a framework that the reader can fill in, and spatial order provides one. When you explain that the window is directly opposite the door, or that the tree is to the right of the brook, or that the museum is on the east side of the park, or that France is part of the northern border of Spain, you are using spatial order.

Use your recognition of the spatial pattern to test your presentation for completeness. Scan the scene yourself, moving in the order you have created. Have you omitted important details? Is there something between France and Spain (like the Pyrenees) that should be mentioned? In short, is your pattern complete?

Note that recognizing spatial order is a liberating discovery, not a confining one. You are now free to devote your energies to selecting vivid details and colorful examples, trusting the pattern to assist the reader's perception of the scene. You are also free to vary the pattern. Moving from left to right, you might choose to leap to a prominent feature near the right edge, or to linger over the description of an unusual object in the center. Understanding your pattern gives you control. Notice how the writer of the example below has organized the details of the scene without rigidly following a simple pattern:

> Directly below my window a sidewalk stretches up to the parking lot behind the dormitory. To the right of the sidewalk a hill rises gradually to a broad plateau, bare except for an old barn made of rough-sawn lumber, its tin roof pitted with rust. To the left of the sidewalk, perhaps a half-mile up a gently sloping hill, is a large white frame farm house with a matching white barn. At the very top of the hill are dense woods.

Comment: The effectiveness of place description often depends on how well the writer handles direction. Expressions like "below," "to the right," and "at the very top" help the reader see each detail in exact relation to other details.

YOUR **TURN**

1. Without preimposing a pattern, list the contents of your room/ closet/desk/purse/bookpack. Look over your list to see if a pattern has emerged. Using your list for reference, describe the contents to another person. Does a pattern emerge as you describe? You can describe orally, or you can write a short description for a reader who then tries to sketch the scene you have depicted. How effective was your description?

2. How many different spatial patterns can you list? Think of patterns suited for small scenes as well as for landscapes or geographic settings.

3. Describing a small scene in front of you logically demands a spatial ordering. Can you think of other descriptions that might use a spatial pattern?

Chronological Order

When you tell a story, you probably order the events by time. You tell what happened first, then what followed, and so on. But chronological order can be a useful pattern in almost any form of writing. Whenever your writing explains or describes activities and events, the pattern most often used is time order. Consider: If you explain the steps in a process, logically you begin with the first step and move through time toward a conclusion. An overview of the Civil War would also be logically ordered by the sequence of important activities. On a smaller scale, an account of a terrifying moment in your life would be arranged in chronological order—first this happened, then that, then the next.

Recognizing that chronological order is the dominant pattern in your writing allows you to review your work for completeness. You can scan the chronology, alert for missing pieces—"Have I omitted any steps?" "Were there other important battles?" "Did anything else happen *before* the lights went out?"

You can also check to make sure that the events on your time line are essential to your discussion. A detailed time line on the Civil War would cover many volumes, so you must make choices. Are you going to include only major battles? Only Northern victories? Only events that involved Robert E. Lee? Recognizing the dominant pattern of the discussion will help you to control your content as well as your organization.

Once you have identified the pattern, checking it for consistency is not difficult. Ask yourself: Are these steps in the proper sequence? Did these events occur in this order?

Organization according to chronology is relatively simple, but you needn't feel locked in to a rigid pattern. When you are in control of the pattern, you can change it for effect. Flashback is often used in novels and short stories to reveal essential information or to develop characters, but you needn't consider it a technique only for fiction. For example, in a history paper you might move back through time to note an earlier event that had an influence on the current one: "His earlier encounter with the Union forces had also ended in disaster, most notably in the Tennessee skirmishes the year before. He was thus determined that the coming battle would end in victory."

Or, you might move the chronology abruptly forward: "Later, my best friend would discover that my brother had engineered the sound effects. At that moment, though, I could not have been more frightened." Understanding a pattern should not mean slavishly following it; instead, use your understanding to control your variations.

Here is an example of chronological ordering:

> The observation area was built shortly after the park was completed, with construction records dating to the early 1870s. For most of the late nineteenth century, the area was frequented by families during the day and young lovers after twilight.
>
> By 1908, the government had established a weather station at the site and the 24-hour staffing effectively ended use of the place for courting purposes. When the station was abandoned in the '50s, an evening crowd developed that made the place too risky for peaceful folk. Soon even daytime visitors were discouraged by rumors of drug dealings. During the '50s and '60s, the observation point was the bane of law enforcement agencies; a lookout could effectively sight any approach to the area and a series of raids ended in frustration.
>
> A preservation fever swept the city in the early '70s, though, and the old observation tower was targeted for "rescue." Fund-raising efforts were successsful and the site was re-opened to the general public in 1976. The city maintains the area now, with an extensive security system and a full calendar of activities for all ages. Nature walks originate at the center and children's "Discovery" classes are on-going. The tower is once again a place for all the people of the city to enjoy.

Comment: Chronological order is not only for stories. If your material stretches over an identifiable period of time, consider ordering it chronologically. Note the frequent references to dates here. It is essential to keep the audience "placed" in your time line. Other helpful phrases include "two weeks later," "one year earlier," "at the same time," and other such transitional expressions.

Y O U R [T U R N]

1. Choose a field such as history or science or art or political science. Make a list of topics that could be developed in chronological order. Any topic that involves events or activities can be used. Remember, too, that chronological order is the dominant pattern, but others might be possible.

2. Bring in news articles or features (nonfiction) that are arranged in chronological order. Identify any variations in the time order such as flashbacks or leaps to a later time.

3. Write a brief history of your educational journey. Where did you begin? Do you see the end of it?

   Note that you will need to make decisions about content—are you going to detail your adventures grade by grade? School by school? Memorable highlights? What variations on time order are there in your discussion?

Order of Importance

Once the pattern is identified, ordering your presentation according to time and space involves few decisions. If you present your ideas in order of importance, however, you will need to make more complex evaluations of your material.

In order of importance, details or arguments are presented in ascending order, from the least important to the most important. Your first evaluations, then, determine the relative importance of your ideas. That hierarchy is greatly influenced by a scale of values. To illustrate, consider a proposal to renovate an empty office complex into shelter for the homeless. Which questions are the most important? To the city, money might be the major obstacle. To the surrounding businesses, fears of vandalism or of atmosphere might be the major concern. The church group proposing such a plan might be most concerned about the needs of the people—will the facility be adequate, convenient, inviting?

Ordering your ideas by importance is a complex activity. It combines a careful study of the audience with thoughtful consideration of purpose. After all, whether you intend to convince your audience, to inform them or to involve them, the knowledge, the opinions and the values of your audience will influence the selection and organization of your material. (For a more thorough consideration of audience, review Chapter 14.)

When you order your ideas by importance, there are a number of common variations. You might begin with a small point, one that your audience can easily understand and accept. You then present ideas of increasing complexity or controversy, leading your audience toward the most difficult or controversial point. (Remember that levels of complexity and controversy are determined by your profile of the audience.) This arrangement subtly suggests that the writer's case is gaining strength as the presentation progresses. In addition, this order places the writer's best point in the final position, the position of greatest emphasis.

It is also possible to present your material in reverse order, with the most important point at the beginning. If your time is short or if the readers' attention span is brief, such an order may be your best choice. Most news articles begin with the most important information first, partially because the newspaper audience tends to scan the headlines and the opening paragraphs for news. This reverse order—the most important point first, the least important last—can also be used when your intention is ironic or humorous. If your treatment of each point is equally serious, the decreasing importance of your material may seem comic, so be sure you control the impact of such a variation.

Another variation from strict order of importance can be effective when the issue is controversial. You might begin not with the least important argument, but with the second most important. You then progress toward a strong conclusion with the most important point. This arrangement is designed to give the reader both a good first impression and a good final impression.

Look carefully at the relative importance of the reasons presented in the following paragraph:

> There are three good reasons for not allowing young children to watch MTV. First, the scenarios often depict bizarre dress and behavior, sometimes with a strongly sexual or violent message. In addition, whereas music by itself stimulates the child's own imagination, MTV provides ready-made images. Finally, and most important, by presenting a new dramatization every three or four minutes, MTV prevents the natural advancement of the child's attention span.

Comment: The first reason is a strong, even frightening allegation, designed to get the attention of the audience. The second is less dramatic, while the third is identified by the writer as "most important."

YOUR TURN

1. List all of the reasons you can to explain why you chose the college you are now attending. Now, arrange the list so that the most convincing reasons are at the end, with your audience being:

a. your parents or other relatives
b. a friend who didn't go to college
c. a friend who chose another school
d. a friend who is choosing for next year
Did your order change with your audience? Why?

2. Find a newspaper article that presents its points using an order of importance. Compare it with an article from a weekly news magazine like *Time* or *Newsweek.* Is the order similar? What changes do you see? Why do you think the order is different?

Ordering by Classification

Sometimes your information will organize into groups. You might recognize that some of your reasons for choosing a college are based on finances, some are based on consideration for your family, and some are based on your own personal feelings. Recognizing that categories are emerging can help you to identify more categories and expand them: "What other financial concerns exist?" "How else will this decision affect my family?"

Classification is also useful whenever you wish to show how you believe individual members of a group should, in your judgment, be grouped according to some organizing principle. You might, for example, classify people according to how chauvinistic they are, or foreign countries according to their relative political stability. Consider the categories in this example of classification:

Notice the consistency of structure here—the dashes and parenthetical comments used in each part of the classification. This aids the reader in understanding the writer's meaning.

> There are three kinds of book owners. The first has the standard sets and best-sellers—unread, untouched. (This deluded individual owns woodpulp and ink, not books.) The second has a great many books—a few of them read through, most of them dipped into, but all of them as clean and shiny as the day they were bought. (This person would probably like to make books his own, but is restrained by a false respect for their physical appearance.) The third has a few books or many—every one of them dog-eared and dilapidated, shaken and loosened by continual use, marked and scribbled in from front to back. (This man owns books.)
>
> (MORTIMER J. ADLER)

In this classification, bookowners are divided according to their attitude toward their books. That attitude is used as the organizing principle, and any further categories should be based on the same principle. A fourth category of "those who prefer science fiction" does not logically belong in this discussion.

Identifying the organizing principle for your categories can help you review your material to be sure all logical categories have been included, and it can help you test the categories to be sure that they are consistent-ly divided. Having a clear organizing principle should also make it easier for you to place further examples. If you find that one example could fit into more than one category, take a close look at the organizing principle. In the book owners passage above, a lover of science fiction might belong in any of the three categories, so the organizing principle has nothing to do with favorite readings.

Classification may be used only in one small section of your paper, or it may be the dominant pattern of the entire work. Where each of the things classified is to be dealt with in some detail, the classification may be bro-ken into several parts. Thus the author of the above passage might have chosen to write, "There are three kinds of book owners. The first . . . ," and then present a paragraph or more of specification, perhaps accompa-nied by some examples. Then he might have turned to the second type, writing, "The second kind of book owner has. . . ." And finally, one or more paragraphs later, he might have written, "The third kind. . . ."

Y O U R   T U R N

1. Look at the following categories. What seems to be the organizing principle of each?
   a. students with new designer wardrobes
   b. students with second-hand jeans and shirts
   c. students with home-made clothes

   a. political leaders elected to power
   b. political leaders who seized power
   c. political leaders born into power
   d. political leaders appointed by council

   a. Sixteenth-century English poets
   b. Seventeenth-century English poets
   c. Eighteenth-century English poets
   d. Nineteenth-century English poets

2. Can you add additional categories to the classifications above? Make sure that each category is based on the same organizing principle, and that it does not overlap with an existing category.

3. Make a list (push for at least ten entries) based on one of the fol-lowing leads:
   a. persons I have dated
   b. athletes I have observed
   c. persons in my classes (any level)
   d. books on my shelves
   e. recreational activities

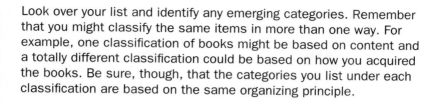

Look over your list and identify any emerging categories. Remember that you might classify the same items in more than one way. For example, one classification of books might be based on content and a totally different classification could be based on how you acquired the books. Be sure, though, that the categories you list under each classification are based on the same organizing principle.

Ordering by Comparison and Contrast

Comparison is useful when you wish to show the important similarities or differences (contrasts) between two or more members of the same class. When you have identified such a pattern in your writing, quickly check two points. First, does this comparison-contrast serve some useful purpose? Does it offer some useful information? It is relatively easy to put together a superficial comparison that describes likes and dislikes or even appearance and image. The test here is whether or not you are analyzing thoughtfully. If anyone else could have produced the same comparison, consider whether you have really explored the subject.

A second legitimate concern is, are the two topics under discussion from the same category? Obviously you wouldn't compare a car to a football, but a "contrast" of two people who have nothing significant in common can be just as useless. Even a good subject can take a wrong turn—while a comparison of the negotiating styles of the U.S. president and the Russian premier might be enlightening, who really cares about their respective tastes in food or movies or recreation?

Similarities are relatively easy to deal with. You can say, for example, "Both boys were talented athletes and superior students." Contrasts, however, are somewhat more difficult. You must choose between an opposing pattern of organization and an alternating pattern.

In an **opposing pattern,** one subject is presented in some detail before the discussion turns to the other. For example, the characteristics of one boy would be described in one or more paragraphs, then a transition would move the discussion to the second boy.

In an **alternating pattern,** each contrast is completed within a sentence or a pair of sentences: "Joe was mild-mannered and easy-going, whereas Bill was aggressive and hot-tempered." Paragraphs are typically divided by the major points being contrasted; that is, after a contrast of the boys' differing temperaments, a new paragraph opens to describe their contrasting plans for the future.

Here is an example of the opposing pattern of comparison:

The casual visitor to a classroom would have difficulty separating the mature students from the immature. At a glance, they may look very much alike in many respects. Either might be tall or short, slender or heavy-set, fair or dark, fashionably or shabbily dressed shy and reserved or bold and bubbly. The visitor would have to know them a little better to recognize the differences.

To begin with, mature students want to get as much from the course as they can, even if it is not one they are intensely interested in. And they expect the burden of the course to fall on them, so their thoughts and conversation tend to focus on what they can do for themselves to improve their performance and grades. From the moment a course begins, mature students listen attentively; when directions are given, they make certain they understand them, and they follow them exactly. . . .

Immature students, on the other hand, are not so much interested in what they can get from a course as what they can get away with in it. They are more concerned with a grade than with learning. In their minds the burden of the course falls on the professor, so they think and talk a lot about what's wrong with the course and how the professor should try to make it more interesting. When explanations or directions are given, they listen absent-mindedly at best, so they frequently do their work in a different way than they are supposed to. . . .

The alternating pattern, as we have noted, would complete each contrast within a sentence or pair of sentences. This pattern poses one problem for the writer—how to keep the sentence structure varied enough to avoid monotony. Here is how the first part of the preceding comparison might be expressed in the alternating pattern.

The casual visitor to a classroom would have difficulty separating the mature students from the immature. At a glance, they may look very much alike in many respects. Either might be tall or short, slender or heavy-set, fair or dark, fashionably or shabbily dressed, shy and reserved or bold and bubbly. The visitor would have to know them a little better to recognize the differences.

To begin with, mature students want to get as much from the course as they can, even if it is not one they are intensely interested in. Immature

> Notice that the sequence of points in each case is the same—that is, attitude toward learning is discussed first in each case, then attention in class, and so on.

students, on the other hand, are not so much interested in what they can get as what they can get away with. They are more concerned with grades than with learning. Mature students expect the burden of the course to fall on them, so their thoughts and conversation tend to focus on what they can do for themselves to improve their performance and grades. Immature students believe the burden of the course falls on the professor, so they think and talk a lot about what's wrong with the course and how the professor should try to make it more interesting.

When explanations are given, mature students listen attentively and make sure they understand; immature students listen absentmindedly at best. When directions are given, mature students follow them exactly, whereas immature students frequently ignore them. . . .

When you have identified a comparison—contrast pattern in your writing, use it to review your work efficiently. To test for completeness, look over your material to make sure that all important points of similarity and difference have been included. Note, too, that you have probably emphasized contrasts or comparisons. Such a focus is logical, but be sure that such emphasis is consistent with your controlling idea and your purpose. For example, if your main idea was that World War II was essentially different in cause and in result from World War I, make sure that you have not spent much time on similarities.

To make sure that you have not altered the pattern without purpose, look over your discussion and list the points covered in each paragraph. You can use that list to identify how points of contrast are grouped and to decide if those points are effectively organized. When you present those points of contrast, you will need to order them according to importance or chronology or even spatial pattern, so look carefully at your list.

YOUR TURN

1. A friend has narrowed his choice of new cars down to two and has asked for your expert advice. Select any two cars from the same class (no fair comparing the Cadillac Seville to the Subaru Justy) and advise your friend about their strengths and weaknesses.

2. Words like communism and socialism are often used interchangeably, but in truth there is a marked difference between the two. List some key differences between any two often-confused

concepts (wealthy/successful; loyalty/blind obedience; mother-
ing/smothering; and so forth.)

3. You want to recommend (or condemn) a movie (book, TV show,
recording) to your friends because it is similar to one they enjoyed
(or hated). List your reasons for the recommendation.

Cause-to-Effect (Effect-to-Cause) Order

Our earliest lessons taught us the pattern of cause-effect: frantic cries
bring help, hot stoves burn fingers, cute performances bring attention.
Our natural fascination with cause-effect relationships continues as we
observe the world around us. In times of tragedy or triumph, we seem
driven to ask, "Why?" Perhaps we think we can understand the causes of
a tragedy and thus avoid a recurrence; perhaps we hope to understand
the forces that resulted in success so that we can repeat. In trying to
understand why we are what we are and why we do what we do, we speculate endlessly about cause and effect. For all these reasons, then, it is
only natural that one of the most common patterns in our writing will be
cause-effect.

In cause-to-effect order, a phenomenon is described and then its effects
are identified. For example, an economics course examination question on
the effects of the Great Depression would be effectively answered by identifying the Great Depression (what it was and when it occurred) and then
examining the various effects it had on different segments of the population, on business and industry, on government and world affairs. If, however, the question called for a discussion of the causes of the Great
Depression, then effect-to-cause order would be used—that is, the Great
Depression would be identified and then the various causes that led to it
would be discussed.

The logical intent of your writing may be to identify the causes of some
phenomenon, or it may be to detail the effects of one. Be aware, too, that
such analysis generally produces complex results. Consequently, no one
single pattern can adequately express all cause-effect relationships. Any
of the following may appear in your work:

- The Single Cause or Single Effect: One of the rarest patterns in
causal analysis is the one that offers a single cause for a phenomenon
or identifies only one effect. If an issue is worthy of careful analysis,
it is probably too complex to resolve with a single point. But do not
overlook the power that such identification could carry. If one dramatic incident turned your life toward the theater (or medicine or
politics), do not be afraid to declare it. And, if there is one major disastrous result to stem from adopting a plan, don't weaken the discussion by fishing around for a few more.

- Multiple Causes: The more complex the phenomenon, the less likely a single cause will answer all questions. Particularly hard to define in a single stroke are questions of human motivation. Why does a person become insane? There might be several factors, including heredity, physical illness, unrelenting financial pressure, disastrous personal relationships—the list may be endless. If there is such a welter of contributing causes, do not oversimplify. Present the major possibilities, selecting an appropriate order—perhaps a chronological series of occurrences, perhaps a survey of the smallest-to-largest pressures, perhaps a geographic ordering of close-to-home catastrophes compounded by political upheavals in remote lands.

- The Domino Effect: Have you ever seen a row of dominos, carefully arranged so that knocking over the first one begins a chain reaction that ends when the last domino falls? Sometimes you will find a single, direct string of causes from Event A to Event Z. A familiar example goes like this:

  > For want of a nail, a shoe was lost;
  > For want of a shoe, a horse was lost;
  > For want of a horse, a rider was lost;
  > For want of a rider, a battle was lost;
  > For want of a victory, a kingdom fell—and all for lack of a nail.

  Certainly such a chain simplifies a complex problem, but there may be times when such simplification is justifiable. An explanation of a scientific phenomenon may be built on just such a chain reaction, for example. There may also be such a chain in your own life, perhaps beginning with some simple choice like choosing to skip one class— which led to X—which led to Y—and ended with some great triumph or catastrophe. Such chains are generally arranged in chronological order, but be aware that B must do more than follow A—it must be *caused* by A. (You probably eat breakfast after sunrise, but you wouldn't argue that it is the rising of the sun that causes you to eat.)

- "Straw That Broke the Camel's Back" Pattern: If you have identified a number of possible causes but are not satisfied that all are of equal importance, remember the story of the camel who bore incredible burdens until the proverbial last straw brought him to his knees. The mother whose control snaps when a child spills cereal probably is not facing the day's first aggravation. Similarly, you probably recognize in yourself that your temper may be hotter when you have already faced a series of frustrations. This pattern is not a chain of events, however, because the spilled cereal was not caused by the earlier disasters. Nor does a failing grade on a test have a direct relationship to a friend asking for a favor. And, in itself, the spilled cereal or the requested favor is probably not enough to cause a dramatic reaction. If you see such a pattern in your material, be sure to identify the background factors as well as the possibly trivial cause of a dramatic event.

Don't overlook the pattern that organizes the effects of some phenomenon. If you begin with the event and are not primarily concerned with its roots, you can identify the effect it has had (or could have) on its environment. You might, for example, analyze the impact of the Great Depression on our current economic policies, or demonstrate that the fall of Vicksburg was a crushing blow to the army of the Confederacy, or project that our abuse of natural resources will create an uninhabitable wasteland. A cause-effect pattern that moves from A to its impact might take several forms:

- Historical Analysis: When you look over your shoulder and identify a significant event, you will often focus on the changes which followed. Significant battles, power struggles and treaties are often discussed in such patterns. Natural disasters like floods and fires also have far-reaching impacts with room for further analysis. Don't forget that your personal history may also be analyzed in this pattern. Consider this controlling idea "My seventh grade math teacher taught me to really play with numbers. Ever since then, I have been obsessed with figures on a page, to the point that my entire life has changed." As the paper develops to show the audience the impact of that one class, the historical analysis will follow the same cause-to-effect pattern as a discussion of the effects of the Norman Conquest of 1066.

- Predictions: If you trace the cause-effect relationship between present circumstances and probable outcomes, you can make predictions. Such predictions need not be random guesses; your knowledge of human nature and historical precedent can give you a basis for reasonable speculation. Political pollsters demonstrate this pattern and candidates may change images and even platforms in response. Scientists who have warned us of the "Greenhouse Effect" for years have used this form of cause-effect pattern. If you wonder about your own future, you are basing your speculations on what you know about yourself, your interests, your abilities, and your resources. All such speculations, while they come with no guarantees, are inviting, interesting, and potentially useful.

- Proposal: When you propose a change of any kind, the audience will expect you to explain the benefits of your plan. When you demonstrate such factors as financial savings and increased efficiency, you are predicting the effects. Such speculation is expected even in informal proposals for a summer vacation. Note that "If we do go on the cruise, you will be able to play golf every morning and lay on the beach every afternoon" follows the same pattern as "The adoption of this evaluation system will provide a consistent record of performance and relieve staff anxiety."

Y O U R   T U R N

1. Examine one of your strongest opinions—on any subject—that has strengthened or changed recently. Can you identify anything that has influenced your opinion?

2. Political candidates often hire image consultants who advise them on ways to appeal to voters. From your observations, what factors influence the way people vote? You can be as specific as you like about the voters' age, region, education, etc.

3. Select a hotly contested battle from any historical period and explain why one side eventually emerged victorious.

   OR

   Select a crucial conflict from any historical period and explain how its outcome affected the events that followed.

4. Monday morning quarterbacks have become something of a cliché, but become one for a moment. Why did Team X win or lose any one game?

   OR

   Recommend a specific change for your favorite team—new player, new coach, new location, etc. What effects would such a change have?

THE PATTERNS IN COMBINATION

In longer works, it is unusual to find one pattern consistently maintained. The more common use of patterns is a combination of two or more; thus causes may be compared or contrasted to other causes, categories may be arranged in order of importance with some attention to the effects of such classification. The following brief student essay will illustrate.

Superwoman

When my youngest child was registered for kindergarten, my husband and I had a family conference. It had long been a dream of mine to return to school to work on a degree in music education, but with young children needing constant supervision, the dream seemed impossible. Someday, I had promised myself, someday . . . and now that someday was here.

"Someday" began to take definite form when I realized that all three children would be out of the house for at least eight hours a day. But I was not fool enough to think that all my responsibilities to the children would climb onto the schoolbus, so I discussed the possibilities with my partner, my helpmate, my husband.

We were both aware that my going back to school would have serious repercussions on family life as we had known it. One immediate effect would be to seriously strain an already tight budget. Tuition, books, transportation and other school expenses would have to be included in our financial plans. We decided, though, that the long term effect of my education would be increased earning potential, something that would affect our daily budget in a relatively short time and would also ease the burden on my husband. We decided that a school loan would be an investment rather than a burden.

It was not as easy to resolve questions about the work load at home. We considered hiring outside help to cover some of my responsibilities, but the cost of a cook, a maid, a chauffeur, a laundry service, and a nanny was obviously beyond our budget. I gamely agreed to carry on as usual, with some extra help on occasion, as I added classes and homework to my now-empty days. I cautioned my husband that things would not be the same—the high standards for housekeeping and nutritious meals we had maintained for the last twelve years were likely to suffer. But both of us were confident that our high hopes and willingness to compromise would see us through the adjustments.

So I began my new career as a college freshman (or is it freshperson these days?). I immediately discovered a world of confusion and frustration. Registration almost sent me home in tears as I stood in line after line (too often the wrong line) and found myself surrounded by strangely-dressed people who spoke a bizarre language. My penny-loafers and skirt and sweater set had looked so perfect at home; now I felt like I was lost in a time warp. I was scared to ask questions

The essay reviews the causal analysis done by the writer and here spouse.

The essay offers specific examples to show that the writer felt out of place.

since all the others seemed to know where they were going, but I discovered that following the crowd around lead me to events like an autograph session with the school mascot and cheerleaders. By the end of the day, I was totally exhausted, physically and emotionally drained of all signs of life.

When I staggered into my house a scant ten minutes ahead of the school bus, I was too numb to realize that my troubles were just beginning. The children descended on me with requests for snacks, with notes to be signed and money to be allotted for gym uniforms and school plays and football equipment. I didn't realize until days later that my eight-year-old daughter was trying out for the football team and that I had signed up (in my own handwriting) to be room mother for kindergarten *and* for second grade. I was too stubborn to admit, even to myself, that my schedule was becoming impossible. Even before my school career began, I would not have been able to head two such committees and drive back to school after practice every day while keeping up with the usual keyboard lessons, Brownie troop activities, dental check-ups and heart-worm treatments (did I mention that we have three dogs?).

But superwoman was just getting into gear. For the next three weeks, I moved through the house like a blur, defrosting with one hand and mopping with the other. I did my homework while the kids did theirs, and I cooked meals for a week ahead on Saturday afternoons. I did the housework after everyone else was in bed; I did the ironing after midnight. I told myself—and everyone who was even remotely interested—that I had everything under control.

But deep inside (all right, not so deep), I knew that I was kidding myself. My life was not just changed; it was destroyed. I looked at my husband one day and realized that we had not had a waking moment alone since the first day of classes, and I was overwhelmed with a surprising mix of emotion. I was guilty and angry and sad and resentful all at once. I remembered our life "b.c." ("before college") and was envious

The writer presents the results of her first day actions.

The transition here picks up the image used in the title and fast-forwards the actions of the essay.

Notice the lists of activities.

of the calmer self who had had it so easy. She had cleaned house in the daylight hours, and she had finished all the ironing before lunch. She had planned menus at leisure, delighting in looking for new recipes and interesting combinations of food. She had had time to read, to keep up with national news and to enjoy novels and magazines. She had gone to the library, to aerobics classes, to her children's school conferences—and to lunch with her husband. None of those things seemed possible for the new me and I began to wonder if my degree was really worth the sacrifices I was making.

The writer contrasts here present life with her former existence.

I would like to tell you that in that moment of revelation I changed my ways, re-ordered my priorities and organized my life and my family. But I can't in all honesty say any such thing. I did sit down with my husband and discuss my feelings, and we did become more realistic in my expectations. He does take charge of dinner three nights a week, and no one complains (much) about take-out pizzas and meals that have to be thawed or unwrapped. I have stepped down to assistant roommother and found a reliable carpool for my quarterback, and I make it to aerobics three times a week (well, almost every week).

The effects of her realization are described.

My schedule is still crazy, but I have resigned myself to a messier house and I have learned to read all notes from school before I sign. I am a wiser woman now, but I sometimes look back to those first few weeks and smile—with just a little more practice, I tell myself, superwoman might have learned to fly.

Notice the conclusion's careful reference to the title.

Notice that this essay does not follow one simple pattern; instead, there are sections that classify the problems the writer and her husband anticipated, sections that describe the effects of her decision, and sections that compare her life before and after she began college.

Most essays that present complex situations use some combination of patterns to reflect that complexity. Be aware that trying to reduce every discussion to a single neat pattern may not always work, nor is it expected to. The key word is control rather than consistency; in other words, it is not recommended that you randomly throw ideas on paper, but it is effective to change patterns when you see a need to do so.

YOUR TURN

1. Select an essay from a popular magazine and analyze the patterns used by the writer. Be prepared to present your analysis for class discussion.

2. Look for an essay that is dominated by one pattern. Are there any other patterns used in the essay? Is it easy to find a "pure" essay?

3. Select one of your own essays and identify combinations of patterns.

ORDERING ASSERTIONS AND EVIDENCE

A special sensitivity to your audience's opinions is needed when you write to convince. One of your goals is to hold the audience's attention without alienating or triggering feelings of alarm. With that aim in mind, look carefully at your persuasive writing to identify the most effective arrangement of ideas. In some cases, you will present your assertion first and then the evidence that supports it. In the following passage, the writer immediately calls on the audience to accept the assertion:

There are many reasons to support the new governor and his proposals, but one of the most compelling is the desperate state of our economy. With our current high rate of unemployment and our projected budget deficits, it is clear that present policies are ineffective. Those policies have not recognized our decreasing role in supplying energy to the world. The governor's proposals sound drastic, but given the support of the people, they can begin the economic turnaround this state so desperately needs.

An alternative is to present the evidence first and conclude the writing with the assertion drawn from it:

It is news to no one that our state is financially desperate. Our unemployment rate is at an all-time high and our state budget faces record deficits within the next year. Our current fiscal policies have been unresponsive to our decreasing role in supplying energy to the world and have been patently ineffective. Given our desperate situation, it is clear that drastic measures are called for. We have elected a new governor with new ideas, and if we continue to support him, he could be the one to turn this state around.

Assertion-to-evidence order is more common because it is clearer. But wherever the readers are likely to respond to the conclusion with disbelief or resistance, evidence-to-assertion order is preferable. In the two passages above, note that supporters of the new governor can rally around the immediate call for cooperation. But opponents might have an immediate negative reaction to such a bold demand. The second passage leads from an unpleasant but accepted description toward the call for support. It may not be a successful call, but it is more likely to be read with an open mind than is the first passage.

YOUR TURN

1. Go through the "Letters to the Editor" section in search of strong opinions. Do the writers begin with the opinion, or do they work toward it? What audience do you see as most responsive to the letter? When you recognize the pattern, try reversing it. Would the reverse order have been more effective?

2. Identify a proposal of your own that would meet with strong resistance from your audience (an inconvenient favor from a casual friend or a major concession from an instructor, for example). Briefly describe approaches that would keep the audience open-minded and receptive as long as possible.

INDUCTIVE AND DEDUCTIVE REASONING

When you examine evidence and look for connections, you are reasoning inductively. For example, if you decide to use the school transit system to get from your home off-campus to your morning class on Monday, you may find that the bus is at least twenty minutes behind schedule. If you discover on Wednesday and on Friday that the bus is behind schedule, you might ask other students to report on their experiences. If you are told that the morning bus has been late for the last three weeks, you should examine the evidence and reach a general conclusion: The bus system is not reliable transportation in the mornings. Reasoning inductively comes naturally to you—it reflects the pattern by which you evaluate both people and experiences in your daily life. Have you discovered that the corner grocery store is especially crowded between 4:00 P.M. and 6:00 P.M.? Or that the bank drive-through lines are longest on Friday afternoons? Or that your older brother cannot keep a secret? You probably reached those conclusions by observing numerous instances yourself and perhaps by hearing other people report on similar observations. Here is an example of inductive reasoning:

The present Student Government Association sees our student fees like a savings account set aside to pay for programming mistakes. Last fall, the country music festival weekend was poorly attended, so the SGA assessed student fees to pay off the debts. Then, the SGA scheduled a Christmas dance the week before final exams. Since ticket sales did not cover expenses, our student fees were used again. Our fees were also used to pay for the softball tournament scheduled during spring break and the benefit dinner attended by only twelve people. The SGA attitude seems to be that any scheduled activity should be guaranteed by student fees, even if it was poorly planned and poorly publicized.

Deductive reasoning often follows from inductive reasoning. When you made a generalization based on specific examples, you reasoned inductively. When you test that generalization against further incidents, you are reasoning deductively. For example, you have decided based on past experiences that your brother cannot be trusted with a secret. The generalization about his unreliable nature is applied when you plan a surprise party for your mother without telling him until the last minute. Here is an example of deductive reasoning:

Ellen Davison will be running for City Council in Murfreestown next month as a Democrat. Her opponents are an Independent candidate and a Republican. Democrats have traditionally done well in local elections in Murfreestown, particularly when the opposition is divided, so Davison should win the election.

The distinction between the two need not be explored at great length here. Just remember that when you look at specific incidents and form a general conclusion, you have reasoned inductively. When you apply that general principle to another incident, you have reasoned deductively.

Both patterns of reasoning can be effective in presenting evidence to your readers. Be wary, though, of errors common to such reasoning. When you look at specific evidence to reach a general conclusion, be sure that your evidence is sufficient to justify your conclusion. If you condemn the school transit system after one bad experience, or if the system is operating short two buses when you take your survey, you may reach a conclusion that is invalid. "Hasty generalization" similarly accounts for many wrong judgments of people we scarcely know. Another problem occurs when we reason without sufficient knowledge. For instance, the analysis of Ellen Davison's political future was based on the observation that Democrats have done well in local elections, but if women have traditionally been defeated at the polls, Davison may not be assured of a win (see Chapter 10 for more detail about logical fallacies).

Y O U R T U R N

1. Look over two or three issues of the same magazine and list the types of articles and advertisements that appear. Reach a conclusion about the nature of the audience of that magazine.
   Have you reasoned inductively or deductively to reach that conclusion?

2. Assume that you are part of an advertising agency that has widely varied accounts. Recommend to your immediate supervisor three or four accounts that he should try to advertise in the magazine you analyzed in #1. In forming your recommendation, have you reasoned inductively or deductively?

3. Look carefully at one person you feel that you know well (fictional characters are acceptable). First, describe the nature of the person. Then, analyze your response: How did you come to such conclusions? Then, consider how your judgment of this person affects your expectations. Do you ever expect certain behaviors in certain situations (for example, "Dr. Huxtable will find a solution to that problem," or, "My father will support new taxes for better health care")? Can you identify inductive and deductive patterns of reasoning?

PATTERNS OF RESPONSE TO OTHER MATERIAL

When you present your material, it is unlikely that your ideas exist in a vacuum. You might be arguing in direct opposition to someone else's written views, or you might be explaining why a prevailing opinion is inadequate or incorrect. Or, you might be reacting to a general statement, providing a specific illustration of the comment. Whether your intent is to involve the emotions of your readers or to inform or convince them, your awareness of other ideas can give shape to your reasoning and your writing. If you are aware that your ideas contradict or enrich other ideas, look over this brief list of patterns that can be formed when your ideas are a response to existing material.

Extension: When your ideas corroborate or exemplify an idea that is familiar to your readers, you can shape your discussion by referring to the prevailing opinion and noting your acceptance of it. A comparison of your ideas and your experiences to the generally accepted principles will organize your presentation.

> A recent poll by *The Daily Sentinel* showed that freshmen on this campus do not use the resources of Student Health Services. Further investigation into that problem might show that first-year students are not even aware of the health services. None of the students in my English class was aware that mental health counseling is available; only one of the students in my community health class knew about the immunizations available on campus; no one in my journalism class even knew where the services are located. Off-campus residents asked if any services were restricted to dormitory residents, and no one knew anything about student insurance if hospitalization were required. In sum, my own informal survey reveals that students don't use the Student Health Services because they know little or nothing about those services.

Refutation: If your ideas are in sharp contrast to existing views, you can develop part or all of your paper by detailing your disagreement. You can challenge the logic, the evidence, the sources and the accuracy of other material. A point-by-point contrast of those views will organize your material logically and effectively.

> There is a persistent stereotype that varsity college athletes are inferior students who got into college only because of their physical abilities. There may be some athletes to whom the stereotype applies, but I have seen many athletes whose dedication to studies was admirable. Today's athletes have to meet admissions requirements, just as other students do, and they are required to earn a minimum number of credits each year. Their "job" requires long and strenuous hours, and their performance is constantly evaluated and criticized. Most of them operate under enormous pressure to maintain grades and to maintain peak performances. I have taught on the college level for twelve years, and it has been my experience that varsity athletes (with some few exceptions) are organized, disciplined, and motivated students.

In response to John David's letter of June 5, I can only wonder where he got his information. David attacks the Women's Escort Program on two grounds, that there are not enough escorts available and that escorts are themselves dangerous. As one of the founders of the program, I would like to answer both charges. First, in spite of David's claims, there are sufficient escorts available. On an average night, twelve escorts are on duty and six more are on call. Not once in five semesters have all twelve escorts been called out at once. Every woman requesting service has been answered. Second, the charge that the escorts are themselves a danger to the women is absurd. Not only are escorts interviewed and screened, each one is a currently registered student and each one must log out each time he goes on assignment. In other words, there is a written record of which escort is to meet every woman who calls. Also, in the program's history, there has never been any kind of complaint lodged against any escort. In short, John David's remarks are uncalled for and unsubstantiated.

Note: refutations can be based on a written text, on an oral presentation, or on generally accepted, prevailing opinions. In each case, it is a good strategy to summarize the opposing views fairly and completely, and to challenge only those points which you have evidence against. Two major weaknesses of refutations occur when the writer has not understood the original material (be wary of ironic or sarcastic discussions like Jonathan Swift's "A Modest Proposal") and when the writer does not have evidence to back the challenge ("Well, I think that claim is just wrong"). Contrast the refutation above with this answer to the same letter:

John David's complaints about the Women's Escort Service are absurd. He obviously knows nothing about the service. The only women who have ever been turned down are those who wanted escorts off campus. And, the idea that escorts are dangerous is foolish. David's charges are totally ridiculous.

Y O U R   T U R N

1. Choose from the "prevailing attitudes" listed here and write a short response that either reinforces or refutes it:
   a. College is a valuable experience for everyone. Even students who do not graduate can benefit from a year or two in the college environment.

    b. Competitive athletics are not good for children. Parents and
      other adults put unhealthy pressure on children to win at all
      costs. Participants are emotionally scarred by the experience.
    c. Politics is a career for the wealthy and the corrupt. It takes a
      great deal of money to get elected, and it takes a willingness to
      compromise values to be successful.

SUMMARY

You recognize and use logical connections between ideas everyday; seeing
those connections as patterns will help you to shape your material as you
draft. Seeing the patterns in your ideas will give you greater control over
your presentation, and it will help you to identify omissions and errors in
thinking.

Additional Readings

*The three essays that follow are examples of logical patterns common to
our thinking and writing: cause/effect, comparison, and classification.*

*How many times have you asked yourself, "But what does that mean to
me? How will I be affected by it?" Letty Cottin Pogrebin's essay, "Feeling
Out 50," answers those questions as she muses on the ways that turning 50
is affecting her thinking.*

*Suzanne Britt illustrates another common approach to ordering life as she
compares two kinds of people. As she describes those who have "That Lean
and Hungry Look" and those who don't, she makes it clear where her sym-
pathies lie.*

*Faced with a variety of frauds to discuss, Jane Bryant Quinn organized
her information by classifying it. In "Phone Fraud's 'Top Ten' Can Rob
Unwary," Quinn groups the material into logical categories.*

Feeling Out 50
Letty Cottin Pogrebin

1   On June 9, I will be 50 years old. I cannot believe it. Fifty is somebody
else's age. It's an abstraction. It belongs to my parents' generation. I don't
act or dress like my mother did at this age. I can't identify with it. I can't
"relate" to it. I certainly don't feel 50. What does 50 feel like? What does
50 *mean*? I don't understand any of this. I just know I don't like it.

2   I've spent most of my life trying to look older. Until age 35, I was often
taken for 18. Well into my forties, bartenders were still asking for my I.D.
Being female, plus looking young, marked two counts against me in my

work life and made it twice as hard to be taken seriously. Now turning 50, I am finally, unequivocally an adult. So why can't I enjoy it? Don't worry, be happy, I tell myself. You're in pretty good shape, you love your work and family; what are you complaining about?

3　　I'm complaining because 50 depresses me. When Gloria Steinem turned 40 and people said she didn't look it, she gave the famous answer, "This is what 40 looks like." On her fiftieth birthday, as gorgeous and youthful as ever, she told interviewers. "I guess 50 is what 40 used to be." But it's not that simple for me. While feminist ideology continues to deconstruct the culture of aging, and many women claim to be growing older with pride and affirmation, I just haven't been able to pull if off. My brain agrees but I can't seem to internalize the message.

4　　"If you don't like aging," people say, "consider the alternative." Okay, I'm grateful for not being dead, but beyond that, positive bromides are cold comfort. Slogans like "She's not getting older, she's getting better" stick in my craw like sour grapes. Better at what? Better than whom? When does positive thinking become pitiful self-deception?

5　　The idea of my "aging gracefully" is a joke. I'm aging about as gracefully as a turnip, bitching every inch of the way. "Older but wiser" likewise falls on deaf ears (more on hearing loss later). I'm no wiser now than I was at 20, only more experienced.

6　　Experience tells me that regardless of her *real* age, every woman has a "true age," one year that feels most authentically, organically in tune with who she is. For no apparent reason, mine is 36. From the inside out, I will be perennially, immutably 36. But from the outside in, certain undeniable changes have come to my attention. For instance, I used to be treated like an enfant terrible. These days, when I do something clever, no one is surprised. I'm *supposed* to be competent by now; if not now, when? Another thing: more and more often I realize I'm the oldest person in the room. By all appearances I fit right in with the thirtysomethings, but then it's clear I'm the only one in the crowd who thinks Bon Jovi is a cheese. I've even started censoring myself; why make a witty reference to Baby Snooks if I have to spend five minutes explaining who she was. (A 1940s radio character played by Fanny Brice. *Please* don't ask me who's Fanny Brice.)

7　　The sneakiest, most subtle changes are the physical ones. I don't mean that I've turned gray or developed dowager's hump. I mean I've noticed that the number of times I've been whistled at on the street has dwindled to a paltry tweet or two per year. Although hardly a feminist measure of self-esteem, that plus the fact that no one tells me I look like my daughters' sister anymore are definite signs of age. Forget about vanity items like wrinkles or unsightly sags, I'm talking here about physical deterioration. Suddenly, I find I have to concentrate to hear voices that never gave me trouble before, and as Woody Allen put it, my eyes are getting so bad I have to wear glasses for sex.

8   I don't miss the street hassles and I can live without the compliments, but I'm not prepared to live in a 50-year-old's skin when I still have this 36-year-old kid inside. It's an out-of-body experience.

9   What bothers me most about turning 50 is its existential weight. Maybe 50 reminds me of dying because my mother died at 53. But even if I get another 30 years, how healthy will I be? Will it be enough time to see how everything turns out: do we finally triumph over the deficit, AIDS, and acid rain? Who will be America's second woman president, Yale's second black president, and the ultimate peacemaker in the Middle East? Can I live long enough to know my grandchildren's lovers? I'm too curious to be an existentialist.

10   Will 30 years be enough to realize my own dreams: learn Russian, write three novels (the "promising" first, the "disappointing" second, and a "fully realized" third), then win the Pulitzer? Or do I have to accept that nobody gets it *all* done?

11   "Not now" used to mean "I'll do it when I grow up," as if I had forever. If 50 means anything, it means that no matter how I look or how others treat me, I am grown up at last. Grown-ups know that time is running out and "not now" is another word for "maybe never." And maybe that's okay too. Ask me at 51.

That Lean and Hungry Look
Suzanne Britt

1   Caesar was right. Thin people need watching. I've been watching them for most of my adult life, and I don't like what I see. When these narrow fellows spring at me, I quiver to my toes. Thin people come in all personalities, most of them menacing. You've got your "together" thin person, your mechanical thin person, your condescending thin person, your tsk-tsk thin person, your efficiency-expert thin person. All of them are dangerous.

2   In the first place, thin people aren't fun. They don't know how to goof off, at least in the best, fat sense of the word. They've always got to be adoing. Give them a coffee break, and they'll fix the screen door and lick S&H green stamps. They say things like "there aren't enough hours in the day." Fat people never say that. Fat people think the day is too damn long already.

3   Thin people make me tired. They've got speedy little metabolisms that cause them to bustle briskly. They're forever rubbing their bony hands together and eying new problems to "tackle." I like to surround myself with sluggish, inert, easygoing fat people, the kind who believe that if you clean it up today, it'll just get dirty again tomorrow.

4   Some people say the business about the jolly fat person is a myth, that all of us chubbies are neurotic, sick, sad people. I disagree. Fat people may not be chortling all day long, but they're a hell of a lot *nicer* than the

wizened and shriveled. Thin people turn surly, mean and hard at a young age because they never learn the value of a hot-fudge sundae for easing tension. Thin people don't like gooey soft things because they themselves are neither gooey nor soft. They are crunchy and dull, like carrots. They go straight to the heart of the matter while fat people let things stay all blurry and hazy and vague, the way things actually are. Thin people want to face the truth. Fat people know there is no truth. One of my thin friends is always staring at complex, unsolvable problems and saying, "The key thing is. . . ." Fat people never say that. They know there isn't any such thing as the key thing about anything.

5   Thin people believe in logic. Fat people see all sides. The sides fat people see are rounded blobs, usually gray, always nebulous and truly not worth worrying about. But the thin person persists. "If you consume more calories than you burn," says one of my thin friends, "you will gain weight. It's that simple." Fat people always grin when they hear statements like that. They know better.

6   Fat people realize that life is illogical and unfair. They know very well that God is not in his heaven and all is not right with the world. If God was up there, fat people could have two doughnuts and a big orange drink anytime they wanted it.

7   Thin people have a long list of logical things they are always spouting off to me. They hold up one finger at a time as they reel off these things, so I won't lose track. They speak slowly as if to a young child. The list is long and full of holes. It contains tidbits like "get a grip on yourself," "cigarettes kill," "cholesterol clogs," "fit as a fiddle," "ducks in a row," "organize" and "sound fiscal management." Phrases like that.

8   They think these 2,000 point plans lead to happiness. Fat people know happiness is elusive at best and even if they could get the kind thin people talk about, they wouldn't want it. Wisely, fat people see that such programs are too dull, too hard, too off the mark. They are never better than a whole cheesecake.

9   Fat people know all about the mystery of life. They are the ones acquainted with the night, with luck, with fate, with playing it by ear. One thin person I know once suggested that we arrange all the parts of a jigsaw puzzle into groups according to size, shape and color. He figured this would cut the time needed to complete the puzzle by at least 50 per cent. I said I wouldn't do it. One, I like to muddle through. Two, what good would it do to finish early? Three, the jigsaw puzzle isn't the important thing. The important thing is the fun of four people (one thin person included) sitting around a card table working a jigsaw puzzle. My thin friend had no use for my list. Instead of joining us, he went outside and mulched the boxwoods. The three remaining fat people finished the puzzle and made chocolate, double-fudged brownies to celebrate.

10   The main problem with thin people is they oppress. Their good intentions bony torsos, tight ships, neat corners, cerebral machinations and

pat solutions look like dark clouds over the loose, comfortable, spread-out, soft world of the fat. Long after fat people have removed their coats and shoes and put their feet up on the coffee table, thin people are still sitting on the edge of the sofa, looking neat as a pin, discussing rutabagas. Fat people are heavily into fits of laughter, slapping their thighs and whooping it up, while thin people are still politely waiting for the punch line.

11   Thin people are downers. They like math and morality and reasoned evaluation of the limitations of human beings. They have their skinny little acts together. They expound, prognose, probe and prick.

12   Fat people are convivial. They will like you even if you're irregular and have acne. They will come up with a good reason why you never wrote the great American novel. They will cry in your beer with you. They will put your name in the pot. They will let you off the hook. Fat people will gab, giggle, guffaw, gallumph, gyrate and gossip. They are generous, giving and gallant. They are gluttonous and goodly and great. What you want when you're down is soft and jiggly, not muscled and stable. Fat people know this. Fat people have plenty of room. Fat people will take you in.

Phone Fraud's "Top Ten" Can Rob Unwary
Jane Bryant Quinn

Combine the dream of get-rich-quick with low long-distance telephone rates and what do you get? A plague of telemarketing scams, fleecing the innocents for millions of dollars every month.

Crooked salespeople can set up phone banks virtually overnight. They prey on the trusting, swipe their money, and vanish before the law can catch them.

Law-enforcement officials have stepped up their struggle against telescams. But they don't have the money or the manpower to chase them all down. Nor do they always have the weapons they need. When a boiler room is kicked out of Florida, it has only to cross into Georgia to be back in business again.

A bill in Congress would give more authority to the law. Sponsored by Rep. Thomas Luken, it would let state attorneys general bring telefraud cases into federal district courts. A federal judge can be crooked business from operating in any state. Therefore, they could be shut down everywhere all at once, Sara Cooper of the National Consumers League told my associate, Virginia Wilson.

The House passed this bill last year, but the Senate didn't. That's a pity. The cops need every bit of help they can get. Here are the top ten frauds to watch for, according to the Alliance Against Fraud in Telemarketing:

1. Prize offers. You get a postcard saying that you're eligible to win (or have already won) one of several rich prizes. It turns out that

you don't get that prize unless you spend $300 to $500 on vitamins, water purifiers, office supplies, or other items. You're then sent a cheap rabbit jacket that sheds, or a diamond chip almost too small to see.

2. Penny stocks. A stockbroker pitches an exciting new company, selling for under $3 a share and guaranteed to go up in price. The company may be sham, but you won't know it. The brokerage firm runs up the stock price artificially. When you try to take your "profits," the broker won't send them to you. Eventually, the stock falls to its natural value—a few cents a share. Your investment is wiped out.

3. Business fraud. Your small company gets a call from someone "conducting a survey" or "checking serial numbers" on office copiers. Armed with information about your copier, you get bills for toner or paper that was never delivered. Your bookkeeper innocently pays them. Sometimes the products are delivered, but they're poor in quality and you're overbilled.

4. Magazines. The caller claims to be doing a survey: Which magazines do you like best? You find yourself billed for subscriptions you didn't really want. Or you buy magazines that you think will cost only a few dollars a week. Instead, you're billed for five-year subscriptions, all to be paid in advance.

5. Credit repair. You respond to a newspaper ad that say, "Erase bad credit." When you respond you're falsely told that—on payment of $200 or more—bankruptcies and judgments can be removed from your credit history. They can't.

6. Gold, oil, coins, gems. Tangible investments are remarkably easy to sell by phone. Investors blindly send in money for oil or silver futures that the broker overprices or just doesn't buy; gold coins sold for three or five times their true market value; piles of dirt that supposedly contain gold. One dirtpile swindler made his phone calls from a Wyoming jail.

7. Travel. You get a postcard, announcing that you've won a free vacation, or huge discounts on your next vacation. To qualify, you have to join a travel club for $250, or purchase a "companion ticket" at an inflated price. There is no free trip. You've paid for it with the purchase.

8. Art. Cash in on the art-investment boom! Buy limited-edition lithographs at $1,000 or more! Except that the lithographs are vastly overpriced and will only fall in value.

9. Business ventures. These also start with a newspaper ad: "Big profits, no experience needed." Or "Make big bucks working part-time at home." You spend a lot of money on business supplies. But the venture is no good.

10. Cellular telephone lottery. You pay $2,000 to $5,000 for someone to enter you into the federal lottery for cellular telephone franchises. You're told you can't lose, because everyone who enters gets a valuable share. Not true.

It's easy to recognize a telecrook. He guarantees profits. He presses for an instant decision. He may not send you any written material. He asks for a credit-card number.

When you get these calls, get the name and phone number of the company. Then call your state's consumer office and turn the blighters in.

CHAPTER TEN

Evaluating Logic

When the patterns of ideas are identified and tested for completeness and control, the connections between the ideas can be tested. This section describes the most common logical weaknesses.

REVISING FOR LOGIC

Patterns emerge because you see ideas in a context, connected to other ideas in logical frameworks like cause-effect and classification. When you are satisfied that the frameworks of your writing are complete and consistent, you should begin a careful review of the logic that connects your ideas.

In Chapter 7 we discussed the importance of evaluating ideas during the planning stage of the writing process. More specifically, we noted the value of maintaining a questioning attitude, of separating fact from opinion and taste from judgment, and of being sensitive to the connections between ideas. In addition, we detailed the questions you should ask about your judgments and the reasoning that underlies them.

Now that you are working with a well-developed draft, it is time to evaluate again: to test the soundness of your ideas, to separate fact from opinion, to scrutinize the logical connections between your ideas. Just as certain patterns occur naturally and frequently in discussions, certain logical errors, or fallacies, seem to follow. When you are aware of these potential weaknesses, you can strengthen the logical structure of your paper.

When you identify a logical fallacy in your paper, remember that you are not necessarily expected to change your judgment. First, you are expected to look carefully at the reasoning behind the judgments. That examination may result in a change of assertion but it may also lead you to more precise word choice or more careful selection of examples. In short, don't dismiss the entire discussion when you find a weak point.

COMMON LOGICAL FALLACIES

The logical fallacies that follow are not the only ones that occur in thinking, but they are the most common ones. Learning to recognize each and eliminate it from your compositions will help you revise your writing to make it reasonable.

Either-Or Thinking

When you see a particular reality solely in terms of opposing extremes, you overlook other possible views. From such a perspective, it is tempting to demand that people choose between the two extremes and your clear if often unstated suggestion is that no third choice is possible. Here is an example of either-or thinking:

Original Passage

The Israelis and the Palestinians are engaged in a titanic power struggle. Which group will emerge victorious is uncertain, but one fact can hardly be doubted. Whomever triumphs, the other will be destroyed.

Analysis

Destruction of one or the other is certainly a possible outcome of the struggle. But it is not the only possibility. Perhaps both will be destroyed. Or perhaps the struggle will be one day transformed into cooperation and neither will be destroyed.

Revised Passage

The Israelis and the Palestinians are engaged in a titanic power stuggle. Perhaps one will emerge victorious over the other. It is impossible to say. But one thing is certain. The situation is extremely dangerous for all concerned.

Comment

This revision is not the only possible one. The controlling idea of the composition may suggest another one. Nevertheless, this revision eliminates the either-or error.

Whenever you encounter either-or thinking in your composition, ask "Why must it be one or the other? Why not both (or neither)?" and revise your composition accordingly.

Stereotyping

Stereotyping is ignoring someone's or something's individuality and focusing instead on some preconceived notion about the person or thing. (It is one of the central features of prejudice.) There are stereotypes about Jews and blacks and atheists and political parties and student athletes and working women and modern art and rock music—in short, about almost everything and everyone. Here is an example:

Original Passage

Giving federal subsidies to today's artists is a waste of money. Modern art is nothing more than a splash of paint on canvas. And today's performance art is vulgar and obscene.

Analysis

To say that all modern art is meaningless or vulgar is to make a sweeping generalization about an entire category. By *some* standards, *some* modern art might be so judged, but the statements here make no allowance for individual evaluation.

Revised Passage

Federal funding for the arts is a questionable practice. Can we justify any amount of money spent on a luxury like the arts when thousands of Americans go without the necessities of shelter and food?

Comment

Whether this is the most reasonable position to take remains debatable. Nevertheless, it is a more responsible position.

Whenever you find yourself expressing a prefabricated assessment of an entire class of people or things, ask "What evidence do I have that the assessment is fair or that it fits all the individual members of that class?" If you have no such evidence, regard the idea as a stereotype and revise it.

Attacking the Person

If an objection to an idea focuses on personal characteristics of its supporter, look carefully at the attack. In most cases, it is not a reasonable approach because an argument's validity does not depend on such factors as the marital history or religious background of its advocates. Be very sure that negative information on the individuals involved is relevant to the issue at hand before you consider it as part of your judgments. Here is an example of attacking the person:

Original Passage

Richard Nixon once suggested that the president of the United States and the leader of Russia should name special individuals to meet regularly and focus exclusively on the relationship between the two countries. I think the president should reject any idea that came from a man who disgraced the presidency and showed himself to be without honor.

Analysis

However disgraceful Richard Nixon's behavior may have been in office, and however lacking he may be in qualities the writer regards as admirable, it is unreasonable to reject his idea on that account. In fact, when it comes to matters such as the one in question, his ideas should be carefully considered because he is an expert in those matters.

Revised Passage

Richard Nixon has suggested that the president of the United States and the Russian leader should name special individuals to meet regularly and focus exclusively on the relationship between the two countries. I think the idea should be rejected, not because that relationship is unimportant, but because it is too important to be entrusted to anyone but the heads of state themselves.

Comment

Whatever value this argument may prove to have, it at least has the virtue of focusing on the issue rather than attacking the person.

Your personal reaction to the speaker should not be a factor in your evaluation of the ideas. Be aware that you can support an idea for the illogical reasons you might attack it. A likable, honorable man can present a weak idea, so your challenge is to keep the focus on relevant issues. Ask yourself "Is what I have said about the person sufficient to evaluate this idea?" If it is not, revise your composition accordingly.

Contradiction

Contradiction occurs when a person makes two assertions that are logically inconsistent with each other. This fallacy may indicate that you are still not clear about your assertion—you need to examine your reasoning to see if you are being honest with yourself about your reasons for the judgment. Here is an example of a contradiction:

Original Passage

Abortion is wrong because it is the taking of a human life. From the moment of conception, human life is present and must be treated with respect. The decision is more difficult if the mother's life is in danger, but the decision should always be made with full regard for the humanity of the baby. If the woman was a victim of rape, however, abortion should be one of her options.

Analysis

First the writer says that abortion is taking of human life and is never justified; then, later, she says that there is a situation in which it is justified. That is a contradiction. This writer needs to think some more about her stand against abortion. A pregnant rape victim is also carrying a human life. Allowing an abortion for a rape victim suggests that the real issue is whether or not a woman had some control over getting pregnant. That is very different from arguing that human life is sacred.

Revised Passage

> Abortion is wrong because it is the taking of a human life. From the moment of conception, human life is present and must be treated with respect. The decision is more difficult if the mother's life is in danger, but the decision should always be made with full regard for the humanity of the baby. Even in cases of rape, the fetus must be recognized as a human being.

Comment

Certainly the stand taken in the revised passage remains controversial, but it is logically consistent.

Emotionally charged issues like abortion are prone to logical fallacies because much of what we feel and believe is not based on logic. If you choose to write on such topics, be warned that your audience will give more attention to reasonable, consistent discussions than to emotional outbursts.

Whenever you encounter a contradiction in your composition, ask "Does the contradiction invalidate my entire argument or only a part of it? And if a part, which part?" Then revise accordingly.

Faulty Analogy

Analogy is a line of reasoning suggesting that things alike in one respect are also alike in other respects. Analogy is a common kind of reasoning and there is nothing wrong with it, as long as the similarities that are claimed are real. An analogy is faulty when the similarities are not real. Here is an example of faulty analogy:

Original Passage

> The government is reportedly requiring that stronger warnings be placed on cigarette packages and in cigarette advertisements. I think it's ridiculous to have even the present warnings. The practice makes no more sense than putting "Warning! Eating too much of

this product may make you a fat slob" on packages of spaghetti or "Warning! Careless use of this instrument may smash your fingers" on hammers.

Analysis

The analogies are vivid, but faulty. Eating spaghetti is good for people if done in moderation. Smoking cigarettes does no comparable good. Similarly, the hammer is a useful tool that can do harm if used carelessly. But cigarettes are not useful and have been shown to do harm no matter how carefully they are used.

Revised Passage

It has been proposed that drugs be legalized and that warning labels be placed on their packaging as a deterrent to drug use. But such a proposal would be no more effective than the warning labels currently placed on cigarette packages.

Comment

Warning labels on drugs and warning labels on cigarettes are comparable, so the conclusion that one will not be effective because the other has not been is reasonable.

Whenever you review any analogy in your compositions, ask "These two things may be similar in certain respects, but are there any significant respects in which they are dissimilar?" If there are, the analogy is probably faulty and should be changed or eliminated.

Faulty Causation

There is a certain amount of speculation whenever you link ideas in cause-effect patterns, so you must look very carefully at the logic of your causal analysis. One of the most common fallacies is based on the conclusion that one thing caused another merely because of their proximity in time or space. (You might have heard lawyers refer to circumstantial evidence.) For example, if a black cat crosses a man's path, and shortly thereafter he has an accident, he might conclude that the cat's crossing his path caused his misfortune.

This error occurs not only in everyday reasoning but in formal reasoning as well. For many years the prevailing medical opinion was that damp night air caused malaria, simply because the onset of the disease occurred after exposure to night air. It was many years before mosquitoes were identified as the primary carriers of the disease.

Evaluations of human motivation are also prone to error. Just as you should separate the person from the issue (see "Attacking the Person"), you should also be wary of confusing a motive with an argument. A presenter may in fact benefit from the proposal, but regardless of his motives, you should evaluate the ideas presented.

Original Passage

One of my professors told the class that he believes the way student evaluations are used on this campus doesn't provide effective evaluations of the quality of teaching. He said the questions themselves are OK, but the evaluation should be made at the end of the semester instead of during the tenth week. He sharply criticized the administration, saying that they are more concerned with suiting their schedules than with getting meaningful input from students.

How reasonable are these arguments? We needn't look far to find an answer. A secretary in the administrative affairs office revealed that the professor himself received a terrible rating on the student evaluations. His argument is clearly self-serving and therefore unreasonable.

Analysis

Perhaps what the secretary allegedly said about the professor's rating is true. And perhaps that is what prompted him to take a critical look at the evaluation procedure. That would be a normal enough reaction. But it is not reason enough to disregard his analysis. While you should look carefully at any source whose self-interest is involved, be sure to concentrate on the evidence that supports or challenges the conclusions.

Other weaknesses in the cause-effect pattern may occur if you oversimplify a complex issue and discuss only the most obvious causes. Ask yourself, "Have I considered all the possible causes here? Should I include other factors?"

Whenever you have said in your composition that one thing has caused another, ask "Is the proximity in time or space evidence of a true cause-and-effect relationship or merely a coincidence?"

Whenever you have approved or rejected a person's view because of his or her motivation, ask "What bearing does the person's motivation have on the quality of the idea?"

Irrational Appeal

When you appeal to the audience to accept your ideas, you try to connect your ideas to something that the audience already accepts. Be aware that there are some connections between ideas and audience that are easily abused. Each of the appeals described here can be appropriate and rational when properly handled, but each can be easily misused to substitute for a rational appeal. Watch for these four potentially flawed appeals: appeal to emotion, appeal to tradition or faith, appeal to moderation, and appeal to authority.

> An appeal to emotion is rational when it accompanies thought and analysis and irrational when it substitutes for them.

> An appeal to tradition or faith is rational when the particular practice or belief is regarded in light of present circumstances and irrational when it means "Let's continue to do (believe) as we have done merely because we have always done so."

> An appeal to moderation is rational when the moderate approach is offered as the best solution to the problem or issue and irrational when moderation is merely a convenient way to avoid offending someone or to evade the responsibility of judging.

> An appeal to authority is rational when it acknowledges the fallibility of people and their institutions and the possibility of differing interpretations; it is irrational when it disallows reasonable questions and challenges. (As used here, authority means not only eminent people but also eminent books and documents, such as the Bible and the U.S. Constitution, and eminent agencies, such as the Supreme Court.)

Here is an example of irrational appeal:

Original Passage

> Recent court decisions that permit teenagers to receive birth control prescriptions from clinics without their parents' knowledge should be vigorously opposed. Our society, indeed the larger European civilization in which it is rooted, has always regarded the family as the essential social unit. Moreover, the Judeo-Christian tradition has always accorded the family a pre-eminent place in the hierarchy of human institutious. All right-thinking people will recognize such court decisions as an assault on our heritage and lend their support to the movement to resist those decisions.

Analysis

There is nothing necessarily wrong with detailing the historical background to an issue or with making a spirited appeal on behalf of a point of view or principle. But here they are used as a substitute for analysis. The writer says, in effect, "We should oppose the decisions because our ancestors would have opposed them," and never offers a rational argument for opposing them.

Revised Passage

Recent court decisions that permit teenagers to receive birth control prescriptions from clinics without their parents' knowledge should be vigorously opposed for two reasons. The first reason is that those decisions undermine the role of parents in the upbringing of children at a time when that role has already been weakened by popular culture. The second and more important reason is that it is unfair for the law to hold parents responsible for their teenagers and yet treat the teenagers as independent in medical matters.

Comment

The view expressed in this passage may, of course, be debated. Nevertheless, its essential appeal is rational rather than irrational—that is, to logic rather than to a feeling of respect for our ancestors.

Hasty Conclusion

A hasty conclusion is one that is drawn without appropriate evidence. In other words, it is a conclusion chosen without sufficient reason from two or more possible conclusions. Hasty conclusions are especially tempting in situations where prior opinions compromise objectivity. Those opinions make a person wish for a particular conclusion to be so, and wishing leads to uncritical acceptance. Here is an example of a hasty conclusion:

Original Passage

We had a great deal in common. We both played in the band, we belonged to the same church, and we both preferred reading books to watching television. Yet despite all that, and despite the fact that I asked her out numerous times, she always refused me. Instead, she went out with Burton Ogilvy, the star athlete in our class. Looking back on that painful experience, I realize that she was a hypocrite, choosing Burton over me not because she cared for him but because he was the "big man" in the class.

Analysis

The hasty conclusion here is that the girl chose Burton because he was a "big man" rather than because she cared for him more than she cared for the author. Nothing the writer offers here demonstrates that this conclusion is the most reasonable interpretation of her behavior.

If the writer has more evidence than presented above, evidence that is adequate to support the conclusions, then he should present it. If he lacks such evidence, he should omit the conclusions from his composition. (To do so, he would only have to change the final sentence to read, "Looking back on that painful experience, I will always wonder whether she really cared for Burton more than for me or whether she went out with him because he was the 'big man' in the class.")

When checking your compositions for logic, note every conclusion and ask "What evidence do I have that this is the most reasonable conclusion?" If you lack sufficient evidence to support your choice, revise the conclusion or eliminate it.

Overgeneralization

A generalization is a judgment about a class of people or things made after observation of a number of members of that class. Over-generalization is generalization based upon insufficient observation. One of the most common errors in argument, overgeneralization may be explained by the natural human tendency to classify sensory data tidily and by the difficulty of determining how much data is necessary to support a generalization. Accordingly, writers often make careless assertions about whole groups of people and things. Here is one example:

Original Passage

I have been at this college a month now and am glad I chose it over other colleges I was considering. The professors here are very helpful and encouraging, and all the professional and service staff go out of their way to help students. The townspeople, however, are not very friendly at all. They seem to resent the college students for some reason. Perhaps some ongoing town-versus-gown conflict is responsible for their behavior, but whatever its cause, I find it disturbing.

Analysis

This writer speaks of the professors, the professional and service staff, and the townspeople in sweeping terms. In order to make such generalizations, he ought to have had many more contacts than a month's stay on a campus could possibly have provided. This passage, therefore, overgeneralizes.

To revise this passage, the writer should change the level of generalization to fit the amount of experience it is based on. That change may be accomplished by using such words as "some" and "certain." For example, the writer could refer to "some professors," and "certain townspeople." But a more substantive change is also desirable. The writer should provide one or more examples of helpfulness, friendliness, and encouragement, so that the passage not only tells but shows the readers her experiences. (Writers who recognize the effectiveness of demonstration and who take care to limit their topics effectively seldom have a problem with overgeneralization.)

Whenever you check your composition for logic and find generalizations, ask "Is the level of generalization here appropriate, given the amount of data I have?" Be particularly suspicious of generalizations for which you have provided little or no evidence.

Oversimplification

It is natural to want to simplify matters—simplification aids understanding and communication. For that reason, simplification is legitimate, as long as it does not distort the reality it describes. When it does, it becomes oversimplification. The most frequent kind of oversimplification in compositions is the presentation of only one side of a two-sided (or three- or four-sided) reality. Here is an example of such oversimplification:

Original Passage

There's been a great deal written recently about the question of paying varsity athletes on scholarship. The argument is that athletes make money for the university and should be compensated for their time. But athletes are already paid. Their tuition, books and room and board are paid by the university. Why should they receive more money?

Analysis

There is some truth in what this writer says. Varsity athletes on scholarship are compensated to some extent for their athletic efforts. But the question is more complex. Athletes work longer hours than average students at demanding, exhausting, physical activities. Their efforts often bring great financial reward to colleges. Their college life is dedicated to preparing for an athletic career, yet their future in professional athletics is bleak. In addition, athletes are not allowed to have part-time jobs, so their pockets are often empty, leaving them vulnerable to offers of illegal cash. To dismiss all question of financial compensation because tuition and room and board are covered is to oversimplify a complex question.

The above analysis should not be taken to mean that the writer is necessarily wrong in arguing against salaries for varsity athletes. That position may be the most reasonable one. The point is that the writer should make whatever case there is without oversimplifying—that is, without distorting the facts or being selective in presenting them. (In addition, the paper would be more persuasive if the writer did a little research and presented statistics in place of supposition.)

There is no easy formula for detecting oversimplification. Your best approach is to be suspicious of any neat description of a complex reality.

When you encounter one, ask "Is the truth really this neat and simple? Is there another side to it that is not represented here?" If there is, revise your composition to acknowledge it.

A BRIEF REVISION GUIDE

To help you apply the approaches discussed in this chapter when you revise your compositions for logic, here is a brief review of common errors:

- **Either-Or Thinking:** Seeing a particular reality only in terms of one extreme or the other.

  Example: Unless this evalaution system is implemented, the education system of the state is doomed to mediocrity forever.

  Ask "Why must it be one or the other? Are these really the only two possibilities?"

- **Stereotyping:** Ignoring reality in favor of a preconceived notion.

  Example: As a football player, Biff Jonson should not take calculus unless he has a private tutor.

  Ask "What evidence do I have that the assessment is fair or that it fits all the individual members of that class?"

- **Attacking the Person:** Disposing of an argument by attacking the person who holds it.

  Example: John Anders has a hot temper. How can we take his proposals about tax increases seriously?

  Ask "Is what I know about the person sufficient to assess the idea? Is it relevant to the question?"

- **Contradiction:** Making two assertions that are logically inconsistent with each other.

  Example: Our schools and our roads are in deplorable shape; I want a candidate who will make these improvements an absolute priority. But Alice Mills supports new taxes; I couldn't possibly vote for her.

  Ask first, "Have I contradicted myself?" then ask, "Why have I contradicted myself? Are my reasons logically consistent? Should I be more precise in my descriptions and definitions? Should I be more careful in allowing exceptions? Do I need to re-think this entire argument?"

- **Faulty Analogy:** Suggesting that things alike in one respect are also alike in other respects when, in fact, they are not.

  Example: Children learn to cheat early. The child who is told to foul another basketball player intentionally learns that breaking rules is acceptable, so that child grows up to cheat on income tax forms.

  Ask, "These two things may be similar in some ways, but are there any differences which are significant to my argument?"

- **Faulty Causation:** Concluding that one thing caused another merely because of their proximity in time or space. Or concluding that a person's motives are the total measure of his or her ideas. Or exploring only the most obvious cause of a phenomenon.

  Example: When Edward Tompson was governor of the state, we had prosperity. We should elect him again to restore our economy.

  Example: Jane Sentel will make money if her property is rezoned, so all of her reasons to support the project must be fraudulent.

  Example: If the driver had been sober, this accident could have been avoided.

  Ask "Is the proximity in time or space evidence of a true cause-and-effect relationship or merely a coincidence?" or "What bearing does the person's motivation have on the quality of the idea?" or "Have I considered all of the possible influences on this event?"

- **Irrational Appeal:** Appealing unreasonably to emotion, tradition or faith, moderation, or authority.

  Example: If Judge Elson is re-elected, neighborhoods will become war zones and your children will not be safe in their own beds.

  Ask whether the appeal is offered in a context of reasoning or as a substitute for reasoning.

- **Hasty Conclusion:** Selecting one conclusion out of two or more possible ones without good reason for doing so.

  Example: The epidemic was caused by an influx of foreigners who carried the measles germ.

  Ask "What evidence do I have that this is the most reasonable conclusion?"

- **Overgeneralization:** Making a judgment about a class of people or things based upon insufficient observation.

  Example: Both of the accidents in the parking lot involved freshmen rushing to school. Freshmen should not be allowed to have cars on campus.

  Ask "Is the level of generalization here appropriate given the amount of data I have?"

- **Oversimplification:** Presenting only one side of a two-sided (or three-or four-sided) reality.

  Example: Raising the drinking age to twenty-five will eliminate the problem of drinking and driving.

  Ask "Is the truth really this neat and simple? Is there another side to it that is not represented here?"

One final note: In revising your compositions for logic, it is possible to adopt two erroneous views. The first is that if you find one or more errors, the entire composition is ruined. The other, perhaps more common, view, is that if you find no errors, the argument your composition presents is the best one. To avoid both errors, keep these principles in mind:

- The presence of an error does not necessarily invalidate an argument. Although errors always weaken an argument, not all errors are equally serious. And even the best argument may contain numerous errors when presented by a careless thinker.

- The absence of error is no guarantee that an argument is the best possible one. It merely establishes the argument as reasonable and worthy of consideration.

Y O U R   T U R N

A. Each of the following passages contains at least one of the fallacies discussed in the chapter. Identify each error and revise each passage, if possible, to eliminate it. You may change the idea as much as you wish, even reversing it if that is appropriate. If you are unable to make a judgment, explain what knowledge you would need to do so. (Caution: Make sure your choices are based on reason and not just your preference for one idea over another.)

1. It is true that physical education instructors often claim that vigorous exercise can eliminate the tension caused by stress. However, physical education instructors have a reputation for being unintelligent, so their testimony is suspect.

2. The idea that smoking cigarettes affects athletic performance is a lot of nonsense. I've smoked since fifth grade and I've always been able to outrun any kid in the school. Even now in college, I can outrun my roommate, who's the fastest guy on the track team.

3. I know that nudists are the target of a lot of jokes, but joking aside, they're sick creatures. I have an uncle who is a member of a nudist colony and when he's visited my home (fully clothed, I might add), he's always ogled my sisters and talked about sex most of the time. Now I'm generally tolerant, but I confess I have little use for perverts. Nudists should be made to undergo psychiatric treatment.

4. Many people believe that astrology is not a science, but they are wrong. Anyone who will take the time to set aside preconceived notions and investigate the subject will come to the same conclusion. I used to be an unbeliever myself, and then I

took the time to read the characteristics of my astrological sign, Gemini, and I was amazed at what I discovered. Geminis are described as mercurial types, with a great range of emotional response. They are two-sided in their natures, capable of both very logical and very creative activity. (A great many artists and writers are Geminis.) That description fit me so perfectly that I knew astrology has to be scientific.

5. I never cease to be amazed at the opinions of some of my classmates. For example, we were discussing sex in my psychology class recently and one student was arguing in favor of virginity before marriage. At first I thought she was joking and would break down and laugh in a minute or two. Then I realized she was serious. She really believes that people should not engage in sex before marriage. The idea is absurd—it's like having a beautiful wardrobe and leaving it to rot in the closet or having a fine automobile and letting it stand until it rusts. Since that day I've wondered what made that girl accept such a foolish idea. I'm convinced it can only be prudishness and fear of sex.

6. Parents are continually pressuring teenagers to accept their values and conform to traditional ways of behaving. They never seem to realize that each generation has its own unique view of life and its own approach to living, and that by honoring the new perspective, their sons and daughters are showing their individuality. What was right twenty years ago is not necessarily right now. If only parents were less anxious over the differences, they would realize that they are only an expression of the age and that in time, perhaps in their grandchildren's day, a cycle will have been completed and the values and standards they believe in will once again return.

7. Television commercials are a gigantic insult to viewers' intelligence. They blare out their deceitful messages every ten or fifteen minutes all day and night, urging us to rush out and purchase some overpriced item that we don't need or that will fall far short of the advertising claim. And the biggest insult of all is that you and I pay for those commercials because their cost is passed on in the price of the product or service. No one has anything good to say about commercials, and yet they survive and even grow in absurdity. How they manage to do so is a mystery to me.

8. For years liberal politicians in this country have deceived us into believing that the welfare system is necessary to combat poverty. The truth is almost exactly the opposite—welfare creates poverty. It does so by making people dependent on government handouts and therefore content to be idle instead of working and being self-sufficient. The proof of this is evident in every community across the nation. Look at the people cashing

welfare checks or using food stamps to buy cigarettes and beer, able-bodied people who could hold a job but don't. And if that isn't proof enough for you, reflect on this fact—during the last ten years, when there were more people on welfare than ever, unemployment increased.

9. In the 1970s television movies explored subjects previously considered taboo for the media, subjects like homosexuality and rape. Some critics protested that those subjects were not fit for viewing. I disagreed because I opposed censorship in any form, believing that no subject should be closed to writers or filmmakers. But developments of recent years have caused me to change my mind. In 1983 NBC presented *Princess Daisy,* a film that explored the issue of brother-sister incest; then in 1984 ABC presented *Something about Amelia,* the subject of which was father-daughter incest. Since such films can only serve to stimulate interest in this reprehensible behavior, and thereby lead to an increase in crimes against children, I believe they should be banned from the air.

B. Analyze the topics below to identify areas likely to tempt the careless thinker into fallacy. For example, if the topic encourages generalizing from experience, you should note that overgeneralization is a temptation. Likewise, if there is any   mention of cause, consider the fallacies that commonly result from faulty causal analysis.

1. Is there a significant difference between male and female athletes in strength, speed, or agility? Explain and support your position and discuss its implications for coeducational sports.

2. What changes do you think are most needed in the fight against crime? In addressing this question, be sure to consider changes in all areas—police work, the courts, probation and parole, and the prison system.

3. In recent years, the world was plagued by a number of incidents in which terrorists or revolutionary groups seized innocent hostages and demanded ransoms or certain actions by governments. What should our government's policy be in dealing with such incidents?

4. The following sayings clash: "The squeaky wheel gets the grease," and "Silence is golden." Which do you believe is better to live by? Why? (Or: "He who hesitates is lost" contradicts "Look before you leap.")

5. The following sayings clash: "Clothes make the man" and "Don't judge a book by its cover." Which do you believe makes more sense? Why?

6. Many students complain that the workload in college is so heavy they cannot keep up with their assignments. Is this true at your college? How heavy is the workload at your college?

7. It is standard practice in medical research to perform experimental surgery on animals. Some people strongly protest this practice, known as vivisection. Do you approve of it?

8. Is it reasonable to require citizens to pass a literacy test before allowing them to vote?

9. Conformity is a very common trait in people. What, in your judgment, causes people to conform? (Be sure to explain the process by which conformity occur.)

Additional Reading

Elizabeth Hoisington, the first woman to be a general in the U.S. Army, offers numerous unsupported opinions and conclusions in the interview reprinted here. As you analyze the logic of the discussion, imagine the kind of audience Hoisington pictured for her words. Do you think she expected her audience to share her views? Did she anticipate close scrutiny of her ideas? In some ways, the material here resembles a rough draft. It contains the ideas the speaker believes, but needs critical examination to identify areas needing additional support or explanation.

As you read, look for signs of the logical fallacies discussed in this chapter. Are the analogies accurate? Are the appeals to emotion justified? Are the conclusions hasty, the solutions over-simplified? Are the writers presenting all of the possibilities, or are they tempting readers to see the issues in a limited way?

Should Women Fight in War?
Interview with Elizabeth Hoisington

Q General Hoisington, why do you oppose assignment of women to combat units in the armed forces?

A If we assign women to combat units, we must accept the inevitability of their going into battle.

I have no personal experience in a combat unit, but my male colleagues tell me—and I believe—"War is hell." Heads are blown off; arms and legs are maimed; suffering is so intolerable it affects men for years. It is bad enough that our men have to endure this. But do we want young women to suffer it, too?

I get fed up with all the studies about *whether* or *how many* women should be assigned combat units. Studies cannot duplicate the realism of a battle in a Vietnam jungle or the cold Korean hills, the trauma from killing, witnessing death and terrible wounds.

I do not doubt the Army has women who can complete a combat course, endure three days or three weeks under field conditions, and shoot as straight as any man. But in my whole lifetime, I have never known ten women whom I thought could endure three months under actual combat conditions in an Army unit.

I think we should continue to have a legal bar against women in combat units—not because they are women but because the average woman is simply not physically, mentally and emotionally qualified to perform well in a combat situation for extended periods. Nor should our country allow women to subject themselves to this experience that is so devastating and leaves such dreadful wounds—mentally and physically.

Q Do you think that putting women into combat units would reduce the effectiveness of our military forces?

A Yes, I do. Women cannot match men in aggressiveness, physical stamina, endurance and muscular strength in long-term situations. In a protracted engagement against an enemy, soldiers with these deficiencies would be weak links in our armor. We cannot build a winning Army if the soldiers in it have no confidence in the long-term mental and physical stamina of their comrades.

Also, we must consider the consequences of mixing men and women in units in a close situation like combat. Man-woman relationships become a problem, and they could cause costly distractions.

Q Would you favor allowing women to serve on combat ships and aircraft, while barring them from combat roles in the infantry or ground forces generally?

A No, I do not think it's practical to make this distinction. Congress decided this question of women serving in combat planes and ships when they passed Public Law 625, the Women's Armed Services Integration Act, in June 1948. They said women will not be assigned to ships or planes that are engaged in combat missions. Congress also made it clear that it expected the Army to keep women out of combat units through its regulations.

Nothing has changed since then to make Congress change its mind. The American people do not want their women in combat units. Only a small, nonrepresentative group of rather noisy women are advocating that women be assigned to combat units.

Congress should *not* change the law. The Army should not change its regulations. They must continue to look at the big picture.

We know some women have the brains, ability and courage to be fighter pilots and part of a missile or ship's crew. But how are the mothers, fathers, husbands and brothers of these women going to feel when the planes and ships go down, the women are killed or taken prisoner? Who then will want to admit it was their idea to change the policy and put women in combat units?

Q Do you oppose such a change because it would alter the traditional role and image of women in American society?

A The crux of this whole thing is that women alone can be mothers. There's no transferring that role.

I think we already have a pretty good plan for the division of responsibility between the sexes. It's pretty plain that God intended women to bear the children and men to be the protectors in our society.

Q Isn't it unfair to limit a woman's job opportunities—to say she cannot become a fighter pilot or a destroyer captain or a platoon leader—simply because of her sex?

A This question cannot be decided on the basis of job opportunities or equal rights. It has to be decided on the basis of whether or not this is the proper thing for women to be doing.

We shouldn't let people who have no knowledge of war or combat duty make the decision. We should listen to men with knowledge and experience in such matters. They alone know the endurance and stamina required. They alone know the reaction to hand-to-hand combat, to bodies and minds being blown apart or crippled forever. Ask any combat-experienced Army officer or NCO (noncommissioned officer) if he wants his daughter assigned to a combat unit.

Q What about the women themselves? Obviously, they might be exposed to physical danger. Do you fear it might be harmful to them in other ways as well?

A Yes, it would be harmful in many ways. If women knew or could even imagine the physical, mental and emotional demands of serving in combat, they would not blithely or bravely volunteer to serve in combat. The peripheral dangers of serving in combat units—being raped by stronger or temporarily crazed comrades; being taken prisoner of war and similarly abused, beaten and starved; being mentally and physically incapable of performing one's assigned duties in combat and being responsible for others being killed or wounded—these are some of the other harmful situations women would experience in combat. There is more to fear in combat than just being killed and not returning to your loved ones at home.

Q Will it be possible for the armed services to continue with the all-volunteer force without using women in combat or, at least, semicombat units?

A Yes, I think so. Just recently, the Secretary of the Army stated that the all-volunteer Army is a success. If this is true, there should be no need to change the policy on using women in combat units.

Presenting Information

In any writing, you present information to your audience, using a variety of techniques. Identifying and practicing those techniques will improve your writing and your confidence.

PRESENTING INFORMATION

Presenting information is at the heart of most writing. You may use that information to recreate vivid scenes, characters or incidents, or you may use that information to explain or to argue a specific idea. Whatever your purpose, though, information should be presented by the most logical and effective methods.

Defining Literally

Regardless of your thesis or purpose, literal definition is used if a term might be new to your readers or if a familiar word is used in an unfamiliar way. Some definitions are brief enough to be worked smoothly into the sentence: "Some of the manuscripts discovered in the old bookstore were palimpsets, **parchments with earlier texts poorly erased and still visible beneath the most recent one.**" A more complex definition might extend through a paragraph, or even an entire composition. Extensive definitions often combine several writing patterns and techniques—description, comparisons, numerous examples, or detailed explanations.

To define literally:

1. Identify the general class to which the term belongs.
2. Identify the special features that differentiate it from the rest of the class.

Thus soccer might be defined as a team sport (general class) in which the object is to kick a round leather ball into the opposing team's goal while preventing them from kicking the ball into your goal (special features). Consult the dictionary to make sure of your definition, but give your readers a more vivid or insightful definition.

Software theft, popularly called "piracy," is the unauthorized duplication of software. It is a federal offense.

The copyright law is clear. Title 17 states that it is illegal to make or distribute copies of copyrighted material without authorization (Section 10G). The owner of a piece of software can make a copy only for archival backup purposes.

There is no distinction between duplicating software for sale or for free distribution. If a copy is made for any purpose other than to backup the user's original, the copier is guilty of "software piracy." Penalties include fines of up to $50,000 and jail terms of up to five years.

Y O U R   T U R N

Write a one-paragraph literal definition of one of the following:

education   democracy   male chauvinism   patriotism
prejudice

Check the dictionary definition, but offer a thoughtful definition that connects the abstract term to real life.

Listing

Sometimes the most efficient presentation of information is a list. Listing can be as simple as single words or phrases, or as complete as grammatical sentences organized into paragraphs. (Using parallel structure to list similar items is also effective; review the appropriate sections in Chapter 17.) Listing is particularly useful to present numerous facts that require little or no explanation, or to provide an overview of such things as resources or organizations. For example, the simplest way to show the research grants awarded to an institution during the past year is to list the grants; no elaborate descriptions or explanations are needed. Similarly, listing could review the officials who served in a given position during the last ten years or to identify community-sponsored day care centers.

Multiple, lengthy lists can overwhelm your readers. However, if your intention is to create that effect (suppose that you are trying to impress someone with the many responsibilities you carry), a massive list may be your best tactic. For the most part, though, listing is used only for brief sections of your writing.

Sample List
Golfers carry a variety of clubs because a typical round of golf will call for a variety of shots. A typical bag contains woods, irons, and utility

clubs. The woods, which are often made of metal, are used to give distance and height to shots. The average golfer carries a 1-wood (or driver), a 3-wood and a 5-wood. The higher the number, the greater the height and the shorter the distance the ball will travel. Irons are similarly numbered from the 1-iron to the 9-iron, but the average golfer probably does not carry a 1-iron or even a 2-iron. Irons with lower numbers (1, 2, or 3) produce long, low shots while irons with higher numbers (7, 8, or 9) produce high, shorter shots. Utility clubs include special chipping clubs and wedges like the pitching wedge, the sand wedge, and the extra-loft wedge. Finally, for the shot that rolls the ball into the hole, all golfers carry some variety of putter.

Y O U R   T U R N

As you organize the factual data on these topics into paragraphs, list the details where appropriate.

1. Consult the current issue of an almanac for information about a country you know little about (population, geography, form of government, economy, and so on). Arrange the information in complete sentences and in paragraph form.

2. Consult the current issue of an almanac for statistical information on one of the following topics: crime, traffic fatalities, disease (maybe a particular disease), marriage and divorce. Arrange the information in complete sentences and in paragraph form.

3. Choose an activity that requires special supplies or equipment and present the information to your readers in paragraph form.

Tracing

Tracing can be used to show the history (that is, the growth and development) of something—for example, the history of the essay, of the American secondary school, or of the idea of free enterprise—if space limitations do not permit detailed treatment. Tracing often makes make great leaps in time and space in moving from one important point to another, but the movement is almost always chronological, thus avoiding any distracting jumps back and forth in time.

If you wish to follow a character or even an entire family through several decades of activity, your method may be closer to narrating than to tracing. Ask yourself, "Am I telling a story that spans a period of time, a story that has a beginning and an ending? Or am I really tracing a trend or an idea or a symbol as it evolves?" (For more discussion of narrating, see Chapter 13.) Remember that tracing is more than a chronological list; it demonstrates the evolution, the progress, or the decline of the subject.

Tracing can be used to inform the audience of the history of a non-controversial topic. On Mickey Mouse's fiftieth birthday, for example, a number of articles traced the evolution of his appearance and personality from the early "Steamboat Willie" character to the modern Mickey. A persuasive paper might trace the evolution of American foreign policy to argue that such policies are becoming dangerously naive. For the most part, though, tracing will help you present large amounts of background information very efficiently. Notice the huge span of time covered in the following passage:

> The principle of poker is very ancient. One of its precursor games, *primero,* appears in literature at least as early as 1526. Around 1700 the betting and bluffing aspect produced the games of brag in England and *pochen* (to bluff) in Germany. The French borrowed from the Germans and created *poche,* which they brought to New Orleans in 1803. During the next several years English-speaking settlers in the Louisiana Territory anglicized *poche* to poker, altered the rules slightly, and created the essential game played today.

This passage includes jumps of two centuries and one century and rapid shifts from England to Germany to France to the United States. Yet it is not at all confusing. As its form makes clear, it is telescoping a long and complex development.

Y O U R   T U R N

Practice tracing with these subjects. (If you use the encyclopedia or some other source, take care not to borrow the phrasing or structure of your source. A good way to avoid heavy influence from your source is to jot down pertinent information in fragmentary form while you are reading, then close the encyclopedia before beginning to write.)

1. Trace the history of bathing.

2. Trace the history of a particular sport.

3. Trace the development of dogs or of a particular breed of dog.

4. Trace your formal education to date.

Presenting a Process

When you need to explain how something works or happens, how it is done or how to do it, you present the information by explaining a process. For example, you can present a process to detail a scientific phenomenon such as the way mountains are formed, or a cultural or religious ritual, or the changing of an automobile tire. As a rule, the steps in the process should be presented in exact chronological order, and no step should be omitted. However, if your purpose is more to interest the readers than to instruct them, this order can be varied.

While process explanations are often written directly to the readers, note that the explanation below is written in third person:

This passage details how something is done rather than how to do it. If the purpose had been to explain how to define a word one's self (as a dictionary editor would), the author would have used the imperative mood—"First do this, then do that."

> To define a word . . . the dictionary editor places before him the stack of cards illustrating that word; each of the cards represents an actual use of the word by a writer of some literary or historical importance. He reads the cards carefully, discards some, rereads the rest, and divides up the stack according to what he thinks are the several senses of the word. Finally, he writes his definitions, following the hard-and-fast rule that each definition must be based on what the quotations in front of him reveal about the meaning of the word. The editor cannot be influenced by what he thinks a given word ought to mean. He must work according to the cards or not at all.

YOUR TURN

Present the processes below, making sure that all steps are included in the proper order. Be sure you have told the reader what the results of the process should be.

1. Using third person, describe the process of buying a car.
2. Using second person, explain to an average student how to prepare for a particular exam, such as history or biology.
3. Using first person, describe the process used in your home to get everyone out of the door in the morning.
4. Experiment by re-writing any of the above passages, changing the person from third to second or first. Discuss the changes in pronoun usage. How does the change affect the tone of the passage?

Using Analogies

An analogy is a reference to a point of similarity between two things of different classes. For example, the human heart can be compared to a mechanical pump. This technique is used whenever you want the reader to see something clearly and the complexity of the matter makes it difficult for you to offer a simple explanation. An analogy can be very vivid and can be useful in situations where exactness is not necessary. But because analogies ignore the differences between things, they should not be used carelessly or as a substitute for more exact techniques. (For potential problems with this technique, see "Faulty Analogy," Chapter 10.)

Additional Reading

Undisciplined Kids Much Like Gamblers
John Rosemond

John Rosemond, an authority on interactions between parents and children, used analogy to explain to a parent why children continue to request privileges or favors, regardless of the firmness or the frequency of the refusals. As you read his explanation, test the analogy: Do you see enough similarity between the two patterns of behavior to accept his comparison?

1   It occurs to me that compulsive gamblers and undisciplined children are very much alike. In spite of evidence to the contrary, they believe they can win.

2   George the gambler bets on everything from horses to numbers, but his favorite vice is the "one-armed bandit," or slot machine, as it is known by the uninitiated. Once a year, at the very least, George makes a pilgrimage to Las Vegas from his home in Atlantic City. There, he cashes in big bills for rolls of quarters and joins fellow fools in the slot machine arcade.

3   In goes a quarter, and then another, and another and another and another and finally, after pumping $10 into the slot, George hits double cherries and wins $2 back. Ten more dollars later, he hits three lemons and wins $5.

4   "I'm on a roll now," thinks George, his skin tingling with excitement. "Hey, hey, jackpot, here I come!"

5   Thirty more quarters and fifteen come back on wild cards. Ten more go in, five come out. Fifty more in, forty out. George is flushed with an adrenalin high, convinced that this is his lucky night. Or is it morning?

6   This goes on (and on) over the next 12 hours. To look at George, anyone would think he was a winner. He's got this wild look in his eyes, and there's a manic excitement to the way he stuffs quarters into the slot and pulls the lever. Yeah, boy, that George sure is on a roll.

7   George feels like a winner, too. That is, until he runs out of money. And there he sits, staring unbelievingly at the machine, trying to figure out what happened. Wasn't he winning? He thought he was. He felt like he was. He even acted like he was. But he wasn't, as evidenced by one empty money clip. The reason George thought, felt and acted like a winner was because the machine paid him off just enough to make him forget his losses.

8   Now, for comparison's sake, let's visit the life of another gambler. This one is 7 years old and her name is Heloise. Heloise gambles that her parents won't make her do what they want her to do. They tell Heloise to do something and she ignores them or does only half or says "In a minute," but the minute never comes.

9   Heloise's parents have a way of dealing with her disobedience. Everytime she fails to do what they tell her to do the first time they tell her to do it, she loses a privilege for the rest of the day and must sit in the downstairs bathroom for 10 minutes. Almost every time, that is. And that's the rub, as we shall see.

10   As we join Heloise and her parents, it's a sunny Saturday morning in Suburbanville, USA. After a cheery breakfast, Heloise's parents tell her to be sure and make her bed and straighten her room before she goes outside to play. Ten minutes later, Heloise joins a group of friends who are riding bikes up and down the street. One hour later, Heloise's parents discover an unmade bed and an unstraight room. They call Heloise in, banish her to the bathroom for 10 and take away her bike for the rest of the day.

11   That afternoon, Heloise ignores her mother's call and again she sits and again a privilege is taken away. Later, for only putting away half of her clean clothes, she loses another 10 minutes and another privilege. Still later, she engaged her mother in an argument over giving the puppy a bath. Ah, but this time her mother says, "I'm tired of arguing with you over every little thing, Heloise, so just go back outside and I'll bathe him myself."

12   And so it goes, day in and day out at Heloise's household. She disobeys an average of four times, her parents punish her an average of three times. Is she winning? Obviously not. Does she stop misbehaving? Obviously not.

13   Why not? For the same reason George doesn't stop priming the slot machine with quarters. Heloise's parents cave in to her disobedience just often enough to keep her from realizing that disobedience is a losing game.

14   The reason that consistency is so important in matters of discipline is that while gamblers eventually run out of money, children never run out of energy.

At times you may be tempted to use two or more analogies in the same passage. This temptation is best resisted. It is extremely difficult to multiply analogies without having them clash. For example, combining the analogy of the gambler in the previous passage with, let's say, the analogy of a person taking a chance on a blind date would obscure rather than illuminate the point being made.

Few devices can make your point so vividly as an apt analogy. Thus you should encourage your creative voice to explore similarities between your subject and other persons or things. If you are describing a man, for example, rather than comparing him to other men, explore unusual directions. If your subject is in motion, explore possible comparisons to other kinds of motion—animal grace or wind-tossed flutters. If you are examining the impact of some event, compare it to influential events from other fields; thus a political regime is compared to a plague or a scientific discovery becomes a tempest. Not all of the images you imagine will be effective in your paper, but that is a critical evaluation to be made *after* the creative voice has supplied them.

Y O U R **T U R N**

Complete the following. Make the analogy effective by saying not only what the thing is like, but also how the two are similar:

a. The taxi driver made his way through traffic like _____.

b. Listening to Professor X lecture is like _____.

c. The sun shining on the lake looked like _____.

d. Waiting in line for dinner in the college cafeteria is like

_____ .

Citing Examples

The technique of citing examples is basic to clear, lively writing. It is the technique through which you make your general statements specific and therefore meaningful to your readers. Consider the following passage: "In addition to having everyday benign uses, cyanide has its sinister uses. History has recorded many cases where it has been the instrument of murder."

By the time a reader has finished reading this, she is not only ready to be offered one or more examples—she expects them. And if you do not offer them, she will be disappointed. When readers can reasonably ask, "Do you have an example of this?" unless you have a compelling reason to move to another point, you should provide one or more examples. Examples need not be extensive, but they should be adequate in number and detail to satisfy the readers' expectation. The essay that follows illustrates the technique of citing examples:

Additional Reading

Grin and Sell It
Molly Ivins

The house had been for sale in a depressed market for some time when the Serious Nibble appeared. Upon the occasion of the Serious Nibble's third visit, the house was immaculate, the kids were at Grandma's, and the owners ready to answer any questions. All went well until the end of the tour when the real estate lady was touting the charms of the backyard, which include a small toolshed. "So handy for your garden tools," enthused the real estate lady, "and a wonderful place to store the children's bikes—look at all this space!" and with that she flung open the door and a little mouse ran out. Anyone can have a little mouse lurking in the toolshed, that's nothing: unfortunately the little mouse was followed by a large rat, which jumped out of the toolshed veritably in front of the Serious Nibble's nose. Before the Nibble could even shriek, the real estate lady said, "And think what a wonderful time your cat will have here!"

Real estate ladies, a plucky and hardy bunch, seldom get the credit they deserve in this world. Never been an epic poem, major novel, or country-western song written about 'em. You don't find the romance, the adventure, the hair-raising thrills of selling real estate celebrated in song or story. Which is a damn shame because we're talking some real heroes here; we're talking wit, grit, and spunk.

The National Association of Realtors estimates there are one million active licensed agents in the country; all are out there selling the most incredible dogs every day. Real estate already has the two-tier system proposed by Felice Schwartz—the "mommy track" is residential property—men sell commercial real estate. The division is not absolute—men who sell homes and women who sell factory sites are not uncommon—but the association says 65 percent of the salespeople are women but only 33 percent of the brokers (owners and operators of offices) are female. Why real estate ladies are still ladies instead of women is one of those mysterious questions—the way the girls in the Miss America Pageant are always girls.

In Dallas, a real estate lady was called upon to show a house that featured a remarkably ugly atrium with a cement floor covered with plastic potted plants, all dusty and covered with cobwebs. All the rooms looked into the atrium, so there was no getting away from it, but the real estate lady continued to burble on cheerfully. One of the advertised attractions of the house was that the dining room table would be sold with the house: that turned out to be because the table was made out of cement and was cemented to the dining room floor. Somewhat discouraged, the real estate lady and her client went out to inspect the backyard, which had, as advertised, a swimming pool, even though it looked like the advanced stage of a nasty biological experiment. While they were standing there surveying this disheartening prospect, the back door blew shut behind them. No way to get back into the house, and the pool was surrounded by eight-foot-tall cement fence. The saleswoman was in her complete Dallas real estate lady costume—heels, hose, Ultrasuede, jewelry, and makeup—but she gamely climbed up that fence anyway and jumped off on the far side, still in her high heels, and broke her ankle. Excruciating pain. The real estate lady had just started to crawl toward the street in search of help when the lawn's automatic sprinkler system came on. And they all have days like that.

Real estate ladies are necessarily masters of the old Roseanne Rosannadanna routine: "Oh, never mind." One thought it a trifle odd to find four pairs of shoes by the front door, but led her client in anyway, which is how they came to discover two couples, quite naked, coupling on the dining room floor. "We'll just come back later," said the real estate lady with a gallant smile. Another real estate lady was talking with a client when he mentioned that he had, many years before, killed his parents. "Well," she said gamely, "these things do happen."

Real estate ladies regularly deal with the oddest excrescences of taste—a million-dollar home that features clear plastic toilet seats stuffed with fake dollar bills: a house crammed with ghastly rococo statues of masturbating nymphs and ladies with clocks in their navels combined with a mock-Italian grape arbor achieved by twining plastic grape leaves around the rafters and sprinkling the whole with tiny Christmas lights.

Bettye Harrison of Chattanooga once sold a local property that belonged to the Sudan interior missions, headquartered in New York. As it happened, the only man with authority to sign the deed was in Africa, so she dispatched runners after him: they went 30 miles into the jungle on foot and came back with a signed deed in two weeks. She says the U.S. Mail has been slower.

Customers do occasionally have the last word. One agent told a client who was enthusiastic about a house, "Now, you do realize, Mrs. Smith, that this is a mixed neighborhood." Mrs. Smith gasped in dismay, "Republicans?"

Y O U R　T U R N

1. Give examples of pranks or practical jokes you've played or seen played.
2. Give examples of embarrassing moments you've experienced.
3. Give examples of politicians that inspire you.
4. Give examples of television commercials that offend or aggravate you.
5. Give examples of short stories about women.
6. Give examples of education curriculum specialties.

Combining Techniques

As you can see in the following passages, discussions of any length or complexity will use techniques in combination:

This passage is a blend of many techniques. The first paragraph cites three *brief examples*. The third example is given slightly expanded treatment, including (in the next-to-last sentence) an *explanation*.

Paper towels were reportedly first developed when a manufacturer got a load of paper too thick for toilet tissue and had to decide what to do with it. The forklift truck was invented when a man saw donuts being lifted out of a bakery oven on steel "fingers." Similarly, Gutenberg, the inventor of the printing press, had long pondered how to achieve quicker book production than carving words laboriously on blocks and rubbing paper against the blocks. Watching a wine-press one day gave him the necessary insight—that the same process could be used in printing. That is, the image could be transferred to paper by pressing an inked lead seal against the paper. Gutenberg, like the inventor of paper towels and the forklift, was being resourceful.

Resourcefulness is the ability to see the connections between things, to improvise, to make new applications. This, research has shown, involves a disposition to search out and try a variety of solutions to a problem, even those that seem irrelevant, to combine things previously uncombined. Edison's success in inventing the phonograph reveals this disposition. Instead of trying to copy the human anatomy of sound production, as others did, he devised a new method. (Incidentally, in the 1860s a man named Faber invented a crude talking machine that did imitate the human speech mechanism.) Similarly, successful airplane inventors such as the Wright brothers got beyond imitating birds flapping their wings.

The second paragraph begins in *literal definition,* then presents *factual informatin* (the reporting of reasearch findings), and finally cites *two brief examples.* The third paragraph begins with *factual assertion,* followed by (in the second sentence) *explanation* and *analogy.* The next sentence is a blend of *factual assertion* and *brief examples.*

At the heart of resourcefulness is another characteristic of creative people—playfulness. It is playfulness that allows a person to arrange and rearrange the elements of a problem and its possible solutions much as a child arranges his building blocks, now in one combination, then in another, taking delight in finding ever new and unexpected combinations. In fact, it may well be that this seemingly frivolous characteristic is one of the most important in the creative process. Einstein thought it was. He once remarked that "combinatory play seems to be the essential feature in productive thought."

It is to this quality of resourcefulness that we owe one of the greatest breakthroughs in the history of medicine, the development of penicillin. Countless lives have been saved over the past three decades by that development, which began when Alexander Fleming noticed what other researchers observed but remained incurious about—the inhibiting effect of molds on staphylococcus colony growth. (At least one of those other researchers regarded what he saw as a mere nuisance.) Fleming was not only unusually observant and curious, but resourceful as well. For he worked out the connection between that action of the molds and the conquering of disease.

Y O U R   T U R N

1. Identify the various techniques used in the following passage:

It is morning at Morris High School, a gothic fortress rising above the ruins of New York City's scarred South Bronx. All but the main entrance is sealed; in front of it is a security guard, ready to turn back anybody who tries to enter without proper identification. Inside, five more guards equipped with walkie-talkies patrol the halls and cafeteria in the 60 percent Hispanic, 39 percent black school. Most classroom doors are locked after classes begin, and study halls, once a favorite spot for fights, have been shut down. The dingy lockers that formerly lined the corridors have been removed. Explains principal Chester Wiggan: "The kids used to store drugs in them and set fires." Four trailers equipped as classrooms, in which pupils who are disciplinary problems study in isolation from the rest of the student body, are parked outside.

The military-camp atmosphere of Morris High is extreme. But increasingly, schools from Memphis to Los Angeles are adopting similar methods—as well as closed-circuit TVs, guards, emergency phones in the classrooms—to combat a violence that was once unheard of.

2. Select a piece of non-fiction you recently read and found interesting. It may be any type of writing—a book, an article, a letter to a newspaper editor. Photocopy a passage from it (at least several paragraphs), noting in the margin the techniques of development the author used.

INFORMATION FROM SOURCES

In much of your academic writing, you will be expected, even required, to use material from sources other than your own memory. Producing researched writing actually involves two stages: First, you collect the material from written sources, field research, or non-print media; next, you incorporate researched material into your writing. Do not think, though, that outside sources are consulted only for formal research papers. When you read a short essay or ask an acquaintance for an opinion, you are conducting research. Should you decide to use material from any research, whether it was brief and informal or extensive and formal, you must be sure to include it skillfully and to document it properly.

Plagiarism

Using information from other sources is a sign that you are well-informed; failing to properly credit your sources can be **plagiarism.** Plagiarism is a kind of academic theft; when you do not credit your sources, you present their ideas and information as your own. Most universities take firm stands against plagiarism, so you should be familiar with its most common forms.

If a paper is copied directly from another, the intent is clearly fraud. No amount of discussion or definition will change such behavior. However, poor documentation of sources can also result in plagiarism. If you have copied a passage from another work, you know that the original source should be credited. Even if you paraphrase the material into your own words, the source must still be given. (The forms of documentation are covered in Chapter 19; additional information is available in most handbooks.) If you extend or develop an idea drawn from your readings, you should indicate the source of the original, making clear what additions and extensions you have made. While common knowledge (facts widely available and known to many) needs no documentation, if you are using the opinions of others, you should at the very least give the name of your source. Remember, if you have noted in the text that "the president once said. . . ." or that "someone on 'Good Morning America' said . . . ," you are perhaps guilty of sloppy documentation, but you are not plagiarizing.

Presenting the Information

Summarizing, quoting, and paraphrasing are commonly used to present information gathered from sources. While a research paper makes extensive use of these techniques, they are not limited to formal research work and may appear in any paper that presents information from sources.

Summarizing

Summarizing is restating something more concisely than it was originally stated, including only the main ideas. This technique is often used at the beginning of scientific and technical articles to give the reader an overview of the content of the articles. But its use is not confined to such writing. Summaries are useful in any relatively long piece of writing (at least several thousand words) when an important idea can be reinforced by reviews of major points.

Summaries are especially valuable when you are citing research data. A single essay, for example, may join data from several different studies.

Sometimes each of the works referred to may be ten times longer than the essay, so your challenge is to present the data without assigning it too much space or allowing it to steal the focus from your main idea. Summarizing can be the solution to this problem. The shorter the summary, of course, the greater the risk of distortion and oversimplification. Nevertheless, if approached with care, even long and complex material can be effectively summarized.

Sample Summary

The essay on resourcefulness, page 293 in this chapter, is summarized below.

Resourcefulness is the ability to see connections between things, and to improvise when the first ideas do not work. It also involves playfulness, looking for unexpected or new connections that may at first seem frivolous. Resourcefulness produced such diverse inventions as paper towels, the printing press, the phonograph, and the airplane. In each case, the inventor went beyond imitation to see new combinations and connections.

Comment

Notice that main ideas and some significant examples are included, but the detail and explanation are omitted.

Y O U R   T U R N

Summarize a magazine or encyclopedia article on a subject of special interest to you OR on one of the following subjects. When you turn in your work, include a photocopy of the original article.

brainwashing	volcanoes	asthma
cancer	photography	superstition
creation	human intelligence	

Quoting and Paraphrasing

To quote is to express another person's idea in exactly his or her words; to paraphrase is to express another person's idea in your words. These techniques show your recognition that other people's ideas and experiences are valuable and can aid in your efforts to understand and communicate. It is possible, of course, to overdo these techniques. But you needn't fear this if you remember to use other people's thoughts to complement and support your own and not to substitute for them.

When should you quote and when should you paraphrase? Professional writers follow this rule:

- Quote whenever the source's wording is so concise or appropriate that a paraphrase would do the idea an injustice
- Quote whenever the source's content is   controversial or inflammatory and a paraphrase might distance it from its source or weaken it in any way
- Paraphrase at all other times

Quoting

You may quote a single word, a phrase or clause, or a paragraph or more. But however brief or long your quote, you should take care to maintain the context—that is, to preserve the meaning of the quoted passage as conveyed in the original material. In addition, you should follow these conventions to ensure correct reading:

Long Quotation—If the quotation runs five or more lines, set it off in a separate, indented paragraph. (In such cases, change to single-spacing and drop the quotation marks.)

Ellipsis—If you omit any words in the quoted material, mark the omission with three spaced periods (four if the omission occurs at the end of a sentence). This punctuation is called an ellipsis.

Brackets—If you are quoting part of a sentence, try to select your sentence structure to fit that of the quoted passage. If for some reason you cannot do so, use brackets to indicate any changes you make. For example, if the verb in the quoted passage was "keep" and you must change it to "keeping" to fit your sentence structure, write "keep[ing]" so the reader will see where you have altered the quote.

Emphasis—If you wish to underline any words that were not underlined in the original version, in order to create emphasis for your own purpose, you may do so provided you say "emphasis added" in parentheses immediately after the end of the quoted material.

Sic—Since the readers will assume that anything within quotation marks is exactly as it appeared in the original, be sure not to change any wording or punctuation inadvertently. If the material contains archaic spelling or errors, copy them exactly as they are, followed immediately by *sic* (Latin for "thus it is") in brackets. This will indicate that the error occurred in the original material.

Sample Passage

In seventeenth-century New England no respectable person questioned that woman's place was in the home. By the laws of Massachusetts as by those of England a married woman could hold no

This passage contains examples of both partial quoting (sentences 4 and 5) and full quoting (the single-spaced, indented parapgraph). Note that the original author footnoted the full quotation though the reference is omitted here.

property of her own. When she became a wife, she gave up everything to her husband and devoted herself exclusively to managing his household. Henceforth her duty was to "keep at home, educating of her children, keeping and improving what is got by the industry of the man." She was "to see that nothing be wasted, or prodigally spent; that all have what is suitable in due season." What the husband provided she distributed and transformed to supply the everyday necessities of the family. She turned flour into bread and wool into cloth and stretched the pennies to purchase what she could not make. Some times she even took care of the family finances. Samuel Sewall, the famous Puritan diarist, recorded on January 24, 1703/4, that he had turned over the cash account to his wife, relying upon her superior financial judgment:

> I paid Capt. Belchar £8-15-0. Took 24s in my pocket, and gave my Wife the rest of my cash £4-3-8, and tell her she shall now keep the Cash; if I want I will borrow of her. She has a better faculty than I at managing Affairs: I will assist her: and will endeavor to live upon my Salary; will see what it will doe. The Lord give his Blessing.

E. MORGAN, 100–01

Paraphrase

Whenever there is no good reason to quote, paraphrase. Paraphrasing is used more often than quoting because, like summarizing, it can reduce long passages to fit briefer treatments. Remember, though, that no two words have precisely the same meaning and that any time you translate another person's words into your own, you run the risk of distortion. Choose your paraphrases with care.

This passage is identical to that on pages 297–298 with one exception—the quotations have been changed to paraphrases. Note that the paraphrases are accurate. The date on which Samuel Sewall wrote in his diary is omitted here because without the actual quotation it would serve no purpose.

Had there been no special advantage to quoting, the closing section of our earlier passage might have been paraphrased as follows:

> . . . She turned flour into bread and wool into cloth and stretched the pennies to purchase what she could not make. Sometimes she even took care of the family finances. Samuel Sewall, the famous puritan diarist, recorded that he had turned over the cash account to his wife, relying upon her superior financial judgment.

E. MORGAN, 42–43

Quoting and paraphrasing are often used in combination. If a lengthy passage contains much material that is useful to your work, quoting the key words and phrases and paraphrasing the other ideas will often be more effective than a lengthy block quote. The examples that follow are based on a passage from "Does Part-Time Pay Off?" a *Ms.* special report by Susan McHenry and Linda Lee Small (March 1989). Study the specific uses of quoting and paraphrasing.

Source Material

Today, at least one in six jobholders in this country works less than 35 hours a week—the most widely accepted boundary distinguishing full- and part-time work—and the increased hiring of part-timers and temporary workers has been seen as one of the most significant changes in today's labor market. Between 1968 and 1985, part-time employment grew faster than full-time. More than 25 percent of the much heralded 10 million jobs created during the Reagan administration were part-time. Part-time was industry's answer to uncertainty in the economic outlook and the trend toward corporate restructuring. Women joined the work force in increasing numbers until, today, an American mother is more likely to be employed than not. (88–89)

Possible References

A combination of paraphrase and direct quote, logically connected to the ideas under discussion:

Many saw Reagan's emphasis on traditional family as an attempt to discourage women from working outside the home; however, during his administration, the numbers of working women continued to increase and, despite Reagan's influence, "an American mother is more likely to be employed than not" (McHenry & Small, 89).

A Paraphrase

Ten million jobs were created during the Reagan administration, but more than a quarter of those jobs were part-time (McHenry & Small, 88).

Direct Quote of Key Words

In the last two decades, industry hiring has shifted toward the part-time worker, a change that McHenry and Small termed "one of the most significant" (88).

Ellipses and Grammatical Change to Integrate Material

In a 1989 study of part-time employment in the United States, McHenry and Small found that "at least one in six jobholders . . . work[ed] less than thirty-five hours a week" (88).

From the Same *Ms.* Report, Note the Combination of Reference Options

A report from the Conference Board, the New York-based nonprofit research organization with a constituency of the nation's largest corporations, conceded that "employers often think people 'really prefer' the only choice available to them." In addition, many working mothers say they "chose" part-time because they have no adequate, affordable child care. According to a report by 9 to 5, National Association of Working Women, nearly 35 percent of women who work part-time said they would be glad to add hours to their workweek if there were better childcare options available (90).

SUMMARY

Presenting information is part of every essay, regardless of the purpose. Information often dictates how it should be presented; for example, words may need to be defined, or necessary supplies may need to be listed or a trend may need to be traced. Having a variety of strategies at your disposal can make such presentations simpler.

YOUR TURN

1. Select one of the following quotations. Then rewrite it in your own words, being careful to avoid distorting the idea.

   a. "Chins are exclusively a human feature, not to be found among the beasts. If they had chins, most animals would look like each other. Man was given a chin to prevent the personality of his mouth and eyes from overwhelming the rest of his face, to prevent each individual from becoming a species unto himself." (Chazal)

   b. "To suppose, as we all suppose, that we could be rich and not behave the way the rich behave, is like supposing that we could drink all day and stay sober." (L. P. Smith)

   c. "The value of philosophy is to be sought largely in its very uncertainty. He who has no tincture of philosophy goes through life imprisoned in the prejudices derived from common sense, from the habitual beliefs of his age or his nation, and from convictions which have grown up in his mind without the cooperation or consent of his deliberate reason. As soon as we begin to philosophize, on the contrary, we find that even the most everyday things lead to problems to which only very incomplete answers can be given. Philosophy, though unable to tell us with certainty what is the true answer to the doubts which it raises, is able to suggest many possibilities which enlarge our thoughts and free them from the tyranny of custom." (Russell)

2. Think of a topic you are interested in but know little about (perhaps an exotic topic like headhunting or cannibalism). Look it up in a

good encyclopedia. To ensure that you do not inadvertently borrow the phrasing and structure of the encyclopedia article, jot down the pertinent information in fragmentary form while you are reading. If you find a particularly vivid or striking description, be sure to copy it exactly as it appears. Then close the encyclopedia before beginning to write. Present the information in your own words and sentence structure. If you do quote directly, be sure to mark the quoted material and to incorporate it smoothly into your text.

3. Select one of the following quotations. Then write a short paragraph, working the quotation in smoothly and grammatically.

   a. "Fanaticism consists in redoubling your effort when you have forgotten your aim." (Santayana)
   b. "A cathedral, a wave of a storm, a dancer's leap, never turn out to be high as we hoped." (Proust)
   c. "The greatest of faults, I should say, is to be conscious of none." (Carlyle)
   d. "People hate those who make them feel their own inferiority." (Chesterfield)
   e. "Men are not punished for their sins, but by them." (Hubbard)
   f. "The magic of first love is our ignorance that it can ever end." (Disraeli).

USING INFORMATION

One political maxim is, "Figures can lie, and liars can figure." Take the implicit warning here and realize that presenting information is only part of your written response. If you do not also explain the significance or relevance of the information, you allow the audience to define the connections and you run the risk of having your ideas misinterpreted. Consider that politicians may use the results of the same poll or the most recent statistics on a social problem to argue two very different positions. Such diverse approaches are possible because information can be interpreted, evaluated, or even challenged as it is presented to an audience.

Interpreting and Evaluating

Whether you use statistics or quotes or personal observations, you must present to your readers your understanding of the material and your evaluation of its accuracy and importance.

When you interpret information, you probe its significance, the assumptions on which it rests, the attitudes it suggests, or its relation to other ideas, statements, or works. It is all very well to say that the

Catholic population in the southwestern part of the United States is on the rise, but what does such a fact mean? Why is the population rising? Is the birth rate higher? Are new immigrants settling near their relatives in that area? How is it affecting the economy or the politics of the area? In other words, how is that information connected to your ideas?

Sometimes interpretation is controversial. Do the latest statistics on poverty in the United States show the effectiveness of the government's efforts to relieve poverty? Or do they reflect a new method of defining the poverty level? The argument is based on interpretation of information. Whenever you explain what something means, you are interpreting for your audience. (Literary works, for example, are often interpreted; the special considerations of interpreting literature are covered in Chapter 20.)

Sample Interpretation

The new City Council policy requiring that all who purchase alcoholic beverages must show a valid picture ID is intended to ease the burden of clerks who complain that they cannot be sure of a purchaser's age. The policy goes into effect at midnight tonight, and it will affect consumers of all ages. Even senior citizens will be required to show identification such as a driver's license which has a recent photograph and a signature. The policy will be in effect for an initial thirty day trial, at which time the council will hear testimony on the effectiveness of the policy and the inconvenience to stores and consumers.

YOUR TURN

1. Choose a recent policy decision or statement by a public official and interpret its meaning for your audience.
2. Interpret the Yiddish proverb, "The girl who can't dance says the band can't play."
3. Interpret Thomas Fuller's assertion, "Travel makes a wise man better but a fool worse."

Evaluation is similar to interpretation. It, too, is used to analyze, but your analysis will involve an added component—judgment. To evaluate is to engage in a critical examination of something, pointing out its strengths and weaknesses or its advantages and disadvantages, and sometimes suggesting an alternative or solution. Note that these two passages not only interpret meaning but also judge:

The new City Council policy requiring that all who purchase alcoholic beverages must show a valid picture ID is intended to ease the burden of clerks who complain that they cannot be sure of a purchaser's age. It is far more likely to create massive inconvenience for those same clerks who must now ask even senior citizens for identification. For those who do not drive and do not possess a driver's license, it poses a further inconvenience. Furthermore, since it allows other picture IDs, the policy will not catch underage consumers who have IDs more easily tampered with. The policy will be in effect for an initial thirty-day trial, at which time the council will surely see that this "solution" is inefficient and impractical.

Telling us to obey instinct is like telling us to obey "people." People say different things: so do instincts. Our instincts are at war. If it is held that the instinct for preserving the species should always be obeyed at the expense of other instincts, whence do we derive this rule of precedence? To listen to that instinct speaking in its own cause and deciding in its own favour would be rather simple minded. Each instinct, if you listen to it, will claim to be gratified at the expense of all the rest. By the very act of listening to one rather than to others we have already prejudged the case. If we did not bring to the examination of our instincts a knowledge of their comparative dignity we could never learn it from them. And that knowledge cannot itself be instinctive: the judge cannot be one of the parties judged: or, if he is, the decision is worthless and there is no ground for placing the preservation of the species above self-preservation or sexual appetite.

C. S. LEWIS

The author made his position clear enough in the first two or three sentences. But had he stopped there, or even after the fifth or sixth sentences, the critical reader would not be so inclined to accept his judgment. For this reason, wise writers take additional time and special care with their evaluations.

YOUR TURN

Offer interpretations if necessary, but also include your judgment of:

a. a particular course you are now taking.
b. an English course taken in high school.
c. a particular television program (or current television programming in general).
d. a proposal for change currently being discussed on your campus or in your town or state.
e. the leadership of any public official.

Speculating

Speculation is used when you wish to project the outcome of a present situation, to make an educated guess about future events. It is, of course, not the same kind of prediction that a seer makes. Rather, it is a suggestion about probabilities. When you use this technique, keep in mind that you are speaking about the future, a matter that is closed to all but the clairvoyant and subject to innumerable variables. Avoid any pretense of certainty; instead, be tentative.

Sample Speculation

Occultism, then, *is likely* to drift toward obsolescence as the enlightenment of scientific research spreads to the dark corners wherein mystery still lurks. Just as the occult practices of astrology gave way to a science of astronomy, occult alchemy turned into scientific chemistry, magical cures were supplanted by sound medicine, witchcraft and fortune-telling yielded to parapsychology, so in time *might* a more reliable foundation supplant the remaining occult systems. An extended psychology and psychiatry, for example, *may* take over the still flourishing practice of exorcising devils and will offer something better. *Probably* many of the more morbid and unsavory derivatives of our religious primitivism that still survive as occult orgies, even in the more sophisticated centers of population, *can be* converted to more hygienic modes of emotional release. Purporting, as it does, to deal with hidden matters, occultism becomes a challenge to the inquiring mind.

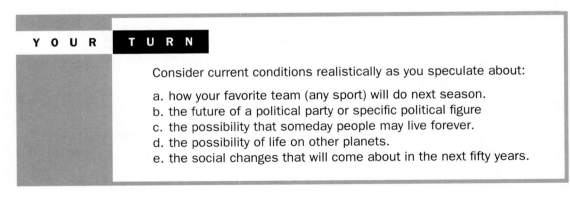

YOUR TURN

Consider current conditions realistically as you speculate about:

a. how your favorite team (any sport) will do next season.
b. the future of a political party or specific political figure
c. the possibility that someday people may live forever.
d. the possibility of life on other planets.
e. the social changes that will come about in the next fifty years.

Explaining

Explaining, giving more information or detail about an idea, is useful whenever the idea or some part of it is apt to confuse the readers or lead them to misinterpret. To use this technique effectively, you must discriminate between ideas that require further elaboration and those that do not. Put yourself in the place of your readers, then read your work with an objective eye. Here is an effective explanation:

> The old warning "Don't believe everything you read in the newspapers" makes a lot of sense. Newspaper reporters and editors may not purposely try to deceive anyone. However, in their rush to make deadlines these busy professionals aren't always able to verify their stories, check their details, study the implications of their headlines. The inevitable errors and unintentional distortions such rushing causes are not always discovered, and even when they are, the corrections are usually printed days or weeks later and seldom in the most prominent place in the newspaper. So cautious readers, while avoiding outright skepticism, maintain a certain mental reservation about the "news."

Notice that explanations like the one above don't try to argue a point; they simply try to clarify it. Explanations generally supply more information; interpretations give the writer's analysis of what has been presented. Establishing a context for information may influence interpretation, but the explanation of background is usually less subjective than interpretation.

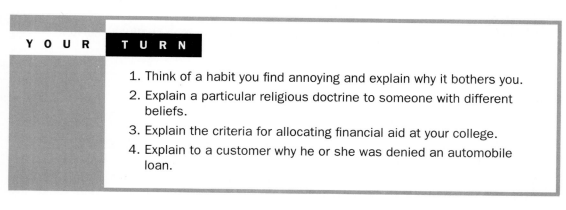

Y O U R   T U R N

1. Think of a habit you find annoying and explain why it bothers you.
2. Explain a particular religious doctrine to someone with different beliefs.
3. Explain the criteria for allocating financial aid at your college.
4. Explain to a customer why he or she was denied an automobile loan.

WRITING TO CONVINCE

As you review the draft of an argumentative paper, look for two frequently used strategies: presenting reasons and challenging information.

Presenting Reasons

Presenting reasons may sound synonymous with explaining, but the phrase is used here to refer specifically to the reasons behind the writer's assertions. This is the most basic of the techniques of persuasive writing because it answers the questions critical readers are most likely to ask about such judgments—"Why does the writer take this view rather than one of the other possible views? What are the writer's reasons for concluding it is the best view?" Presenting your reasons is one of the most effective ways of demonstrating that your judgments are not arbitrary. Here is an example of this technique:

> I oppose increases in military spending not because I believe the Russians pose no threat to our nation's security, nor because I believe our military might is invincible, but because the defense budget has never been purged of waste, inefficiency, and unnecessary duplication of equipment and services. Thus the Administration should be able to make a significant cut in the defense budget without reducing our defense capability.

Y O U R   T U R N

For each question, give your opinion and your reasons for it:

a. Do you believe that the death penalty should be abolished?
b. Should a student who cheats on an examination receive a grade of F in the course?
c. Do you believe that women are equal to men in athletic ability?
d. Do you believe in life after death?

Challenging Information

As you gather information about a subject, you may find that some of it is contradictory. By evaluating the material, you will make reasonable decisions about what to include in your discussion, but do not discard the contradictory material too soon—it may give you a focus for your essay. By asking questions about material and then answering them for the audience, you can supply information and, at the same time, dispel commonly held but inaccurate beliefs. By pointing out the misconceptions and inadequate analysis of other writing, you can effectively present your own interpretation and evaluation. Note the technique of challenging information in the passage below:

> Many people in this community believe that a group home for retarded citizens would be an undesirable addition to this neighborhood. The arguments against the home here are much like arguments used in other communities: The residents would be a danger

to the children in the neighborhood, they would not properly maintain the home to the standards of the neighborhood, they would create a continuing disturbance in the neighborhood, and so on. But a careful examination of similar group homes in similar neighborhoods shows the truth. The residents of such homes are carefully selected and supervised. They are not perverts; to the contrary, they are generally peaceful and productive citizens who function well on a slightly different level. And the group homes in other areas are well-maintained and indistinguishable from other residences. Finally, the only disturbance created by the resident homes have been initiated by the so-called "normal" neighbors who protest and picket in the area.

When you decide to challenge information, be sure that you do so thoroughly. You should either explore the information in doubt and verify it, or reject it and replace it with more accurate material.

Y O U R   T U R N

Try the technique of challenging information by identifying contradictory views and presenting further analysis to reject one side or to resolve the contradiction.

1. Has the current administration (city, state, national) been effective?
2. Is a varsity sports program essential to a major college?
3. Can a woman reasonably expect to balance a career, a marriage, and children?
4. Are teenagers more likely than adults to be involved in alcohol-related automobile accidents?

Sample Composition

This essay is a formal, informative discussion of an environmental concern. The writer has done some reading about the topic but has not researched it to any great depth; nonetheless, sources are cited in the text and in a bibliography, just as would be done in a longer research paper (Documentation here follows MLA guidelines; for further discussion of documentation styles, see Chapter 19). Also note that, while the topic is controversial, the paper is classified as informative. An effective persuasive paper could certainly be written on this subject, but in this example, the writer has not taken sides; instead, there is consideration for all points of view.

Poison from the Skies

Note that the title foreshadows the controlling idea expressed in the final sentence of the first paragraph and that the introduction stimulates readers' interest by dramatically contrasting traditional associations with the present reality.

The second parapgraph, like most paragraphs in the composition, presents factual data, arranged for clarity and interest.

The warm spring rain falls gently on the forest, spilling from leaf to leaf and then to the forest floor, where it seeps into the ground or runs in quiet rivulets into a nearby creek or lake. The scene has traditionally held only pleasant, poetic associations—nature renewing itself. Yet today scientists warn that rain can be a poison that harms virtually everything it touches.

The harmful phenomenon is known as acid rain. Rainwater, like any chemical, is measured on the pH scale, which measures hydrogen ion concentration. The scale extends from 0 to 14, with the lower end representing extreme acidity. Distilled water measures 7; normal rainwater, 5.6. Since the scale is logarithmic, a small change in the pH reading reflects a significant change in acidity. For example, rainfall that measures 5.5 is ten times more acidic than normal rainfall. To appreciate the extent of the danger posed by acid rain, we need only consider that pH values of less than 4.0 have been recorded from water samples taken from certain Adirondack Mountain ponds ("Acid Rain," p. 6).

Acid rain results from the release of sulfur oxide and nitrogen oxide into the upper atmosphere. Though automobile exhaust fumes contribute to the formation of acid rain, its main source is smoke from coal-burning or electric power plants, which rises into the upper atmosphere, where its pollutants combine with water vapor and are carried hundreds and even thousands of miles, eventually falling to earth as rain or snow.

The damage caused by acid rain is staggering. Though this damage is centered in the northeastern United States and Canada, an area of at least 2 1/4 million square miles, its effects are felt throughout those countries and far beyond them to the outermost reaches of prevailing winds. In Eastern Europe, for example, acid rain has endangered an estimated 2 1/2 million acres of forest ("Flacke Charges," p. 8).

Although some plants thrive on high acidity, many others cannot tolerate it. The Argonne National Laboratory estimates that 5 percent of the nation's soybean crop has been lost to acid rain ("Acid Rain"). Moreover, acid rain sterilizes the seeds of hardwood trees. In the period from 1956 to 1965, tree growth in the White Mountains declined by 18 percent ("Flacke Charges," p. 8). Nor is the harm done to plants alone. Acid rain pollutes rivers and streams and poses a double danger to fish by increasing the acidity of the water and causing soil reactions that release large quantities of aluminum. Thus the fish either die from a lack of oxygen at lower depths or from high acidity or aluminum poisoning near the surface ("Flacke Charges," p. 9).

Here the writer turns to the effects of acid rain on people. (Note also the brief presentation of the process by which objects are harmed.)

Buildings, monuments, bridges, and outdoor sculpture also suffer ill effects. The rain leaves a crusty deposit on them, which in time washes off, taking layers of stone with it. But none of the damage done to buildings, nor even that to lakes, forests, crops, and such industries as lumber, paper, and tourism, is as ominous as one effect whose extent is as yet undetermined—the leeching of acid rain into ground water and the resulting contamination of drinking water.

This paragraph presents factual data.

Public concern about the acid rain problem has understandably mounted over the past decade. Among the suggested remedies that have been proposed are strengthening the U.S. Clean Air Act by setting emissions limits for sulfur dioxide from coal-fired power plants and closely monitoring actual emissions; a program requiring high-sulfur coal to be cleaned before burning; and installation of low-nitrogen-oxide burners on existing power plants to cut down emissions ("Three Proposed," p. 7). A number of bills have been presented before Congress to reduce acid rain ("Three Proposed," p. 8), and a number of agreements have been signed between northeastern states and Canadian provinces to help standardize research methods and coordinate clean-up efforts ("New York").

Despite such efforts to solve the problem, complications remain. The dramatic rise in oil prices over the past dozen years has driven many industries to convert from oil to coal, thus adding to the acid rain problem ("Acid Rain"). In addition, because there are at least three groups involved with the problem—coal-burning factories and plants, the Environmental Protection Agency (EPA), and the affected downwind areas—resolution is often slow and difficult ("Flacke Charges," p. 9). Sometimes

The writer here presents general and specific examples of the complications that arise.

one party is forced to go to court to get action. Such was the case in Jefferson County, Kentucky, when the Air Pollution Control District filed suit against the EPA for failing to reduce sulfur emission from an Indiana power plant ("Flacke Charges," p. 9).

Not everyone agrees about the seriousness of the problem or the course of action that should be taken. Anne M. Burford, former head of the EPA, argues that more research data is needed. "The current question before us," she argues, "is will the basis for future measures to control acid deposition be blind groping in response to media and political emotionalism, or the result of rigorous scientific analysis that can define some kind of significant benefit?"

Here the writer uses the techniques of quotation and paraphrase. Note that the writer presents each side objectively without taking sides.

John Roberts, Canada's Minister of Environment, disagrees, calling acid rain "cancer of the biosphere" and arguing that since more than 3,000 research studies have demonstrated that it is a "clear and present danger," immediate and decisive action is necessary. "I say we do have enough information to act," he says. "It's not a matter of science any longer; it's a matter of political will."

The one point everyone seems agreed on is that the problem of acid rain is likely to continue challenging our ingenuity throughout the 1980s and perhaps much longer.

Works Cited

"Acid Rain." *New York State Environment* 10 Feb. 1981 : 6–8.

Burford, Anne McGill, and John Roberts. "Acid Rain: International Irritant." Debate. *American Forests* May 1983: 12–13.

"Flacke Charges EPA Indifferent to Acid Rain." *New York State Environment* 24 Dec. 1981: 8–9.

"New York and Ontario Sign Acid Rain Agreement." *New York State Environment* 18 May 1983: 7.

"Three Proposed Amendments: Acid Rain." New York State Environment 29 March 1982 : 7–8.

Strengthening Arguments

The differences between writing to convince and writing to inform are in the nature of your thesis and its relationship to your audience. Your thesis is controversial; that is, there is logical opposition to it. And, the intention to convince your readers indicates that they might not readily accept your ideas. In short, you must prove to a skeptical audience that your assertions are reasonable.

Like other writing, argument should be logically organized and carefully explained so that your audience understands your ideas. But the skepticism of your audience requires that you do more than explain and illustrate your ideas; you are expected to be convincing as well as clear so that your audience both understands and accepts your points. As a result, you must do more than give examples; you must offer evidence that is reliable, current, relevant, and sufficient. You must also consider the issues raised by your opposition, conceding when necessary and refuting whenever possible. Finally, you must be sensitive to your readers, anticipating their opinions and questions and responding not only to their interests but to their needs and to their feelings. The material in this chapter will help you in all of these areas.

EVALUATING EVIDENCE

In arguments, you must be sure that readers understand your points. But clarity alone will not suffice. Skeptical readers will examine your assertions critically and ask for evidence that proves your claims (see Chapter 4 for a detailed discussion of claims). When you draft arguments, you establish a logical framework for your assertions and fill in that framework with evidence. Pay close attention to the nature and quality of your evidence. In particular, ask yourself, "Does this evidence come from a reliable source? Is it relevant to the issues raised? Is it current? Is it sufficient?" Remember that your audience is likely to ask the same questions, so be sure that you can answer them.

Reliability

When you question the reliability of your evidence, you are testing the source. Take a careful look at the people who are making statements, at the agencies conducting polls, at the organization printing the material. Sources can be unreliable for several reasons, some of them sinister and some of them quite innocent. Consider the following criteria:

Is the source unbiased? If the source is financially involved in the issue, you should at the very least be suspicious about opinions, reports, or even statistics issued. A passenger who will be compensated by an insurance company if the other driver is at fault is not an unbiased source. A survey taken by the Citizens for David Jones should not be accepted at face value. The testimony of friends and relatives is also likely to be highly subjective. Should you discard evidence from a potentially biased source? You will have to decide how much subjectivity has influenced the material, but remember that your audience will be asking the same questions. Do not arbitrarily discard material that seems plausible even if it comes from biased sources; however, try to verify such material from other sources.

Is the source credible? More directly, can you trust this source? It is more likely that you can believe stories in *National Geographic* than stories in *The National Enquirer*. Reputation plays a large part in determining credibility, and reputation can be a fragile thing. A rape case in Illinois created headlines some years back when the young woman involved recanted her story. Her alleged assailant was not freed immediately because the legal system operated on the principle that the source of the new story (the young woman) was a self-confessed liar and could not be believed. In short, she was no longer a credible source and any story she told could not be trusted as evidence. However convincing it might seem, material from a source that cannot be trusted should be discarded.

Is the source qualified to make these statements? It is entirely possible that an unbiased, sincere source can still provide unreliable evidence. Imagine that you are invited to observe a heart surgeon's innovative surgical techniques. Could you offer reliable testimony? Only if your credentials qualify you to judge would your observations be useful. Lack of knowledge or ability can disqualify a source. Consider the witness with poor eyesight or the referee who was out of position or the child without the capacity to understand; all should be disqualified as primary sources of evidence. However, consider the possibility that such sources can corroborate other evidence. If you can verify the observations from other sources, unqualified comments may still be of limited use. Consider, too, that a source qualified in one area may not be qualified in another. Henry

Kissinger may be an expert on foreign affairs; do we accept his qualifications on laboratory tests on animals? If your source does in fact have less well known qualifications, be sure to let the reader know, too: "Wayne Newton, better known for his Las Vegas shows, is also a long-time breeder of Arabian horses. Newton believes that the best horses come from. . . ."

Relevance

An additional test of evidence is its relevance to current issues. If you are evaluating a political candidate, do you want information about athletic ability? If you are proposing an expensive community art appreciation program, should you include discussions of tax increases? If you watch courtroom dramas on television, you will hear one lawyer argue that a question is not "relevant," and the other lawyer will assure the court that the connections will soon become clear. Ask yourself the same questions about your evidence: "Is it relevant? Is the connection to my assertions clear?"

Two further considerations in evaluating relevance are these:

- Relevance itself can be an arguable question. When Gary Hart campaigned for the presidency in the late 1980s, his personal life became an issue when his marital infidelity was made public. Many argued that Hart's personal life had no bearing on his qualifications to be president of the United States, citing the infidelities of previous leaders. Others argued that his personal life was an indication of the man's character and thus relevant to the question of his fitness to serve. You may need to decide if material is relevant, and you may need to explain, even to justify, the connections.

- Relevance can be confused because of inadequate transitions. Remember that transitional devices provide guides for your readers, indicating the logical relationships between ideas. If you have omitted or misused words like "because" or "in contrast" or "an exception is . . ." or "in addition," your readers might fairly ask, "What does that have to do with the issue?" Your creative strategy might be innovative and convincing without being obvious, so be sure to demonstrate—with explicit transitional devices—the relevance of your evidence to your claim (review transitional devices in the Chapter 16 discussion of paragraph coherence).

Currency

Evidence should also be evaluated for its currency. "Currency" is a relative concept, for it is closely connected to the nature of your material. Most discussions of research and technology are out of date within a few years, so a ten-year-old article on space exploration or on AIDS research has limited value. Before you discard all such material, though, examine it for historical value; that is, does the early work reveal the attitudes of the time toward space travel or toward victims of the disease? Consider, too, that tracing the background of current thought will require such earlier material. For the most part, though, be cautious of using material that has been called into question by later findings.

There are, however, many topics which do not go out of date so quickly. Samuel Johnson's observations on Shakespeare are 200 years old and still of value to Shakespearian scholars. Analyses of historical events that are contemporary with the events or that follow within a few years offer a perspective that should not be ignored, and evaluations of historical figures by those who knew them (biographies and autobiographies) will remain timely and immediate.

In short, check the dates of your material (the original dates if it has been reprinted), but consider the nature of your subject before you discard older information.

Sufficiency

The simple guideline here is, "Be sure that you have supplied enough evidence to convince your readers." The question of sufficiency, though, is a bit more complicated. Are three pieces of evidence *enough?* Would five pieces be too many? Will one good quotation suffice, or should you use all three that you have found? The maddening answer is, "It depends." It depends on the nature of your work, and it depends on the status of your source, and it depends on your audience. While it is not practical to compile a chart that details how much evidence to use in every imaginable circumstance, you can review some guidelines:

- Sufficiency is affected by the work at hand. As you investigated your subject, did you find that most experts agreed with your claim? If you are supporting the prevailing opinion, the widely accepted stand, you need not smother the issue with evidence. You must still offer evidence, perhaps testimony from an expert or the results of a major study, but you need not belabor the point with example after example. Consider, too, the nature of your paper: a long, formal research paper is expected to provide extensive documentation; a brief introduction to a question is not.

- Sufficiency is affected by the status of your source. If your evidence comes from a well-recognized and well-respected source, you will not need to verify it at great length. In contrast, if your source is potentially biased or somewhat unreliable, you should supply additional verification whenever possible. The opinion of a well-known spokesperson is more effective than the opinion of an obscure junior researcher; be aware of the "weight" carried by your source.

• Sufficiency is affected by the attitude of your audience. When you profile an audience (see Chapter 4, "Writing to Convince the Audience," and Chapter 14, "Connecting Audience, Content and Purpose"), you speculate about their opinions. Remember that your argument rarely addresses an audience that is already enthusiastic about your subject—such an audience would need little or no evidence. Conversely, an audience that is totally hostile to your views is unlikely to be convinced by anything you say. Your most likely audience is one that has not yet formed strong opinions. For such readers, you should supply evidence to show that you are well informed and that your assertions are logical and reasonable.

Y O U R   T U R N

Evaluating the evidence used by other writers is often easier than evaluating your own material. But if you practice critical thinking by evaluating other writing, you will become aware of common errors and will be better able to recognize your own.

1. Look carefully at the interview with General Elizabeth Hoisington. Using the guidelines in this chapter, evaluate the evidence she offers to support her claims.

2. Suppose that the Hoisington interview is presented to conservative Army administrators. Do you think it likely that such an audience would agree with her or not? How would that audience affect her use of evidence? How would you expect her to change her presentation for an audience of feminist supporters?

3. Make a list of ten or more magazines readily available on public newsstands. How would you rate these magazines as reliable, credible sources? Are all credible magazines equally reliable on all issues? Explain.

4. Look over one of your working drafts. Evaluate the sources of your information for reliabilty, credibility and currency.

ANALYZING THE OPPOSITION

When you write arguments, be aware of opposing viewpoints. Such views might be personified in a spokesperson who has expressed them. There may be a written text which you are refuting, or there may be a prevailing attitude to which you are responding (see Chapter 9, "Identifying Patterns" for a discussion of responding to other material). The opposition to your claim might be poorly defined or it might be anticipated and not yet articulated. But regardless of the form, opposing views deserve consideration as you review your draft. Specifically, you should be aware of the definitions used, you should understand the issues raised, and you should recognize the strengths and weaknesses contained in such views.

DEFINING TERMS

Effective argument depends on clear, mutual definition of terms. If you have ever presented compelling arguments only to have your opposition announce, "But that is not what I meant at all," you already understand the need for mutual definition. Such misunderstandings may be unintentional, with each side sincerely believing that all terms are mutually understood. But it is also possible that vague terminology has been used to obscure an issue or to direct the opposition away from crucial matters. Read George Orwell's essay, "Politics and the English Language" for "a catalogue of swindles and perversions" that occur when "the person who uses them has his own private definition, but allows his hearer to think he means something quite different."

Your challenge in reviewing your presentation is to be aware of potentially ambiguous terms and to be sure that you and your opposition are using them in the same way. If you use terminology like "the government should . . ." or "the people say . . ." or "progress demands. . . ," be sure that you have made clear the specific part of government to be responsible and the exact group of people whose opinions are cited and the specific developments labelled "progress." Resist the temptation to leave such vague terms undefined, and demand of your opposition that all definitions be clear.

UNDERSTANDING THE ISSUES

All terminology in argument should be mutually agreed upon to provide a solid base for further discussion. It is equally important that you understand the issues raised in opposing views. Some study may be needed, but it is crucial to your own writing that you be fully aware of the specifics and the implications of opposing views. Without a clear understanding, you run the risk of wasting time at best and of looking foolish at worst. Consider what happened on a recent talk show when the audience railed angrily against a proposed kindergarten for four-year-olds. Speaker after speaker argued that most four-year-olds are not ready for structured programs until, three-quarters of the way through the program, one mother loudly insisted, "No one can make me send my baby to your program." Project administrators looked at each other in surprise and quickly explained that the program was entirely voluntary and that no child would be *required* to attend. The audience visibly relaxed and began to see the flexibility and the objectives of the plan.

What happened to waste the time and energies of so many people? From the beginning, there was a misunderstanding of the proposal. Perhaps the administrators did not make the specifics clear, or perhaps the audience did not listen carefully, but the end result was a tremendous outpouring of wasted energy.

Another kind of misunderstanding occurs when irony or sarcasm is used. If you do not recognize the misdirection implicit in such work, you may find yourself arguing vehemently against someone who actually shares your views. Read Jonathan Swift's "A Modest Proposal" and realize that many of his readers were horrified at his insensitivity to the problems of the Irish; in fact, Swift was appalled at the conditions in Ireland and worked actively for their improvement. If you read carefully, you will often find places where the writer's "mask" slips. Swift, for example, says that the English landlords have already "devoured" their Irish tenants. The accusation is a clue that he is really sympathetic to the Irish cause.

A writer using irony may also create a persona who is unmistakably obnoxious. The opinions offered by the obnoxious persona should be recognizable as distinct from the opinions of the author. Look at the examples below to see how the persona and his or her views are presented ironically.

Sample

> No one is more compassionate than I am. I love animals, small children, and Salvation Army Santas. What I can't abide are self-righteous do-gooders who try to convince me to give money for genetic research. What difference does it make to me if doctors learn to test for genetic diseases in a fetus? I'm not going to have a baby. Research that does not directly benefit humanity is a waste of money and time. I think it's time all such "charities" were exposed.

Comment

The narrow-mindedness and self-centeredness of this self-proclaimed "compassionate" speaker are a clue that the observations are not to be taken at face value.

Sample

> Legalizing drugs will provide tremendous benefits to society. Users will not have to sneak around anymore; they can poison their bodies in public without fear of legal intervention. Neighborhood drugstores can perform a real service to their patrons, saving them trips

into dangerous neighborhoods. Best of all, the government can make money by taxing drugs instead of spending money trying to enforce hopelessly inadequate laws.

Comment

Does this passage support the idea that society will indeed benefit, or that users will be done a real service? The difference between the supposed benefits and the impression created by diction like "poison their bodies" creates irony and clues the readers that the writer's statements should not be accepted at face value.

RECOGNIZING STRENGTHS AND WEAKNESSES

When you understand the issues and their implications, you can evaluate strengths and weaknesses. Remember that your audience often expects you to explain why your ideas are more reasonable than the opposing views. At the very least, the audience expects you to show that you are aware of and understand the opposition. To satisfy such audience expectations, follow these guidelines:

Attack the weak points. One way to demonstrate the strength of your stand is to explain the weakness of your opposition. Review the material in this chapter on evaluating evidence and in Chapter 10, "Evaluating Logic." If you find serious flaws in the thinking or in the presentation of the opposition, consider using those findings.

Identify the strongest points. If it is possible, avoid discussing the strengths of the opposition. However, if the point raised is obvious and unavoidable, you will look ill-prepared if you ignore it. When you must mention a strong opposing point, soften the impact with these approaches:

1. Reduce the point in importance. "This proposal will take money, but more importantly, it will save lives." Or, "It is true that our school district has a high rate of teenage pregnancy, but more importantly, those teenagers are staying in school and earning their diplomas."

2. Concede the point graciously and *briefly*. Give it no more space than you must, and turn attention quickly to another point. "This will be an expensive program, but it will be an effective one. Two other districts with similar programs report that. . . ."

Whether your argument will be a direct response to the opposition or not, it is important that you understand its terminology, issues, and proposals. Knowing the strengths and weaknesses of the opposition can help you to strengthen your own presentation.

Y O U R   T U R N

1. Read George Orwell's "Politics and the English Language." In your own words, explain his categories of misused language. Can you supply recent examples of the problems he describes?

2. One way to be sure that you understand the issues of an argument is to summarize it. Read "Letter from a Birmingham Jail" by Michael Levin and summarize the main points. Compare your summary with several others; are there any differences? Have any of the summaries omitted or misunderstood any points?

3. In the two essays above, how would you rate the points from strongest to weakest? Compare your list with your classmates'. Have you all agreed upon the rankings? Does it matter that you do?

4. Summarize the points you made in any of your working drafts. Looking over the list, rank the points from strongest to weakest. What can you do to strengthen the weaker ones? Have you emphasized the strengths of your argument?

Additional Reading

Politics and the English Language
George Orwell

George Orwell wrote this essay nearly fifty years ago, analyzing language that fails to communicate clearly. What are some of the explanations Orwell offers for ambiguous language? Do the same motives apply today?

1   Most people who bother with the matter at all would admit that the English language is in a bad way, but it is generally assumed that we cannot by conscious action do anything about it. Our civilization is decadent and our language—so the argument runs—must inevitably share in the general collapse. It follows that any struggle against the abuse of language is a sentimental archaism, like preferring candles to electric light or hansom cabs to aeroplanes. Underneath this lies the half-conscious belief that language is a natural growth and not an instrument which we shape for our own purposes.

2   Now, it is clear that the decline of a language must ultimately have political and economic causes: it is not due simply to the bad influence of this or that individual writer. But an effect can become a cause, reinforcing the original cause and producing the same effect in an intensified

form, and so on indefinitely. A man may take to drink because he feels himself to be a failure, and then fail all the more completely because he drinks. It is rather the same thing that is happening to the English language. It becomes ugly and inaccurate because our thoughts are foolish, but the slovenliness of our language makes it easier for us to have foolish thoughts. The point is that the process is reversible. Modern English, especially written English, is full of bad habits which spread by imitation and which can be avoided if one is willing to take the necessary trouble. If one gets rid of these habits one can think more clearly, and to think clearly is a necessary first step towards political regeneration: so that the fight against bad English is not frivolous and is not the exclusive concern of professional writers. I will come back to this presently, and I hope that by that time the meaning of what I have said here will have become clearer. Meanwhile, here are five specimens of the English language as it is now habitually written.

3   These five passages have not been picked out because they are especially bad—I could have quoted far worse if I had chosen—but because they illustrate various of the mental vices from which we now suffer. They are a little below the average, but are fairly representative samples. I number them so that I can refer back to them when necessary:

1. I am not, indeed, sure whether it is not true to say that the Milton who once seemed not unlike a seventeenth-century Shelley had not become, out of an experience ever more bitter in each year, more alien [*sic*] to the founder of that Jesuit sect which nothing could induce him to tolerate.

Professor Harold Laski
(Essay in *Freedom of Expression*)

2. Above all, we cannot play ducks and drakes with a native battery of idioms which prescribes such egregious collocations of vocables as the Basic *put up with* for *tolerate* or *put at a loss* for *bewilder*.

Professor Lancelot Hogben
(*Interglossa*)

3. On the one side we have the free personality: by definition it is not neurotic, for it has neither conflict nor dream. Its desires, such as they are, are transparent, for they are just what institutional approval keeps in the forefront of consciousness; another institutional pattern would alter their number and intensity; there is little in them that is natural, irreducible, or culturally dangerous. But *on the other side,* the social bond itself is nothing but the mutual reflection of these self-secure integrities. Recall the definition of love. Is not this the very picture of a small academic? Where is there a place in this hall of mirrors for either personality or fraternity?

Essay on psychology in *Politics*
(New York)

4. All the "best people" from the gentlemen's clubs, and all the frantic fascist captains, united in common hatred of Socialism and bestial horror of the rising tide of the mass revolutionary movement, have turned to act of provocation, to foul incendiarism, to medieval legends of poisoned wells, to legalize their own destruction of proletarian organizations, and rouse the agitated petty-bourgeoisie to chauvinistic fervour on behalf of the fight against the revolutionary way out of the crisis.

Communist pamphlet

5. If a new spirit *is* to be infused into this old country, there is one thorny and contentious reform which must be tackled, and that is the humanization and galvanization of the B.B.C. Timidity here will bespeak canker and atrophy of the soul. The heart of Britain may be sound and of strong beat, for instance, but the British lion's roar at present is like that of Bottom in Shakespeare's *Midsummer Night's Dream*—as gentle as any sucking dove. A virile new Britain cannot continue indefinitely to be traduced in the eyes or rather ears, of the world by the effete languors of Langham Place, brazenly masquerading as "standard English." When the Voice of Britain is heard at nine o'clock, better far and infinitely less ludicrous to hear aitches honestly dropped than the present priggish, inflated, inhibited, school-ma'amish arch braying of blameless bashful mewing maidens!

Letter in *Tribune*

4 Each of these passages has faults of its own, but, quite apart from avoidable ugliness, two qualities are common to all of them. The first is staleness of imagery; the other is lack of precision. The writer either has a meaning and cannot express it, or he inadvertently says something else, or he is almost indifferent as to whether his words mean anything or not. This mixture of vagueness and sheer incompetence is the most marked characteristic of modern English prose, and especially of any kind of political writing. As soon as certain topics are raised, the concrete melts into the abstract and no one seems able to think of turns of speech that are not hackneyed: prose consists less and less of *words* chosen for the sake of their meaning, and more and more of *phrases* tacked together like the sections of a prefabricated henhouse. I list below, with notes and examples, various of the tricks by means of which the work of prose-construction is habitually dodged:

5 *Dying metaphors.* A newly invented metaphor assists thought by evoking a visual image, while on the other hand a metaphor which is technically "dead" (e.g. *iron resolution*) has in effect reverted to being an ordinary word and can generally be used without loss of vividness. But in between these two classes there is a huge dump of worn-out metaphors which have lost all evocative power and are merely used because they save people the trouble of inventing phrases for themselves. Examples

are: *Ring the changes on, take up the cudgels for, toe the line, ride roughshod over, stand shoulder to shoulder with, play into the hands of, no axe to grind, grist to the mill, fishing in troubled waters, on the order of the day, Achilles' heel, swan song, hotbed.* Many of these are used without knowledge of their meaning (what is a "rift," for instance?), and incompatible metaphors are frequently mixed, a sure sign that the writer is not interested in what he is saying. Some metaphors now current have been twisted out of their original meaning without those who use them even being aware of the fact. For example, *toe the line* is sometimes written *tow the line.* Another example is *the hammer and the anvil,* now always used with the implication that the anvil gets the worst of it. In real life it is always the anvil that breaks the hammer, never the other way about: a writer who stopped to think what he was saying would be aware of this, and would avoid perverting the original phrase.

6   *Operators* or *verbal false limbs.* These save the trouble of picking out appropriate verbs and nouns, and at the same time pad each sentence with extra syllables which give it an appearance of symmetry. Characteristic phrases are *render inoperative, militate against, make contact with, be subjected to, give rise to, give grounds for, have the effect of, play a leading part (role) in, making itself felt, take effect, exhibit a tendency to, serve the purpose of,* etc., etc. The keynote is the elimination of simple verbs. Instead of being a single word, such as *break, stop, spoil, mend, kill,* a verb becomes a *phrase,* made up of a noun or adjective tacked on to some general-purpose verb such as *prove, serve, form, play, render.* In addition, the passive voice is wherever possible used in preference to the active, and noun constructions are used instead of gerunds (*by examination of* instead of *by examining*). The range of verbs is further cut down by means of the *-ize* and *de-* formations, and the banal statements are given an appearance of profundity by means of the *not un-* formation. Simple conjunctions and prepositions are replaced by such phrases as *with respect to, having regard to, the fact that, by dint of, in view of, in the interests of, on the hypothesis that;* and the ends of sentences are saved from anticlimax by resounding common-places as *greatly to be desired, cannot be left out of account, a development to be expected in the near future, deserving of serious consideration, brought to satisfactory conclusion,* and so on and so forth.

7   *Pretentious diction.* Words like *phenomenon, element, individual* (as noun), *objective, categorical, effective, virtual, basic, primary, promote, constitute, exhibit, exploit, utilize, eliminate, liquidate,* are used to dress up simple statements and give an air of scientific impartiality to biased judgments. Adjectives like *epoch-making, epic, historic, unforgettable, triumphant, age-old, inevitable, inexorable, veritable,* are used to dignify the sordid process of international politics, while writing that aims at glorifying war usually takes on an archaic colour, its characteristic words being: *realm, throne, chariot, mailed fist, trident, sword, shield, buckler, banner, jackboot, clarion.* Foreign words and expressions such as *cul de sac,*

ancien régime, deus ex machina, mutatis mutandis, status quo, gleich-schaltung, weltanschauung, are used to give an air of culture and elegance. Except for the useful abbreviations. *i.e., e.g.,* and *etc.,* there is no real need for any of the hundreds of foreign phrases now current in English. Bad writers, and especially scientific, political and sociological writers, are nearly always haunted by the notion that Latin or Greek words are grander than Saxon ones, and unnecessary words like *expedite, ameliorate, predict, extraneous, deracinated, clandestine, subaqueous* and hundreds of others constantly gain ground from their Anglo-Saxon opposite numbers.[1] The jargon peculiar to Marxist writing (*hyena, hangman, cannibal, petty bourgeois, these gentry, lacquey, flunkey, mad dog, White Guard,* etc.) consists largely of words and phrases translated from Russian, German or French; but the normal way of coining a new word is to use a Latin or Greek root with the appropriate affix and, where necessary, the *-ize* formation. It is often easier to make up words of this kind (*deregionalize, impermissible, extramarital, non-fragmentary,* and so forth) than to think up the English words that will cover one's meaning. The result, in general, is an increase in slovenliness and vagueness.

8   *Meaningless words.* In certain kinds of writing, particularly in art criticism and literary criticism, it is normal to come across long passages which are almost completely lacking in meaning.[2] Words like *romantic, plastic, values, human, dead, sentimental, natural, vitality,* as used in art criticism, are strictly meaningless, in the sense that they not only do not point to any discoverable object, but are hardly ever expected to do so by the reader. When one critic writes, "The outstanding feature of Mr. X's work is its living quality," while another writes, "The immediately striking thing about Mr. X's work is its peculiar deadness," the reader accepts this as a simple difference of opinion. If words like *black* and *white* were involved, instead of the jargon words *dead* and *living,* he would see at once that language was being used in an improper way. Many political words are similarly abused. The word *Fascism* has now no meaning except in so far as it signifies "something not desirable." The words *democracy, socialism, freedom, patriotic, realistic, justice,* have each of them several different meanings which cannot be reconciled with one

---

[1]An interesting illustration of this is the way in which the English flower names which were in use till very recently are being ousted by Greek ones, *snapdragon* becoming *antirrhinum, forget-me-not* becoming *myosotis,* etc. It is hard to see any practical reason for this change of fashion: it is probably due to an instinctive turning-away from the more homely word and a vague feeling that the Greek word is scientific.

[2]Example: "Comfort's catholicity of perception and image, strangely Whitmanesque in range, almost the exact opposite in aesthetic compulsion, continues to evoke that trembling atmospheric accumulative hinting at a cruel, an inexorably serene timelessness. . . . Wrey Gardiner scores by aiming at simple bull's-eyes with precision. Only they are not so simple, and through this contented sadness runs more than the surface bitter-sweet of resignation." *(Poetry Quarterly.)*

another. In the case of a word like *democracy,* not only is there no agreed definition, but the attempt to make one is resisted from all sides. It is almost universally felt that when we call a country democratic we are praising it: consequently the defenders of every kind of régime claim that it is a democracy, and fear that they might have to stop using the word if it were tied down to any one meaning. Words of this kind are often used in a consciously dishonest way. That is, the person who uses them has his own private definition, but allows his hearer to think he means something quite different. Statements like *Marshal Pétain was a true patriot, The Soviet Press is the freest in the world, The Catholic Church is opposed to persecution,* are almost always made with intent to deceive. Other words used in variable meanings, in most cases more or less dishonestly, are: *class, totalitarian, science, progressive, reactionary, bourgeois, equality.*

9   Now that I have made this catalogue of swindles and perversions, let me give another example of the kind of writing that they lead to. This time it must of its nature be an imaginary one. I am going to translate a passage of good English into modern English of the worst sort. Here is a well-known verse from *Ecclesiastes:*

> I returned and saw under the sun, that the race is not to the swift, nor the battle to the strong, neither yet bread to the wise, nor yet riches to men of understanding, nor yet favor to men of skill, but time and chance happeneth to them all.

10   Here it is in modern English:

> Objective consideration of contemporary phenomena compels the conclusion that success or failure in competitive activities exhibits no tendency to be commensurate with innate capacity, but that a considerable element of the unpredictable must invariably be taken into account.

11   This is a parody, but not a very gross one. Exhibit (3), above, for instance, contains several patches of the same kind of English. It will be seen that I have not made a full translation. The beginning and ending of the sentence follow the original meaning fairly closely, but in the middle the concrete illustrations—race, battle, bread—dissolve into the vague phrase "success or failure in competitive activities." This had to be so, because no modern writer of the kind I am discussing—no one capable of using phrases like "objective consideration of contemporary phenomena"—would ever tabulate his thoughts in that precise and detailed way. The whole tendency of modern prose is away from concreteness. Now analyse these two sentences a little more closely. The first contains forty-nine words but only sixty syllables, and all its words are those of everyday life. The second contains thirty-eight words of ninety syllables: eighteen of its words are from Latin roots, and one from Greek. The first sentence contains six vivid images, and only one phrase ("time and

chance") that could be called vague. The second contains not a single fresh, arresting phrase, and in spite of its ninety syllables it gives only a shortened verison of the meaning contained in the first. Yet without a doubt it is the second kind of sentence that is gaining ground in modern English. I do not want to exaggerate. This kind of writing is not yet universal, and outcrops of simplicity will occur here and there in the worst-written page. Still, if you or I were told to write a few lines on the uncertainty of human fortunes, we should probably come much nearer to my imaginary sentence than to the one from *Ecclesiastes*.

12   As I have tried to show, modern writing at its worst does not consist in picking out words for the sake of their meaning and inventing images in order to make the meaning clearer. It consists in gumming together long strips of words which have already been set in order by someone else, and making the results presentable by sheer humbug. The attraction of this way of writing is that it is easy. It is easier—even quicker, once you have the habit—to say *In my opinion it is not an unjustifiable assumption that* than to say *I think*. If you use ready-made phrases, you not only don't have to hunt for words; you also don't have to bother with the rhythms of your sentences, since these phrases are generally so arranged as to be more or less euphonious. When you are composing in a hurry—when you are dictating to a stenographer, for instance, or making a public speech—it is natural to fall into a pretentious, Latinized style. Tags like *a consideration which we should do well to bear in mind* or *a conclusion to which all of us would readily assent* will save many a sentence from coming down with a bump. By using stale metaphors, similes and idioms, you save much mental effort, at the cost of leaving your meaning vague, not only for your reader but for yourself. This is the significance of mixed metaphors. The sole aim of a metaphor is to call up a visual image. When these images clash—as in *The Fascist octopus has sung its swan song, the jackboot is thrown into the melting pot*—it can be taken as certain that the writer is not seeing a mental image of the objects he is naming; in other words he is not really thinking. Look again at the examples I gave at the beginning of this essay. Professor Laski (1) uses five negatives in fifty-three words. One of these is superfluous, making nonsense of the whole passage, and in addition there is the slip *alien* for *akin,* making further nonsense, and several avoidable pieces of clumsiness which increase the general vagueness. Professor Hogben (2) plays ducks and drakes with a battery which is able to write prescriptions, and, while disapproving of the every day phrase *put up with,* is unwilling to look *egregious* up in the dictionary and see what it means; (3), if one takes an uncharitable attitude towards it, is simply meaningless: probably one could work out its intended meaning by reading the whole of the article in which it occurs. In (4), the writer knows more or less what he wants to say, but an accumulation of stale phrases chokes him like tea leaves blocking a sink. In (5), words and meaning have almost parted company. People who write in this manner usually have a general emotional

meaning—they dislike one thing and want to express solidarity with another—but they are not interested in the detail of what they are saying. A scrupulous writer, in every sentence that he writes, will ask himself as least four questions, thus: What am I trying to say? What words will express it? What image or idiom will make it clearer? Is this image fresh enough to have an effect? And he will probably ask himself two more: Could I put it more shortly? Have I said anything that is avoidably ugly? But you are not obliged to go to all this trouble. You can shirk it by simply throwing your mind open and letting the ready-made phrases come crowding in. They will construct your sentences for you—even think your thoughts for you, to a certain extent—and at need they will perform the important service of partially concealing your meaning even from yourself. It is at this point that the special connection between politics and the debasement of language becomes clear.

13   In our time it is broadly true that political writing is bad writing. Where it is not true, it will generally be found that the writer is some kind of rebel, expressing his private opinions and not a "party line." Orthodoxy, of whatever colour, seems to demand a lifeless, imitative style. The political dialects to be found in pamphlets, leading articles, manifestos, White Papers and the speeches of under-secretaries do, of course, vary from party to party, but they are all alike in that one almost never finds in them a fresh, vivid, home-made turn of speech. When one watches some tired hack on the platform mechanically repeating the familiar phrase—*bestial atrocities, iron heel, bloodstained tyranny, free peoples of the world, stand shoulder to shoulder*—one often has a curious feeling that one is not watching a live human being but some kind of dummy: a feeling which suddenly becomes stronger at moments when the light catches the speaker's spectacles and turns them into blank discs which seem to have no eyes behind them. And this is not altogether fanciful. A speaker who uses that kind of phraseology has gone some distance towards turning himself into a machine. The appropriate noises are coming out of his larynx, but his brain is not involved as it would be if he were choosing his words for himself. If the speech he is making is one that he is accustomed to make over and over again, he may be almost unconscious of what he is saying, as one is when one utters the responses in church. And this reduced state of consciousness, if not indispensable, is at any rate favorable to political conformity.

14   In our time, political speech and writing are largely the defence of the indefensible. Things like the continuance of British rule in India, the Russian purges and deportations, the dropping of the atom bombs on Japan, can indeed be defended, but only by arguments which are too brutal for most people to face, and which do not square with the professed aims of political parties. Thus political language has to consist largely of euphemism, question-begging and sheer cloudy vagueness. Defenseless villages are bombarded from the air, the inhabitants driven out into the countryside, the cattle machine-gunned, the huts set on fire with

incendiary bullets: this is called *pacification*. Millions of peasants are robbed of their farms and set trudging along the roads with no more than they can carry: this is called *transfer of population* or *rectification of frontiers*. People are imprisoned for years without trial, or shot in the back of the neck or sent to die of scurvy in Arctic lumber camps: this is called *elimination of unreliable elements*. Such phraseology is needed if one wants to name things without calling up mental pictures of them. Consider for instance some comfortable English professor defending Russian totalitarianism. He cannot say outright, "I believe in killing off your opponents when you can get good results by doing so." Probably, therefore, he will say something like this:

> While freely conceding that the Soviet régime exhibits certain features which the humanitarian may be inclined to deplore, we must, I think, agree that a certain curtailment of the right to political opposition is an unavoidable concomitant of transitional periods, and that the rigours which the Russian people have been called upon to undergo have been amply justified in the sphere of concrete achievement.

15   The inflated style is itself a kind of euphemism. A mass of Latin words falls upon the facts like soft snow, blurring the outlines and covering up all the details. The great enemy of clear language is insincerity. When there is a gap between one's real and one's declared aims, one turns as it were instinctively to long words and exhausted idioms, like a cuttlefish squirting out ink. In our age there is no such thing as "keeping out of politics." All issues are political issues, and politics itself is a mass of lies, evasions, folly, hatred and schizophrenia. When the general atmosphere is bad, language must suffer. I should expect to find—this is a guess which I have not sufficient knowledge to verify—that the German, Russian and Italian languages have all deteriorated in the last ten or fifteen years, as a result of dictatorship.

16   But if thought corrupts language, language can also corrupt thought. A bad usage can spread by tradition and imitation, even among people who should and do know better. The debased language that I have been discussing is in some ways very convenient. Phrases like *a not unjustifiable assumption, leaves much to be desired, would serve no good purpose, a consideration which we should do well to bear in mind,* are a continuous temptation, a packet of aspirins always at one's elbow. Look back through this essay, and for certain you will find that I have again and again committed the very faults I am protesting against. By this morning's post I have received a pamphlet dealing with conditions in Germany. The author tells me that he "felt impelled" to write it. I open it at random, and here is almost the first sentence that I see: "[The Allies] have an opportunity not only of achieving a radical transformation of Germany's social and political structure in such a way as to avoid a nationalistic reaction in Germany itself, but at the same time of laying the foundations of a

co-operative and unified Europe." You see, he "feels impelled" to write—feels, presumably, that he has something new to say—and yet his words, like cavalry horses answering the bugle, group themselves automatically into the familiar dreary pattern. This invasion of one's mind by ready-made phrases *(lay the foundations, achieve a radical transformation)* can only be prevented if one is constantly on guard against them, and every such phrase anaesthetizes a portion of one's brain.

17   I said earlier that the decadence of our language is probably curable. Those who deny this would argue, if they produced an argument at all, that language merely reflects existing social conditions, and that we cannot influence its development by any direct tinkering with words and constructions. So far as the general tone or spirit of a language goes, this may be true, but it is not true in detail. Silly words and expressions have often disappeared, not through any evolutionary process but owing to the conscious action of a minority. Two recent examples were *explore every evenue* and *leave no stone unturned,* which were killed by the jeers of a few journalists. There is a long list of flyblown metaphors which could similarly be got rid of if enough people would interest themselves in the job; and it should also be possible to laugh the *not un-* formation of our existence,[3] to reduce the amount of Latin and Greek in the average sentence, to drive out foreign phrases and strayed scientific words, and, in general, to make pretentiousness unfashionable. But all these are minor points. The defence of the English language implies more than this, and perhaps it is best to start by saying that it does *not* imply.

18   To begin with it has nothing to do with archaism, with the salvaging of obsolete words and turns of speech, or with the setting up of a "standard English" which must never be departed from. On the contrary, it is especially concerned with the scrapping of every word or idiom which has outworn its usefulness. It has nothing to do with correct grammar and syntax, which are of no importance so long as one makes one's meaning clear, or with the avoidance of Americanisms, or with having what is called a "good prose style." On the other hand it is not concerned with fake simplicity and the attempt to make written English colloquial. Nor does it even imply in every case preferring the Saxon word to the Latin one, though it does imply using the fewest and shortest words that will cover one's meaning. What is above all needed is to let the meaning choose the word, and not the other way about. In prose, the worst thing one can do with words is to surrender to them. When you think of a concrete object, you think wordlessly, and then, if you want to describe the thing you have been visualizing you probably hunt about till you find the exact words that seem to fit it. When you think of something abstract you are more inclined to use words from the start, and unless you make a conscious effort to prevent it, the existing dialect will come rushing in and do the

---

[3]One can cure oneself of the *non un-*formation by memorizing this sentence: *A not unblack dog was chasing a not unsmall rabbit across a not ungreen field.*

job for you, at the expense of blurring or even changing your meaning. Probably it is better to put off using words as long as possible and get one's meaning as clear as one can through pictures or sensations. Afterwards one can choose—not simply *accept*—the phrase that will best cover the meaning, and then switch round and decide what impression one's words are likely to make on another person. This last effort of the mind cuts out all stale or mixed images, all prefabricated phrases, needless repetitions, and humbug and vagueness generally. But one can often be in doubt about the effect of a word or a phrase, and one needs rules that one can rely on when instinct fails. I think the following rules will cover most cases:

(i) Never use a metaphor, simile or other figure of speech which you are used to seeing in print.
(ii) Never use a long word where a short one will do.
(iii) If it is possible to cut a word out, always cut it out.
(iv) Never use the passive when you can use the active.
(v) Never use a foreign phrase, a scientific word or a jargon word if you can think of an everyday English equivalent.
(vi) Break any of these rules sooner than say anything outright barbarous.

These rules sound elementary, and so they are, but they demand a deep change of attitude in anyone who has grown used to writing in the style now fashionable. One could keep all of them and still write bad English, but one could not write the kind of stuff that I quoted in those five specimens at the beginning of this article.

19   I have not here been considering the literary use of language, but merely language as an instrument for expressing and not for concealing or preventing thought. Stuart Chase and others have come near to claiming that all abstract words are meaningless, and have used this as a pretext for advocating a kind of political quietism. Since you don't know what Fascism is, how can you struggle against Fascism? One need not swallow such absurdities as this, but one ought to recognize that the present political chaos is connected with the decay of language, and that one can probably bring about some improvement by starting at the verbal end. If you simplify your English, you are freed from the worst follies of orthodoxy. You cannot speak any of the necessary dialects, and when you make a stupid remark its stupidity will be obvious, even to yourself. Political language—and with variations this is true of all political parties, from Conservatives to Anarchists—is designed to make lies sound truthful and murder respectable, and to give an appearance of solidity to pure wind. One cannot change this all in a moment, but one can at least change one's own habits, and from time to time one can even, if one jeers loudly enough, send some worn-out and useless phrase—some *jackboot, Achilles' heel, hotbed, melting pot, acid test, veritable inferno* or other lump or verbal refuse—into the dustbin where it belongs.

ACCOMMODATING THE AUDIENCE

In understanding your opposition, you reviewed terminology and issues, but one further question must be answered: Are the audience and the opposition the same?

Sometimes you will present your argument to an audience with opposing views. If the agency with the power to make a decision opposes your request, audience and opposition are the same. Your writing must be sensitive to the demands of that situation as you work to counter arguments without alienating your audience. If an agent is rejecting your insurance application or questioning your expense vouchers or auditing your tax return, you must recognize that the audience is also raising opposing views.

On the other hand, many of your arguments will be addressed to a third party that you hope to convince of the reasonableness of your stand. If you think of the courtroom again, you will see lawyers for the plaintiff (the one who presses a claim), the defendant (the one who refutes the claim), and the audience (a judge and often a jury, too). The plaintiff and defendant rarely address each other; instead, each seeks to convince the audience of the reasonableness of the arguments. Each side is more concerned with the audience's perception of the argument than with the opposition's.

When you review your work, look closely at your audience and your opposition. If they are in fact one and the same, your material and your presentation must accommodate. If the opposition is not the audience, then you can make the same distinction made in the courtroom. In either case, as you review your draft, you must be keenly aware of your audience. Be sure that your material accommodates the expectations of both a neutral and an opposing audience.

Understanding Interests

Your analysis of your audience provides much information about the background and attitude of your audience. Does your presentation use that knowledge? Have you referred to their areas of interest? Have you demonstrated that you are aware of their lifestyles? If you are asking for money, for example, have you explained how it will be spent to benefit this audience?

Evaluating Knowledge

Accommodating your audience also means being aware of their knowledge about your subject. Reviewing your work from the readers' perspective, be sure that you have explained unfamiliar terminology and that you have offered examples relevant to their experience. If you suspect that no one in your audience is familiar with creationism, explain the concept carefully. In addition, examples should be familiar enough that the audience can see your point. Comparing the exploits of a modern-day general to Civil War officer J.E.B. Stuart will be meaningless unless your audience knows something about Stuart. Finally, anticipate the questions this audience might raise and provide reasonable answers. Will they be concerned about money? Will they understand the financing options you are describing? Will they see the comparisons that you are making? Not only will the information strengthen your paper, but supplying detail as your audience becomes aware of a need for explanation will make you look knowledgeable and concerned.

Acknowledging Position

You can also recognize the knowledge of your readers by recognizing their positions. To show that you are aware of their ideas, offer explicit observations like, "We are all concerned about the effect of this development on existing drainage systems," or "This investigation will include all of the employees, part-time and full-time, who have been with the company for at least three years." Such assurances will show your audience that you are interested in their point of view. Making explicit efforts to look at issues from all sides will improve your relationship with your audience; in addition, it will improve your understanding of the subject.

Recognizing Emotions

Because you are working so hard to be reasonable and logical, you might assume that your audience is reflecting thoughtfully on the issues. But if you expect readers to be completely rational in their responses to your ideas, you could be making a mistake. As you consider knowledge and attitudes, you should also be sensitive to the emotional reactions of your readers: their hopes, their angers, and their fears.

Reassuring readers that their emotions are recognized will encourage their acceptance of your ideas. Even if you have no answers for emotional responses, offering written recognition will make your persona seem understanding and credible. Phrasing like, "Sweeping changes like these may initially be met with understandable anger. But careful analysis of the proposition will show. . . ." can defuse anger and encourage readers to look carefully at proposals. Similarly, acknowledging that fear or uncertainty is legitimate will reassure readers that they are respected and important. Your efforts to understand and to acknowledge the emotional reactions of your audience can be as important to your argument as the evidence you bring.

SUMMARY

Writing that seeks to convince the audience requires special consideration of audience and opposition, and careful evaluation of issues, evidence, and terminology. You must be alert to the weaknesses of your case before you present it to an audience.

YOUR TURN

Read Martin Luther King, Jr.'s "Letter from Birmingham Jail," looking for ways in which King acknowledges the audience. Make a list of specific explanations, reassurances, or diction choices that show King understands his audience.

Additional Reading

Letter from Birmingham Jail
Martin Luther King, Jr.
April 16, 1963

Written in the Birmingham, Alabama, jail in 1963, to the eight clergymen named a the beginning of the letter. King had been jailed, along with his supporters, for demonstrating against the segregation of the city's lunch counters.

> *Bishop* C. C. J. Carpenter
> *Bishop* Joseph A. Durick
> *Rabbi* Milton L. Grafman
> *Bishop* Paul Hardin
> *Bishop* Nolan B. Harmon
> *The Rev.* George M. Murray
> *The Rev.* Edward V. Ramage
> *The Rev.* Earl Stallings

My dear Fellow Clergymen,

1   While confined here in the Birmingham City Jail, I came across your recent statement calling our present activities "unwise and untimely." Seldom, if ever, do I pause to answer criticism of my work and ideas. If I sought to answer all of the criticisms that cross my desk, my secretaries would be engaged in little else in the course of the day and I would have no time for constructive work. But since I feel that you are men of

genuine good will and your criticisms are sincerely set forth, I would like to answer your statement in what I hope will be patient and reasonable terms.

2   I think I should give the reason for my being in Birmingham, since you have been influenced by the argument of "outsiders coming in." I have the honor of serving as president of the Southern Christian Leadership Conference, an organization operating in every Southern state with headquarters in Atlanta, Georgia. We have some eighty-five affiliate organizations all across the South—one being the Alabama Christian Movement for Human Rights. Whenever necessary and possible we share staff, educational, and financial resources with our affiliates. Several months ago our local affiliate here in Birmingham invited us to be on call to engage in a nonviolent direct action program if such were deemed necessary. We readily consented and when the hour came we lived up to our promises. So I am here, along with several members of my staff, because we were invited here. I am here because I have basic organizational ties here. Beyond this, I am in Birmingham because injustice is here. Just as the eighth century prophets left their little villages and carried their "thus saith the Lord" far beyond the boundaries of their home town, and just as the Apostle Paul left his little village of Tarsus and carried the gospel of Jesus Christ to practically every hamlet and city of the Graeco-Roman world, I too am compelled to carry the gospel of freedom beyond my particular home town. Like Paul, I must constantly respond to the Macedonian call for aid.

3   Moreover, I am cognizant of the interrelatedness of all communities and states. I cannot sit idly by in Atlanta and not be concerned about what happens in Birmingham. Injustice anywhere is a threat to justice everywhere. We are caught in an inescapable network of mutuality tied in a single garment of destiny. Whatever affects one directly affects all indirectly. Never again can we afford to live with the narrow, provincial "outside agitator" idea. Anyone who lives inside the United States can never be considered an outsider anywhere in this country.

4   You deplore the demonstrations that are presently taking place in Birmingham. But I am sorry that your statement did not express a similar concern for the conditions that brought the demonstrations into being. I am sure that each of you would want to go beyond the superficial social analyst who looks merely at effects, and does not grapple with underlying causes. I would not hesitate to say that it is unfortunate that so-called demonstrations are taking place in Birmingham at this time, but I would say in more emphatic terms that it is even more unfortunate that the white power structure of this city left the Negro community with no other alternative.

5   In any nonviolent campaign there are four basic steps: (1) collection of the facts to determine whether injustices are alive; (2) negotiation; (3) self-purification; and (4) direct action. We have gone through all of these steps in Birmingham. There can be no gainsaying of the fact that racial

injustice engulfs this community. Birmingham is probably the most thoroughly segregated city in the United States. Its ugly record of police brutality is known in every section of this country. Its unjust treatment of Negroes in the courts is a notorious reality. There have been more unsolved bombings of Negro homes and churches in Birmingham than any city in this nation. These are the hard, brutal, and unbelievable facts. On the basis of these conditions Negro leaders sought to negotiate with the city fathers. But the political leaders consistently refused to engage in good faith negotiation.

6

Then came the opportunity last September to talk with some of the leaders of the economic community. In these negotiating sessions certain promises were made by the merchants—such as the promise to remove the humiliating racial signs from the stores. On the basis of these promises Rev. Shuttlesworth and the leaders of the Alabama Christian Movement for Human Rights agreed to call a moratorium on any type of demonstrations. As the weeks and months unfolded we realized that we were the victims of a broken promise. The signs remained. As in so many experiences of the past we were confronted with blasted hopes, and the dark shadow of a deep disappointment settled upon us. So we had no alternative except that of preparing for direct action, whereby we would present our very bodies as a means of laying our case before the conscience of the local and national community. We were not unmindful of the difficulties involved. So we decided to go through a process of self-purification. We started having workshops on nonviolence and repeatedly asked ourselves the questions, "Are you able to accept blows without retaliating?" "Are you able to endure the ordeals of jail?"

7

We decided to set our direct action program around the Easter season, realizing that with the exception of Christmas, this was the largest shopping period of the year. Knowing that a strong economic withdrawal program would be the by-product of direct action, we felt that this was the best time to bring pressure on the merchants for the needed changes. Then it occured to us that the March election was ahead, and so we speedily decided to postpone action until after election day. When we discovered that Mr. Connor was in the run-off, we decided again to postpone action so that the demonstrations could not be used to cloud the issues. At this time we agreed to begin our nonviolent witness the day after the run-off.

8

This reveals that we did not move irresponsibly into direct action. We too wanted to see Mr. Connor defeated; so we went through postponement after postponement to aid in this community need. After this we felt that direct action could be delayed no longer.

9

You may well ask, "Why direct action? Why sit-ins, marches, etc.? Isn't negotiation a better path?" You are exactly right in your call for negotiation. Indeed, this is the purpose of direct action. Nonviolent direct action seeks to create such a crisis and establish such creative tension that a community that has constantly refused to negotiate is forced to confront the issue. It seeks so to dramatize the issue that it can no longer be ignored. I just referred to the creation of tension as a part of the work of the nonviolent resister. This may sound rather shocking. But I must confess that I am not afraid of the word tension. I have earnestly worked and preached against violent tension, but there is a type of constructive nonviolent tension that is necessary for growth. Just as Socrates felt that it was necessary to create a tension in the mind so that individuals could rise from the bondage of myths and half-truths to the unfettered realm of creative analysis and objective appraisal, we must see the need of having nonviolent gadflies to create the kind of tension in society that will help men rise from the dark depths of prejudice and racism to the majestic heights of understanding and brotherhood. So the purpose of the direct action is to create a situation so crisis-packed that it will inevitably open the door to negotiation. We, therefore, concur with you in your call for negotiation. Too long has our beloved Southland been bogged down in the tragic attempt to live in monologue rather than dialogue.

10   One of the basic points in your statement is that our acts are untimely. Some have asked, "Why didn't you give the new administration time to act?" The only answer that I can give to this inquiry is that the new administration must be prodded about as much as the outgoing one before it acts. We will be sadly mistaken if we feel that the election of Mr. Boutwell will bring the millennium to Birmingham. While Mr. Boutwell is much more articulate and gentle than Mr. Connor, they are both segregationists dedicated to the task of maintaining the status quo. The hope I see in Mr. Boutwell is that he will be reasonable enough to see the futility of massive resistance to desegregation. But he will not see this without pressure from the devotees of civil rights. My friends, I must say to you that we have not made a single gain in civil rights without determined legal and nonviolent pressure. History is the long and tragic story of the fact that privileged groups seldom give up their privileges voluntarily. Individuals may see the moral light and voluntarily give up their unjust posture; but as Reinhold Niebuhr has reminded us, groups are more immoral than individuals.

11   We know through painful experience that freedom is never voluntarily given by the oppressor; it must be demanded by the oppressed. Frankly I have never yet engaged in a direct action movement that was "well timed," according to the timetable of those who have not suffered unduly from the disease of segregation. For years now I have heard the word "Wait!" It rings in the ear of every Negro with a piercing familiarity. This "wait" has almost always meant "never." It has been a tranquilizing thalidomide, relieving the emotional stress for a moment, only to give birth to all ill-formed infant of frustration. We must come to see with the distinguished jurist of yesterday that "justice too long delayed is justice denied." We have waited for more than three hundred and forty years for our constitutional and God-given rights. The nations of Asia and Africa are moving with jet-like speed toward the goal of political independence,

and we still creep at horse and buggy pace toward the gaining of a cup of coffee at a lunch counter.

12   I guess it is easy for those who have never felt the stinging darts of segregation to say wait. But when you have seen vicious mobs lynch your mothers and fathers at will and drown your sisters and brothers at whim; when you have seen hate filled policemen curse, kick, brutalize, and even kill your black brothers and sisters with impunity; when you see the vast majority of your twenty million Negro brothers smothering in an air-tight cage of poverty in the midst of an affluent society; when you suddenly find your tongue twisted and your speech stammering as you seek to explain to your six-year-old daughter why she can't go to the public amusement park that has just been advertised on television, and see tears welling up in her little eyes when she is told that Funtown is closed to colored children, and see the depressing clouds of inferiority begin to form in her little mental sky, and see her begin to distort her little personality by unconsciously developing a bitterness toward white people; when you have to concoct an answer for a five-year-old son asking in agonizing pathos: "Daddy, why do white people treat colored people so mean?"; when you take a cross country drive and find it necessary to sleep night after night in the uncomfortable corners of your automobile because no motel will accept you; when you are humiliated day in and day out by nagging signs reading "white" men and "colored"; when your first name becomes "nigger" and your middle name becomes "boy" (however old you are) and your last name becomes "John," and when your wife and mother are never given the respected title "Mrs."; when you are harried by day and haunted by night by the fact that you are a Negro, living constantly at tiptoe stance never quite knowing what to expect next, and plagued with inner fears and outer resentments; when you are forever fighting a degenerating sense of "nobodiness";—then you will understand why we find it difficult to wait. There comes a time when the cup of endurance runs over, and men are no longer willing to be plunged into an abyss of injustice where they experience the bleakness of corroding despair. I hope, sirs, you can understand our legitimate and unavoidable impatience.

13   Your express a great deal of anxiety over our willingness to break laws. This is certainly a legitimate concern. Since we so diligently urge people to obey the Supreme Court's decision of 1954 outlawing segregation in the public schools, it is rather strange and paradoxical to find us consciously breaking laws. One may well ask, "How can you advocate breaking some laws and obeying others?" The answer is found in the fact that there are two types of laws. There are *just* laws and there are *unjust* laws. I would be the first to advocate obeying just laws. One has not only a legal but moral responsibility to obey just laws. Conversely, one has a moral responsibility to disobey unjust laws. I would agree with Saint Augustine that "An unjust law is no law at all."

14   Now what is the difference between the two? How does one determine when a law is just or unjust? A just law is a man-made code that squares with the moral law or the law of God. An unjust law is a code that is out of harmony with the moral law. To put it in the terms of Saint Thomas Aquinas, an unjust law is human law that is not rooted in eternal and natural law. Any law that uplifts human personality is just. Any law that degrades human personality is unjust. All segregation statutes are unjust because segregation distorts the soul and damages the personality. It gives the segregator a false sense of superiority and the segregated a false sense of inferiority. To use the words of Martin Buber, the great Jewish philosopher, segregation substitues an "I-it" relationship for the "I-thou" relationship, and ends up relegating persons to the status of things. So segregation is not only politically, economically, and sociologically unsound, but it is morally wrong and sinful. Paul Tillich has said that sin is separation. Isn't segregation an existential expression of man's tragic separation, an expression of his awful estrangement, his terrible sinfulness? So I can urge men to obey the 1954 decision of the Supreme Court because it is morally right, and I can urge them to disobey segregation ordinances because they are morally wrong.

15   Let us turn to a more concrete example of just and unjust laws. An unjust law is a code that a majority inflicts on a minority that is not binding on itself. This is *difference* made legal. On the other hand a just law is a code that a majority compels a minority to follow that it is willing to follow itself. This is *sameness* made legal.

16   Let me give another explanation. An unjust law is a code inflicted upon a minority which that minority had no part in enacting or creating because they did not have the unhampered right to vote. Who can say the legislature of Alabama which set up the segregation laws was democratically elected? Throughout the state of Alabama all types of conniving methods are used to prevent Negroes from becoming registered voters and there are some counties without a single Negro registered to vote despite the fact that the Negro constitutes a majority of the population. Can any law set up in such a state be considered democratically structured?

17   These are just a few examples of unjust and just laws. There are some instances when a law is just on its face but unjust in its application. For instance, I was arrested Friday on a charge of parading without a permit. Now there is nothing wrong with an ordinance which requires a permit for a parade, but when the ordinance is used to preserve segregation and to deny citizens the First Amendment privilege of peaceful assembly and peaceful protest, then it becomes unjust.

18   I hope you can see the distinction I am trying to point out. In no sense do I advocate evading or defying the law as the rabid segregationist would do. This would lead to anarchy. One who breaks an unjust law must do it *openly, lovingly* (not hatefully as the white mothers did in New

Orleans when they were seen on television screaming "nigger, nigger, nigger") and with a willingness to accept the penalty. I submit that an individual who breaks a law that conscience tells him is unjust, and willingly accepts the penalty by staying in jail to arouse the conscience of the community over its injustice, is in reality expressing the very highest respect for law.

19   Of course there is nothing new about this kind of civil disobedience. It was seen sublimely in the refusal of Shadrach, Meshach, and Abednego to obey the laws of Nebuchadnezzar because a higher moral law was involved. It was practiced superbly by the early Christians who were willing to face hungry lions and the excruciating pain of chopping blocks, before submitting to certain unjust laws of the Roman Empire. To a degree academic freedom is a reality today because Socrates practiced civil disobedience.

20   We can never forget that everything Hitler did in Germany was "legal" and everything the Hungarian freedom fighters did in Hungary was "illegal." It was "illegal" to aid and comfort a Jew in Hitler's Germany. But I am sure that, if I had lived in Germany during that time, I would have aided and comforted my Jewish brothers even though it was illegal. If I lived in a Communist country today where certain principles dear to the Christian faith are suppressed, I believe I would openly advocate disobeying these antireligious laws.

21   I must make two honest confessions to you, my Christian and Jewish brothers. First I must confess that over the last few years I have been gravely disappointed with the white moderate. I have almost reached the regrettable conclusion that the Negroes' great stumbling block in the stride toward freedom is not the White Citizens' "Counciler" or the Ku Klux Klanner, but the white moderate who is more devoted to "order" than to justice; who prefers a negative peace which is the absence of tension to a positive peace which is the presence of justice; who constantly says "I agree with you in the goal you seek, but I can't agree with your methods of direct action"; who paternalistically feels that he can set the time-table for another man's freedom; who lives by the myth of time and who constantly advises the Negro to wait until a "more convenient season." Shallow understanding from people of good will is more frustrating than absolute misunderstanding from people of ill will. Lukewarm acceptance is much more bewildering than outright rejection.

22   I had hoped that the white moderate would understand that law and order exist for the purpose of establishing justice, and that when they fail to do this they become the dangerously structured dams that block the flow of social progress. I had hoped that the white moderate would understand that the present tension in the South is merely a necessary phase of the transition from an obnoxious negative peace, where the Negro passively accepted his unjust plight, to a substance-filled positive peace, where all men will respect the dignity and worth of human personality. Actually, we who engage in nonviolent direct action are not the creators

of tension. We merely bring to the surface the hidden tension that is already alive. We bring it out in the open where it can be seen and dealt with. Like a boil that can never be cured as long as it is covered up but must be opened with all its pus-flowing ugliness to the natural medicines of air and light, injustice must likewise be exposed, with all of the tension its exposing creates, to the light of human conscience and the air of national opinion before it can be cured.

23   In your statement you asserted that our actions, even though peaceful, must be condemned because they precipitate violence. But can this assertion be logically made? Isn't this like condemning the robbed man because his possession of money precipitated the evil act of robbery? Isn't this like condemning Socrates because his unswerving commitment to truth and his philosophical delvings precipitated the misguided popular mind to make him drink the hemlock? Isn't this like condemning Jesus because His unique God consciousness and never-ceasing devotion to His will precipitated the evil act of crucifixion? We must come to see, as federal courts have consistently affirmed, that it is immoral to urge an individual to withdraw his efforts to gain his basic constitutional rights because the quest precipitates violence. Society must protect the robbed and punish the robber.

24   I had also hoped that the white moderate would reject the myth of time. I received a letter this morning from a white brother in Texas which said: "All Christians know that the colored people will receive equal rights eventually, but is it possible that you are in too great of a religious hurry? It has taken Christianity almost 2000 years to accomplish what it has. The teachings of Christ take time to come to earth." All that is said here grows out of a tragic misconception of time. It is the strangely irrational notion that there is something in the very flow of time that will inevitably cure all ills. Actually time is neutral. It can be used either destructively or constructively. I am coming to feel that the people of ill will have used time much more effectively than the people of good will. We will have to repent in this generation not merely for the vitriolic words and actions of the bad people, but for the appalling silence of the good people. We must come to see that human progress never rolls in on wheels of inevitability. It comes through the tireless efforts and persistent work of men willing to be co-workers with God, and without this hard work time itself becomes an ally of the forces of social stagnation.

25   We must use time creatively, and forever realize that the time is always ripe to do right. Now is the time to make real the promise of democracy, and transform our pending national elegy into a creative psalm of brotherhood. Now is the time to lift our national policy from the quicksand of racial injustice to the solid rock of human dignity.

26   You spoke of our activity in Birmingham as extreme. At first I was rather disappointed that fellow clergymen would see my non-violent efforts as those of the extremist. I started thinking about the fact that I stand in the middle of two opposing forces in the Negro community. One

is a force of complacency made up of Negroes who, as a result of long years of oppression, have been so completely drained of self-respect and a sense of "somebodiness" that they have adjusted to segregation, and of a few Negroes in the middle class who, because of a degree of academic and economic security, and because at points they profit by segregation, have unconsciously become insensitive to the problems of the masses. The other force is one of bitterness and hatred and comes perilously close to advocating violence. It is expressed in the various black nationalist groups that are springing up over the nation, the largest and best known being Elijah Muhammad's Muslim movement. This movement is nourished by the contemporary frustration over the continued existence of racial discrimination. It is made up of people who have lost faith in America, who have absolutely repudiated Christianity, and who have concluded that the white man is an incurable "devil." I have tried to stand between these two forces saying that we need not follow the "do-nothingism" of the complacent or the hatred and despair of the black nationalist. There is the more excellent way of love and nonviolent protest. I'm grateful to God that, through the Negro church, the dimension of non-violence entered our struggle. If this philosophy had not emerged I am convinced that by now many streets of the South would be flowing with floods of blood. And I am further convinced that if our white brothers dismiss us as "rabble rousers" and "outside agitators"—those of us who are working through the channels of nonviolent direct action—and refuse to support our nonviolent efforts, millions of Negroes, out of frustration and despair, will seek solace and security in black nationalist ideologies, a development that will lead inevitably to a frightening racial nightmare.

27   Oppressed people cannot remain oppressed forever. The urge for freedom will eventually come. This is what has happened to the American Negro. Something within has reminded him of his birthright of freedom; something without has reminded him that he can gain it. Consciously and unconsciously, he has been swept in by what the Germans call the *Zeitgeist*,[1] and with his black brothers of Africa, and his brown and yellow brothers of Asia, South America, and the Caribbean, he is moving with a sense of cosmic urgency toward the promised land of racial justice. Recognizing this vital urge that has engulfed the Negro community, one should readily understand public demonstrations. The Negro has many pent-up resentments and latent frustrations. He has to get them out. So let him march sometime; let him have his prayer pilgrimages to the city hall; understand why he must have sit-ins and freedom rides. If his repressed emotions do not come out in these nonviolent ways, they will come out in ominous expressions of violence. This is not a threat; it is a fact of history. So I have not said to my people, "Get rid of your discontent." But I have tried to say that this normal and healthy discontent can be channeled through the creative outlet of nonviolent direct action. Now this approach

[1]The predominant outlook or spirit of a time or a generation.

is being dismissed as extremist. I must admit that I was initially disappointed in being so categorized.

28   But as I continued to think about the matter I gradually gained a bit of satisfaction from being considered an extremist. Was not Jesus an extremist in love? "Love your enemies, bless them that curse you, pray for them that despitefully use you." Was not Amos an extremist for justice—"Let justice roll down like waters and righteousness like a mighty stream." Was not Paul an extremist for the gospel of Jesus Christ—"I bear in my body the marks of the Lord Jesus." Was not Martin Luther an extremist—"Here I stand; I can do none other so help me God." Was not John Bunyan an extremist—"I will stay in jail to the end of my days before I make a butchery of my conscience." Was not Abraham Lincoln an extremist—"This nation cannot survive half slave and half free." Was not Thomas Jefferson an extremist—"We hold these truths to be self evident that all men are created equal." So the question is not whether we will be extremist but what kind of extremist will we be. Will we be extremists for hate or will we be extremists for love? Will we be extremists for the preservation of injustice—or will we be extremists for the cause of justice? In that dramatic scene on Calvary's hill three men were crucified. We must never forget that all three were crucified for the same crime—the crime of extremism. Two were extremists for immorality, and thus fell below their environment. The other, Jesus Christ, was an extremist for love, truth, and goodness, and thereby rose above His environment. So, after all, maybe the South, the nation, and the world are in dire need of creative extremists.

29   I had hoped that the white moderate would see this. Maybe I was too optimistic. Maybe I expected too much. I guess I should have realized that few members of a race that has oppressed another race can understand or appreciate the deep groans and passionate yearnings of those that have been oppressed, and still fewer have the vision to see that injustice must be rooted out by strong, persistent, and determined action. I am thankful, however, that some of our white brothers have grasped the meaning of this social revolution and committed themselves to it. They are still all too small in quantity, but they are big in quality. Some like Ralph McGill, Lillian Smith, Harry Golden, and James Dabbs have written about our struggle in eloquent, prophetic, and understanding terms. Others have marched with us down nameless streets of the South. They have languished in filthy, roach-infested jails, suffering the abuse and brutality of angry policemen who see them as "dirty nigger lovers." They, unlike so many of their moderate brothers and sisters, have recognized the urgency of the moment and sensed the need for powerful "action" antidotes to combat the disease of segregation.

30   Let me rush on to mention my other disappointment. I have been so greatly disappointed with the white Church and its leadership. Of course there are some notable exceptions. I am not unmindful of the fact that each of you has taken some significant stands on this issue. I commend

you, Rev. Stallings, for your Christian stand on this past Sunday, in welcoming Negroes to your worship service on a nonsegregated basis. I commend the Catholic leaders of this state for integrating Springhill College several years ago.

31   But despite these notable exceptions I must honestly reiterate that I have been disappointed with the Church. I do not say that as one of those negative critics who can always find something wrong with the Church. I say it as a minister of the gospel, who loves the Church; who was nurtured in its bosom; who has been sustained by its spiritual blessings and who will remain true to it as long as the cord of life shall lengthen.

32   I had the strange feeling when I was suddenly catapulted into the leadership of the bus protest in Montgomery[2] several years ago that we would have the support of the white Church. I felt that the white ministers, priests, and rabbis of the South would be some of our strongest allies. Instead, some have been outright opponents, refusing to understand the freedom movement and misrepresenting its leaders; all too many others have been more cautious than courageous and have remained silent behind the anesthetizing security of stained glass windows.

33   In spite of my shattered dreams of the past, I cam to Birmingham with the hope that the white religious leadership of the community would see the justice of our cause and, with deep moral concern, serve as the channel through which our just grievances could get to the power structure. I had hoped that each of you would understand. But again I have been disappointed.

34   I have heard numerous religious leaders of the South call upon their worshippers to comply with a desegregation decision because it is the law, but I have longed to hear white ministers say follow this decree because integration is morally right and the Negro is your brother. In the midst of blatant injustices inflicted upon the Negro, I have watched white churches stand on the sideline and merely mouth pious irrelevancies and sanctimonious trivialities. In the midst of a mighty struggle to rid our nation of racial and economic injustice, I have heard so many ministers say, "Those are social issues with which the Gospel has no real concern," and I have watched so many churches commit themselves to a completely other-worldly religion which made a strange distinction between body and soul, the sacred and the secular.

35   So here we are moving toward the exit of the twentieth century with a religious community largely adjusted to the status quo, standing as a tail light behind other community agencies rather than a headlight leading men to higher levels of justice.

36   I have travelled the length and breadth of Alabama, Mississippi, and all the other Southern states. On sweltering summer days and crisp autumn mornings I have looked at her beautiful churches with their

[2]In 1955–56 King led a boycott by Montgomery, Alabama blacks against the city's segregated buses, advocating a policy of passive resistance to segregation. The desegregation of Montgomery buses in 1956 was a major victory for the civil rights movement.

spires pointing heavenward. I have beheld the impressive outlay of her massive religious education buildings. Over and over again I have found myself asking: "Who worships here? Who is their God? Where are their voices when the lips of Governor Barnett[3] dripped with words of interposition and nullification? Where were they when Governor Wallace[4] gave the clarion call for defiance and hatred? Where were their voices of support when tired, bruised, and weary Negro men and women decided to rise from the dark dungeons of complacency to the bright hills of creative protest?"

37   Yes, these questions are still in my mind. In deep disappointment, I have wept over the laxity of the Church. But be assured that my tears have been tears of love. There can be no deep disappointment where there is not deep love. Yes, I love the Church; I love her sacred walls. How could I do otherwise? I am in the rather unique position of being the son, the grandson, and the great grandson of preachers. Yes, I see the Church as the body of Christ. But, oh! How we have blemished and scarred that body through social neglect and fear of being nonconformist.

38   There was a time when the Church was very powerful. It was during that period when the early Christians rejoiced when they were deemed worthy to suffer for what they believed. In those days the Church was not merely a thermometer that recorded the ideas and principles of popular opinion; it was a thermostat that transformed the mores of society. Wherever the early Christians entered a town the power structure got disturbed and immediately sought to convict them for being "disturbers of the peace" and "outside agitators." But they went on with the conviction that they were a "colony of heaven" and had to obey God rather than man. They were small in number but big in commitment. They were too God-intoxicated to be "astronomically intimidated." They brought an end to such ancient evils as infanticide and gladiatorial contest.

39   Things are different now. The contemporary Church is so often a weak, ineffectual voice with an uncertain sound. It is so often the arch-supporter of the status quo. Far from being disturbed by the presence of the Church, the power structure of the average community is consoled by the Church's silent and often vocal sanction of things as they are.

40   But the judgment of God is upon the Church as never before. If the Church of today does not recapture the sacrificial spirit of the early Church, it will lose its authentic ring, forfeit the loyalty of millions, and be dismissed as an irrelevant social club with no meaning for the twentieth century. I am meeting young people every day whose disappointment with the Church has risen to outright disgust.

41   Maybe again I have been too optimistic. Is organized religion too inextricably bound to the status quo to save our nation and the world? Maybe

[3]Ross Barnett, governor of Mississippi, in 1962 ordered resistance to the registration of a black student, James Meredith, at the University of Mississippi.

[4]George Wallace, governor of Alabama, stood in a doorway of the University of Alabama in a symbolic effort to block the registration of two black students in 1963.

I must turn my faith to the inner spiritual Church, the church within the Church, as the true *ecclesia*[5] and the hope of the world. But again I am thankful to God that some noble souls from the ranks of organized religion have broken loose from the paralyzing chains of conformity and joined us as active partners in the struggle for freedom. They have left their secure congregations and walked the streets of Albany, Georgia, with us. They have gone through the highways of the South on torturous rides for freedom. Yes, they have gone to jail with us. Some have been kicked out of their churches and lost the support of their bishops and fellow ministers. But they have gone with the faith that right defeated is stronger than evil triumphant. These men have been the leaven in the lump of the race. Their witness has been the spiritual salt that has preserved the true meaning of the Gospel in these troubled times. They have carved a tunnel of hope through the dark mountain of disappointment.

42

I hope the Church as a whole will meet the challenge of this decisive hour. But even if the Church does not come to the aid of justice, I have no despair about the future. I have no fear about the outcome of our struggle in Birmingham, even if our motives are presently misunderstood. We will reach the goal of freedom in Birmingham and all over the nation, because the goal of America is freedom. Abused and scorned though we may be, our destiny is tied up with the destiny of America. Before the pilgrims landed at Plymouth, we were here. Before the pen of Jefferson etched across the pages of history the majestic words of the Declaration of Independence, we were here. For more than two centuries our foreparents labored in this country without wages; they made cotton "king"; and they built the homes of their masters in the midst of brutal injustice and shameful humiliation—and yet out of a bottomless vitality they continued to thrive and develop. If the inexpressible cruelties of slavery could not stop us, the opposition we now face will surely fail. We will win our freedom because the sacred heritage of our nation and the eternal will of God are embodied in our echoing demands.

43

I must close now. But before closing I am impelled to mention one other point in your statement that troubled me profoundly. You warmly commended the Birmingham police force for keeping "order" and "preventing violence." I don't believe you would have so warmly commended the police force if you had seen its angry violent dogs literally biting six unarmed, nonviolent Negroes. I don't believe you would so quickly commend the policemen if you would observe their ugly and inhuman treatment of Negroes here in the city jail; if you would watch them push and curse old Negro women and young Negro girls; if you would see them slap and kick old Negro men and young Negro boys; if you will observe them, as they did on two occasions, refuse to give us food because we wanted to sing our grace together. I'm sorry that I can't join you in your praise for the police department.

[5] "assembly of the people"

44   It is true that they have been rather disciplined in their public handling of the demonstrators. In this sense they have been rather publicly "nonviolent." But for what purpose? To preserve the evil system of segregation. Over the last few years I have consistently preached that nonviolence demands that the means we use must be as pure as the ends we seek. So I have tried to make it clear that it is wrong to use immoral means to attain moral ends. But now I must affirm that it is just as wrong, or even more so, to use moral means to preserve immoral ends. Maybe Mr. Connor and his policemen have been rather publicly nonviolent, as Chief Prichett was in Albany, Georgia, but they have used the moral means of nonviolence to maintain the immoral end of flagrant racial injustice. T.S. Eliot has said that there is no greater treason than to do the right deed for the wrong reason.

45   I wish you had commended the Negro sit-inners and demonstrators of Birmingham for their sublime courage, their willingness to suffer, and their amazing discipline in the midst of the most inhuman provocation. One day the South will recognize its real heroes. They will be the James Merediths, courageously and with a majestic sense of purpose, facing jeering and hostile mobs and the agonizing loneliness that characterizes the life of the pioneer. They will be old, oppressed, battered Negro women, symbolized in a seventy-two year old woman of Montgomery, Alabama, who rose up with a sense of dignity and with her people decided not to ride the segregated buses, and responded to one who inquired about her tiredness with ungrammatical profundity: "My feets is tired, but my soul is rested." They will be young high school and college students, young ministers of the gospel and a host of the elders, courageously and nonviolently sitting in at lunch counters and willingly going to jail for conscience sake. One day the South will know that when these disinherited children of God sat down at lunch counters they were in reality standing up for the best in the American dream and the most sacred values in our Judeo-Christian heritage, and thus carrying our whole nation back to great wells of democracy which were dug deep by the founding fathers in the formulation of the Constitution and the Declaration of Independence.

46   Never before have I written a letter this long (or should I say a book?). I'm afraid that it is much too long to take your precious time. I can assure you that it would have been much shorter if I had been writing from a comfortable desk, but what else is there to do when you are alone for days in the dull monotony of a narrow jail cell other than write long letters, think strange thoughts, and pray long prayers?

47   If I have said anything in this letter that is an overstatement of the truth and is indicative of an unreasonable impatience, I beg you to forgive me. If I have said anything in this letter that is an understatement of the truth and is indicative of my having a patience that makes me patient with anything less than brotherhood, I beg God to forgive me.

48   I hope this letter finds you strong in the faith. I also hope that circumstances will soon make it possible for me to meet each of you, not as an

integrationist or a civil rights leader, but as a fellow clergyman and a Christian brother. Let us all hope that the dark clouds of racial prejudice will soon pass away and the deep fog of misunderstanding will be lifted from our fear-drenched communities and in some not too distant tomorrow the radiant stars of love and brotherhood will shine over our great nation with all of their scintillating beauty.

Yours for the cause of
Peace and Brotherhood

MARTIN LUTHER KING, JR.

Recreating Experience

Recreating experience is a method, not a purpose. You can use a vivid scene or incident to reach your readers' imaginations, to give them information, or to convince them to accept your ideas.

When you recreate experiences for your readers, you do so for any number of reasons. If you want to involve your readers imaginatively—to invite them to share the emotions you associate with a particular person or place or incident—recreating your subject is good strategy. But recreating experience is also an effective way to give information. For example, you can explain to your readers the options available to a pregnant teenager, or you can frame your presentation of options by telling the story of one young woman who faces the problem and explores her choices. Television docudramas often provide information about a subject by showing realistic characters who must cope with problems like Alzheimer's disease, AIDS, or mental illness. Sometimes such recreations are used to move the audience to certain actions or attitudes: support, compassion, financial aid. The purposes can be varied; the common denominator is the strategy: the recreation of experience. When you decide that your audience will respond to such an approach, the techniques in this chapter will help you to improve your presentation.

DESCRIBING

One of the qualities of vivid writing is that it does not merely tell the audience about a subject—instead, it works to show the readers what scenes and characters are like. You will use such descriptions when you want your readers to share a moment or a scene, when you want them to laugh or to empathize or even to mourn with you. Description is also an effective tool when you want to paint vivid scenes for readers to increase their understanding or to encourage change in their attitudes or behavior. Regardless of your purpose, description should create a sensory impression for your readers—to enable them to see, hear, taste, smell, or touch the subject you are describing. It may also be used to convey thoughts, feelings, impressions, and states of mind.

Helpful Strategies

The heart of description is concrete detail—that is, detail that can be known through sensory experience and that produces images in your readers' minds. A general guide for deciding how much detail to include is that important matters are given more space than less important ones. Bear in mind, too, that most beginning writers have a dangerous tendency to give too little detail, expecting the readers to fill in what is left unsaid. Notice how the details below help you to see the character and the setting:

Describing People
This example describes a person as she usually appeared. Sometimes it is useful to describe someone as she appeared on a particular occasion.

She was about five feet nine inches tall and must have weighed at least 195 pounds. Her eyes were beady and very suspicious, her nose absurdly tiny for such a broad face. The corners of her mouth dipped in a perpetual frown, and her normal speaking voice was a low hiss. Her figure resembled a German tank on stilts—large and shapeless, with skinny, stick-shaped legs and big, long, flat feet.

Here direction is not so important. The focus is not on the arrangement of the furnishings but on their bizarre character.

His twelve feet by five feet room was originally planned to be a closet. The furniture consists of a sofa with three pillows and a twelve inch portable TV that refuses to work. Two hundred sixty beer cans are piled on top of one another to form a pyramid running the entire width of the room. A dozen mobiles made from popsicle sticks and empty six-pack cartons hang from the ceiling.

Describing Thoughts
The writer used this description because it was an *inaccurate* depiction of college life—that is, because it permitted her to show (later) how mistaken she had been.

Before I entered college, my thoughts of college life were rather stereotyped—cobblestone paths; tall, dark, suave, handsome men speeding about in little red sports cars; distinguished professors graying at the temples, dressed in tweed, puffing on pipes, and speaking polysyllabically.

When you offer physical description of a person or place, consider what your audience already knows. The search party seeking a missing child may need a detailed physical description, but if you are describing a person or place that the readers know be sure to focus on images or details that offer something new. Why repeat that your best friend has brown hair? Is there something unique about her hair? Can you offer a vivid comparison to help the audience really see her hair? If physical details are obvious or well-known, would your time be better spent describing her weird sense of humor or her penchant for collecting used toothpicks?

YOUR TURN

When you practice drawing vivid verbal pictures, remember that it is easier to edit excess detail than it is to add more. So, experiment with sensory images—describe each subject below with details that appeal to sight, sound, taste, touch, and smell. You can ask the critical voice to choose the best images later. Write a brief description of:

a. a very peaceful place
b. an eccentric but harmless person
c. a place of unusual activity and confusion (for example, the team locker room after an important win, or the dressing room between acts of the college play or your household on a typical morning)
d. how you feel when you have to go to the doctor or dentist (You may speak about how you always feel or how you felt on a particular occasion.)

NARRATING

At the center of a narrative is a story—a real-life character or characters involved in some kind of actual incident. While many narratives follow chronological order, it is also possible to present the events without adhering to a strict time line. You may vary the sequence with flashbacks, leaps into the future, or presentations of simultaneous occurrences. The narrative may span a few moments (an assassination, for example) or several decades (one man's rise toward political power).

What does not vary in narratives is the immediacy of the story. We are discussing non-fiction narratives, of course, but you will still present characters involved in incidents. (If you are presenting information in chronological order but do not have characters involved, see the section in Chapter 11, "Tracing.") First-person narratives feature you, your family and your friends, while other narratives might present scientists researching a vaccine for the AIDS virus or the governor hearing last-minute appeals from death-row inmates or an aborigine from the Australian outback setting up a temporary shelter.

Narratives are a logical choice when you want your readers to get involved in an incident. Most jokes are told using narrative techniques, and your amusing or frightening account of a wild ride through the mountains also uses narrative. But don't limit the technique to writing that invites the reader to share an experience. You can also use narrative to inform the readers of a process by showing a specific person appealing a traffic ticket or buying a car. You might narrate the experience of a victim whose attacker was freed to argue for more stringent penalties for assault, or you might narrate the story of a now-homeless family's eviction to encourage your audience to support a particular charity. In each case, the narrative provides characters who can be loved or hated by the audience, and it shows those characters involved in some incident that has a natural stopping point. Even a continuing story, such as research still in progress, has such stopping points (for example, a successful application for a grant, or a line of research that is proven faulty and abandoned). As you develop a narrative, keep two things in mind:

1. Include details to recreate the experience for the readers. Select details carefully, omitting those that do not contribute to your intended effect. So, while it may be true that Uncle Harry's youngest son was killed in an automobile accident, such information should not be included if your story about Uncle Harry is intended to be light-hearted amusement.

2. Include a climactic moment or "high point" when conflict is resolved or understanding is reached. Since the composition builds toward this climactic moment, the narrative should end shortly after it is reached.

Helpful Strategies

Since the bare bones of a story are rarely sufficient to support a paper, narratives usually involve other techniques like dialogues and descriptions. You can make your narratives more effective by practicing these techniques, and you can also use strategies that many professional writers use in their work. Here are five:

1. Make a chronological list of every incident. With the list on paper, you can make clearer judgments about the importance of events and about possible variations in the time line. You will also allow your creative voice to generate material about each event without the burden of ordering it sequentially. A time line that puts the earliest event at the far left and the most recent at the far right can also help you to see the sequence clearly.

2. Get into the narrative quickly. If you are unsure of the best place to begin, it is tempting to start at a point well before the actual incident. Note that professional writers waste no time getting the narrative under way. An amateur writing about the time he was on a small pleasure craft and got caught in an ocean storm, for example, might recount two weeks of preparations for the trip. By the time he'd get around to the experience of riding out the storm, he'd be several hundred words into the composition.

A professional, in contrast, might begin like this: "The sky had suddenly grown ominous and the swells began to toss the boat maliciously. . . ." If prior events were worth including, he would work them in later in a flashback sentence like this: "When we had planned the trip two weeks earlier, we'd never realized the danger of a summer storm, so we were unprepared for what was about to happen." Even third-person narratives of historical events can begin with a dramatic moment and establish background through flashbacks.

> When King Henry VIII renounced the Catholic Church in 1534 and established himself as the head of the Church of England, his overwhelming desire to legitimize a relationship that might produce a son was clear. The irony of Henry's abolition of English Catholicism should not be lost; less than twenty years before, Henry had refused to support the Protestant Reformation and in 1517 was called "the Defender of the Faith" by the Pope.

3. Use flashbacks with precision. Flashbacks will strengthen your narrative when you use them to contrast the present with an earlier state or to suggest causal connections. Be sure to cue the audience that you are tampering with chronological order; transitions will not only identify the jump but can also show its logical connection to the present. Some sample connectors:

> As she examined the microbes on the latest slide, Dr. Elston remembered where she had seen that pattern before. Three years earlier, while working on the epidemic in Philadelphia, she had first encountered. . . .

> As I stared into his hate-twisted face, I realized that he had stored every slight, every insult, from the last few years. And I remembered the moment when our relationship first began to crumble. . . .

> Such decisions were not easily made. The cold realities of political office had not yet removed the idealism that fired his early campaign, and he often thought of his younger self, a man who. . . .

As appealing as flashbacks can be, though, be warned. Over-used, they become tiresome and irritating. Don't fall for the trap of sticking in a flashback just because you forgot to say something earlier.

4. Pace the narrative according to the importance of the moments by giving each part of the experience the space it deserves, no more and no less. It is not unusual in an effective narrative treatment of, say, seven paragraphs to find one paragraph skimming the events of several days, and two or three paragraphs detailing the events of a single hour. A general rule is to reserve detailed descriptions and dialogue for the more significant moments in the story.

5. End the narrative quickly and naturally. Once you have presented the climactic moment of the experience or situation, you will be writing on borrowed time. Your readers will know that the story is

essentially over and will therefore be expecting you to end the composition quickly. Don't be tempted to add several paragraphs of interpretation. If the narrative isn't clear, your commentary won't substitute for careful revision.

Devise a brief and graceful closing. In a narrative about the final sickness of a loved one, that closing might be as simple as "Early on the morning of July 24, my sister died." If you feel it important to include the significance of her death to you, you might add another sentence, such as "I have been told that time eases sorrow, but after four years I still find myself thinking that I must call Marian, and the realization that I cannot brings back a pain that is as sharp as though she had died last week."

Y O U R   T U R N

1. Look through newspapers and magazines to find information presented using narrative techniques. Write a short analysis of the sample that

    a. identifies it as writing that intends to inform or persuade or involve the audience,
    b. identifies the character(s) in the narrative, and
    c. identifies the time span of the narrative.

2. Practice your own narrative technique by writing brief accounts of dramatic moments. Be sure to use specific characters throughout the incident.

    a. Write a narrative account of the strangest experience you've ever had.
    b. Write a narrative account of the first fight you had as a child.
    c. Write a narrative account of a current event (local, state, national, or international level).

USING DIALOGUE

Dialogue is the technique used to recreate conversation. It is an especially effective way of conveying a sense of reality and immediacy. Nevertheless, it should be used sparingly, because it takes up more space than other techniques and because it can wear on readers' patience if it is extended unreasonably or includes material that is not relevant. Be sure to use dialogue in your compositions only when it will make a positive contribution. In addition, be sure to compress it as much as you can by eliminating nonessential comments or relegating them to brief explanatory passages.

It is conventional to begin a new paragraph with every change of speaker in dialogue. This approach enables you to eliminate unnecessary designations of speaker. In using it, however, remember that your readers will expect a change of paragraph in the dialogue to signal a change of speaker, and any lapse of consistency on your part will confuse them and undermine the effectiveness of your writing. Here is an example of effective dialogue:

> The secretary gave me a vacant half-smile and said, "The dean will not be able to see you now."
>
> "But I had an appointment."
>
> "Something important came up. I'll reschedule you for tomorrow."
>
> I decided to try the forceful approach. "Look, I've been waiting to see him for a week. That's long enough. I want to see him today."
>
> She gave me a long, withering look and then said, matter-of-factly, "He's free at 11 A.M. and 2 P.M. tomorrow. Which time shall I put you down for?"
>
> "I guess 2 P.M. will be OK."
>
> As I rode down on the elevator, I decided that my forceful approach still needed work.

Y O U R T U R N

Practice this technique by writing short dialogues, punctuated and paragraphed carefully, for each of the following situations:

    a. a disagreement you had with someone
    b. a conversation in which someone revealed a secret to you
    c. an unusual or otherwise interesting conversation you heard two other people engage in

"But You Promised," told here by Iron-Eyes Cody, makes a dramatic point by involving the readers in a situation. Cody uses description, narrative, and dialogue to recreate an event for the readers. As you read, consider whether these strategies are effective. Does the dialogue sound "real" to your ears? Does the narrative move the action at an appropriate pace? Is the description sufficient to frame the story, or is it excessive, slowing the pace of the story to a tedious crawl?

Additional Reading

"But You Promised"
Condensed from *Guideposts*
Iron Eyes Cody

1   As an actor in Hollywood films, I have played many American Indian roles—warrior, medicine man, chief. And in a TV spot for the Keep America Beautiful campaign, I was an Indian drifting alone in a canoe. As I saw how our waters were being polluted, a single tear rolled down my cheek, telling the whole story. Now I have another story to tell, a legend I heard in my youth.

2   Many years ago, Indian braves would go away in solitude to prepare for manhood. One hiked into a beautiful valley, green with trees, bright with flowers. There, as he looked up at the surrounding mountains, he noticed one rugged peak, capped with dazzling snow.

3   *I will test myself against that mountain*, he thought. He put on his buffalo-hide shirt, threw his blanket over his shoulders and set off to climb the pinnacle.

4   When he reached the top, he stood on the rim of the world. He could see forever, and his heart swelled with pride. Then he heart a rustle at his feet. Looking down, he saw a snake. Before he could move, the snake spoke.

5   "I am about to die," said the snake. "It is too cold for me up here, and there is no food. Put me under your shirt and take me down to the valley."

6   "No," said the youth. "I know your kind. You are a rattlesnake. If I pick you up you will bite and your bite will kill me."

7   "Not so," said the snake. "I will treat you differently. If you do this for me, I will not harm you."

8   The youth resisted awhile, but this was a very persuasive snake. At last the youth tucked it under his shirt and carried it down to the valley. There he laid it down gently. Suddenly the snake coiled, rattled and leaped, biting him on the leg.

9   "But you promised—" cried the youth.

10   "You knew what I was when you picked me up," said the snake as it slithered away.

11   And now, wherever I go, I tell that story to young people who might be tempted by drugs. Remember the words of the snake: "You knew what I was when you picked me up."

DEFINING FIGURATIVELY

Figurative definition differs from literal definition (see Chapter 11) in that it deals with subjective, rather than objective, meaning. While the literal definition of a word does not change from person to person, your figurative definition conveys your impression of something and thus may be completely different from someone else's. Such a definition often uses figures of speech to suggest a creative comparison to something essentially unlike the object but sharing some quality (for example, "His car was his pampered baby, nurtured and sheltered and exhibited with great pride—when he dared to bring it out."). Contrast the literal definition of "concentration camp"—"a prisonlike place where people are incarcerated, usually without due process of law"—with its meaning to people who lost their loved ones in such a camp. To such people, a concentration camp is a diabolical place, the product of insane minds filled with blind, irrational malice, a place where every vestige of human decency is forgotten in an orgy of senseless pain and persecution, a place of supreme insult to God and humanity alike.

As this definition suggests, where the thing being defined arouses powerful emotions in people, literal definition cannot convey ideas adequately. In such cases, you should consider using figurative definition. Note the comparisons in the figurative definitions below:

> To the old man, the child seemed a messenger from another world. Even the dirty clothes served to hide her ethereal qualities from casual observers. She was his link to a better time, a reminder that all that was good and pure and innocent was still alive—somewhere.

> My friends, the opposition party's proposal is nothing short of monstrous. If we allow such fiscal policies to hatch, the beast will turn on us and consume the very economy it is purported to protect!

Figurative definition is a showcase for your creative perceptions. Anyone can describe a budgetary proposal as "bad," but a description like the following is more vivid and more effective in its opposition:

> The current suggestion that aid for prenatal care be eliminated is a cancer that seems at first innocuous. But as it spreads, its effects will be felt at every level of society. . . .

Because figurative definition calls up emotional reactions to images, it is often used in promotion and advertising. This definition of a baseball glove was offered by the Rawlings Sporting Goods Company in 1985:

What Is a Baseball Glove?

A baseball glove is a beginning and an ending: a child's first sure step toward adulthood; their final, lingering hold on youth; it is promise . . . and memory.

A baseball glove is the dusty badge of belonging, the tanned and oiled mortar of team and camaraderie; in its creases and scuffs lodge sunburned afternoons freckled with thrills, the excited hum of competition, cheers that burst like skyrockets.

A baseball glove is Babe Ruth, Stan Musial, Mickey Mantle, Reggie Jackson, Keith Hernandez and a thousand-and-one names and monuments strung like white and crimson banners in the vast stadium of memory.

A baseball glove is the leather of adventure, worthy successor to the cowboy's holster, the trooper's saddle and the buckskin laces of the frontier scout; it is combat, heroics, and victory . . . a place to smack a fist or snuff a rally.

Above all, a baseball glove is the union of family recreation and togetherness; it is union beyond language, creed or color.

Figurative definition employs the same kind of creative exploration used to shape analogies.

Y O U R   T U R N

As you write a figurative definition for each of the following, remember to go beyond a literal description. Try to capture the essence, the feeling, that will make the concept "breathe" for your readers.

a. Define what home means to a person who has been away for several months (a college student, a newlywed, a soldier).
b. Define what freedom means to a person who has recently acquired it after many years (released prisoner, political emigrant).
c. Define what Mother's Day means to someone whose mother has just died.
d. Define what a job means to an unemployed man or woman with a large family.

SUMMARY

Recreating experiences can inform, involve, or convince your readers. Regardless of your purpose, awareness of effective strategies will improve your writing, making the events or scenes or people more vivid in your own mind and in your readers.

COMBINING TECHNIQUES

So far we have examined techniques as they are used singly. More commonly, however, they are used in combination. In other words, a narrative might include dialogue, figurative definition or description of a person, place, thing, or emotion. Many times description is woven into the fabric of the narrative itself, so that the readers receive vivid sensory impressions while the narrative continues. Here are some examples of effective combinations of techniques:

The writer begins with a lead-in explanation specifying his reason for offering the narrative. Then he explains the particulars of the assignment.

When Henry Brooke Carter died recently, the news stories in all the media included highlights from his long and distinguished career in journalism. But for those of us who studied journalism with him, the anecdote that will perhaps be longest remembered is the following one, which I offer here as a personal footnote to the record:

The assignment was to be done during the semester break and would serve as our lead-in to the second semester. There was a month to complete it—nevertheless it was difficult. We were to obtain an interview with someone who had just made the front page of a daily newspaper and write a lively account of the person's reactions to being in the spotlight. The instructor explained that the person's story needn't have been glamorous—it could have been just a slender human interest affair. What was important was the person's reactions and how well we could commit them to words. For most of us the vacation passed swiftly. When we returned to campus, a single question was on everyone's lips—"What did you get?"

Here he recounts what happened after the semester break.

The answers drew varying responses, from polite nods and ho-hum expressions to excited requests to explain every detail.

"What did you get?"

"Queen of the County Fair."

"Uh huh."

"How about you?"

"A man attacked by a pig."

"Really? Attacked? By a pig?"

Note the use of broken time order (flashback) here. The writer takes Henry's experience out of the natural sequence of events and places it at the end to give it emphasis.

And so on through a small catalogue of events, many predictable, a few bizarre. But the one that earned the admiration and awe of all of us was Henry Carter's. For it revealed a preview of that rare combination of good fortune, nerve, and ingenuity that mark the superlative newsman. And we didn't have to ask him about it. We'd read about it in the papers.

Henry had spent the first three weeks of the semester break enjoying himself—skiing, dancing, playing ball. Only at the beginning of the fourth week did he begin to develop the slightest concern about the assignment, reading the newspapers every day but finding nothing that interested him. Then one day he was talking to a friend on a downtown corner of his city when a masked man ran out of a nearby bank and bumped into Henry. Reacting quickly, Henry grabbed the bandit's arm and twisted it, wrestling him to the ground and immobilizing him. The driver of a car that had apparently been waiting for the robber paused only long enough to survey the situation. The he sped away. A moment later the police arrived.

When the man was identified as a well-known bank robber, wanted in several states, Henry's face and story made national headlines. And Henry completed the journalism assignment by interviewing *himself.*

Y O U R   T U R N

1. Photocopy an effective presentation of an experience. In the margins or on a separate sheet of paper, identify the individual techniques and combinations of techniques the writer used.

2. Write several paragraphs on one of the following topics. Use a combination of techniques.

   a. Your first (or most significant) encounter with prejudice.
   b. The most impressive act of sportsmanship you ever witnessed.
   c. An experience in which you made an important discovery about a friend.
   d. An experience in which you made an important discovery about yourself.

Sample Composition

The sample below will demonstrate the combination of techniques typical of most essays. Note that the essay offers no life-enhancing information and argues no controversial assertion, but it does attempt to draw the audience into the action, to recreate an experience so that the readers can share the feelings of a character.

MY RACING DEBUT

The writer gets into the narrative quickly, working in necessary background information skillfully.

More than 2,500 auto-racing fans had gathered on that warm June evening in 1983. Mid-State racetrack had never had a bigger crowd on opening night. I had a special reason for being there—I was about to drive my first professional race. Even in grade school my friend Charlie and I had been interested in cars and racing. We read racing magazines, watched mechanics work, and went to the racetrack whenever we could.

Then when we were a little older and learned to drive, we entered some local amateur racing competitions. It wasn't surprising, then, that we decided in the summer of '83 to buy a 1975 Chevy, rebuild it to racing specifications, and apply to race at Mid-State.

The opening night festivities seemed to take forever. The local high school band marched to the infield playing a John Philip Sousa classic. Next an overweight soprano sang the "Star Spangled Banner" slightly off key but with great enthusiasm. And then came the speakers—the mayor, followed by the president of the racing association. Finally, we were ready to race.

The call came for the drivers to take the track and warm up. The announcer introduced us one at a time. "'Boswick . . . Shaver . . . Reilly . . . Seaver . . . .'" I grew nervous, wondering if my name had been left off the list. "Edwards. . . ." That was it. As I drove onto the track a big cheer went up from the crowd. I smiled, realizing that I had a lot of friends out there, and a lot of family—my mom, dad, and sisters, and even my aunt and uncle who had always thought me lacking in ability. "Tonight I'll not only make my family proud," I thought, "but I'll make believers out of my aunt and uncle too. . . ." Completing my warm-up laps, I left the track for a few last-minute adjustments to the engine and one last strategy session. As Charlie and I talked, I could see he had the jitters, and I wondered if he could see that I did too.

"Remember, you've got the pole position, so that gives you a big advantage," Charlie reminded me.

"I know, I know, all I've got to do is get the jump on them."

"Right. Get the quick start and then just let'er out. You've got the horses to hold the lead, and. . . ."

"Gentlemen, take your positions," the announcer interrupted.

I gave Charlie the thumbs-up sign and eased out on to the track. As I sat at the pole revving my engine and waiting for the flag, I glanced around the stands. People were waving and shouting. Though I couldn't hear my

---

Here and elsewhere the writer presents descriptive details not merely for their own sake but to recreate the experience as he wants the readers to see it.

Note the description of his thoughts and feelings.

Note the use of dialogue.

Here the details are carefully selected to make the climax more effective.

name, I knew my buddies were chanting "Edwards, Edwards, Edwards" as they had said they would. I'd soon give them something to cheer about.

The climactic moment is not merely stated but dramatized.

Now I kept my eyes on the starter. "Vroom, vroom," I revved the car again and again. There it was, the green flag. All in one smooth motion I let the clutch up and jammed the gas pedal down, bracing myself against the seat for the car to surge forward.

Instead, the car lurched ahead a few feet, and then the engine sputtered and died. Ram! Bam! Crash! The car behind me rammed into me and several other cars rammed the cars in front of them.

Because the readers will have questions about subsequent events, the writer provides answers, but ends the composition as quickly and naturally as possible.

I couldn't believe it. I wanted to die. I had stalled the car in my first professional race. It turned out that no real harm had been done, though, so the starter lined us up again. That time I started all right, and though I lost the race, I won a nickname that will probably last a lifetime: "Stall."

CHAPTER FOURTEEN

Connecting Audience, Content, and Purpose

This chapter explains the importance of considering your readers and profiling their knowledge and opinions about your topic. It explains the relationship between your knowledge of audience and your presentation of a credible writing self. Finally, it directs the analysis of a reader-directed draft using peer evaluations.

❏ The Third Decision: To Review the Work in Progress

When you have a complete draft, you may feel that your work is finished. But careful writers know that putting ideas on paper is a beginning, not an end. Before you label a piece of writing "finished," you should encourage your editorial voice to review the work—first content and framework, and finally elements like paragraphs, sentences, and diction.

This third decision seems to move you away from developing ideas. But do not make the mistake of closing off such considerations. Many writers find that the creative voice continues to supply ideas and the critical voice continues to press for clarification every time a work is reviewed. For that reason, some writers refuse to allow anyone else to type their final drafts, arguing that each time they go over the material, they see ways to improve. You, too, should remain alert to new ideas as you revise and edit your writing.

This section directs your review on two levels. First, it reconsiders the relationship between audience and content to make sure that your work is presented specifically for your readers. Then, it examines the framework (introductions, conclusions, and titles), logical paragraphing, effective sentence structures, and careful diction.

EARLY AWARENESS OF AUDIENCE

The first impulse to write often carries with it an awareness of the rhetorical situation—you not only have something to say; you also want to say it *to someone.* Consider the example of the parking lot filled with potholes. You want to protest so that someone will fix the problem. Even if your concept of your audience is somewhat fuzzy, you are aware that someone in authority should read your words.

A vague idea of your audience is enough when you first began to write. But when you have explored your subject and drafted your response, it is time to examine the audience in some detail. Whether you want to engage the imagination of your readers or to broaden their understanding or to persuade them to accept your assertions, careful analysis of the connections between your ideas and your audience will improve your draft.

THE EFFECTS OF DETAILED CONSIDERATION OF AUDIENCE

To say that your material will be influenced by your awareness of audience is to say nothing startling. You already know that some of your jokes will not be funny to some of your friends, so you select the material and adapt the language as needed. You also know that some details are best omitted when you write home about your college career—better to focus on your scholarly endeavors than your frustrations with the computer if you want to reassure your family that you are handling your role with grace.

Considering the audience of your writing, then, is simply a matter of transferring the skills you already have. The basic questions will remain the same: "What will it take to reach this audience emotionally—to make them laugh or cry or rage?" "What information do they need to better understand this subject?" "What will it take to convince them that this assertion deserves serious consideration?" Thinking about these questions will remind you that writing is not done in a vacuum.

A careful analysis of audience will influence your writing in three ways:

1. **It will help the creative voice generate new ideas.** Your creative voice can help you see the subject through the eyes of your audience. That new vision can mean new insights, new approaches, new ideas. As a result, your desire to communicate effectively with an audience inevitably leads you to further explorations of the subject. Consideration of audience, then, is a tool for creative discovery of new ideas.

2. **It will help the critical voice select the most effective material.** Examine an ad campaign and you will see that the scenery, the people and the language are all aimed at a specific audience—perhaps one that loves to party, or one that has unlimited funds, or one that is impressed by glamorous images. Similarly, identifying an audience for your work will help you select words and images more effectively.

3. **It will help both voices shape the most effective persona, the self-image you present to your readers.** As you identify the background and attitudes of the audience, you should ask yourself, "what kind of person can best present this material to this audience?" Your persona should not be created without any regard for your own feelings or ideas; just as you are serious and conscientious

when addressing the IRS auditor and silly when you entertain at a child's birthday party, your persona varies as you address different audiences for different purposes. Your critical voice will analyze the needs and expectations of this audience so that you can present the most effective persona. But remember, whatever "face" you present to your audience should be a part of you.

PROFILING YOUR AUDIENCE

You do not need an extensive biography of your audience. In fact, you need only the information that will make your writing most effective. That information will vary, depending on the purpose of your work. Consider that a thorough analysis of the political stance of the Committee for Governmental Quality is essential if your request that they fund your campaign is to be effective. In contrast, you need only know how Aunt Agatha feels about off-color humor before you decide what to include in your account of "growth experiences" at the university.

Your analysis of your audience may vary in its depth, but regardless of the rhetorical situation, it should include consideration of similar questions:

- What knowledge does my audience already have?
- What opinions does my audience already hold?
- What tone and diction will this audience expect?

A SAMPLE AUDIENCE PROFILE

Remember that in most cases *you* designate the audience for your writing. You send the letter to a specific person or to the editor of a specific publication with a predictable readership. You send memos to specific persons and articles to specific magazines. It is possible, then, for you to form a relatively precise image of your intended audience.

Suppose that you are writing a letter praising a particular political candidate. Designate an audience, familiar or unfamiliar, and profile it, using the sample questions that follow. If you do not know an answer, feel free to speculate. Obviously not all of the information is relevant for every paper, but answering these questions will help you develop a sense of your audience as a real person or group of people.

General Information

- Is your audience a specific person? Give the name and/or job description of that person.
- Is your audience an organized group, like the Men's Club at your church or the League of Women Voters?

- Estimate the age (or average age) of your audience. If you give an age span, try to be as specific as possible—for example, "Most are between twenty and thirty, with a few of them as old as forty," rather than "The group ranges in age from twenty to forty."
- Do you know of a religious preference? A political party?
- Does the audience tend to be liberal? Conservative? Somewhere in between?
- What does your audience do for an income?
- Estimate the income of your audience. If you can't give a dollar figure, label them as upper, middle, or lower class.
- Is your audience male or female? Married? Single? Divorced? Childless?
- Does your audience live in this country? What area? Urban or rural or other? Native to that area or just moved in?
- Would this audience expect a formal tone? Would it be offended by a familiar one?

Connections to This Topic

- Do you know anyone personally who fits this profile? If so, how would that person react to your ideas? Are there sensitive areas to treat carefully or avoid altogether?
- Is this audience likely to know anything about this topic? Is there obscure background data that must be provided or special vocabulary to be explained?
- Has this audience previously expressed a direct opinion on this or similar topics?
- What resources are available to this audience? Television? Newspapers? Libraries? Speakers? Debates?
- Has anything happened in this geographic area that was related to this topic? How did this community react? How did this audience react?

If you make an effort to profile your audience in this kind of detail, you may find that the faces become individuals and the voices clearer. You will also find it easier to speculate about opinions or beliefs—even to hear your audience respond when you ask a question. Imagine that you are a political candidate who has been asked to address a group. Wouldn't you want to know as much as possible about the group and its opinions as you prepare your speech?

SPECULATING ABOUT YOUR AUDIENCE

Much of the effectiveness of your writing will depend on how well you answer these questions. However, it is impossible to really know or predict another person's mind, so your answers are bound to be imperfect.

The best you can do is speculate. If you examine your experience with people and are willing to do some research on your audience, you can turn that speculation into an educated guess.

Familiar Audiences

At times you will know your audience fairly well. For example, you may write a letter to your brother disagreeing with his assessment of a particular high school teacher. Even though you will be unable to predict your brother's thinking exactly, you will at least be relatively sure of most of his ideas. Whenever you write for a familiar audience, consider the following:

1. Have you ever discussed this or similar topics? Has your audience said anything that might indicate feelings or opinions about this topic? Does this audience have much knowledge about this subject?

2. How does this audience usually react? Is the first response calm and rational or is it highly emotional? Are new ideas grasped quickly, or will comprehension be slow? Is the attention span fairly long? Is this audience impatient with detail? Respectful of authority? Quick to jump to conclusions? Easily bored? Easily confused? What kinds of examples and analogies will be meaningful to them?

Unfamiliar Audiences

Sometimes your readers will be unfamiliar faces without names or personalities. It is more difficult to determine what they know about the subject and where they are most likely to disagree with your views. But it is not impossible. And you do not have to limit your approach to blind guessing.

The key to effective speculation about unfamiliar audiences is understanding that most of what people think and say and believe is not fresh and original at all. It is a reflection of what they have heard others say. As a result, you can predict with reasonable accuracy how most audiences will react to various ideas. You must simply be alert to what you see and hear. Here's how to put this understanding to use in considering your audience:

1. Designate yourself a typical member of the audience and reflect on your experience with the subject or issue. What have you seen or read about this topic? How did you react? What reactions or opinions are shared by others that you know? Reactions common to you and to people you know are likely to be common to your audience as well.

2. Recall the views you have heard expressed: not just those in conversation, but also those in books, magazines, and newspapers, in soap opera dialogue, and so on. The more frequently an idea or argument is expressed, the more likely it is that your readers have been influenced by it.

Consider that much has been said and written about schoolchildren with AIDS. You (and your audience) have heard about communities that banned the children from school and other communities that threatened them and their families. You have heard the issues discussed and are aware that much of the fear comes from ignorance—both scientists' ignorance about the disease and community ignorance about what is known. Analyzing your own knowledge about the subject and your opinions about the issues (as well as the reactions you have heard from friends and family and feature interviews) will allow you to speculate about the knowledge and opinions of your designated audience.

Speculation, of course, carries with it some risk of error. (In the case of schoolaged AIDS victims, some readers might base their opinions on something besides the commonly presented reasons.) But if you can relate your audience to yourself and to those you know, your speculation will be accurate enough to direct your decisions about content and persona.

Y O U R T U R N

For each of the following ideas, decide how well the specified audience is likely to understand the issue and where and to what extent they are likely to disagree with the point of view. (If you know people who could be classified as members of the audience, consider what attitudes and habits might affect their view of the issue.)

1. Idea: A part-time or summer job can help a teenager prepare for adulthood.
   Audience: A group of young teenagers who have never had a job.

2. Idea: Jobs are available to teenagers if they know how to seek them out and present themselves to employers.
   Audience: A group of older teenagers who, because of their appearance or manner, have never been able to get a job.

3. Idea: In many American schools, teachers have difficulty maintaining discipline and creating an atmosphere conducive to learning.
   Audience: People from a foreign country where teachers, indeed all adults, are treated with respect and where rules are obeyed.

Additional Readings

"To His Coy Mistress" by Andrew Marvell is an example of an argument tailored to a particular audience. Notice that the first verse paragraph praises the young lady at length, reinforcing that her appearance is a thing of great worth. It also presents the speaker as a man who would relish the opportunity to worship her at great length. The second section, then, has an even greater impact as the speaker changes tone to warn her of impending disaster. Imagine her own shift of attitude as she is first praised lavishly, then warned that worms will soon devour her in a lonely tomb! If the speaker has indeed read his audience well, and if his words have had the desired effect, his illogical suggestion that only his love can save her from such a fate is unlikely to be critically evaluated.

To His Coy Mistress
Andrew Marvell

Had we but world enough, and time,
This coyness, lady, were no crime.
We would sit down, and think which way
To walk, and pass our long love's day.
5   Thou by the Indian Ganges' side
Should'st rubies find: I by the tide
Write love poems   Of Humber would complain. °I would
Love you ten years before the Flood,
And you should, if you please, refuse
10   Till the conversion of the Jews.
i.e,   My vegetable° love should grow
Unconsciously Vaster than empires, and more slow.
growing   An hundred years should go to praise
Thine eyes, and on thy forehead gaze:
15   Two hundred to adore each breast,
But thirty thousand to the rest.
An age at least to every part,
And the last age should show your heart.
For, lady, you deserve this state,
20   Nor would I love at lower rate.
    But at my back I always hear
Time's wingèd chariot hurrying near;
And yonder all before us lie
Deserts of vast eternity.
25   Thy beauty shall no more be found,
Nor in thy marble vault shall sound
My echoing song: then worms shall try
That long preserved virginity,

And your quaint honor turn to dust,
30 And into ashes all my lust.
The grave's a fine and private place,
But none, I think, do there embrace.
    Now therefore, while the youthful hue
Sits on thy skin like morning dew,
35 And while thy willing soul transpires
At every pore with instant fires,
Now let us sport us while we may;
And now, like am'rous birds of prey,
Rather at once our time devour,
40 Slowly   Than languish in his slow-chapt° power,
  devouring   Let us roll all our strength, and all
Our sweetness up into one ball;
And tear our pleasures with rough strife
Through   Thorough° the iron gates of life.
45   Thus, though we cannot make our sun
Stand still, yet we will make him run.

Few writings are more closely connected to audience than are personal letters. In the two examples that follow, notice that the letter writers seem well aware of their readers and the probable reactions of those readers. Dickens, for example, signals that he expects his wife to read in haste: "If you have hurried on thus far without quite understanding (apprehending some bad news) I rely on your turning back and reading again." He anticipates her fears, assuring her that the sick child is in no pain, and tries to prepare her for the worst possible news. Notice diction like: "I have perfect confidence . . ." and "I rely on . . ." and "do your duty . . ." and "show yourself worthy of the great trust." He is appealing to her feelings and her values in a way that shows his understanding of her nature.

Bryant, too, writes to a woman whom he knows well. As he addresses his mother, notice how he first creates an atmosphere of dread, counting on her motherly feelings of concern to build to a fever pitch. The news he actually brings is in such contrast to the foreboding tone that we can almost feel her relief. Having pulled her emotional strings, he then appeals to her compassionate nature to accept his new wife, and cautions her that some things cannot be fought against. Does he anticipate that she would resent his marriage, particularly since it was done without her knowledge? Notice the diction used to create the opening sense of melo-drama: "melancholy intelligence," "what has happened to me," "pale, thin, with a solemn countenance, hooked nose and hollow eyes," "cabalistical expressions," "too much frightened."

In each letter, the writers present images of themselves that are expected to have an effect on their readers. Dickens shows his own concern for the child, but also expresses his care and his confidence about his wife's feel-ings. Bryant shows himself first as a frightened child at the mercy of forces surrounding him, then turns to a more adult persona who trusts his moth-er to welcome and accept his new bride.

Letters

from Charles Dickens

Devonshire-terrace
Tuesday morning, 15th April, 1851

My dearest Kate—Now observe, you must read this letter very slowly and carefully. If you have hurried on thus far without quite understand-ing (apprehending some bad news) I rely on your turning back and read-ing again.

Little Dora, without being in the least pain, is suddenly stricken ill. There is nothing in her appearance but perfect rest—you would suppose her quietly asleep, but I am sure she is very ill, and I cannot encourage myself with much hope of her recovery. I do not (and why should I say I do to you, my dear?) I do not think her recovery at all likely.

I do not like to leave home, I can do no good here, but I think it right to stay. You will not like to be away, I know, and I cannot reconcile it to myself to keep you away. Forster, with his usual affection for us, comes down to bring you this letter and to bring you home, but I cannot close it without putting the strongest entreaty and injunction upon you to come with perfect composure—to remember what I have often told you, that we never can expect to be exempt, as to our many children, from the afflic-tions of other parents, and that if—if when you come I should even have to say to you, "Our little baby is dead," you are to do your duty to the rest, and to show yourself worthy of the great trust you hold in them.

If you will only read this steadily I have a perfect confidence in your doing what is right.

Ever affectionately,
Charles Dickens

from William Bryant
[June, 1821]

Dear Mother:

I hasten to send you the melancholy intelligence of what has lately happened to me.

Early on the evening of the eleventh day of the present month I was at a neighboring house in this village. Several people of both sexes were assembled in one of the apartments, and three or four others, with myself, were in another. At last came in a little elderly gentleman, pale, thin, with a solemn countenance, hooked nose, and hollow eyes. It was not long before we were summoned to attend in the apartment where he and the rest of the company were gathered. We went in and took our seats; the little elderly gentleman with the hooked nose prayed, and we all stood up. When he had finished, most of us sat down. The gentleman with the hooked nose then muttered certain cabalistical expressions which I was too much frightened to remember, but I recollect that at the conclusion I was given to understand that I was married to a young lady of the name of Frances Fairchild, whom I perceived standing by my side, and I hope in the course of a few months to have the pleasure of introducing to you as your daughter-in-law, which is a matter of some interest to the poor girl, who has neither father nor mother in the world. . . .

I looked only for goodness of heart, an ingenuous and affectionate disposition, a good understanding, etc., and the character of my wife is too frank and single-hearted to suffer me to fear that I may be disappointed. I do myself wrong; I did not look for these nor any other qualities, but they trapped me before I was aware, and now I am married in spite of myself.

Thus the current of destiny carries us along. None but a madman would swim against the stream, and none but a fool would exert himself to swim with it. The best way is to float quietly with the tide. . . .

Your affectionate son,
William

CREATING A PERSONA

If you have ever been invited to a social event without knowing how to dress for it, you already understand the relationship between audience and persona. For an unfamiliar social occasion, you want information that will help you present an appropriate image, an image largely determined by appearance. In a similar manner, information about your audience will help you present the image most appropriate and most acceptable to the situation.

You should not manufacture a whole new personality here; you need only to emphasize qualities which you expect this audience to respect. You create your persona by the decisions you make: **choice of person**—first, second, third; **selection of details**—personal material, scholarly testimony, complex data; **level of language**—scholarly, informal, familiar; and **choice of tone**—sympathetic, authoritative.

When you apply for a bank loan, you emphasize your persona's competence, independence, and maturity. In contrast, when you request money from your parents, you might present yourself as a devoted child who needs their assistance. Both images are real; you merely emphasize the facets that suit the rhetorical situation.

In your writing, then, you present the persona likely to get the best hearing from your audience. You might emphasize your knowledge of research and current philosophies if your audience expects a scholarly discussion. You might stress your own experiences if your audience is likely to identify with you. You might even conclude that your audience will best be reached by a direct focus on the material without a visible persona at all. Such decisions show that you understand the guiding principle of personas: **The presence of your persona should be subordinate to your purpose.** In other words, if presenting yourself to the readers will advance your purpose, then you do so. But if you feel a visible persona would detract from the material, you become as unobtrusive as possible.

Establishing a persona (or softening the persona's voice) is largely influenced by the point of view you choose. Let's see how your choices might affect the audience.

First Person: Using "I/me/my/mine" or even "we/our/us" puts a great deal of emphasis on the persona. That can be an advantage if you want the readers to identify strongly with you, to share your feelings and your thoughts and to learn what you learn. Be cautious, though, about letting the "I" dominate the writing. The observations and the realizations are the real star of the discussion. The following passages show how an I-dominated passage can be changed.

Self-Dominating First Person

I was having a sandwich in the college snack bar when I saw her enter. I was struck by her incredible beauty. I saw that she was about five feet eight inches tall. I was especially taken by her hair, a deep chestnut brown with natural red highlights. I could hear her clear, firm voice from my corner in the shop, and I watched her has she walked decisively to a table. I knew I would have to meet her that very day.

Self in Background

I was having a sandwich in the college snack bar when she entered. She was incredibly beautiful—about five feet eight inches tall, with stunningly attractive hair—a deep chestnut brown with natural red highlights. Her voice was firm and clear as she placed her order, and she walked like a person who knew exactly what she wanted. I knew I would have to meet her that very day.

Second Person: Addressing the readers as "you" can work to get the attention of the audience. It often gives the feeling that you have put a hand on the readers' shoulders to direct them through your discussion.

Such intimacy can backfire, though, if you are describing problem behaviors and offering solutions. For example, you might write, "Your voting record as college students has not been impressive. Polls show that you tend to support candidates who are attractive and who smile appealingly." Be aware that your readers may not want to be associated so directly with weak-minded voting habits, and that your direct approach may seem hostile and offensive.

Accusing Second-Person

When you waste most of your out-of-class hours, you should expect to fail most of your classes. But it is never too late for you to change from an irresponsible, disorganized student into a productive scholar.

Revision to Neutral Stance

If a student has not used out-of-class hours wisely, failing grades may be the result. But it is never too late to change from a disorganized student into a productive scholar.

Third Person: Third person point of view has the effect of distance and objectivity. You are not pushing yourself to the foreground, nor are you directly associating the readers with the topic. Consider the short passage on college voting patterns above, re-written to desensitize the criticism: "College students as a whole have not compiled an impressive voting record. Polls show that they tend to support candidates who smile often and present attractive images." Your audience is now free to admit. "Yes, I have been guilty of such behavior" or to say, "Yes, I have known people like that." The criticism is less personal because it is less direct.

Third person, then, is a good choice if you do not wish to get to close to the readers. It is also effective when you want the material to stand on its own, without the distractions of "I think" or "I feel." Notice in the example below that the first person point of view keeps emphasis on the writer's feelings rather than on the material, and note that the third person point of view sounds more authoritative and scholarly.

Too Personal, Intrusive Voice

I think the siege at Vicksburg was a turning point in the Civil War. It seems to me that if the South had been able to hold the city, it would have been able to control the Mississippi River. I have often wondered what would have happened if Vicksburg had not fallen. I guess that the war would have been longer.

Focus on Material Itself

The siege at Vicksburg was a turning point in the Civil War. If the South had been able to hold the city, it would have been able to control the Mississippi River. If Vicksburg had not fallen, the war would probably have been much longer.

Y O U R   T U R N

1. Select passages from several published works and identify the voice as first, second or third person. Rewrite the passages from a different point of view. How does the effect of the passage change?
2. Select several paragraphs from your own work, either a draft in progress, an earlier work, or a short piece that appeals to you. Rewrite the passage at least three times, trying out the different points of view described here. Can you identify different effects of the variations? Share the passages with a friend and ask if such differences are apparent.

IDENTIFYING AN INDIRECT AUDIENCE

There is one final consideration in identifying and describing an audience. You should be aware that sometimes your writing is not addressed directly to its audience. A "Letter to the Editor" of a newspaper is addressed to the editor but is actually aimed at the readership of the newspaper. Similarly, an information sheet about a summer camp might address an audience of children while supplying information for the parents. Some writing, such as essay examinations or research papers, appear to have no direct audience, yet you are aware that your writing must demonstrate to the instructor your knowledge of the material.

Such considerations of indirect audiences need not be complex. Once you have recognized that you are directing your writing to one audience while addressing another, you can adjust your diction as needed (that is, to the level of the child who will first see the camp brochure) and offer the information expected (that is, about safety measures or fee structures).

Keep in mind that whether the audience is being addressed directly or indirectly, and whether it is one person or many people, the basic questions you must consider are the same:

What do they know about the subject or issue?
Where and to what extent are they likely to disagree with your view?
What voice will they be most likely to accept?

YOUR CONTRACT WITH YOUR READERS

Knowing your audience will help you to create a persona and to tailor your presentation to the knowledge and opinions of your readers. But directing your content to your audience is not sufficient. You must also be sensitive to the attitude your writing conveys. If your attitude is, "Here's a rough statement of my ideas—if the readers want to understand it, let them figure it out," you should not be surprised if your readers feel insulted and decide they can't spare the time to struggle with your message.

The safest and most realistic approach to writing is the attitude that you owe the readers something, not the reverse. When you write for readers, you are making a claim on their time; therefore, you owe them a careful effort to make your thoughts clear and meaningful. When you write for yourself, make the same demands as any reader would. Clear, meaningful discussion will help you discover more about your knowledge and your attitudes, so demand full explanations of yourself as writer regardless of the audience you picture.

Think of your relationship with your readers as a contractual one: You offer, in return for their attention, a worthwhile and pleasurable experience. With this perspective, you will not be likely to take your readers for granted.

PRODUCING EFFECTIVE READER-DIRECTED WRITING

Knowing your readers and creating an appropriate persona are crucial links between writing that is self-directed and writing that is reader-directed. But it is not always easy to evaluate the effectiveness of your own ideas or presentation. As a result, it is good strategy to combine self-evaluation with peer evaluation to get additional feedback from another perspective. However, simply handing your draft to a reader rarely produces useful criticism. Getting useful feedback requires some preliminary effort on your part.

First, make sure that you have ready a reader-oriented draft. Your earliest drafts are writer-oriented; that is, you have written primarily for yourself as investigation and as exploration. But when you have made some decisions about controlling idea and purpose, and when you have defined and described your audience in some detail, it is time to produce another draft that is specifically directed to that audience.

At this point, review your early writings, including whatever explorations you did in the early stages. For this scan, look over the material with a clear eye to your audience's knowledge and attitudes, and produce a draft that is aimed at your audience, not yourself. The test questions become, "Will my audience understand this?" and "Will my audience find this convincing?"

When you read over this draft, read from the perspective of your audience, trying to separate your own knowledge and attitude from the reader's probable point of view.

Guidelines for Peer Evaluation

Peer evaluation can provide invaluable feedback. Before you hand over that draft, though, lay some groundwork. The kind of peer review sheets instructors hand out can give you some good ideas here, but the best review sheets come directly from the writer. Your task for this paper is to develop reviewer's guidelines that point the reader where you need him or her most. Requesting specific information is far more likely to produce helpful feedback than is a vague request like "Tell me what you think." Three simple guidelines can make peer evaluation more useful:

1. **Make clear to the reviewer that you do not expect editing.** Many people who claim to be "so bad in English" are nervous about their knowledge of grammar and mechanics—areas that you are not yet addressing. Emphasize that you want evaluation of your ideas.

2. **Ask your reviewer to play the role of your intended audience.** Naturally, you should supply information about that audience. Describe your audience, naming names if possible (for example, "my lab supervisor, Mrs. Benton"). Give your reviewer any details about that audience that might be relevant to your topic. In some cases, that might include religious affiliation, marital status, age, sex, educational background, or political leanings. Consider your topic as you prepare your description. If a project costing money is involved, you might need to consider your audience's fiscal standing (for example, can the University afford your proposal? Is money an issue at all?). Some consideration of values might be needed: Does the audience respect your subject? Is reform a priority? Is there much interest in this topic? Any information which could affect the audience response is relevant, so make your description as complete as possible.

3. **Provide a list of specific areas to be reviewed.** That list should reflect areas in which you most want feedback. For instance, if your topic is relatively technical, a reasonable request would be, "Are there any terms here which need further explanation?" You might ask the reviewer to identify your main points, which will assure you that your primary claims are clear (or warn you that you are not communicating). If you are comfortable with your main support, ask the reviewer to identify your evidence— "What examples are offered here? Are the examples good support for the points?" You might ask, too, if the reviewer (assuming the role of audience) would expect to hear certain points discussed. Are there any obvious areas that should be considered? For example, if the cost of your proposal is high, you might ask if the reviewer is satisfied with your discussion of funding.

A peer evaluation sheet for a paper intended to involve the audience's imagination might look something like this one:

Comment Sheet: Embarrassing Incident

To the reviewer: Please answer the following questions from the perspective of the audience. The paper contains terminology about maneuvers on the field, but it is written for a group of student musicians who have marched at school football games for several years. They are familiar with the technical side of both music and marching.

1. What is the main idea of this paper?
   [An obvious, but useful, question—if the answer surprises you, you may have wandered too far from your controlling idea.]
2. Briefly list the main events in the order they are presented here.
3. When you read the description of the concert hall, can you see the relative positions of the orchestra leader, the first violinist, and me? If you need more information about setting or characters, please mark the section with a question mark.
4. Does the description of my reaction to the collision show my feelings clearly? Do you see what I was feeling at that point? Do you understand why I thought it necessary to stay on the stage instead of running for the door?

Notice that the writer wants feedback only about the presentation of the incident. All of the questions ask the reader to consider the presentation of the incident; none is directed toward style, diction, or grammar.

Here is a second sample, based on an informative paper:

Comment Sheet: The Siege of Vicksburg

To the reviewer: Please answer the following questions from the perspective of the audience. The paper is written for a group of American history students who have not studied the details of the Civil War but are aware of it.

1. Does this paper explain or give information about this subject that could be argued, or is it an explanation that will probably be accepted?
2. Did you know something about the Vicksburg conflict before reading this? What information was new?
3. Is the discussion of the behavior of the townspeople clear? Should I give more information about the shelling or the caves dug as shelter?
4. Do you understand why Vicksburg was important to the South? Is the effect of the loss on the outcome of the war made clear?

Notice that the comment sheet is again brief and specifically focused on content. Your comment sheet should be tailored to the specific writing situations, so it might be useful to include a question or two about writing technique. If your class has been working on clear use of pronouns, or on transitional phrases, you might include guidelines like these:

Have I used "they" only with a clear antecedent?
Underline the transitional expressions used to connect paragraphs to each other.

As you list reviewer guidelines, remember that asking a reader to discuss more than four or five areas may result in shallow responses. If you have more questions, go through the peer evaluation exercise several times, giving different reviewers different questions. Another legitimate concern is that the reviewer's responses may not be serious or accurate; one safeguard is to get responses from several reviewers and compare the answers. Remember, too, to trust your instincts when it is time to act on the suggestions received. You are not required to accept the comments; you are expected only to consider the areas targeted by responses.

In review, then, your part in the peer evaluation exercise is as follows:

1. Create a reader-directed draft.
2. Define, in writing, the role you wish the reviewer to assume.
3. Ask a few specific questions about areas of the draft.
4. Select a reviewer and give assurances that editing is not expected.
5. Review the comments, revise the draft as needed, and repeat the process if desired.

Y O U R   T U R N

Develop a review sheet for a paper in progress (any topic will work here). Assuming that you have with you a reader-directed draft, define (on the review sheet) your audience and formulate four or five questions that will target specific areas of the draft.

SUMMARY

Considerations of audience will help you produce more effective writing that builds on the knowledge of the readers while responding to their opinions and expectations. Peer evaluations can provide useful feedback once you have produced a reader-directed draft.

Y O U R   T U R N

1. For each of the subjects below, identify possible papers that would inform, convince, or involve your readers. Then, designate an audience for one paper of each kind and describe it in some detail, using the lists of questions from this chapter. For example, if you pick the subject "Traffic Tickets" you might produce a humorous account of yourself arguing with a policeman over a ticket, directed toward a group of close friends who have been sharing similar stories. Or, you might produce an informative paper for a driver's education class about the process of challenging a ticket, or you might produce an argument against a particular regulation that you were once ticketed for breaking, directed to the traffic board that could change the rule. For each paper, picture your readers and their knowledge and opinions.

   a. A bartender serves alcohol to a person who later causes an automobile accident.
   b. The rules of the Olympics do not permit the participation of professional athletes.
   c. Music videos have an unhealthy influence on children.
   d. There might be a monster in Loch Ness, Scotland.
   e. Team X (any sport) has a chance for a winning season this year.

2. Select someone whose judgments you trust and explain the connections between audience and topic that you identified in exercise 1. Ask your friend to help you evaluate the completeness and the soundness of your ideas. If you have developed your ideas in a draft, ask the friend to evaluate the draft. Be sure to use the guidelines presented in this chapter as you set up the peer evaluation exercise.

3. If you are currently working on an essay, ask a friend to evaluate a draft. Be sure to follow the guidelines explained in this chapter as you set up the peer evaluation exercise.

Beginnings and Endings

After you have compiled an organized, logical draft that is tuned to your specific audience, you should turn your attention to the "packaging" of the essay: the introduction, the conclusion, and the title.

Only when you have a complete draft of your discussion should you focus specifically on the beginning and end of your work. The title and the introduction of your paper play a crucial role in reaching the audience and your conclusion should make a strong final impression. Because your selection of ideas and details and even your selection of audience and thesis may shift as you work on your draft, it is far more logical to wait until such areas are set before turning to introductions, conclusions, and titles. When your material is complete and you are satisfied with the presentation of your ideas, it is time to look carefully at the parts of your writing that first attract your readers and at the part that leaves the final impression. This chapter will review techniques for improving the beginnings and the endings of your paper.

INTRODUCING YOUR PAPER

When you write for your readers instead of for yourself, remember that your audience must be invited, even enticed to read your writing. That invitation is usually found in your opening paragraph.

The first realization about introductions (and conclusions) is that there is no one "proper" length. Instead of counting words or sentences, think of introductions and conclusions as logical units. Each is designed to serve a purpose, and when that purpose has been served, the unit should end—after one sentence or after twenty.

An introduction should do two things: **interest the readers and indicate the topic of the paper.** To illustrate the proper function of an introduction, consider this example of a poor one seen on a notice posted in the lobby of a busy classroom building. At the top, in bold, dark letters, was the word **"SEX."** The introduction certainly intrigued readers who crowded around the notice—but only briefly. The next line read, "Now that I have your attention, the Young Politicians Committee for Social

Justice will meet Thursday. . . ." Many of the readers walked off in disgust, muttering about a "cheap trick."

The introduction to the notice really was nothing more than a cheap trick. It interested the readers, but it had nothing to do with the contents of the notice. It not only turned readers away, it made them feel cheated and angry. Could anyone call such an introduction effective?

Consider, now, the overused introduction that begins, "In this paper I am going to explain the way that billboards are made. First I will talk about. . . ." No one could accuse this writer of subterfuge—the readers know exactly what this paper will cover. But are the readers interested? Unless there is already interest in the topic itself, it is unlikely that this introduction will do much to stimulate any.

The counsel here, then, is that you keep in mind both objectives of an introduction: to intrigue the readers *and* to identify the subject. While you need not announce the most controversial aspect of your stand, you should in all fairness indicate the subject of your discussion. And, while you should not resort to cheap theatrics, you should make an effort to appeal to the interests of your audience, at least enough to draw them to your writing.

Intriguing the Readers

Writing an introduction that indicates the topic is not terribly difficult. With little creative effort, you can produce a basic statement of your controlling idea that will tell your readers what your paper discusses. Enticing the audience to begin reading eagerly is more challenging, but remember that the introduction gives readers their first impression of your work. It is worth your time and effort to make that impression a good one.

Here are some suggestions:

1. **Find a starting point.** Since you have already profiled your audience in some detail (see Chapter 14), you have a good idea of their interests and their concerns. Finding an effective approach, then, is a matter of matching the contents of your work with the nature of your audience. Even if you don't know much about the audience, there are some areas that arouse interest in most human beings and at least get their initial attention. Two such areas that fit the "What's in it for me?" category are these:

    "How will reading this help me to survive?" Survival is one of the strongest instincts of the human species. If your discussion has information that could increase health and safety or save a life, say so immediately. Information about CPR or AIDS or nuclear disarmament could be introduced by ringing a warning bell, but so could subjects like aerobics, nutrition, social welfare programs, child care, or even sunglasses. Use your creative thinking skills to explore the topic, looking for links to health, fitness, and safety at any level from individual to global.

One caution: Use the dramatic emphasis appropriate to the occasion. One writer introduced a paper on changing a tire by warning his audience that without such knowledge, they were at the mercy of rapists and murderers who roamed the highways looking for stranded motorists. The effect was ludicrous rather than dramatic.

"How will this affect my bank balance?" Since our world virtually demands financial resources for survival, you can show your readers a direct benefit if you connect your discussion to their money. Look for an angle that will result in short- or long-term financial gain, either by generating more income or by direct savings. Obvious topics suited to this approach include using coupons, understanding the stock market, being your own tutor (or trainer, gardener, tailor, financial planner, analyst), and electing a candidate whose fiscal programs will boost your investments. Explore your topic for possible angles on financial benefit to your readers, and you may find a strong "hook" to catch and hold their interest.

2. **Use your knowledge of the audience.** Your understanding of your audience will identify more angles of approach. If you know that your audience has strong fears, deep loyalties, or intense feelings of love or hostility, your knowledge might suggest an effective starting point.

3. **Select a technique.** When you have decided to open with an emphasis on survival, finances, fears, or feelings, you are ready to choose your opening technique. In many cases, the draft you have been working on will suggest the form for its introduction; for instance, a paper that uses the narrative technique might be logically introduced by opening with a moment of dramatic intensity. Similarly, a surprising or fascinating quote from a source might catch the readers' interest. Or, a paper that analyzes the differences between two historical figures might begin with a description of similarities to explain why the two figures are in the same discussion (conversely, a study of similarities might open with a survey of the vast differences that have obscured the essential likenesses). If you are challenging a traditional assertion, you might begin by describing the commonly held belief, then shift into your analysis and rejection of it.

Your draft, then, is the best place to begin your search for an introduction. It will often suggest both the content and the form of your opening passage.

If your previous work does not bring inspiration, read over this list to see if something stirs you.

Ask a question. Openings like, "What would happen if . . .?" or "Will the candidate's policies really prove to be the solution to . . ?" are a natural draw because they invite the readers to answer. Be careful to guide the readers toward your own answers; you don't want them to answer with a discussion-ending, "No."

Personify the problem. Most people are intrigued by glimpses into the lives of others, and are more likely to respond to individuals than to faceless crowds. Note the appeals used to generate sponsors for needy children: The story of a single child who needs your help has proved to be the most effective method. Identify in your discussion an individual who represents those affected by your topic and open with a brief scene (but don't let the scene run away with the paper—keep it short). You can use a "typical" person rather than an actual one if you are careful to label him or her as such. Your introduction might read:

Susannah sits and stares at the wall in disbelief. Her carefully planned life seems suddenly a horrible joke. The student government elections—the sorority picnic—the registration for fall semester—all are suddenly remote and meaningless. Susannah, a sophomore with a long list of extracurricular activities, has just added one more detail to her autobiography. She is pregnant—and unmarried and confused.

Susannah is not an actual person, but she represents one of the fastest growing problem segments of the American population.

Use a quote. Conventional sources like books of quotations are always handy, but expand your search by thinking of song lyrics or dialogue from movies or even slogans from commercials. If the quote is readily recognizable by your audience, you need only the briefest of citations ("Guns don't kill people," assure the bumper stickers; "people kill people"). If you are not sure that the audience will recognize the quote, name the singer, the songwriter and/or the song. Name the character and, if necessary, the movie. Caution: Be sure that the quote has a direct connection to the discussion; if it is even a little "off," save it for another paper.

Say something startling. Vivid statistics or images will often catch the readers' interest long enough for your sparkling style to take hold, so look for something surprising or shocking.

Two football fields could fit, end to end, in the Cathedral of St. John the Divine. And the awe-inspiring Rose Window, more than twenty-five feet in diameter, appears smaller only because it is approximately eight stories above us.

In this city, one child is beaten savagely every four hours, six children every day. At least one of those children will require immediate medical attention, and too often one of those children will die, beaten to death by someone who is supposed to love and care for a helpless child.

This is by no means an exhaustive list of techniques. It is intended only to stimulate your creative mind, to open possibilities that you can tailor to fit your discussion and your audience. Regardless of the opening you finally develop, remember to test it for two functions:

Does it accurately indicate the topic?
Does it catch the readers' interest?

If either function is weak, devote some time and energy to improving it. If your readers are not interested at the beginning, it is difficult if not impossible to keep them reading. If your audience does not have the option of setting your work aside, the weak beginning will create a negative first impression that will influence how the rest of the work is perceived.

Indicating the Topic

If you have asked an appropriate question or used a relevant quote, incident, or statistic, you have already given the readers an indication of your topic. Only a brief clarification is needed here.

The introduction is expected to identify the subject. It is not required to identify your opinion of that subject. You can, of course, begin with a bold statement of your assertion. But you have other options. If, for example, you wish to propose a controversial solution to the problems of the homeless in your community, you might want to first show the magnitude of the problem and the ineffectiveness of existing programs. Your introduction need only identify your topic as "the homeless in this community"; you can develop the topic (and your solution) as the discussion progresses.

The thesis statements of papers that inform and papers that involve audience imaginatively may also be expressed later in the text; the expectations of the introduction are usually fulfilled if the readers are made aware of the general subject area to be discussed.

Y O U R   T U R N

1. "Practicing" introductions without a paper in progress is an awkward exercise at best. You can, however, increase your own hoard of techniques by looking through current magazines and

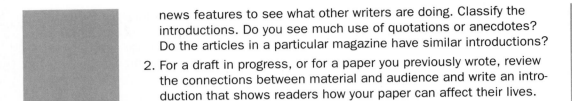

news features to see what other writers are doing. Classify the
introductions. Do you see much use of quotations or anecdotes?
Do the articles in a particular magazine have similar introductions?

2. For a draft in progress, or for a paper you previously wrote, review
the connections between material and audience and write an introduction that shows readers how your paper can affect their lives.
Be direct about life- or money-saving results.

3. Try a variety of introductory techniques for the same draft. If you
have trouble deciding which ones are most effective, ask a friend
to comment on your work.

CONCLUDING THE DISCUSSION

Have you ever wanted to end a conversation with someone but didn't
know how? You hang in an awkward limbo, looking for a graceful exit,
suspecting that the other person, too, is finished, but not knowing what to
say to close the encounter. The end of a written discussion may be similarly vague. You have presented your ideas and want nothing more than
to have the readers ponder your words. But you can't seem to find just the
right close, so you ramble on a bit, weakening the impact of your presentation by bringing up new ideas or even contradicting yourself. Even the
liveliest writing can mire in such a swamp, leaving a final impression of
confusion and chaos.

But it doesn't have to end this way. Concluding a paper, like introducing one or presenting ideas or describing a scene, is a skill. It can be
learned and practiced and polished, with rapid improvement very quickly. Let's look at what conclusions are supposed to do, and some methods
to accomplish those ends.

A conclusion's primary goal is to provide a sense of closure. It signals
the readers that you have indeed finished, that there are no further
points to cover or examples to add. As you might suspect, once you have
given such a signal, your audience begins to shuffle its mental papers and
close its briefcase. So keep your closing words to a minimum.

A conclusion can have other effects. It can reassert your strongest or
most vivid point; it can comment on the aftermath of an incident; it can
shift the burden to the audience, in effect saying "Now it's your move."
Decide what your conclusion needs to do, then decide what method you
will use. Look over the following list to encourage creative conclusions:

**Signal that you are finishing by using transitional words or
phrases.** A handbook will supply a longer list, but such transitions
as "In conclusion," "Finally," "In sum," "As a final result," and "To
reiterate" will let the audience know that the end is near.

Review the list of techniques suggested for introductions. Close with an appropriate quotation or an intriguing question; use an anecdote or a startling statistic.

Review your discussion. You might summarize your main ideas, or you might choose to reiterate your strongest point. Such repetition is more effective in a paper longer than 500 words.

Look at your introduction. Sometimes you can use a similar technique to conclude your discussion, almost like a pair of bookends. If you asked a question to open the discussion, repeat it and summarize your answer:

> Again, then, the question arises: "Why should anyone care about these children?" And the answer becomes clear: Because they are the future, and their health and education will become the health and education of the nation.

If you began with an incident, pick up the same characters and comment on their fate:

> For Susannah, it is too late for preventive measures like education. But a community action program like the proposed Caretime can reach girls like Susannah to help them understand that their lives have not ended because a new life has begun.

You can give the next line of the song, or extend the quotation used to begin, or incorporate your startling opening into a closing reference:

> The Cathedral has been the site of stirring rhetoric by diverse speakers like Jesse Jackson and Desmond Tutu, and it has sheltered Episcopalians, Catholics, Hindus, and Jews. It has even seen the blessing of a procession of zoo animals—but no football games have yet been played in its stadium-sized interior.

Connect the discussion to the audience. Remember that matters of survival and finance push buttons for the average reader, and that you have analyzed the needs and wants of your audience; use that knowledge to show the readers that this topic has an impact on their lives. Note the link to the readers' self-interest:

> Even if you live in a small and isolated community, AIDS will soon touch your life. One estimate is that within the next five years, every person in the United States will lose at least one relative, friend, neighbor, schoolmate or co-worker to the disease. So do not think that education about AIDS is unnecessary. The disease is coming, and your best defense will be knowledge.

Challenge the audience to make the next move. You can call on your readers to re-think a position or to take direct action (write a letter, make a phone call, send a check, enroll in a class):

That such a problem can exist on American soil is horrifying. That American children are living under bridges and in cardboard boxes is appalling. What is your community doing to reach these children? Contact your local United Care office today. Your time and your resources are needed. A child is calling.

As you work on your conclusion, make sure that it clearly tells the readers that you are finished. If it also sums up or calls for action, be sure that you do not introduce new ideas or begin another paper. Be brief—the signal has been given and the audience is preparing to leave.

YOUR TURN

1. Review current magazines for illustrations of varied conclusions. Classify the conclusions you find. Do essays in particular magazines tend to end in similar ways?

2. Look over a draft in progress or a previously written paper. Write a conclusion that "matches" the introduction, answering a question or mentioning the same characters.

3. Try a variety of endings on the same paper. End with a quote or a call to action or a summary of main points. If you are unsure of the most effective endings, ask a friend to comment on your work.

FINDING A TITLE

It may seem strange to wait until such a late stage to choose a title. But you must wait until your rough drafts have taken shape to be able to choose an appropriate title for your work. By now you know that writing evolves, and what you started out to say may have changed several times. But you are now ready to make a more informed decision about your title.

Be wary of using a topic as your title. A title like " Four Reasons to Go to College" can sound as foolish as calling your paper "A Narrative Composition" (and almost as foolish as naming a child "Boy" or "Girl"). But don't discard such a title without looking at it—the dramatic intensity of such a simple statement is sometimes (though rarely) effective.

Look closely at the discussion to find a unique perspective or an apt description. A paper that recreated your adventures in an ocean storm might use a thought that ran through your mind during the experience, such as "My God, I'm Drowning!" or even a line of actual dialogue, such as "Help! Man Overboard!" Look for a possible play on words or the possible fresh application of a cliché; "Teaching New Tricks to Old Dogs" might work for an account of the installation of computers in a traditional military prep school, and a dual meanings of a title like "Terminal Illness" might suggest the serious nature of computer-related health problems.

Whatever title you select, remember that, like your introduction, it should reflect the content of your discussion (although it may do so very subtly) and it should stimulate your readers' curiosity. Since it is the first impression on your readers, spend as much time as you need to find a lively, effective title for your work.

Sample Passages

When Fat Was in Fashion

The occasion of this article was Flemish artist Rubens' four-hundredth anniversary. The article is both a discussion of Rubens' art and a comment on changing tastes in body size and shape. The conclusion speculates about future tastes in figures, at the same time referring to the article's focus on Rubens' art.

Somewhere in the first fifteen minutes of North by Northwest, Cary Grant pats his stomach, frowns, and tells his secretary to make a note: "Think thin!" Everybody in the audience laughs in instant sympathy—we are all patting our stomachs and thinking thin as hard as we can. One glance at the art of Rubens, however, shows that this was not always so—obviously, thinking fat used to be the thing. The opulent fleshy beauty of Rubens' women probably made the leaner ladies of his day frown when they patted their own meager stomachs, and wish they could compete in the big leagues.

Yet today the very name of Rubens is apt to produce a reaction of disgust. Those puffy knees, those bumps and hills of flesh have never had less fashionable appeal than right now, in the very year of Rubens' four-hundredth anniversary. . . .

Recent movie images, mostly imported from Italy, may foster a new change in visual taste. The enormously ample women in Fellini and Wertmuller films could create a new standard of sexual desirability. Just as the perverse taste for scrawny, hollow-cheeked, morbid images during the Romantic era gradually generated a new ideal image, so the perversely fascinating fatties in the new movies may start an underground vogue which will surface in the future as an acknowledged ideal. In fact, at this present thin-conscious moment, fat beauty has all the edge—all the more chance to be the newest, most outrageous avant-garde trend in erotic taste. We have already had some models to admire: Mama Cass in the '60s, Barbara Cook in the '70s. It may even be that the memory of Zero Mostel's vast grace will bring about the epoch of the desirable fat man. Other big figures, such as James Coco and Robert Morley, have already expressed personal pleasure in their own size. One of these days, the bulk of us may be on the way to Fat City—just in time, and in better shape for the next celebration of the art of Rubens.

The Mystery of the Missing Bones

This informative article begins with a narrative, pauses to report some background facts, then resumes the narrative. The conclusion first heigtens the sense of mystery by reminding the readers of the unanswered questions and then emphasizes the unusual interest the case continues to generate.

At 9:30 A.M. on June 9, 1972, the phone rang in Christopher Janus' room at New York's Harvard Club. When the 62-year-old millionaire business-man picked it up, a husky-voiced woman with a foreign accent was on the line: "Mr. Janus, I am not an eccentric," she began. "I'm the widow of a U.S. marine who was serving in North China when World War II broke out, and I have the bones."

Janus had just returned from Peking, where the director of the Peking Man Museum and officials of the People's Republic of China had asked him to recover the more than 500,000-year-old fossilized remains of Peking man—China's most precious anthropological treasure, which van-ished some time after December 8, 1941. Janus was offering a $5,000, no-questions-asked reward for information leading to recovery of the bones.

The caller declined Janus' invitation to come to see him. . . .

Does the woman in black hold the missing piece to the puzzle? Why has she not contacted Janus again? Why did the Chinese select him as their intermediary? And what about the bones themselves? Buried for half a million years, exposed for less than 20, they still grip men's imaginations by their absence as strongly as they did by their presence.

The title is in quotation marks only because it is a statement people often make.

"Hey, You Ought to Sue the Doctor"

Only the most misanthropic doctor could be pleased by the news that teachers, as well as physicians, are now being sued for malpractice. I am not the most misanthropic of physicians (had I been sued a couple of times, especially by educators, I might be) and therefore am saddened by this new development. As a member of a profession which has just begun to work its way out of a genuine malpractice crisis, I can, however, give my friends in teaching some advice. . . .

There is one final consolation for teachers as they face potential malpractice suits, and that is my mordant observation that in twentieth-century America, you know that people take your work seriously only when they are willing to sue you about it.

SUMMARY

The title and the introduction will give your reader the first impression of your draft, and the conclusion will provide the last, lingering effect of your message. Leaving these important structural elements until you have completed the body of your paper will give you a chance to craft the most effective beginning and ending for your paper.

YOUR TURN

Knowing that titles are the first invitation to a reader, you can understand why magazines sold on newsstands list titles on their covers. Bring in a variety of publications to compare the featured titles. Be sure to include publications like *National Enquirer* as well as more conservative publications like *Good Housekeeping*. Magazines like *Reader's Digest* that anthologize many articles each month are also good sources for this kind of survey.

EDITING TEXT

When you feel that your ideas are complete and your presentation is organized, your editorial voice is ready to review some of the specific elements of the work. In some ways the loudest of the three, the editorial voice, is concerned with correctness and clarity, with elegance and economy. It marks errors and suggests changes in diction, in phrasing, in paragraphing. The editorial voice needs little encouragement; however, it does need direction. The next three chapters will explain principles of paragraphing, methods for improving sentence structures, and criteria for effective diction.

A final level of editing, the review of grammar, spelling, punctuation, and capitalization, should not be neglected. In no other area is general advice quite so useless. Each writer tends to repeat specific mistakes; for example, you probably have a mental list of words that are difficult for you to spell, and you already know whether you tend to misuse semicolons or forget when to use quotation marks. In other words, your editorial voice has become alert to the kinds of errors that you most frequently make. And that is a logical way to approach final editing. As you work on your writing, keep a list of the errors you make (grammatical, spelling, and mechanical) and use that list to direct your editorial review.

As you identify errors, you can find help in correcting them. Your handbook provides reviews not only of the proper rules but also of the most common errors and corrections. If spelling is your problem, invest in a good dictionary. You might also find help in a misspeller's dictionary, a book listing words by common misspellings. If you have access to word-processing software, find out if it has a spell-checker built into it. Some software reviews sentence structure for possible grammatical problems. Keep in mind, though, that relying on mechanical help will not improve your in-class work and that nothing will be as attuned to your personal needs as your own editorial voice.

Improving Paragraphs

This chapter explains the fundamentals of paragraphing. It also demonstrates how to edit paragraphs for effective length and improved coherence.

BUILDING BLOCKS

The largest structural unit of your text is the paragraph. Since the editorial voice will often decide to transfer or to eliminate parts of paragraphs, you should make those decisions before you focus on sentences or phrases. As strong as the editorial voice is, it is also very possessive—once you have corrected the spelling of a word or re-arranged an awkward sentence, the editorial voice is reluctant to change or eliminate what has been "fixed." Therefore, it is more effective to edit the larger block of text and then to look carefully at the remaining smaller structures. To accomplish that task you need to understand the dynamics of paragraphing.

When you speak, you gesture, raise and lower your voice, and pause for shorter or longer periods of time. In addition, you watch your audience to gauge reactions and if you see any sign of confusion or misunderstanding, you clarify your point.

Such devices are not available to you in writing, so you must make your message clear in other ways. Paragraphing is one of your most effective tools because it:

- Breaks your ideas into easily digestible pieces.
- Signals how your thoughts are being grouped.
- Marks your turning from one idea to another.

THE DIALOGUE CONTINUES

Once the editing voice begins to speak, continuing input from the creative and the critical voices may be drowned out. But that input continues, even if it is in a whisper. As you look over the structural units of the text, be aware of the inner promptings which still say, "Can you explain *A* in more detail?" or "What does *B* mean to the audience?" or even, "Should there be a discussion of the background here?" Trust your ability to work on more than one level, and jot down any ideas or questions. However, if you can, save those notes for later and continue to concentrate on the editorial task at hand. If the questions are persistent and compelling, though, consider dismissing the editor for a time and turning again to a concentration on content rather than text.

BASIC PARAGRAPH PATTERNS

Traditionally, the paragraph has been approached as a mini-composition with a specific task (for example, to describe, narrate, or define); a controlling idea, called a topic sentence; and systematic development. Here is an example of a paragraph developed as a mini-composition:

> **The search for principle is the essence of the judicial process.** It can never be enough for a court to say, as a legislature properly can, "X wins the case because he has more votes behind him." Especially in the Supreme Court, which must find in the vague words of our fundamental law the guideposts for a nation, every decision should be supported by reasons that appeal to the intellect and to the ethical sense of Americans. The requirement that a court give reasons for its judgments is a basic safeguard as the country began to realize belatedly during that shameful era when men were labeled "security risks" by boards of quasi-judges who gave no reasons at all and thus avoided responsibility for their conclusions.

Although the topic sentence may be placed anywhere in the paragraph, it is often placed at the beginning to provide an immediate signal to the readers of what ideas will be developed. Following are three of the most common patterns with topic sentences marked.

Cross-Reference: For a more complete presentation of patterns, see Chapter 9. Such logical frameworks as cause-effect, chronology, and classification can be effectively used for paragraphs as well as for longer presentations.

Generalization Followed by Specific Details

> **Nowhere is the refugee impact more starkly evident than in Dade County, Florida, which was inundated by 153,000 Cubans and Haitians during an 18-month period in 1980 and 1981.** Although most of the Mariel boat-lift refugees from Cuba have been assimilated, they account for 16 percent of the total felony arrests in Dade, and jailing these refugees and other Latin-Caribbean aliens accused of crimes is costing Dade taxpayers more than $6 million a year. Further, the federal government has refused

to reimburse the county for the estimated $130 million spent on health, education, police protection and social services for refugees.

Statement of Opinion Followed by Cases-in-Point That Support It

Of the world's exaggerators, none surpasses the Arabs, whose language is a symphony of poetical excess. A Cairo gas station attendant greets his co-workers in the morning: "May your day be scented with jasmine." Sometimes the exaggerations that are inherent in Arabic can be dangerous. Saudi Arabia's late King Saud once told a visiting group of Palestinian journalists that "The Arabs must be ready to sacrifice a million lives to regain the sacred soil of Palestine." It was rhetoric, a flourish; Arabs hearing it would no more take it literally than would an American football crowd hearing "Rip 'em up, tear 'em up." But the words made headlines all over the world as a statement of bloody Saudi intent.

Personal Perspective Followed by Reasons to Explain It

. . . Third, I worry about the private automobile. It is a dirty, noisy, wasteful, and lonely means of travel. It pollutes the air, ruins the safety and sociability of the street, and exercises upon the individual a discipline which takes away far more freedom than it gives him. It causes an enormous amount of land to be unnecessarily abstracted from nature and from plant life and to become devoid of any natural function. It explodes cities, grievously impairs the whole institution of neighborliness, fragmentizes and destroys communities. It has already spelled the end of our cities as real cultural and social communities, and has made impossible the construction of any others in their place. Together with the airplane, it has crowded out other more civilized and more convenient means of transport, leaving older people, infirm people, poor people, and children in a worse situation than they were a hundred years ago. It continues to lend a terrible element of fragility to our civilization, placing us in a situation where our life would break down completely if anything ever interfered with the oil supply.

If you decide to place the topic sentence later in the paragraph, or if you decide to omit it entirely, remember that effective paragraphs are purposeful and controlled, not random. Even if you do not express it to your readers, the topic sentence should be clear to you, clear enough to control the content and the arrangement of the paragraph. Note the varied handling of the topic sentences in the paragraphs below:

As a child, Woodstone was shy, almost pathologically so. He rarely spoke, even to his own family, and he was terror-stricken in the presence of strangers. His teachers thought him rather dull, one writing in his record that he was "quintessentially mediocre." He had no hobbies, no diversions, and certainly no passions. **In short, there was not the slightest clue from his early years that he would emerge from his cocoon as one of the world's premiere Shakespearean actors.**

Comment: Saving the topic sentence for last allows the writer to duplicate the sense of the paragraph with the structure. The pattern of Woodstone's life did not reveal his talent until late, and neither does the pattern of the paragraph.

Paragraphs without topic sentences are often controlled by a vivid image, so vivid that any further comment would be superfluous.

Clothes were scattered on the floor, the desk, the chair, even the window sill. And these were the clean clothes, the ones she had considered and discarded as she prepared for her battle against the day. Makeup too reflected agonies of indecision: not one but several shades of lipstick smeared on blotting tissue, polish remover uncapped in the midst of a frenzied clutter of shades. From the closet to the edge of the bed there ran a trail of shoes, doubtless tested against a multitude of outfits with much anguished and anxious soul-searching. Even her jewelry box had been ransacked for the perfect finish to the perfect look.

Comment: Unless there is some ironic contradiction to be noted, this passage might be weakened by unnecessary general comments. Do you need an overt statement that the room described above is a mess?

YOUR TURN

Choose five of the following sentences and let each serve as the topic sentence of a separate paragraph. Vary the paragraph pattern by following a generalization with details, or a statement of opinion by cases-in-point, or a personal perspective by reasons for it. Consider placing the topic sentence late in the paragraph, or omitting it entirely.

1. You can keep your fine restaurants—I prefer fast-food places.
2. The political process in this country leaves a lot to be desired.
3. Concern for the environment is (not) a priority for the current federal administration.
4. You're never more alone than when you're out of money.
5. Emotional abuse of children can be even more damaging than physical abuse.
6. Television commercials present warped views of American life.

7. When the subject turned to religion, the discussion became heated.

8. Thoreau was right when he called Spring "an experience in immortality."

9. Rising tuition costs will soon make college unavailable to middle-class Americans.

10. Perhaps might doesn't make right, but it gives a person a powerful advantage.

EDITING FOR LENGTH

When you edit paragraphs for length, remember that a paragraph is designed as a logical unit. When it has satisfied the logical needs of the discussion, it should end. If you give logical function priority, you will find that fully developed paragraphs vary in length, ranging from a single sentence paragraph used for transition to a page-long paragraph of narrative that takes the reader for a breathtaking ride. Your editorial eye, then, should be looking for the most logical places to divide your presentation. Here are some natural junctures:

1. Between Techniques of Development

A natural paragraph break may occur whenever you end a description and begin an analysis, or turn from interpretation to evaluation, or finish an explanation and start a narration. Here is an example.

This passaage begins with a quotation, a factual assertion about the book, and an evaluation of the book's quality. The second paragraph moves to facutal information about the man and his time. (Notice how, out of the mass of information that could have been included, the information here is carefully

Shortly before he died, Russell Davenport wrote a friend: "I have worked out my 'philosophy,' have developed a coherent approach to the whole problem of freedom, and rough-drafted about three-quarters of a first book." This volume is that three-quarters, carried as far toward a conclusion as his notes would permit. Even in its unfinished form, it is the best thing Davenport ever wrote. How good that is, and how relevant to current American thinking, can be better appreciated with some knowledge of his life and previous work.

Russell Wheeler Davenport was born July 12, 1899, in South Bethlehem, Pa., and died in New York City April 19, 1954 (the anniversary of "the shot heard round the world"). His mature life, brief as it was, spanned a period of nearly unprecedented change in the patterns of American life and the direction of American national policy. In these changes Davenport participated as an intensely committed citizen and some of them he directly influenced as a publicist. While America was groping reluctantly for the role of successful world leadership, Davenport was groping for the ideas and policies that would support this role.

selected to create a focus on the writer's particular interest.) The third paragraph moves to a judgment about the man's personal qualities, followed by a paraphrase.

The qualities he brought to his search were among the best qualities that America was at the same time bringing to her ordeal. They were the qualities that George Santayana once touched on in a classic description of the Yale man. . . .

2. When There Is a Change in Time, Place, or Focus

In a comparison between two people, you might discuss their behavior in class, their behavior out of class, and their general attitude toward others. All these characteristics would be part of the same comparison. Yet each is a separate aspect, and each marks an appropriate place for starting a new paragraph. Here is an example of breaking paragraphs at an appropriate place.

Sometimes, watching television helps you learn to think on your feet. Like an old friend of mine named Shakey, who once escaped from the North Dakota State Penitentiary. While he hid in the basement of a private residence, they were putting up roadblocks all around the city of Bismarck. But Shakey was smart. He knew that there had to be some way for him to extricate himself from this mess. Then, all of a sudden it occurred to him: Shakey remembered a caper film he had seen on television once, in which a fugitive had managed to breach several roadblocks by using an emergency vehicle.

With this basic plan in mind, he proceeded to the Bismarck City Hospital and, pretending to be hysterical, he stammered to the first white-coated attendant he met that his brother was lying trapped beneath an overturned farm tractor about 12 miles or so from town. He then climbed into the back of the ambulance, and with red lights blazing and siren screaming, the vehicle drove right through two roadblocks—and safely out of Bismarck.

Two days or so later, Shakey arrived back on the same ranch in Montana where he'd worked before his jail sentence. The foreman even gave him his job again. But Shakey was so proud of what he'd done that he made one big mistake: He boasted about his escape from the North Dakota state prison, and in the end he was turned over to the authorities, who sent him back to North Dakota—and prison.

3. Between Speakers in Dialogue

This kind of paragraph break is not distracting to readers even if there is a change of speaker after every few words, because it provides them with a guide to who is speaking without repeating "John said" and "Bill replied" over and over. Here is an example of such paragraphing:

After the first speaker is identified (". . . John offered"), there is no need for further

As they shuffled along the street, eyes cast down as if looking for money, John and Bill grappled with the problem of what to do that night.

"How about checking out the dance?" John offered.

"Nah. Bunch of creeps there."

identification. In
a longer dialogue,
there might be
such a need. A
dialogue with
three or more
speakers requires
additional
identification.
How much would
be required
varies depending
on how clear the
changes in
speakers were.

Here the same
paragraphing
rule is used even
though
technically there
is no dialogue
(only the
headmaster
speaks).
Nevertheless, the
narrator's own
unexpressed
thouht are
recorded in
response to the
headmaster's
comments as if
they were
spoken.

"Then how about a movie?"

"Nothin' good's playin."

"We could go to the rec center."

"No way. Art's always there and I owe him money."

"I don't know what to do then."

"Come on. Think of somethin'. I don't want to walk around the street all night."

Here is a slightly different variation of the same kind of paragraphing.

I had better explain that I was a frequent visitor to the headmaster's study, because of the latest thing I had done or left undone. As we now say, I was not integrated. I was, if anything, disintegrated; and I was puzzled. Grown-ups never made sense. Whenever I found myself in a penal position before the headmaster's desk, with the statuettes glimmering whitely above him, I would sink my head, clasp my hands behind my back, and writhe one shoe over the other.

The headmaster would look opaquely at me through flashing spectacles.

"What are we going to do with you?"

Well, what were they going to do with me? I would writhe my shoe some more and stare down at the worn rug.

"Look up, boy! Can't you look up?"

Then I would look up in the cupboard, where the naked lady was frozen in her panic and the muscular gentleman contemplated the hindquarters of his leopard in endless gloom. I had nothing to say to the headmaster. His spectacles caught the light so that you could see nothing human behind them. There was no possibility of communication.

"Don't you ever think at all?"

No, I didn't think, wasn't thinking, couldn't think—I was simply waiting in anguish for the interview to stop.

"Then you'd better learn—hadn't you?"

On one occasion the headmaster leaped to his feet, reached up, and plonked Rodin's masterpiece on the desk before me.

"That's what a man looks like when he's really thinking."

I surveyed the gentleman without interest or comprehension.

"Go back to your class."

Y O U R   T U R N

The following passages are unparagraphed. Read them carefully. Then, in light of the guidelines explained in the chapter, decide how they should be paragraphed and write them out. For each division, briefly explain what juncture you see.

1. When Arthur was in the first grade, the teacher directed the class to "think." "Now, class," she said,"I know this problem is a little harder than the ones we have been doing, but I am going to give you a few extra minutes to think about it. OK? Now start thinking." It was not the first time Arthur had heard the word used. He had heard it many times at home. But never quite this way. The teacher seemed to be asking for some special activity, something he should know how to start and stop. Like his father's car. "Vroom-m-m," he muttered half aloud. Because of his confusion, he was unaware he was making the noise. "Arthur, please stop making noises and start thinking." Embarrassed, and not knowing quite what to do, he looked down at his desk. Then out of the corner of his eye he noticed that the little girl next to him was staring at the ceiling. "Maybe that's the way you start thinking," he guessed. He decided the others had probably learned how to do it last year, that time he was home with the measles. So he stared at the ceiling. As he progressed through grade school and high school, he heard that same direction hundreds of times." No, that's not the answer, you're not thinking—now think!" And occasionally, from a particularly self-pitying teacher given to talking to himself aloud: "What did I do to deserve this? Don't they teach them anything in the grades anymore? Don't you people care about ideas? Think, dammit, THINK." So Arthur learned to feel somewhat guilty about the whole matter. Obviously this thinking was an important activity that he'd failed to learn. Maybe he lacked the brain power. But he was resourceful enough. He watched the other students and did what they did. Whenever a teacher started in about thinking, he screwed up his face, furrowed his brow, scratched his head, stroked his chin, stared off into space or up at the ceiling, and repeated silently to himself, "Let's see now, I've got to think about that, think, think (I hope he doesn't call on me), think." Though he didn't know it, that's just what the other students were saying to themselves. Since Arthur's situation is not all that uncommon, your experience may have been similar. That is, many people have told you to think, but no one ever explained what thinking is, how many kinds of thinking there are, and what qualities a good thinker has that a poor thinker lacks.

2. Dying is an integral part of life, as natural and predictable as being born. But whereas birth is cause for celebration, death has become a dreaded and unspeakable issue to be avoided by every means possible in our modern society. Perhaps it is that death reminds us of our human vulnerability in spite of all our technological advances. We may be able to delay it, but we cannot escape it. We, no less than other, nonrational animals, are destined to die at the end of our lives. And death strikes indiscriminately—it

cares not at all for the status or position of the ones it chooses; everyone must die, whether rich or poor, famous or unknown. Even good deeds will not excuse their doers from the sentence of death; the good die as often as the bad. It is perhaps this inevitable and unpredictable quality that makes death so frightening to many people. Especially those who put a high value on being in control of their own existence are offended by the thought that they too are subject to the forces of death. But other societies have learned to cope better with the reality of death than we seem to have done. It is unlikely that any group has ever welcomed death's intrusion on life, but there are others who have successfully integrated the expectation of death into their understanding of life. It is difficult to accept death in this society because it is unfamiliar. In spite of the fact that it happens all the time, we never see it. When a person dies in a hospital, he is quickly whisked away; a magical disappearing act does away with the evidence before it could upset anyone. But, as you will read later in various contexts, being part of the dying process, the death, and the burial including seeing and perhaps interacting with the body is an important part of coming to grips with death—that of the person who has died and your own. We routinely shelter children from death and dying, thinking we are protecting them from harm. But it is clear that we do them a disservice by depriving them of the experience. By making death and dying a taboo subject and keeping children away from people who are dying or who have died, we create fear that need not be there. When a person dies, we "help" his loved ones by doing things for them, being cheerful, and fixing up the body so it looks "natural." Again, our "help" is not helpful; it is destructive. When someone dies, it is important that those close to him participate in the process; it will help them in their grief, and it will help them face their own death more easily.

3. My older sister, Ann, and my younger sister, Martha, always think they are right. They are so stubborn! They fight over the silliest things. I remember hearing them fight last year over the rain. They were watching television with my cousin when he commented that it was raining out. Ann said she knew it was raining, that it had been pouring for a half hour. Martha looked out and said it wasn't pouring, but only sprinkling. In a few minutes they were screaming at each other about how hard or lightly it was raining. My cousin's TV viewing was ruined. Another of their dumb fights occurred last month. Ann had just returned home from staying overnight at a friend's house. Her clothes lay strewn on the couch. Martha saw the clothes and told Ann to pick them up because we were going to have company for dinner. Ann ignored her. About a half hour later, Ann looked on the couch for the clothes, but didn't find them there. She looked all around the room and then happened to

glance out the window—there were the clothes, strewn across the yard (where Martha had obviously thrown them). Ann said nothing. She walked upstairs, went into Martha's room, took all her clothes out of the drawers, and threw them out the window. Nor was that enough for Ann. She then went downstairs and began arguing with Martha. The battle raged for more than an hour. Finally, Ann stormed out of the house. When she returned later that evening, Ann found the door locked. (Martha had decided that was a good way to get the last "word.") She was forced to spend the night at a friend's house. But even that was not the most ridiculous fight they ever got into. The most ridiculous one was over a tuna fish sandwich. I was in the living room with my boyfriend at the time. My sisters were in the kitchen. All of a sudden we heard Martha yelling at Ann and calling her a pig. I rushed to the kitchen to see what was going on. Ann was trying to leave the room with her tuna fish sandwich. Martha was holding on to her, shouting that she would let go only when Ann got a plate to put under the sandwich. They both stood there for about fifteen minutes . . . until Martha got tired and let Ann go. Ann walked into the living room, put her sandwich on the coffee table, and turned on the TV set. When she turned around to pick up the sandwich, there was Martha standing in front of her, sandwich in hand. And in a flash she had squashed the sandwich in Ann's surprised face.

EDITING FOR COHERENCE

Coherence in writing means that your ideas and your sentences follow each other in a logical, almost inevitable order. Sentence 3, for example, should be the best, if not the only, possible sentence to follow Sentence 2, and it should be followed just as inevitably by Sentence 4. The readers should not notice the orderly patterns but should focus undisturbed on the discussion. Chapter 9 presented a basic way to make your writing coherent—by arranging the ideas in your composition in the most logical and easy to follow order. Even the most carefully arranged paper, however, will often need improvement in coherence. Following are four strategies for improving the connections within and between your paragraphs.

Use Pronouns Effectively

Pronouns, words that stand in place of nouns, provide a subtle way of keeping your subject in clear focus without repeating it again and again. They include *I, me, mine, you, yours, it, its, we, us, ours, they, them, theirs, this, that, who, whom, whoever, someone, anyone,* and *no one.* Here is an example of their use:

> I came to marvel at John F. Kennedy's ability to look at his own strengths and weaknesses with utter detachment, his candid and objective responses to public questions, and his insistence on cutting through prevailing bias and myths to the heart of a problem. He had a disciplined and analytical mind. Even his instincts, which were sound, came from his reason rather than his hunches. He hated no enemy, he wept at no adversity. He was neither willing nor able to be flamboyant or melodramatic.

Repeat Words Skillfully

Undoubtedly you were warned against repetitious writing. Such warnings are justified, for repetition can as easily be a vice as a virtue. The trick is to avoid using it as a cover for poverty of thought, and instead to use it judiciously to reinforce the connections between ideas. Consider this passage:

> Philosophy is the love of wisdom. There are many who believe that for a red-blooded man there are better things to love than wisdom. It seems to be supposed by such persons that wisdom is an abstraction that one can best find when he manages to get lost from life. However, one cannot be on good terms with wisdom and on bad terms with life, for we would hardly call a man wise who did not get along well with life. If one really wishes to understand philosophy, it is not enough to learn to pass formal examinations in this subject; one must also learn to face the tests of living. If one has knowledge of the truth as an intellectual matter but does not live it, then this knowledge is shallow and incomplete; if a philosopher speaks about the truth and yet fails to make it a part of his existence, his words have a hollow ring.

In the twenty odd paragraphs that follow this quoted paragraph, the author discusses various philosophers and holy men from ancient times to the present, pointing out the particular ways in which they manifested their love of wisdom. And every couple of paragraphs or so—whenever he feels the readers could benefit from a reminder of the central focus of his ideas—the author repeats the key phrase "love of wisdom." For example, he writes, "Yet even in this century the love of wisdom has not been entirely eroded and has remained strong in some of our great philosophers, such as the French philosopher Henri Bergson." And later, "Just as Bergson in France managed to love wisdom in this war-torn century, Bertrand Russell in England did so too." And still later, "The love of wisdom embraces the love of peace, and perhaps no human being better exemplified this love than Mahatma Gandhi."

Use Echo Words

Echo words are words that do not exactly repeat what was said, but whose sense is so nearly the same that they recall what was said. In the passage about love of wisdom, for example, the author used numerous echo words in the paragraphs following the one quoted above. These included "to know the truth," "love, truth, and justice," "the highest values," and "truth, justice, and virtue."

Use Relationship Words

Relationship words (also called "transitions") signal that a change of some sort is about to occur in the idea. Such words show exactly how a group of subsequent words relates to a group of preceding words. The following types of relationship words are used for this purpose.

Words for Adding   Whenever another example or case in point is being added, or further details are being provided, or additional development in the same vein as previous development is being presented, there is a potential for misunderstanding. The readers may wonder, "Is this new material more evidence of the same kind or contrasting evidence?" The use of one or more relationship words will answer the question. You may choose from a number of words that show you are adding a point—*also, first (second, third, and so on), in addition, next, further, finally, lastly, besides, another, still another*. However, the most common and simplest adding word is *and*.

From the time you were in grade school, you probably were taught that you should not begin a sentence with *and*, but there is no foundation for such a rule. Like any opening, it can be monotonous if overused, but it is also an effective tool. Here are just a few examples from the works of respected twentieth-century writers:

> The music of poetry, then, must be a music latent in the common speech of its time. **And** that means also that it must be latent in the common speech of the poet's place.

> Even supposing that all teachers were willing and able to exact vigilance over written work, there would still be many practical problems of detail. **And** first, what motive for writing well can the student be made to feel?

> When one watches some tired hack on the platform mechanically repeating the familiar phrases—bestial atrocities, iron heel, blood-stained tyranny, free peoples of the world, stand shoulder-to-shoulder—one often has a curious feeling that one is not watching a live human being but some kind of dummy: a feeling which suddenly

becomes stronger at moments when the light catches the speaker's spectacles and turns them into blank discs which seem to have no eyes behind them. **And** this is not altogether fanciful.

If these examples are not enough to persuade you that it is perfectly proper to use *and* to begin a sentence, pay a quick visit to your library and check further. And don't look only at books; look at current magazines and newspapers, including *Time* and *Newsweek* and the *New York Times.* You'll find more than enough evidence that and is not only acceptable, but one of the most natural and helpful connectives available to you as a writer.

Caution: Even if you accept this use of *and*, be sensitive to an audience that might find it awkward. It is an effective tool, but not the only one.

Words for Intensifying Whenever you are adding something that is more important than preceding points, you need a relationship word that both signals adding and increases the emphasis on what follows, intensifying it. The most common words that achieve both aims are *moreover, more (most) important, more (most) significant, above all, mainly,* and *principally.*

Words for Illustrating Whenever you turn from an assertion to a point of evidence that supports it, you need words that signal what you are illustrating your idea. You may choose *for example, for instance, to illustrate,* or *a case in point,* to name a few popular phrases.

Words for Changing Time or Place Whenever you progress or switch from one time or place to another, you need to signal the exact change you are making. Sometimes a simple expression like *afterward, later, then, soon, now, before,* or *eventually* will suffice. At other times a more specific reference will be necessary, such as *at nine o'clock, the following Thursday, in Oakdale,* or *when we finished.*

Words for Contrasting Whenever you turn from one idea to an opposing idea, you need a word that signals that opposition or contrast. For example, in "I went to the movie, but I didn't enjoy myself," the *but* alerts the reader that the expected reaction (the writer's enjoyment) did not occur. Some common expressions used to signal contrast are *however, nevertheless, yet, or, on the other hand, in contrast, to be sure, unexpectedly, surprisingly,* and *still.* But the most frequently used is *but.*

Unfortunately, many people have been taught not to begin a sentence with *but.* That prohibition is as unfounded as the prohibition concerning *and.* The word *but* has been used to begin sentences since Anglo-Saxon times. And a check of current books, magazines, and newspapers will reveal that no other connective, with the possible exception of *and,* is used so often in this way. Here are a few examples of its occurrence in the work of respected writers.

When the churchwardens apply to me at the usual seasons I contribute; and when the hat goes round for special expenses for repairs to the building, I pay my share of what may be necessary to keep it standing. I am on intimate terms with the rector. I am, in short, a local pillar of the church; and I visit it occasionally. **But** I have never attended a service there. Whether from defect or excess of intellect, I cannot use the Church of England ritual either as spiritual food or to express and demonstrate my religion. The last time I tried it was when my mother died. She was not a Church of England ritualist; but she had no prejudices nor bigotries . . . And so the Church of England burial service was read. **But** I found it morbid and heathenish. It was all wrong for my mother and all wrong for me.

I have noticed that, as a class, it is the rich who are especially anxious to be loved for themselves alone. The fact is understandable since they are no doubt particularly likely to be imposed upon. **But** it tends to become an obsession and is one of their less attractive traits.

Words for Drawing a Conclusion   Whenever you are pointing out cause-and-effect relationships or drawing a conclusion from the evidence you have presented, you need a word that emphasizes the reasoning you are doing. You may choose from *therefore, so, for this reason, consequently, in conclusion, accordingly, thus, hence, as a result, it follows that, because of this,* and *for* (in the sense of *because*). The last word, *for,* has been subject to the same misunderstanding as *and* and *but.* It too is completely acceptable at the beginning of a sentence, as these examples demonstrate.

But the joke is one for the white man to ponder. For it frees him, too: from the need to "love" in order not to lynch.

Bellamy's *Utopia* now reads so strangely, not through the absurdities of his prophecies, but because of the humane hopes that he attached to their fulfillment. **For** despite his compassion and his democratic ideals, Bellamy unguardedly embraced, under the rubric of the general welfare, the implacable totalitarian features that Bulwer-Lytton shrank from.

Words for Comparing   Whenever you compare one thing with another, you need a word that signals that a comparison is being made. Choose from *like, as, just as, just like,* and *similarly.*

Words for Summarizing   Whenever you draw a piece of writing to a close and wish to bring together in a concise way some or all of the points you made earlier, use an expression like one of these: *to repeat, to sum up, in summary.*

Longer Connectives   Often a single word or a short expression is not adequate to signal the relationship involved. In such cases, longer connectives are necessary. These may be a clause, a whole sentence, or even, in some cases, a paragraph in length. Here are two examples of such longer connectives.

Another example of Ed's cruelty to his wife, not physical in this case but mental, occurred last week.

These are the proposals that have been made. All of them, as we have seen, are reasonable. But which of them offers the best prospect of success?

A SAMPLE PASSAGE How important is it, really, to connect your ideas effectively? Let's look at a brief passage that contains a number of connectives and decide how large their contribution is to its meaning. Each of the underlined words or phrases is a connective of one of the four main types explained above.

Something has to be done about the number of violent criminals, many of them teenagers (in some cases, even children) who prey on law-abiding citizens. These sociopaths are seldom imprisoned for any length of time. Even when they are caught and convicted of a violent crime, the law seems weighted in their favor, and because of their youth or some legal technicality or the judge's leniency, they are soon free to victimize others again. For example, a convicted felon was recently released in his parents' custody after being found guilty of a sex crime. Within a month he had raped and murdered another young woman. Moreover, he was tried on a lesser charge and, as a result, got a lighter sentence. So in seven or eight years he may be walking the streets again. Nor is his situation all that uncommon. Reduced charges, light or suspended sentences, and early parole seem to be the dominant pattern in today's courts. Something must be done to change this pattern. The answer, of course, is not a merciless, repressive legal system. Neither is it vigilante action. Those solutions would be little better than the problem itself. Surely our democratic principles demand that the rights of suspects be upheld and that humane treatment be given even the most vicious unrepentant criminal. But those considerations must no longer be allowed to obscure the first and most

<u>important</u> reason for any law—to protect the rights of the honest, the responsible, and the innocent.

Without the connective words and phrases, the passage would still be intelligible. But the connections allow an easier reading of the passage, giving the readers a better understanding of its meaning. In addition, connectives subtly increase the readers' confidence in the writer by demonstrating that the writer has control over his or her ideas and is fully aware of their interrelationships.

A word of caution is in order here. Be sure to choose your connectives with care. The wrong ones can be worse than none at all, for they will not only make reading difficult, but also actually set up misinterpretation. So don't just sprinkle in your connectives indiscriminately. Make them fit the relationships and convey the meaning you intend.

Y O U R   T U R N

1. Reread the paragraph above about violent crime and the need for reform of the legal system. Classify each of the underlined words or phrases as one of the following kinds of connectives: repeated words, echo words, pronouns, or relationship words. In the case of relationship words, indicate the kind of relationship shown.

2. Read each of the following passages closely. List each connective word or phrase in the passage. Then classify each as you did in Exercise 1 (above).

   a. Standing on our microscopic fragment of a grain of sand, we attempt to discover the nature and purpose of the universe which surrounds our home in space and time. Our first impression of the universe is something akin to terror. We find the universe terrifying because of its vast meaningless distances, terrifying because of its inconceivably long vistas of time, which dwarf human history to the twinkling of an eye, terrifying because of our extreme loneliness and because of the material insignificance of our home in space—a millionth part of a grain of sand out of all the sea-sand in the world. But above all else, we find the universe terrifying because it appears to be indifferent to life like our own; emotion, ambition and achievement, art and religion, all seem foreign to its plan. Perhaps, indeed, we ought to say it appears to be actively hostile to life like our own.

b. With few exceptions, modern authorities have accepted [Studies of a Reclining Male Nude] as a study by Michelangelo for the figure of Adam in the "Creation of Adam" section of the Sistine Chapel ceiling. But is it really one of Michelangelo's drawings? Bernard Berenson once doubted it. He thought it more likely a very accomplished contemporary copy of a Michelangelo drawing now lost to us. Then, as sometimes happens with even the greatest connoisseurs, Berenson reversed himself. He elevated it from "School of Michelangelo" to a work by the master himself. Yet he continued to harbor doubts about it.

c. Next morning my wife slipped out of the hotel successfully. The train was about an hour late in starting. I filled in the time by writing a long letter to the Ministry of War, telling them about Kopp's case—that without a doubt he had been arrested by mistake, that he was urgently needed at the front, that countless people would testify that he was innocent of any offense, etc., etc., etc. I wonder if anyone read that letter, written on pages torn out of a notebook in wobbly handwriting (my fingers were still partly paralyzed) and still more wobbly Spanish. At any rate, neither this letter nor anything else took effect. As I write, six months after the event, Kopp (if he has not been shot) is still in jail, untried and uncharged. At the beginning we had two or three letters from him, smuggled out by released prisoners and posted in France. They all told the same story—imprisonment in filthy dark dens, bad and insufficient food, serious illness due to the conditions of imprisonment, and refusal of medical attention. I have had all this confirmed from several other sources, English and French. More recently he disappeared into one of the "secret prisons" with which it seems impossible to make any kind of communication. His case is the case of scores or hundreds of foreigners and no one knows how many thousands of Spaniards.

3. Look over several of your own passages, at least several paragraphs in length. Mark the logical junctures of your ideas and note the transitional words or phrases (if any) that you used. Is there a need for more such signals?

SUMMARY

Paragraphing is one way to clarify written material. It is a visual clue to new ideas and to new techniques. Paragraph length is determined by logical divisions in material, but coherence can be aided by specific techniques.

Improving Sentences

This chapter explains the fundamentals of sentence style, including combining and expanding sentences, using coordination and subordination, maintaining clarity with parallel structures, and varying word order and voice.

Effective sentences do not just happen. You must design them. Your creative voice often supplies you with vivid descriptions and phrasing, so your drafting has probably produced many fine passages. Once you have arranged your ideas and your paragraphs carefully, you can direct your editorial voice to sentence structure. The pace, the rhythm, even the length of your sentences will reflect your own creativity and style, but there are some traditional rhetorical strategies to be considered in this polishing stage. Let's look more closely at the fundamentals of sentence style and then turn to specific strategies for solving common sentence problems.

THE SIMPLE SENTENCE

There are six basic sentence patterns for the simple English sentence. Although you may have forgotten the terms traditionally assigned to these patterns, you will surely find the patterns themselves familiar.

They are as follows:

Subject/Verb
The heat shields disintegrated.
The director resigned.

Subject/Verb/Object
Seat belts save lives.
George chomps his food.

Subject/Verb/Indirect Object/Direct Object
Bill owes the store a thousand dollars.
Insensitive people cause others embarrassment.

Subject/Verb/Direct Object/Objective Complement
The team elected Jasper captain.
Arthur had his nose broken.

Subject/Linking Verb/Noun
Time is money.
College can be a grind.

Subject/Linking Verb/Adjective
Jan is beautiful.
Taxes are eternal.

The basic patterns are not prescriptions; rather, they are descriptions based on the way we actually use language. But your sentences are not limited to the basic patterns. Instead, you are free to add art to function and make your sentences pleasing to read. Consider, for example, the following passage. It is made up entirely of basic patterns of the simple sentence.

> The Greco-Roman civilization was efficient. It was productive. It was intelligent. It was tasteful. It was literate. Except in bad reigns it was filled with spiritual and personal liberties. It was in most ways the greatest success in social living that our Western world has seen. Far more people could read and write in A.D. 150 than in 1550. Perhaps more people could read and write in A.D. 150 than in 1750 and 1850. Schools were nearly everywhere. Europe was filled with books and libraries. So was northern Africa. So was Egypt. The Near East was, too. There was free movement of thought. Over thousands of square miles the travelling teachers moved. They went from city to city. So did the philosophers and orators. The religious and social propagandists did, too. They were all freely explaining. And they were eloquently disputing.

This passage is technically correct, and it contains a great deal of significant detail. Yet it is a chore to read. Compare that passage with the following.

> Efficient, productive, intelligent, tasteful, literate, and, except in bad reigns, filled with spiritual and personal liberties, the Greco-Roman civilization was in most ways the greatest success in social living that our Western world has seen. Far more people could read and write in A.D. 150 than in 1550, or perhaps in 1750 and 1850. . . .
>
> Schools were nearly everywhere. Europe and northern Africa and Egypt and the Near East were filled with books and libraries. There was free movement of thought. Over thousands of square miles, from city to city, moved the travelling teachers, the wandering philosophers and orators, the religious and social propagandists—all freely explaining and eloquently disputing.

This passage has the same material as the first and essentially the same order of ideas. Yet it is more enjoyable to read because it is written in a more mature style, a style that is not difficult to learn.

EXPANDING YOUR SENTENCES

An important skill in composing sentences is the skill of expanding basic sentence patterns. This is done by adding words to them. Let's begin our consideration of this process by clarifying three important terms: **base clause, free modifiers,** and **texture.**

The **base clause** is the main unit of a sentence. It appears in any of the forms detailed at the beginning of this chapter. **Free modifiers** are any words, phrases, or clauses that can be set off from the base clause by punctuation. They are sometimes related to the subject of the base clause and sometimes to the verb. **Texture** refers to the number of free modifiers present in a sentence. If relatively few free modifiers are present, the texture is said to be thin; if many, dense. Let's now examine several sentences and see how these terms apply.

Base Clause:	The old man wheezed each breath laboriously.
Base Clause with one free modifier; texture, thin:	The old man wheezed each breath laboriously, a rattling noise providing rhythmic accompaniment.
Base Clause with numerous free modifiers; texture, dense :	His body frail, gray, and listless, his head barely denting the mattress, the old man breathed laboriously, a rattling noise providing rhythmic accompaniment and signalling that the end was near.

Free modifiers may be added to any one of three places—before the base clause, within the base clause, or after the base clause. In sentences with a very rich texture they are frequently found in all three places. Here are some examples of the modification that can be used in each place. (The base clause in each case is underlined.)

Modification before the Base Clause

Suddenly, before anyone in the car realized what was happening, the driver slumped over the wheel and veered off the road into the ditch.

With heart pounding and eyes darting nervously from left to right, Jennifer entered the darkened hallway.

The moment he was handed the letter, he knew the news was bad.

Modification within the Base Clause

<u>He thought to himself,</u> tentatively at first, and then with increasing conviction, <u>that she had cheated him.</u>

<u>The economy,</u> which every candidate for high office has a plan to control, <u>may very well be uncontrollable.</u>

<u>The party,</u> unless I am mistaken, <u>is closed to everyone but dormitory residents.</u>

Modification after the Base Clause

<u>The sisters left home at the same time</u>—Jane to get married, Agnes to join the Navy, and Marie to study law.

<u>He dribbled the basketball the length of the concrete court,</u> water splashing up with every bounce.

<u>Down the block from my house is a park</u> with an Olympic-size swimming pool, eight tennis courts, and twelve acres of picnic area with tree-lined walks, fireplaces, and picnic tables.

Although free modifiers may be placed in any or all of the three positions in a sentence, they are most frequently placed at the end. The typical base clause used by professional writers is general or abstract and is followed by free modifiers that add specific, concrete detail. The resulting sentence is called a cumulative sentence (like the three sentences just above). Here is another example:

> <u>On that evening she began her relationship with cocaine,</u> a relationship that would cost her tens of thousands of dollars, a career, two marriages, and her self-respect, a relationship from which she is only now, a decade later, beginning to escape.

A Strategy for Expanding Sentences

An effective way to decide when and how to expand your sentences is to ask appropriate questions about them, the kinds of questions an interested person might ask to obtain more information. Here are some examples of this questioning strategy:

Base Clause

The left fielder caught the fly ball.

Appropriate Questions

How deep was he in left field? Did he have to move to the ball? How exactly did he catch it? What did he do after he caught it?

Resulting Sentence

After racing back almost to the left centerfield wall and leaping high in the air, the left fielder caught the fly ball with a stabbing motion, then rifled the ball to second base to catch the runner for a double play.

Base Clause

Sally could be a world-class runner.

Appropriate Questions

What talents does she have that suggest this conclusion? Are there any conditions she will have to meet in order to realize her potential?

Resulting Sentence

A gifted performer with a long, loping stride, unusual stamina, and a formidable finishing kick, Sally could be a world-class runner if she would accept the difficult regimen required for successful competition at that level.

Base Clause

Three deer walked into the open meadow.

Appropriate Questions

How exactly did they walk? Were they bucks or does?
Did they seem afraid? If so, why?

Resulting Sentence

Three deer, a buck and two does, walked noiselessly into the open meadow, listening and sniffing cautiously, their senses sharpened by a week of shotgun blasts, ready to dart for the safety of the woods at the first hint of danger.

Y O U R T U R N

Select five of the following sentences and expand each using the strategy explained in the preceding pages. You may insert modification before, within, or after the base clause, or (if appropriate) in all three places. Read the resulting sentences aloud to be sure they are neither awkward nor confusing.

The divorce was bitter.
We walked quietly along the deserted beach.

Hockey is a violent sport.
He sat in the church and prayed.
We argued about whether the drinking age should be raised.
They met under unusual circumstances.
He sat thinking of his wedding vows.
She promised her mother she would study medicine.
"A fool and his money are soon parted."
I love to ski.
The race was disappointing.
Being alone can be painful.
Agnes gave Charlie her pen.
Betty dyed her hair brown.
The food tasted awful.
Peace of mind must be earned.
Few dentists work painlessly.
Swimming is an excellent form of exercise.
I hate losing.
Rationalizing is a sign of insecurity.
The best part of being in love is the sharing.
Failing is no fun.
She jogs five miles every day.
My car stopped.
The sign said "10-percent discount for cash."
Blind dates are risky.
We must not forget the persecuted people of the world.
The two boys were led to the principal's office.

Using Coordination and Subordination

Coordination and subordination are methods of combining two or more simple sentences into a single sentence unit. **Coordination** leaves each of the original sentence units grammatically independent of the others, capable of standing alone as a complete thought. **Subordination,** on the other hand, makes one or more of the original sentence units dependent on one or more of the others. The following examples further clarify this distinction:

Simple Sentences

The United States should not permit its environment to be treated as an endlessly renewable resource.
Also, it should not stand idly by while wildlife and natural resources are sacrificed in the name of progress.

Revision

The United States should not permit its environment to be treated as an endlessly renewable resource, nor should it stand idly by while wildlife and natural resources are sacrificed in the name of progress. (**Coordination**—each of the two sentence units could stand alone as a complete thought.)

Simple Sentences

He didn't get the job. He made a very poor impression on the interviewer.

Revision

He didn't get the job because he made a very poor impression on the interviewer. (**Subordination**—the word "because" makes the second clause incapable of standing alone as a complete thought.)

Simple Sentences

I've wasted enough time this term. From here on I'm going to be a model student.

Revision

I've wasted enough time this term; from here on I'm going to be a model student. (**Coordination**)

Simple Sentences

The twins were sleeping soundly. Meanwhile their brother Tim got up, tiptoed to the kitchen, and ate the rest of the cake.

Revision

While the twins were sleeping soundly, their brother Tim got up, tiptoed to the kitchen, and ate the rest of the cake. (**Subordination**)

When you use coordination and subordination to combine simple sentences, you are doing more than varying sentence structure and length. Effective sentence structure is not arbitrary; it is determined by the logical connections between ideas and by your decisions about their relative importance. Thus a main clause should contain a main idea, with a subordinate (or dependent) clause expressing an idea that is less important. Consider the following examples:

Simple Sentences

The game seemed out of reach for the visiting team. Then in the final minute and a half they scored six unanswered baskets to win by a single point.

Revisions

The game seemed out of reach for the visiting team, but in the final minute and a half they scored six unanswered baskets to win by a single point. (**Coordination:** the ideas are considered equally important.)

or

Although the game seemed out of reach for the visiting team, in the final minute and a half they scored six unanswered baskets to win by a single point. (**Subordination:** the comeback win is given more emphasis.)

Simple Sentences

The first treaty to divide the western territory was not a fair treaty. It was ignored. Thirteen years of war followed. Hundreds of deaths were recorded on both sides. A more equitable treaty was signed. Both sides wanted peace. The second treaty was honored.

Revision

Because the first treaty to divide the western territory was unfair, it was ignored. But after thirteen years of war and hundreds of deaths had been chronicled, both sides wanted peace. Because of these desires, a more equitable treaty was signed and honored.

Comment: The second passage is better partly because the sentence structure is varied and sophisticated, but also because the sentence structure shows the logical connections between the ideas. The three main clauses tell us that the first treaty was ignored, that both sides wanted peace, and that a better treaty was signed and honored. The other clauses and phrases are secondary ideas. They explain why the main actions occurred—because the first treaty was unfair, because there were years of bloody war, because peace became a priority. By subordinating the explanatory ideas, the writer has created a more precise and more effective passage.

In addition to being used individually, coordination and subordination may also be used together:

Simple Sentences

Some people do all their own car repairs. I don't do any. I can't tell a fan belt from a fuel pump.

Revision

Some people do all their own car repairs, but I don't do any because I can't tell a fan belt from a fuel pump.

Comment: The first two clauses are coordinate because the two contrasted ideas are equally important; the one beginning with "because" is subordinate because the idea it contains is explanation for the one it follows.

When you combine ideas using coordination and subordination, you must first decide which ideas are of equal "rank" and which are explanatory. Use your sentence structures to reflect the logical contents of your work. Small details can be reduced to modifying phrases or even single words. As you connect clauses, be precise about the logical connections between your ideas. (Words that show relationships, discussed in Chapter 16, will help you show those connections to your readers.)

YOUR TURN

Combine each of the following groups of sentences using coordination and/or subordination.

1. We must address the problem and at least make an effort to solve it. Otherwise it will grow in size and complexity. In time it will do irreparable harm.

2. I've had my fill of listening to him boast about his accomplishments. I've also had my fill of seeing him misuse other people. From now on I'm avoiding him.

3. Calling long-distance is a good cure for loneliness. However, it isn't recommended for those on a budget. Time, as the saying goes, is money.

4. My sister bought a new car last year. She paid as much for it as my parents paid for their house. They bought the house twenty years ago.

5. A series of short sentences seems choppy. A series of long sentences, on the other hand, can seem formidable. Writers who wish to be read avoid both extremes. They strive for variety of sentence length.

USING PARALLEL STRUCTURE

As you move beyond basic sentence patterns to combined and expanded patterns, many of your sentences will become longer. Moreover, the relationships between the parts of those sentences will grow more complicated. This will increase the danger of lapses in coherence and will necessitate your taking steps to maintain clarity. Parallel structure is an invaluable aid in such situations.

Parallel structure is a kind of repetition. However, it is not repetition of words, but repetition of grammatical form. The kinds of parallelism range from the simple pairing of two or more adjectives, nouns, verbs, or adverbs to the more complex repetition of phrase or clause structure. Here are just a few examples of parallel structure:

Parallel Adjectives

> The creative person is not only imaginative and flexible but conscientious and persevering.

Parallel Nouns and Past-Tense Verbs

> Whenever she entered a room, conversation stopped, heads turned, and eyes followed her every movement.

Parallel Gerund Phrases

> Getting up late in the morning, relaxing on the beach in the forenoon, playing tennis in the afternoon, and dancing until late at night—that's my idea of a vacation.

Parallel Adjective Clauses

> This is the roommate who uses my aftershave lotion and never replaces it, who gets my clothes dirty and never cleans them, who borrows my money and never repays it.

Parallel structure helps you maintain sentence clarity in two ways. First, its consistency of form provides the reader with signposts that show the relationships among the parts of the sentence. Because structure echoes sense, ideas linked together in parallel structures should be of equal importance. Minor details become a pair or series of adjectives or prepositional phrases; two reasons are expressed as two clauses. Here is an example of this effect.

> Let the word go forth from this time and place, to friend and foe alike, that the torch has been passed to a new generation of Americans, born in this century, tempered by war, disciplined by a hard and bitter peace, proud of our ancient heritage, and unwilling to witness or permit the slow undoing of those human rights to which this nation has always been committed, and to which we are committed today, at home and around the world.

Second, parallel structure permits the expression of ideas in balanced form, as these examples illustrate:

> The more I watch him humiliate his wife, the more I appreciate the importance of respect in marriage.

Either she will begin living up to her end of the agreement we made at the beginning of the semester, or I will stop living up to mine.

Here is a passage that demonstrates both effects of parallel structure; that is, it makes clear the relationships among the ideas and presents the ideas in balanced form.

The tragedy of life is not in the hurt to a man's name or even in the fact of death itself. The tragedy of life is in what dies inside a man while he lives—the death of genuine feeling, the death of inspired response, the death of the awareness that makes it possible to feel the pain or the glory of other men in oneself. [Albert] Schweitzer's aim was not to dazzle an age but to awaken it, to make it comprehend that moral splendor is part of the gift of life, and that each man has unlimited strength to feel human oneness and to act upon it. He proved that although a man may have no jurisdiction over the fact of his existence, he can hold supreme command over the meaning of existence for him. Thus, no man need fear death; he need fear only that he may die without having known his greatest power—the power of his free will to give his life for others.

Y O U R   T U R N

Each of the statements below expresses an idea that can be more effectively expressed using parallel structure. Rewrite each, making it more effective. (Where two or more sentences are present, consider combining them.)

1. If you can't let me be free, then you might as well kill me.

2. When you have a cold, you should eat more than you usually do, but with a fever you are better off not eating at all.

3. If you don't try to do things, you have no chance of succeeding.

4. I would rather you do what I tell you to do than have you imitate me.

5. If you don't like the deal I'm offering you, you don't have to accept it.

6. He left town a villain, but when he returned he was considered to be heroic.

7. She was born in Chicago but spent her childhood and teenage years in New York and went to England to attend college.

8. That family survived poverty; they also had to overcome prejudice; and personal tragedy was another obstacle they met successfully.

9. An educated person should be able to get beyond his personal feelings and make decisions objectively. Deferring judgment until he has considered evidence and choosing the course of action that is most beneficial or least harmful are also important qualities he should have.

10. A teacher's greatest reward is to see students learn that hardships can be overcome, it is worthwhile to put forth effort, and they can make succeeding a habit.

VARYING WORD ORDER

We have seen how you can relieve monotony in your sentences as well as make your sentence structure reflect your content by combining and expanding the basic sentence patterns. A third way to ensure that your writing is precise and enjoyable to read is by adding variety to your word order. Not every word order, of course, is acceptable, because not every word order makes sense. Consider the sentence "I will miss her when she's gone." It can also be written, "When she's gone, I will miss her." But "Gone her I will when miss she's" is absurd, and "Miss her I will when she's gone" would only work in certain contexts. Note too that even slight shifts in word order can alter meaning. "We are thinking of going to Disney World again" does not mean the same thing as "We are thinking again of going to Disney World." So effective variation of word order demands some sensitivity to language.

The list of all possible pattern variations would be too long to include here. Nevertheless, we can identify some of the most common ways to vary basic patterns.

Invert Subject-Verb Order

Originals
The stranger came softly.
The security of the world depends on the restraint of a handful of
    political leaders.
The team charged onto the field chanting "We're number one!"

Revisions
Softly came the stranger.
On the restraint of a handful of political leaders depends the security of the world.
Onto the field charged the team chanting "We're number one!"

Open with a Prepositional Phrase

Originals
Few teachers in my high school gave regular homework assignments.

He tried with all his strength to resist the muggers.
I really believed, for one brief moment, that she cared for me.

Revisions
In my high school few teachers gave regular homework assignments.
With all his strength he tried to resist the muggers.
For one brief moment, I really believed that she cared for me.

Open with an Adjective

Originals
The girl was dejected and sat in the corner by herself all evening.
The driver, weak from his accident, crawled out of the car and stumbled across the high way.
The challenger, taller and more muscular than the champion, seemed a good bet to take the title.

Revisions
Dejected, the girl sat in the corner by herself all evening.
Weak from his accident, the driver crawled out of the car and stumbled across the highway.
Taller and more muscular than the champion, the challenger seemed a good bet to take the title.

Open with an Adverb

Originals
My grandfather usually visits us for the holidays.
We entered the haunted house cautiously looking quickly from side to side and listening intently.

Revisions
Usually my grandfather visits us for the holidays.
Cautiously we entered the house, looking quickly from side to side and listening intently.

Open with a Participle

Originals
Mrs. Murphy, outraged at the implicit insult, shouted an obscenity.
The big dog edged toward me threateningly, its head lowered and teeth bared.
Agnes, dazzling in her floor-length sequined gown, drew the attention of every man in the room.

Revisions
Outraged at the implicit insult, Mrs. Murphy shouted an obscenity.
Head lowered and teeth bared, the big dog edged toward me threateningly.
Dazzling in her floor-length sequined gown, Agnes drew the attention of every man in the room.

Open with an Infinitive Phrase

Originals

He scaled the side of a five-story building to prove his courage to his roommates.

Her dream is to become president of the United States.

It is both foolish and dangerous to try to lose all that weight in just a few weeks.

Revisions

To prove his courage to his roommates, he scaled the side of a five-story building.

To become president of the United States is her dream.

To try to lose all that weight in just a few weeks is both foolish and dangerous.

Change the Order of Clauses in a Complex Sentence

Originals

We plan to travel to Europe this summer, if we can afford to go.

She did well in that course, even though she lacked the background for it.

Try studying when all else fails.

Revisions

If we can afford to go, we plan to travel to Europe this summer.

Even though she lacked the background for that course, she did well in it.

When all else fails, try studying.

Y O U R   T U R N

1. Each of the following sentences is acceptable as written. But the word order could be varied to relieve monotony and create additional interest. Rewrite each sentence using a different word order.
   a. The city of Oneonta, New York, sits in a scenic valley in the Catskill Mountains midway between Albany and Binghamton.
   b. The bright sunlight made her hair shine as she stood before the class with her head tilted toward the window.
   c. Just like the three famous monkeys, they heard no evil, saw no evil, and spoke no evil.
   d. She would have had a 4.0 grade point average last semester if she hadn't gotten a B in Health.
   e. His thoughts were filled with memories of her.
   f. Agatha, confused about the purpose of the assignment, asked the teacher to explain further.

g. He called his girlfriend every night to be sure she was not out with someone else.

h. He was elated over his acceptance into graduate school and treated himself to filet mignon and a bottle of champagne.

i. She approached her father fearfully expecting to be punished for borrowing the car without permission.

2. Practice the techniques of sentence composition you learned in this chapter by rewriting the following passages.

a. Jupiter has four moons. Their names are Io, Europa, Ganymede, and Callisto. Galileo discovered them. This happened in 1610. They were the first bodies in the solar system to be discovered by telescope.

b. Charles Atlas' real name was Angelo Siciliano. He was a ninety-seven-pound weakling in real life. He was beaten up by another boy. Then he became obsessed with physical strength. He watched a tiger in a zoo. He marveled at its sleek power. He decided that its conditioning was achieved by pitting muscle against muscle. Thus Atlas developed his body-building method. He called it dynamic tension. Its present, more scientific name is isometrics.

c. Power over words gives a person a sense of confidence. That sense of confidence projects to others. It projects as competency. Power over words helps a person overcome tension and frustration, too. It does this by allowing an adequate outlet for thoughts and feelings. It also aids the person's understanding. It does this by providing a means of dealing with complexity and confusion.

d. Sex discrimination means unfairness to individuals, It also means a denial of Constitutional guarantees. But it means more. It means a loss of half the talents our society possesses. It means the loss of half the wisdom. It means the loss of half the ingenuity. It means the loss of half the creativity. It means the loss of half the leadership. All of industry is impoverished by that loss. So is all of government. And so are all of the arts and sciences. Each of us is victimized. The old and the young are victimized. The rich and the poor are victimized. Men and women are victimized.

3. Look over some of your own passages to see if the sentence structures are varied and precise reflections of meaning. Find areas to revise, then explain your revisions. Why was each change made?

CHOOSING ACTIVE OR PASSIVE VOICE

Active voice preserves the natural order of action: "Joe failed the test."
Passive voice inverts the natural order: "The test was failed by Joe." In
certain situations, passive voice may be more appropriate than active
voice; for example, when you focus on what was done rather than on who
did it, and when you either do not know who acted or do not want to
say. Thus it would be appropriate to say, "The crime was committed last
Thursday," and "The department store was invaded by a horde of bargain
hunters." But in most other cases, active voice sets a livelier pace for your
readers. "Joe failed the test" is immediately clear. The emphasis is on the
actor and the action, creating an energetic sentence. Remember, though,
that you select the voice of the verb, and if you want to slow the pace or
emphasize the result over the actor, passive voice may be a better choice.

YOUR TURN

1. Review the passage below, noting that the passive voice creates
   wordy, sometimes awkward sentences. Rewrite it in active voice. Is
   your version shorter than the original?
   An investigation of the community center financial affairs was
   conducted by city officials. It was determined by them that the
   bank account had been used by the officers of the center as a
   source of personal loans. It was revealed by the investigation that
   the mismanagement and fraud that was found was the fault of the
   center director. All of the money transfers had been signed by him,
   and all of the missing amounts were curiously similar to amounts
   that had been deposited by him in his own account.

2. Choose a narrative passage of any length and rewrite it using
   exclusively active voice. Then re-write it entirely in the passive
   voice. Which passage "moves" more rapidly? Are there awkward
   spots in either passage that might be strengthened by changing
   voice? Try a passage that uses both voices to see how the pace
   changes.

SUMMARY

Sentence structure can be grammatically correct without being varied or
precise. You can improve sentence structure by using coordination, subordination, and parallelism to make the grammatical structure of your sentences reflect the logical structure of your ideas, and by varying word
order, length, and voice.

Additional Readings

I Have a Dream
Martin Luther King, Jr.

Martin Luther King's "I Have a Dream" is a speech rather than an essay. If you have heard it (it is readily available on videotape and is often replayed on television), you will remember the sound of the sentences as they washed across the Washington, D.C., crowd. As you read it now, listen to your inner voice as it falls into the cadences of the speech.

Then analyze the sentences to see how King used parallelism and repetition to weave his ideas into an integrated whole. Notice that his opening words and images echo Lincoln's. Do you think that the echo is a coincidence?

Identify images that recur through several paragraphs. For example, King says in paragraph three that the gathering is an attempt to "cash a check." Where else does he refer to the idea that something is owed and should be paid?

Look too at the rhythms created by the parallel structures. Notice when the structure is varied. How do the structures of the sentences reflect the meaning?

1 Five score years ago, a great American, in whose symbolic shadow we stand, signed the Emancipation Proclamation. This momentous decree came as a great beacon light of hope to millions of Negro slaves who had been seared in the flames of withering injustice. It came as a joyous daybreak to end the long night of captivity.

2 But one hundred years later, we must face the tragic fact that the Negro is still not free. One hundred years later, the life of the Negro is still sadly crippled by the manacles of segregation and the chains of discrimination. One hundred years later, the Negro lives on a lonely island of poverty in the midst of a vast ocean of material prosperity. One hundred years later, the Negro is still languishing in the corners of American society and finds himself an exile in his own land. So we have come here today to dramatize an appalling condition.

3 In a sense we have come to our nation's Capitol to cash a check. When the architects of our republic wrote the magnificent words of the Constitution and the Declaration of Independence, they were signing a promissory note to which every American was to fall heir. This note was a promise that all men would be guaranteed the unalienable rights of life, liberty, and the pursuit of happiness.

4 It is obvious today that America has defaulted on this promissory note insofar as her citizens of color are concerned. Instead of honoring this sacred obligation, America has given the Negro people a bad check; a check which has come back marked "insufficient funds." But we refuse to believe that the bank of justice is bankrupt. We refuse to believe that there are insufficient funds in the great vaults of opportunity of this nation. So we have come to cash this check—a check that will give us

upon demand the riches of freedom and the security of justice. We have also come to this hallowed spot to remind America of the fierce urgency of *now*. This is no time to engage in the luxury of cooling off or to take the tranquilizing drug of gradualism. *Now* is the time to make real the promises of Democracy. *Now* is the time to rise from the dark and desolate valley of segregation to the sunlit path of racial justice. *Now* is the time to open the doors of opportunity to all of God's children. *Now* is the time to lift our nation from the quicksands of racial injustice to the solid rock of brotherhood.

5   It would be fatal for the nation to overlook the urgency of the moment and to underestimate the determination of the Negro. This sweltering summer of the Negro's legitimate discontent will not pass until there is an invigorating autumn of freedom and equality. 1963 is not an end, but a beginning. Those who hope that the Negro needed to blow off steam and will now be content will have a rude awakening if the nation returns to business as usual. There will be neither rest nor tranquility in America until the Negro is granted his citizenship rights. The whirlwinds of revolt will continue to shake the foundations of our nation until the bright day of justice emerges.

6   But there is something I must say to my people who stand on the warm threshold which leads into the palace of justice. In the process of gaining our rightful place we must not be guilty of wrongful deeds. Let us not seek to satisfy our thirst for freedom by drinking from the cup of bitterness and hatred. We must forever conduct our struggle on the high plane of dignity and discipline. We must not allow our creative protest to degenerate into physical violence. Again and again we must rise to the majestic heights of meeting physical force with soul force. The marvelous new militancy which has engulfed the Negro community must not lead us to a distrust of all white people, for many of our white brothers, as evidenced by their presence here today, have come to realize that their destiny is tied up with our destiny and their freedom is inextricably bound to our freedom. We cannot walk alone.

7   And as we walk, we must make the pledge that we shall march ahead. We cannot turn back. There are those who are asking the devotees of civil rights, "When will you be satisfied?" We can never be satisfied as long as the Negro is the victim of the unspeakable horrors of police brutality. We can never be satisfied as long as our bodies, heavy with the fatigue of travel, cannot gain lodging in the motels of the highways and the hotels of the cities. We cannot be satisfied as long as the Negro's basic mobility is from a smaller ghetto to a larger one. We can never be satisfied as long as a Negro in Mississippi cannot vote and a Negro in New York believes he has nothing for which to vote. No, no, we are not satisfied, and we will not be satisfied until justice rolls down like waters and righteousness like a mighty stream.

8   I am not unmindful that some of you have come here out of great trials and tribulations. Some of you have come fresh from narrow jail cells. Some of you have come from areas where your quest for freedom left you

battered by the storms of persecution and staggered by the winds of police brutality. You have been the veterans of creative suffering. Continue to work with the faith that unearned suffering is redemptive.

9   Go back to Mississippi, go back to Alabama, go back to South Carolina, go back to Georgia, go back to Louisiana, go back to the slums and ghettoes of our northern cities, knowing that somehow this situation can and will be changed. Let us not wallow in the valley of despair.

10   I say to you today, my friends, that in spite of the difficulties and frustrations of the moment I still have a dream. It is a dream deeply rooted in the American dream.

11   I have a dream that one day this nation will rise up and live out the true meaning of its creed: "We hold these truths to be self-evident: that all men are created equal."

12   I have a dream that one day on the red hills of Georgia the sons of former slaves and the sons of former slaveowners will be able to sit down together at the table of brotherhood.

13   I have a dream that the state of Mississippi, a desert state sweltering with the heat of injustice and oppression, will be transformed into and oasis of freedom and justice.

14   I have a dream that my four little children will one day live in a nation where they will not be judged by the color of their skin but by the content of their character.

15   I have a dream today.

16   I have a dream that the state of Alabama, whose governor's lips are presently dripping with the words of interposition and nullification, will be transformed into a situation where little black boys and black girls will be able to join hands with little white boys and white girls and walk together as sisters and brothers.

17   I have a dream today.

18   I have dream that one day every valley shall be exalted, every hill and mountain shall be made low, the rough places will be made plain, and the crooked places will made straight, and the glory of the Lord shall be revealed, and all flesh shall see it together.

19   This is our hope. This is the faith with which I return to the South. With this faith we will be able to hew out of the mountain of despair a stone of hope. With this faith we will be able to transform the jangling discords of our nation into a beautiful symphony of brotherhood. With this faith we will be able to work together, to pray together, to struggle together, to go to jail together, to stand up for freedom together, knowing that we will be free one day.

20   This will be the day when all of God's children will be able to sing with new meaning.

21

    My country, tis of thee
    Sweet land of liberty,
        Of thee I sing:
    Land where my fathers died,

Land of the pilgrims' pride,
From every mountainside
    Let freedom ring.

22   And if America is to be a great nation this must become true. So let freedom ring from the prodigious hilltops of New Hampshire. Let freedom ring from the mighty mountains of New York. Let freedom ring from the heightening Alleghenies of Pennsylvania!

23   Let freedom ring from the snowcapped Rockies of Colorado!

24   Let freedom ring from the curvaceous peaks of California!

25   But not only that; let freedom ring from Stone Mountain of Georgia!

26   Let freedom ring from Lookout Mountain of Tennessee!

27   Let freedom ring from every hill and molehill of Mississippi. From every mountainside, let freedom ring.

28   When we let freedom ring, when we let it ring from every village and every hamlet, from every state and every city, we will be able to speed up that day when all of God's children, black men and white men, Jews and Gentiles, Protestants and Catholics, will be able to join hands and sing in the words of the old Negro spiritual, "Free at last! free at last! thank God almighty, we are free at last!"

CHAPTER EIGHTEEN

Improving Diction

Word choice should be examined by the editorial voice to evaluate the exactness of the diction. The effect of diction choices on economy and on liveliness should also be reviewed.

The words you select to convey ideas influence not only your readers' understanding of your ideas, but also your readers' attitude toward your material. Word choice also influences sentence structure; choosing the exact word will not only make your meaning clearer, it may also make your sentences cleaner and livelier. Serious attention, then, should be directed to your word choices (or diction) when you edit the text. Your editorial concerns should be directed toward three areas: the exactness, the economy, and the liveliness of your choices.

EDITING FOR EXACTNESS

Precise diction conveys ideas with complete accuracy. To be exact would not be a difficult task if language were fixed and stable. But language changes. New words are added, archaic terms become obscure, familiar words acquire unfamiliar meanings. Shakespeare's language is difficult to understand fully without extensive footnotes, and words of our own time like space shuttle and penicillin would be equally obscure to his sixteenth-century audience.

Invention and discovery are two obvious causes of changes in language. But there are other causes as well. Terms like cold war and Watergate owe their existence to particular historical events. Still another cause is the shift in people's awareness and knowledge and interest and attitude toward things. Is it a blessing or a curse to be labelled a liberal? The attitude toward that word has undergone several changes in the last twenty years. Is a nonconformist a creative force in society or a destructive one?

Finally, a gradual awareness of the effects of sexist stereotyping in language is complicating word choices. Thoughtful readers are aware that the use of the third person masculine pronouns does not uniformly include females, but old habits are not easy to break. Today's audience will expect you to have checked your work carefully for unconscious exclusion of the female sex.

Editing for precise diction, then, presents challenges. It is further complicated by the fact that our own knowledge of language changes as we develop more ways to convey the finest shades of meaning. But exact word choice is a major factor in accurate communication with readers. In addition, precise diction can eliminate awkward, wordy sentences and create lively, informative images. Regardless of the challenges, then, the editorial voice is expected to review word choice.

Two Kinds of Meaning: Denotation and Connotation

In editing your sentences for exactness, you must be sensitive to the meaning of your words. There are two kinds of meaning: denotative meaning and connotative meaning.

Denotative meaning is the direct, explicit, literal meaning of a word. Many words have similar meanings, but few, if any, have exactly the same denotative meaning, For example, conscious, aware, and cognizant are often used interchangeably. Yet there are subtle differences among them. Conscious refers to an inner realization, aware to sensory realization, and cognizant to reasoning about sensory realization. Similarly, the words unbelief and disbelief both signify not believing. But unbelief refers to simple absence of belief, and disbelief to refusal to believe. Consider, too, that you would want your case to be heard by a disinterested judge but not an uninterested one.

Connotative meaning is implied or associative meaning, the favorable or unfavorable aura that surrounds denotation's meaning. For example, thrifty and stingy have similar denotative meanings. But thrifty implies a positive kind of frugality and stingy a negative kind. This is true to such an extent that thrift is regarded as a virtue, stinginess a vice! Similarly, to say someone planned what she did is a compliment, whereas to say she schemed is an insult. And a statesman and a politician are both engaged in the same line of work, but the former term is more favorable. You might admire a persistent child but be aggravated by a stubborn one. Though the denotative meanings are quite similar, the connotative meanings differ greatly.

Not all terms have strong connotations, however. Sometimes a term has a relatively neutral one. Consider, for instance, these sentences:

> George manages the financial records at Hill's Book Bin.
> George manipulates the financial records at Hill's Book Bin.
> George handles the financial records at Hill's Book Bin.

The word "manage" has a slightly favorable connotation, suggesting competency. The word "manipulate" is strongly negative, to the point of implying some criminal activity. But the word "handle" is almost neutral.

How Inexactness Occurs

Your editing is likely to be most effective if you are alert to the common enemies of exactness—similar-sounding words, empty expressions, and vogue expressions. Let's examine each more closely.

The first great enemy of exactness is confusion between words that look or sound alike but have widely different meanings. The writer who uses "censure" (to disapprove or condemn) instead of "censor" (to suppress something believed to be objectionable) is not likely to impress educated readers. If the writer says home wrecker (one who breaks up others' marriages) instead of house wrecker (one who demolishes houses), considerable misunderstanding could result. And if there are more than a few such mistakes—for example, confusing ingenious and ingenuous, or counsel and council—the writer will not only jar the readers' sensibilities, break their concentration, and distract them; the writer will also probably lose the readers' confidence and kill their interest in the material. See your handbook for a glossary of commonly confused words.

The second enemy of exactness is the overworked or empty expression. You will recognize these examples of overworked expressions (called clichés): *couldn't care less, burn the midnight oil, a crying shame, last but not least, sink or swim, toe the line, make your mark, low man on the totem pole, sneaking suspicion, the other side of the coin, truth is stranger than fiction, a fight to the finish, be there for someone,* and *up for it* (as in "The Bloomville Bombers are really *up for* today's game against the Bovina Bonzos").

Originally such expressions were fresh and vivid. The problem is that most people have heard them so often in so many contexts that they have lost their power to illuminate any particular context.

Empty expressions are substitutes for exactness. Whenever you say something is *cute* or *great* or *good* or *pretty good* or *really good* or *bad* or *lovely* or *beautiful* or *wonderful* or *fine,* you have not described anything. You have merely pretended to describe, given a broad clue to a description you might have given. Now there are occasions when that is enough, when time or space do not allow more precise and meaningful statement. But usually it is not enough and is the result of laziness rather than necessity. Similarly, when you speak of "stuff" or "things," you are identifying only in the broadest and least helpful sense. Writing that is filled with such generalities cheats readers and, not infrequently, bores them.

Be especially careful of fashionable expressions that become popular for a time and are quickly killed by overuse. You might know some of these expressions that have recently been in vogue: *go with the flow, I hear you, ego trip, mellow, in touch with yourself, wasted, getting your head together, unreal, I know where you're coming from, up front, put it all together, hang-up, relevant, meaningful, uptight, the name of the game, goes with the territory, laid back, I can't relate to it, into* (as in, "I'm really *into* dominoes lately"), and *bottom line.* Writers who use such expressions in their writing risk anesthetizing their readers.

FOUR IMPORTANT CONCERNS

The four basic areas you must consider to achieve exactness in your sentences are **level of diction, degree of clarity, degree of concreteness and specificity,** and **use of sexist language.**

Level of Diction

There are three broad levels of diction: standard written (formal), standard conversational (informal), and colloquial/slang. All three are appropriate when used in their place. Since colloquialism and slang are seldom appropriate in writing, except in dialogue, we will concentrate on the first two categories. The line between them was until recently quite sharply drawn. But a recent trend toward informality in all areas of living is now reflected in a tendency toward conversational diction in writing. Many respected writers today use a casual, informal style. Yet there remain occasions in which formality is preferred. Let's consider some examples of each style:

Standard Written	Standard Conversational
purchase	buy ("I plan to buy a car.")
demonstrate	show ("She will show you how.")
approximately	about ("It has been about a year.")
inquire	ask ("Tell him to ask in a letter.")
complete	finish ("We will finish the job.")
assist	help ("Can you help us?")
difficult	hard ("The course was hard.")
prepare	do ("I will do my tax return.")
obtain	get ("Did you get permission?")
forward	send ("Please send me a copy.")
contribute	give ("She gives a lot to charity.")
sufficient	enough ("Enough time has elapsed.")
initial	first ("The first step is easy.")
do not	don't ("Please don't be late.")
cannot	can't ("They can't help us.")
should not	shouldn't ("We shouldn't go.")

There is no absolute rule as to when conversational diction is permissible in writing. The best guide is this approach—when the piece of writing is formal (a scholarly article, a business letter to someone you don't know), use standard written diction; at most other times choose the simpler and more economical conversational diction.

The diction in each of the following examples is appropriate to the occasion and audience. Notice that the first is formal without being stuffy or inflated, and the second is informal without being chummy or impolite.

> Because I have had some difficulty obtaining the information necessary to complete form 32986S, as you requested, I will be unable to submit it by November 30. I therefore request a one-month extension of the deadline.
> —from a letter to the
> Internal Revenue Service

> I've had some trouble getting the information necessary to finish the form you asked for, so I won't be able to send it by November 30. I'd appreciate your giving me an extra month to do it.
> —from a letter to a
> business colleague

Degree of Clarity

Normally you will want your writing to be as clear as possible. In most situations ambiguity (openness to more than one interpretation) is a fault. Yet there are situations where ambiguity is intended. And where this is so, you should choose wording that retains just the degree of ambiguity you wish. For example, in the sentence "Bertha did not at that time show malice," the key words are "at that time." The sentence is open to the interpretation that at other times, perhaps usually, Bertha does show malice. In other words, the sentence is ambiguous. (Whether this ambiguity is desirable depends on the writer's intention.)

A caution is necessary here. The careful reader will recognize ambiguity and realize you are consciously or unconsciously avoiding an issue. So unless you have good reason to be ambiguous, strive to be clear.

Degree of Concreteness and Specificity

There are many times when you will want to speak about abstract and general matters. Abstract words deal with concepts that cannot be touched, seen, or heard. (For example, **justice** is an abstract word, while **payment for injuries** is concrete.) General words embrace all the members of a concrete class or group rather than particular ones. (Thus **human beings** is a general term; **Americans,** a more specific one; **Irish-Americans,** still more specific; and **James Murphy,** very specific.)

If your discussion is about abstract or general matters, there is certainly nothing wrong with it. The problem is that most of us tend to speak more abstractly than we really need to or intend to. It's often easier to use abstract terms than to think of exactly what we want to say. Be aware of this tendency and control it by using concrete, specific words as often as possible.

Here are some examples of varying degrees of concreteness and specificity:

From the General and Abstract . . . to the Specific and Concrete:

- responsibility > taking care of business > paying bills > paying the electric bill
- man > Oriental man > Chinese man > young Chinese man > twenty-year-old Chinese man
- city > New York City > Queens County > Jackson Heights > the corner of 82nd Street and Roosevelt Avenue.
- car > General Motors car > Chevrolet > 1977 Chevrolet Nova > dark blue 1977 Chevrolet Nova with a cream vinyl top

In each of the above cases the more specific and concrete reference makes it easier for the readers to visualize what you are speaking of. Such references, then, make your writing more real to them. This is true not only of the nouns you use but also of the verbs. For even the smallest, most mundane of activities there are numerous verbs. You don't have to say someone **put** food into her mouth. You can say she **shoveled** or **crammed** or **stuffed** or **slopped** it in (assuming such description is accurate). Nor need you be limited to saying a baseball player **hit** the ball. You can say he **slapped** it, **punched** it, **slugged** it, **swatted** it, **clouted** it, **stroked** it, **belted** it, **pounded** it, **whacked** it, **walloped** it, or **tapped** it.

The same principle applies to adjectives and adverbs. There is a rich choice of precise words to select from. With a little effort and imagination, you can transform **funny** into **droll, farcical, amusing, ludicrous, laughable, comical, rollicking, hilarious, diverting, jocular, witty, humorous, entertaining,** or, if delicacy is not important, **gutbusting.** Similarly, **hot** can become **blistering, boiling, sweltering, sultry, muggy, suffocating, steamy, wilting,** or **scorching.** And **slowly** can become **ploddingly, deliberately, leisurely, laggardly, haltingly, stumblingly,** and so on.

Sexist Language

Make sure that your diction is free from unconscious sexist stereotyping. Thoughtful readers are aware that the use of the third person masculine pronouns does not uniformly include females, and they will expect you to choose your references carefully.

For many years the use of "man" and the appropriate pronouns was generally thought to mean "humanity." But today there is a general acknowledgment that such masculine references are not consistently meant to include all human beings. Persistent references to doctors and lawyers and politicians as "he" are now seen as a reflection of an outdated mindset that does not fully acknowledge women's roles in society. Thus you should check your work carefully to eliminate unconscious sexist stereotypes. Consider that in areas where men and women work or play together, sexist language may be ambiguous. For example, an amateur golf tournament billed as a "four-man scramble" may or may not be open to female golfers. When you edit your work for sexist stereotypes, consider the following suggestions:

- Avoid masculine nouns and pronouns when you wish to refer to both sexes.

  Sample adjustments:

man/mankind	person/human beings
policeman	police officer
businessman	business executive
he/his/him	he or she
	(drop the possessive
	entirely or rewrite
	in the plural)
a student/he	students/they

- Avoid stereotyping or trivializing women; refer to men and women in the same way whenever possible.

  Sample adjustments:

coed	student
stewardess	flight attendant
lady lawyer	lawyer
authoress	writer

- Avoid unconscious gender references like this one, found in an advertisement for a festival: "Fun for folks of all ages—grab your wife and kids and come to the fair this weekend." Despite the copywriter's best intentions, this pitch is not directed to women.

Your word choice should, of course, depend on the context of your writing. You cannot base your selection merely on the appeal of the word itself. Rather, the word must fit the composition form, the controlling idea, and the audience. Obviously these are complex considerations, and successful handling of them will depend on your skill in writing. But that skill will come to you if you make your choices with care.

Y O U R   T U R N

1. Look up each word in each of the following sets of words in a good dictionary. Note and explain any significant differences in denotation or connotation.

reserved, secretive, aloof
loquacious, garrulous, talkative, verbose
clever, crafty, wily, astute
persevering, stubborn, adamant, inflexible
eccentric, weird, strange, uncommon
comrade, colleague, collaborator, accomplice
obedient, servile, slavish, fawning
develop, invent, create, discover, find
stupid, ignorant, unschooled, dense

2. The following sets of words are often confused with each other. Look up each word as necessary. Then explain the differences in meaning.

misplaced, displaced
practical, practicable
phase, faze
raze, raise
complement, compliment
misdirected, undirected
ascent, assent
misinformed, uninformed
dissent, descent
dying, dyeing
respectfully, respectively
credible, creditable

3. Each of the following sentences is in standard written English. Each would be appropriate in relatively formal writing, but not in informal writing. Rewrite each, making it suitable for informal prose.
   a. Senator Smith's aversion to debate may be prompted more by his ignorance of the issue than by his busy schedule.
   b. Should you fail to respond by July 15, I shall be forced to turn the matter over to my attorney.
   c. I am pleased to recommend John E. Begood for this position without reservation.

4. Each of the following sentences is written in standard conversational English. Each would be appropriate in relatively informal writing, but not in formal writing. Rewrite each, making it suitable for formal prose. Be on the alert for stuffiness.
   a. I heard you got the promotion you've been hoping for. Congratulations. You really deserve it. And I know you'll be the best regional manager in the company.
   b. I'd like to thank your foundation for the scholarship you gave me. I'm sure I couldn't have attended Splendor University without that $5,000 a year. I'm going to work my hardest to show my appreciation.

    c. Dinosaurs are gone now, but no one really knows why. Maybe it got too cold, or maybe they just died out because they couldn't find enough food.

    d. Chemical plants dump stuff into the river and the air and the soil. People who live near the plants are worried because their kids will breathe the dirty air. Sometimes the drinking water smells bad and there are even things floating in it.

5. Each of the following words is rather general and abstract. Think of at least three concrete substitutes for each. Use your specific terms in sentences.

Example: walked

    The little girl *skipped* lightly across the room.

    Angrily Maria *stomped* into the office, demanding change.

    Jonathan *strolled* along the bank, idly tossing pebbles into the stream.

looked	ran	sat
went	heavy	dirty
said	happily	beautifully

6. Review the following sentences for sexist diction stereotypes. How would you edit each?

    a. The financial difficulties of this parish will remain until every man realizes his fiscal obligation to the church.

    b. Man will continue to advance as long as he is able to recognize his limitations and willing to work to overcome them.

    c. The lady doctor told her nurse that no new patients could be accepted unless referred by another doctor.

    d. The busy executive told his male secretary that all incoming calls were to be held until further notice.

7. Consult the sports pages of a newspaper. Find as many terms as you can that mean either *win* or *beat*. Add any others you can think of to the list.

8. Revise the following passage, making it more interesting by substituting more concrete and/or specific words for the italicized words. You may add or omit words if you wish.

    The night club was *crowded,* the air *hot and stale.* A *large* man *entered* the *room* from the bar. The lights *went off.* Then a spotlight *went on.* The man *walked* over to the stage, *went up* the steps, *picked up* a banjo lying next to a chair, and *sat down* on the chair. The *noise* of the crowd *stopped.* Everyone was *watching* the man. He *picked casually* at the banjo a few times, his eyes *looking* around the room, his mouth *closed* tightly around a well-chewed cigar. Then he *took* the cigar from his mouth, *placed* it gently on the floor beside him, *took a long breath,* and began *playing* in earnest.

9. Call on the editorial voice to review some of your own work for concrete, specific diction. Identify general and abstract terms, and substitute or add concrete, specific words.

10. Select several passages from your own work and experiment with levels of diction. Write each passage using standard written diction, then re-write using conversational English. What changes did you make?

EDITING DICTION FOR ECONOMY

Economy and its related quality, simplicity, are recognized as two indicators of competency, excellence, and eloquence in writing. "The language of truth," said Marcellinus Ammianus, fourth-century Roman historian, "is unadorned and always simple." In our own time the message is the same. Sir Winston Churchill had little patience with linguistic barbarism. On one occasion he delivered this attack on it:

> I hope you have all mastered the official socialist jargon which our masters, as they call themselves, wish us to learn. You must not use the word "poor"; they are described as "the lower income group." When it comes to a question of freezing a workman's wages the Chancellor of the Exchequer speaks of "arresting increases in personal income". . . . Sir Stafford Cripps does not like to mention the word "wages," but that is what he means. There is a lovely one about houses and homes. They are in future to be called "accommodation units." I don't know how we are to sing our old song "Home, sweet Home." (He then began singing.) "Accommodation unit, sweet accommodation unit, there's no place like our accommodation unit." I hope to live to see the British democracy spit all this rubbish from their lips.

Such reactions to inflated and pretentious writing are almost universal (except among those who commit it). The reason for this is not difficult to grasp: Simplicity and economy make writing easier to understand, more accessible to the readers. (Read George Orwell's "Politics and the English Language," for the assertion that obscure language is often used deliberately.) Moreover, they make it easier for readers to retain the ideas. Memorable writing is often brief and simple: "The only thing we have to fear is fear itself"; "Ask not what your country can do for you; ask what you can do for your country." The Gettysburg Address contains a total of 267 words. Of those, 217—or 81 percent—are words of one syllable. And another 32 are two-syllable words.

The Basic Principles

Choose the word that most exactly expresses your thought. If you need a long word, it would be foolish to substitute a shorter, less accurate word. But, unless the idea or the audience or the occasion demands the long word, use the short one.

Similarly, in the words of George Orwell, "Never use a foreign phrase, a scientific word, or a jargon word if you can think of an everyday English equivalent." If the foreign or scientific or jargon word is the only one that fits, then by all means use it. But first look for the simple word.

Moreover, remember that length by itself is no index of economy. A relatively short piece of writing can be very bloated, whereas an entire volume on so limited a topic as the courtship practices of the earthworm can be admirably brief, given the amount and complexity of information it conveys. You achieve economy by saying whatever you have to say—however much or little—in as few words as possible. To do so, eliminate unnecessary words and, without sacrificing effectiveness, reduce a clause to a phrase, a phrase to a word.

Following these principles will free your writing from excess baggage and encourage you to develop a precise and exciting writing style. As hard as it may be to trim anything from your draft, remember that most of your audiences will read for ideas, not for the pleasure of your prose.

Three Diction Problems

Now let's examine some problem passages and see how they can be improved by applying the basic principles of simplicity and economy. The first is a letter expressing interest in a job opening:

Dear Mr. Wemple:

With the presentation of these lines, I herewith evidence an occupational interest in the accounting department of Wemple Industries. Realizing that your schedule is a crowded one, I shall endeavor to be concise.

I am a graduate of the South Central University's School of Business, having earned the bachelor's degree in accounting. Twelve hours of graduate study were completed at the same institution.

Since earning my degree I have been employed at Amalgamated Acme Corporation as a junior assistant accountant. This position has been a source of considerable gratification to me. However, for a considerable number of years I have nurtured the hope of one day securing employment with a large international corporation, hence the purpose of these lines.

An opportunity to meet and discuss with you the prospect of my joining the Wemple accounting staff would be most appreciated.

Thanking you for the consideration I am sure you will render these lines, I am,

Sincerely yours,

Radley Harper

The problem here is **pretentiousness.** The writer may have meant to sound serious and respectful, but he manages to sound only stuffy. In fact, some of his phrasing is so overly formal ("With the presentation of these lines," "Hence, the purpose of these lines") that it almost makes him seem insincere. How much better his letter would have been had he written it like this:

Dear Mr. Wemple:

I would like to be considered for a position in the accounting department of Wemple Industries. Here are my credentials in brief.

I hold a bachelor's degree in accounting from South Central University's School of Business. In addition, I completed twelve hours of graduate study at South central.

Since I graduated, I have worked for Amalgamated Acme Corporation as a junior assistant accountant. The work has been interesting, but for many years I have looked forward to working for a large international corporation like Wemple.

I would appreciate the opportunity to meet with you and discuss the possibility of my joining the Wemple accounting staff.

Sincerely,

Radley Harper

Here is another passage to consider:

> For the period of June through August of last year I was employed at an eating establishment called the Surf Inn for the purpose of getting some experience in my field, which is restaurant management. In view of the fact that I had no experience prior to that time, I was assigned to do the most menial tasks—that is, those in connection with cleaning the kitchen, washing dishes, and scrubbing pots and pans. The manager, however, made me a promise that in the event that I did a good job, he would give consideration to promoting me to waitress. And he made me a further promise that, in the event that I did a good job as a waitress, he would give consideration to letting me work as hostess during the regular host's day off. These promises gave me encouragement. . . .

The problem here is not pretentiousness. It is simple **wordiness.** Many of the expressions that contain three or four words could be replaced by one or two words. And the unnecessary repetition could be removed. The result would be the following.

> Last summer I worked at a restaurant, the Surf Inn, to get some experience in my field, restaurant management. Because I had no previous experience, I was assigned to cleaning the kitchen, washing dishes, and scrubbing pots and pans. The manager, however, promised that if I did a good job, he would consider promoting me to waitress and maybe even to hostess during the regular host's days off. These promises encouraged me. . . .

In addition to pretentiousness and wordiness is a third common problem, **jargon,** which is the technical terminology used in various fields (law, medicine, the social sciences). The problem is usually compounded by the long, involved sentence structure that often accompanies such terminology. Here is an example of jargon:

> There has come to be associated and blended with the traditional objective that the aim of all pedagogical systems is to stimulate the learner's apprehension of factual and theoretical knowledge and develop his or her cognitive processes, the more recent, sociologically prompted objective of personal adjustment to environment and the development of highly individualized value-focuses. The attendant ascendency of the affective dimension of learning has eroded the position of the cognitive sufficiently as to transmogrify the reality of contemporary education and create certain diriment impediments to effective integration of competing goals in the foreseeable future.

Jargon, unlike pretentiousness and wordiness, can seldom be corrected by changing a word here and a phrase there. Because it is not merely inflated but overly abstract, sometimes to the point of obscurity, it must be rewritten entirely. And particular care must be taken to clarify all obscure parts. Here is a revision of the above passage.

Traditionally the aim of education was to instill knowledge and develop intellectual skills in students. But in recent years other aims have been pursued, notably helping students adjust to the world around them and choose their own values. The emphasis on feeling, however, has so weakened the place of thought that the two may not be effectively integrated for some time.

Y O U R   T U R N

1. Examine each of the following passages carefully. Decide whether it suffers from pretentiousness, wordiness or jargon. Then rewrite it in a simple, economical style. (Remember that jargon usually requires not just minor changes but complete revision.)
   a. For value received, the undersigned jointly and severally promise(s) to pay the sum of five hundred dollars.
   b. Due to the fact that your office experienced a delay in mail service, it is the decision of this committee to extend your allocation of time for the completion of your report one full month from the originally assigned completion date.
   c. All employees are urged to extinguish the illumination in all rooms and facilities not in use so that the maximum benefit of our energy-saving potential may be realized by this company.
   d. Tom is of the opinion that we are not in a position to make contact with any amateur player for the purpose of recruiting him for our professional team without coming into violation of the latest N.C.A.A. directive.

2. Each of the following sentences contains an inflated expression. Rewrite each sentence, substituting a more economical expression. Be sure not to change the meaning of the sentence.
   a. He sent me a check in the amount of twenty dollars.
   b. Please call Agnes in connection with that overdue loan.
   c. I'd like to meet you sometime next week and speak with respect to the proposal you made.
   d. On the occasion of his eighteenth birthday, he celebrated for a week.
   e. We'll be able to take a vacation in the near future.
   f. Enclosed you will find my application form.
   g. He is an expert in the area of civil rights.
   h. I would like to request that you get here on time.
   i. Judging on the basis of the available evidence, I'd say he's guilty.
   j. Henry made inquiry regarding the job.
   k. There are many cases in which students succeed without trying.
   l. I am not able to do it at this time.

m. See if you can make contact with him before Wednesday.
n. Rainy days afford me an opportunity to get my housework done.
o. The report was of a confidential nature.
p. Maybe we'll be able to hold a meeting next week.
q. My English teacher offered instruction to more than 150 students last semester.

3. The words and expressions below are acceptable in many contexts. Yet each has a simpler, more everyday equivalent. Write that equivalent for each.
a. fracture
b. undulate
c. emancipate
d. rancor
e. avarice
f. edifice
g. veracious
h. instructional activity

4. Revise the following letter to make it more effective with its audience. (Don't be afraid to make radical changes if necessary.)

Dear Mr. Fetish:

Persistence is an admirable trait in, for, and of human beings because it inherently implies a willingness on the part of the individual to pursue his or her obligations with fervor and zeal. I am hopeful that I am the possessor of this quality.

A year has passed since I had the opportunity to meet with you and discuss the English program offerings. The passing of this year has not dimmed my enthusiasm for and my desire to become a staff member of the department, certainly I have continued to grow professionally during the past twelve months. These lines would not have been forwarded to you if I did not feel able to make a substantial contribution to the program offerings at Blatchford College. Vital teaching is an end result of professional growth and experience. Good teaching is more than a chronological acquisition of credit hours; my past experience is replete with first hand experiences and know-how. Teaching is, has been, and always will be my vocation.

I would be most happy to, once again, come to Blatchford to discuss, at your convenience, job possibilities for the forthcoming academic year.

Thanking you for the consideration I am sure you will render these lines, I am,

Yours most cordially,

Parker P. Parker

5. Review some of your own work, either a draft in progress or an earlier work, to see if you have been guilty of the errors described here. What corrections can you make.

Substitute Vivid Words for Bland Words

Vivid words are dramatic. They make an ordinary passage come alive for the readers. They stimulate the readers' imaginations and heighten their interest. To appreciate what they contribute to a piece of writing, you need only compare the following bland and vivid passages.

Bland Version
I listen hard but unsuccessfully for the sound of bugles playing reveille, of drums playing the long roll. In my dreams I hear again the noise of guns and muskets and of people on the battlefield.

Vivid Version
I listen vainly, but with thirsty ear, for the bewitching melody of faint bugles blowing reveille, of far drums beating the long roll. In my dreams I hear again the crash of guns, the rattle of musketry, the strange, mournful mutter of the battlefield.

Bland Version
It was a time when a simple refrain could make successes out of untalented singers.

Vivid Version
It was a time when five dums and a doobie-doobie could make chart busters out of incompetent hog callers with a three-note range.

Is it possible to overdo vividness or to use it inappropriately? Of course, but the opposite problem—not being vivid enough—is much more common. If you keep your audience and purpose in mind, there is little danger that you will overdo.

Substitute Figurative for Literal Language

Figurative language is language that employs the devices of literature, particularly poetry. Because figurative language looks past the literal, it can offer readers a fresh description or comparison in creative, lively prose. Here are some of the most common figures of speech.

Simile   A simile is an imaginative comparison of one thing to another, very different thing. It can be recognized by the use of the word like or as. For example, in the sentence "Leonard was like a lion in the office but like a mouse at home," the lion and mouse references are similes. No meaningful literal comparison can be made between a man and a lion because they are different species. The similes suggest another level where the traits of Leonard, the lion and the mouse can be compared concisely and poetically.

Metaphor   A metaphor is much like a simile, except that it is more than an imaginative comparison of two different things. By omitting "like" or "as," the metaphor becomes an imaginative identification of such things. Thus in "Leonard was a lion in the office, but a mouse at home," the lion and mouse references are metaphors. Here are some other examples of metaphors: "Her daily run became an exhilarating flight from the worries and cares lurking inside the walls"; "Betrayed and insulted, Alan snarled angrily at all who approached"; "He entered the torture chamber, prepared to test himself against the machines until his muscles were unresponsive jelly."

Personification   Because personification identifies something non-human with human capabilities or qualities, it is a special kind of metaphor. For example, in the sentence "The factory whistles screamed their defiance into the night sky," the whistles are identified as human things with feelings and voices. Because such metaphorical identification is so common, it has been labelled separately as personification. Identify the assignment of human qualities in each of the following: "The storm wept in frenzied passion, throwing its tears and its anguish into the teeth of the wind and spending itself in a final dance of destruction"; "The old car groaned and wheezed as it dragged up the hill, coming to rest in the driveway with an audible sigh of relief"; "Spring emerged shyly, almost reluctantly, peeking out from behind clouds and disappearing whenever we stepped out without our jackets."

Understatement   Understatement, as the term suggests, is the expression of an idea with considerably less force than might be reasonably expected. To say that Julius Erving is a fair basketball player is understatement because Julius Erving is an unusually gifted basketball player. And to say that Aleksandr Solzhenitsyn has had some acquaintance with the forces of repression is understatement because most of his life was spent suffering under those forces. Understatement works best when the audience is aware of the true extent of the thing described. For instance, to say that Cary Grant "made a few movies" is easily recognized as understatement; it is an unexpected way to describe his illustrious career and thus gets the attention of the audience.

Metonymy and Synecdoche   The closely related techniques of metonymy and synecdoche are, respectively, using the name of one thing for another closely related thing, and using the part to stand for the whole or the whole for the part. Instead of saying that a judge retired and his judicial responsibilities were assumed by someone else, we might say that "the gavel was passed" from one to the other. Similarly, we might say we wrote to a college concerning admission, meaning we wrote to the admissions director of the college. Here are other examples of these techniques: "His bat is as much a threat today as it was ten years ago"; "The United States has made its position clear—now it is Iraq's turn to do likewise"; "Give us this day our daily bread"; "The White House has issued a special report."

When used with some originality, all of the devices of figurative language have one thing in common—they offer unexpected insight or perspective on the subject, creating livelier content and livelier style.

SUMMARY OF EDITING STRATEGIES

To assist you in applying the approaches to editing discussed in this chapter, here is a brief summary:

To Edit for Exactness

- Be sensitive to denotative and connotative meaning.
- Be careful with words that sound alike but have different meanings, and avoid both overworked or empty expressions and vogue expressions.
- Choose your level of diction, degree of clarity, and degree of concreteness and specificity with care.
- Check for sexist references or stereotypes.

To Edit for Economy

- Check for pretentiousness.
- Check for wordiness.
- Check for jargon.

To Edit for Liveliness

- Substitute vivid words for bland words.
- Substitute figurative for literal language.

Y O U R T U R N

1. Read each of the quoted passages carefully. Then identify the various wars in which the author has made the writing lively.
   a. Convicts' paranoia is as thick as the prison wall—and just as necessary. Why should we have faith in anyone? Even our wives and lovers whose beds we have shared, with whom we have shared the tenderest moments and most delicate relations, leave us after a while, put us down, cut us clean aloose and treat us like they hate us, won't even write us a letter, send us a Christmas card every other year or a quarter for a pack of cigaretes or a tube of toothpaste now and then. All society shows the convict its ass and expects him to kiss it: the convict feels like kicking it or putting a bullet in it. A convict sees man's fangs and claws and learns quickly to bare and unsheath his own, for real and final. To maintain a hold on the ideals and sentiments of civilization in such circumstances is probably impossible.
   b. On Wednesday morning at a quarter past five came the earthquake. A minute later the flames were leaping upward. In a dozen different quarters south of Market Street, in the working-class ghetto, and in the factories, fires started. There was no opposing the flames. There was no organization, no communication. All the cunning adjustments of a twentieth-century city had been smashed by the earthquake. The streets were humped into ridges and depressions and piled with debris of fallen walls. The steel rails were twisted into perpendicular and horizontal angles. The telephone and telegraph systems were disrupted. And the great water mains had burst. All the shrewd contrivances and safeguards of man had been thrown out of gear by thirty seconds' twitching of the earth's crust.

2. The following details are from an account of the Wright brothers' historic first flight. Work them into a lively account, applying what you have learned in the chapter.
   The place: Kitty Hawk, North Carolina
   The men: Wilbur Wright—well groomed, 5' 6", 150 pounds, straight black hair, blue eyes, long and sharp nose, swarthy complexion, Orville Wright—blond, shorter but huskier than his brother, black eyes, fair complexion
   The beach: Quiet and secluded
   Wind: 21 miles per hour
   Plane was three years in the making
   Brothers financed work themselves
   U.S. had spent thousands on rival project by Prof. Langley of Smithsonian Institute

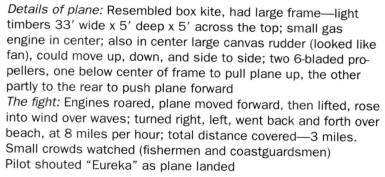

Details of plane: Resembled box kite, had large frame—light timbers 33′ wide x 5′ deep x 5′ across the top; small gas engine in center; also in center large canvas rudder (looked like fan), could move up, down, and side to side; two 6-bladed propellers, one below center of frame to pull plane up, the other partly to the rear to push plane forward

The fight: Engines roared, plane moved forward, then lifted, rose into wind over waves; turned right, left, went back and forth over beach, at 8 miles per hour; total distance covered—3 miles. Small crowds watched (fishermen and coastguardsmen)

Pilot shouted "Eureka" as plane landed

3. Select some of your own writing and edit for exactness, economy, and liveliness. Bring some of your original prose to class and present your edited version for comparison.

SUMMARY

Diction has a major influence on your readers' understanding and acceptance of your ideas. Edit carefully for precise denotative and connotative meaning, and work to avoid problems like wordiness, pretentiousness, jargon, and sexist language.

Additional Readings

A Semantic Parable
S. I. Hayakawa

S. I. Hayakawa's "Semantic Parable" is an illustration of the importance of careful labelling. Can you supply other examples of programs whose images are/were affected by their titles?

Samuel Ichiye Hayakawa was born in Vancouver, British Columbia, and educated at the University of Wisconsin. He was president of San Francisco State College from 1969 to 1973 and U.S. Senator from California From 1977 to 1983. His works include Language in Action (1939) and Language in Thought and Action (1978), from which this selection was taken.

In "A Semantic Parable," S. I. Hayakawa suggests what can result when people feel labeled. He also shows how words inevitably lead to quarrels when each of the arguing parties bestows a different meaning on the words used in the argument.

1   Once upon a time (said the Professor), there were two small communities, spiritually as well as geographically situated at a considerable distance from each other. They had, however, these problems in common: Both were hard hit by a depression, so that in each of the towns there were about one hundred heads of families unemployed. There was, to be sure, enough food, enough clothing, enough materials for housing, but these families simply did not have money to procure these necessities.

2   The city fathers of A-town, the first community, were substantial businessmen, moderately well educated, good to their families, kindhearted, and sound-thinking. The unemployed tried hard, as unemployed people usually do, to find jobs; but the situation did not improve. The city fathers, as well as the unemployed themselves, had been brought up to believe that there is always enough work for everyone, if you only look for it hard enough. Comforting themselves with this doctrine, the city fathers could have shrugged their shoulders and turned their backs on the problem, except for the fact that they were genuinely kindhearted men. They could not bear to see the unemployed men and their wives and children starving. In order to prevent starvation, they felt that they had to provide these people with some means of sustenance. Their principles told them, nevertheless, that if people were given something for nothing, it would demoralize their character. Naturally this made the city fathers even more unhappy, because they were faced with the horrible choice of (1) letting the unemployed starve, or (2) destroying their moral character.

3   The solution they finally hit upon, after much debate and soul-searching, was this. They decided to give the unemployed families relief of fifty dollars a month; but to insure against the pauperization of the recipients, they decided that this fifty dollars was to be accompanied by a moral lesson, to wit: the obtaining of the assistance would be made so difficult, humiliating, and disagreeable that there would be no temptation for anyone to go through the process unless it was absolutely necessary; the moral disapproval of the community would be turned upon the recipients of the money at all times in such a way that they would try hard to get off relief and regain their self-respect. Some even proposed that people on relief be denied the vote, so that the moral lesson would be more deeply impressed upon them. Others suggested that their names be published at regular intervals in the newspapers, so that there would be a strong incentive to get off relief. The city fathers had enough faith in the goodness of human nature to expect that the recipients would be grateful, since they were getting something for nothing, something which they hadn't worked for.

4   When the plan was put into operation, however, the recipients of the relief checks proved to be an ungrateful, ugly bunch. They seemed to resent the cross-examinations and inspections at the hands of the relief investigators, who, they said, took advantage of a man's misery to snoop into every detail of his private life. In spite of uplifting editorials in A-town *Tribune* telling how grateful they ought to be, the recipients of the

relief refused to learn any moral lessons, declaring that they were "just as good as anybody else." When, for example, they permitted themselves the rare luxury of a movie or an evening of bingo, their neighbors looked at them sourly as if to say, "I work hard and pay my taxes just in order to support loafers like you in idleness and pleasure." This attitude, which was fairly characteristic of those members of the community who still had jobs, further embittered the relief recipients, so that they showed even less gratitude as time went on and were constantly on the lookout for insults, real or imaginary, from people who might think that they weren't as good as anybody else. A number of them took to moping all day long, the thinking that their lives had been failures; one or two even committed suicide. Others found that it was hard to look their wives and kiddies in the face, because they had failed to provide. They all found it difficult to maintain their club and fraternal relationships, since they could not help feeling that their fellow citizens despised them for having sunk so low. Their wives, too, were unhappy for the same reasons and gave up their social activities. Children whose parents were on relief felt inferior to classmates whose parents were not public charges. Some of these children developed inferiority complexes which affected not only their grades at school, but their careers after graduation. Several other relief recipients, finally, felt they could stand their loss of self-respect no longer and decided, after many efforts to gain honest jobs, to earn money by their own efforts, even if they had to go in for robbery. They did so and were caught and sent to the state penitentiary.

5   The depression, therefore, hit A-town very hard. The relief policy had averted starvation, no doubt, but suicide, personal quarrels, unhappy homes, the weakening of social organizations, the maladjustment of children, and, finally, crime, had resulted. The town was divided in two, the "haves" and the "have-nots," so that there was class hatred. People shook their heads sadly and declared that it all went to prove over again what they had known from the beginning, that giving people something for nothing inevitably demoralizes their character. The citizens of A-town gloomily waited for prosperity to return, with less and less hope as time went on.

6   The story of the other community, B-ville, was entirely different. B-ville was a relatively isolated town, too far out of the way to be reached by Rotary Club speakers and university extension services. One of the aldermen, however, who was something of an economist, explained to his fellow aldermen that unemployment, like sickness, accident, fire, tornado, or death, hits unexpectedly in modern society, irrespective of the victim's merits or deserts. He went on to say that B-ville's homes, parks, streets, industries, and everything else B-ville was proud of had been built in part by the work of these same people who were now unemployed. He then proposed to apply a principle of insurance: If the work these unemployed people had previously done for the community could be regarded as a form of premium paid to the community against a time of misfortune,

payments now made to them to prevent their starvation could be regarded as insurance claims. He therefore proposed that all men of good repute who had worked in the community in whatever line of useful endeavor, whether as machinists, clerks, or bank managers, be regarded as citizen policyholders, having claims against the city in the case of unemployment for fifty dollars a month until such time as they might again be employed. Naturally, he had to talk very slowly and patiently, since the idea was entirely new to his fellow aldermen. But he described his plan as a "straight business proposition," and finally they were persuaded. They worked out the details as to the conditions under which citizens should be regarded as policyholders in the city's social insurance plan to everybody's satisfaction and decided to give checks for fifty dollars a month to the heads of each of B-ville's indigent families.

7   B-ville's claim adjusters, whose duty it was to investigate the claims of the citizen policyholders, had a much better time than A-town's relief investigators. While the latter had been resentfully regarded as snoopers, the former, having no moral lesson to teach but simply a business transaction to carry out, treated their clients with businesslike courtesy and got the same amount of information as the relief investigators with considerably less difficulty. There were no hard feelings. It further happened, fortunately, that news of B-ville's plans reached a liberal newspaper editor in the big city at the other end of the state. This writer described the plan in a leading feature story headed "B-VILLE LOOKS AHEAD. Great Adventure in Social Pioneering Launched by Upper Valley Community." As a result of this publicity, inquiries about the plan began to come to the city hall even before the first checks were mailed out. This led, naturally, to a considerable feeling of pride on the part of the aldermen, who, being boosters, felt that this was a wonderful opportunity to put B-ville on the map.

8   Accordingly, the aldermen decided that instead of simply mailing out the checks as they had originally intended, they would publicly present the first checks at a monster civic ceremony. They invited the governor of the state, who was glad to come to bolster his none-too-enthusiastic support in that locality, the president of the state university, the senator from their district, and other functionaries. They decorated the National Guard armory with flags and got out the American Legion Fife and Drum Corps, the Boy Scouts, and other civic organizations. At the big celebration, each family to receive a social insurance check was marched up to the platform to receive it, and the governor and the mayor shook hands with each of them as they came trooping up in their best clothes. Fine speeches were made; there was much cheering and shouting; pictures of the event showing the recipients of the checks shaking hands with the mayor, and the governor patting the heads of the children, were published not only in the local papers but also in several metropolitan picture sections.

9   Every recipient of these insurance checks had a feeling, therefore, that he had been personally honored, that he lived in a wonderful little town,

and that he could face his unemployment with greater courage and assurance, since his community was back of him. The men and women found themselves being kidded in a friendly way by their acquaintances for having been "up there with the big shots," shaking hands with the governor, and so on. The children at school found themselves envied for having had their pictures in the papers. All in all, B-ville's unemployed did not commit suicide, were not haunted by a sense of failure, did not turn to crime, did not get personal maladjustments, did not develop class hatred, as the result of their fifty dollars a month. . . .

10   At the conclusion of the Professor's story, the discussion began:

11   "That just goes to show," said the Advertising Man, who was known among his friends as a realistic thinker, "what good promotional work can do. B-ville's city council had real advertising sense, and that civic ceremony was a masterpiece . . . made everyone happy . . . put over the scheme in a big way. Reminds me of the way we do things in our business: as soon as we called horse-mackerel tuna-fish, we developed a big market for it. I suppose if you called relief 'insurance,' you could actually get people to like it, couldn't you?"

12   "What do you mean, 'calling' it insurance?" asked the Social Worker. "B-ville's scheme wasn't relief at all. It *was* insurance. That's what all such payments should be. What gets me is the stupidity of A-town's city council and all people like them in not realizing that what they call 'relief' is simply the payment of just claims which those unemployed have on a community in a complex interdependent industrial society."

13   "Good grief, man! Do you realize what you're saying?" cried the Advertising Man in surprise. "Are you implying that those people had any *right* to that money? All I said was that it's a good idea to *disguise* relief as insurance if it's going to make people any happier. But it's still relief, no matter what you *call* it. It's all right to kid the public along to reduce discontent, but we don't need to kid ourselves as well!"

14   "But they *do* have a right to that money! They're not getting something for nothing. It's insurance. They did something for the community, and that's their prem—"

15   "Say, are you crazy?"

16   "Who's crazy?"

17   "You're crazy. Relief is relief, isn't it? If you'd only call things by their right names. . . ."

18   "But, confound it, insurance is insurance, isn't it?"

19   (Since the gentlemen are obviously losing their tempers, it will be best to leave them. The Professor has already sneaked out. When last heard of, not only had the quarrelers stopped speaking to each other, but so had their wives—and the Advertising Man was threatening to disinherit his son if he didn't break off his engagement with the Social Worker's daughter.)

20   This story has been told not to advance arguments in favor of "social insurance" or "relief" or for any other political and economic arrangement, but simply to show a fairly characteristic sample of language in action.

Do the words we use make as much difference in our lives as the story of A-town and B-ville seems to indicate? We often talk about "choosing the right words to express our thoughts," as if thinking were a process entirely independent of the words we think in. But is thinking such an independent process? Do the words we utter arise as a result of the thoughts we have, or are the thoughts we have determined by the linguistic systems we happen to have been taught? The Advertising Man and the Social Worker seem to be agreed that the results of B-ville's program were good, so that we can assume that their notions of what is socially desirable are similar. Nevertheless, they *cannot agree.*

21   Alfred Korzybski, in his preface to *Science and Sanity,* . . . asks the reader to imagine what the state of technology would be if all lubricants contained emery dust, the presence of which had never been detected. Machines would be short-lived and expensive; the machine age would be a dream of the distant future. If, however, someone were to discover the presence of the emery, we should at once know *in what direction to proceed* in order to release the potentialities of machine power.

22   Why do people disagree? It isn't a matter of education or intelligence, because quarreling, bitterness, conflict, and breakdown are just as common among the educated as the uneducated, among the clever as the stupid. Human relations are no better among the privileged than the underprivileged. Indeed, well-educated people are often the cleverest in proving that insurance is *really* insurance and that relief is *really* relief—and being well educated they often have such high principles that nothing will make them modify their position in the slightest. Are disagreements then the inevitable results of the nature of human problems and the nature of man? Possibly so—but if we give this answer, we are confessing to being licked before we have even started our investigations.

23   The student of language observes, however, that it is an extremely rare quarrel that does not involve some kind of *talking.* Almost invariably, before noses are punched or shooting begins, *words are exchanged*—sometimes only a few, sometimes millions. We shall, therefore, look for the "previously undetected emery dust" (or whatever it is that heats up and stops our intellectual machinery) in *language*—that is to say, *our linguistic habits* (how we talk and think and listen) and *our unconscious attitudes toward language.* If we are even partially successful in our search, we may get an inkling of the *direction in which to proceed* in order to release the now imperfectly realized potentialities of human co-operation.

24   P.S. Those who have concluded that the point of the story is that the Social Worker and the Advertising Man were "only arguing about different names for the same thing," are asked to reread the story and explain what they mean by (1) "only" and (2) "the same thing."

"You Call This Adorable?"
Felicia Halpert

Felicia Halpert's letter to the producer of NBC Sports ("You Call This Adorable?") identifies a recurring pattern in sports broadcasting. Listen to announcers covering women's events to hear the kind of diction Halpert objects to. Does it also offend you? Why or why not?

Dear Michael Weisman:

1   This letter is a follow-up to our recent telephone conversation. In the course of that interview, there wasn't time to fully air my opinions, so I decided to write. I figured, if you knew this letter would be read by thousands of women—many of whom watch NBC to catch the Olympics— you'd be glad to hear me out.

2   Television's sports coverage can be dazzling, Michael, no doubt about it. What you can show with your Minicams and "super slo mo" often defies description. But as much as I am anticipating the visual display, judging from what your commentators and analysts have said about women competitors in the past, I am also weary.

3   Calling 27-year-old females "girls," while referring to 19-year-old males as "men," is only the tip of the iceberg. At the 1987 Pan Am basketball games, as U.S player Jennifer Gillom brought the ball upcourt, CBS commentator Billy Packer turned to his colleague and said, "Doesn't Gillom remind you of a lady who someday is going to have a nice large family and is going to be a great cook? Doesn't she look like that? She's got just a real pleasant face."

4   We see on our screens amazing feats of female strength, speed, and endurance. Yet there's a persistent buzz to suggest that this athleticism is somehow atypical, indeed abnormal. At the opening of the women's downhill skiing competition in Calgary, as a montage of female athletes flashed on the screen, ABC's Al Trautwig chose to observe, "At some point these women were all normal little girls. Somewhere along the way they got sidetracked."

5   Sidetracked?!

6   Having put his foot in his mouth, Trautwig then went in for the whole leg. He pressed his point that female athletes could even be pretty, referring to "glamorous" Maria Walliser, whose "strikingly pretty face has made her a European cover girl." Michaela Gerg from West Germany, he informed us, "had a confidence problem. But she's been seeing a psychologist who has put some confidence in those strikingly blue eyes of hers."

7   Trautwig isn't the only offender. In reviewing coverage from past Olympics I found plenty of babble on women's appearance, their unhappy personal lives, their vulnerabilities and jealousies—images that undermine their physical achievement.

8

Reporters and commentators still haven't discovered that women can compete, and so they always throw cattiness into their journalistic formula. In the competition between figure skaters Debi Thomas and Katarina Witt the media kept telling us of the great animosity between them, though it was hardly evident. In fact, Margot Adler, a reporter who covered the Calgary Games for National Public Radio, recalls that "the emphasis on cattiness was played up by everybody. But I didn't see it." Most of the time, she added, Witt and Thomas "didn't interact with each other at all. They went about their own business."

9   Then, in the downhill skiing competition between Michela Figini and Maria Walliser, ABC's Trautwig reported: "There were rumors that they hated each other and avoided each other." But when asked whether she disliked Walliser, Figini replied, of course not. To which Trautwig retorted, "But do they *hate* each other?"

10   These same journalists are able to appreciate, even applaud, honorable competition between men. When skaters Brian Orser and Brian Boitano were locked in a duel for the man's singles title in 1988, their friendship was consistently emphasized by the press.

11   I grant you, Michael, that television isn't the only culprit. After all, it was *Time* magazine that said of Romanian gymnast Ecaterina Szabo, "Little Szabo looks like she would sooner fall off the balance beam than neglect eye shadow."

12   In her study of media coverage of the '76 and '84 Olympics, Assistant Professor Margaret Carlisle Duncan of the University of Wisconsin found that "Olympic sportswomen were portrayed in two quite opposing ways, one way emphasizing women's strength and the other focusing on women's weakness. And more often than one would think, these themes of strength and weakness appeared in bizarre combinations within a single article. Writers veered wildly between describing women athletes as powerful, precise, courageous, skillful, purposeful, and in control—and as cute, vulnerable, juvenile, manipulating, and toy- or animal-like."

13   This kind of ambiguity was amply demonstrated on ABC during the recent Calgary Games. ABC skating analyst Dick Button praised Midori Ito's spectacular skating as "a triumph of athleticism," adding, "she is adorable!" Button was also wild about Brian Orser form Canada, but he described his style as "brilliant, really fine" and added that he is a "wonderfully confident and controlled skater." Meanwhile, at the conclusion of American skater Caryn Kadavy's program, he said, "She is so lovely. You know she really has a vulnerability that makes your heart warm to her." To which Jim McKay added. "It fits her personality. A very appealing and vulnerable person."

14   Part of the problem, as you've agreed, is that women's sports aren't covered much during the year, and commentators do not develop much knowledge about women players. What's more, women are rarely recruited for the anchor booth, in part because of attitudes like those of Jim Spence, former vice president of ABC Sports, who wrote in his book, *Up Close and Personal: The Inside Story of Network Television Sports,* "There

is no reason why an audience, whatever its makeup, should be required to tolerate an announcer with a very shallow level of knowledge or feeling for sports. And that, of course, is the main reason we have had 99 percent of our sports dealt to us by men."

15   The networks claim they only want experienced people to cover the Olympics. But then how does one explain Kathy Lee Gifford, whose sports background prior to the '88 Games was minimal at best? Nevertheless she was paired with her husband football player-turned-commentator Frank Gifford, for the late-night recap on ABC. In that role she contributed such gems as "for a girl who eats ice cream every day," Katarina Witt looks fabulous.

16   After Donna de Varona, swimming medalist and now ABC commentator, concluded a segment on 16-year-old Soviet skater Yekaterina Gordeyeva that described her as "an extraordinary athlete with a simple secret, a ponytail, and a dream," Kathy couldn't help but add, "and she's adorable," Needless to say, "adorable" and "lovely" were popular words in Calgary.

17   Obviously, it's not the sex of the commentator that counts but his or her appreciation of the strength and ability involved in being a world-class performer. Eric Heiden, a former multiple gold medal winner in speed skating, demonstrated that understanding when he commented on gold medalist Bonnie Blair. As she rounded the speed-skating oval, Heiden called her "a fantastic skater. She's got great determination, great technique. And she's such a good corner skater. Look at that tiger look! She really comes in there with a look of determination."

18   Ironically, some of the best-remembered Olympians have been women: Olga Korbut, Nadia Comaneci, Dorothy Hamill, and Mary Lou Retton. But their visibility was a by-product of media coverage that transforms the Games into the athletic equivalent of the Miss World beauty pageant. Every four years we have the crowning of a bright, enthusiastic girl; usually a pixie, always white, who has won our hearts with her "spunky" performance and "winning smile." We are charmed by her youth, her immaturity. Often, more mature female competitors receive uncomplimentary coverage, even in victory.

19   For example, when Margaret Murdock, 33, became the first woman ever to win a silver medal in the mixed-sex shooting competition, *Sports Illustrated* described her as "nunnish . . . a shambling figure in a faded orange sweatshirt and baggy jeans, with short graying hair curling around orange ear protectors and silver-rimmed glasses, she showed the beginnings of a double chin."

20   Olga Korbut, who won adoration and acclaim in 1972 as the heartwarming four foot eleven gymnast from the Soviet Union, was described four years later in *Time* as "haggard," in *Newsweek* as "old" and "strained," and as one who had "tried too hard—for too long." She was 21.

21   Over the years, the media have played a significant role in increasing the visibility of female athletes. The airing of the first Olympic marathon for women in 1984 provided an unforgettable opportunity to watch them

compete in a grueling test of endurance. The TV audience rightly heard ABC commentators Al Michaels and Jim Lampley describe this as "a dramatic and historic event," and a "great moment for women runners, women athletes, and women in general."

22   But even in this admirable display of reportorial fairness, all was not perfect. When Swiss runner Gabriela Andersen-Schiess staggered into the stadium and began listing from side to side, medical attendants surrounded her but they didn't touch her. To do so would have disqualified her from finishing. The stadium crowed urged her on, and she never stopped moving forward.

23   But in the broadcast booth, Marty Liquori reacted strongly, repeatedly saying, "In my opinion, someone should take charge and stop her—. . . . Someone should walk out there and take responsibility and grab her."

24   Andersen-Schiess finished and recovered physically two hours after the race. The next day, Liquori's commentary received high praise from most of the press. His reasoning for wanting Andersen-Schiess removed was that "there's nothing to be accomplished," presumably because she wasn't going to win any medals.

25   But as Scott Ostler in the Los Angeles *Times* noted, "Nothing to be accomplished? How about finishing? . . . They only hold the first Olympic women's marathon once. If a woman wants to push herself beyond sanity and reality, isn't that in the Olympic tradition? . . . Why is it that women have to cross the finish line with their hair neatly combed and their makeup fresh? Why can't they gasp and sweat and stagger, just like the guys do? Amid all the pixies and sweethearts comes a Swiss marathoner who stumbles and staggers and somehow finishes. If she were a man, they would salute her courage. But she is a woman and the TV people wonder why the officials don't grab this poor girl and help her."

26   Michael, NBC has a unique opportunity to improve the coverage of women during these Olympics. I spoke with Gayle Gardner, a sports reporter for your network who will co-anchor some of the coverage. Her assessment of what we can expect is guarded, but she says, "There are women working on this who will not allow the performances (of women athletes) to be undercut."

27   I hope she is right. The Olympics is one of the rare events where female athletes are seen by millions of Americans. We watch women who have spent countless hours perfecting their skills, determined to excel during those few brief moments when they face a judge's scrutiny, leap over a barrier, or race toward a ribbon. At their best the Games are a testament to the spirit of physical achievement. It's time television gave us the appropriate words to back up the poetry we're seeing.

Sincerely,

Felicia E. Halpert

POLISHING A DRAFT: GUIDELINES FOR REVISION AND EDITING _____

After you have explored a subject and developed a draft or two, you are left with an important but potentially exhausting task: reviewing the content and the form of the text to identify areas needing improvement. If you are reluctant to begin this polishing, do something concrete to get yourself started. You might begin by gathering materials—the draft, some clean paper, a dictionary, a thesaurus, and pens or pencils. A different ink or highlighter might help you visualize changes. When you sit down to work on a draft that felt, at one time, relatively complete, it is a good idea to set some goals that will keep your attention on specific tasks. For example, setting out "to improve this paper" is unlikely to promote effective change. In contrast, deciding that you will "identify all cohesive devices to see if the paper is structurally glued together" will give your work a specific focus. When you are ready to polish a draft, then, consider these guidelines:

1. Read over the draft, then read over any teacher comments or peer evaluations. Have you been given some specific criticisms about ideas or passages? Make a list of the areas needing attention.

2. Look over the list. Are there any duplications; that is, did more than one reader target the same area? Can you make distinctions between major problems and minor ones? Plan your attack and make a new list that orders your priorities. For example, "First I will review support for my second point. Two readers thought it was weak. Then, I need to look at my conclusion to see if I changed the topic."

3. If you don't have evaluations, or if they were not specific, create your own checklist. Start by writing down (yes, again) the controlling idea, the purpose, and the audience of this paper. Having a visual reminder may help you stick to the topic. It is a good idea to ask yourself, now that you're a little distant from the original writing sessions, if your paper really fulfills that purpose. If it seems to do something else, can you define the new purpose? As the reader now, how do you respond to the paper? If the paper's overall effect is not exactly what you intended, what should you do? If you think the paper works as is, re-consider the controlling idea or purpose.

4. When you feel that you have a clear statement of thesis and purpose (original or revised), measure each paragraph against those statements. If you have a question about a point's relationship to thesis or purpose, mark the section. If you feel that a section is particularly clear, mark that too. Get an idea of the paper's strong areas. If parts of the paper don't seem to fit the thesis or purpose, try to figure out what elements change the direction of the paper. Does something need to be condensed? Look at the parts you feel work toward the stated purpose. Are those parts clear? Can you give those sections more emphasis?

5. When you feel that you have cleared out extraneous comments, look carefully at your remaining work. Underline the main point of each section. Those points should have a clear relationship to your overall purpose. Now look at the development of those points. Have you explained the idea (not repeated it)? Are examples appropriate? What have you done to support and develop each point? If you find that you have repeated the idea in different words, clean house. Can you underline or number specific things that develop the idea? Do you need another example? Another testimony? Another detail?

6. Look at the introduction. Does it accurately reflect the content of your paper? Does it make a conscious effort to "hook" the reader? What did you do to catch attention or create interest? Can you improve the introduction? Is it too wordy? Awkward? Is it clear? Remember, this section provides the first impression of the paper. How do you sound? Informed? Pompous? Uncertain? Check your image here.

7. Now look at the conclusion. Does it affirm the purpose of the paper? Does it reflect the content of this paper? Does it refer to incidents or ideas in the paper? Is it somehow connected to the introduction?

8. When (*and only when*) you are satisfied with the content, you are ready to edit text. You may want to edit at another time; take a break and wait until you are rested and sharp. Then, pull out the dictionary and the handbook and anything else that will help you find and correct errors. List mistakes you made on other pieces of writing. Then, turn to the last page of your paper and begin reading from the bottom up. For some reason, errors blend beautifully with the text of a paper, and reading the paper in reverse tends to break up the old familiar pattern.

   Check for major errors: fragments, fused sentences, comma splices, gross agreement errors. Check for any constructions you've had trouble with: parallel structures, dangling modifiers. Circle any word that might be misspelled. Check the spelling. (Note: If it's not in your dictionary, ask a friend for an alternate spelling.) If you have a spelling problem, start a list of your most common errors. (Know your instructor's policy about computer-assisted editing. Can you use a spell-checker, grammar-prompt, or other program?) Check obvious punctuation errors. Have you used question marks as needed? If you've revised part of a sentence, does the rest of it still fit? (Verbs and pronouns must agree, so any changes may have repercussions.)

9. Read over the corrected draft to see if you have been consistent. If you are writing from first person, is the entire work consistently from the "I" perspective? Does it shift unnecessarily to "we"? Or to

"you"? If you used "he or she" once, did you use it everywhere? Is verb tense consistent? Are there unnecessary shifts between past tense and present tense?

10. Check for cohesion. Have you used pronouns accurately? Did you repeat key words? Structures? Did you repeat too much? Check between paragraphs. Mark your transitional devices. Have you varied them?

11. Give it a final read to see if the paper has a consistent tone. Is the diction consistently formal? Pompous? Chatty? For most papers, eliminate all slang.

PART FOUR

Special

Invitations

Much of your writing is voluntary, a response to situations that prompt you to put your ideas on paper. But on the job and in the classroom, there are assignments that do not leave you the option of declining the invitation. The discussions of writing to inform, to convince, and to involve your readers will guide you through most writing situations. There are, however, some special kinds of writing that require additional considerations. Researched writing, literary interpretations, and essay examinations are all invitations that command your response. As you gather material, draft prose paragraphs, and review your writing, look over these chapters for advice.

Writing a Research Paper

Writing from sources includes exploring a topic, drafting and reviewing, but it also involves two special skills: the ability to locate material and the ability to document sources. The discussion of locating material includes field work like surveys and observations as well as library research, and the documentation section includes information about MLA, APA, and number styles. Two sample research papers illustrate persuasive and informative writing, presented in two distinct formats and documented in two distinct styles.

Much of your writing relies on research to supply information, information that sketches background about a subject, explains specific procedures or policies, or gives the thinking of experts in the field. When you collect and organize such information, you inform not only the readers but yourself as well.

The idea of research may sound intimidating, but remember that a research paper is not substantively different from other kinds of writing. As you have probably concluded, the biggest difference is the source of information for the paper. You are expected to provide a thorough analysis of the current thinking on a subject—expanding the discussion beyond personal response. Not surprisingly, such a thorough presentation is usually longer than a personal response paper. Other predictable differences are the more formal tone and the need for thorough, precise documentation of sources.

But the differences between research papers and other written responses are less important than the similarities. Like other writing, research papers serve different purposes. Some are informative, presenting factual information without taking sides. Others are persuasive, presenting and defending judgments about a researched subject. Both kinds of papers will be discussed in this chapter.

❑ The First Decision: To Accept the Invitation to Write

Some research papers are responses to academic assignments that make the decision to write for you. You may also follow your interest in a topic into a library or a museum or out into the field. Your job may require that you research a problem. Perhaps your investigation will end when your curiosity is satisfied. Or, the results of your research may be intriguing enough that you want to share them. Whether your decision to write is forced by the classroom or whether it is one you make for yourself, the process outlined in this book will produce a thoughtful, logical research paper just as it produces effective personal essays and literary analyses.

Just as you do with any written response, you begin by gathering raw materials. An obvious place to begin is the library, but do not confine your efforts to the most obvious. Expand your approach to include field research like interviews, polls, site visits, and observations. Some strategies for research are outlined here.

LIBRARY RESEARCH

If you have had little experience with your college library, it can seem an intimidating place. Remember, though, that it is meticulously organized and designed to be easy to use.

Some colleges require a "Books and Libraries" course that will introduce the resources and the layout of the facility, and some libraries provide extensive written materials and even orientation tours. In addition, the personnel will be able to direct you to reference materials and explain how to use special resources like computer-aided research services. Every book, record, tape, and other source of information stored in the library has a special identification code that makes it available to you. So approach the library with the idea that you will find what you need.

Expect to find general collections that include the books you might want to check out, reference works and periodicals that you will need to use in the library (or photocopy—most libraries provide inexpensive photocopying facilities), government publications that may be set aside, and nonprint materials like records, films, and videotapes.

If you are having trouble locating materials, always ask for assistance—the library may have older periodicals bound in hardcover or stored in microform. Most libraries also participate in interlibrary loans; you can then request a copy of a book or a journal article that your library does not have.

All of the time spent reading about libraries in general will not substitute for direct contact. Even if you have never used the resources of the campus library, researching a specific topic will help you to learn about your library as you find material for your paper.

The Library Classification System

Libraries in the United States use either the Dewey Decimal system or the Library of Congress system to catalogue their holdings. Books are assigned a code number and grouped with similar works. The code numbers (and thus the location of the books) can be found through reference catalogues of the library holdings. Larger libraries provide maps of their floorplans with information about the classification system and the location of materials. Check your own library for information about the system in use.

The Library Catalogue

The library catalogue usually provides you with three different ways to access the library's holdings: by author, by title, and by subject. You can use the catalogue to determine what materials are available on a specific subject without knowing any particular author or title. Or, if you know the title or author's name, you can use the catalogue to determine exactly where a work is shelved. (See Figures 19.1 and 19.2)

The traditional catalogue, the "card catalogue," consists of drawers of three- by five-inch cards containing the information shown on the samples below. However, you may find that your library's catalogue is on microfilm, on microfiche, or even in a computer. Your librarian will explain which system is in use.

Becoming familiar with your library means more than understanding its general arrangement. It means learning its specific holdings in the

Figure 19.1   Author Card

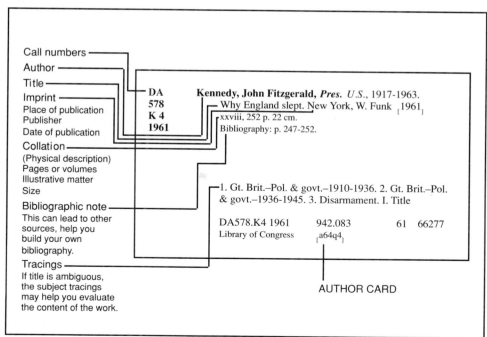

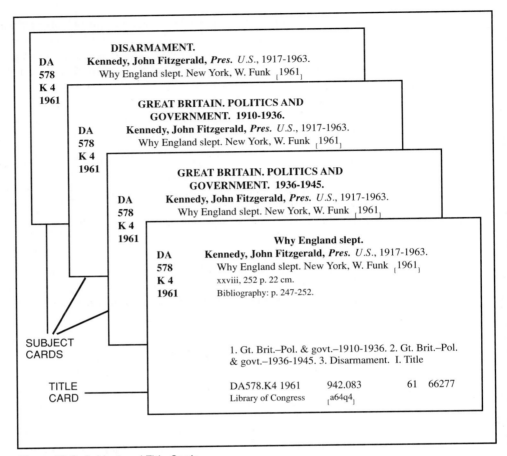

Figure 19.2 Subject and Title Cards

subject area in which you will be doing your research. Does the library have extensive book holdings in that subject, or will you likely have to send for the books you need through interlibrary loan? What periodicals (journals and magazines) does it subscribe to, and how many years of back issues are on file? Knowing the answers to these questions before you begin your research will enable you to allow sufficient lead time for receiving materials and to save time in using the periodical indexes.

A Strategy for Research

Calling on the creative voice to supply information will not produce effective research papers. Instead, use your creative energies to explore the resources of the library. Library personnel can give you some information about standard available reference works, but you will often find other useful sources in the footnote or bibliographic references in the works you consult. Keep handy a list of works to consult, and add to it as often as you can.

To begin such a list, you must find a starting point. Leslie McDaniels, whose research strategy is described here, began with the broad subject "The Occult."

1. Leslie began in the reference section of the library with a good general encyclopedia. Encyclopaedia Britannica and Encyclopedia Americana are among the best. She consulted the Micropaedia volume of Britannica and the index volume of Americana.
   Encyclopaedia Britannica is divided into two sets of books: the Macropaedia set, containing fully detailed articles on a limited number of subjects; and the Micropaedia set, containing brief articles and cross-references on a large number of subjects. The Micropaedia set functions very much like the single-volume index of Americana.

She found these entries:

Britannica, Micropaedia Volume VII, p. 469
one celestial body or an observer's view of another body. See eclipse, occultation, and transit.

occultism, a general designation for various theories, practices, and rituals based on esoteric knowledge, especially alleged knowledge about the world of spirits and unknown forces of the universe. Devotees of occultism strive to understand and explore these worlds, often by developing the higher powers of the mind. To this end they frequently study very early writings in the belief that such secrets were known to ancient civilizations and can be repossessed. A favorite text is the Chinese *I Ching* ("Classic of Changes").

Occultism covers such diverse subjects as Satanism, astrology, Kabbala, Gnosticism, theosophy, divination, witchcraft, and certain forms of magic.
   —mystical function and ambiguous utility 12:786f
   —Odin as Norse patron 8:36g
   —Taoist and Confucian views 17:1034e
   —theosophic affirmation of supernatural 18:276f

Americana, index (Volume 30), p. 588

OCCULTATION (atron.) 20–608
   Eclipse 9–582

OCCULTISM (mysticism) 20–609
   See also Devil, The; Divination; Extrasensory perception; Magic; Witchcraft
   Astrology 2–557
   Cabala 5–108
   Demonology 8–699; 9–36

Evil Spirit 10–733
Extrasensory Perception (ESP) 10–804
Fortune-Telling 11–628; 9–196
Ghost 12–724
Magic 18–117
Numerology 20–543
Parapsychology 21–287
Psychokinesis 22–721
Rosicrucians 23–701
Spiritualism 25–514
Superstition 26–35

Note that both entries list other related subjects and give volume and page references.

2. Next, Leslie determined that her interest was not in the broad topic of occultism. After reading the list of related subjects she decided that astrology was her real interest and consulted the appropriate volumes of *Britannica* (Macropaedia, Vol. 2, p. 219) and *Americana* (Vol. 2, p. 557, as noted in the entry). She found an excellent brief overview of the subject (more scholarly and detailed in *Britannica,* but more concise and readable in *Americana*).

3. Leslie then looked for a subject encyclopedia.

There are various encyclopedias available in each of the following areas: art, astronomy, biology, chemistry, computer science, dance, earth sciences, economics, education, film, history, law, literature, mathematics, medicine, music, philosophy, physics, psychology, religion, science and technology, and the social sciences.

She checked N. Devore's *Encyclopediae of Astrology* and the psychology and religion encyclopedias.

Recommended readings are found at the end of an encyclopedia article.

4. Leslie looked for other reference books on her topic. By consulting a guide to reference materials, such as Eugene O. Sheehy's *Guide to Reference Books,* she found bibliographies and other reference books on her topic. Guides to reference materials also answer such questions as the following:

- **Where can I find miscellaneous facts and statistics?** Sheehy lists *The World Almanac, Information Please Almanac, The New York Times Encyclopedic Almanac,* and *The People's Almanac,* among other sources.
- **Where can I find information about specific people?** Sheehy lists *Who's Who (British), Who's Who in America,* and *Who's Who in the World,* among other sources.

- **Where can I find information about the English language?** Sheehy lists the *Oxford English Dictionary,* Eric Partridge's *Dictionary of Slang and Unconventional English,* and *Webster's New Dictionary of Synonyms,* among other sources.
- **Where can I find significant quotations?** Sheehy suggests E. M. Beck's *Familiar Quotations* and George Seldes's *The Great Quotations,* among other sources.
- **Where can I find publishing information about books that were or are still in print?** Sheehy lists *Cumulative Book Index, Books in Print,* and *Paperback Books in Print,* among other sources.

5. Leslie also checked the library catalogue. She looked in the author and title catalogues for the books recommended in the bibliographies listed above. Sometimes a book will be listed in one catalogue section but not in another, so consult both.

   Some of the books listed in the bibliographies she consulted were not in the library, so she requested them through interlibrary loan. But interlibrary loan told her the material might take several weeks to arrive, so Leslie was forced to look for other sources available on campus. She made a mental note that next time she would start a little earlier. The subject catalogue gave her additional sources under both the general heading of "Occultism" and the specific heading of "Astrology."

6. The librarian directed Leslie to the periodical indexes in the reference section of the library and suggested that she check both the *Reader's Guide to Periodical Literature* (the basic reference to nontechnical articles) and also the *Humanities Index* since the *Reader's Guide* should not be the sole or primary tool for a college research paper.

   A number of indexes are also available for specialized and technical subjects. The following are among the most commonly used:

   Applied Science and Technology Index
   Art Index
   Biography Index
   Biological and Agricultural Index
   Book Review Index
   Business Periodicals Index
   Education Index
   Engineering Index
   General Science Index
   Humanities Index
   Index to Legal Periodicals
   MLA International Bibliography
   Magazine Index

Music Index
Philosopher's Index
Religion Index One: Periodicals
Social Sciences Index

Here is one of the listings Leslie found:

The Humanities Index, April 1975–March 1976, p. 41
    Wettiin. Sov Lit nos: 116-41 '75
First night back; tr. by A. Shkarovsky-Raffe.
    Sov Lit no 1:3-29 '75
ASTBURY, R.
    Juvenal 10, 148-50. *Mnemosyne* 28 fasc 1:40-6 '75
ASTRODYNAMICS
    See also Astronautics
ASTROLOGY
    Astrology as popular culture. M. Truzzi, *J Pop Cult* 8:906–11
        Spr '75
    Astrology: magic or science? L. E. Jerome. *il Humanist* 35:
        10-16 S '75
    Critical look at astrology. B. J. Bok. *il Humanist* 35:6-9 S '75
    My flirtation with astrology. C. Lamont. *il Humanist* 35:16 S '75
    Objections to astrology: a statement by 186 leading scientists.
        il Humanist 35:4-6 S '75
    Science and religion in the writings of Dr. William Fulke, R.
        Bauckham. *Brit J Hist Sci* 8:17-31 Mr '75
    See also
    Occult sciences
ASTROLOGY in literature
    Astrology and the Wife of Bath: a reinterpretation. B. F. Ham-
        lin. *Chaucer R* 9:153-65 Fall '74
    Chapman's Byron and Bartholomaeus Anglicus. G. F. Freije,
        Eng Lang Notes 12:168-71 Mr '75
    Satan in orbit and medieval demonology (*Paradise Lost,* IX: 64-
        66) J. M. Steadman, *Eng Lang Notes* 12:161-3 Mr. '75
ASTRONAUTICS
    See also
    Space flight

The article entries are presented in abbreviated form. But that form
is easy to decipher. The first article entry is read as follows: Title:
"Astrology as Popular Culture." Author: M. Truzzi. Journal: Journal
of Popular Culture. Volume: 8. Pages: 906–11. Issue: Spring 1975.

If an abbreviation puzzles you, look for the explanation of the
entry code at the beginning of the index volume.

Note that at the end of the listing of articles is a cross-reference
to a related heading, "Occult Sciences," and that the next heading

covers a more specialized aspect of the subject, "Astrology in Literature." Leslie copied the entries of articles she wished to read. Then, she checked the periodical index of her library to find out which journals and magazines (and which back issues) were on file. Most of the journals she needed were listed in the index, but when she tried to find the articles, she discovered that one journal was missing and another had important pages missing. Leslie thought about making a trip to the state university library; it was two hours away, but she hoped to find more complete holdings to make the trip worthwhile.

7. For this project, Leslie decided not to use the *New York Times Index.*

The *New York Times Index* is the standard newspaper index for the United States. It covers all stories that appeared in that newspaper from 1851 to the present. Most libraries will have in their microfilm collection any *Times* story you wish to read.

8. She did check to see if her library had access to computer data bases and abstracting services.

Data bases are especially helpful when you are having difficulty finding information on your subject. Abstracting services such as *Psychological Abstracts, Sociological Abstracts,* and *America: History and Life* offer helpful summaries of journal articles. *Dissertation Abstracts International* provides summaries of doctoral dissertations.

9. Finally, Leslie compared the code numbers of the books she wanted to the library guide posted in the lobby. The guide told her which floors and even which parts of the room to check for the books and journals.

Some of the books were not on the shelves, but she discovered that once she had found the proper shelf, there were other books on the subject that looked useful. Before she carried the entire stack back to her dorm, though, she checked the index and the table of contents to see which pages of the books were most relevant to her topic. Then she scanned those pages. Some works seemed directly relevant; those she decided to borrow. Others had only a few pages that seemed useful, so she photocopied those sections and made careful notes about the author, title, publisher, and date of publication on the photocopies. Since journals and magazines are rarely allowed out of the library, she did the same with articles, photocopying parts of some and all of others, noting author, article title, publication title, volume, number, and date on all of her copies. Thus she carried a much smaller stack of material across campus to her dorm.

Not all of your research projects will parallel Leslie's investigations. But whatever sources you consult as you gather materials, keep your purpose larger than merely acquiring information. Research, as Leslie found, can add to your list of sources. While a lengthy bibliography is no substitute for critical judgment, it does indicate to your readers that you are a credible, informed writer. But a much more important goal is to deepen your understanding, to see the connections among ideas and grasp the significance of the information. The aim here, in short, is to stimulate your thinking. Read actively, keeping a list of ideas that are triggered by the author's words, scribbling a question or a note of agreement or disagreement for future reference. Most important, whenever an author offers an interpretation or judgment, ask appropriate questions, such as "What other interpretations or judgments are possible here?" "How substantial is the evidence offered in support?" and "how reasonable is the author's position?"

Taking Notes

One of the most time-consuming parts of research is note-taking. Photocopying is probably the fastest and most accurate shortcut, but make sure that you copy with selectivity. It is easy to photocopy pages and pages of material without really reading; in spite of the bulk of material, your

Figure 19.3 Bibliography Card

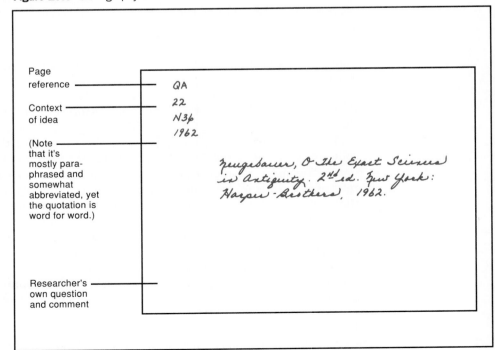

Page reference

Context of idea

(Note that it's mostly paraphrased and somewhat abbreviated, yet the quotation is word for word.)

Researcher's own question and comment

QA
22
N36
1962

Neugebauer, O. *The Exact Sciences in Antiquity.* 2nd ed. New York: Harper-Brothers, 1962.

research has barely begun. Also, documenting sources thoroughly as you use them will save return trips to the library. When you cannot photocopy, follow these suggestions to make note taking as efficient as possible:

1. Make a bibliography card for every work you decide is useful to you and make it the first time you handle the work. Be sure to include all relevant information. Figure 19.3 illustrates a bibliography card.

2. Make a separate note card for every idea. When arranging your ideas, it is much easier to shuffle cards than to recopy notes. (See Figure 19.4 for a sample note card.)

3. Condense the material as much as possible. Never quote a long passage unless it is so important and so concise that a paraphrase would be unacceptable. And take the time to be sure the paraphrase does not lean too heavily on the author's phrasing. By condensing, limiting your quotations, and paraphrasing carefully, you will reduce the chances of committing unintentional plagiarism when you are writing the paper.

4. Recheck for accuracy. When you have finished taking notes on a source, check to be sure that you have not misinterpreted the source's statement or quoted out of context. Check, too, that what you have written is clear enough that you will not be confused about

Figure 19.4 Note Card

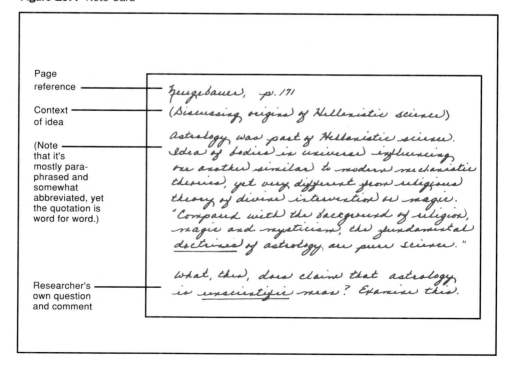

Page reference

Context of idea

(Note that it's mostly paraphrased and somewhat abbreviated, yet the quotation is word for word.)

Researcher's own question and comment

it when you are writing the paper. (A note that is meaningful today can be very puzzling two weeks from now.) A brief remark about the context in which the statement was made or your reaction to the statement can help provide that clarity.

RESEARCH IN THE FIELD

When you think of researching a topic, you probably think first of the library. But there is another kind of research that can prove invaluable as you gather information about a topic: field research.

Field research can take several forms. You can visit relevant sites or conduct random samples or interview experts. All such research can add to your understanding of a subject and improve both your thinking and your writing.

Personal Observation

If you are writing about the lifestyle of another era, field research might consist of a visit to an historic preservation area or to an historic home. Visits to special exhibits or collections are also field research. Such personal expeditions can be cited in your writing to verify your observations.

Before you research a site, you should do some preliminary research. If you are not sure what to expect, call the museum or the site or even the tourist bureau in the area to find out what the exhibits will cover. Ask about information available at the site. Even if you are told that the exhibits will be well-documented and self-explanatory, do some reading about the subject of the exhibit or about the lifestyle in the era of the place you are to visit. Look over the material you have already gathered to find emerging areas of emphasis.

Suppose that you are planning to visit a living history museum where you will watch typical rural workers of the nineteenth century as they work near their homes. Since most of the workers at such museums are prepared to discuss their activities, you might decide ahead of time to focus on the women in the family. Planning ahead, you prepare a list of questions about their typical day's work, including questions about food preparation, clothing manufacture, and home maintenance. If you ask about women's responsibilities, you might be surprised to learn that rural women often worked in the fields with their husbands and that many provided the medical care for their own families and for their neighbors. By choosing a focus ahead of time, you are ready to ask particular questions. (A tape recorder is also useful when you interview, but be sure to ask permission before you record any conversation.)

You should also be prepared when you go into the field. A notebook and pencil are essential, but you may also want to bring photographic equipment to document your observations. Even if you do not use visual aids in your final project, photographs will record details of architecture or layout without overlooking significant detail.

Surveys and Polls

Another kind of field research is the random sample. If you are planning to comment on the general opinions of a particular population, it is sound practice to verify your observations with some simple surveys. To begin, select and define a particular population. You might define your group as "freshmen living in Williams Hall." You might choose "female athletes on the varsity track squad." Or you might define a population in your off-campus community, such as "residents of Afton Oaks Apartments" or "mothers of pre-schoolers at Kinder-Care #19" or even "teenagers in the Kenilworth Subdivision."

When you have defined your group, estimate its size. To have any validity, a random sample must include a significant portion of the population, but there is considerable leeway in defining "significant portion." If the group is composed of people of similar attitude and background, a small sample (5-10 percent) will suffice. If your random sample uncovers widely varying attitudes, however, you must be prepared to sample until you feel a pattern is emerging. Remember that no one expects you to sample everyone (think of the word "sample" here), but you are expected to include a realistic cross-section of opinions.

If your population is small and easily accessible, you might distribute questionnaires. Even without 100 percent response, you will probably get enough answers to make reasonable generalizations about the desire for quiet hours in the dorm or the resistance to a swimming pool at the day-care center.

With a larger, more varied population, your goal is a cross-section. A reasonable approach to surveying the student body at your school might be to conduct brief surveys of students as they leave a much-frequented spot. You could station yourself at the exit to the student union with a clipboard and a pen, or you could set up at the door to the library or to a snack bar. Remember that your location is a key to the accuracy of the cross-section. If you are stationed outside of the engineering building, or if you are set up at a dorm-connected cafeteria, you will poll only a select population. So, take the nature of your defined population into consideration when you establish poll sites.

Some final cautions in using surveys and polls:

- Look carefully at the population and at the sample responses before you make generalizations. Logic demands that you tread lightly when asserting that "all" or "a majority" or "many" or "few" or "hardly any" have a certain opinion.

- Be sure that you have taken an adequate sample and that you have reached a reasonable cross-section before you make any kind of generalizations.
- Be prepared to explain your method of polling to your readers so that they will have confidence in your methods as well as in your reasoning.

Interviews

Another productive method of field research is the interview. To find a person whose knowledge or experience could add to your understanding of a subject and to your presentation, you can check a campus directory or a current university catalogue for a list of faculty and their specialties. Depending on your subject, the yellow pages of the local telephone book is also organized by occupation. In addition to finding experts through their jobs, you can often find them through mention in the local newspaper. Some will register with a speakers' bureau (contact the local university, the Chamber of Commerce, and the public library) in their areas of interest, including both careers and avocations. You can also check with specific interest groups like a local photographic society or a smockers' guild to find experts in specific areas.

Once you have identified a potential expert to interview, contact the person. If you are reluctant to call without prior introduction, send a letter explaining your interest and requesting the interview. In the letter, indicate that you will call to make arrangements. You can ask the person to contact you, but make such contact as simple as possible. Remember who is doing whom the favor here.

When you schedule the interview, you should ask if the person objects to a tape recorder. If the answer is yes, you must respect the person's wishes. Even if you do tape the interview, bring pencil and paper to make notes as you talk.

You should also bring a list of questions. You might find that only one question is needed to start the person talking, but be prepared to ask questions that focus on your specific needs. Bring more questions than you can imagine needing (but don't insist that all be answered).

To formulate questions, do some background reading on your topic. Basic information about dates or places should be available from any source, so do not ask the person to do your background research for you. In your preliminary reading, make notes about areas that are not clear to you or that intrigue you. For instance, you might read that one general refused to come to the aid of another during a battle. During the interview, you can mention that detail and ask the expert for an analysis.

Sample Questions:

> Queen Elizabeth I must have known that she would die one day and leave her country without an heir. Why did she not marry?

One of the shocking statements about the Love Canal toxic waste problem is that both government and industry were aware of the health hazards in the community but did not take action. Why do you think that nothing was done to protect the people of the area until they began to protest?

I know that much news space has been given to insider trading on Wall Street, but I'm not clear on how it works. What does "insider trading" mean, and what's wrong with it?

The "Indiana Jones" character makes archaeology look exciting. Is field work usually so adventurous? What goes on during a typical field investigation?

Your department is responsible for investigating complaints of child abuse and neglect. How do you decide if a complaint is justified, and what do you do if you think a child is being abused or neglected?

Begin the interview by explaining briefly your particular project. If you provide a context for the interview, the person might be able to supply answers to questions that you did not know enough to ask. Listen carefully and be flexible about the direction of the interview, even though you have a list of questions with you. Take notes carefully and don't hesitate to ask for clarification of details or for accurate spellings. Watch interviews on television to see how one question might suggest another. The expert might say, "I'm not really sure why the disaster occurred. The warning signs were given, but no one heeded them." The interviewer quickly responds, "What were those signs?" And, after the answer, "Who should have heeded them?" Transcripts of interviews also appear in newspapers and magazines. Look carefully to see how interviewers ask for clarification or for further information.

Be considerate of the person's time and resources. If you have done some preliminary work on the subject and have prepared a list of questions, the interview will move smoothly. When your time is up, be sure to ask the person if you can quote him or her directly. You might also ask if the person would like to see a copy of your final work. Finally, verify information on full name and on credentials (not necessarily with the person) before you leave.

Two variations on the face-to-face interview are the telephone interview and the written questionnaire. In either case, set up the contact just as you set up the face-to-face interview. The same considerations about taping, quoting and verification of information apply.

Finally, when you prepare your draft, be sure to document all sources, written and oral.

❏ The Second Decision: To Draft the Response

Drafting research papers is not unlike drafting other kinds of writing. When you have collected your notes, you review them and compile material into an early rough draft. That draft will take shape as you hear the dialogue between the creative and critical voices. The creative voice will help you find approaches that do more than re-cover familiar ground. The critical voice will help you identify background information, continuing puzzles, contrasting opinions, and logical patterns like cause/effect, comparison or classification.

You will be able to identify a thesis just as you did in other papers, by finding the recurring ideas and unique approaches. With your thesis, you can identify material that can be eliminated as well as material that needs further research. Expect that you may need to do further research if your critical voice identifies incomplete discussions.

As you draft, you will shape your response according to your purpose. As noted earlier in this chapter, a research paper may be written either to inform or to persuade. Let's look more closely at each kind so that you can make a choice about your own.

THE INFORMATIVE RESEARCH PAPER

The purpose of the informative research paper is to present the facts about an issue or scholarly topic as objectively as possible. When you write an informative paper, you should only report what you found in your research. You do not attempt to analyze or evaluate the data, nor do you offer your opinion about the issue. Where controversy exists and the sources you have consulted disagree in their interpretations, you can describe the disagreement and present relevant details about it, but refrain from taking sides. Though it is impossible to be totally objective, you should strive to be as dispassionate and impartial as you can. Your aim is not to persuade but to inform.

Make your paper informative if either of these circumstances applies:

- After completing your research, you find that you have no strong view about any of the controversial aspects of the subject, or that your view is not substantial enough to be the focal point of the paper. (Note: Do not confuse this with a situation in which you do have a strong view but are timid about expressing it.)
- Your subject is a rather technical one about which you lack the competency to make an informed judgment, even after completing your research.

THE PERSUASIVE RESEARCH PAPER

Like the informative research paper, the persuasive research paper presents research findings. Nevertheless, its larger purpose is not to inform but to persuade the readers. Therefore, when you write a persuasive research paper, you not only report what you have found in your research; you also offer your own interpretation of those findings. Where controversy exists and the sources consulted disagree in their judgments, you should weigh each side and explain which you find more reasonable and why.

Make your research paper persuasive if you have a significant judgment to make and you have the competency to make it. If you have done your research well and are willing to exercise care in evaluating your own arguments and those of others, you should be able to make significant judgments about all but the most technical matters.

DECIDING ON FORMAT

Choosing your purpose will shape the contents of your draft, and deciding on format will influence the organization. There are two formats commonly used in research papers. Either format may be used with either informative or persuasive research papers, but be aware that, for academic papers or particular journals, the format is often designated. Know the expectations of your audience.

The Separated Format

The divisions of the paper in the separated format are as follows:

I. Presentation of the issue or topic
II. Presentation of your research data
III. Presentation of your sources' interpretations and judgments of the data
IV. Your interpretations and judgments (This division is included only if the paper is persuasive.)

One advantage of the separated format is that it helps you avoid much of the confusion involved with handling detailed or complicated material. You don't have to decide where to put a particular bit of information— what it is determines where it goes. Still another advantage of this format is that it helps you distinguish between your source's judgments and your own judgments and thereby avoid plagiarism (presenting as your own the ideas or words of someone else). (A lengthier discussion of plagiarism can be found in Chapter 11.)

The Integrated Format

The integrated format employs the standard essay form of introduction—body—conclusion. Instead of demanding a strict separation of your research data from your sources' interpretations, and of your sources' interpretations from your own interpretations, it allows you to blend the material as you wish. You may, for example, take one item from the data, offer your sources' interpretations of it, discuss where you agree and disagree, and then move on to another item.

The principal advantage of the integrated format is that it offers you greater freedom to arrange your material to advantage, to be persuasive, to put more of your personality and style into your paper. The principal disadvantage is that it demands careful transitions and documentation to separate your judgments from those of your sources.

❏ The Third Decision: To Review the Work in Progress

The effectiveness of a research paper is measured in much the same way as the effectiveness of other writing. The presentation of the material must be clear with adequate definitions, examples, explanations, and descriptive details to make it understandable to the reader, and it must be so arranged and expressed that it is easy to follow. But the persuasive paper has an additional challenge. Since it argues for your own interpretations and opinions, you must be sure that it satisfies the demands for clear assertions, sound logic, and adequate evidence that are common to all arguments.

EVALUATING THE RESEARCH

In addition to the usual measures of good writing, the research paper is also measured by the quality of the research. Your sources should be varied to ensure a balanced presentation of the facts. Your experts should be accepted, credible authorities whose opinions are respected even by their opposition. Be wary of a narrow list of sources and a limited number of similar opinions; both are signs that you have not adequately researched your subject. An additional consideration is the age of your information. "Current" is a term best defined by the subject matter. Consider that critical commmentary on Charles Dickens from the nineteenth century might be useful to show how his contemporaries viewed his work, but an opinion from that era would be virtually useless if it concerned any branch of science.

MANUSCRIPT MECHANICS

When you are ready to edit the text, consult your instructor (or your editor) for details about manuscript preparation. These guidelines, based on the *MLA Handbook* guidelines, are often used:

Materials

For handwritten manuscripts, use standard 8-1/2 x 11-inch notebook paper with wide spaces between lines. (Do not use paper torn out of a spiral notebook.) Use a good pen with black or blue ink, and write neatly and legibly, taking care not to run your words together.

For typewritten manuscripts, use standard type on 8-1/2 x 11-inch typing paper. (Do not use onionskin paper or erasable bond.) Write or type on only one side of the paper.

Margins, Indentation, and Spacing

Use a one-inch margin on all sides. Indent the first word of each new paragraph five spaces. When quoting prose passages of more than four lines, block the quote and indent the entire block ten spaces. When quoting poetry of more than three lines, indent each line ten spaces. Double space all text, including blocked quotes. However, if the poem was originally presented with unusual margins or indentation, follow the original.

Hyphenation

Avoid breaking a word at the end of a line. You can divide hyphenated words such as mother-in-law, ill-suited, and president-elect only where they are already hyphenated.

Page Numbers

Number all pages consecutively throughout the manuscript. Place each number in the upper right-hand corner, one-half inch from the top. From page 2 on write your last name before the page number to safeguard against misplaced pages. Use no punctuation marks with page numbers.

Tables and Illustrations

Place all tables and illustrations as close as possible to the section of the text they are related to. Label all tables "Table" plus an arabic numeral, and add a title. Both labels and titles should be placed flush left on separate lines.

Titles and Other Headings

Follow your instructor's specifications. When a separate title page is not required, a common format directs that you type your name in the upper right-hand corner of the first page, and below that type your professor's name, the course title, and the date, each on a separate line. Next, double-space twice and type your title in the center of the page, then double-space again and begin the first paragraph.

Capitalize only the initial letter of each important word in your title. (Do not capitalize the initial letters of articles, or those of brief conjunctions and prepositions, except when such words appear at the beginning of the title.)

Do not underline your title or put quotation marks around it. Those devices are used only in your references to other people's titles. However, if your title includes a reference to another person's title, use the appropriate device for that person's title, as illustrated in the following examples:

Correct: What's Wrong with My Home Town
Correct: An Analysis of T. S. Eliot's "Ash Wednesday"
Correct: Hawthorne's Sources for *The Scarlet Letter*

If your paper contains subheadings, type them as you do your title, with double-spacing before and after to separate them from the text.

Abbreviations

In formal writing, abbreviations are usually avoided. There are, however, several exceptions to this rule. The abbreviations of personal titles or designations occurring before or after a name, such as Ms., Dr., or Ph.D., are acceptable, as are references to specific times (10:45 P.M., A.D. 1066) and Latin abbreviations (i.e. for "that is"; e.g. for "for example"; etc. for "and so forth").

Corrections

Corrections are acceptable in a manuscript as long as they are neatly made and are not so numerous as to be distracting. Minor changes may be made by crossing out the word or words to be deleted and printing or typing the corrections directly above it, using a caret (^) to indicate where the correction goes. Never make corrections in the margins.

DOCUMENTATION

Reviewing the form of the manuscript also includes a careful look at documentation. Since much of your material is drawn from other sources, you must document extensively and accurately. Let's look at the process closely.

Documentation Defined

Documentation is acknowledgment. It strengthens your credibility because it tells your readers that you have consulted the accumulated knowledge and interpretation of the experts in forming your views. More-over, it provides your readers with the necessary information should they wish to pursue the subject further themselves. In short, it enhances your paper.

Knowing When to Document

Documentation helps the reader separate source material from your own observations. In general, you will document all direct use of material, including quotes, tables, graphs, or charts. In addition, material that is used indirectly (summarized or paraphrased) must be credited to its origi-nal source. Be particularly careful to credit controversial opinions or alle-gations; it is important that the reader be able to identify the source and the context of such remarks. Finally, any idea that is not widely known or that is the subject of dispute should be credited.

But not every thought that comes to you in the course of your research needs to be documented. You need to acknowledge only the thoughts of others that are not common knowledge. How can you identify these ideas? The question is not nearly so difficult as it may seem.

To begin with, your creative voice will help you to develop ideas of your own as you are reading the ideas of another person. "This author's conclu-sion about the issue is exactly opposite that of the previous author I con-sulted." Or, "This interpretation is not correct—it omits an important consideration." These ideas are yours. Even though they came to you as you read other ideas and may even have been prompted by those ideas, it would be incorrect to credit them to another writer because no one else expressed them.

Another kind of idea that need not be credited is **common knowledge.** Common knowledge is that which is accepted by those who are familiar with the subject, the kind of idea you would find expressed in most books and articles on the subject despite the differences in the authors' views. For example, the fact that Thomas Jefferson wrote the Declaration of Inde-pendence is, like the purpose and historical significance of the document, common knowledge. No reference to such a fact needs to be credited.

The careful writer tries to avoid both underdocumentation and over-documentation by keeping in mind that the purpose of documentation is to signal the readers that an idea belongs to someone else. Whenever a situation arises in which you are not really sure how to classify the idea, ask yourself whether the idea came from one specific source that you con-sulted. If so, document it. If it came from a number of sources, then it is probably common knowledge. If it was not expressed in any of your sources, you can claim it as your own. In neither of these cases does the idea need to be documented.

Finally, if you are in doubt, it is best to credit the source. Over-zealous documentation is a minor problem; sloppy scholarship and plagiarism are not.

Kinds of Documentation

Documentation may first suggest bibliography. But a closing list of works is not the only documentation expected in a research paper. You will be expected to acknowledge sources in the text of the paper, and you may need to use additional bibliographic or explanatory notes (footnotes at the bottom of the page or endnotes ["Notes"] in a separate list immediately before the full bibliography.) Each kind of documentation has its own purpose and form. The details of form will be illustrated later in the chapter, but consider the following guidelines as you prepare your text.

Bibliographies

You are probably familiar with the list of works at the end of an article or text. This list, often titled "Bibliography" or "Works Cited" or even "Works Consulted," is only one kind of documentation. As the names imply, the list may contain all of the sources you consulted or it may be limited to the sources you actually cite in the paper. There may also be a list of sources designated "For Further Reading," references which were not used for the paper but are good sources of additional information.

Text Citations

Text citations acknowledge the source of specific information and tell the reader exactly where it can be located. The citation should include enough information to locate the work in the bibliography, and additional references specific enough to locate the information in the original source (usually page references). If you include any or all of this information in the text, you can omit it from the citation. For example, if you write, "Long, in his 1987 acceptance speech, said that. . . ." (16), you have identified the source and need only give a page reference (here, page 16) to complete the citation. You may have seen this kind of information supplied in footnotes or endnotes, but the current style of documentation is to use internal text citations whenever possible.

Notes

Bibliographic and explanatory notes are used when the citation is either lengthy or peripheral and would interrupt the flow of the text. Such notes might begin "Similar views can be found in. . . ." or "Prior to this incident, the Senator's record on right-to-work was labor-oriented. See Jones, 23-35 for additional information."

For all of these citations, there are several kinds of documentation styles in use today. Some of them are specific to a particular journal or newspaper and can be identified by studying those specific publications or requesting specific guidelines from the editors of those works. Three of the most common forms of documentation are the Modern Language Association (MLA) style, the American Psychological Association (APA) style, and the number system. MLA style is used for many academic research papers in the humanities; APA, for psychology and other social science disciplines; the numbering system, for the sciences.

Don't think that documentation is either complicated or mysterious. Proper form is no more than attention to detail, a time-consuming but relatively simple matter of looking at an example and duplicating its form. Proper documentation style is a courtesy to your readers because you give them information in the format they are most familiar with, but it is also a statement about your own credibility. It says that you understand the language and expectations of the field, and that you are knowledgeable and conscientious enough to use it.

Studying the forms of citations is an empty exercise until you are ready to use them. Because the documentation styles are so different, it is essential that you know which style your audience expects. You can then pay careful attention to the details of form like spacing, capitalization, parentheses, commas and periods for the appropriate style. More information can be found in the following works:

> MLA Handbook for Writers of Research Papers. 3rd. ed. New
> York: Modern Language Assn. of America, 1988.
> Publication Manual of the American Psychological Association.
> 3rd. ed. Washington, D.C.: American Psychological Assn.,
> 1984.
> CBE Style Manual: A Guide for Authors, Editors, and Publishers
> in the Biological Sciences. 5th ed. Bethesda: Council of Biology Editors, 1983.

These references will describe the styles for any conceivable source, including personal contact and nonprint resources. Such a detailed presentation is beyond the scope of this book, but it does provide a brief reference of three major styles.

MLA STYLE

The MLA recommends that two kinds of documentation be used in a research paper. The first is **brief parenthetical documentation within the paper.** It tells readers (1) that material has been borrowed, (2) from whom it has been borrowed, and (3) exactly where the original can be found. The second, **a closing list of the works cited in the paper,** provides relevant publication information about the sources of borrowed material.

Guidelines for Brief Documentation

As you document sources within the text, remember that your purpose is to aid your readers, not to distract them. To that end, your citations should be as brief as accuracy and clarity will permit, and they should be as close as possible to the borrowed material. As you study the form of the examples below, note that each points clearly to a specific source and identifies the specific location of borrowed material. When you use similar citations, duplicate the format as closely as possible.

Documentation with author's name given in text:

Carol Tavris explains how Freudianism has confused us about the nature of anger (36–39).

Documentation with author's name not given in text:

Though the system of the form of psychotherapy known as logotherapy is often associated with existentialism, its founder has not been uncritical of existentialism (Frankl 13).

Documentation of work by two authors:

Among the purposes of rumor is the justification of feelings we might otherwise feel guilty of harboring (Allport and Postman 37).

Documentation of work by author with two or more works cited in works cited list (To avoid confusion, the title of the work or a shortened version of it should be added just before the page reference in the brief parenthetical citation, as shown.):

Rollo May calls creativity "the struggle against disintegration," (Courage to Create 140).

Documentation of quoted material:

According to Carol Tavris, "the decision about whether or not to express anger rests on what you want to communicate and what you hope to accomplish, and these are not necessarily harmonious goals" (123).

Citation of anonymous works:

"Nights of Grief" argues that no one should ignore such warning signs (14).

OR

Under no circumstances should such warning signs be ignored ("Nights of Grief" 14).

Citation of an entire work (*No* parenthetical documentation is needed.):

The pamphlet "Nights of Grief" is invaluable reading for the parents of troubled teenagers.

Guidelines for the Works Cited List

Works Cited need not include works that were consulted but contributed nothing to the research paper; however, it must include all works that contributed ideas or information to the paper. It should begin on a new page immediately following the last page of the text, continuing the page-numbering sequence and format of the text. The heading "Works Cited" should be centered one inch from the top of the first page of the list. The first line of each new entry should begin flush with the left margin, with any subsequent lines indented five spaces from the left margin. All entries should be alphabetized by the author's last name or, in the case of anonymous works, by the first word in the title other than "A," "An," or "The." Double-spacing should be used throughout. Study the examples below for internal spacing and punctuation of entries.

The list may include many kinds of materials, but the guidelines here illustrate the most common sources, books and articles, with some attention to other sources. Because this list is limited to coverage of fundamentals, you should consult the *MLA Handbook,* 3rd edition (1988) for unusual citations.

Citing Books

Most book citations are relatively simple, needing only author, title, and publication information. Following is a list of all the information that could be required. Seldom, if ever, will you need to cite all this information, but if you do, study the list and the example below for the proper sequence and form.

Author's Name: Last name first, followed by a comma, exactly as it appears on the title page.

Title of a Part of the Book: When you are citing a work that appears in a larger work (for example, an essay or a poem in an anthology) enclose the part title in quotation marks.

Title of the Book: Full title. Separate any subtitle by a colon and two spaces; underline the title and subtitle.

Name of the Editor, Translator, or Compiler: Abbreviate the word "editor" and place a period after it: Ed. John Harrison.

Edition Used

Number of Volumes

Name of the Series

Place of Publication, Name of the Publisher, Date of Publication: Use an appropriately shortened version of the publisher's name. For example, use Knopf for Alfred A. Knopf, Inc., and Oxford UP for Oxford University Press. If several cities are listed, give only the first, and include state or country only if the location is ambiguous (for example, Birmingham, Eng.).

Page Numbers: Include only when citing part of a work: (for example, a short story in an anthology). Cite the beginning and ending pages for the part.

Here is a fictitious sample citation illustrating how all the above information would appear. Note carefully the punctuation and spacing.

> Werblow, Stanley F. "Self-Knowledge and Self-Deception." <u>Reflective Thinking: A Symposium.</u> Ed. Freeman Sage. 3rd ed.
> Vol. 3 of <u>Philosophy in Everyday Life</u>. New York : Harper, 1982. 12-41.

Note that if a work has two authors, the name of the second author is presented in normal, rather than reverse, order. In the above case the citation would begin as follows: Werblow, Stanley F., and Ralph M. Patterson. Note, too, that if two or more works by Werblow were being cited, the second and subsequent references would not begin with his name but with three unspaced hyphens followed by a period or comma, as in these samples:

> --- . <u>Thinking of Thinking</u>. New York: Holt, 1968.
> ---, ed. <u>Essays on Productive Thinking.</u> New York: Harper, 1977.

Articles from well-known encyclopedias need minimal citation. Since the reference work is arranged alphabetically, no page numbers need be cited:

> "Occultism." <u>Encyclopaedia Britannica: Macropaedia</u>. 1985 ed.

Citing Periodical Articles

Periodical article citations, like book citations, identify author, title, and publication information. Following is a list of all the information that could be required. Observe the order and the form indicated when preparing your citations of periodical articles.

Author's Name: As for books.

Title of the Article: In quotation marks.

Name of the Periodical: Underlined.

Series Number: If there has been more than one.

Volume Number: If there is a volume number, give the number without volume.

Date of Publication: Year in parentheses, followed by colon, space, and page numbers.

Page Numbers: For the entire article. If the article does not appear on consecutive pages, give the first page number followed by a plus sign: for example, 192 +.

Here is a sample entry illustrating how all the above information would appear. Note carefully the punctuation and spacing.

> Johnson, Michael P. "Runaway Slaves and the Slave Communities in South Carolina, 1799–1830." <u>William and Mary Quarterly</u> 3rd ser. 38 (1981): 418–41.

Because there are a number of different kinds of periodical publications (quarterly journals, weekly magazines, daily newspapers, etc.), there are variations in citation form for periodical articles. These are some of the most common:

From a journal that pages each issue separately:

> Lyon, George Ella. "Contemporary Appalachian Poetry: Sources and Directions." <u>Kentucky Review</u> 2.2 (1981): 3–22.

(If a journal numbers the issues of an entire volume in sequence, you can omit the issue number: *Review* 2 (1979): 261-275.)

An article from a weekly or bi-weekly periodical:

> Friedrich, Otto. "Saying What You Mean." <u>Time</u> 9 Apr. 1984: 78.

A newspaper article (use the name of the newspaper as it appears on the masthead, but omit the article "The"; if the name of the city is not included in the newspaper's name, include it in square brackets, without underlining, immediately after the name. Give the date, edition, section and page.):

> Brody, Jane E. "Kinsey Study Shows Deep Predisposition." <u>New York Times</u> 23 Aug. 1981, late ed.: 1 +.

An editorial (Add the author's name if known, the title, and the label "Editorial."):

> "Business Need City's People, Too." Editorial. <u>Sunday Press</u> [Binghamton, NY] 23 Oct. 1983: E2.

A letter to the editor: (Note that "N. pag." is used to signify that the letters section of the magazine was unpaginated.)

> Stewart, Douglas J. Letter. <u>National Geographic</u> 165 (May 1984): N. pag.

Citing Nonprint Materials

The MLA Handbook gives examples of non-print-material citations. The following are among the most frequently used:

A radio or television program: Include the following information in the order shown: the title of the program, underlined; the names of the director, narrator, and producer (if relevant); the network; the local station and its city; the date of the broadcast.

> The First Americans. Narr. Hugh Downs. Writ. and prod. Craig
> Fisher. NBC News Special. KNBC, Los Angeles. 21 Mar. 1968.

An interview on radio or television: Begin with the name of the person interviewed. If the interview is the entire work, underline the title. If the interview is untitled, use the word Interview. Next give the name of the interviewer if this information is pertinent (for example, With Mike Wallace), the network, the local station and its city, and the date of the interview.

> Gordon, Suzanne. Interview. All Things Considered. Natl. Public
> Radio. WNYC, New York. 1 June 1983.

An interview you conduct personally (Label it "Personal interview" or "Telephone interview."):

> Warren, Nathan E. Personal interview. 18 Sept. 1984.

A lecture, speech, or address (If the presentation was untitled, use an appropriate descriptive label [Lecture, Address, etc.]):

> Ciardi, John. Address. Opening General Sess. NCTE Convention.
> Washington, D.C. 19 Nov. 1982.

Computer Software:

> WordPerfect 5.0 Computer software. WordPerfect, 1988. IBM
> PC/XT/AT.

APA STYLE

The American Psychological Association is an organization of social scientists. APA style is expected by most departments in the social sciences, so check with your psychology and sociology instructors and refer to this section when necessary.

Brief Documentation

A text reference in APA style should include the author, the year of publication, and the page number. If part of the information is included in the text, the reference can omit it.

Sample Text References:

These references are taken from the first sample research paper.

Works with one author:

> The astrological systems used by today's astrologers are variations on Greek astrology (Jerome, 1975, p. 10).

> As Derek Parker, a defender of astrology admits, "Some astrologers still seek to preserve its past links with magic," and astrology remains "dear to those who are interested in the occult" (1970, p. 70).

If an author has two or more works cited in the works cited list, they are listed according to earliest publication date; the date is part of the text citations and will make the reference clear. If two works have the same publication date, they are listed alphabetically and are designated in the list and in the references by "a" or "b" after the year (for example, 1979a).

Works with two authors:

> Others go even further in their agreement, stating flatly that "however astrology may be viewed today, it was the earliest exact science in history" (Cazeau and Scott, 1979, p. 227).

Works with no author identified:

> It was part of the "magical world view" prevalent at the time, when people did not comprehend the great distances between us and the stars and regarded them as the homes or possessions of the gods (Statement, 1978, p. 9).

Guidelines for the Works Cited List

Any source referred to in the text of your paper should be included in this list. As you review the samples below, note the changes from MLA style, particularly in the position of dates and in the capitalization of titles. Note, too, that works are listed alphabetically by author, with these exceptions:

- Works by a single author are listed before works by that same author and a co-author.
- Works by the same author are arranged according to earliest publication date. If two works have the same publication date, they are arranged alphabetically and designated like this: 1979a and 1979b.

Citing Books

Logically enough for a scientific format, APA style emphasizes the date of publication by including it in parentheses immediately after the author's name. (If a work has two authors, both names are included in full and both are listed last name first.) Title information follows, with volume and edition numbers enclosed in parentheses. The city and publisher are included in as brief a form as possible.

Sample References:

> Jones, Marc Edmund (1969). <u>Astrology: How and why it works.</u> New York: Penguin.
>
> Neugebauer, O. (1952). <u>The exact sciences in antiquity (2nd ed).</u> New York: Harper.
>
> Cazeau, Charles J. & Scott, Stuart D. (1979). <u>Exploring the unknown: Great mysteries re-examined.</u> New York: Plenum.
>
> <u>Encyclopedia of occult sciences.</u> (1968). New York: Tudor.

Citing Periodical Articles

Periodical article citations, like book citations, identify author, title, and publication information. Following is a list of all the information that could be required. Observe the order and the form indicated when preparing your citations of periodical articles:

Author's Name: As for books.

Date of Publication: Year in parentheses, followed by a period.

Title of the Article: Capitalize only the first word; do not use quotation marks.

Name of the Periodical: Underlined.

Volume Number: Underlined.

Issue Number: If each issue is paged separately, the issue number follows the volume number and is enclosed in parentheses.

Page Numbers: For the entire article. Use "pp." for newspaper or magazine references, but not for journal articles.

Articles from journals:

> Roll, W. G. (1973, June). Science looks at the occult. Psychic, 4, 50–55.
>
> Silverman, T. I., and Whitmer, M. (1974, May). Astrological indicators of personality. Journal of Psychology, 89, 259–260.

An article from a magazine:

> Friedrich, Otto (1984, April 9). Saying what you mean. Time, p. 78.

A newspaper article (use the name as it appears on the masthead, but omit the article "The"; if the name of the city is not included in the newspaper's name, include it in square brackets, without underlining, immediately after the name. Give the date, edition, section and page.):

> Brody, Jane E. (1981, August 23). Kinsey study shows deep predisposition. New York Times (late), p.1.

NUMBER SYSTEM

The number system of documenting sources is used in the sciences. The works consulted are listed at the end of the paper and are numbered (1), (2), etc. In the text itself, sources are identified according to those numbers and, if necessary, a specific page.

Sample Text References:

> No one has yet successfully disputed these claims (1), nor is it likely that a successful challenge will be made in the future (2, p. 123).

Citations on the closing list are brief, including author, date, title and publication information but typically allowing short forms and abbreviations. The entries may be ordered alphabetically (expected in the fields of biology and mathematics) or according to the order in which sources are cited in your paper (expected in physics, engineering, and chemistry). Since there is such variety in the number format, you should check with your instructor for specific instructions about style.

SUMMARY

Writing a research paper may seem like a mammoth task, but the writing strategies that have worked for informative and persuasive writing will also work when you research to find material. Some attention to the resources available to you and to the expected forms of documentation will result in effective research papers, both those that inform and those that convince.

Sample Research Papers

To help you understand the principles and approaches explained above, two annotated sample research papers follow. Both deal with the same topic, astrology, and the same essential question—is it science or superstition? In addition, both use the same research data. But one is intended to inform, the other to persuade. And, each illustrates a different format and a different style of documentation.

An Informative Research Paper

The following paper is informative and is written in a separated format. The form of the title page for this paper was specified by the instructor, who also defined page number placement. Some instructors also require formal outlines preceding the text itself. Note that text citations and closing list follow the APA style recommendations.

Astrology: Science or Superstition

by
Leslie McDaniels

English 101
Professor James Pelletier
November 30, 1988

Notice how the author has kept the focus on informing the reader about what her research disclosed. Nowhere does she include her interpretation and judgment. Though the subheadings refer to specific points made in the paper rather than as general divisions, close examination of the grouping of ideas will reveal that the format here is the separated format and its general divisions are followed.

Astrology: Science or Superstition?

The widespread modern interest in astrology raises once again a very old question: Is there any scientific basis for astrology or is it essentially superstition? The question is important because if astrology is scientific, then the scoffers and the skeptics are denying themselves a means of making their lives happier, more successful, and more productive. On the other hand, if astrology is unscientific, then those who are influenced by it are being deceived, perhaps even harmed. A review of what knowledgeable people are saying about the question is in order.

History of Astrology

Astrology began in Babylonia and Egypt, at approximately the same time, as a system of omen reading to predict the fates of kings (Jerome, 1975, p. 10). Some scholars believe it was an aspect of star worship, since the word "astrology" (of Greek origin) means "discourse or doctrine about the stars" (Thompson, 1969, pp. 18–19). Others believe it was less

McDaniels 2

By placing your name at the top of each page you ensure that if a page or two gets spearated from your paper your professor will be able to tell whose it is.

formalized and more a kind of wonder; one writer calls it "an amazed and quasi-religious meditation, a vast dream in which principles and laws were slowly sketched out" (Encycl. occult, 1968, p. 45). In any case, it was part of the "magical world view" prevalent at the time, when people did not comprehend the great distances involved between us and the stars and regarded them as the homes or possessions of the gods (Statement, 1978, p. 9).

The Greeks borrowed their earliest notions about astrology from the Babylonians and the Egyptians. Later they combined the elements of both and developed them into a more complex and mathematical system that expressed their theory of the universe. The astrological systems used by today's astrologers are variations on Greek astrology (Jerome, 1975, p. 10).

Note that this list of names is abstracted from twenty pages of source material.

The list of famous people in Western history who reportedly accepted astrology in some form is long indeed. It includes not only literary figures, philosophers, and religious thinkers, but scientists as well. That list includes Plato and Aristotle, St. Augustine, Chaucer, Boccaccio, Jewish scholar Ibn Ezra, Albert the Great, St. Thomas Aquinas, Nostradamus, Roger Bacon, Duns Scotus, Johannes Kepler, and at least a dozen popes (Crow, 1968, pp. 179–98).

From the earliest times until the end of the sixteenth century, astrology was used in medicine to aid physicians in diagnosing illness and prescribing treatment (Thompson, 1969, p. 103). Yet this aspect of astrology, like others, continued to be intertwined with magic at least through the Middle Ages. Talismans--objects used to attract the influence of a particular planet or of the moon or sun--were still common in the sixteenth century. Julianus Ristorus, for example, a professor at Pisa University at that time, carried two rings engraved with astrological inscriptions, one to ward off mosquitoes and the other to cure ailments of the shins and feet (Encycl. occult, 1968, p. 220). Nor is astrology completely free of magic even in contemporary times. As Derek Parker, a defender of

McDaniels 3

astrology, admits, "Some astrologers still seek to preserve its past links
with magic," and astrology remains "dear to those who are interested in
the occult" (1970, p. 70).

Claims and Counterclaims

The most basic tenets of astrology, which all the sources listed at the
end of this paper acknowledge, are the following: (a) the sun, moon, and
planets exert great forces on human beings; (b) the exact force of each
heavenly body differs from that of all other bodies; and (c) the exact
moment of decisive influence is the moment of birth. Let us consider what
scientists say of each of these tenets.

The Exerting of Great Forces

Scientists are divided on this question. Most seem to believe that any
force exerted by the planets is at best insignificant (Thompson, 1969, p.
284). One writer expresses his denunciation of the idea dramatically:
because of the vast distances involved, Bart J. Bok says, the "gravitation-
al forces at birth produced by the doctor and nurse and by the furniture
in the delivery room far outweigh the celestial forces" (1975, p. 30). Yet
other scientists disagree. Charles J. Cazeau and Stuart D. Scott, Jr.,
believe it is not entirely impossible that cosmic energy may have effects
on us that we are not aware of. They suggest that there is already hard
scientific evidence of such energy, citing the fact that radio astronomers
have demonstrated that distant nebulae and galaxies do emit tremendous
radio-frequency energy, one known galaxy (M 87) emitting 1,000 times
more than our own galaxy. The astrological notion that the planets affect
us, they say, "is indeed fantastic but is it more so than splitting and joining atoms, television, or trips to the moon?" (1979, p. 234).

Different Planets, Different Forces

The scientists agree that it is unlikely that different planets represent
different forces. Bok points out that it is now known that all heavenly

*Note how
information from
different sources
is combined in
one paragraph.
The key to doing
this effectively is
to plan carefully,
arranging your
research data so
that related
points are
grouped together.*

McDaniels 4

bodies are made of the same basic ingredients. Accordingly, he finds it unreasonable to believe that the same ingredients could exert vastly different forces and achieve vastly different effects, as astrologers claim (1975, pp. 30–31). Further evidence that this claim of astrologers is questionable is offered by Cazeau and Scott. They point out that three of the known planets were only discovered in recent times (Uranus in 1781, Neptune in 1846, and Pluto in 1930). If each planet really did have a special influence, they reason, wouldn't astrological predictions made before their discovery have been in error? The authors believe so, despite the fact that they have never heard this conclusion expressed by astrologers (1979, p. 232).

The Influence at Birth

The science of genetics has established that at the moment of conception the genetic package is complete. Thus a person's eye color, body type, and hundreds of other characteristics are determined then (subject, in some cases, to later environmental influences). If there were one special moment in which cosmic forces were exerted, why, Bok asks, wouldn't it be the moment of conception? Why the moment of birth, which science has shown to be of relatively little significance? (1975, p. 31). Other scientists consulted agree with this line of reasoning without exception.

The Evidence

To support their contention that astrology is a science, its defenders argue that even in ancient times astrology was based on careful observation and reasoning. This fact, they believe, becomes blurred by the fact that the ancients lacked adequate technology to make accurate judgments and the knowledge necessary to keep their data free of superstition and pagan religion. The result, according to one source, was "a science at bottom confused, vitiated by errors and childishness, yet rich in astounding intuitions, in millions of confirmations, and in all kinds of other knowledge. . . ."

(Encycl. occult, 1968, p. 46). It was an imperfect science, in other
words, but a science nonetheless. Then, in the Middle Ages, the scientific
nature of astrology became even more blurred by a split in science
itself into an official side--exact, emphasizing careful experimentation
and calculation--and an outlaw side composed of those disciplines that
refused to give up past links with the occult (Encycl. occult, 1968,
p. 46).

Some scientists tend to agree with this argument. Science historian
O. Neugebauer, for example, says the idea of ancient astrologers that
heavenly bodies exert influence on human beings was very different from
the idea of the gods determining fate or of people influencing events by
magic. Thus, though he notes that the line between "rational science and
loose speculation" was not clear, causing astrology to promote magic and
superstition, he suggests that it is not incorrect to call ancient astrology
scientific (1952, p. 171). Gazeau and Scott go even further in their agreement, stating flatly that "however astrology may be viewed today, it was
the earliest exact science in history" (1979, p. 227).

Most opponents of astrology reject this view. Lawrence Jerome, for
instance, argues that Greek astrology was not a science at all. It came to
the Greeks as a "full-blown magical system, its assumptions and operating principles unquestioned." Nor, he adds, did the idea of the stars influencing human lives arrive through scientific observation, Rather, it was
based on the magical "principle of correspondences," wherein what is
seen as being like something else or reminiscent of it is considered to
have the same properties (Jerome, 1975, pp. 11–12).

This principle, according to Jerome, worked as follows. The ancients
noted that a particular planet had a reddish cast, so in their primitive
minds it became associated with blood, war, aggressiveness. Accordingly,
they named it Mars after the god of war. Later, they linked other things
associated with war--iron, for example,--with the planet. Similarly, the
planet Venus was named after the goddess of love, and all the mythology

connected with her--beauty, sensitivity, and so on--became associated with the planet and to those born under its influence (1977, pp. 70–71).

Jerome admits that a detailed horoscope not only looks scientific, but actually is scientific in the sense of its intricate plottings and calculations of the stars, moon and sun. But he stresses that the key point many people fail to notice is that all these plottings and calculations take place "against an arbitrary framework of signs rather than real stars." Hence in the most meaningful sense, in Jerome's view, astrology is decidedly not a science (1977, p. 79).

In light of the duration and passion of the debate over whether astrology is science or superstition, there has been surprisingly little experimental research to test the matter. And what little there has been has resulted in mixed findings. One researcher, Michael Gauqelin, studied the backgrounds of 576 members of the French Academy of Medicine and another group of 508 famous physicians and found a strong statistical correlation between astrological predictions of success in medicine and actual success (Cazeau and Scott, 1979, p. 235). Yet two other studies -- J. E. Barth and J. T. Bennett's study of the influence of Mars on military careers, and Bart J. Bok's study of scientists' times of birth --reported no correlation between astrological prediction and reality (Jerome, 1975, p. 15).

Still another experiment tested the accuracy of astrological indicators of personality. This study took 130 college students whose exact birth times were available. Each of the students and one of his/her friends was asked to rate the student's aggressiveness, ambition, creativity, intuitiveness, and extroversion. In addition, each of the 130 was given a standard personality inventory test. The results of the ratings and inventories were compared with the students' horoscopes. The study showed "that the astrological indicators of personality were not related to either self or friends' descriptions of the subjects' personalities." Though the experimenters did not include all astrological indicators of personality, and therefore state that their findings do not prove that astrology cannot predict personality, they conclude that their failure to find correlations in the most important astrological indicators "reduces the likelihood of this possibility being true" (Silverman and Whitmer, 1974, p. 94).

Conclusions of the Authorities

Predictably, the judgments of the authorities on whether astrology is a science are mixed. O. Neugebauer, in his discussion of ancient science, states that "compared with the background of religion, magic, and mysticism, the fundamental doctrines of astrology are pure science" (1952, p. 171). Building on the same perspective, Zolar offers a forceful argument for the affirmative position:

> The astrological outlook came to light as a set of attractive scientific hypotheses displacing whatever beliefs preceded them and filling a vacancy in the mind of man. These hypotheses have endured for three or two [sic] millennia, though repeatedly challenged. They have outlasted many irrelevant, purely emotional and prejudiced beliefs that conflicted with more materialistic and fatalistic tenets and they have found their supporters among the learned and the great as among the common people. Within the womb of astrology, astronomy was bred and nourished, and there never was any competition or conflict between them. Astrology is neither stupidity nor superstition. No hero of astronomy fought it as a scientific St. George; no movement of pioneers of progress speeded it toward death. No, most of the great astrologers are better known to the average person as astronomers or mathematicians. The history of astronomy is really only the history of astrology from a slightly different viewpoint (1972, p. viii).

Note how this quotation is more than five lines is handled (spacing, margin and so on). It is significant that there is only one such long quote in this paper—the emphasis is rightly on the expression of the writer of the research paper and not on the expression of her sources. Wherever possible paraphrase or quote briefly reserving such lengthy quotations as this for those rare occasions where their significance and compactness warrant using them.

Yet Richard Cavendish, in his comprehensive study of the occult, classifies astrology as "essentially a magical art" (1967, p. 219). Further, a statement signed by 192 leading scientists calls astrologers "charlatans" and warns that "those who wish to believe in astrology should realize that there is no scientific foundation for its tenets" (Statement, 1975, p. 9). And a statement endorsed by the Society for the Psychological Study of Social Issues brands astrology "a magical practice that has no shred of justification in scientific fact" (Bok, 1975, p. 32).

For C. J. S. Thompson the matter comes down to a lack of demonstration on the part of astrologers. "No proof has ever yet been furnished," he declares, "that the movements or positions in the heavens of the planets and stars can influence the life and destiny of any human being, or that they are able to impart special properties to vegetable life." For this reason, he concludes, astrology "must likewise be banished with other ancient cults to the realms of romance" (1969, p. 284, p. 288).

Is astrology science or superstition? Despite the passions of those on either side of the question, the issue is yet unsettled. Nor is it likely to be until the claims and methods of astrology are subjected to close scrutiny under the best experimental conditions.

Reference List

Bok, Bart J. (1975). A critical look at astrology. Objections to astrology.
(pp. 30–36). Buffalo: Prometheus.

Cavendish, Richard (1967). The black arts. New York: Capricorn.

Cazeau, Charles J. and Scott, Stuart D. (1979). Exploring the unknown:
Great mysteries re-examined. New York: Plenum.

Crow, W. B. (1968). A history of magic, witchcraft and occultism.
London: Aquarius.

Encyclopedia of occult sciences. (1968). New York: Tudor.

Jerome, Lawrence E. (1975, Sept–Oct.). Astrology: Magic or science?
Humanist, pp. 10–16.

Jerome, Lawrence E. (1977). Astrology disproved. Buffalo: Prometheus.

Jones, Marc Edmund (1969). Astrology: How and why it works. New
York: Penguin.

Mark, Alexandra (1970). Astrology for the aquarian age. New York:
Essandra.

Neugebauer, O. (1952). The exact sciences in antiquity. (2nd ed.) New
York Harper.

Parker, Derek (1970). Astrology in the modern world. New York:
Taplinger.

Roll, W. G. (1973, June). Science looks at the occult. Psychic, 4, 50–55.

Silverman, T. I. and Whitmer, M. (1974, May). Astrological indicators of
personality. Journal of Psychology, 87, 89–95.

Snyder, C. R. (1974). Why horoscopes are true: The effects of specificity
on acceptance of astrological interpretations. Journal of Clinical
Psychology, 30, 577–80.

Standen, Anthony (1975). Is there an astrological effect on personality?
Journal of Psychology, 89, 259–60.

Statement by 192 leading scientists. (1975). Objections to astrology.
Buffalo: Prometheus.

Thompson, C. J. S. (1969). The mystery and romance of astrology. New
York: Brentano's.

Zolar (1972). The history of astrology. New York: Arco.

A Persuasive Research Paper

The following paper is persuasive rather than informative and is written in an integrated rather than a separated format. However, it is based on the same research as the preceding paper and uses many of the same passages of information. These similarities between the two papers will make the essential difference—the inclusion of the writer's own interpretations and judgments—all the more prominent.

The form of the paper reflects MLA guidelines: no title page, no outline, name and page number of each page. However, your instructor may modify the form, so be sure to check specific guidelines for your own assignment. Note that text citations and closing list follow the MLA style recommendations.

William J. Murphy

Professor Pelletier

English 101

November 30, 1988

Astrology: Science or Superstition?

Compare the introduction, conclusion, and format of this paper with those of the preceding paper. Note how this paper fits the description of the integrated format on page 480.

Astrology is very fashionable today. Newspapers and magazines carry regular horoscope columns, and respected publishing houses publish books explaining the wisdom of consulting the stars as a guide to daily living. Celebrities on television talk-shows speak enthusiastically of astrology and tell of its helpfulness in their lives. The range of areas in which astrologers offer guidance is virtually limitless. When to marry, have children, take a vacation, buy stocks and bonds, and socialize are all covered. Some astrologers even predict the most favorable days for making an appointment with a doctor or dentist.

As in any essay, the writer makes the paper's controlling idea clear early in his presentation. In addition, the way the idea is presented communicates that the presentation is persuasive.

This belief that the sun, moon, and planets influence the lives of people is not new at all. It dates from the time of ancient Babylonia and Egypt where it was associated with a system of omen reading to predict the fates of kings. The Greeks borrowed the idea and fashioned it into a more complex and mathematical system that expressed their theory of the universe. Today's astrological systems are variations of the Greek system (Jerome, "Magic" 10).

Murphy 2

Despite astrology's long history, it still arouses controversy. Is it science or superstition? There continues to be too much disagreement among authorities to say the matter is fully settled. Yet the evidence accumulated to date suggests strongly that it is <u>not</u> a science. That is the position this paper will present.

In ancient times astrology does seem to have been an advanced idea. Science historian O. Neugebauer says that the idea of the sun, moon, and planets influencing human lives was very different from--and much more scientific than--the then-prevalent ideas of the gods determining fate and of people influencing events by magic (171). And at least two scientists state without qualification that "however astrology may be viewed today, it was the earliest exact science in history" (Cazeau and Scott 227).

Part of the problem many people have in accepting such judgments is that they conceive of science solely in modern terms and forget that it was once quite primitive and inexact. In ancient times all the sciences were lacking in technology and their approaches and data were mingled with notions of superstition and pagan religion (<u>Encycl. Occult</u> 46). For the critics of astrology to point to the imperfections of astrology at that time and close their eyes to the identical imperfections in other areas of science would be unfair.

Another reason for classifying ancient astrology--and, for that matter, astrology through the period of the Middle Ages--as a science is that many of the greatest thinkers in history, including great scientists, accepted it as a science and often practiced it in one form or another. Among those supporters of astrology were Plato, Aristotle, St. Augustine, Chaucer, Boccaccio, Jewish scholar Ibn Ezra, Albert the Great, St. Thomas Aquinas, Nostradamus, Roger Bacon, Duns Scotus, Johannes Kepler, and at least a dozen popes (Crow 179–98).

These arguments for classifying ancient astrology as a science do not persuade everyone. One critic of astrology, for example, maintains that

This passage represents the author's own judgment. Note the pattern used here—the presentation of one or more items of data followed by the author's interpretation or judgment. This pattern, a standard one in persuasive writing, is repeated in subsequent pages.

The writer concedes a point here to those who disagree with him. This willingness to admit the complexity of the issue is characteristic of the balanced, mature thinker. (Note the pattern of presentation of data followed by interpretation and judgment.)

astrology cannot be so classified because it came to the Greeks as a "full-blown magical system, its assumptions and operating principles unquestioned" (Jerome, "Magic" 11). Yet even if that is true and the arguments cited above are less than compelling, they are nevertheless strong arguments. And since the case against astrology can be made on more substantive grounds, this writer is inclined to concede that <u>ancient</u> astrology <u>was</u> a science.

This conclusion (it is the author's own, and not that of his sources) is impressive because it makes a useful distinction between past and present "links" with magic.

From the beginning, astrology has had strong ties with magic and the occult. As late as the sixteenth century, astrology was used in medicine to aid physicians in diagnosing illness and prescribing treatment (Thompson 103). And talismans--objects used to attract the influence of a particular planet or of the moon or sun--were used as preventatives. Julianus Ristorus, for example, a sixteenth-century professor at Pisa University, carried two rings engraved with astrological inscriptions, one to ward off mosquitoes and the other to cure ailments of the shins and feet (<u>Encycl. Occult</u> 220). Nor is astrology completely free of magic even in contemporary times. As Derek Parker, a defender of astrology, admits, "Some astrologers still seek to preserve its past links with magic." adding that astrology remains "dear to those who are interested in the occult" (70). While the ancient link with magic may be forgiven as one of the imperfections of a primitive discipline, the modern link cannot be dismissed so easily. Science, after all, concerns itself with the natural world, and magic deals with the supernatural.

We noted earlier that the idea of heavenly bodies influencing human beings is considered by some scientists to have been a valuable and scientific idea in ancient times. Somewhat more surprising, perhaps, is the fact that some scientists regard the idea as <u>still</u> within the realm of possibility, even given modern scientific knowledge and perspectives. (Others, of course, and they may be a majority, scoff at the idea.) Cazeau and Scott, for example, believe it is not entirely impossible that cosmic energy may have effects on us we are not aware of. They suggest that there is already hard scientific evidence of such energy, citing the fact that radio astronomers have demonstrated that distant nebulae and galaxies do emit tremendous radio-frequency energy, one known galaxy (M87) emitting 1,000 times more than our own galaxy. The astrological notion that the planets affect us, they say, "is indeed fantastic but is it more so than splitting and joining atoms, television, or trips to the moon?" (234).

Yet if the idea of celestial influence has met some scientific acceptance, two closely related astrological ideas have not fared so well. One is the idea that the exact force of each heavenly body differs from that of all other bodies. The scientists consulted for this paper are in agreement that it is highly unlikely that different planets would have different forces. Bart J. Bok points out that it is now known that all heavenly bodies are made of the same basic ingredients. Accordingly, he finds it unreasonable to believe that the same ingredients could exert vastly different forces and achieve vastly different effects (30–31).

The author's comment here reinforces the source's judgment and at the same time goes beyond it.

Even Cazeau and Scott, who are eminently fair-minded in their dealing with astrology, question how astrologers can have avoided making errors in their calculations before 1781, since three planets--Uranus, Neptune, and Pluto--were discovered after that time. They also question why astrologers do not now admit that such errors must have existed before 1781 (232). Their criticisms seem reasonable. The failure of astrologers

Note that in this judgment, as in his other judgments, the author does not parrot his source's ideas— rather, he contributes ideas, valuable ideas, of his own. This is the mark of a good persuasive paper.

to note such errors and address themselves to them does not build confidence in their claim to being scientific.

The second astrological idea that does not bear scrutiny well is that the stars work their influence at the moment of birth. The science of genetics has established that at the moment of conception the genetic package is complete. Thus a person's eye color, body type, and hundreds of other characteristics are determined then (subject in some cases, to later environmental influences). If there were one special moment in which cosmic forces were exerted, why, Bok asks, wouldn't it be the moment of concep-tion? Why, instead, the moment of birth, which science has shown to be of relatively little significance (31)? Other scientists consulted for this paper agree with this line of reasoning without exception. It seems clear that the ancients committed an understandable, but crucial, error in assigning so much importance to the moment of birth. But however great that error, the error of modern astrologers in refusing to admit it is far greater. For being scientific seems to demand, at very least, addressing the matter and either correcting it or showing why it does not need correction.

Lawrence E. Jerome has argued persuasively that the idea that the stars influence human lives, the central premise of astrology, did not come to the ancients through scientific observation at all. Rather, he explains, it was based on the magical "principle of correspondences," wherein what is seen as being like something else or reminiscent of it is considered to have the same properties ("Magic" 11–12). This principle, according to Jerome, worked as follows. The ancients noted that a partic-ular planet had a reddish cast, so in their primitive minds it became asso-ciated with blood, war, aggressiveness. Accordingly, they named it Mars after the god of war. Later, they linked other things associated with war--iron, for example--with the planet. Similarly, the planet Venus was named after the goddess of love, and all the mythology connected with her--beauty, sensitivity, and so on--became associated with the planet and to those born under its influence (Disproved 70–1).

Here the author's helpful comment shows his grasp of the issue by explaining what a response by astrologers would have to consist of to answer Jerome satisfactorily.

This magical basis of astrology's central premise, Jerome believes, is itself enough to disqualify any claim astrology might have to being a sci-ence. The argument seems compelling. And Jerome has stated it in at least two publications. Surely it has come to the attention of astrologers. The only effective response to Jerome's argument is a demonstration that the observed effects of the planets on human beings predated the assigning of mythological notions, the effects of the planets claimed by astrology actually do occur--in other words, that Mars really does have an effect on human aggressiveness, Venus on love, and so on. Lacking such a demonstration--and it has not been forthcoming--Jerome's argument seems unassailable.

One of the most important considerations in deciding whether astrology is a science is the testimony of scientists. As we noted earlier, scientists are not all in agreement on the question. Some continue to take a favorable attitude toward astrology. O. Neugebauer, for example, states that "compared with the background of religion, magic, and mysticism, the fundamental doctrines of astrology are pure science" (171). Yet that position is clearly a minority view. Richard Cavendish, in his comprehensive study of the occult, classifies astrology as "essentially a magical art" (219). A statement signed by 192 leading scientists calls astrologers "charlatans" and warns that "those who wish to believe in astrology should realize that there is no scientific foundation for its tenets" ("Statement" 9). And a statement endorsed by the Society for the Psychological Study of Social Issues brands astrology "a magical practice that has no shred of justification in scientific fact" (Bok 32). The scientific community, it is safe to say, is generally opposed to considering astrology a science.

The several reasons cited so far in this paper are sufficient to support the tentative conclusion that astrology is not a science. But there is an even better reason. It does not fit the contemporary definition of science. Though the terms <u>knowledge</u> and <u>science</u> are sometimes used interchangeably, the latter is a more restrictive category:

> [The term <u>science</u>] ordinarily . . . applies only to a body of systematized knowledge dealing with facts gathered over a long period of time and by numerous persons as a result of observation and experiment and with the general truths or laws derived by inference from such facts. The term usually connotes more exactness and more rigorous

Here is the most impressive contribution of the author. He takes the initiative, follows what he believes to be a sound approach not found in the sources he consulted, and considers the issue from a different perspective—that of definition. (It is possible, of course, to write an effective analytical research paper without taking such bold initiative, but excellence in analysis does depend on the author's making at least some significant contribution of his or her own to the discussion.)

testing of conclusions than <u>knowledge</u> does and therefore is often used to denote knowledge whose certainty cannot be questioned (<u>Webster's New Dictionary of Synonyms</u>).

Considerable confusion seems to center around the <u>history</u> of astrology. Defenders say that astrology once fit the definition of science completely and was accepted by the most eminent thinkers as a science. And that is true. The problem comes when they reason that because it was once a science, it must <u>still</u> be a science. That is incorrect. To be judged a science today, astrology must meet today's definition. That definition is more restrictive than the definition in earlier times, and if the supporters of astrology wish it to be applied, then they must address the serious questions critics have raised and demonstrate their case. The burden of proof is on them.

In conclusion, reasonable people remain ready to consider impartially any new evidence advanced for astrology. But until such evidence is presented, they are justified in regarding astrology with skepticism, preferring, instead, Shakespeare's perspective on human fortunes: "The fault, dear Brutus, is not our stars, but in ourselves. . . . " (<u>Julius Caesar</u> 1.2).

Note that the author does not evade the issue. Rather, he offers his considered judgment, carefully expressed to reflect the evidence presented in the paper.

Works Cited

Bok, Bart J. "A Critical Look at Astrology." <u>Objections to Astrology</u>.
    Buffalo: Prometheus, 1975. 30–36.

Cavendish, Richard. <u>The Black Arts</u>. New York: Capricorn, 1967.

Cazeau, Charles J. and Stuart D. Scott. <u>Exploring the Unknown: Great
    Mysteries Re-examined</u>. New York: Plenum, 1979.

Crow, W. B. <u>A History of Magic, Witchcraft and Occultism</u>. London:
    Aquarius, 1968.

<u>Encyclopedia of Occult Sciences</u>. New York: Tudor, 1968.

Jerome, Lawrence E. <u>Astrology Disproved</u>. Buffalo: Prometheus, 1977.

---."Astrology: Magic or Science?" <u>Humanist</u> Sept-Oct. 1975 : 10–16.

Jones, Marc Edmund. <u>Astrology: How and Why It Works</u>. New York:
    Penguin, 1969.

Mark, Alexandra. <u>Astrology for the Aquarian Age</u>. New York: Essandra,
    1970.

Neugebauer, O. <u>The Exact Sciences in Antiquity</u> 2nd ed. New York:
    Harper, 1952.

Parker, Derek. <u>Astrology in the Modern World</u>. New York: Taplinger,
    1970.

Roll, W. G. "Science Looks at the Occult." <u>Psychic</u> 4 (June 1973) : 50–55.

Silverman, T. I. and M. Whitmer. "Astrological Indicators of Personality."
    <u>Journal of Psychology</u> 87 (May 1974) : 89–95.

Snyder, C. R. "Why Horoscopes Are True: The Effects of Specificity on
    Acceptance of Astrological Interpretations." <u>Journal of Clinical
    Psychology</u> 30 (1974) : 577–80.

Standen, Anthony. "Is There an Astrological Effect on Personality?"
    <u>Journal of Psychology</u> 89 (1975) : 259–60.

"Statement by 192 Leading Scientists." <u>Objections to Astrology.</u> Buffalo :
    Prometheus, 1975.

Thompson, C. J. S. <u>The Mystery and Romance of Astrology</u>. New York:
    Brentano's, 1969.

Zolar. <u>The History of Astrology</u>. New York : Arco, 1972.

SUGGESTED TOPICS FOR A RESEARCH PAPER _____

Each of the topic ideas presented here should be regarded as an idea starter rather than as a refined topic:

Nutrition: When did this science begin? What are the most important events in its development? What do nutritionists say about the current dieting craze? About specific diets? About "junk food"?

Intuition: Is there such a phenomenon as intuition, or is it a figment of people's imagination? What do the various schools of psychology say about it? (Be sure to consult humanistic as well as behavioristic schools of psychology.)

The Insanity Plea: What is the legal definition of insanity? Under what conditions may a plea of insanity be entered? What is the philosophical basis of the plea? What do judges, lawyers, psychologists, and ethicists think about the wisdom of discontinuing the insanity plea?

The Good Old Days: When were the good old days? What were the conditions then? Were they better or worse than conditions now? Why do people remember times past with such fondness? How accurate is human memory in such matters?

Prisons: What are the most pressing problems besetting our prison system? Do other countries have such problems? If not, why not? What do penologists believe are the causes of and solutions to these problems?

Mental Institutions: How did society treat the insane in centuries past? What was its understanding of mental health and illness? How has the increase in knowledge about insanity affected the conditions in mental institutions and the treatment of the inmates? What reforms do the experts believe are still needed?

Confucianism or Buddhism or Mohammedanism: How does this religion differ from Christianity and Judaism? What does it have in common with them? Where did it originate and what have been the important events in its history? In what ways, if any, does it differ today from when it was founded?

Solar Energy: What are the physical principles on which the idea of solar energy is founded? How does solar energy work? What do the experts say about the advantages and disadvantages of solar energy compared to other forms of energy?

America: Was Columbus the first non-native to visit the western hemisphere? What evidence is there that others preceded him? How reliable is that evidence? If others are thought to have preceded

Columbus, how, when, and from where are they believed to have traveled?

Prohibition: Whose idea was Prohibition? Who supported it, who opposed it, and how did the idea become law? What were the effects of Prohibition on American life?

Isaac Asimov (the most prolific American writer): What was Asimov's background? How many books did he write? In how many fields? Where did he get the ideas for his books? What were his work habits? What do those who knew him think of his work? Have there ever been any writers more prolific than Asimov?

Marriage: How does marriage in other cultures differ from marriage in our culture? (Consider such customs as courtship, engagement, the giving of a dowry, and arranged marriages.) How does marriage in our culture today differ from marriage in our culture 100 or 200 years ago?

Hobbies: What are some of the most unusual or dangerous or expensive hobbies people pursue? How do hobbies today compare with hobbies in colonial times or hobbies in ancient Rome?

Writing about Literature

Writing about literature can mean reporting, reviewing, or interpreting elements of a work. This chapter analyzes various contexts of writing about literature and reviews basic elements of literature often considered. An overview of the process and models of students working will also illustrate the similarities between writing about literature and writing about other subjects.

Reading literary works often stimulates thinking—you identify with a character's dilemma and wonder how she will act; you recognize a character as similar to someone you know; you decide that this book is better than the last one by the same author; you look back over a story to find out why the ending was such a shock; you see similarities between one work and another, or between the world in the work and the world as you know it.

In all of these reactions, your reading sparks a response. But will you put the response into writing? If you keep a journal or a reading log, you might record your reactions. If you write to a friend soon after your reading, you might send your responses. You might also contribute a review of a work to a newspaper or magazine. Or, the decision to respond in writing might be made for you when an instructor assigns a paper. Whatever the impetus that moves you from reaction to written response, using what you know about writing as a process can help you when your subject is literature.

TRUSTING YOUR OWN REACTION

Whether you read poems or prose fiction or drama, your response is both intellectual and emotional. It is also your own. No one can tell you what you are supposed to feel about a work; no one should ever tell you that your response is not valid. Tillie Olsen's short story "I Stand Here Ironing" is one that prompts differing responses from readers. In the story, a mother is thinking as she irons that her first born has not had an easy life, and many readers respond to her recollections with great sympathy for the daughter. But other readers see the mother's pain as she thinks of her daughter's difficult life, and they argue that the sympathy should be for her. Is one reaction more valid than the other? Both are based on careful and accurate readings of the story, so neither one can be discounted. A reaction is shaped by the reader's background and experiences, so it is unrealistic and unproductive to expect all readers to respond in the same way.

A creative response to literature starts with your willingness to trust your own responses. If you do not, you will be tempted to produce dull and predictable writing that echoes what everyone else has already thought.

To hear your creative voice, read the story actively, pen in hand. After each paragraph, think about your reactions. Do you like these characters? Can you hear their voices in the dialogue? Do you know anyone like this? Can you see this place? Is it like any other? Do you find anything puzzling or mysterious? Use your pen to highlight vivid sections and to record your reactions. When you have finished a work, reflect on the ending. Does it leave you satisfied? Do you know enough about what has happened to each character? Did each character deserve his or her fate? Think about your own reactions. Does the work make you feel sad? angry? resentful? Why do you think you feel that way? What associations have you brought to the work?

Some readers keep reading logs reserved exclusively for reactions to literature. You might find such a log useful, or, if you keep a journal, you can record your reactions to a work and try to explain to yourself why you are feeling as you do.

One student wrote, in response to Kate Chopin's "The Story of an Hour":

I was really angry when Louise Mallard died. She had finally begun to live. I had a relationship with a girl once who dominated everything we did. She made all the decisions about our time together. She called me all the time to find out what I was doing. I felt like I had to answer to her for everything. When we broke up, I felt like I had just started to live again. When your life is dominated by someone else, it's really not a life at all.

Another student wrote about the same story:

It's hard for me to imagine that one person could let another make decisions for her. My mother and my grandmother were both really strong women, even though my grandmother was sick most of the time I knew her. She was in control of her life. She and my grandfather had a really good relationship. They talked to each other a lot before they made any decisions. I couldn't really get involved with Louise Mallard's character. She was weak.

Y O U R   **T U R N**

1. To identify your own responses to literature, keep a reading log.
   a. Make entries immediately after you read a work, then go back later, after class discussion or after a second reading, and record any changes in your response.
   b. Record a passage that moves you to some emotion. Then, record your feeling and explain it.
2. To encourage creative responses, "play" with a literary work or character:
   a. Imagine interviewing one of the characters in the work. What would you like to ask? Would you be in any danger?
   b. Write a letter to the author, explaining how you felt about a work and why.
   c. Write to a character, explaining why you think a particular act was wrong. OR Write a defense or an explanation of some negative action by a character. OR In the voice of a character, explain why you took some particular action.
   d. If you could change the ending of the work, what would you write? You can end the work earlier, alter the outcome, or continue it past the current ending.

UNDERSTANDING THE CONTEXTS OF WRITTEN RESPONSE

When you move from reaction to written response, be sure that you understand the context of the writing and the expectations of your audience. Some situations will require that you work very closely with the text, and others will encourage you to explore your personal reactions. Are you writing for yourself or for others? Is your work an academic interpretation of the text or some element of it? Have you been assigned to explore your own response in a personal essay? Are you writing a newspaper column to help readers anticipate their own reactions? Are you describing for an audience that knows little about the work? Be sure that you understand any limits imposed by these varied contexts.

Some writing about literature is intended to give information to readers unfamiliar with the work. If you are preparing an annotated booklist, a quick summary of the primary text (the piece of literature to be discussed) will give readers enough information to make a decision to continue. If your analysis compares a work to a less familiar piece, your readers need information about the second work to understand your discussion.

Most writing about literature, though, is intended for readers who already know something about the subject. Your demonstration of knowledge about a work should convince an instructor that you understand the material. Your review should convince your readers that your evaluation is sound. Your analysis should convince readers that your reading of the work is reasonable. When you understand that your purpose is usually to convince readers to accept your credentials, your judgment, or your interpretation, you will also recognize the needs common to all arguments: the need to formulate a clear thesis, the need to supply appropriate evidence, and the need to accommodate the audience.

In short, contexts vary. With that variation come changes in the relationship between your material, your purpose, and your audience. That relationship should be examined when you are expected to demonstrate knowledge of a work, to evaluate it, or to interpret it.

Reporting on a Work

When you are asked to provide information about the primary text or about its author or background, be sure that you know what you are expected to do, for whom, and for what purpose. Your writing can focus on information about the plot, identify the setting, or discuss the place of this work within a larger context of similar works or works by the same author. Many assignments designate the subject for you, so be sure that you understand exactly what is expected of you. Look at these two samples to see how students responded to requests for specific information:

As a library aide, Barry was asked to provide summaries of five popular children's books for the library's summer reading list. He realized that both children and their parents would look at the list, and that they did not expect him to tell the story so completely that all surprises would be gone. His entries were supposed to indicate the contents of the books so that readers could make informed choices. Here are some of the samples Barry produced:

CHARLOTTE'S WEB

Charlotte's Web by E. B. White is the story of a likable pig named Wilbur and a unique spider named Charlotte. Wilbur will become breakfast food unless Charlotte can think of some way to save his life. She rallies the barnyard animals to save Wilbur, to the delight of Fern, the little girl who raised Wilbur from a piglet. A full-length animated movie was based on this book.

STUART LITTLE

E. B. White, the author of *Charlotte's Web,* also wrote about a strange little boy who looks remarkably like a mouse. His human parents and brother devise clever ways for Stuart to get around the house and the city, and Stuart has numerous adventures related to his size and appearance. His sworn enemy is, of course, the family cat, and his best friend, a lovely bird who saves his life and finally leads Stuart on the journey of his life.

Chandra was also asked for a report, but in her case the situation was an in-class reading quiz. Chandra realized that her answers were expected to demonstrate to the instructor that she was familiar with the assigned reading, so she made sure to include specific details and she did not worry about giving away too much of the story. Here are some questions and answers from Chandra's quiz:

Q: Explain the circumstances of "My Last Duchess."

A: "My Last Duchess," by Robert Browning, is a dramatic monologue spoken by the Duke of Ferrara to an emissary sent to discuss the terms of the Duke's coming marriage. The two men are walking apart from the other guests in a section of the castle filled with art treasures, including a portrait of the Duke's last Duchess. He points out the painting and talks about the Duchess, saying that she made him jealous by smiling at everyone. He also says that he gave commands and all smiles stopped, so he apparently had her killed. Then he turns to the emissary, whose replies are not given, and suggests that they return to the guests.

Q: Why is Mrs. Drover in "The Demon Lover" returning to an empty house?

A: "The Demon Lover" by Elizabeth Bowen is set in England during World War II. Mrs. Drover and her family have left the town of London because of the bombings and have gone to live in the country near the city. Mrs. Drover has returned during the day to pick up some things that had been left behind. She also wants to check on the condition of the house.

Notice that each student has suited the response to the audience and to the situation. Barry's summaries are careful to leave the details of the plot to the readers, but Chandra's detailed answers show that she wants her instructor to recognize her knowledge. None of these responses is controversial, so none requires extensive support to persuade the audience to accept it.

Purpose and Audience

Most reports will be intended to provide information rather than to persuade. If you report on the historical backgrounds of the work, or present a chronology of the author's work, or describe the contents of the work, your primary audience does not expect controversial assertions and evidence; instead, you will supply information that might be unfamiliar but is probably not controversial.

In an academic setting, your audience always includes your instructor. Even if your report is presented to your classmates, the instructor is nonetheless an audience with expectations. You can prove to your instructor that you know the material by including specific detail and referring to particular elements of the work. Meeting your instructor's expectations also requires careful examination of the assignment. Have you been directed to discuss the author? Is reference to other works of literature or to secondary criticism expected? Should you give the background of this work or concentrate solely on the primary text? Should you summarize the plot, list the main characters or describe the setting?

Knowing the expectations of your instructor includes knowing the expected form of the presentation. Does your instructor expect work to be formal in tone? Are contractions or first person acceptable? What documentation, if any, is expected? Should the paper be typed?

Whenever you are asked to demonstrate knowledge of a work, remember that your information itself is not controversial. If your presentation is accurate and complete, it will also be convincing.

Reporter's Checklists

Identifying Context

- What information is requested?
- Who will read this presentation?
- What information will the readers expect?
- What will readers do with this information?

Drafting a Response

- What do I want to focus on for this writing?
- Have I presented specific detail?
- Are my examples accurate?
- Does my presentation consider the complete work?

Reviewing a Work

Like reports, evaluations must be based on knowledge of the work. Without accurate presentation of details, your observations will not be taken seriously by your readers. But a review is expected to do more than simply report contents. It is expected to evaluate it, to judge technique or effectiveness or worth.

Purpose and Audience

Academic writers evaluate either complete works or specific elements of works. Newspapers and magazines also present reviews of books, plays, and movies. These two contexts present audiences with varying knowledge of the subject and with different expectations of the review. The situations below will illustrate:

David, who writes the movie review column for the student newspaper, is aware that people often read reviews before deciding to read a work or see a performance. He knows that his readers expect guidance, including information about the type of work, the themes it explores, the techniques it uses, the quality it achieves. In his review of *Indiana Jones and The Last Crusade,* he includes such information but is careful to reserve details about plot that might ruin suspense. Here is his review:

If you liked the first Indiana Jones movie and were a little disappointed by the second, *The Last Crusade* just might restore your enthusiasm. Indy is back, and of today's action/adventure movie heroes, he is again the best. If you want adventure, you will not be disappointed. The action is fast-paced and the perils are deadly as Indy, in pursuit of the mystical Holy Grail, follows his father into a Nazi trap that includes a face-to-face encounter with Adolf Hitler and a daring escape from a dirigible in a plane that neither man knows how to land. The tension builds to a breath-holding climax as Indy must solve ancient riddles to find the Grail in time to save his father's life.

But *The Last Crusade* offers more than exciting adventure. One of the best features of this movie is Indy's relationship with his father, painted with deft strokes that will touch your emotions without becoming maudlin. Indy does not at first appear to be close to his father, but when his father is in danger, it is Indy to the rescue, into the depths of a Nazi stronghold without hesitation. The elder Dr. Jones, played to perfection by Sean Connery, is not surprised at his son's appearance, but, to the amusement of the audience, is repeatedly astonished at his performance. "Look what you did!" he murmurs in amazement as the two escape over multiple Nazi corpses. Connery and Ford regard each other with impatience, with astonishment, and finally with reluctant tenderness, forcing us to see Indy as a vulnerable, confused, and loving part of an appealing and believable father-son relationship.

If you like adventure movies, *The Last Crusade* is a breathtaking roller-coaster ride from beginning to end. And if you want more than larger-than-life comic book heroes, Indy and his father will make you care about them while you gasp at their adventures. It's worth seeing—more than once.

In contrast to the newspaper review, academic reviews or evaluations are often directed to readers who know the work (including any shocking surprises) and are expecting judgment and opinions of it. The reviewer is not relieved of the obligation to know the work thoroughly; if anything, knowledgeable readers expect absolute accuracy and quickly spot errors that undermine credibility. Emily, a student in an Introduction to Fiction class, recognized the need to do more than demonstrate knowledge of the work when she evaluated "The Demon Lover" in response to an assignment. She assumed that her audience, which included the instructor, was familiar with the work and would not be disappointed if she revealed the ending. Here is an excerpt from her paper:

A ghost story should never answer all questions about strange encounters. It should leave the readers still searching for some logical explanations to seemingly supernatural incidents. By refusing to supply answers, the story leaves the readers in a state of puzzled uncertainty. That effect lingers long after shocking scenes have faded from memory.

"The Demon Lover" is a fine example of just that kind of unanswered question. When Mrs. Drover looks into the face of the taxi driver and begins to scream, the reader is left to decide if her mind has snapped or if there is indeed a demon at the wheel. All of the details of the story— the mysterious letter appearing under impossible circumstances, the chilly draft of wind, even the unsettling memories of the fiance—invite the readers to supply logical explanations. The simplest explanation is supernatural forces. But the woman and her life and her errand seem so normal that the readers hesitate. That hesitation, the tension between the reluctance to accept a supernatural explanation and the impossibility of anything else, keeps the readers involved with the story long after Mrs. Drover has gone screaming to an unknown destination.

In each of these two situations, the writer offers a clear judgment of the effectiveness of the work and is aware of the background of the readers and responsive to their expectations.

Using Evidence

As you collect information for your review, remember that the context often directs evaluations to focus on specific areas like the realism of the characters, the effectiveness of the first-person point of view, the talents of the lead actress, or the relative merits compared with an earlier work. Assertions in any of these areas should be developed and supported with textual evidence. While a plot summary is either accurate or inaccurate, an evaluation of effectiveness or quality is an arguable assertion to be explained and supported. Look at Roy Blount, Jr.'s evaluation of the characters' language in the novel *High Hearts:*

> The dialogue would chip a beaver's teeth. One belle to another: "Sin-Sin was impressed when Evangelista guided her through your labyrinthine closets and showed her every gown for which you've marked a card stating when you wore it, where you wore it, and what shoes, hat, gloves and parasol you wore with it."

Blount does not simply tell us that the dialogue is unrealistic; he cites an example from the novel to show us the awkwardness of the conversations between characters.

Unless the instructor expects you to research other commentaries, the primary text or texts will supply the evidence to support your assertions. Your citations should be accurate and should fairly reflect the tone and the style of the work; if you can find only a single example of awkwardness in 500 pages, it would be misleading to cite that example as typical.

Using Comparison

When you draft your review, expect it to emerge as a comparison. Even if you do not compare one character to another or one work to another, your review will compare the work or some aspect of it to standards understood by you and your readers. For example, Blount's comment on the tongue-tangling dialogue of *High Hearts* is a comparison to the implicit standard that characters should speak like real human beings. The review of "The Demon Lover", also compares the work to a standard; in this case, the essay begins with the criteria for a good ghost story.

Evaluations often involve comparisons of characters or of works that are similar in some significant respect (same author, same setting, same subject); these comparisons are readily organized by discussion of shared or contrasting qualities (see Chapter 9 for further consideration of logical patterns). Look at these evaluative comparisons in excerpts from student papers:

"Bells for John Whiteside's Daughter" ("Daughter") is more effective in conveying real grief than is the poem "To a Dead Child" ("Child"). "Child" gets its emotional impact from a lengthy description of the child in the coffin. The description is detailed but full of cliches like "the roses bloom no more in her cheeks." In contrast, "Daughter" expresses shock at seeing the busy child so still, describing her lively assault on the geese to create a vivid picture of her in motion before she was "so primly propped." The sorrow is not centered on the corpse, but on the living spirit that has gone. The emotion called up by the description of the child in death is shallow and fleeting, but the sense of loss and astonishment evoked by the glimpses of the child in motion is lasting. It echoes in the heart, an expression of the pain and disbelief felt when any child dies.

Of the four Compson children in *The Sound and the Fury,* only Benjy is capable of real love. Jason, of course, has feelings only for money. But Quentin's idea of love, passionate as it is, depends on image and not on reality. His confusion over his sister's emerging sexuality shows his inability to love his sister as she really is. And Caddy, who loves so intensely and so completely at first, is finally driven to find temporary comfort in strange beds. It is only Benjy, whose forever childlike mind protects him from the twisted influence of his mother, who is able to love blindly and simply, without reservation or judgment. Hearing golfers call "Caddy," Benjy remembers her loving presence vividly ("Caddy smells like trees") and does not understand the futility of his feelings. Benjy's love for his sister Caddy remains unspoiled by her absence or by the hell around him; locked in perpetual childhood, he alone maintains the ability to give pure, unconditional, uncomplicated love.

Reviewer's Checklists

Identifying Context

- What will the readers know about this work?
- Should any surprises be left concealed?

- Is a specific approach defined by the context?
- Do the standards need explanation?
- Are the standards generally accepted?

Drafting a Response

- Is there a direct comparison to standards?
- Do those standards need explanation?
- Is there a comparison to other works?
- Do the comparisons contain clear judgments?
- Are the assertions appropriate to the context?
- Are the assertions supported by evidence?
- Is the evidence accurate and relevant?
- Are examples typical of the work?

Additional Reading

Rita Mae Brown's Battle Hymn of the Ridiculous
Roy Blount, Jr.

1   My daddy down in Georgia told me, "Son, take pride in your work, don't honk at old people and never read a Civil War novel longer than *The Red Badge of Courage.*"

2   So I never did. Until *High Hearts* by Rita Mae Brown. I'd been meaning to read her earlier novels which I'd heard were roguish and good. The premise of this one seemed promising: Geneva, the heroine, cuts her hair and enlists in the Confederate cavalry as a man so that she can be near her husband, who turns out not to be her equal as a warrior. Threatening to me, as a former indifferent male soldier; but hey, I can be threatened.

3   I've heard that Rita Mae Brown is a witty and engaging speaker, and in her pictures she looks like she'd be a fun person to be in the cavalry with. Daddy can't have anticipated a writer who used to keep company with the best women's tennis player in the world; who is on record as also liking men; who helped found the radical feminist group, Redstockings; who had an Amish father and a Southern mother; who studied English and classics at NYU; who served on the Literature Panel of the National Endowment for the Arts; who holds a Ph.D. from the Institute for Policy Studies.

4   So I broke Daddy's rule.

5   I read faster and faster, wishing I could read faster still; driving, driving; wiping away bad black English, caked blood, good Virginia soil and bad white English, pausing only to note that at three different points in the first 81 pages someone was described as not having the sense God gave a goose. It's a good expression, but it can be overworked.

6   So can dangling modifiers. If you took them out of the following passage, I realize, you would have to go in and completely rewrite, thereby endangering several subtle inadvertent effects:

7   "Steam moistened Geneva's nostrils as she gulped her hot chocolate. Expensive and delicious, Geneva preferred this luxury to jewelry, but Lutie assured her that as she grew older, she'd develop a taste for stones."

8   But you don't want to run dangling modifiers into the ground, page in and page out. "Shod a week ago, the shoes fit him perfectly." I wonder whether any former member of the Literature Panel of the National Endowment for the Arts has shod shoes, publicly, before.

9   Geneva gets to do a lot of neat stuff (which she later comes to recognize as part of man's inhumanity to man): engage in fistfights, blow Yankees away, chop down telegraph poles. In battle, the good guys tend to have catlike reflexes. I kept being reminded of baseball books for boys. I have never read a novel by John Jakes, but this is what I imagine one is like. You have heard about the influence of movies on the novel. This is an example of the influence of miniseries.

10   The dialogue would chip a beaver's teeth. One belle to another. "Sin-Sin was impressed when Evangelista guided her through your labyrinthine closets and showed her every gown for which you've marked a card stating when you wore it, where you wore it, and what shoes, hat, gloves and parasol you wore with it."

11   This is the only novel I have ever read in whose acknowledgments cats are thanked ("my mews: Cazenovia, Sneaky Pie, Pewter, and Buddha") *and* in whose text a mother, unhinged by grief, seizes her son's severed head and tries to eat it. Trying times.

12   Another character makes a true observation: "Man can live without pleasure, but doan know if he can live without the future." Not for long, anyway.

13   You are young. I have lived through 464 pages of the past and the past perfect, indiscriminately mixed. *Listen to me.* I don't care who wrote it, don't read a Civil War novel longer than *The Red Badge of Courage.*

Interpreting a Work

One of the most common expectations of writing about literature is that it will **explain** some aspect of the work. Instructors often assign interpretations of theme or character motivation or use of symbol. The interpretation should, of course, demonstrate knowledge of the work, but it is not expected to judge relative merit.

Purpose and Audience

Those who read interpretations of literature are usually familiar with the primary work. If you include other works in comparative discussions, it is good strategy to summarize them briefly, but it is not expected that you summarize your primary text. Instead, you will explain what both you and the reader have observed. A reasonable analogy is a guided tour of an historic district. The audience would feel annoyed and short-changed if the guide merely described the homes: "Here we have a two-story blue house with a broad front porch and two side entrances." The expectation is that the guide describes only enough to identify before moving to interpretation: "The two-story blue house on the corner was built by Thomas Allen in 1868. He was the first in this area to use gas lighting inside the home, and for the first year, even his family refused to stay overnight for fear of fire."

Similarly, your interpretation of a work should describe enough to identify a work but then move quickly on to interpretation. Look closely at the two passages below:

Emily Grierson grew up in a large white house in a neighborhood that was once "select." But now the house is in decay and the neighborhood is filled with gas stations and cotton gins. It is described as "an eyesore among eyesores."

Emily Grierson's house, its paint peeling and its wood rotting, stands in a neighborhood shifting slowly from residential to commercial. It is a relic of a bygone era. Like the Grierson family, it is not the splendid thing it once was. Like Miss Emily's, its exterior is decaying and its foundations are weakening.

The description of the house should be familiar to readers; the interpretation of its significance makes the discussion worth reading.

In an interpretation, then, you know that your readers expect you to explain what they have already observed. The context of your writing may direct you to interpret a particular element of the work, like theme, or setting, or use of symbols. As you define your thesis, test it against the specifics of the assignment to make sure that it is an appropriate response.

Potential Problems

Your interpretation of the work should be supported by the work itself. It is often tempting to include personal reactions to a work, but you must be sure that the primary text supports your interpretation. Consider the interpretations offered in these passages:

Mathilde Loisel was not treated fairly in "The Necklace." Her sins were minor, but her entire life is ruined by little mistakes. At the end, when her friend reveals the truth about the necklace, Mathilde is probably very angry with her. In fact, Mathilde and her husband will probably sue the woman to recover damages.

Before he is killed by Beowulf, Grendel terrorizes Hrothgar's hall because his lands have been stolen. He was living in the area before the hall was built and has a prior claim to the land. The new hall violates his property and he has every right to attack the hall.

In the first example, the writer has gone beyond the text of the story to speculate about Mathilde Loisel's reactions. In fact, the story ends when her friend reveals the truth about the necklace. There has been nothing in the story to suggest that Mathilde is capable of great anger, and the speculation about a lawsuit reveals more about modern America than about the primary text. In the second passage, the writer's sympathy for Grendel is not supported by the text of *Beowulf*. The idea that a monster could own property or even claim land is not suggested in the poem, and nothing in the work suggests that Grendel has any justification for his attacks. Both passages, in fact, reflect the writers' beliefs rather than the works under discussion.

Speculating about the characters in a work may lead you to observations that cannot be supported by evidence in the text. Another kind of problem is created if you develop an assertion that is contrary to such evidence. When your readers realize that you have ignored or altered incidents or characters that would weaken your assertion, they will rightly question your credibility. The interpretations below will illustrate:

The Duke of Ferrara, narrator of "My Last Duchess," has apparently grown tired of his wife and has sent her off to a convent. He has kept a painting to remember her lovely self, but he no longer wishes to see her smiling at everyone else. Shut up in a convent, she will not be able to annoy him by paying attention to other men.

The Awakening is a story of triumph against repression. Edna learns to live her own life in spite of her restricted environment. She manages to escape the demands of husband and society to become her own person, working to improve her art.

In the first sample, the writer has not considered the circumstances of the poem: The Duke is discussing marriage terms with his guest. In Renaissance Italy, divorce would have been unthinkable, so it is unlikely that his last wife is alive. The second sample suggests that the writer does not know that Edna swims to her death at the end of the novel. Her death might arguably represent escape from repression, even, perhaps, a kind of triumph. But the passage above leaves the distinct impression that Edna is alive and well and working at her painting. In each of the samples, the writers have ignored elements of the stories, leaving their readers to question the value of the interpretations.

The problematic interpretations discussed here should caution you about the expectations of interpretation. While you should discuss specifics of the work, you are expected to explain rather than merely describe the story. In addition, your explanations must be supported by the text and they must not ignore significant elements of the work.

A final caution in interpreting literature is to be aware of irony. Irony exists when there is a contrast between intention and effect. When a gruesome execution takes place on a sunny June day, the contrast between expectations and reality is ironic. When one character announces that events will occur "Over my dead body," and the audience knows that his murder is being plotted, the contrast between the audience's knowledge and the character's knowledge is ironic. And, if a character attempts to clear her name but manages only to muddy it further, her actions are ironic.

Irony can exist when two characters have differing expectations or levels of knowledge. It can also exist when the discrepancy is between the knowledge or attitude of characters and audience. In Edgar Allan Poe's "The Cask of Amontillado," Montresor lures his "friend" Fortunato into the catacombs to entomb him. As they descend, Fortunato coughs and Montresor professes deep concern. Fortunato says that the cough is nothing; "I shall not die of a cough," he says. Montresor replies, "True—true," and warns Fortunato to use proper caution. The conversation is, on one level, a normal exchange between friends. But "I shall not die of a cough" means different things to Montresor and to Fortunato (and to the readers). The different meanings attached to that statement enable readers to recognize the irony in Montresor's concern for Fortunato's health.

Irony can be verbal or situational, conscious or unconscious. It can also be humorous, though it is just as often grim, even tragic. But when you interpret a work, irony undetected can misdirect you.

Interpreter's Checklists

Identifying the Context

- Does the assignment define a controlling idea?
- Does the audience know this work?
- What else is the audience likely to know?
- What does the audience expect from my writing?

Drafting the Response

- Have I described specific elements of this work?
- Do my descriptions move on to interpretation?
- Is my interpretation supported by the text?
- Have I ignored any significant elements of the work?
- Have I identified and considered ironic situations, dialogue or commentary?
- Have I brought in works unknown to the audience?
- Is any summary necessary to this discussion?
- Is my discussion appropriate to this context?

THE PROCESS OF WRITING ABOUT LITERATURE

Understanding the expectations of the writing situation provides a starting point for your written response. It triggers the dialogue between creative and critical voices that shapes your process of writing. It directs your creative voice in explorations of the topic as you gather material and make decisions about purpose, audience, and controlling idea and begin to draft your response. And, as you review your work, your knowledge of the expectations of the assignment and the readers helps your critical voice suggest appropriate changes. Look at one student's response to a class assignment to see how writing about literature parallels writing about other subjects.

Additional Reading

The Lottery
Shirley Jackson

1   The morning of June 27th was clear and sunny, with the fresh warmth of a full-summer day; the flowers were blossoming profusely and the grass was richly green. The people of the village began to gather in the square, between the post office and the bank, around ten o'clock; in some towns there were so many people that the lottery took two days and had to be started on June 26th, but in this village, where there were only about three hundred people, the whole lottery took less than two hours, so it could begin at ten o'clock in the morning and still be through in time to allow the villagers to get home for noon dinner.

2   The children assembled first, of course. School was recently over for the summer, and the feeling of liberty sat uneasily on most of them; they tended

Reprinted with the permission of Farrar, Straus & Giroux, Inc. from *The Lottery* by Shirley Jackson, Copyright 1948, 1949 by Shirley Jackson, copyright renewed 1976 by Laurence Hyman, Barry Hyman, Mrs. Sarah Webster, and Mrs. Joanne Schnurer; *"The Lottery"* originally appeared in *The New Yorker*.

to gather together quietly for a while before they broke into boisterous play, and their talk was still of the classroom and the teacher, of books and reprimands. Bobby Martin had already stuffed his pockets full of stones, and the other boys soon followed his example, selecting the smoothest and roundest stones; Bobby and Harry Jones and Dickie Delacroix—the villagers pronounced this name "Dellacroy"—eventually made a great pile of stones in one corner of the square and guarded it against the raids of the other boys. The girls stood aside, talking among themselves, looking over their shoulders at the boys, and the very small children rolled in the dust or clung to the hands of their older brothers or sisters.

3 Soon the men began to gather, surveying their own children, speaking of planting and rain, tractors and taxes. They stood together, away from the pile of stones in the corner, and their jokes were quiet and they smiled rather than laughed. The women, wearing faded house dresses and sweaters, came shortly after their menfolk. They greeted one another and exchanged bits of gossip as they went to join their husbands. Soon the women, standing by their husbands, began to call to their children, and the children came reluctantly, having to be called four or five times. Bobby Martin ducked under his mother's grasping hand and ran, laughing, back to the pile of stones. His father spoke up sharply, and Bobby came quickly and took his place between his father and his oldest brother.

4 The lottery was conducted—as were the square dances, the teen-age club, the Halloween program—by Mr. Summers, who had time and energy to devote to civic activities. He was a round-faced, jovial man and he ran the coal business, and people were sorry for him, because he had no children and his wife was a scold. When he arrived in the square, carrying the black wooden box, there was a murmur of conversation among the villagers, and he waved and called, "Little late today, folks." The postmaster, Mr. Graves, followed him, carrying a three-legged stool, and the stool was put in the center of the square and Mr. Summers set the black box down on it. The villagers kept their distance, leaving a space between themselves and the stool, and when Mr. Summers said, "Some of you fellows want to give me a hand?" there was a hesitation before two men, Mr. Martin and his oldest son, Baxter, came forward to hold the box steady on the stool while Mr. Summers stirred up the papers inside it.

5 The original paraphernalia for the lottery had been made with some pieces of the box that had preceded it, the one that had been lost long ago, and the black box now resting on the stool had been put into use even before Old Man Warner, the oldest man in town, was born. Mr. Summers spoke frequently to the villagers about making a new box, but no one liked to upset even as much tradition as was represented by the black box. There was a story that the present box had been made with some pieces of the box that had preceded it, the one that had been constructed when the first people settled down to make a village here. Every year, after the lottery, Mr. Summers began talking again about a new box, but every year the subject was allowed to fade off without anything's being

done. The black box grew shabbier each year; by now it was no longer completely black but splintered badly along one side to show the original wood color, and in some places faded or stained.

6   Mr. Martin and his oldest son, Baxter, held the black box securely on the stool until Mr. Summers had stirred the papers thoroughly with his hand. Because so much of the ritual had been forgotten or discarded, Mr. Summers had been successful in having slips of paper substituted for the chips of wood that had been used for generations. Chips of wood, Mr. Summers had argued, had been all very well when the village was tiny, but now that the population was more than three hundred and likely to keep on growing, it was necessary to use something that would fit more easily into the black box. The night before the lottery, Mr. Summers and Mr. Graves made up the slips of paper and put them in the box, and it was then taken to the safe of Mr. Summers' coal company and locked up until Mr. Summers was ready to take it to the square next morning. The rest of the year, the box was put away, sometimes one place, sometimes another; it had spent one year in Mr. Graves's barn and another year underfoot in the post office, and sometimes it was set on a shelf in the Martin grocery and left there.

7   There was a great deal of fussing to be done before Mr. Summers declared the lottery open. There were the lists to make up—of heads of families, heads of households in each family, members of each household in each family. There was the proper swearing-in of Mr. Summers by the postmaster, as the official of the lottery; at one time, some people remembered, there had been a recital of some sort, performed by the official of the lottery, a perfunctory, tuneless chant that had been rattled off duly each year; some people believed that the official of the lottery used to stand just so when he said or sang it, others believed that he was supposed to walk among the people, but years and years ago this part of the ritual had been allowed to lapse. There had been, also, a ritual salute, which the official of the lottery had had to use in addressing each person who came up to draw from the box, but this also had changed with time, until now it was felt necessary only for the official to speak to each person approaching. Mr. Summers was very good at all this; in his clean white shirt and blue jeans, with one hand resting carelessly on the black box, he seemed very proper and important as he talked interminably to Mr. Graves and the Martins.

8   Just as Mr. Summers finally left off talking and turned to the assembled villagers, Mrs. Hutchinson came hurriedly along the path to the square, her sweater thrown over her shoulders, and slid into place in the back of the crowd. "Clean forgot what day it was," she said to Mrs. Delacroix, who stood next to her, and they both laughed softly. "Thought my old man was out back stacking wood," Mrs. Hutchinson went on, "and then I looked out the window and the kids was gone, and then I remembered it was the twenty-seventh and came a-running." She dried her hands on her apron, and Mrs. Delacroix said, "You're in time, though. They're still talking away up there."

9   Mrs. Hutchinson craned her neck to see through the crowd and found her husband and children standing near the front. She tapped Mrs. Delacroix on the arm as a farewell and began to make her way through the crowd. The people separated good-humoredly to let her through; two or three people said, in voices just loud enough to be heard across the crowd, "Here comes your Missus, Hutchinson." and "Bill, she made it after all." Mrs. Hutchinson reached her husband, and Mr. Summers, who had been waiting, said cheerfully, "Thought we were going to have to get on without you, Tessie." Mrs. Hutchinson said, grinning, "Wouldn't have me leave m'dishes in the sink, now, would you, Joe?," and soft laughter ran through the crowd as the people stirred back into position after Mrs. Hutchinson's arrival.

10   "Well, now," Mr. Summers said soberly, "guess we better get started, get this over with, so's we can go back to work. Anybody ain't here?"

11   "Dunbar," several people said. "Dunbar, Dunbar."

12   Mr. Summers consulted his list. "Clyde Dunbar," he said. "That's right. He's broke his leg, hasn't he? Who's drawing for him?"

13   "Me, I guess," a woman said, and Mr. Summers turned to look at her. "Wife draws for her husband," Mr. Summers said. "Don't you have a grown boy to do it for you, Janey?" Although Mr. Summers and everyone else in the village knew the answer perfectly well, it was the business of the official of the lottery to ask such questions formally. Mr. Summers waited with an expression of polite interest while Mrs. Dunbar answered.

14   "Horace's not but sixteen yet." Mrs. Dunbar said regretfully. "Guess I gotta fill in for the old man this year."

15   "Right," Mr. Summers said. He made a note on the list he was holding. Then he asked, "Watson boy drawing this year?"

16   A tall boy in the crowd raised his hand. "Here," he said. "I'm drawing for m'mother and me." He blinked his eyes nervously and ducked his head as several voices in the crowd said things like "Good fellow, Jack," and "Glad to see your mother's got a man to do it."

17   "Well," Mr. Summers said, "guess that's everyone. Old Man Warner make it?"

18   "Here," a voice said, and Mr. Summers nodded.

19   A sudden hush fell on the crowd as Mr. Summers cleared his throat and looked at the list. "All ready?" he called. "Now, I'll read the names—heads of families first—and the men come up and take a paper out of the box. Keep the paper folded in you hand without looking at it until everyone has had a turn. Everything clear?"

20   The people had done it so many times that they only half listened to the directions; most of them were quiet, wetting their lips, not looking around. Then Mr. Summers raised one hand high and said, "Adams." A man disengaged himself from the crowd and came forward. "Hi, Steve," Mr. Summers said, and Mr, Adams said, "Hi, Joe." They grinned at one another humorlessly and nervously. Then Mr. Adams reached into the

black box and took out a folded paper. He held it firmly by one corner as he turned and went hastily back to his place in the crowd, where he stood a little apart from his family, not looking down at his hand.

21   "Allen," Mr. Summers said. "Anderson. . . . Bentham."

22   "Seems like there's no time at all between lotteries any more," Mrs. Delacroix said to Mrs. Graves in the back row. "Seems like we got through with the last one only last week."

23   "Time sure goes fast," Mrs. Graves said.

24   "Clark. . . . Delacroix."

25   "There goes my old man," Mrs. Delacroix said. She held her breath while her husband went forward.

26   "Dunbar," Mr. Summers said, and Mrs. Dunbar went steadily to the box while one of the women said, "Go on, Janey," and another said, "There she goes."

27   "We're next," Mrs. Graves said. She watched while Mr. Graves came around from the side of the box, greeted Mr. Summers gravely, and selected a slip of paper from the box. By now, all through the crowd there were men holding the small folded papers in their large hands, turning them over and over nervously. Mrs. Dunbar and her two sons stood together, Mrs. Dunbar holding the slip of paper.

28   "Harburt. . . . Hutchinson."

29   "Get up there, Bill," Mrs. Hutchinson said, and the people near her laughed.

30   "Jones."

31   "They do say," Mr. Adams said to Old Man Warner, who stood next to him, "that over in the north village they're talking of giving up the lottery."

32   Old Man Warner snorted. "Pack of crazy fools," he said. "Listening to the young folks, nothing's good enough for *them*. Next thing you know, they'll be wanting to go back to living in caves, nobody work any more, live *that* way for a while. Used to be a saying about 'Lottery in June, corn be heavy soon.' First thing you know, we'd all be eating stewed chickweed and acorns. There's *always* been a lottery," he added petulantly. "Bad enough to see young Joe Summers up there joking with everybody."

33   "Some places have already quit lotteries," Mrs. Adams said.

34   "Nothing but trouble in *that*," Old Man Warner said stoutly. "Pack of young fools."

35   "Martin." And Bobby Martin watched his father go forward. "Overdyke. . . . Percy."

36   "I wish they'd hurry," Mrs. Dunbar said to her older son. "I wish they'd hurry."

37   "They're almost through," her son said.

38   "You get ready to run tell Dad," Mrs. Dunbar said.

39   Mr. Summers called his own name and then stepped forward precisely and selected a slip from the box. Then he called, "Warner."

40   "Seventy-seventh year I been in the lottery," Old Man Warner said as he went through the crowd. "Seventy-seventh time."

41   "Watson." The tall boy came awkwardly through the crowd. Some-one said, "Don't be nervous, Jack," and Mr. Summers said, "Take your time, son."

42   "Zanini."

43   After that, there was a long pause, a breathless pause, until Mr. Sum-mers, holding his slip of paper in the air, said, "All right, fellows." For a minute, no one moved, and then all the slips of paper were opened. Sud-denly, all the women began to speak at once, saying, "Who is it?," "Who's go it?," "Is it the Dunbars?," "It it the Watsons?" Then the voices began to say, "It's Hutchinson. It's Bill," "Bill Hutchinson's got it."

44   "Go tell you father," Mrs. Dunbar said to her older son.

45   People began to look around to see the Hutchinsons. Bill Hutchinson was standing quiet, staring down at the paper in his hand. Suddenly, Tessie Hutchinson shouted to Mr. Summers, "You didn't give him time enough to take any paper he wanted. I saw you. It wasn't fair!"

46   "Be a good sport, Tessie," Mrs. Delacroix called, and Mrs. Graves said, "All of us took the same chance."

47   "Shut up, Tessie," Bill Hutchinson said.

48   "Well, everyone," Mr. Summers said, "that was done pretty fast, and now we've got to be hurrying a little more to get done in time." He con-sulted his next list. "Bill," he said, "you draw for the Hutchinson family. You got any other households in the Hutchinsons?"

49   "There's Don and Eva," Mrs. Hutchinson yelled. "Make them take their chance!"

50   "Daughters draw with their husbands' families, Tessie," Mr. Summers said gently. "You know that as well as anyone else."

51   "It wasn't fair," Tessie said.

52   "I guess not, Joe," Bill Hutchinson said regretfully. "My daughter draws with her husband's family, that's only fair. And I've got no other family except the kids."

53   "Then, as far as drawing for families is concerned, it's you," Mr. Sum-mers said in explanation, "and as far as drawing for households is con-cerned, that's you, too. Right?"

54   "Right," Bill Hutchinson said.

55   "How many kids, Bill?" Mr. Summers asked formally.

56   "Three," Bill Hutchinson said. "There's Bill, Jr., and Nancy, and little Dave. And Tessie and me."

57   "All right, then," Mr. Summers said. "Harry, you got their tickets back?"

58   Mr. Graves nodded and held up the slips of paper. "Put them in the box, then," Mr. Summers directed. "Take Bill's and put it in."

59   "I think we ought to start over," Mrs. Hutchinson said, as quietly as she could. "I tell you it wasn't fair. You didn't give him time enough to choose. *Every*body saw that."

60   Mr. Graves had selected the five slips and put them in the box, and he dropped all the papers but those onto the ground, where the breeze caught them and lifted them off.

61   "Listen, everybody," Mrs. Hutchinson was saying to the people around her.

62   "Ready, Bill?" Mr. Summers asked, and Bill Hutchinson, with one quick glance around at his wife and children, nodded.

63   "Remember," Mr. Summers said, "take the slips and keep them folded until each person has taken one. Harry, you help little Dave," Mr. Graves took the hand of the little boy, who came willingly with him up to the box. "Take a paper out of the box, Davy," Mr. Summers said. Davy put his hand into the box and laughed. "Take just one paper," Mr. Summers said. "Harry, you hold it for him." Mr. Graves took the child's hand and removed the folded paper from the tight fist and held it while little Dave stood next to him and looked up at him wonderingly.

64   "Nancy next," Mr. Summers said. Nancy was twelve, and her school friends breathed heavily as she went forward, switching her skirt, and took a slip daintily from the box. "Bill, Jr.," Mr. Summers said, and Billy, his face red and his feet overlarge, nearly knocked the box over as he got a paper out. "Tessie," Mr. Summers said. She hesitated for a minute, looking around defiantly, and then set her lips and went up to the box. She snatched a paper out and held it behind her.

65   "Bill," Mr. Summers said, and Bill Hutchinson reached into the box and felt around, bringing his hand out at last with the slip of paper in it.

66   The crowd was quiet. A girl whispered, "I hope it's not Nancy," and the sound of the whisper reached the edges of the crowd.

67   "It's not the way it used to be," Old Man Warner said clearly. "People ain't the way they used to be."

68   "All right," Mr. Summers said. "Open the papers. Harry, you open little Dave's."

69   Mr. Graves opened the slip of paper and there was a general sigh through the crowd as he held it up and everyone could see that it was blank. Nancy and Bill, Jr., opened theirs at the same time, and both beamed and laughed, turning around to the crowd and holding their slips of paper above their heads.

70   "Tessie," Mr. Summers said. There was a pause, and then Mr. Summers looked at Bill Hutchinson, and Bill unfolded his paper and showed it. It was blank.

71   "It's Tessie," Mr. Summers said, and his voice was hushed. "Show us her paper, Bill."

72   Bill Hutchinson went over to his wife and forced the slip of paper out of her hand. It had a black spot on it, the black spot Mr. Summers had made the night before with the heavy pencil in the coal-company office. Bill Hutchinson held it up, and there was a stir in the crowd.

73   "All right, folks," Mr. Summers said. "Let's finish quickly."

74   Although the villagers had forgotten the ritual and lost the original black box, they still remembered to use stones. The pile of stones the boys had made earlier was ready; there were stones on the ground with the blowing scraps of paper that had come out of the box. Mrs. Delacroix selected a stone so large she had to pick it up with both hands and turned to Mrs. Dunbar. "Come on," she said. "Hurry up."

75   Mrs. Dunbar had small stones in both hands, and she said, gasping for breath, "I can't run at all. You'll have to go ahead and I'll catch up with you."

76   The children had stones already, and someone gave little Davy Hutchinson a few pebbles.

77   Tessie Hutchinson was in the center of a cleared space by now, and she held her hands out desperately as the villagers moved in on her. "It isn't fair," she said. A stone hit her on the side of the head.

78   Old Man Warner was saying. "Come on, come on, everyone." Steve Adams was in the front of the crowd of villagers, with Mrs. Graves beside him.

79   "It isn't fair, it isn't right," Mrs. Hutchinson screamed, and then they were upon her.

❏ Invitation to Write: The Assignment

Margaret Daniels, a student in a freshman composition class, was given this assignment for an out-of-class essay on Shirley Jackson's "The Lottery":

> Most readers are shocked by the ending of "The Lottery." What makes it so difficult for anyone to foresee the ending? Explain to readers who know the story in an essay 300–500 words in length.

Margaret's response to the assignment provides a working model of writing about literature as a process. Let's examine the decisions Margaret made and the activities that resulted to see how the process can work.

❏ The First Decision: To Accept the Invitation to Write

Margaret had not yet read "The Lottery," but the assignment actually made the first decision for her. Her first step was to preview the story carefully, giving some thought to the positive expectations created by the title. She knew from her assignment that the ending was shocking, so even though she let her creative voice react freely to the story, she found herself looking for signs that something terrible was going to happen.

Comment: However the decision to write is made, the gathering of material begins with the primary text. Preview the work by reading any introductory notes about the writer or the work and by considering your reaction to the title. What do you expect of a work called "The Demon Lover"? What does "The Chaser" suggest to you? Read the work through to the end, paying careful attention to details and thinking about your responses. In this first reading, try to let the creative voice react without critical guidance.

    After your first reading, you should understand the work, its form, its background, its main ideas. Then, take a careful look at your reason for writing. Should you produce a report or description? Should you evaluate this work as it stands or in comparison to other works? Should you interpret a particular aspect of the work?

Margaret knew from the assignment that she was expected to analyze the story's effect on readers. She thought first about her own response and realized that, like other readers, she had been unprepared for the violent, ritualistic execution. With the assignment to direct her, she began to think about why she had found no warning in the story itself.

Comment: You should trust your own reactions to a work. If your response is based on an accurate reading of the text, it is legitimate.

Do not limit your response to something safe and predictable; if the villain seems much like the hero, if the narrator's judgment seems questionable, if you suspect the obvious motives, explore that reaction. Verify it against the text itself (Can it be supported? Does it ignore anything major?) and do not worry if no one else seems to see it your way.

Margaret found only a few details in the story that seemed connected to the ending. Since she knew that her reaction was similar to the reactions of other readers, it occurred to her that the writer had planned to shock, and that the story deliberately avoided any clues to the ending. She decided to test her theory by making two lists, one list of possible clues to the ending and one list of elements that might actually misdirect the reader. Her first lists looked like this:

Theory: "The Lottery" ends with a gruesome, shocking stoning of a woman.

The reader is given no warning and is actively misled by the story.

Misdirections	Possible Clues
the title: a prize	the piles of rocks
Mr. Summer's name	Mr. Graves' name
the setting:	nervous people
June day	the black box
sun, flowers	other villages' ending
kids playing	the lottery
rural village	
the box underfoot	
normal conversation	

Comment: As you continue to explore the work, a good thought to keep in mind is that literature is crafted by an artist, not spewed forth at random, and the artist makes choices that determine the form and the effect of the work. The point of view, the details of setting, and the actions of characters are the results of those choices and should be examined.

You need not concern yourself with the writers' reasons for making particular choices; even if you do read something about one writer's intentions, remember that intentions are far less important than outcome. If a football play is intended to gain one or two yards for a first down, the team gets credit only for what actually happens. If the play is a failure, or if it turns into a touchdown, the original intention is irrelevant to the outcome. Similarly, a work intended to shock the readers that amuses them instead is judged by its effect rather than by the writer's intentions. So, instead of trying to second-guess the writer, focus on the work itself.

Margaret's first list convinced her that her initial theory was promising. She decided to explore the work by cubing with the elements of fiction, using each one to ask, "Does the _____ misdirect the reader?" Her cube produced the following:

Did the *plot* misdirect the readers?
> Expecting a lottery on a summer day—expecting a happy winner
> People gather—normal people talking about dishes in the sink, tractors, taxes

Did the *characters* misdirect the readers?
> All the characters are everyday, normal people.
> The man who conducts the lottery ritual does the Halloween program and the teenage dances.
> The kids are out of school, playing in the sun.

Did the *setting* misdirect the readers?
> Sunny summer day—flowers, green grass, rural village, ordinary people, noon gathering in the town square, children playing
> Black box is underfoot all year, doesn't seem threatening to anyone

Did the *point of view* misdirect the readers?
> Objective point of view used—no one's thoughts are revealed; no revealing comments are made by the narrator.
> No clues about feelings at all, just report of action.
> First person or omniscient narrators would have shown the nervousness to be fear.
> First person—who? Mrs. H? story would end with her death
> Objective permits details to be concealed.

Comment: Many academic assignments specify evaluation or analysis of particular elements like plot, point of view, characterization, setting, or theme. As you examine the text, let the specific demands of this rhetorical situation direct your exploration.

Margaret reviewed her notes and her ideas, and decided that her original theory was correct. It could be supported by the text, and it did not require speculation or omission of significant incidents. She formulated this thesis statement:

The readers of "The Lottery" are lead to believe that there will be a

happy winner of a game of chance; as a result, the shock of the grisly

conclusion is intensified.

With her controlling idea in writing, Margaret looked over her notes and decided that the areas of point of view and setting needed the most attention. She also wrote her ideas out in prose passages, explaining fully and listing details from the text.

> **Comment:** When you have explored the primary text, you should explain your first ideas in prose passages. As you review your notes, consider: What are your observations about plot or point of view? What is your opinion of the characters? What connections do you see between setting and plot or setting and characters? What themes are illustrated by the work?
>
> Reviewing your ideas before you begin to draft will also give you a chance to mark those that look promising, those that were not immediately obvious but now seem logical and are well-supported with textual evidence.
>
> With a prose explanation of your ideas in hand, you can evaluate your ideas for logic and accuracy and relevance to the context of your writing.
>
> Have you presented incidents as they happened? Have you overlooked important details? Are there further examples of your character's childishness or heroism, or is there contradictory evidence that makes your interpretations shaky? In addition, you should look again at the assignment or other stimulus for this response. Were you expected to report or to review or to interpret? What information best suits your purpose? Were you expected to concentrate on a specific element like point of view or setting? What information or approaches should be saved for another paper?
>
> Remember, though, as you begin to draft your response, that none of these decisions is final. If any direction seems unproductive or confusing, it is never too late to re-direct your discussion. Save your notes.

❏ The Second Decision: To Draft a Response

When Margaret decided that she was ready to draft, she examined her material for logical connections. The assignment cued her to look for a cause-effect pattern, but she was not sure of the best order for the points she would discuss. For her first draft, she decided to start with the earliest detail that misdirects the reader, the title. She also decided that the least obvious technique of misdirection was the point of view, and she planned to end her discussion by explaining that technique.

Margaret also needed more information about her own audience, so she went back to her instructor to make sure that her approach was appropriate for the assignment and to ask about the audience's knowledge of the work. The instructor told her to assume that her audience knew the plot of the story and cautioned her to avoid summarizing. Reassured, Margaret organized her material into a rough draft.

Comment: As you prepare to draft, direct your critical voice to look for connections between ideas that might organize your drafts.

As you do with other subjects, use the patterns to explore further, looking for more causes or additional points of comparison or further examples of types. A combination of patterns can be an effective strategy; the point to check is whether the variations in pattern are unintentional or deliberate. Review the discussion of patterns in Chapter 9; as you will see here, patterns like chronology, cause and effect, comparison, and classification are particularly useful when writing about literature.

Patterns of Response

Chronology   There are two chronologies to consider here. One is the chronology of events in the story. If you have read carefully, you are aware of any variations in the time line of the story's events. "A Rose for Emily" is a good example of a story whose incidents are not presented in chronological order.

But you can also order your own paper chronologically by discussing the events in the order in which they are presented to you. If you are tracing a character's development or the evolution of the work itself, chronology is often the logical choice. Any discussion that covers the work from beginning to end might be presented chronologically, but be aware that chronological presentation of details often turns into summary, so use it sparingly.

Cause–Effect   Within the text, you might discuss the motivation of incidents or their effects on later incidents. Characters can be examined for their motives or for the forces that shaped them or for their impact on other characters. If you are asked to study the work in a larger context, you might discuss the effect of culture or cultural events on a work, or you might see causal connections between a writer's life and the incidents in the work. Be wary of oversimplification, particularly if you try to connect the writer to the work, and review your causal analysis for logic and completeness as you review all such connections.

Comparison–Contrast   Comparisons of character's various stages of development, or comparisons to other characters, are often insightful. You might also compare or contrast the work to another that shares some significant characteristic (author, subject, technique). Be sure that your analysis covers significant points and that there are reasonable grounds for comparison.

Classification A classification of the work itself might be useful, but within the text a classification of the symbols used or of the types of characters is more likely. Classification can also be used to organize other discussions; for example, a classification of causes would be useful if there are several.

Drafting includes writing for yourself to make ideas clear and writing for your audience to satisfy expectations.

❏ **The Third Decision: To Review the Work in Progress**

With a draft in hand, Margaret needed to review her work. Her thesis was appropriate, and she made sure that she had included enough detail to support her points and to show the instructor that she understood the story. She made a rough outline of points and supporting evidence, and decided that her presentation was logical and complete. But when she asked a friend to evaluate the draft, he did not understand her discussion of point of view. He also noted that the description of setting was a lengthy summary of the opening paragraphs of the story. Margaret agreed, making the following changes:

Rough draft The point of view conceals details from the readers. It tells nothing about the characters or the plot.

Revision The objective point of view reports on actions but does not reveal thoughts or feelings. If the readers knew what even one character was thinking, they would know that the characters are afraid and that something dreadful is coming.

Rough draft The story opens on a clear, sunny summer morning. Flowers are blooming and grass is growing. The people of the small village gather in the square, expecting to get home for dinner. Children are recently out of school and they play in groups, the boys collecting rocks and the girls talking in groups and watching the boys. The men gather in groups, talking of planting and rain, and the women greet each other quietly as they gather with their husbands.

Revision All of the details of the setting suggest a normal, even wholesome atmosphere. The images are of growing, living things—flowers, grass, and children, all in a small town atmosphere lit by warm summer sun. The activities are ordinary: children play, men talk of crops and weather, women gossip. There is nothing in their actions to suggest that these ordinary people expect to commit a monstrous act of violence before lunchtime.

Comment Peer evaluations can be helpful when you are reviewing your draft; as noted in Chapter 14, be sure to tell your reviewer about audience expectations and be sure to ask for specific feedback rather than a general response.

A second reviewer liked Margaret's discussion, but asked her about the stones and the black box. Didn't those details foreshadow (give hints or clues about) the ending? Margaret thought about the comment and decided to add a discussion of the details that might hint at the ending.

The Manipulation of the Reader in "The Lottery"

When Tessie Hutchinson's family and neighbors end the morning's activities by stoning her to death, most readers are stunned. A common question is "What did I miss?" But readers have missed nothing. The ending of "The Lottery" is shocking, and Shirley Jackson has created a short story that misdirects the readers and deliberately conceals any warning of what is to come. As a result, the feeling of shock at the violent ending is intensified.

The title of the story is the first misdirection. A lottery suggests a game of chance with a happy winner. The expectations created by the title are deliberately sustained until Mrs. Hutchinson's family draws the special marker. Her bitter refusal to accept the results is a complete surprise to the readers.

The setting of the story, drawn carefully in the opening paragraphs, plays a major part in the readers' expectations. All of the details of the setting suggest a normal, even wholesome atmosphere. The images are of growing, living things—flowers, grass, and children, all in a small town atmosphere lit by warm summer sun. The activities are ordinary: children play, men talk of crops and weather, women gossip. There is nothing in their actions to suggest that these ordinary people expect to commit a monstrous act of violence before lunchtime.

The story is told from the third-person objective point of view. This point of view reports on actions but does not reveal thoughts or feelings. If the readers were shown what even one character was thinking, they would know that the characters are afraid and that something dreadful is coming. But the choice of objective point of view is a deliberate strategy to conceal such information from the readers.

There are details in the story that do connect to the ending. The boys gather rocks in the opening paragraphs, and the ominous black box and ritual are associated with a man named "Graves." Should alert readers recognize these warnings? Small boys often play with rocks and the "ominous" black box is shabby and familiar. It spends the rest of the year, readers are told, in ordinary places like the barn, the post office, and a shelf in the grocery store. The deadly-sounding Mr. Graves is identified as the postmaster; he first appears carrying an ordinary three-legged stool. After the readers know the ending, the rocks and the names and the color of the box become important, but there is no reason to be alarmed or warned by these details on the first reading.

The ending of the story is shocking, and it is also a shock to the readers. That effect is deliberate, intensified by manipulating the readers to expect a happy ending. The title, the setting, and the point of view work deliberately to lead away from the reality of the final grisly scene.

> **Comment** Maintain the attitude that your choices about content and organization are not permanent. Remember that material can be deleted or added or moved at any point, so if you think of additional evidence or a stronger point, include it.

Margaret felt that her presentation was complete and well-organized, and she was confident that it was clear to her readers. Before she labelled it finished, though, she called on her editorial voice. In addition to reviewing grammar and spelling, she was conscious of specific editorial concerns:

- **Does the introduction name both the literary work and the author (if known), even if the title of the paper includes that information?** Novels and longer works are underlined but short stories and most poems (epics like *The Iliad* are an exception) are framed by quotation marks. It is good practice to refer to the genre early in the discussion, including brief tags like "Faulkner's novel *The Sound and the Fury*. . ." or " 'My Last Duchess,' a narrative poem by Robert Browning, . . ."
- **Is the material presented from the third-person point of view?** The writing should emphasize the literary work, not the writer's feelings. With few exceptions, then, first person is inappropriate. An essay is, by definition, an opinion, so it is redundant to say, "It is my opinion that the novel is one of his best." A direct statement, "The

novel is one of his best," is not only more concise; it is also more forceful and more precisely focused on the idea.

- **Is verb tense consistent?** The story was written in the past, so "the
  author wrote. . ." or "the first critical reviews were. . ." But the story
  and characters have an on-going existence, so "the narrative illustrates . . ." and "Mr. Summers says. . ." and "the townspeople are. . ."
  Be alert to the temporal relationship between events in the story that
  creates tense sequences like "Mrs. Hutchinson argues that the selection was unfair."
- **Are words like "clearly" or "obviously" used with caution?** If
  the material is indeed clear and obvious, the discussion might be
  unnecessary. If the material is not so clear or obvious, telling the
  reader that it is merely begs the question and does not substitute for
  explanation and evidence.

When she was satisfied with the content and the form of her writing,
Margaret turned in the paper.

CATALOGUE OF APPROACHES TO ANALYZING LITERATURE

The study of various literary genres could become a lifetime's work, but
this introduction to analyzing and writing about literature can cover only
a few basic considerations. The elements of narrative (prose, poetic, or
dramatic form) covered here can be aids to your pre-writing explorations
of a work. Or, if you have been assigned to evaluate or interpret specific
elements of the work, you can read the appropriate sections.

Plot and Narrative Structure

Not all literature is about a story, but narratives in prose fiction, drama,
and poetry are centered on a series of events. If you are summarizing a
work or reporting on its main events, you must understand the "plot" of
the work.

Causality

It takes more than a record of events to make a plot. E. M. Forster offered
a clear distinction when he wrote, "A plot is also a narrative of events, the
emphasis falling upon causality. 'The king died and then the queen died'
is a story. 'The king died and then the queen died of grief' is a plot. The
time-sequence is preserved, but the sense of causality overshadows it"
(*Aspects of the Novel*, p. 86, HBJ, 1982). When you examine the plot of the
work, then, be sure to look at the connections between actions as closely
as you look at the actions themselves.

Structure

As you study causality, expect to find that the narrative includes some kind of background information or explanation of the opening circumstances, some complication of the opening situation, and some resolution of the problems. There is usually a dramatic moment when the direction of the story is determined; key information is revealed, characters reach significant understandings, or solutions are found. The climax, as such a moment is called, is not necessarily the end of the story. The characters must demonstrate their new-found courage or confront the old enemy or work out the details of the marriage, but the final outcome has been determined at the climax. It is usually followed by the "denouement," as the solutions are implemented, the villains finally dispatched, the remaining details put into place. In actuality, there may be little explanation given and the story may end abruptly, but if you allow for variation, you can find these broad outlines in most narratives. Remember that the pattern of opening situation/complication/resolution indicates logical rather than chronological order. Thus the action might begin with a major problem and shift back to provide background the circumstances. In a short work, expect one major complication and resolution, but in longer works like novels or epic poems, the pattern might be repeated any number of times.

Conflict

Another useful exploration is a study of the kinds of complications that arise in a narrative. Most of the tensions can be placed in one of the following categories ("Character" is used here in the broadest sense. It can designate persons of either gender or nonhuman characters like animals or robots or any character personified with motives.):

Character versus Self The character's primary struggle is inner. It is often a struggle against an emotion like fear or panic, an attempt to maintain (or to establish) control over the self. Struggles to answer questions about religion or about one's place in the universe or to make ethical decisions or to accept the realities of life are also inner conflicts with the self.

Character versus Character Two characters are in direct opposition, perhaps in open physical combat, perhaps in a struggle for emotional control, perhaps in some kind of race or contest. The opposition is personal, but it may or may not be hostile. Such conflicts are usually resolved with the defeat or surrender of one character.

Character versus Society The character struggles against an established authority such as a government, a computer, a military bureaucracy. The opponent is not personal, although it may be personified by a "type" character who, if destroyed, is replaced by another. The conflict might also be with a societal attitude like prejudice; if there is an opposing character who personifies the attitude, any "defeat" is not final because another character will simply step into the conflict.

Character versus Nature The character struggles against natural forces like bitter cold or powerful storms or vast oceans. Struggles against illness or disease can be included here. Expect also struggles with the self against panic or fear and with society against ignorance or fear of a disease.

Character versus the Supernatural Conflicts with demonic forces or with ghostly figures would fit this category. Be alert to hallucinations (conflicts with the self) or human manipulations (conflicts with other characters). Science fiction characters are not supernatural; in fact, most illustrate very human qualities and should be included in the other categories.

When you classify the conflicts of the narrative, remember that combinations of conflicts are not unusual. A character in conflict with a ghost may also struggle with personal fears, with the skepticism of another character or with the restrictions of a bureaucracy.

Chronological Order

As you look at logical patterns and conflicts, you should also consider the chronological order of events. The events of a story occur chronologically (some of them, perhaps, simultaneously), but the story may not have been told chronologically. Remember that the writer makes the decisions about order, so it might be significant that a flashback to a childhood trauma precedes a character's violent behavior in the present. "A Rose for Emily," for example, begins with a death and flashes back to report incidents from Emily's life. But the reminiscences do not occur in chronological order, challenging the reader to sort out events that might have led to other events. The disorder of the events influences the readers' perceptions of the story and thus becomes an area to examine.

Checklists for Exploring Plot

Causality

- Why did X happen?
- Is there a logical explanation?
- Are there coincidences that could have been engineered?
- Who was involved?
- How did various characters feel about X?
- Did anyone influence the event?
- Did other events lead to it?

- What followed from X?
- Did anyone profit by it?
- Who was hurt by it?

Logical Structure

- What is the opening situation?
- Who are the characters?
- What are their emotional connections?
- Financial circumstances?
- What is going on?
- What complications alter the opening circumstances?
- Who arrives?
- What questions are raised?
- What tensions become evident?
- To identify the dramatic turning point or climax, first examine the end of the story. How are problems solved?
- What is the outcome of tensions or conflicts or relationships?
- Then, work backward: At what point did the lovers reach an understanding?
- At what point were the answers to questions first clear?
- At what point did you predict the ending? (Do not be surprised if your answer is, "Not until it happened.")

Conflict

- What tensions are evident in the narrative?
- Are the main struggles internal?
- Does the main character face direct, personal opposition?
- Is the opponent faceless and impersonal, perhaps a power structure or a widespread attitude?
- Are there natural elements to overcome, including climate or terrain or health?
- Are there supernatural forces at work?
- Is there any human explanation for those forces?

Chronological Structure

- In what order do events actually occur?
- In what order are the events presented to the readers?
- What differences are there between the two lists?
- Is there any possible explanation for the differences?
- Is it difficult to put the chronological sequence together?
- Is there a connection between the events that are presented out of order?
- Does the presentation affect understanding of the plot?

1. Read "A Rose for Emily" and list the incidents in chronological order. What connections become clearer as you sort out time frame?

2. Identify the conflicts in "A Rose for Emily." Classify them, using the types discussed here.

3. The logical structure of "The Story of an Hour" follows a standard pattern of background/complication/resolution. Trace that structure.

Additional Readings

A Rose for Emily
William Faulkner

I

1   When Miss Emily Grierson died, our whole town went to her funeral: the men through a sort of respectful affection for a fallen monument, the women mostly out of curiosity to see the inside of her house, which no one save an old manservant—a combined gardener and cook—had seen in at least ten years.

2   It was a big, squarish frame house that had once been white, decorated with cupolas and spires and scrolled balconies in the heavily lightsome style of the seventies, set on what had once been our most select street. But garages and cotton gins had encroached and obliterated even the august names of that neighborhood; only Miss Emily's house was left, lifting its stubborn and coquettish decay above the cotton wagons and the gasoline pumps—an eyesore among eyesores. And now Miss Emily had gone to join the representatives of those august names where they lay in the cedar-bemused cemetery among the ranked and anonymous graves of Union and Confederate soldiers who fell at the battle of Jefferson.

3   Alive, Miss Emily had been a tradition, a duty, and a care; a sort of hereditary obligation upon the town, dating from that day in 1894 when Colonel Sartoris, the mayor—he who fathered the edict that no Negro woman should appear on the streets without an apron—remitted her taxes, the dispensation dating from the death of her father on into perpetuity. Not that Miss Emily would have accepted charity. Colonel Sartoris invented an involved tale to the effect that Miss Emily's father had

loaned money to the town, which the town, as a matter of business, preferred this way of repaying. Only a man of Colonel Sartoris' generation and thought could have invented it, and only a woman could have believed it.

4   When the next generation, with its more modern ideas, became mayors and aldermen, this arrangement created some little dissatisfaction. On the first of the year they mailed her a tax notice. February came, and there was no reply. They wrote her a formal letter asking her to call at the sheriff's office at her convenience. A week later the mayor wrote her himself, offering to call or to send his car for her, and received in reply a note on paper of an archaic shape, in a thin, flowing calligraphy in faded ink, to the effect that she no longer went out at all. The tax notice was also enclosed, without comment.

5   They called a special meeting of the Board of Aldermen. A deputation waited upon her, knocked at the door through which no visitor had passed since she ceased giving china-painting lessons eight or ten years earlier. They were admitted by the old Negro into a dim hall from which a stairway mounted into still more shadow. It smelled of dust and disuse—a close, dank smell. The Negro led them into the parlor. It was furnished in heavy, leather-covered furniture. When the Negro opened the blinds of one window, they could see that the leather was cracked; and when they sat down, a faint dust rose sluggishly about their thighs, spinning with slow motes in the single sun-ray. On a tarnished gilt easel before the fireplace stood a crayon portrait of Miss Emily's father.

6   They rose when she entered—a small, fat woman in black, with a thin gold chain descending to her waist and vanishing into her belt, leaning on an ebony cane with a tarnished gold head. Her skeleton was small and spare; perhaps that was why what would have been merely plumpness in another was obesity in her. She looked bloated, like a body long submerged in motionless water, and of that pallid hue. Her eyes lost in the fatty ridges of her face, looked like two small pieces of coal pressed into a lump of dough as they moved from one face to another while the visitors stated their errand.

7   She did not ask them to sit. She just stood in the door and listened quietly until the spokesman came to a stumbling halt. Then they could hear the invisible watch ticking at the end of the gold chain.

8   Her voice was dry and cold. "I have no taxes in Jefferson. Colonel Sartoris explained it to me. Perhaps one of you can gain access to the city records and satisfy yourselves."

9   "But we have. We are the city authorities, Miss Emily. Didn't you get a notice from the sheriff, signed by him?"

10   "I received a paper, yes." Miss Emily said. "Perhaps he considers himself the sheriff. . . . I have no taxes in Jefferson."

11   "But there is nothing on the books to show that, you see. We must go by the—"

12   "See Colonel Sartoris. I have no taxes in Jefferson."

13   "But, Miss Emily—"

14   "See Colonel Sartoris." (Colonel Sartoris had been dead almost ten years.) "I have no taxes in Jefferson. Tobe?" The Negro appeared. "Show these gentlemen out."

II

15   So she vanquished them, horse and foot, just as she had vanquished their fathers thirty years before about the smell. That was two years after her father's death and a short time after her sweetheart—the one we believed would marry her—had deserted her. After her father's death she went out very little; after her sweetheart went away, people hardly saw her at all. A few of the ladies had the temerity to call, but were not received, and the only sign of life about the place was the Negro man—a young man then—going in and out with a market basket.

16   "Just as if a man—any man—could keep a kitchen properly," the ladies said; so they were not surprised when the smell developed. It was another link between the gross, teeming world and the high and mighty Griersons.

17   A neighbor, a woman, complained to the mayor, Judge Stevens, eighty years old.

18   "But what will you have me do about it, madam?" He said.

19   "Why, send her word to stop it," the woman said. "Isn't there a law?"

20   "I'm sure that won't be necessary," Judge Stevens said. "It's probably just a snake or a rat that nigger of hers killed in the yard. I'll speak to him about it."

21   The next day he received two more complaints, one from a man who came in diffident deprecation. "We really must do something about it, Judge. I'd be the last one in the world to bother Miss Emily, but we've got to do something." That night the Board of Aldermen met—three graybeards and one younger man, a member of the rising generation.

22   "It's simple enough," he said. "Send her word to have her place cleaned up. Give her a certain time to do it in, and if she don't. . . ."

23   "Dammit, sir," Judge Stevens said, "will you accuse a lady to her face of smelling bad?"

24   So the next night, after midnight, four men crossed Miss Emily's lawn and slunk about the house like burglars, sniffing along the base of the brickwork and at the cellar openings while one of them performed a regular sowing motion with his hand out of a sack slung from his shoulder. They broke open the cellar door and sprinkled lime there, and in all the outbuildings. As they recrossed the lawn, a window that had been dark was lighted and Miss Emily sat in it, the light behind her, and her upright torso motionless as that of an idol. They crept quietly across the lawn and into the shadow of the locusts that lined the street. After a week or two the smell went away.

25   That was when people had begun to feel really sorry for her. People in our town, remembering how old lady Wyatt, her great-aunt, had gone

completely crazy at last, believed that the Griersons held themselves a little too high for what they really were. None of the young men were quite good enough for Miss Emily and such. We had long thought of them as a tableau, Miss Emily a slender figure in white in the background, her father a spraddled silhouette in the foreground, his back to her and clutching a horsewhip, the two of them framed by the backflung front door. So when she got to be thirty and was still single, we were not pleased exactly, but vindicated; even with insanity in the family she wouldn't have turned down all of her chances if they had really materialized.

26 When her father died, it got about that the house was all that was left to her; and in a way, people were glad. At last they could pity Miss Emily. Being left alone, and a pauper, she had become humanized. Now she too would know the old thrill and the old despair of a penny more or less.

27 The day after his death all the ladies prepared to call at the house and offer condolence and aid, as is our custom. Miss Emily met them at the door, dressed as usual and with no trace of grief on her face. She told them that her father was not dead. She did that for three days, with the ministers calling on her, and the doctors, trying to persuade her to let them dispose of the body. Just as they were about to resort to law and force, she broke down, and they buried her father quickly.

28 We did not say she was crazy then. We believed she had to do that. We remembered all the young men her father had driven away, and we knew that with nothing left, she would have to cling to that which had robbed her, as people will.

III

29 She was sick for a long time. When we saw her again, her hair was cut short, making her look like a girl, with a vague resemblance to those angels in colored church windows—sort of tragic and serene.

30 The town had just let the contracts for paving the sidewalks, and in the summer after her father's death they began the work. The construction company came with niggers and mules and machinery, and a foreman named Homer Barron, a Yankee—a big, dark, ready man, with a big voice and eyes lighter than his face. The little boys would follow in groups to hear him cuss the niggers, and the niggers singing in time to the rise and fall of picks. Pretty soon he knew everybody in town. Whenever you heard a lot of laughing anywhere about the square, Homer Barron would be in the center of the group. Presently, we began to see him and Miss Emily on Sunday afternoons driving in the yellow-wheeled buggy and the matched team of bays from the livery stable.

31 At first we were glad that Miss Emily would have an interest, because the ladies all said, "Of course a Grierson would not think seriously of a Northerner, a day laborer." But there were still others, older people, who said that even grief could not cause a real lady to forget noblesse oblige—without calling it noblesse oblige. They just said, "Poor Emily. Her kinsfolk should come to her." She had some kin in Alabama; but years ago her

father had fallen out with them over the estate of old lady Wyatt, the crazy woman, and there was no communication between the two families. They had not even been represented at the funeral.

32   And as soon as the old people said, "Poor Emily," the whispering began. "Do you suppose it's really so?" they said to one another. "Of course it is. What else could. . . ." This behind their hands; rustling of craned silk and satin behind jalousies closed upon the sun of Sunday afternoon as the thin, swift clop-clop-clop of the matched team passed: "Poor Emily."

33   She carried her head high enough—even when we believed that she was fallen. It was as if she demanded more than ever the recognition of her dignity as the last Grierson; as if it had wanted that touch of earthiness to reaffirm her imperviousness. Like when she bought the rat poison, the arsenic. That was over a year after they had begun to say "Poor Emily," and while the two female cousins were visiting her.

34   "I want some poison," she said to the druggist. She was over thirty then, still a slight woman, though thinner than usual, with cold, haughty black eyes in a face the flesh of which was strained across the temples and about the eyesockets as you imagine a lighthouse-keeper's face ought to look. "I want some poison," she said.

35   "Yes, Miss Emily. What kind? For rats and such? I'd recom——"

36   "I want the best you have. I don't care what kind."

37   The druggist named several. "They'll kill anything up to an elephant. But what you want is——"

38   "Arsenic," Miss Emily said. "Is that a good one?"

39   "Is . . . arsenic? Yes, ma'am. But what you want——"

40   "I want arsenic."

41   The druggist looked down at her. She looked back at him, erect, her face like a strained flag. "Why, of course," the druggist said. "If that's what you want. But the law requires you to tell what you are going to use if for."

42   Miss Emily just stared at him, her head tilted back in order to look him eye for eye, until he looked away and went and got the arsenic and wrapped it up. The Negro delivery boy brought her the package; the druggist didn't come back. When she opened the package at home there was written on the box, under the skull and bones: "For rats."

IV

43   So the next day we all said, "She will kill herself"; and we said it would be the best thing. When she had first begun to be seen with Homer Barron, we had said, "She will marry him." Then we said, "She will persuade him yet," because Homer himself had remarked—he liked men, and it was known that he drank with the younger men in the Elks' Club—that he was not a marrying man. Later we said, "Poor Emily" behind the jalousies as they passed on Sunday afternoon in the glittering buggy, Miss Emily with her head high and Homer Barron with his hat cocked and a cigar in his teeth, reins and whip in a yellow glove.

44   Then some of the ladies began to say that it was a disgrace to the town and a bad example to the young people. The men did not want to interfere, but at last the ladies forced the Baptist minister—Miss Emily's people were Episcopal—to call upon her. He would never divulge what happened during that interview, but he refused to go back again. The next Sunday they again drove about the streets, and the following day the minister's wife wrote to Miss Emily's relations in Alabama.

45   So she had blood-kin under her roof again and we sat back to watch developments. At first nothing happened. Then we were sure that they were to be married. We learned that Miss Emily had been to the jeweler's and ordered a man's toilet set in silver, with the letters H.B. on each piece. Two days later we learned that she had bought a complete outfit of men's clothing, including a nightshirt, and we said, "They are married." We were really glad. We were glad because the two female cousins were even more Grierson than Miss Emily had ever been.

46   So we were not surprised when Homer Barron—the streets had been finished some time since—was gone. We were a little disappointed that there was not a public blowing-off, but we believed that he had gone on to prepare for Miss Emily's coming, or to give her a chance to get rid of the cousins. (By that time it was a cabal, and we were all Miss Emily's allies to help circumvent the cousins.) Sure enough, after another week they departed. And, as we had expected all along, within three days Homer Barron was back in town. A neighbor saw the Negro man admit him at the kitchen door at dusk one evening.

47   And that was the last we saw of Homer Barron. And of Miss Emily for some time. The Negro man went in and out with the market basket, but the front door remained closed. Now and then we would see her at the window for a moment, as the men did that night when they sprinkled the lime, but for almost six months she did not appear on the streets. Then we knew that this was to be expected too; as if that quality of her father which had thwarted her woman's life so many times had been too virulent and too furious to die.

48   When we next saw Miss Emily, she had grown fat and her hair was turning gray. During the next few years it grew grayer and grayer until it attained an even pepper-and-salt iron-gray, when it ceased turning. Up to the day of her death at seventy-four it was still that vigorous iron-gray, like the hair of an active man.

49   From that time on her front door remained closed, save during a period of six or seven years, when she was about forty, during which she gave lessons in china-painting. She fitted up a studio in one of the downstairs rooms, where the daughters and granddaughters of Colonel Sartoris' contemporaries were sent to her with the same regularity and in the same spirit that they were sent to church on Sundays with a twenty-five-cent piece for the collection plate. Meanwhile her taxes had been remitted.

50   Then the newer generation became the backbone and the spirit of the town, and the painting pupils grew up and fell away and did not send

their children to her with boxes of color and tedious brushes and pictures cut from the ladies' magazines. The front door closed upon the last one and remained closed for good. When the town got free postal delivery, Miss Emily alone refused to let them fasten the metal numbers above her door and attach a mailbox to it. She would not listen to them.

51   Daily, monthly, yearly we watched the Negro grow grayer and more stooped, going in and out with the market basket. Each December we sent her a tax notice, which would be returned by the post office a week later, unclaimed. Now and then we would see her in one of the downstairs windows—she had evidently shut up the top floor of the house—like the carven torso of an idol in a niche, looking or not looking at us, we could never tell which. Thus she passed from generation to generation—dear, inescapable, impervious, tranquil, and perverse.

52   And so she died. Fell ill in the house filled with dust and shadows, with only a doddering Negro man to wait on her. We did not even know she was sick; we had long since given up trying to get any information from the Negro. He talked to no one, probably not even to her, for his voice had grown harsh and rusty, as if from disuse.

53   She died in one of the downstairs rooms, in a heavy walnut bed with a curtain, her gray head propped on a pillow yellow and moldy with age and lack of sunlight.

V

54   The Negro met the first of the ladies at the front door and let them in, with their hushed, sibilant voices and their quick, curious glances, and then he disappeared. He walked right through the house and out the back and was not seen again.

55   The two female cousins came at once. They held the funeral on the second day, with the town coming to look at Miss Emily beneath a mass of bought flowers, with the crayon face of her father musing profoundly above the bier and the ladies sibilant and macabre; and the very old men—some in their brushed Confederate uniforms—on the porch and the lawn, talking of Miss Emily as if she had been a contemporary of theirs, believing that they had danced with her and courted her perhaps, confusing time with its mathematical progression, as the old do, to whom all the past is not a diminishing road but, instead, a huge meadow which no winter ever quite touches, divided from them now by the narrow bottleneck of the most recent decade of years.

56   Already we knew that there was one room in that region above stairs which no one had seen in forty years, and which would have to be forced. They waited until Miss Emily was decently in the ground before they opened it.

57   The violence of breaking down the door seemed to fill this room with pervading dust. A thin, acrid pall as of the tomb seemed to lie everywhere upon this room decked and furnished as for a bridal: upon the valance curtains of faded rose color, upon the rose-shaded lights, upon the

dressing table, upon the delicate array of crystal and the man's toilet things backed with tarnished silver, silver so tarnished that the monogram was obscured. Among them lay a collar and tie, as if they had just been removed, which, lifted, left upon the surface a pale crescent in the dust. Upon a chair hung the suit, carefully folded; beneath it the two mute shoes and the discarded socks.

58   The man himself lay in the bed.

59   For a long while we just stood there, looking down at the profound and fleshless grin. The body had apparently once lain in the attitude of an embrace, but now the long sleep that outlasts love, that conquers even the grimace of love, had cuckolded him. What was left of him, rotted beneath what was left of the nightshirt, had become inextricable from the bed in which he lay; and upon him and upon the pillow beside him lay that even coating of the patient and biding dust.

60   Then we noticed that in the second pillow was the indentation of a head. One of us lifted something from it, and leaning forward, that faint and invisible dust dry and acrid in the nostrils, we saw a long strand of iron-gray hair.

The Story of an Hour
Kate Chopin

1   Knowing that Mrs. Mallard was a afflicted with a heart trouble, great care was taken to break to her as gently as possible the news of her husband's death.

2   It was her sister Josephine who told her, in broken sentences: veiled hints that revealed in half concealing. Her husband's friend Richards was there, too, near her. It was he who had been in the newspaper office when intelligence of the railroad disaster was received, with Brently Mallard's name leading the list of "killed." He had only taken the time to assure himself of its truth by a second telegram, and had hastened to forestall any less careful, less tender friend in bearing the sad message.

3   She did not hear the story as many women have heard the same, with a paralyzed inability to accept its significance. She wept at once, with sudden wild abandonment, in her sister's arms. When the storm of grief had spent itself she went away to her room alone. She would have no one follow her.

4   There stood, facing the open window, a comfortable, roomy armchair. Into this she sank, pressed down by a physical exhaustion that haunted her body and seemed to reach into her soul.

5   She could see in the open square before her house the tops of trees that were all aquiver with the new spring life. The delicious breath of rain was in the air. In the street below a peddler was crying his wares. The notes of a distant song which some one was singing reached her faintly, and countless sparrows were twittering in the eaves.

6   There were patches of blue sky showing here and there through the clouds that had met and piled one above the other in the west facing her window.

7   She sat with her head thrown back upon the cushion of the chair, quite motionless, except when a sob came up into her throat and shook her, as a child who has cried itself to sleep continues to sob in its dreams.

8   She was young, with a fair, calm face, whose lines bespoke repression and even a certain strength. But now there was a dull stare in her eyes, whose gaze was fixed away off yonder on one of those patches of blue sky. It was not a glance of reflection, but rather indicated a suspension of intelligent thought.

9   There was something coming to her and she was waiting for it, fearfully. What was it? She did not know; it was too subtle and elusive to name. But she felt it, creeping out of the sky, reaching toward her through the sounds, the scents, the color that filled the air.

10   Now her bosom rose and fell tumultuously. She was beginning to recognize this thing that was approaching to possess her, and she was striving to beat it back with her will—as powerless as her two white slender hands would have been.

11   When she abandoned herself a little whispered word escaped her slightly parted lips. She said it over and over under her breath: "free, free, free!" The vacant stare and the look of terror that had followed it went from her eyes. They stayed keen and bright. Her pulses beat fast, and the coursing blood warmed and relaxed every inch of her body.

12   She did not stop to ask if it were or were not a monstrous joy that held her. A clear and exalted perception enabled her to dismiss the suggestion as trivial.

13   She knew that she would weep again when she saw the kind, tender hands folded in death; the face that had never looked save with love upon her, fixed and gray and dead. But she saw beyond that bitter moment a long procession of years to come that would belong to her absolutely. And she opened and spread her arms out to them in welcome.

14   There would be not one to live for her during those coming years; she would live for herself. There would be no powerful will bending hers in that blind persistence with which men and women believe they have a right to impose a private will upon a fellow-creature. A kind intention or a cruel intention made the act seem no less a crime as she looked upon it in that brief moment of illumination.

15   And yet she had loved him—sometimes. Often she had not. What did it matter! What could love, the unsolved mystery, count for in face of this possession of self-assertion which she suddenly recognized as the strongest impulse of her being!

16   "Free! Body and soul free!" she kept whispering.

17   Josephine was kneeling before the closed door with her lips to the keyhole, imploring for admission. "Louise, open the door! I beg; open the

door—you will make yourself ill. What are you doing, Louise? For heaven's sake open the door."

18   "Go away. I am not making myself ill." No; She was drinking in a very elixir of life through that open window.

19   Her fancy was running riot along those days ahead of her. Spring days, and summer days, and all sorts of days that would be her own. She breathed a quick prayer that life might be long. It was only yesterday she had thought with a shudder that life might be long.

20   She arose at length and opened the door to her sister's importunities. There was a feverish triumph in her eyes, and she carried herself unwittingly like a goddess of Victory. She clasped her sister's waist, and together they descended the stairs. Richards stood waiting for them at the bottom.

21   Some one was opening the front door with a latchkey. It was Brently Mallard who entered, a little travel-stained, composedly carrying his grip-sack and umbrella. He had been far from the scene of accident, and did not even know there had been one. He stood amazed at Josephine's piercing cry; at Richards' quick motion to screen him from the view of his wife.

22   But Richards was too late.

23   When the doctors came they said she had died of heart disease—of joy that kills.

Point of View/Persona

One of the choices made by a writer is the point of view from which the story is told. Should a character involved in the story tell what happens? Should a bystander? Should a third-person narrator explain the events? The options include a first-person narrator who is directly or indirectly involved in the story, an omniscient third-person narrator who explains not only action but also thoughts and feelings of all characters, a third-person narrator whose knowledge is limited to one character's thoughts and feelings, and an objective third-person narrator who reports observable details without explaining the inner workings of any characters. Since stage plays present incidents from the fourth class, with only the characters' observable actions and speeches for information, the objective point of view is also called "dramatic."

At stake is more than a choice of pronouns. Each point of view has its own relationship to the work and to the readers. As you examine literature to identify point of view, consider the effect that choice of narrator can have on the work and on the readers' perceptions of it:

First-Person Easily recognized by its use of "I" and "we" pronouns, first-person point of view presents the material from the perspective of a character who is directly or indirectly involved in the action. The first-person perspective involves readers with a first-hand participant.

It tends to create a bond between reader and narrator, often arousing sympathy for a likable narrator and intensifying the readers' reactions to the story. If the narrator is unpleasant, readers may feel repelled, even disgusted, by the whole story. If the narrator feels indignation or pity, readers are subtly encouraged to react the same way.

When you identify a first-person perspective, be aware of the tendency to identify with the narrator. Also be aware that such a narrator is limited. A participant in the story cannot logically be everywhere or know everything, so you will see or hear only what that narrator would logically encounter. The narrator is also limited by the nature of the character, by factors like age, stability, intelligence, background, and maturity. For example, a small child cannot understand the complexities of actions that he reports, and a madwoman cannot be expected to narrate logically or accurately. Writers are of course aware of these limitations when they select first-person perspective. You may be expected to read between the lines to learn what the narrator is not able to realize.

Third-Person Omniscient The narrator who sits somewhere above the action and moves freely through the minds of all characters and behind closed doors is almost god-like. This narrator presents the feelings of characters or incidents from various locations without limitations.

This point of view has three readily observable effects on the readers. First, there is also an aura of credibility attached to such a narrator. A first-person narrator might hallucinate or be misled; an omniscient narrator's report is not suspect. If one character manufactures a ghostly apparition, the omniscient narrator is aware of the pretense. If characters are acting in conflict with their feelings, the omniscient narrator knows.

A second effect follows logically from this unquestioned credibility. Using the omniscient point of view reveals all to the readers. Plot twists or shocking revelations must come from a new development because the narrator has had access to thoughts and feelings of all characters.

A third effect is that the third-person narrator is somewhat distanced from the readers. The omniscient perspective does not create the emotional bond that the first-person does; the narrator is not a character that becomes "real" to the readers. Such emotional distance is neither advantage nor disadvantage. It is simply a variation that must be considered in a thorough discussion of point of view.

Limited Omniscient It is easier to define this perspective by contrasting it to the omniscient. The narrator here does not have total access to all incidents or to the inner workings of all characters. The most common limitation is that the narrator reports what is known or felt by only one character. The point of view is similar to the first-person in that it presents the narrative from one person's perspective, but it retains the aura of credibility and the emotional distance of the omniscient view.

Objective The objective narrator has no emotional connection to any character or access to any inner mental processes. Instead, like a fly on the wall, this narrator describes what can be seen or heard. You will recognize that dramatic performances use this perspective. Even a stage character's soliloquy may not accurately represent inner reactions, so you are left to make decisions about motive or nature or ethics based on what you observe. The objective narrator leaves you with a similar responsibility. Without commentary on the characters or incidents, you must be an active participant in the narrative, interpreting and reacting to what you are told. The writer, of course, will influence your reaction by the selection of details, but you are led to a judgment rather than told what to think.

An immediate effect of this perspective is that the writer can easily conceal information from the readers. Strange occurrences or odd gatherings are described but not interpreted, making it possible for the writer to surprise, even shock with an unforeseen ending.

Most discussions of point of view include more than identification. Notice that the sample below also considers the relationship between reader and material.

The third-person narrator in "The Demon Lover" creates an air of credibility that the first-person narrator of "The Yellow Wall-Paper" does not. The first-person narrator is descending into madness, and as soon as the reader recognizes her fragile mental state, her interpretations of incidents and even her descriptions of the woman crawling about in the garden are not accepted at face value. In contrast, the third-person narrator of "The Demon Lover" is thoroughly credible. The letter on the hall table, for example, might be explained as hysterical hallucination if a first-person narrator had reported it. But the reader believes, without any hesitation, that the letter is real and that its appearance is mysterious.

When you identify the point of view of a work, in all cases it is important that you distinguish the **narrator** from the writer. The narrator, also called the **persona,** may be similar to the writer but is not identical. The persona is created by the writer, designed to suit the purposes of the narrative. Even if the character is expressing the feelings of the narrator, there is a separation between the two that must be recognized.

Checklists for Exploring Point of View

Identify

First-Person

- Does the narrator use first-person pronouns like "I" or "we"?
- Is the narrator part of the action or an observer?
- Is the observer one of the minor characters?
- Does the observer seem to be watching from inside or outside of the action?
- Is the narrator reminiscing about past events or reporting on current incidents?
- Can the narrator be believed?
- Is the narrator old enough or mature enough or intelligent enough or sane enough to understand the narrative?
- Does the narrator have any biases or any desire to conceal something from the audience?

Omniscient

- If the narrator is not first-person, what knowledge does the narrator have?
- Does he/she seem to know what characters are thinking?
- Does he/she present information from varied situations?
- Does he/she seem to be present at all of these events?

Limited Omniscient

- Does the third-person narrator present information from only one character's inner self?
- Is the information limited to one perspective?
- Are the pronouns third person, like "she" or "he" or "they"?

Objective

- Does the narrator report and describe only what could be seen?
- Are the characters' feelings or thoughts expressed only by the characters?
- Are the readers left to label the characters' behavior or personalities?

Analyze

- Is there a situation defining speaker/audience in the work?
- Is it addressed to someone?
- Is it a journal or diary or letter?
- Is someone telling the story to an identified audience?
- Do I trust this narrator?
- Do I believe the reports?

- Do I see anything that the narrator has not connected or has tried to conceal from the audience?
- How do I feel about this narrator?
- Do I respect/pity/love/hate this narrator?
- Do I care about the outcome of the situation?
- How does the narrator seem to feel about the characters or incidents reported?
- Have the narrator's feelings influenced mine?
- Has this point of view kept information from the readers?
- Has any information vital to the outcome of the story been concealed?
- Was the concealment consistent with this perspective?
- What was the effect of such concealment?
- Was the reader forced to read more actively?
- Was the ending surprising?
- How might the narrative have changed with a different point of view?
- What information would have been known or unknown?

Y O U R   T U R N

1. Identify the points of view in the passages below. Try rewriting the passages from different perspectives. Is the effect of the new passage any different?

   a. She had never been so angry in her life. He sat before her, looking smug and complacent, and she knew that he was very pleased with himself. She wondered what he would do next, now that he had managed to get the office next to hers. Would he take advantage of their old relationship to make her days a series of snide, knowing remarks? She quickly stifled her impulse to do something childish, but she had more trouble resisting violence. Mustering her self-control, she opted for a sweeping but dignified retreat that totally ignored his presence.

   b. That's my last Duchess painted on the wall,
   Looking as if she were alive. I call
   That piece a wonder, now; Fra Pandolf's hands
   Worked busily a day, and there she stands.
   Will't please you sit and look at her?. . .

   c. At first he sat, calmly looking at his hands and occasionally picking at invisible lint on his cuffs. He was the model of polite expectancy, seeming alert to his surroundings yet showing no signs of boredom. He sat on the bench for almost thirty minutes before standing, stretching slightly, and walking to the window. Returning to the sitting area, he scanned the reading material but tossed each ancient magazine onto the table with a quick slapping motion. His image began to show signs of strain, the eyes flickering quickly each time noises from the hall intruded on the silence. He shifted in his seat and began to sigh with increasing frequency.

d. Each of them had separate plans for the money. Jamie saw the family at the beach. He could picture the children in the waves, fearful at first but soon oblivious to the salty splashing. Eleanor had different ideas. Her vision was a mountain retreat with clear, icy cold streams tumbling over rocks. She could feel the late spring chill as she scrambled over the rocky crossing, and she shivered with anticipation.

2. Identify the point of view in "A Rose for Emily." How does that narrator's knowledge limit the story? How does that narrator's feeling about Miss Emily affect the readers' feelings about her?

3. Identify the narrator of "My Last Duchess." How does that narrator rate as a reliable narrator? Give examples of the narrator's observations that should not be accepted at face value.

Additional Readings

The Demon Lover
Elizabeth Bowen

1   Towards the end of her day in London Mrs. Drover went round to her shut-up house to look for several things she wanted to take away. Some belonged to herself, some to her family, who were by now used to their country life. It was late August; it had been a steamy, showery day: at the moment the trees down the pavement glittered in an escape of humid yellow afternoon sun. Against the next batch of clouds, already piling up ink-dark, broken chimneys and parapets stood out. In her once familiar street, as in any unused channel, an unfamiliar queerness had silted up: a cat wove itself in and out of railings, but no human eye watched Mrs. Drover's return. Shifting some parcels under her arm, she slowly forced round her latchkey in an unwilling lock, then gave the door, which had warped, a push with her knee. Dead air came out to meet her as she went in.

2   The staircase window having been boarded up, no light came down into the hall. But one door, she could just see, stood ajar, so she went quickly through into the room and unshuttered the big window in there. Now the prosaic woman, looking about her, was more perplexed than she knew by everything that she saw, by traces of her long former habit of life—the yellow smoke-stain up the white marble mantelpiece, the ring left by a vase on the top of the escritoire; the bruise in the wallpaper where, on the door being thrown open widely, the china handle had always hit the wall.

The piano, having gone away to be stored, had left what looked like claw-marks on its part of the parquet. Though not much dust had seeped in, each object wore a film of another kind; and, the only ventilation being the chimney, the whole drawing-room smelled of the cold hearth. Mrs. Drover put down her parcels on the escritoire and left the room to proceed upstairs; the things she wanted were in a bedroom closet.

3   She had been anxious to see how the house was—the part-time care-taker she shared with some neighbors was away this week on his holiday, known to be not yet back. At the best of times he did not look in often, and she was never sure that she trusted him. There were some cracks in the structure, left by the last bombing, on which she was anxious to keep an eye. Not that one could do anything—

4   A shaft of refracted daylight now lay across the hall. She stopped dead and stared at the hall table—on this lay a letter addressed to her.

5   She thought first—then the caretaker must be back. All the same, who, seeing the house shuttered, would have dropped a letter in at the box? It was not a circular, it was not a bill. And the post office redirected, to the address in the country, everything for her that came through the post. The caretaker (even if he were back) did not know she was due in London today—her call here had been planned to be a surprise—so his negligence in the manner of this letter, leaving it to wait in the dusk and the dust, annoyed her. Annoyed, she picked up the letter, which bore no stamp. But it cannot be important, or they would know . . . She took the letter rapidly upstairs with her, without a stop to look at the writing till she reached what had been her bedroom, where she let in light. The room looked over the garden and other gardens: the sun had gone in; as the clouds sharp-ened and lowered, the trees and rank lawns seemed already to smoke with dark. Her reluctance to look again at the letter came from the fact that she felt intruded upon—and by someone contemptuous of her ways. However, in the tenseness preceding the fall of rain she read it: it was a few lines.

> Dear Kathleen: You will not have forgotten that today is our anniversary, and the day we said. The years have gone by at once slowly and fast. In view of the fact that nothing has changed, I shall rely upon you to keep your promise. I was sorry to see you leave London, but was satisfied that you would be back in time. You may expect me, therefore, at the hour arranged. Until then . . .
>
> K.

Mrs. Drover looked for the date: it was today's. She dropped the letter on to the bed-springs, then picked it up to see the writing again—her lips, beneath the remains of lipstick, beginning to go white. She felt so much the change in her own face that she went to the mirror, polished a clear patch in it, and looked at once urgently and stealthily in. She was con-fronted by a woman of forty-four, with eyes starting out under a hat-brim that had been rather carelessly pulled down. She had not put on any more powder since she left the shop where she ate her solitary tea. The pearls her husband had given her on their marriage hung loose around her now rather thinner throat, slipping in the V of the pink wool jumper her sister knitted last autumn as they sat round the fire. Mrs. Drover's most normal expression was one of controlled worry, but of assent. Since the birth of the third of her little boys, attended by a quite serious illness, she had had an intermittent muscular flicker to the left of her mouth, but in spite of this she could always sustain a manner that was at once energetic and calm.

6   Turning from her own face as precipitately as she had gone to meet it, she went to the chest where the things were, unlocked it, threw up the lid, and knelt to search. But as rain began to come crashing down she could not keep from looking over her shoulder at the stripped bed on which the letter lay. Behind the blanket of rain the clock of the church that still stood struck six—with rapidly heightening apprehension she counted each of the slow strokes. "The hour arranged . . . My God, " she said, "what hour? How should I . . .? After twenty-five years . . ."

7   The young girl talking to the soldier in the garden had not ever completely seen his face. It was dark; they were saying goodbye under a tree. Now and then—for it felt, from not seeing him at this intense moment, as though she had never seen him at all—she verified his presence for these few moments longer by putting out a hand, which he each time pressed, without very much kindness, and painfully, on to one of the breast buttons of his uniform. That cut of the button on the palm of her hand was, principally, what she was to carry away. This was so near the end of a leave from France that she could only wish him already gone. It was August 1916. Being not kissed, being drawn away from and looked at intimidated Kathleen till she imagined spectral glitters in the place of his eyes. Turning away and looking back up the lawn she saw, through branches of trees, the drawing-room window light: she caught a breath for the moment when she could go running back there into the safe arms of her mother and sister, and cry: "What shall I do, what shall I do? He has gone."

8   Hearing her catch her breath, her fiancé said, without feeling: "Cold?"
9   "You're going away such a long way."
10   "Not so far as you think."
11   "I don't understand?"
12   "You don't have to," he said. "You will. You know what we said."
13   "But that was—suppose you—I mean, suppose."
14   "I shall be with you," he said, "sooner or later. You won't forget that. You need do nothing but wait."
15   Only a little more than a minute later she was free to run up the silent lawn. Looking in through the window at her mother and sister, who did not for the moment perceive her, she already felt that unnatural promise drive down between her and the rest of all human kind. No other way of

having given herself could have made her feel so apart, lost and foresworn. She could not have plighted a more sinister troth.

16   Kathleen behaved well when, some months later, her fiancé was reported missing, presumed killed. Her family not only supported her but were able to praise her courage without stint because they could not regret, as a husband for her, the man they knew almost nothing about. They hoped she would, in a year or two, console herself—and had it been only a question of consolation things might have gone much straighter ahead. But her trouble, behind just a little grief, was a complete dislocation from everything. She did not reject other lovers, for these failed to appear: for years she failed to attract men—and with the approach of her thirties she became natural enough to share her family's anxiousness on this score. She began to put herself out, to wonder; and at thirty-two she was very greatly relieved to find herself being courted by William Drover. She married him, and the two of them settled down in this quiet, arboreal part of Kensington: in this house the years piled up, her children were born, and they all lived till they were driven out by the bombs of the next war. Her movements as Mrs. Drover were circumscribed, and she dismissed any idea that they were still watched.

17   As things were—dead or living the letter-writer sent her only a threat. Unable, for some minutes, to go on kneeling with her back exposed to the empty room, Mrs. Drover rose from the chest to sit on an upright chair whose back was firmly against the wall. The desuetude of her former bedroom, her married London home's whole air of being a cracked cup from which memory, with its reassuring power, had either evaporated or leaked away, made a crisis—and at just this crisis the letter-writer had, knowledgeably, struck. The hollowness of the house this evening canceled years on years of voices, habits, and steps. Through the shut windows she only heard rain fall on the roofs around. To rally herself, she said she was in a mood—and for two or three seconds shutting her eyes, told herself that she had imagined the letter. But she opened them—there it lay on the bed.

18   On the supernatural side of the letter's entrance she was not permitting her mind to dwell. Who, in London, knew she meant to call at the house today? Evidently, however, this had been known. The caretaker, had he come back, had had no cause to expect her: he would have taken the letter in his pocket, to forward it, at his own time, through the post. There was no other sign that the caretaker had been in—but, if not? Letters dropped in at doors of deserted houses do not fly or walk to tables in halls. They do not sit on the dust of empty tables with the air of certainty that they will be found. There is needed some human hand—but nobody but the caretaker had a key. Under circumstances she did not care to consider, a house can be entered without a key. It was possible that she was not alone now. She might be being waited for, downstairs. Waited for—until when? Until "the hour arranged." At least that was not six o'clock: six has struck.

19   She rose from the chair and went over and locked the door.

20   The thing was, to get out. To fly? No, not that: she had to catch her train. As a woman whose utter dependability was the keystone of her family life she was not willing to return to the country, to her husband, her little boys, and her sister, without the objects she had come up to fetch. Resuming work at the chest she set about making up a number of parcels in a rapid, fumbling-decisive way. These, with her shopping parcels, would be too much to carry; these meant a taxi—at the thought of the taxi her heart went up and her normal breathing resumed. I will ring up the taxi now; the taxi cannot come too soon: I shall hear the taxi out there running its engine, till I walk calmly down to it through the hall. I'll ring up—But no: the telephone is cut off . . . She tugged at a knot she had tied wrong.

21   The idea of flight . . . He was never kind to me, not really. I don't remember him kind at all. Mother said he never considered me. He was set on me, that was what it was—not love. Not love, not meaning a person well. What did he do, to make me promise like that? I can't remember—But she found that she could.

22   She remembered with such dreadful acuteness that the twenty-five years since then dissolved like smoke and she instinctively looked for the weal left by the button on the palm of her hand. She remembered not only all that he said and did but the complete suspension of her existence during that August week. I was not myself—they all told me so at the time. She remembered—but with one white burning blank as where acid has dropped on a photograph: *under no conditions* could she remember his face.

23   So, wherever he may be waiting, I shall not know him. You have no time to run from a face you do not expect.

24   The thing was to get to the taxi before any clock struck what could be the hour. She would slip down the street and round the side of the square to where the square gave on the main road. She would return in the taxi, safe, to her own door, and bring the solid driver into the house with her to pick up the parcels from room to room. The idea of the taxi driver made her decisive, bold: she unlocked her door, went to the top of the staircase, and listened down.

25   She heard nothing—but while she was hearing nothing the passé air of the staircase was disturbed by a draught that traveled up to her face. It emanated from the basement: down there a door or window was being opened by someone who chose this moment to leave the house.

26   The rain had stopped; the pavements steamily shone as Mrs. Drover let herself out by inches from her own front door into the empty street. The unoccupied houses opposite continued to meet her look with their damaged stare. Making towards the thoroughfare and the taxi, she tried not to keep looking behind. Indeed, the silence was so intense—one of those creeks of London silence exaggerated this summer by the damage of war—that no tread could have gained on hers unheard. Where her street

debouched on the square where people went on living, she grew conscious of, and checked, her unnatural pace. Across the open end of the square two buses impassively passed each other: women, a perambulator, cyclists, a man wheeling a barrow signalized, once again, the ordinary flow of life. At the square's most populous corner should be—and was— the short taxi rank. This evening, only one taxi—but this, although it presented its blank rump, appeared already to be alertly waiting for her. Indeed, without looking round the driver started his engine as she panted up from behind and put her hand on the door. As she did so, the clock struck seven. The taxi faced the main road: to make the trip back to her house it would have to turn—she had settled back on the seat and the taxi had turned before she, surprised by its knowing movement, recollected that she had not "said where." She leaned forward to scratch at the glass panel that divided the driver's head from her own.

27   The driver braked to what was almost a stop, turned round, and slid the glass panel back: the jolt of this flung Mrs. Drover forward till her face was almost into the glass. Through the aperture driver and passenger, not six inches between them, remained for an eternity eye to eye. Mrs. Drover's mouth hung open for some seconds before she could issue her first scream. After that she continued to scream freely and to beat with her gloved hands on the glass all round as the taxi, accelerating without mercy, made off with her into the hinterland of deserted streets.

My Last Duchess
Robert Browning

Town in Italy	Ferrara°
	That's my last Duchess painted on the wall,
	Looking as if she were alive. I call
A fictitious painter	That piece a wonder, now; Frà Pandolf's° hands
	Worked busily a day, and there she stands.
5	Will't please you sit and look at her? I said
	"Frà Pandolf" by design, for never read
	Strangers like you that pictured countenance,
	The depth and passion of its earnest glance,
	But to myself they turned (since none puts by
10	The curtain I have drawn for you, but I)
	And seemed as they would ask me, if they durst,
	How such a glance came there; so, not the first
	Are you to turn and ask thus. Sir, 'twas not
	Her husband's presence only, called that spot
15	Of joy into the Duchess' cheek; perhaps
	Frà Pandolf chanced to say "Her mantle laps
	Over my Lady's wrist too much," or, "Paint
	Must never hope to reproduce the faint

Half-flush that dies along her throat." Such stuff

20
Was courtesy, she thought, and cause enough
For calling up that spot of joy. She had
A heart—how shall I say?—too soon made glad,
Too easily impressed; she liked whate'er
She looked on, and her looks went everywhere.

25
Sir, 'twas all one! My favor at her breast,
The dropping of the daylight in the west,
The bough of cherries some officious fool
Broke in the orchard for her, the white mule
She rode with round the terrace—all and each

30
Would draw from her alike the approving speech,
Or blush, at least. She thanked men—good! but thanked
Somehow—I know not how—as if she ranked
My gift of a nine-hundred-years-old name
With anybody's gift. Who'd stoop to blame

35
This sort of trifling? Even had you skill
In speech—(which I have not)—to make your will
Quite clear to such an one, and say, "Just this
Or that in you disgusts me; here you miss,
Or there exceed the mark"—and if she let

40
Herself be lessoned so, nor plainly set
Her wits to yours, forsooth, and made excuse,
—E'en then would be some stooping; and I choose
Never to stoop. Oh, Sir, she smiled, no doubt,
Whene'er I passed her; but who passed without

45
Much the same smile? This grew; I gave commands;
Then all smiles stopped together. There she stands
As if alive. Will't please you rise? We'll meet
The company below, then. I repeat,
The Count your master's known munificence

50
Is ample warrant that no just pretense
Of mine for dowry will be disallowed;
Though his fair daughter's self, as I avowed
At starting, is my object. Nay, we'll go
Together down, Sir. Notice Neptune, though,

55
Taming a sea-horse, thought a rarity,
A fictitious sculptor   Which Claus of Innsbruck° cast in bronze for me!

Characters and Characterization

When you examine the characters of a work, whether they are human beings, animals, mythical demons, or space creatures, there are some standard considerations of their roles and some typical methods of characterization that can be reported, evaluated, or interpreted.

Flat or Round?

Characters are often labeled as flat or round. A well-rounded character is presented as a complex personality, a fully-developed being whose actions and reactions are presented to the readers for scrutiny. In contrast, a flat character is one-dimensional; that is, he/she is a simple, often predictable character briefly described and easily understood.

Static or Dynamic?

Another approach labels characters as static or dynamic. A static character remains unchanged throughout the work while a dynamic character alters perceptibly. Comparing the character as first presented with that same character later in the work and again at the end will help you distinguish the static from the dynamic. An additional consideration is the nature of the changes: Has the character grown and matured in predictable ways, or has the character undergone some distinct change? For example, an ambitious but desperately poor young man who becomes rich and powerful and less ambitious as he matures has grown, but has his life really changed directions? Ebenezer Scrooge in Charles Dickens' "A Christmas Carol" undergoes distinct personality changes after his visits from Christmas spirits. The course of his life and his relationships with people are radically altered by his encounters with the Christmas ghosts. In contrast, the medieval Sir Gawain is a wiser man after meeting the Green Knight, but what has changed is his understanding of himself and his limitations. His nature and the direction of his life have not changed.

Relationship to Plot

Exploring a character involves more than describing personality and personality changes. Look carefully at the character's role in the narrative. What effect does the character have on the plot? Is he/she actively involved in making things happen, or is the character a passive character to whom things happen? Is the character a catalyst of some kind, motivating others to some action just by being present?

Sources of Evidence

As you gather information about characters, pay attention to the sources of your material within the text. There may be direct description of a character, description from the character's own words or from other characters or from the narrator. You should also expect to see the character in action and to test the descriptions you have been given against the behavior of the character. If you are told, for example, that the character is childish and irresponsible, observe his/her behavior to see if that opinion is valid. If it is not, the discrepancy between perception and reality could be significant. Collect material for your analysis by looking for direct descriptions of the character, reactions of other characters to the primary subject, and behavior of the character throughout the work.

Potential Problems

Two familiar cautions apply to studies of characters and characterization. First, be sure that your conclusions about childish or evil or heroic behavior can be supported by evidence from the text. Second, be sure that you have indeed considered all significant evidence. Remember that characters do grow and change, and you must be sure that thesis and support cover the same material. If you are discussing the young Mr. Brown, you should draw evidence from only his early life; a discussion of Mr. Brown in general should be careful to include his later life as well.

Checklists for Exploring Character

Identifying Character

- Is this character presented as a complex personality?
- Is he/she described in detail in a variety of situations?
- What does this character look like?
- What kind of person is this character? Kind? Unethical? Intelligent?
- Does the writer give direct information about the nature of this character?
- Do the other characters comment on this one?
- Does this character talk about himself/herself? About hopes or fears or plans?
- Does this character act as expected?
- Are actions or words a better indication of personality?

Evaluating Character

- Does this character act in a realistic way?
- Does he/she talk and think as a person in his/her position can be expected to talk and think?
- Are the character's knowledge, motivation, environment, grammar appropriate?

Interpreting Character

- Does this character change during the narrative?
- Are the changes expected from the very beginning, or does something happen to alter the pattern of growth?
- Does the character know or understand more or feel different than would have been expected from just time passing?
- What has been learned? How?
- Is this character what he/she seems to be on the surface?
- Is appearance a reflection or a distortion of what is underneath?
- Does the character try to conceal the true self? Why?

1. Read "The Necklace," stopping as soon as Mathilde Loisel has borrowed the necklace from her friend. How would you describe her at this point? Identify the sources of your information.

2. Finish the story and describe Mathilde Loisel as she appears at the end. Be sure to consider her inner self as well as her outer self. How has she changed? Has she simply matured, or has her character developed into something it was not originally?

3. What kind of character is Mathilde? Flat or round? Static or dynamic? What about her husband? Her rich friend?

4. It is always tempting to speculate about what characters will do next. What do you think will happen next to the Loisel family? How would your ending affect the reading of the story? If your interpretation is affected by speculations about the ending, is your interpretation still valid? Why or why not?

5. Compare the characters of Lot and his wife in Kristine Batey's poem, "Lot's Wife." What apparently concerns each of them? Which would you prefer as a neighbor? Why?

6. Look up the biblical narrative and compare the characterizations of Lot and his wife with the characterizations in the poem. How has Batey changed the image and the evaluation of Lot's wife?

Additional Readings

The Necklace
Guy De Maupassant

1   She was one of those pretty, charming young ladies, born, as if through an error of destiny, into a family of clerks. She had no dowry, no hopes, no means of becoming known, appreciated, loved and married by a man either rich or distinguished; and she allowed herself to marry a petty clerk in the office of the Board of Education.

2   She was simple, not being able to adorn herself, but she was unhappy, as one out of her class; for women belong to no caste, no race, their grace, their beauty and their charm serving them in the place of birth and family. Their inborn finesse, their instinctive elegance, their suppleness of wit, are their only aristocracy, making some daughters of the people the equal of great ladies.

3   She suffered incessantly, feeling herself born for all delicacies and luxuries. She suffered from the poverty of her apartment, the shabby walls, the worn chairs and the faded stuffs. All these things, which another woman of her station would not have noticed, tortured and angered her. The sight of the little Breton, who made this humble home, awoke in her sad regrets and desperate dreams. She thought of quiet antechambers with their oriental hangings lighted by high bronze torches and of the two great footmen in short trousers who sleep in the large armchairs, made sleepy by the heavy air from the heating apparatus. She thought of large drawing rooms hung in old silks, of graceful pieces of furniture carrying bric-à-brac of inestimable value and of the little perfumed coquettish apartments made for five o'clock chats with most intimate friends, men known and sought after, whose attention all woman envied and desired.

4   When she seated herself for dinner before the round table, where the tablecloth had been used three days, opposite her husband who uncovered the tureen with a delighted air, saying: 'Oh! the good potpie! I know nothing better than that,' she would think of the elegant dinners, of the shining silver, of the tapestries peopling the walls with ancient personages and rare birds in the midst of fairy forests; she thought of the exquisite food served on marvelous dishes, of the whispered gallantries, listened to with the smile of the Sphinx while eating the rose-colored flesh of the trout or a chicken's wing.

5   She had neither frocks nor jewels, nothing. And she loved only those things. She felt that she was made for them. She had such a desire to please, to be sought after, to be clever and courted.

6   She had a rich friend, a schoolmate at the convent, whom she did not like to visit; she suffered so much when she returned. And she wept for whole days from chagrin, from regret, from despair and disappointment.

7   One evening her husband returned, elated, bearing in his hand a large envelope.

8   'Here,' he said, 'here is something for you.'

9   She quickly tore open the wrapper and drew out a printed card on which were inscribed these words:

10   *The Minister of Public Instruction and Madame George Ramponneau ask the honor of M. and Mme Loisel's company Monday evening, January 18, at the Minister's residence.*

11   Instead of being delighted, as her husband had hoped, she threw the invitation spitefully upon the table, murmuring:

12   'What do you suppose I want with that?'

13   'But, my dearie, I thought it would make you happy. You never go out, and this is an occasion, and a fine one! I had a great deal of trouble to get it. Everybody wishes one, and it is very select; not many are given to employees. You will see the whole official world there.'

14   She looked at him with an irritated eye and declared impatiently:

15   'What do you suppose I have to wear to such a thing as that?'

16   He had not thought of that; he stammered:

17   'Why, the dress you wear when we go to the theater. It seems very pretty to me.'

18   He was silent, stupefied, in dismay, at the sight of his wife weeping. Two great tears fell slowly from the corners of her eyes toward the corners of her mouth; he stammered: 'What is the matter? What is the matter?'

19   By a violent effort she had controlled her vexation and responded in a calm voice, wiping her moist cheeks:

20   'Nothing. Only I have no dress and consequently I cannot go to this affair. Give your card to some colleague whose wife is better fitted out than I.'

21   He was grieved but answered:

22   'Let us see, Matilda. How much would a suitable costume cost, something that would serve for other occasions, something very simple?'

23   She reflected for some seconds, making estimates and thinking of a sum that she could ask for without bringing with it an immediate refusal and a frightened exclamation from the economical clerk.

24   Finally she said in a hesitating voice:

25   'I cannot tell exactly, but it seems to me that four hundred francs ought to cover it.'

26   He turned a little pale, for he had saved just this sum to buy a gun that he might be able to join some hunting parties the next summer, on the plains at Nanterre, with some friends who went to shoot larks up there on Sunday. Nevertheless, he answered:

27   'Very well. I will give you four hundred francs. But try to have a pretty dress.'

28

The day of the ball approached, and Mme Loisel seemed sad, disturbed, anxious. Nevertheless, her dress was nearly ready. Her husband said to her one evening:

29   'What is the matter with you? You have acted strangely for two or three days.'

30   And she responded: 'I am vexed not to have a jewel, not one stone, nothing to adorn myself with. I shall have such a poverty-stricken look. I would prefer not to go to this party.'

31   He replied: 'You can wear some natural flowers. At this season they look very chic. For ten francs you can have two or three magnificent roses.'

32   She was not convinced. 'No,' she replied, 'there is nothing more humiliating than to have a shabby air in the midst of rich women.'

33   Then her husband cried out: 'How stupid we are! Go and find your friend Madame Forestier and ask her to lend you her jewels. You are well enough acquainted with her to do this.'

34   She uttered a cry of joy. 'It is true!' she said. 'I had not thought of that.'

35   The next day she took herself to her friend's house and related her story of distress. Mme Forestier went to her closet with the glass doors, took out a large jewel case, brought it, opened it and said:

36   'Choose, my dear.'

37   She saw at first some bracelets, then a collar of pearls, then a Venetian cross of gold and jewels and of admirable workmanship. She tried the jewels before the glass, hesitated, but could neither decide to take them nor leave them. Then she asked:

38   'Have you nothing more?'

39   'Why, yes. Look for yourself. I do not know what will please you.'

40   Suddenly she discovered in a black satin box a superb necklace of diamonds, and her heart beat fast with an immoderate desire. Her hands trembled as she took them up. She placed them about her throat, against her dress, and remained in ecstasy before them. Then she asked in a hesitating voice full of anxiety:

41   'Could you lend me this? Only this?'

42   'Why, yes, certainly.'

43   She fell upon the neck of her friend, embraced her with passion, then went away with her treasure.

44   The day of the ball arrived. Mme Loisel was a great success. She was the prettiest of all, elegant, gracious, smiling and full of joy. All the men noticed her, asked her name and wanted to be presented. All the members of the Cabinet wished to waltz with her. The minister of education paid her some attention.

45   She danced with enthusiasm, with passion, intoxicated with pleasure, thinking of nothing, in the triumph of her beauty, in the glory of her success, in a kind of cloud of happiness that came of all this homage and all this admiration, of all these awakened desires and this victory so complete and sweet to the heart of woman.

46   She went home toward four o'clock in the morning. Her husband had been half asleep in one of the little salons since midnight with three other gentlemen whose wives were enjoying themselves very much.

47   He threw around her shoulders the wraps they had carried for the coming home, modest garments of everyday wear, whose poverty clashed with the elegance of the ball costume. She felt this and wished to hurry away in order not to be noticed by the other women who were wrapping themselves in rich furs.

48   Loisel detained her. 'Wait,' said he. 'You will catch cold out there. I am going to call a cab.'

49   But she would not listen and descended the steps rapidly. When they were in the street they found no carriage, and they began to seek for one, hailing the coachmen whom they saw at a distance.

50   They walked along toward the Seine, hopeless and shivering. Finally they found on the dock one of those old nocturnal coupés that one sees in Paris after nightfall, as if they were ashamed of their misery by day.

51   It took them as far as their door in Martyr Street, and they went wearily up to their apartment. It was all over for her. And on his part he remembered that he would have to be at the office by ten o'clock.

52   She removed the wraps from her shoulders before the glass for a final view of herself in her glory. Suddenly she uttered a cry. Her necklace was not around her neck.

53   Her husband, already half undressed, asked: 'What is the matter?'

54   She turned toward him excitedly:

55   'I have—I have—I no longer have Madame Forestier's necklace.'

56   He arose in dismay: 'What! How is that? It is not possible.'

57   And they looked in the folds of the dress, in the folds of the mantle, in the pockets, everywhere. They could not find it.

58   He asked: 'You are sure you still had it when we left the house?'

59   'Yes, I felt in the vestibule as we came out.'

60   'But if you had lost it in the street we should have heard it fall. It must be in the cab.'

61   'Yes. It is probable. Did you take the number?'

62   'No. And you, did you notice what it was?'

63   'No.'

64   They looked at each other, utterly cast down. Finally Loisel dressed himself again.

65   'I am going,' said he, 'over the track where we went on foot, to see if I can find it.'

66   And he went. She remained in her evening gown, not having the force to go to bed, stretched upon a chair, without ambition or thoughts.

67   Toward seven o'clock her husband returned. He had found nothing.

68   He went to the police and to the cab offices and put an advertisement in the newspapers, offering a reward; he did everything that afforded them a suspicion of hope.

69   She waited all day in a state of bewilderment before this frightful disaster. Loisel returned at evening, with his face harrowed and pale, and had discovered nothing.

70   'It will be necessary,' said he, 'to write to your friend that you have broken the clasp of the necklace and that you will have it repaired. That will give us time to turn around.'

71   She wrote as he dictated.

72   At the end of a week they had lost all hope. And Loisel, older by five years, declared:

73   'We must take measures to replace this jewel.'

74   The next day they took the box which had inclosed it to the jeweler whose name was on the inside. He consulted his books.

75   'It is not I, madame,' said he, 'who sold this necklace; I only furnished the casket.'

76   Then they went from jeweler to jeweler, seeking a necklace like the other one, consulting their memories, and ill, both of them, with chagrin and anxiety.

77 In a shop of the Palais-Royal they found a chaplet of diamonds which seemed to them exactly like the one they had lost. It was valued at forty thousand francs. They could get it for thirty-six thousand.

78 They begged the jeweler not to sell it for three days. And they made an arrangement by which they might return it for thirty-four thousand francs if they found the other one before the end of February.

79 Loisel possessed eighteen thousand francs which his father had left him. He borrowed the rest.

80 He borrowed it, asking for a thousand francs of one, five hundred of another, five louis of this one and three louis of that one. He gave notes, made ruinous promises, took money of usurers and the whole race of lenders. He compromised his whole existence, in fact, risked his signature without even knowing whether he could make it good or not, and, harassed by anxiety for the future, by the black misery which surrounded him and by the prospect of all physical privations and moral torture, he went to get the new necklace, depositing on the merchant's counter thirty-six thousand francs.

81 When Mme Loisel took back the jewels to Mme Forestier the latter said to her in a frigid tone:

82 'You should have returned them to me sooner, for I might have needed them.'

83 She did open the jewel box as her friend feared she would. If she should perceive the substitution what would she think? What should she say? Would she take her for a robber?

84 Mme Loisel now knew the horrible life of necessity. She did her part, however, completely, heroically. It was necessary to pay this frightful debt. She would pay it. They sent away the maid; they changed their lodgings; they rented some rooms under a mansard roof.

85 She learned the heavy cares of a household, the odious work of a kitchen. She washed the dishes, using her rosy nails upon the greasy pots and the bottoms of the stewpans. She washed the soiled linen, the chemises and dishcloths, which she hung on the line to dry; she took down the refuse to the street each morning and brought up the water, stopping at each landing to breathe. And, clothed like a woman of the people, she went to the grocer's, the butcher's and the fruiterer's with her basket on her arm, shopping, haggling to the last sou her miserable money.

86 Every month it was necessary to renew some notes, thus obtaining time, and to pay others.

87 The husband worked evenings, putting the books of some merchants in order, and nights he often did copying at five sous a page.

88 And this life lasted for ten years.

89 At the end of ten years they had restored all, all, with interest of the usurer, and accumulated interest, besides.

90 Mme Loisel seemed old now. She had become a strong, hard woman, the crude woman of the poor household. Her hair badly dressed, her

skirts awry, her hands red, she spoke in a loud tone and washed the floors in large pails of water. But sometimes, when her husband was at the office, she would seat herself before the window and think of that evening party of former times, of that ball where she was so beautiful and so flattered.

91   How would it have been if she had not lost that necklace? Who knows? Who knows? How singular is life and how full of changes! How small a thing will ruin or save one!

92   One Sunday, as she was taking a walk in the Champs-Elysées to rid herself of the cares of the week, she suddenly perceived a woman talking with a child. It was Mme Forestier, still young, still pretty, still attractive. Mmd Loisel was affected. Should she speak to her? Yes, certainly. And now that she had paid, she would tell her all. Why not?

93   She approached her. 'Good morning, Jeanne.'

94   Her friend did not recognize her and was astonished to be so familiarly addressed by this common personage. She stammered:

95   'But, madame—I do not know—You must be mistaken.'

96   'No, I am Matilda Loise.'

97   Her friend uttered a cry of astonishment: 'Oh! my poor Matilda! How you have changed.'

98   'Yes, I have had some hard days since I saw you, and some miserable ones—and all because of you.'

99   'Because of me? How is that?'

100   'You recall the diamond necklace that you loaned me to wear to the minister's ball?'

101   'Yes, very well.'

102   'Well, I lost it.'

103   'How is that, since you returned it to me?'

104   'I returned another to you exactly like it. And it has taken us ten years to pay for it. You can understand that it was not easy for us who have nothing. But it is over, and I am satisfied.'

105   Mme Forestier stopped short. She said:

106   'You say that you bought a diamond necklace to replace mine?'

107   'Yes. You did not perceive it then? They were just alike.'

108   And she smiled with a proud and simple joy. Mme Forestier was touched and took both her hands as she replied:

109   'Oh, my poor Matilda! Mine were false. They were not worth over five hundred francs!'

Lot's Wife
Kristine Batey

While Lot, the conscience of a nation,
struggles with the Lord,
she struggles with the housework.

The City of Sin is where
5   she raises the children.
Ba'al or Adonai—
Whoever is God—
the bread must still be made
and the doorsill swept.
10   The Lord may kill the children tomorrow,
but today they must be bathed and fed.
Well and good to condemn your neighbors' religion;
but weren't they there
when the baby was born,
15   and when the well collapsed?
While her husband communes with God
she tucks the children into bed.
In the morning, when he tells her of the judgment,
she puts down the lamp she is cleaning
and calmly begins to pack.
20   In between bundling up the children
and deciding what will go,
she runs for a moment
to say goodbye to the herd,
gently patting each soft head
25   with tears in her eyes for the animals that will not understand.
She smiles blindly to the woman
who held her hand at childbed.
It is easy for eyes that have always turned to heaven
not to look back;
30   those that have been—by necessity—drawn to earth
cannot forget that life is lived from day to day.
Good, to a God, and good in human terms
are two different things.
On the breast of the hill, she chooses to be human,
35   and turns, in farewell—
and never regrets
the sacrifice.

Setting

The setting of the work is most obviously the immediate physical surroundings, the room or the patch of grass or the street corner. It is also
the broader physical context; that is, the town, the country, the planet.
Setting includes details of weather, of time of day, of season, of historical
era. Specific items like furniture or jewelry or clothing are also included,
and background items such as pets or cars or photo albums are part of
the setting. The concept of setting is thus a broad one, incorporating any

aspect of the environment that cannot be labelled a character (a pet like Lassie is more than setting, and Stephen King has shown us that cars can indeed be characters).

Deliberate Details

When you explore setting, remember that the writer chose to include particular details. Young Goodman Brown has a wife named "Faith," not "Penny." Emily Grierson lives in a big decaying house in a decaying society, not in a condominium. Sometimes details are included to create a realistic background for a narrative, but it is reasonable to assume that some details have a greater significance. For example, if an element of setting is spotlighted in the title or is repeatedly mentioned in the work, you should examine symbolic connotations. "The Necklace" is about a piece of jewelry that does more than advance the plot; the jewelry also represents the inability of the character to recognize true value.

You can recognize the connotations of names like Faith or Graves or Summer. The association of colors with traits or feelings is also familiar— red is courage or passion, white is often innocence, black is mystery or evil or death. (Be careful, though—the connotations of color should be consistent with the rest of the work. Also remember that color connotations differ from culture to culture, so a work in translation should be approached carefully.) Springtime and sunrise can both suggest new beginnings; winter and sunset tell of endings; moonlight is both less reliable and less harsh than sunlight.

Must every detail of setting be studied at length? Certainly not every tree has individual significance, and minute scrutiny can become tedious, even ridiculous. At the same time, the tree that was planted when a child was born and withered on the day he died should not be treated like just another tree. And if a character sits at sunrise on the first day of spring at the crest of the hill with home at her back, you should be alert to the messages in the setting.

Relationship to Plot

Another way to look at setting is to consider its relationship to the plot. Does the setting create an atmosphere that signals what is to come? Look at Edgar Allan Poe stories to see gloom and horror written into the very cracks in the walls. In contrast, Stephen King often sets his stories in ordinary places that do nothing to warn you of the horrors to come. Look, too, at the relationship between setting and characters. Is there something in the setting that parallels a character? Emily Grierson in "A Rose for Emily" might be reflected in her house—old, out-of-date, fallen from glory, even decaying. Does the setting suggest order or strength or complexity? In short, does the setting reinforce some aspect of the narrative? Does it, perhaps, present a contrast?

Not every writer creates tapestries of setting rich with symbolic detail. But your exploration of a work should include the possibility that such details are there.

Checklists for Exploring Setting

Context

- Where do the incidents of the narrative take place?
- What does the room look like?
- Is the setting rural or urban?
- What is the nearest town or city?
- What details are mentioned by the writer?
- What is the time of day?
- The time of year?
- The historical era?
- What is the weather like?
- Is there a storm brewing?
- Is it sunny or rainy or overcast?
- Is it hot or cold?

Connections

- How does the setting affect the plot?
- Does it change plans?
- Complicate travel?
- Terrify a character?
- Conceal a murder?
- Trigger a crisis?
- Inspire heroics?
- Do any details of setting reveal aspects of character?
- Is a particular item or color associated with a character?
- Is there any significance to names of characters?
- If the setting does not reflect plot or character, does it show contrast?
- Does the contrast mislead you in any way?
- Is the contrast deliberate?

Y O U R   T U R N

1. In "The Story of an Hour," Louise Mallard retreats to her room after hearing tragic news. Her "storm of grief" has passed. Look closely at the details of setting in the next passage. Why does she sit at a window? Has she ever done it before? What is the sky like on this occasion? What else does she see and hear? What do those details suggest? How does the setting indicate her state of mind?

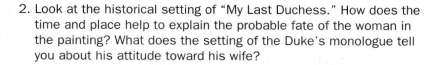

2. Look at the historical setting of "My Last Duchess." How does the time and place help to explain the probable fate of the woman in the painting? What does the setting of the Duke's monologue tell you about his attitude toward his wife?

Theme

When you are asked to discuss the meaning of a story, you should focus on the theme, the comment the narrative makes about human nature in general. The characters and their actions are seen as examples of the way people behave, and the theme is the statement of the way people behave.

The examples below illustrate both a summary and a discussion of theme. Note that both pieces identify the work and mention specifics of the story, but the second paragraph connects the characters to humanity in general.

"The Chaser," a short story by John Collier, is the story of a man who is hopelessly in love with a woman. He goes to a mysterious old man who sells him a love potion that will make the young lady worship and adore him for as long as she lives. The love potion costs only a dollar, but the old man also shows a potion that is very expensive, a potion that will cause death without leaving any trace. There is a suggestion that the young man will grow tired of such endless devotion and will return for the poison. When Alan says, "Goodbye," the old man answers, "Au revoir," literally, "'Til I see you again."

John Collier's short story "The Chaser" is about man's pursuit of happiness. The story illustrates a human tendency to want a thing without fully realizing what getting it could mean. Alan, the main character, describes the love he wishes to receive from the young lady; it is a love, however, that his audience—both the old man and the readers—knows he will soon resent. In short, what Alan thinks he wants will not bring him happiness. His problem, common to many human beings who think they know what they want, is that he has not fully considered the implications of getting what he wants. As the audience knows, Alan will soon return to the old man for "The Chaser," a drink of poison to follow the love potion he is not seeking.

Notice that the second passage discusses theme, assuming that its audience is familiar with the story, while the first summarizes the plot. Plot is one particular narrative involving one set of characters and their interaction. In contrast, theme focuses on a larger human truth. Should you write your own story using the same plot line, you would rightly be called a plagiarist. The theme, however, can be illustrated again and again, using different characters and different situations. For example, a story about a child who wanted a puppy until he actually got one and discovered the work it involved would illustrate the same theme as the story described above. Think also of the countless variations of the theme that poor communication creates serious problems between people.

Multiple Themes

Keep in mind that complex works often illustrate more than a single theme. "The Lottery," for example, can be seen as an illustration of the human tendency to follow traditions without questioning their purpose or origins. But it also shows the human tendency to do things in a group that would be repugnant to individuals. And it shows that human beings will often follow the group without protest until their own lives and property are at stake. If you identified any of these observations as the theme of "The Lottery," you would not be wrong. It might be good practice, then, to talk about "a" theme found in the work rather than "the" theme.

Checklists for Exploring Theme

Identifying Theme

- In what ways is the behavior of the characters typically human?
- Do you understand their actions, even if you do not approve?
- Can you complete this statement: "Human beings, like Character X, have a tendency to ____"?
- Is there an illustration of obstacles to good relationships?
- Of misleading appearances?
- Of human reactions to stress or pressure?
- Of human desires for success or challenge or self-preservation?

Discussing Theme

- Does the discussion talk about this story in particular or about human nature in general?

- Does it connect specific behaviors or thoughts or motives of these characters to the larger context of human nature?
- To be sure that you are discussing theme, can you think of other narratives or situations that illustrate the same theme?

Y O U R   T U R N

1. Identify some general human tendencies illustrated in "The Necklace." How does Mathilde Loisel react to the invitation her husband brings home? How does her husband react to the news that the necklace is missing? How do they both react to the monumental task of replacing it? Are their reactions in any way typical of human behavior?

2. Look again at "A Rose for Emily." Notice that the narrator comments, when she denies her father's death, ". . . we knew that with nothing left, she would have to cling to that which had robbed her, *as people will* (emphasis added)." What is Emily clinging to? How has it robbed her? Is her response typical of human behavior? How else does this same story illustrate the theme of people clinging to something that has somehow robbed them?

3. Look at Margaret Atwood's "Siren Song." What does the siren understand about human nature? What is the secret of the irresistible song?

Additional Readings

The Chaser
John Collier

1. Alan Austen, as nervous as a kitten, went up certain dark and creaky stairs in the neighborhood of Pell Street, and peered about for a long time on the dim landing before he found the name he wanted written obscurely on one of the doors.

2. He pushed open this door, as he had been told to do, and found himself in a tiny room, which contained no furniture but a plain kitchen table, rocking chair, and an ordinary chair. On one of the dirty buff-colored walls were a couple of shelves, containing in all perhaps a dozen bottles and jars.

3. An old man sat in the rocking chair, reading a newspaper. Alan, without a word, handed him the card he had been given. "Sit down, Mr.

Austen," said the old man very politely. "I am glad to make your acquaintance."

4   "Is it true," asked Alan, "that you have a certain mixture that has—
er—quite extraordinary effects?"

5   "My dear sir," replied the old man, "my stock in trade is not very
large—I don't deal in laxatives and teething mixtures—but such as it is,
it is varied. I think nothing I sell has effects which could be precisely
described as ordinary."

6   "Well, the fact is—" began Alan.

7   'Here, for example," interrupted the old man, reaching for a bottle from
the shelf. "Here is a liquid as colorless as water, almost tasteless, quite
imperceptible in coffee, milk, wine, or any other beverage. It is also quite
imperceptible to any known method of autopsy."

8   "Do you mean it is a poison?" cried Alan, very much horrified.

"Call it cleaning fluid if you like," said the old man indifferently. "Lives
need cleaning. Call it a spot-remover. 'Out, damned spot!' Eh? 'Out, brief
candle!'"[1]

9   "I want nothing of that sort," said Alan.

10   "Probably it is just as well," said the old man. "Do you know the price
of this? For one teaspoonful, which is sufficient, I ask five thousand dollars. Never less. Not a penny less."

11   "I hope all your mixtures are not as expensive," said Alan apprehen-
sively.

12   "Oh, dear, no," said the old man. "It would be no good charging that
sort of price for a love potion, for example. Young people who need a love
potion very seldom have five thousand dollars. Otherwise they would not
need a love potion."

13   "I'm glad to hear you say so," said Alan.

14   "I look at it like this," said the old man. "Please a customer with one
article, and he will come back when he needs another. Even if it *is* more
costly. He will save up for it, if necessary."

15   "So," said Alan, "you really do sell love potions?"

16   "If I did not sell love potions," said the old man, reaching for another
bottle, "I should not have mentioned the other matter to you. It is only
when one is in a position to oblige that one can afford to be so confidential."

17   "And these potions," said Alan. "They are not just—just—er—"

18   "Oh, no," said the old man. "Their effects are permanent, and extend
far beyond the mere casual impulse. But they include it. Oh, yes, they
include it. Bountifully. Insistently. Everlastingly."

19   "Dear me!" said Alan, attempting a look of scientific detachment. "How
very interesting!"

20   "But consider the spiritual side," said the old man.

21   "I do, indeed," said Alan.

---

[1]Lines are from Shakespeare's *Macbeth*. (Editors' note)

22   "For indifference," said the old man, "they substitute devotion. For scorn, adoration. Give one tiny measure of this to the young lady—its flavor is imperceptible in orange juice, soup, or cocktails—and however gay and giddy she is, she will change altogether. She'll want nothing but solitude, and you."

23   "I can hardly believe it," said Alan. "She is so fond of parties."

24   "She will not like them any more," said the old man. "She'll be afraid of the pretty girls you may meet."

25   "She'll actually be jealous?" cried Alan in a rapture. "Of me?"

26   "Yes, she will want to be everything to you."

27   "She is, already. Only she doesn't care about it."

28   "She will, when she has taken this. She will care intensely. You'll be her sole interest in life."

29   "Wonderful!" cried Alan.

30   "She'll want to know all you do," said the old man. "All that has happened to you during the day. Every word of it. She'll want to know what you are thinking about, why you smile suddenly, why you are looking sad."

31   "That is love!" cried Alan.

32   "Yes" said the old man. "How carefully she'll look after you! She'll never allow you to be tired, to sit in a draft, to neglect your food. If you are an hour late, she'll be terrified. She'll think you are killed, or that some siren has caught you."

33   "I can hardly imagine Diana like that!" cried Alan.

34   "You will not have to use your imagination," said the old man. "And by the way, since there are always sirens, if by any chance you *should*, later on, slip a little, you need not worry. She will forgive you, in the end. She'll be terribly hurt, of course, but she'll forgive you—in the end."

35   "That will not happen," said Alan fervently.

36   "Of course not," said the old man. "But, if it does, you need not worry. She'll never divorce you. Oh, no! And, of course, she herself will never give you the least grounds for—not divorce, of course—but even uneasiness."

37   "And how much," said Alan, "how much is this wonderful mixture?"

38   "It is not so dear," said the old man, "as the spot remover, as I think we agreed to call it. No. That is five thousand dollars; never a penny less. One had to be older than you are, to indulge in that sort of thing. One has to save up for it."

39   "But the love potion?" said Alan.

40   "Oh, that," said the old man, opening the drawer in the kitchen table, and taking out a tiny, rather dirty-looking phial. "That is just a dollar."

41   "I can't tell you how grateful I am." said Alan, watching him fill it.

42   "I like to oblige," said the old man. "The customers come back, later in life, when they are rather better off, and want more expensive things. Here you are. You will find it very effective."

43   "Thank you again," said Alan. "Goobye."

44   "*Au revoir*," said the old man.

Siren Song
Margaret Atwood

This is the one song everyone
would like to learn: the song
that is irresistible:

the song that forces men
5   to leap overboard in squadrons
even though they see the beached skulls

the song nobody knows
because anyone who has heard it
is dead, and the others can't remember.

10   Shall I tell you the secret
and if I do, will you get me
out of this bird suit?

I don't enjoy it here
squatting on this island
15   looking picturesque and mythical

with these two feathery maniacs,
I don't enjoy singing
this trio, fatal and valuable.

I will tell the secret to you,
20   to you, only to you.
Come closer. This song

is a cry for help: Help me!
Only you, only you can,
you are unique

25   at last. Alas
it is a boring song
but it works every time.

SUMMARY

Writing about literature is essentially like writing about other subjects. You will consider the context of the writing and the expectations of the audience. As you write, you will gather material, aided by consideration of elements of narratives; you will shape a draft, and you will revise and edit until you are satisfied with the logic, accuracy, and completeness of your work.

ADDITIONAL INVITATIONS

1. After reading "My Last Duchess," think about the context: the narrator, his audience, his purpose in speaking so freely to the Count's emissary. Adopt the persona of the emissary and write a report to the Count, your master, in which you explain your perceptions of the man and the planned marriage. You can make recommendations about the new wife's conduct or about the marriage itself.

2. In "The Story of an Hour," Louise Mallard dies abruptly at the end of the story. Imagine that you are a close friend who really knew her well. Would you accept the explanation that she died of joy, "the joy that kills"? Write a letter to Brently Mallard in which you explain what you think really killed his wife. Let your letter demonstrate your feelings—sadness, guilt, anger, whatever.

3. "The Chaser" describes a young man's quest for a perfect love. Assume that the love potion has worked as anticipated, and, in the persona of Alan, write a journal entry that explains your feelings about your perfectly devoted wife after ten years of marriage.

4. When the title character of "Lot's Wife" stands on the "breast," she looks back and chooses to be "human." Imagine what it would have been like to live next door to Lot and his wife. Assume the persona of one of the neighbors who has known the couple for years. Write to a friend who knew them long ago but moved away and describe the current state of the zealous Lot and his wife. Your letter should be sent just before Lot plans his escape from the wicked city.

5. You have just read about "The Lottery" in your local newspaper and you are stunned that such a ritual has taken place in the twentieth century so near your town. But, as you think about it, you realize that your own community participates in similarly destructive "rituals" in the name of tradition. Write an editorial for the local newspaper in which you explain the destructive nature of some traditional practice in your community. It need not be a bloody ritual, but it should be some traditional attitude or practice that hinders the growth of the community or the opportunities of its people, something that people will not relinquish because "we've always done it this way."

6. After attending the funeral of Emily Grierson, you hear that the locked room in her house has been opened, and you hear of the grisly spectacle within. As a citizen of the town who has known Emily since she was a child, you suddenly feel guilty about the way she

lived her life. In your diary, speculate about what you and the other townfolk (her own family included) could have done to make Emily's life more normal. Talk about actions, but be sure to explain how attitudes could have been different.

7. "Siren Song" ends with the comment that the song works every time. Have you ever responded to such a song? Is there a particular siren song that works on you every time? Tell a friend about a personal experience where you were lured by a "song" but ended up crashed on the rocks. Be sure to draw out of the experience some knowledge of what it is that makes you "fall" for this kind of song.

8. In "The Demon Lover," Mrs. Drover tries to shake off her uneasiness as she leaves the house. Suppose that she stopped long enough to write a letter explaining her feelings, just in case. . . . What would that letter say? To whom would she write?

Writing Essay Examinations

Taking essay exams can be a nerve-wracking experience, but you can improve your performance by studying your audience, your material, and the test itself. Using what you know about writing as a process will help you gather material, analyze it for logical connections, and prepare a written response on demand.

If you have come to this section looking for a magic formula that will simplify essay examinations, you will be disappointed. There is no quick fix, no easy approach, to answering essay questions. There are, however, some attitudes and activities that can help you approach such examinations with more confidence.

First, you should know that there are two main causes for disastrous performance on essay examinations: **lack of knowledge** and **inability to present knowledge.** This chapter can't supply you with answers to solve the first problem, but it will offer a plan for preparing for essay exams. The second problem, inability to present what you do know, may stem from poor writing skills; if skills are the problem, what you know about writing as process can be applied to the essay examination to improve your ability to gather, organize, and present your responses.

But there is an additional obstacle to demonstrating knowledge on essay examinations: an acute attack of test anxiety. Unfortunately, we don't know a cure for test anxiety. But we do know that it is a common problem, shared by students of all ages, abilities, and educational backgrounds. While adequate preparation paired with confidence in your writing skills can help, severe test anxiety often needs additional attention. If your panic at test time is frequent and severe, help is available for you. Most colleges offer workshops on coping with stress in general and with test anxiety in particular, so check with your own school for more information. Resident Housing, Freshman Division, the Student Government Association, Special Services, the Dean of Students' office—all of these are potential sponsors of such workshops. You can also check with other campus affiliates like religious student centers to see what counseling programs are available.

But remember that stress levels are highest when you do not feel adequately prepared for a test. To reduce the stress that comes from inadequate preparation, you can study your audience, study the material, and study the test itself.

STUDYING THE AUDIENCE

Studying your audience doesn't mean taking your instructor out to dinner, but it does mean understanding what he or she considers important. That understanding can provide clues about the nature of the test and about the expectations of the audience.

Knowledge about the format and the emphasis of the test can come from the instructor, from former students, or from campus test files. If your instructor gives any information about the form of the test or the material it will cover, take careful notes. In addition, ask questions; the worst that will happen is that the instructor will refuse to give out more information.

If it is possible, ask former students about this instructor's testing. Few instructors give the same tests semester after semester, but most instructors will emphasize the same material and will construct tests that are similar in form to their earlier exams. You might also find out if the instructor expects masses of details, or if spelling of names is crucial to your grade.

Also, check with Freshman Division and your campus library about files of old exams. Because if such files are maintained by the university, the instructor is aware of them and you should not expect an identical test. But you may find out something about the format or the emphasis of your instructor's exams. Identification items and short answer questions require knowledge of specific facts, while longer questions ask you to see relationships between facts. Do old tests provide any clues?

Investigating test format may also give you information about the material your instructor considers most important. Your own notes on class discussions and lectures will give additional clues. Some instructors give introductory lectures that point out areas to be studied; others include such material on course syllabi. As you review your notes for a class, look at topics which have received major emphasis. Does your instructor favor a particular explanation or analysis? Your notes will also show if the instructor has emphasized certain names and dates and specific terminology. Some instructors write key information on the board; others use handouts or overhead projectors. Review the class material for clues to what the instructor considers important.

Finally, remember that the overriding purpose of your answers is to convince the audience (the grader) that you understand the material. Answers are judged not by length but by relevance to the question and by accuracy and completeness. Few instructors expect you to repeat memorized blocks of material. Instead, your answers should show that you understand the material well enough to select appropriate data. They should also be complete and accurate. For example, on a history test covering Civil War battles, the audience (the grader) knows the details of the siege of Vicksburg, but you must not assume that the audience will fill in details for you. It is essential that you remember your purpose—to demonstrate to the grader your own knowledge of the material.

Preparing for an essay examination, then, involves something other than memorizing vast amounts of material. Your consideration of the expectations of the audience is also important.

STUDYING THE MATERIAL

Ideally, when you begin to prepare for any test, you have before you complete and accurate class notes and a text that you have already read. Ideally, you have several days to review the material.

In reality, you will sometimes be forced (for whatever reasons) into intense, limited study sessions. Additional factors like the importance of the test, the amount of material to be covered, your workload, your reading speed, and your understanding of the material are elements that only you can evaluate. The study strategies outlined here are flexible enough to suit most situations, so modify or condense these procedures as needed.

Gather and Review Materials

Set aside a working area and make sure that you have pencil, paper, notes, texts, study guides, and any other material to be reviewed for the test. If you are missing notes, contact a classmate for help.

Your initial goal is to be sure that you comprehend the material. Read it over quickly, marking areas you expect to be tested. After the first read-through, look up definitions of unfamiliar words and review sections that are not clear. If you do not understand something, ask your instructor or a classmate or a tutor for additional help. (Sometimes group study sessions are useful because notes from several students can be compared. But be clear about the nature of the group; will weaker students be tutored?) Review the material until you understand it; it is not yet time to memorize.

Identify Logical Frameworks

There are two kinds of knowledge about material. One kind is knowledge of facts; that is, you know lists of component parts and names and dates and terminology. The second kind is knowledge of frameworks; it is recognizing how facts relate to each other. Thorough preparation for a test will give you both kinds.

Look over your materials again, this time in search of logical patterns or connections. Some of the most common are described here (If you need a detailed review of common patterns, check Chapter 9).

Chronology

- Is there a series of events that can be arranged in chronological order?
- Someone's accomplishments?
- The evolution of an idea or the story of a discovery?
- A sequence of events?
- A series of steps?
- Historical backgrounds?

Cause–Effect

- Is there a simple cause–effect relationship between two events?
- Is there an important event or discovery produced by the efforts of many or a combination of luck and hard work?
- Was there a chain of events?
- Are there several possible causes?
- What resulted from an event or a discovery or an achievement?
- Did it have effects on individual people?
- On communities?
- On countries? Did other things follow from it?
- Is there some trend or condition that can be traced to its causes?

Comparison–Contrast

- Are there two people or events that are comparable to each other?
- From the same background?
- Achieved similar goals?
- Had similar causes or effects?
- Faced each other in key battles?
- Assumed leadership roles under similar conditions?
- Are there two people or events in direct contrast to each other?
- In terms of background or achievement or effectiveness or leadership?
- Two trends or political movements?

Classification

- Are there types of people or problems or approaches or concerns or causes or questions or solutions?
- Consider categories based on levels, like local/state/federal, or individual/community/global or boss/employee/customer.
- Consider categories like financial/legal/personal or childhood/adulthood/old age.

As you look for connections, write down lists or outlines of the frameworks that you see. The most obvious advantage to writing such notes is that you will not forget good ideas that are recorded on paper. But there are other good reasons to work on paper. What is written, experts tell us, stays in the memory longer that what is simply thought about. In addition, outlines and lists make it easier for you to review what you have covered.

As you look for logical connections, think of your analysis of lectures and class discussions. Was there emphasis placed on causes or effects of an event? Was a particular leader discussed in detail? Were leaders or events compared or contrasted to other events? Are there clues to logical frameworks in your lecture notes? Look for instructor comments like, "Three main reasons . . ." or "A similar problem occurred in . . ." or "Problems of various types . . ."

By recognizing logical connections, you are practicing to answer questions on the exam. It is not necessary to write out lengthy responses, but it is good practice to prepare a rough outline or a quick list of what you would discuss if such questions were asked.

Identifying frameworks or logical patterns is a demonstration of one kind of knowledge. If your study plan allows time, it is a good idea to walk away from your material and let your subconscious assimilate the logical patterns for a while. But resist the temptation to call your preparation complete. Most instructors will recognize the general nature of these frameworks and will expect you to supply facts to develop or support these outlines.

Review Specific Details

When you review specific details, you have two goals: to identify short answer items like dates or events or particular works, and to see the details in connection to logical frameworks.

As you review your notes for specific details, keep pen and paper handy. Compile a list of terms and dates and names that might show up on the test. If you anticipate short answer questions as well as essays, mark potential topics and connect details like dates, principal persons involved, and importance to the field.

Items that might be part of a longer answer should be labelled or listed according to your outlines from the last session. You might, for example, highlight in yellow everything that relates to the siege of Vicksburg. Or, you might put a star next to everything connected to the discovery of DNA. Don't be surprised if one detail appears on several of your lists; you are looking for as many connections as possible, hoping to identify the same ones that will appear in the test questions.

Formulate Practice Questions

As a last step in your review of material, make up a test. List probable identification questions like "Who (or what) is X?" "Why is X important?"

"Where can X be found?" Identify good topics for one-paragraph answers, and note topics that need several paragraphs for complete discussion.

Your decision to write out practice answers really depends on the time you have and on your most effective study habits. Remember that your outlines and lists cover more material than a test will, so it is not necessary to write out lengthy responses to every question. In addition, responding to questions mentally allows you to review more material than does responding on paper. The most important concern is that you approach the test itself with confidence that you can discuss material from a number of angles.

STUDYING THE TEST

If you have formed practice questions and have identified logical connections between your material, you have already begun to analyze the format of the test. When you sit down with the actual test, though, spend another five minutes to study the test itself. Read over the entire test before you begin to write.

First, check the point values of each question. Point value is an excellent gauge for the amount of time and space to give an answer. And, since many tests start with short questions and conclude with the longest essay, knowing the point values will help you plan your time. How much time should you spend on each question? Where should you be half-way through the time period? What is the latest time to start the final essay?

Second, be sure you understand the expected format of each answer. Must you answer identifications in complete sentences? Is list form acceptable? Should all answers be in paragraph form? If the information is not on the test itself, ask the instructor.

Third, as you read over the test, identify questions that cover familiar subjects. If you have the option to answer questions in any order, start where you are most confident. In addition, note questions that might help you answer other questions. The correct spelling of a person's name or the date of an event might be given in the identification section, or a short answer question might point to a logical relationship between ideas.

Finally, be sure you understand all directions. Can you write on the test itself? Should you skip lines? Are you allowed to write on the back? Is pencil acceptable? How should you scratch out or add material to your answers? If any directions seem unclear, ask the instructor or test proctor for help.

If any of these considerations seem petty, remember that your careful attention to directions and to format makes an additional statement about you as a student.

RESPONDING TO ESSAY QUESTIONS

When you begin your response, use what you know about the process of writing. The activities of gathering and planning were part of your preparation, but do not neglect to plan your specific response. Regardless of the answers you have practiced, a basic requirement of essay questions is that you respond directly to the question. So, study the question carefully. Does it ask for specific information, or does it leave you to formulate your own thesis? Does it ask for causal connections? Or for comparisons? Look for clues signalling comparison/contrast discussions like "Distinguish between . . ." or "How was X like . . ." or "What did X and Y have in common?" If you are asked to examine "the impact of . . ." or "the influences on . . ." or "the outcome of . . . ," you are probably expected to discuss cause/effect connections. Additional clues to cause–effect patterns are "backgrounds," "foundations," "significant factors," "implications," and "consequences." Questions about "accuracy" or "importance" or "value" often expect an evaluation or comparison to standards. Always be sure that your answer closely follows instructions like "identify" or "list" or "evaluate" or "explain."

When you have identified the expectations of the question, formulate a thesis statement as the opening sentence of your response. Use the wording of the question as much as possible.

> *Question:* Both Sir Gawain and Beowulf are considered heroes of their people, but are they really alike?

> *Student's Analysis:* The question asks for a comparison or contrast of the two figures as they appear in the literature studied for this class.

> *Appropriate Response:* Sir Gawain and Beowulf are both heroes to their own cultures, but those cultures are so different that the two figures have very little in common. (A discussion of the differences between the two figures would follow.)

> *Inappropriate Response:* Beowulf faces three great foes: Grendel, Grendel's mother, and the dragon. He is a hero because, in each fight, he shows his courage and his love of glory . . .

Note

The question already acknowledged that Beowulf was a hero. This answer may eventually get to the point, but it wastes valuable time and energy. It also shows no sign that the student will compare the two characters.

> *Question:* The fall of Vicksburg is called the beginning of the end of the Civil War. Why?

> *Student's Analysis:* The question does not ask for details of the battle. Instead, it asks for an analysis of the effect that the fall of the city had on the outcome of the war.

> *Appropriate Response:* When Vicksburg fell, the backbone of the South was broken. The Mississippi River was then controlled by the Union forces and. . . . (The student does not discuss the battle itself,

but begins immediately to analyze what the loss of Vicksburg did to the Southern efforts.)

Inappropriate Response: Vicksburg fell because of in-fighting and jealousy between the southern leaders. . . .

Note

This response ignores the question's focus on the results of the fall of Vicksburg. A discussion of the causes of the fall signals the instructor that this student does not know the material well enough to answer the question.

Question: Compare the main features and outcome of the "Investiture Conflict" with the nature and consequences of Boniface VIII's struggle with European rulers.

Student's Analysis: The answer should demonstrate knowledge of both conflicts and their effects. In addition, it should compare and contrast the two conflicts.

Appropriate Response: The "Investiture Conflict" between Gregory and the Roman Emperor Henry IV, like Boniface's struggles with other European rulers, was a conflict between church and civil authorities. Boniface, though, based his stand on the dying tradition of feudalism. His failure to recognize the strength of the nationalist philosophy made his tactics largely ineffective. In contrast, Gregory's challenge resulted in. . . . (a lengthy essay that systematically described the main features of the first conflict and its outcome, then contrasted those points with the features and outcome of the second should follow).

Inappropriate Response: The "Investiture Conflict" had similar features to the conflict between Boniface and European rulers. Both conflicts had effects on history, and both involved much struggle and bitterness. . . .

Note

In the opening lines, the answer has managed to give no information whatsoever. Even if the answer eventually works its way to an actual response, this vague opening will have given the instructor a strong negative impression.

When you understand the direction of the question, give some thought to the expected thoroughness of your answer. A short answer worth five points does not demand the time or detail of a question worth twenty-five points. Remember that you must satisfy the instructor that you know the material well enough to select the most important and the most appropriate details.

Question: Explain the problems faced by a scholar who wishes to study original manuscripts of Old English literature. (5 points)

Analysis: A 5 point answer generally calls for a brief overview with minimal specific detail.

Response: The few surviving Old English manuscripts are in poor condition. The pages are crumbling and the writing is faded, often in a cramped and illegible hand. The language is radically different from Modern English.

Question: Explain the problems faced by a scholar who wishes to study original manuscripts of Old English literature. (30 points)

Analysis: Since the point value is greater, the question demands greater detail and explanation. The response given above, while not incorrect, is simply too sketchy for a 30-point answer.

Response: Few Old English manuscripts survive. Much of the literature was oral and the early Christian scribes worked mostly on religious matter. A secular work had to be significant and lucky to even be written down; even then, the survival of manuscripts from 1,000 years ago is almost miraculous. *Beowulf,* for example, is found in only one manuscript (MS Cotton Vitellius AXV) and two transcriptions based on that manuscript.

The few surviving manuscripts are in poor condition. In addition to the effects of age and wear, many suffered fire and water damage when Sir Robert Cotton's library, which housed one of the greatest early collections of medieval manuscripts, burned in the eighteenth century. Most of the *Beowulf* manuscript survived that fire, but it was damaged by heat and water and the edges have continued to crumble away.

An additional problem facing scholars is the cramped and varied handwritings. The very letters are unfamiliar to modern readers and the limited materials encouraged scribes to squeeze as much as possible into small spaces. Most words and sentences run together even in the clearest manuscripts; other manuscripts are obscured by fading inks, unusual handwritings, and inaccurate scribal work.

If scholars do find and decipher the manuscript, the language itself is an obstacle. Varied dialects and erratic spellings leave scholars guessing about many a line.

In sum, scholars wishing to study original manuscripts must have access to the few surviving works, good eyesight and great patience to identify the letters and translate the words.

Before you begin to write an essay response, make a brief list of points to be covered. Look over your list and number the points in order of importance. If you run out of time, you can then be sure that you have covered the major issues.

Unless the instructor gives you other directions, skip lines as you write. There will be no time to recopy, so leaving space for revision is good strategy. As you work through your list of points, answer directly without an effort to sound profound. You have no time for padded, wordy responses, so present your main points and provide specific details to fill in the logical framework. Check the clock to pace yourself. If you are taking too much time, consider moving on to the next question, but starting each new answer on a new page. Then, if you do have time to come back, you will have space to add to your answer.

Leave time to read over your responses for errors and omissions. If you need to add details to an earlier point, use the skipped line. In most cases, instructors are lenient about form, expecting legibility but not demanding clean copy. Know your instructor's policy about scratch-outs (usually a single line with the correction above it will suffice) and about additions that spill over to the back of the page (most instructors agree that an awkward inclusion is better than a missing point). As you review your content, check that:

- The question has been answered directly
- Major points have been covered
- Appropriate details are included
- Scratch-outs and additions are clear and legible
- Errors are corrected

SUMMARY

No one denies that essay examinations can be a test of nerves. But if you have studied the audience, the material, and the test itself, you are ready to respond to the essay questions. The same strategies that help you gather, plan, draft, and review other kinds of writing will work here, too.

Y O U R   T U R N

These questions were taken from recent exams at a major state university. Analyze the wording to identify the logical pattern expected in the response.

1. Introduction to Child Psychology: Bruno Bettelheim argues that children need fairy tales. How are fairy tales useful to children?

2. American Government: American political parties are often characterized as unstable and undisciplined. Write an essay in which you examine this characterization. Is it accurate? Why or why not?

3. Survey of British Literature: How does the Shakespearean or English sonnet use standard sonnet form? How is the Italian sonnet form different?

4. Environmental Toxicology: Concern has been expressed regarding the chronic exposure of humans to lead. Outline the health effects that have been identified and the reason for our concern.

5. Environmental Toxicology: Distinguish between active transport and facilitative diffusion.

6. Marine Microbiology: Discuss the significance of (and implications to marine microbiology) of the deep-sea thermal vents and chemosynthetic activity.

7. History of Western Civilization: What did Alfred the Great's England have in common with the Barbarian kingdoms of the Early Middle Ages?

8. History of Western Civilization: Evaluate Asser's *Life of Alfred* and its value to the historian.

9. Experimental Statistics: Discuss the pairs of concepts in each set below. Your discussion should include some basic definition of the concepts as well as all similarities and differences. Be complete yet concise:
   a. null hypothesis, alternative hypothesis
   b. critical region, acceptance region
   c. point estimation, interval estimation

PART FIVE

Handbook

EDITING THE COMPOSITION

Amateur writers sometimes regard editing as opposed to creativity. "If I concern myself with mechanical matters like grammar, spelling, and usage," they reason, "then my creativity will suffer." Like most erroneous views, this idea contains an element of truth. Thinking about editing during the planning or writing stage of the composition process can detract from creativity. The larger truth, however, is that in its proper place, editing enhances creativity. Mechanical errors not only call attention to themselves and thus distract readers from the writer's message, they also suggest that the writer is a careless person — the kind of person whose ideas readers often dismiss summarily.

Experienced writers invest the time to edit their work not because they value creativity any less than other writers, but because they value it more. They refuse to take the chance of having their message rejected because they did not bother to correct run-on sentences or punctuate correctly.

To become an effective editor, you must learn the important conventions of grammar, punctuation, spelling, manuscript mechanics, and usage that are detailed in the pages that follow. Even more important, you must develop skill in finding errors in your writing. There is no simple formula for doing so, but these two tips will help you:

1. *Become familiar with the kinds of errors you characteristically make. When your instructor discusses a particular error in class and you recognize it as one you have committed in the past, write it down in your notebook. When your instructor makes reference to something in this handbook when he or she returns your composition, read the appropriate section and add the error to the list in your notebook.*

2. *Whenever you write a composition, allow yourself adequate time to edit it. And don't make the mistake of looking for a number of errors at once. If you have problems with subject-verb agreement, comma splices, and pronoun reference, for example, read through your paper three times,* once for each kind of error. *In addition, be sure to notice what you* actually said, *as opposed to what you* intended *to say. The time it takes for the extra reading will be negligible, and you will be increasing your chances of finding all your errors.*

There will, of course, be occasions when the time you have to devote to editing will be severely restricted. The most common of those occasions will be when you are taking an essay exam. But even though you will be forced to streamline your editing efforts on such occasions, you should still use the basic approach outlined above.

Be aware that your writing already has a distinguishable style. Your instructor recognizes your preferred sentence patterns, your vocabulary, and your own "voice" in your writing. He or she also can predict what errors you are most likely to make. By making a list of the typical errors you make, you too can anticipate problem areas and correct your papers before you submit them. If you will be diligent about analyzing your errors and routinely search them out and correct them, you will make correct writing a habit in far less time than you imagined.

The handbook that follows is organized to make your editing easy. It begins with the grammar of words and sentences and follows with tips to improve spelling and the rules for punctuation and mechanics. It also includes material to help you avoid sexist language and a glossary of usage. Review the alphabetized correction and revision symbols listed on the inside front cover and familiarize yourself with what the handbook section can do to help you improve your writing.

Handbook

1 VERBS

Verbs are words that indicate the action or state of being of a subject. A verb that shows action and has an object is *transitive*—"I *bought* the Corvette." A verb that does not have an object is *intransitive*—"The Corvette's engine *broke down*." A verb that connects the subject with a noun or adjective that describes or renames it is a *linking* verb—"I *was* angry."

Because the form of a verb often changes when the subject of the action changes, errors in verb form can occur easily. The strategies we will discuss will help you solve your verb problems.

Principal Parts of Verbs

1 a KNOW THE PRINCIPAL PARTS OF THE VERBS YOU USE

The principal parts of a verb are the three forms from which the various tenses are constructed, *the present infinitive, the past tense,* and *the past participle.* Most English verbs are regular—that is, their tenses and past participles are formed by adding *-d* or *-ed* to the present infinitive. For example, the principal parts of the verb *to agree* are *agree, agreed, agreed;* the principal parts of the verb *to play* are *play, played, played.*

However, a number of English verbs do not follow this pattern. These irregular verbs form their past tenses and past participles differently, often by changing an internal vowel. Here are the principal parts of the most commonly used irregular verbs. Check this list for the verbs you are not familiar with and write their forms down several times so that you will remember them. Also check this list for the verbs you are likely to use. Highlight them, and use this chart as a resource when you discover you regularly misuse one of them.

Infinitive	*Past Tense*	*Past Participle*
arise	arose	arisen
be	was	been
beat	beat	beaten
become	became	become
begin	began	begun
bet	bet	bet

Infinitive	*Past Tense*	*Past Participle*
bid	bid	bid
bite	bit	bitten, bit
blow	blew	blown
break	broke	broken
bring	brought	brought
burst	burst	burst
buy	bought	bought
catch	caught	caught
choose	chose	chosen
come	came	come
cut	cut	cut
dive	dived, dove	dived
do	did	done
draw	drew	drawn
dream	dreamed, dreamt	dreamed, dreamt
drink	drank	drunk
drive	drove	driven
eat	ate	eaten
fall	fell	fallen
find	found	found
flee	fled	fled
fly	flew	flown
forget	forgot	forgotten, forgot
forgive	forgave	forgiven
freeze	froze	frozen
get	got	got, gotten
give	gave	given
go	went	gone
grow	grew	grown
hang*	hung	hung
hear	heard	heard
hid	hid	hidden
hurt	hurt	hurt
keep	kept	kept
know	knew	known
lay (to place)	laid	laid
lead	led	led
leave	left	left
let	let	let
lie (to recline)	lay	lain
lie (to tell an untruth)	lied	lied
lose	lost	lost

*Note: These are the forms of the verb *to hang* when it means *to suspend* (as with a ceiling fixture). When it means *to execute,* the forms are *hang, hanged, hanged.*

Infinitive	*Past Tense*	*Past Participle*
make	made	made
mean	meant	meant
pay	paid	paid
prove	proved	proved, proven
read	read	read
ride	rode	ridden
ring	rang, rung	rung
rise	rose	risen
run	ran	run
say	said	said
see	saw	seen
set	set	set
shake	shook	shaken
shine	shone	shone
sing	sang, sung	sung
sink	sank, sunk	sunk
sit	sat	sat
slide	slid	slid
speak	spoke	spoken
spin	spun	spun
spring	sprang, sprung	sprung
stand	stood	stood
steal	stole	stolen
strike	struck	struck
swear	swore	sworn
swim	swam	swum
swing	swung	swung
take	took	taken
teach	taught	taught
tear	tore	torn
tell	told	told
think	thought	thought
throw	threw	thrown

1 b AUXILIARIES USED TO FORM VERB TENSES

Learn the four auxiliary verbs used to form verb phrases. There are four auxiliaries which combine with a main verb to form verb phrases. These auxiliaries may be used singly with the main verb or they may combine to suggest various meanings.

The **be** auxiliary has eight forms (**am, is, are, was, were, be, being, been**). It is followed by either the present or past participle form of the verb.

Robin is leaving for California next week.
My income tax was figured for me by my nephew Jeff.
I am aware that you don't want to study any longer.
Charlie is being difficult about my loan.

The **modal auxiliaries (will, would, can, could, shall, should, may, might, must)** combine with other auxiliaries or with a main verb to indicate special meanings.

Necessity: You must go quickly while there is still time.
Obligation: I should let Alice know I don't intend to help her.
Possibility: I might get a car and drive through Yorkshire.
Ability: She can type your paper if she has the time.

1 c FORMATION AND USES OF TENSES

Use the principal parts of verbs to form tenses. Tense refers to the form of the verb used to indicate something about the time at which an action takes place. The verb may either be a single word or it may be a verb phrase consisting of one or more auxiliaries and a main verb. There are three simple tenses and three perfect tenses.

The Simple Tenses

Present tense is used to show action is occuring now, indicate habitual or repetitive action, state a fact, summarize plots or describe art, indicate future time.

I see you are wearing green.
I eat six small meals a day.
Water freezes at 32 degrees F.
Sammy quits his job and leaves.
Finals begin tomorrow.

Past tense indicates action occured in the past

I went home after John said he wouldn't help.

Future tense indicates that the action will occur in the future.

I will test the results soon.

The Perfect Tenses

Present perfect tense indicates that the action was begun in the past but is completed in the present. (Or that the action was begun in the past and continues in the present.)

I have run in all the River Road marathons.
I have always enjoyed your company.

Past perfect tense indicates that the action was completed in the past before some other past action.

I had heard that she was in town when I made these plans.

Future perfect tense indicates that the action will be completed before some future time.

I will have worked out my problems by the time Matt gets there.

Exercise

In the blanks below, write the correct form of the verb or verbs indicated in parentheses. Be sure to use the correct principal part of the verb and the appropriate helping verb if it is needed.

Sample: Last week I _____ in the garden and _____ house. (work, clean—both past tense)

Response: Last week I worked in the garden and cleaned house.

1. If we _____ earlier, I wouldn't be asking you to stop now. (eat—past perfect)
2. David _____ his undergraduate degree by next summer. (complete—future perfect)
3. We didn't know anyone who _____ in the new pool, so we _____ to swim in the old one. (swim—past perfect; decide—past)
4. If Al _____ what he said, we _____ sumptuously tonight. (mean—past; dine—future)
5. Once Lois _____ the list, we _____ the job of addressing invitations. (bring—past; tackle—past)
6. The ballerina _____ effortlessly as the music _____ to a crescendo. (spin—past; rise—past)
7. Jane _____ her novel by the time I _____ my short story. (write—future perfect; finish—past)
8. If only I _____ how exhausting ten miles of jogging would be, I would have found an excuse not to do it. (know—past perfect tense)
9. Henry is taking bets that we _____ State College by at least ten points next week. (beat—future tense)
10. After Edna _____ this semester, she plans to transfer to Yale. (complete—present tense)
11. Eloise _____ thirty minutes on a task that should _____ five. (spend—past; take—present perfect)
12. Agnes did nothing to her roommate, and yet her roommate _____ to criticize her to others. (continue—present)
13. He _____ the books on the table when the phone rang. (lay—past tense)
14. Roger _____ every afternoon after work. (gamble—present tense)
15. Because he was suspected of nonpayment of taxes, the IRS _____ his bank account. (freeze—past tense)
16. Angered by the taunts of his classmates, John _____ his arms about wildly, hoping to hit someone. (swing—past tense)
17. If Judy scores a total of eighty more points in the remaining games this season, she _____ seventeen points a game for her college career. (average—future perfect)

18. Naturally, the overweight man _____ in the flimsy antique chair. (sit—past tense)
19. The sun _____ brightly on the polished silver bowl. (shine—past tense)
20. Judy _____ to close the door before the cat _____ out. (spring—past tense; scamper—past tense)

1 d FORMATION AND USES OF PROGRESSIVE FORMS

Understand the make-up and uses of the progressive forms. The three simple tenses and the three perfect tenses may take progressive forms. The progressive forms are made up of the auxiliary **be** and the present participle (the **-ing** form) of the main verb. Here are examples of the various forms and uses of the progressive.

The Progressive Form of Simple Tenses

Present progressive form indicates action in progress in the present, also action in the future (formed with **is/am/are** plus present participle).

I am working 8 hours a day and taking 15 hours this semester.

He is flying to Los Angeles later tonight.

Past progressive form indicates action in progress in the past (formed with **was/were** plus present participle).

Sally was helping her mother move when John appeared.

Future progressive form indicates action that will be on going, (formed with **will be** plus present participle).

Monroe will be trying to find a job next summer.

The Progressive Form of the Perfect Tenses

Present perfect progressive form indicates action begun in the past and continuing to the present (formed with **have/has** plus **been** plus present participle.

The legislature has been considering the bill all night.

Past perfect progressive form indicates action that was in progress before some other action occurred (formed with **had** plus **been** plus present participle).

Aline had been working at Harry's for two weeks before she learned what to do.

EXERCISE

Identify the tense of the progressive verb forms in the following
sentences.

1. Sheila had been working at her job for three months before she
   realized she just didn't like it that much.
2. When I looked up, Mary Sue was driving off in the wrong direction.
3. I am trying to learn how to make bread.
4. Ronnie has been running every morning for a week.
5. My favorite boutique will be having a sale next week.
6. Bill will have been scrubbing his boat for two hours when you get
   there.
7. The police were questioning two suspects at the corner when I
   passed by.
8. I hope all our guests appreciate this meal; Ellen has been cooking
   all afternoon.
9. In my dream, I was screaming for help, but no one came.

1 e CORRECT USE OF **-S** AND **-ED** ENDINGS

Use -s and -ed endings correctly. When we conjugated the irregular
verb *to see,* you might have noticed that the third person singular
form of the present tense is different from the other present tense
forms. We say *I see, you see, he (she, it) sees, we see, you see,* and
they see. The difference is not peculiar to this verb—standard
English requires the *-s* or *-es* ending for the third person singular
form of the present tense of all verbs. Here are some examples of
the correct form with other verbs:

I go	We go
You go	You go
He (she, it) **goes**	They go
I do	We do
You do	You do
He (she, it) **does**	They do
I aggravate	We aggravate
You aggravate	You aggravate
He (she, it) **aggravates**	They aggravate

Even the verb *to be,* which changes in the second person singular as well as the third person singular, follows this rule. Note also
that in the conjugation of the verb *to be,* which follows, the -s ending is *not* used for the second person singular.

I am	We are
You **are**	You are
He (she, it) **is**	They are

Standard English also requires the *-ed* ending for all past tense forms of regular verbs. Thus it would be incorrect to say "I *use* to eat a lot of candy." The correct form is "I *used* to eat a lot of candy." Here are two additional examples of the correct form with different verbs:

I asked	We asked
You asked	You asked
He (she, it) asked	They asked

I poisoned	We poisoned
You poisoned	You poisoned
He (she, it) poisoned	They poisoned

EXERCISE

In the blanks below, write the correct form of the verb or verbs indicated in parentheses. Be sure to observe the *-s* and *-ed* rules where they apply.

1. Sammy _____ to hunt and fish. (love—present tense)
2. David's pizza _____ everybody else's taste bad. (make—present tense)
3. When I _____ her to dance, she _____ and _____ back to her mother. (ask, refuse, walk—all past tense)
4. _____ thanking me now make up for your negligence last night? (do—present tense)
5. José _____ the second round pick and _____ his mother. (accept, call—past tense)
6. Our team _____ Coach Sims and _____ him back. (miss, want—present tense)
7. It's the holiday season, and most people are happy, but Alice _____ depressed. (feel—present tense)
8. We _____ we had lost our maps and didn't know where we were. (discover—past tense)
9. When I was walking home last night, my brother _____ out from behind a bush and _____ me. (jump, scare—past tense)
10. He usually _____ coffee after dinner, but last night he _____ for tea. (order—present tense; ask—past tense)

1 f SUBJECT AND VERB AGREEMENT

1) Make subjects and verbs agree. A singular subject takes a singular form of the verb; a plural subject takes a plural form. This rule presents relatively little difficulty when the subject is a single word and is immediately followed by the verb. Few writers make the mistake of saying "The runners is crossing the line now" or "Even daily quizzes makes me nervous." However, not all sentence constructions are quite so simple. Following are the occasions in which subject-verb agreement errors most commonly occur.

- *When the subject and verb are separated by other words.* In many sentences the verb does not follow the subject immediately. In such cases it is easy to mistake the word closest to the verb for the subject. Consider this case:

Incorrect Verb Form	One of those kidnappers are certain to be arrested soon.
Correct Verb Form	One of those kidnappers is certain to be arrested soon. (*One* is the subject of the verb, not *kidnappers,* which is object of the preposition *of.*)
Incorrect Verb Form	Thanh, along with three other players, were honored at the football banquet.
Correct Verb Form	Thanh, along with three other players, was honored at the football banquet. (*Thanh* is the subject of the sentence and not *players* which is object of the preposition *along with.*)

In editing your compositions be sure your verb choices fit the real subjects and not merely the closest noun.

- *When the words* each *or* every *precede a compound subject.* The words *each* and *every* refer to each part of the compound subject as an *individual* person or unit. Therefore the singular form of the verb should be used. Here are some examples:

Incorrect	Every man and woman in the office *are* expected to contribute for the manager's Christmas gift.
Correct	Every man and woman in the office *is* expected to contribute for the manager's Christmas gift.
Incorrect	Each of the choir members *have* a degree in music.
Correct	Each of the choir members *has* a degree in music.

- *When the parts of a compound subject are joined by* or *or* nor. Sometimes the subject of a sentence has two or more parts. When the word that joins those parts is *and,* there is little confusion because the sense is usually plural, as in *"John and Andy were* the first students to submit their compositions." However, when the word that joins the parts of the subject is *or* or *nor,* the sense is different. The rule that applies in such cases is this: if all parts of the subject are singular, make the verb form singular; if all parts are plural, make the verb form plural; if one part is singular and another is plural, let the part of the subject closest to the verb govern the form of the verb.

Correct   Either Agnes or her sister *is* the one responsible for the damage. (Both parts of the subject are singular.)

Correct   Neither his friends nor his relatives *recognize* his talent. (Both parts of the subject are plural.)

Correct   Neither her shoes nor her blouse *matches* her suit. (*Shoes* is plural and *blouse* singular, so the nearer one governs the form of the verb.)

In editing your compositions, be alert for the words *or* and *nor.* When you find one of them, check to be sure you have chosen the correct verb form.

- *When the subject is a noun with plural form but singular meaning, an indefinite pronoun, a collective noun, or a relative pronoun.* A number of nouns that are plural in form usually have singular meanings and therefore take a singular form of the verb. *Athletics, mathematics, economics, physics, measles,* and *statistics* are examples of such nouns. Indefinite pronouns— that is, pronouns that do not refer to a specific person or thing— are also usually singular in meaning and therefore take a singular form of the verb. Examples of indefinite pronouns include *anyone, anybody, everyone, everybody, everything, each, either, neither, nobody, one, no one, someone, somebody,* and *something.* (The pronouns *all, some, any,* and *none* are exceptions to this rule and may take either a singular or a plural verb form depending on the sense of the word they refer to.)

Incorrect   *Measles are* a more serious disease than most people realize.

Correct   *Measles is* a more serious disease than most people realize.

Incorrect   I checked the house again and *everything were* in order.

Correct   I checked the house again and *everything was* in order.

A collective noun is singular in form, but it refers to a group of individual people or things. These nouns may take either a singular or a plural verb form, depending on whether they refer to the group as a whole or to each individual member of the group.

Committee, jury, council, family, group, team, panel, and *audience* are examples of collective nouns. Similarly, the relative pronouns *who, which,* and *that,* when used as subjects, take either singular or plural verb forms, depending on the sense of the sentence, and the sense of the particular nouns they refer to.

Correct	Judging by their applause, the *audience endorses* the idea. (The audience here is referred to as a single group.)
Correct	The *committee are* in disagreement about the issue. (The group here is referred to as a collection of individuals.)
Correct	The piranha is the only *fish that displays* a total disregard of mealtime restraint. (The singular form *displays* matches the singular form *fish.*)
Correct	There are few *people* I know *who are* as two-faced as Martha. (The plural form *are* matches the plural form *people.*)

- *When the subject is a gerund.* A gerund is a verbal noun—that is, a noun made by adding *-ing* to a verb. *Dancing, sweating,* and *collapsing* are examples of gerunds. Because gerunds look like verbs, you may fail to recognize them as the subjects of sentences. When you edit your compositions, be alert for gerunds that serve as subjects and check to be sure the form of their verbs is singular.

Incorrect	Jogging with others *help* me forget the pain involved. (*Jogging,* not *others,* is the subject of the sentence, so the verb form should be singular.)
Correct	Jogging with others *helps* me forget the pain involved.
Incorrect	Copying the ideas of other writers without crediting those writers *are* both morally and legally wrong. (*Copying,* not *writers,* is the subject of the sentence, so the verb should be singular.)
Correct	Copying the ideas of other writers without crediting those writers *is* both morally and legally wrong.

EXERCISE

Edit each of the following sentences for subject-verb agreement. If the sentence is correct as written, so indicate. If it is incorrect, revise the verb to make it correct.

1. A collection of brass and silver candlesticks were visible through the glass door.

2. Neither my aunt nor my grandparents is happy about my situation.
3. All of the apples looks spoiled.
4. Every student and instructor were called into the auditorium.
5. Statistics baffle me.
6. Running three miles in three days is my goal.
7. The only one of my friends who always goes an extra mile is Margaret.
8. Watching horror movies alone late at night when imagination plays its little deceptions are inadvisable, at least for nervous individuals.
9. Bob, surrounded by five new sisters-in-law, was happy to pose for a family photo.
10. Some of the people at our church object to the young people selling raffle tickets.
11. I know I have to take another course in my field, but economics are not all that interesting to me.
12. Neither prayer nor all-night cramming sessions the last week of the course is going to compensate for fifteen weeks of neglecting homework.
13. Athletics are the only reason Darrell came to this campus in the first place.
14. In today's world critical thinking skills are a definite requirement for effective leadership.
15. Dominic, Dewanda, and Linda (the mayor's daughter) is trying out for the cheerleading squad this year.
16. Neither the mayor nor the councilmen drives big cars.
17. None of my texts explains the material well.
18. Creating and drafting are two crucial stages of the writing process.
19. The musicians along with the soloist depends on a forceful conducter.
20. Walking ten blocks to classes are not my idea of a good parking place.

1 g SEQUENCE OF TENSES IN COMPLEX SENTENCES

Make the tense of the verbs in complex sentences reflect the sense of the sentence. In complex sentences, which have one main clause and at least one subordinate clause, it is important to make the tenses of the verbs in the clauses reflect the sense of the sentence.

Here are some examples of tense sequences with comments following them:

Correct   Lucille *realizes* that a career in mathematics *offers* more job security than one in drama. (The sequence of present tense followed by present tense conveys the meaning that Lucille *now realizes* that a math career *now offers* greater security.)

Correct   I *know* the service station attendant *cheated* me. (The sequence of present and then past tense conveys the meaning that the writer *at present* knows that the attendant cheated him *at some past time.*)

Correct   If I *get* a 70 or better on today's exam, I *will get* a B in the course. (The sequence of present and then future tense conveys the meaning that if the writer gets a 70 on *the present* exam, she will get a B *at some future time,* when grades are submitted.)

Correct   Last week on my soap opera my favorite character *learned* that her husband *cheats* on her. (The sequence of past followed by present tense conveys the meaning that the character *at some past time* learned that her husband *regularly* cheats on her.)

Correct   He *swore* that he *loved* her more than life itself. (The sequence of past tense followed by past tense conveys the meaning that *at some past time* he swore that, *at that very time,* he loved her more than life itself.)

Correct   She *lamented* that she *had been* foolish to marry for money. (The sequence of past and then past perfect tense conveys the meaning that *at some past time* she regretted that she had *at some previous time* decided to marry for money.)

EXERCISE

For each of the following sentences, choose the form of the verb that expresses the meaning specified in parentheses.

1. Esther knows she _____ backers before she can start her business. (Use the verb **to need** and convey the idea that she has this knowledge now.)
2. When I told her about Jim's good news, she _____ for joy. (Use the verb **to shout** and convey the idea the context clearly implies.)
3. By the time my father makes up his mind, I _____ too old to care. (Use the verb **to be** and convey the idea the context clearly implies.)
4. I gave him advice because he _____ for it. (Use the verb **to ask** and convey the idea that the request came before the advice was given.)

5. Sarah finally concluded that her roommate _____ two-faced. (Use the verb **to be** and convey the idea that being two-faced is a habit with the roommate.)

6. Laura refuses to acknowledge that she _____ a psychiatrist. (Use the verb **to visit** and convey the idea that she continues to visit the psychiatrist.)

1 h MEANING AND FUNCTION OF MOOD

The mood of the verb indicates the writer's attitude toward the statement. There are three moods in English: the indicative, the imperative, and the subjunctive. The first two are used far more frequently than the third and seldom cause writers confusion.

1) Use the indicative mood to state a fact or judgment or ask a question:

Mark volunteers his evenings to the Red Cross. (fact)

They deserve to be punished for drinking and driving. (judgment)

Why do you keep trying to persuade him to move out?

2) Use the imperative mood to give a direction or command (Note: The word *you* is understood but not expressed in the imperative mood):

Mark all sentence errors in your paper first.

Always wait until you have polished your ideas to begin editing.

3) The third mood, the subjunctive, is undoubtedly less familiar to you although you hear it and use it occasionally in such expressions as "The politicians be damned" or "Come hell or high water." Since these expressions come to us ready-made in our language, you don't have to be concerned about writing them incorrectly in your papers. However, you do need to understand the form and uses of the subjunctive. In the present tense, it differs from the indicative mood in that it uses only the plain form of the verb regardless of the subject. For example, whereas the present tense indicative mood of the verb *to go* is *I go, you go, he (she, it)* **goes,** *we go you go, they go,* the present tense subjunctive mood is *I go, you go, he (she, it)* **go,** we go, you go, they go. The present subjunctive form of the verb *to be* is *be* for all persons (rather than *am, is,* or *are*). Similarly, the past subjunctive form of the verb *to be* is *were* for all persons.

There are two common uses of the subjunctive mood:

- *Use the subjunctive mood in* **that** *clauses after verbs expressing commands, requests, or recommendations:*

The dean suggested that Roger withdraw from college.

Maggie demanded that Lola be on time to study for the final.

My literature course requires that a student write at least two critical papers.

- *Use the subjunctive form* **were** *in clauses beginning with* **if** *or expressing a wish if the idea being expressed is contrary to fact:*

David wishes Robin were able to be here tonight.

If I were the Dean, I would make an exception in José's case.

Note that not every **if** clause expresses an idea that is contrary to fact. For example, in the sentence "If John accepts the job in Detroit, he won't be able to attend the reunion," the idea being expressed may possibly become a reality, so the indicative mood form **accepts** is correct.

EXERCISE

Check each of the following sentences to determine whether the subjunctive mood is correctly used. Correct those that are in error.

1. I only wish I was in charge; I would give everybody a holiday.
2. Marie resents her parents demand that she quits smoking.
3. If Rosebud were registered, I would enter her in the cat show.
4. My parents asked that my brother fills the gas tank whenever it registers below half full.
5. I couldn't love Rover more than I do if he was purebred.
6. The jury found him guilty as charged and recommended that he receives the death penalty.
7. I wish my roommate was here now—I'd tell him what I think about his lousy housekeeping.
8. The manager recommended that Marcie is given a leave of absence to have her baby.
9. If he was more diligent in searching, he could get a job that would allow him to attend college in the mornings.
10. Politics be dammed! The governor is a good man.

2   PRONOUNS (PRON)

Pronouns have no meaning in themselves. They derive their meaning from the nouns they refer to, which are called antecedents. There are three broad kinds of pronoun error—incorrect case, faulty reference, and pronoun/antecedent agreement.

2 a PRONOUN CASE FORMS (CASE)

The case form of a pronoun matches its function in the sentence. There are three pronoun cases—subjective, objective, and possessive. The following chart shows the correct form of pronouns in each.

Subjective	Objective	Possessive
I	me	my, mine
you	you	your, yours
he	him	his
she	her	her, hers
it	it	its
we	us	our, ours
they	them	their, theirs
who	whom	whose

To avoid using the incorrect pronoun case, observe the following rules:

1) Use the subjective case if the pronoun is the subject of a clause, a complement after any form of the verb **to be** (**is, was, shall be,** etc.), or an appositive of the subject. If the subject, complement, or appositive has two or more parts, use the subjective case for each part. If the pronoun follows the conjunction **than** or **as** and is the subject of an implied verb, use the subjective case.

Subject of a Clause	My sister is prettier than I (am). She runs the sandwich shop, while he goes to the bank.
Complement after a Form of the Verb **to be**	It is he who must be responsible for this mess. If anyone deserves a break, it is they.
Appositive of the Subject	Only two people—he and Bonnie—were ever there when I needed them. Three instructors were rehired: Carsten, Elizabeth, and I.

EXERCISE

Examine each of the following sentences for errors in pronoun case. Correct the errors you find and be prepared to explain your reasoning.

1. No one regrets this more than me.
2. Two officers, Melanie and me, were re-elected.
3. Nobody knew it was him until it was too late.
4. Her and Clinton drove to the coast to see the pelicans.
5. Him and Bob caught 20 pounds of redfish.

6. Jake, Arthur, and me plan to go to Florida during semester break.
7. In my family the one whom finished dinner last had to clear the table.
8. Her mother and she look very much alike.
9. I wish I were as tall as him.
10. The boys called to say that them and their sister will be picking you up at nine o'clock.

2) Use the objective case if the pronoun is the direct object, the indirect object, or the object of a preposition. Also, use the objective case if the pronoun is the object of an unstated but understood verb.

Direct Object	Aunt Margaret treats Jim better than (Aunt Margaret treats) me.
	This test placed her in the top 20 in the country.
Indirect Object	Granny gave me her wedding ring.
	This job offers him the chance of a lifetime.
Object of a	Go with me to the drugstore.
Preposition	Jackie sat between Bertie and me.

Note: Speakers seldom use the form whom; however, careful writers choose it when the objective case is called for.

Exercise

Examine each of the following sentences for errors in pronoun case. Correct the errors you find and be prepared to explain your reasoning.

1. Who are you going to the dance with?
2. Mother gave Mary and I a piece of her mind.
3. Let's keep what we learned about Edna between we club members.
4. It wasn't me who chased the dog out of the classroom.
5. Careful attention must be paid to him while he is on this drug.
6. Anyone could do this job as well as me.
7. They frequently forget Wanda and I when we need them the most.
8. If Claudia hadn't been there, me and Susan would have been stranded.
9. I wanted to ask their clients and they if they'd be attending the dinner.
10. Whom did you think would type all night to get this done?

3) Use the possessive case if the pronoun shows possession or if it precedes a gerund. (A gerund is a verb ending in **-ing** that is used as a noun.)

Possession	Her necklace cost a fortune.
	Your work is cut out for you.
	My term of office is up.
Preceding a	Their shopping every day annoys mother.
Gerund	His complaining is getting on my nerves.
	The key to her great success is her refusing to yield to difficulty.

EXERCISE

Examine each of the following sentences for errors in pronoun case. Correct the errors you find and be prepared to explain your reasoning.

1. There is a reason for him eating late every night.
2. You having to take all the responsibility for the wreck is not fair.
3. The police report noted him weaving in and out of traffic.
4. You marking all the pages is a great help to the editor.
5. Him running out of money every month made starting a savings account impossible.

2 b PRONOUN REFERENCE (REF)

Because pronouns have no meaning in themselves but derive their meaning from their antecedents, their reference to those antecedents must be clear.

1) Make a pronoun refer clearly to one antecedent.

Confusing	When Marie introduced Agatha to Tom, she had no idea that she would marry him. (Does the second **she** refer to Marie or to Agatha? There is no way to be sure.)
Clearer	When Marie introduced Agatha to Tom, she had no idea that Agatha would marry him.

2) Be sure a pronoun refers to a word that is actually expressed in the sentence, and not merely implied.

Confusing	In my psychology professor's lecture, he mentioned the work of Viktor Frankl. (**He** logically refers to professor, but that word is not expressed in the sentence.)
Clearer	In his lecture today, my professor mentioned the work of Viktor Frankl.

3) Avoid using the pronouns **this, that, which,** and **it** to refer loosely to whole statements.

Loose Reference   My sister and her husband are planning to
                   take an extended vacation to Europe this
                   summer, which angers my father because
                   they've owed him money for several years.
                   (Here **which** refers loosely to the entire first
                   clause.)

Clearer   My sister and her husband are planning to
                   take an extended vacation in Europe this
                   summer, a fact that angers my father because
                   they've owed him money for several years.

4) Avoid using the pronoun **they** vaguely without a specific
antecedent.

Vague   I'm really disappointed with the health care in this
                   community. They really should do something to
                   improve it. (Who should do something? The pro-
                   noun **they** here has no specific antecedent.)

Improved   I'm really disappointed with the health care in this
                   community. Interested citizens and groups should
                   do something to improve it.

EXERCISE

Examine each of the following sentences for errors in pronoun
reference. Correct the errors you find and be prepared to explain your
reasoning.

1. Marcia wrote to Mary Ann every day when she was in Europe.
2. When Mark's first book came out, he autographed it for me.
3. Although Margaret had evidence to prove it, Henry thought the
   fantastic story was a lie, which was true.
4. The rivalry between the Tigers and the Bulldogs did not end until
   they had won seven games in a row.
5. I didn't invite Helen to the cookout, which was a big mistake.
6. Gladys told Marcia she was a disappointment as an actress.
7. After the principal's announcement on the microphone, he went to
   lunch.
8. Margaret and Clinton work jigsaw puzzles by the hour, which is
   amazing to me.
9. The policemen's arrival was delayed, so when they got to the scene
   of the crime, no witnesses were there.
10. She said she'd have to date more people before she could be sure
    we were right for each other, stressing that marriage for her would
    be a lifetime commitment. I strongly objected to that.

2 c PRONOUN AND ANTECEDENT AGREEMENT (AGR)

A pronoun agrees in number with its antecedent. Singular pronouns refer to a singular antecedent, and plural pronouns refer to plural antecedents.

1) Use singular pronouns to refer to indefinite pronouns (such as *each, every, anyone, anybody, everybody, everything, no one, each, every, either,* and so on) or to a plural antecedent prefaced by the word *each* or *every.*

Faulty Agreement	Every student in this class is expected to do a ten-page research paper on a topic of their choosing.
Improved	Every student in this class is expected to do a ten-page research paper on a topic of his or her choosing.
Alternative	Students in this class are expected to do a ten-page research paper on a topic of their choosing. (Make the antecedent plural when the passage would require repeated use of **he** or **she** or **his** or **her**.)

2) When the antecedent is a collective noun, one that can be either singular or plural (army, team, committee, panel), use either a singular or a plural pronoun depending on the meaning.

Correct	The panel made their decision based on their research.
Correct	The team discussed their demands before they left.

3) Use a singular pronoun to refer to singular antecedents joined by **or/nor;** use a plural pronoun to refer to plural antecedents joined by **or/nor;** make the pronoun agree with the antecedent nearest when a singular subject is joined to a plural subject by **or/nor.**

Correct	Neither the bird nor the squirrel would move from its perch.
Correct	Neither the doctors nor the nurses would accept the credit for their marvelous fundraising efforts.
Correct	Either Johnny or his buddies will tell me what happened to their wallets.

Exercise

Examine each of the following sentences for errors in pronoun agreement. Correct the errors you find and be prepared to explain your reasoning.

1. No one in the company I used to work for gave more than two weeks' notice when they quit.

2. Everyone on the team did their best.
3. The school board will announce their decision on the bond issue tomorrow.
4. Neither the choir nor the soloist are responsible for the failure of the performance.
5. Each person must do their best to bring about agreement.
6. The panel wants their decision upheld at the business meeting.
7. Every student must turn in their homework before leaving today.
8. Either the workmen or their boss are responsible for explaining why the work has been delayed.
9. If any one of the children needs a ride, they can call me.
10. Neither the coach nor the players mentioned the injury when he talked to the press.

3   ADJECTIVES AND ADVERBS (ADJ/ADV)

Both adjectives and adverbs modify (describe) other parts of speech, but they do not modify the same parts of speech. In addition, most adverbs end in *-ly,* but not all do; moreover, some adjectives end in *-ly.* For these reasons, adjectives and adverbs are sometimes confused.

3 a DIFFERENCES BETWEEN ADJECTIVES AND ADVERBS

Learn to distinguish adjectives from adverbs. The key to distinguishing adjectives from adverbs is to examine the function of the word that is being modified. Adjectives modify nouns or pronouns—that is, they provide descriptive detail about a person, place, or thing. Here are some examples of adjectives.

My brother enjoys *frozen* pizza, but I can't stand it. (The word *frozen* describes the word *pizza,* a noun, so it is an adjective.)

The *tall brunette* woman by the door is in my *poetry* class. (*Tall* and *brunette* modify *woman,* a noun, so they are adjectives. In addition, *poetry* modifies *class,* a noun, so it too is an adjective.)

He was *hard-working* and *deserving,* but his employer gave the promotion to someone else. (*Hard-working* and *deserving* describe *he,* a pronoun, so they are adjectives.)

Adverbs, on the other hand, modify verbs, adjectives, and other adverbs, usually answering where, when, how, or to what extent. Here are some examples of adverbs.

He ate the pizza *greedily.* (*Greedily* modifies *ate,* a verb, by telling the manner in which he ate, so it is an adverb.)

We waited a half-hour for her and *then* decided she wasn't coming. (*Then* modifies *decided,* a verb, by telling when.)

He is *very* anxious about his future with the company. (*Very* modifies *anxious,* an adjective. *Very* is therefore an adverb.)

The band I heard tonight played *really* well. (*Really* modifies *well,* an adverb, so it is an adverb.)

EXERCISE

Each of the italicized words in the following sentences is either an adjective or an adverb. Decide which each word is by examining the word it modifies, as shown in the above examples. Be prepared to explain your choice.

1. He came toward me with a *frowning* face.
2. He addressed the crowd *loudly,* then sat down to *scattered* applause.
3. Drinking and driving is a *deadly* practice.
4. I hope you will answer me *truthfully* so that I can get a *realistic* picture of what I have to face.
5. The *ragged* roses bloomed through the summer heat waiting *patiently* for the rain to come.

3 b USES OF ADJECTIVES AND ADVERBS

Use adjectives and adverbs correctly. Choosing the correct form of a word for your own writing is somewhat more difficult than being able to identify the form when you see it written. Yet if you exercise care and are willing to look up an occasional word in the dictionary, you will not find it a burdensome task. Many of the errors that occur with these two parts of speech involve relatively few words that people stubbornly resist learning. The following are among the most common:

Incorrect	He plays the guitar *good.* (The word *good* is used here to modify *plays,* a verb. But *good* is an adjective. An adverb is needed.)
Correct	He plays the guitar *well.*
Also Correct	He is a good guitarist. (The word *guitarist* is a noun, so it is proper to use the word *good* to modify it.)
Incorrect	We got home from the dance *real* late. (*Late* is an adverb signifying when, so it is incorrect to use the adjective *real* to modify it. An adverb is needed.)
Correct	We got home from the dance *really* late. (*Really* is an adverb, so it is the correct form here. *Very* is another adverb and might have been substituted for it.)

3 c COMPARATIVE AND SUPERLATIVE FORMS

Use comparative and superlative forms correctly. Often we use adjectives comparatively. For example, we don't just say that Tim is *strong,* but that he is *stronger* than Pat, or the *strongest* in his grade. Many adjectives follow this progression, forming the comparative degree by adding *-er* and the superlative by adding *-est.* Others add the word *more* instead of the suffix *-er,* and *most* instead of *-est.* For example, we say *difficult, more difficult,* and *most difficult.* Words in both these categories are called regular adjectives.

Many other adjectives, however, follow a different progression. They form their comparative and superlative degrees not by adding a suffix or a word, but by changing to a different form altogether. *Good* is an example of such an *irregular* adjective. We don't say *good, gooder, goodest,* but *good, better, best.* Here are some further examples of both regular and irregular adjectives.

Regular Adjectives

Positive	Comparative	Superlative
dark	darker	darkest
tall	taller	tallest
swift	swifter	swiftest
angry	angrier	angriest
healthy	healthier	healthiest

Irregular Adjectives

Positive	Comparative	Superlative
many	more	most
little	less	least
bad	worse	worst

Most adverbs are regular, progressing to comparative and superlative forms by adding *more* and *most* to the positive forms. However, some progress irregularly by means of internal changes.

Regular Adverbs

Positive	Comparative	Superlative
pleasantly	more pleasantly	most pleasantly
sorrowfully	more sorrowfully	most sorrowfully
quickly	more quickly	most quickly
carefully	more carefully	most carefully

Irregular Adverbs

Positive	Comparative	Superlative
well	better	best
badly	worse	worst

In choosing comparative and superlative adjective and adverb forms, keep these rules in mind:

- The comparative degree is appropriate whenever the comparison involves *two* people, places, things, or actions; the superlative, when the comparison involves *more than two*.

- It is never correct to use both the word *more* and the *-er* ending (as in *more friendlier*) or to use both the word *most* and the *-est* ending (as in *most friendliest*).

- It is incorrect to use comparative or superlative forms with words that do not logically permit comparison. Examples of such words are *real, unique, perfect, round, square, empty,* and *dead*. (Something cannot be more real than something else, nor can anything be most dead. It is either real or unreal, dead or alive.)

EXERCISE

1. Decide whether each of the following words is an adjective or an adverb by determining whether it would make sense modifying a noun or pronoun, on the one hand, or a verb, adjective, or adverb, on the other. Then use each word correctly in a sentence. (If you have difficulty classifying a word, consult your dictionary.)

   willingly   heavy   sad
   certain   quickly   gracefully
   hard   lovely   terrible
   clumsily   picturesque   tactful

2. Read the following sentences carefully to determine whether the adjectives and adverbs are used correctly. If you find an error, rewrite the sentence to eliminate it.
   a. Sometimes a little advice sure does help.
   b. Doug took me serious and learned to play the guitar good.
   c. Everything happened very sudden.
   d. I find her painting to be the most unique I have ever seen.
   e. My roommate plays the piano real well.
   f. He talks very loud when things are not going good.

4 SENTENCES

Up to this point in the handbook, we have considered word-level problems. Now we will consider problems that occur at the sentence level. The most serious of these are sentence fragments, run-on sentences and comma splices. However, such errors as faulty predication, faulty modification, mixed or incomplete constructions, faulty parallelism, and unnecessary shifts in person, tense, or number also cause problems in clear communication of ideas.

4 a SENTENCE FRAGMENTS (FRAG)

Learn to distinguish sentence fragments from complete sentences and avoid them, except for special effects. A sentence fragment is a group of words that is punctuated as if it were a sentence but does not have all the grammatical elements necessary to make it a complete sentence, or a group of words that is introduced by a subordinating conjunction and standing alone. If you have a sentence fragment problem, it is probably because you have difficulty distinguishing a phrase or a subordinate clause from a complete sentence. Here's how to do so. First check to be sure that the group of words in question has both a subject and a verb. If it does, then check to be sure that no introductory word makes it grammatically dependent on some other group of words. Any group of words that has a subject and verb and is not introduced by such a subordinating word is a complete sentence. Let's see how this simple test can be applied to actual cases:

Words in Question	*Analysis*
Sam and I look forward to swimming in the campus pool. At least once a week.	The first group of words set off as a sentence has both a subject and verb *(Sam and I* and *look forward)* and has no introductory subordinating word. Therefore it is a complete sentence. But the second group of words has no verb; thus it is a fragment and should not be set off as a sentence. The passage should be revised to read: "Sam and I look forward to swimming in the campus pool at least once a week."
The dean spoke sharply to the students. Revealing her anger over the incident in the cafeteria.	The first group of words has a subject and a verb *(dean* and *spoke)* and is not introduced by a subordinating word. It is therefore a complete sentence. The second group of words, however, has neither subject nor predicate. (Though *revealing* is formed from the verb *to reveal,* it is a participle, not a verb.) The passage should be revised to read, "The dean

spoke sharply to the students, revealing her anger over the incident in the cafeteria."

I love winter. Although I hate driving on slippery winter roads.

Despite its brevity, the first group of words is a complete sentence because it has a subject *(I)* and a verb *(love)* and is not introduced by a subordinating word. The second group of words, however, is not a complete sentence. Even though it has a subject *(I)* and a verb *(hate)*, the introductory word *although* makes it dependent on the previous sentence. The passage may be revised to read, "I love winter, although I hate driving on slippery winter roads," or "I love winter. However, I hate driving on slippery winter roads." (The word *however,* unlike *although,* does not subordinate what follows it.)

Following are additional examples of sentence fragments. Each of them can be identified by using the approach demonstrated. Use that approach with each to understand why each is a fragment. (In each group of words the fragment is italicized.)

Fragment	Sentence fragments are easy to find. *If you know what to look for.*
Correction	Sentence fragments are easy to find if you know what to look for. (Or, "Sentence fragments are easy to find. You just have to know what to look for.")
Fragment	Sandy has to take her car to the garage tomorrow. *To get the front end aligned.*
Correction	Sandy has to take her car to the garage tomorrow to get the front end aligned.
Fragment	Please wait here for me. *While I run into the bank and get my check cashed.*
Correction	Please wait here for me while I run into the bank and get my check cashed.

Fragment	There is one ingredient of success more important by far than talent. *A willingness to persevere until the job is done.*
Correction	There is one ingredient of success more important by far than talent—a willingness to persevere until the job is done. (Or, "There is one ingredient of success more important by far than talent. That ingredient is a willingness to persevere until the job is done.")
Fragment	I wouldn't let anyone borrow my clothes. *Especially someone like Lisa, who doesn't even take care of her own things.*
Correction	I wouldn't let anyone borrow my clothes, especially someone like Lisa, who doesn't even take care of her own things.

Many professional writers use sentence fragments on occasion for special rhetorical effects. Such use is justified because those writers have enough writing experience to distinguish between effective and ineffective (awkward) fragments. As an amateur writer, you should avoid the use of sentence fragments in all situations except those in which you are answering your own question, as in these examples:

Acceptable Fragment	Should a professor be expected to tolerate rudeness in class? *No, never.*
Acceptable Fragment	Will I accept her apology if she decides to offer one? *Of course.*

Exercise

Check each of the following groups of words to determine if it contains a sentence fragment. If it does, rewrite the passage to eliminate the fragment.

1. What we need is a new governor. A governor with intelligence and guts.
2. She returned the shorts and requested a refund. Which she never got.
3. L. L. Bean is my favorite mail order company. Although their sizes sometimes don't match what I am accustomed to.
4. Aunt Rita had a severe heart attack. When she saw a strange face at her window.
5. Clinton decided to mow his lawn last week. While Richard was mowing ours.

6. I've decided to cancel my membership in the book club. Because they keep sending me books after I haved mailed back the cards with "send no selection" checked.

7. Traveling with someone else is enjoyable. However, traveling alone is boring.

8. Some people will resort to all kinds of deceptions rather than apologize. The most pathetic of which is pretending that they have been offended.

9. There are no uninteresting subjects. Only uninterested people.

10. Many people favor the banning of pornographic magazines and films. Claiming that even if such material does not lead directly to sex crimes, it nevertheless fosters immature and potentially dangerous attitudes toward women.

4 b RUN-ON SENTENCES AND COMMA SPLICES (RUN-ON, CS)

Learn to recognize run-on sentences and comma splices. These errors consist of running two grammatically complete thoughts together, either without any punctuation (a run-on sentence) or with only a comma (a comma splice). Such errors usually occur because the writer fails to recognize that each thought is grammatically independent of the other. Both errors may be corrected in one of the following ways:

1) Separate the independent thoughts with a comma plus a coordinating conjunction (and, but, or, nor, for, so, or yet).

Run-on Sentence	I know it's foolish to remain faithful to her when she is unfaithful to me I just can't make myself go out with anyone else.
Correction	I know it's foolish to remain faithful to her when she is unfaithful to me, but I just can't make myself go out with anyone else.
Comma Splice	That man is not fit to hold elective office, he certainly won't get my vote.
Correction	That man is not fit to hold elective office, so he certainly won't get my vote.

2) Separate the independent thoughts with a semicolon.

Run-on Sentence	The study of history is not for me I don't do well with names and dates.
Correction	The study of history is not for me; I don't do well with names and dates.
Comma Splice	I went water skiing for the first time yesterday, unfortunately, in three hours I never made it to my feet once.

Correction   I went water skiing for the first time yester-
              day; unfortunately, in three hours I never
              made it to my feet once.

3) Express each independent thought in a separate sentence.

Run-on Sentence   After two days of hoping that the throbbing
                   in my tooth would go away by itself, I made
                   the decision I had resisted I would visit the
                   dentist.

Correction   After two days of hoping that the throbbing
                   in my tooth would go away by itself, I made
                   the decision I had resisted. I would visit the
                   dentist.

Comma Splice   "Diamonds are forever" sounds nice, I doubt,
                   though, that it applies if you don't keep up
                   the payments.

Correction   "Diamonds are forever" sounds nice. I doubt,
                   though, that it applies if you don't keep up
                   the payments.

4) Subordinate one of the thoughts by adding an introductory
word, such as *although, if, when, since,* or *because.* Or change the
construction of the sentence—for example, by revising "She
dropped the tray, then she started crying" to "She dropped the
tray, then started crying."

Run-on Sentence   I know what it means to operate on a sched-
                   ule I worked in a fast-food restaurant for
                   two years.

Correction   I know what it means to operate on a sched-
                   ule because I worked in a fast-food restau-
                   rant for two years.

Comma Splice   He wanted to remember his uncle as he had
                   known him, he never visited the funeral
                   home.

Correction   Because he wanted to remember his uncle as
                   he had known him, he never visited the
                   funeral home.

E X E R C I S E

Check each of the following passages to determine if it contains a run-
on sentence or a comma splice. If it does, rewrite the sentence to
eliminate the error.

1. I have learned that I do have choices in the past I have acted as if I didn't.
2. Research shows that child abusers usually were themselves abused as children I can't understand that at all I'd think that the experience of being abused would make a person less likely to abuse others.
3. Your anxiety is caused from your not accepting the possibility that life may not turn out as you want it to, you want a guarantee that you will get your way.
4. I still observe important occasions of the year, such as birthdays, Thanksgiving, and Christmas, in the way my family observed them, I believe one of the most precious gifts I can give my children is training in the art of celebrating with loved ones.
5. You learn to write by writing, not reading, until you believe this, you will keep putting off the moment to begin.
6. I've learned not to expect recognition for my successes, if I did I'd have spent most of my life in disappointment.
7. To overcome dependency and become independent is the main challenge of life it begins at birth.
8. I'm constantly surprised at the number of people in pain who don't take action that is within their control to reduce their pain, excessive weight, for example, is painful in many ways, yet many people don't work on reducing.
9. Less than a mile from my house is a nuclear power plant, unlike many people, though, I'm not in the least concerned about an accident.
10. She had driven away all who cared for her by her devotion to her ego, now in old age, when she desperately wanted someone to be close to, no one was there.

E X E R C I S E

Following is a letter of application written by a student for her business writing class. Revise each fragment, comma splice, and run-on sentence.

Dear Mr. Thompson:

I read in the February 12, 1989 <u>Times-Picayune/States Item</u> that you are looking for prospective employees, therefore I am applying for a position as a counter salesperson. Because of my coursework and job experience in communications and sales. I am able to bring various skills to your company, Budget Rent-A-Car.

I am presently majoring in International Trade and Finance at LSU. Expecting to graduate in May, 1991. I have been a member of the International Association of Students in Economics and Business Management and the French Club. I can bring communication skills to your company that I have learned in speech fundamentals. Also in speech communication for business and the professions, and business writing.

Not only do I have the communications skills specified in your advertisement, but I also have sales skills as well. As a sales associate at Macy's, I sold men's and women's merchandise, and took inventory, as a salesperson at Xanadu, I sold housewares and gift items.

I would very much like to discuss my qualifications with you in an interview. Would you please write me at the above address? Being available for interviews in the afternoon from May 13 through May 30.

Yours truly,

Mary Dixon

4 c FAULTY PARALLELISM (/ /)

Learn to recognize faulty parallelism. Parallelism is the use of similar grammatical structures for words, phrases, or clauses in a series and for coordinated or paired items.

> After inviting the guests, I got busy making *sandwiches, dips,* and *cookies.* (nouns)

> You should know that this job requires you *to write letters and reports, to make proposals,* and *to survey customer preferences.* (phrases)

> *What I do with my money, what I do with my time,* and *what I do with my talents* is my own business. (clauses)

Dewanda will either take *German* or *Italian.* (paired words)

Carlos *can go to graduate school* or *he can go to work for Exxon.* (paired phrases)

Not only do *we wash windows,* we also *wax floors.* (paired clauses)

EXERCISE

Revise the following sentences which contain faulty parallelism. Put a check by those that are correct.

1. This piece is easy to play and which is beautiful to listen to.
2. They had planned to meet at Marcy's, pack a lunch, and leave before sunup.
3. Ben likes to ride motorcycles and playing baseball.
4. Sheila refused to learn word processing and keeping books.
5. The new clerk is enthusiastic, knowledgeable, and dependable.
6. Students fall naturally into three types: the achievers, the over achievers, and those who under achieve.
7. What could Alice tell you about disappointment and grieving over lost chances?
8. In her dorm room, she felt lonely and without a friend.
9. David planned to study all this week for his ACT and working on his tennis game next week.
10. I find your negative attitude, your complaining, and your refusal to cooperate grounds for dismissal.

4 d FAULTY PREDICATION (PRED)

Make sure the subject and predicate of the sentence make logical sense. Faulty predication occurs when the subject and predicate do not make logical sense. That is, the meaning of the subject is not directly related to the meaning of the predicate. Consider this sentence: "The meaning of the flower in the story symbolizes youth and vitality." The predication here is faulty because, though a flower can symbolize something, a meaning cannot. The sentence should be revised to read, "The flower in the story symbolizes youth and vitality."

Faulty predication often occurs with forms of the verb to be (**is, were, are,** and so on.) Because this verb links the subject of the sentence with its complement, creating a kind of equation, the subject and complement must fit together both logically and grammatically. Thus in the sentence "My broken typewriter is the reason I didn't complete the assignment" the predication is faulty. A typewriter can't be a reason—though, of course, the breakdown of a typewriter can be. Or consider this sentence: "Faulty predication is when a subject and verb do not fit logically and grammatically."

The verb **is** should be followed by a noun that renames or by an adjective which describes it.

To correct faulty predication, re-phrase the sentence to make the subject and verb, or the subject and its complement, fit together logically. Here are some examples of such revision:

Faulty Predication	Flattery is when you praise someone with an ulterior motive. (Flattery is not a time, as the word **when** indicates. Further, the **when clause** is an adverb, not a noun or an adjective.)
Revision	Flattery is praise with an ulterior motive.
Faulty Predication	Her only objection was the price of the tickets. (The price itself cannot constitute the objection, though the **unreasonableness** of the price can.)
Revision	Her only objection was that the price of the tickets was excessive.
Faulty Predication	The actor's strong voice was an outstanding performance. (A **voice** is not a performance.)
Revision	The actor's strong voice contributed to his outstanding performance.

EXERCISE

Check the predication in each of the following sentences. If it is faulty, revise it.

1. Her main trait is talking too much.
2. Prejudice is when you have a preconceived opinion about something or somebody.
3. Prayer in the schools is an argument people get very excited about.
4. Rock music creates negative attitudes in children.
5. Plagiarism is where you quote a source without documenting it.
6. Clean air and economic recovery are problems for this president.
7. The choice of Edgar as class president was chosen without regard for experience and ability.
8. The activities for the elderly are a swimming pool and pool table.
9. The list of reasons you shouldn't stay here is numerous.

4 e FAULTY MODIFICATION (MOD)

Make a modifier refer clearly to another word or phrase in the sentence. Faulty modification exists whenever a modifier does not clearly modify the word it was intended to modify. There are three types of faulty modification: *squinting*, *dangling*, and *misplaced*.

1) Modification is *squinting* if the reader cannot tell whether the modifier refers to the preceding or the following word. For example, in the sentence "I explained last week I would be absent from class," it is not clear whether the explanation was given last week or whether the absence was to have occurred then. To correct squinting modification, rephrase the sentence to make the intended modification clear. In the above case, the corrected sentence might read, "Last week I explained that I would be absent from class," or "I explained I would be absent from class last week." Here are some additional examples.

Squinting	The inn I work at often has a band playing on weekends. (Does the writer work there often, or does a band play often?)
Correction	The inn I often work at has a band playing on weekends.
Squinting	The material he had memorized completely failed to come to mind during the exam. (Did he memorize it completely or did his effort to remember it fail completely?)
Correction	He had memorized the material, but he completely failed to recall it during the exam.

2) A modifier is *dangling* if it does not logically modify some word in the sentence. This error usually occurs in sentences with introductory participial, prepositional, or infinitive phrases. It can be corrected by placing the words you intend the phrase to modify directly after the phrase. Here are some examples of dangling modification:

Dangling	Sprinting toward the finish line, Ace's feet got tangled and he fell on his face. (Who was sprinting? Ace, not just Ace's feet.)
Correction	Sprinting toward the finish line, Ace got his feet tangled and fell on his face.
Dangling	While driving on Interstate 95, a terrible accident happened. (Who was driving? Surely not the accident.)
Correction	While driving on Interstate 95, I saw a terrible accident happen.
Dangling	To be fully awake for my eight o'clock class, six-thirty is the latest I can get up. (Who is awake? You or six-thirty?)
Correction	To be fully awake for my eight o'clock class, I can't get up any later than six-thirty.

The error of misplaced modification can also occur with prepositional phrases or adjective clauses. Such phrases and clauses are usually understood to modify the word (or words) that immediately precede them. If that word is not the one the writer intended to modify, confusion will result. To correct misplaced modification, move the misplaced word, phrase, or clause so that it conveys the meaning you intend.

Misplaced Phrase	We had just finished dinner when the doorbell rang on the patio.
Revised	We had just finished dinner on the patio when the doorbell rang.
Misplaced Clause	The blue car belongs to my brother that was parked in front of my house.
Revised	The blue car that was parked in front of my house belongs to my brother.

3) Modification is *misplaced* if the word modified is not the one the writer intended to modify. This error frequently occurs with such words as *almost, even, exactly, hardly, just, simply, nearly,* and *only,* which modify the word or words immediately following them. Notice how the meaning of the following sentences is affected by the position of the word *only:*

She *only* smiled to him as she passed him in the hall. (She didn't speak to him; she only smiled.)

She smiled *only* at him as she passed him in the hall. (She didn't smile at anyone else, only at him.)

She smiled at him *only* as she passed him in the hall. (She never smiled at him anyplace else, only in the hall.)

EXERCISE

Check each of the following sentences to determine if it contains squinting, dangling, or misplaced modification. If it does, rewrite the sentence to eliminate the error.

1. Using a well-tested recipe, most casseroles can easily be made.
2. While stirring the boiling fudge, my cat walked into the kitchen and asked for her tuna.
3. My gym teacher said I was a 150-pound weakling with a smile.
4. When discussing the latest box office favorite, the actor's ability to act interests the movie critic the most.
5. The roller skates nearly cost $50.
6. David bought a new tire in a little store in New Roads that cost $29.95.

7. George had fifty cents in his pocket exactly.
8. Traveling only thirty miles an hour, a blowout caused our car to swerve into an oncoming truck.
9. Robin almost worked five hours preparing dinner for us.
10. I found the diamond necklace John gave me in the wastebasket.
11. While eating their lunch, the superintendent told them they would have to work overtime.
12. While dancing with another guy, my boyfriend walked into the room.
13. A song played on the radio frequently reminds me of a particular person or incident.
14. The expensive watch drew admiring glances from everyone in the office that Jim's wife had gotten for his birthday.
15. As a rule, people who only think now and then think poorly.

4 f MIXED OR INCOMPLETE CONSTRUCTION (CON)

1) Mixed construction occurs when two incompatible grammatical constructions are used together in a sentence. In such a sentence the writer begins to express a thought one way and then shifts to another way in mid-sentence, thereby violating grammar and making the meaning unclear.

Given the fact that ideas often come to us in rapid succession, it is understandable that from time to time two slightly different ideas will compete for expression in a single sentence. Here's how that can happen. A writer is thinking of these two thoughts simultaneously: "Although Sam is not an honor student, he is very conscientious" and "The fact that someone is not an honor student does not necessarily mean that he or she is irresponsible." But when the writer expresses the thoughts, she does not state one and then the other. Instead, she writes this mixed construction: "Although Sam is not an honor student does not mean he is irresponsible."

Not all mixed constructions, however, occur because the writer combined two separate thoughts. Sometimes they occur because the writer failed to choose between two ways of expressing a single thought. Here are two examples of this error:

Mixed	Because of his recent surgery is the reason he couldn't complete the physical education requirement.
Correction	Because of his recent surgery, he couldn't complete the physical education requirement.
Alternative Correction	His recent surgery is the reason he couldn't complete the physical education requirement.

Mixed	By doing it this way is the fastest way to achieve our goal.
Correction	Doing it this way is the fastest way to achieve our goal.
Alternative Correction	By doing it this way we can achieve our goal most quickly.

2) Incomplete construction occurs when the writer omits one or more words necessary to convey the meaning intended or required by the sense of the sentence. Not all omissions are errors, of course. Here are some examples of acceptable omissions:

Acceptable Omission	My life has been easy; my sister's, hard. (The omission of the words *life has been* in the second half of the sentence is acceptable because they are stated in the first half and the omission causes no confusion.)
Acceptable Omission	Some people prefer Italian food, others Chinese, and still others French. (The omission of the verb *prefer* from the middle and end of the sentence is acceptable because it is the correct form for each of the three parts of the sentence and is clearly implied by the sentence structure.)

The omission of *necessary* words, on the other hand, is an error. Here are some examples of such incomplete construction:

Incomplete	Marie needs twelve more hours of social science; Susan and I, nine each. (The omission of the verb in the second half of the sentence implies that the verb *needs* is intended. However, unlike the subject *Marie,* the subject *Susan and I* is plural, and so requires the plural form of the verb, *need.*)
Correction	Marie needs twelve more hours of social science; Susan and I need nine each.
Incomplete	I like Brunhilda better than Yvonne. (Expressed this way the sentence is confusing. Does the writer like Brunhilda better than she likes Yvonne, or better than Yvonne likes Brunhilda?)
Correction	I like Brunhilda better than Yvonne likes her. (Or ". . . better than I like Yvonne.")
Incomplete	My group had fewer cavities. (Fewer cavities than during the last testing period? Fewer cavities than other groups? Fewer cavities than a dog has fleas? The comparison must be completed to be meaningful.)

Correction   My group had fewer cavities this year than last year.

When editing your composition for mixed or incomplete constructions, be sure to look closely at what you actually said, instead of merely letting your eyes scan the paper as you think of what you *meant* to say.

EXERCISE

Check each of the following sentences to determine if it is a mixed or incomplete construction. If it is, rewrite it to eliminate the error.

1. Because one leg is shorter than the other makes her back hurt.
2. By talking too much gets George in trouble.
3. When Lisa studies with her boyfriend causes her grades to fall.
4. The supermarket near my house has better fruit.
5. Esther enjoys an evening at home with a good book better than her sister.
6. After jogging for six miles every day is the time I enjoy a tall glass of lemonade.
7. By saving some money monthly is the best way to get enough for a down payment on your house.
8. He was a very excitable person and not because he was really lying was the reason he failed the lie detector test.
9. Even though you like a subject does not mean it represents a good career choice for you.
10. He comes from a poor family is the reason he appreciates things the rest of us take for granted.

4 g UNNECESSARY SHIFTS IN PERSON OR TENSE (SHIFT)

Shifts in person or tense often cause difficulties for beginning writers. Some shifts cannot be avoided—the thought being expressed demands them. For example, if you were writing about automobile accidents and turned from one involving several friends to one in which you alone were involved, you would have to shift from "my friends" to "I." Similarly, if you were contrasting the attitude you had toward studying in high school with your present attitude, you would correctly begin with past tense and then, at the appropriate time, switch to present tense.

Not all shifts in person or tense are necessary, however, as these examples illustrate:

Unnecessary Shift   Travelers should always carry traveler's
in Person   checks because you might lose your wallet. (Unnecessary shift from third to second person.)

Correction	You should always carry traveler's checks when traveling because you might lose your wallet.
	or
	Travelers should always carry traveler's checks; they might lose their wallets.
Unnecessary Shift in Tense	Al enjoys baking bread since he has retired. He often takes a loaf to his hostess when he is invited out to dinner. Even if he had other things to do, he would take the time to make a special loaf and presents it proudly as he arrived. (Unnecessary shift from present to past.)
Correction	Al enjoys baking bread since he has retired. He often takes a loaf to his hostess when he is invited out to dinner. Even if he has other things to do, he takes the time to make a special loaf and presents it proudly as he arrives.

EXERCISE

Check each of the following for unnecessary shifts in person or tense. If you find any, revise them to eliminate the error.

1. Many students on this campus lack table manners. You will see them shovel food into their mouths without pausing to breathe, reach across someone else's tray for the salt, talk with their mouths full of food, and burp at their neighbors.
2. We waited four hours for the match to begin, and then Boris walks on the court and proceeds to beat Michael three straight sets.
3. Many travelers wait too late to make their plans. You should not procrastinate if you want good reservations.
4. As the day wore on, Marcie starts complaining and makes herself a nuisance.
5. Most people join the Y for fitness programs. You can take classes or work out alone.
6. Larry and I talked and tried to understand each other, and then he begins accusing me of neglecting him.

5   SPELLING (SP)

Even though misspelling is largely a thing of the past for writers who have access to word processors, those who do not must still learn strategies for dealing with the problem. Many poor spellers regard their problem as a challenge to become excellent spellers.

They try to memorize spelling rules and keep a dictionary handy to look up every word they are unsure of. Some succeed with this approach, but others soon grow weary of forgetting the rules, becoming confused in applying them, or spending much valuable time flipping through the dictionary. Frequently, these people eventually admit defeat and resign themselves to producing writing filled with spelling errors and receiving low grades.

If you are growing weary of the effort to become a good speller, or if you have already abandoned hope, then this spelling section is designed for you. It does not aim to teach you how to write without committing spelling errors. Instead, it aims to teach you how to correct your errors, quickly and effectively, after you have made them. In other words, it treats spelling not as a writing problem but as an editing problem.

In the pages that follow, you will find no specific spelling rules to memorize (though if you already have learned such rules, you should certainly go on using them). Nor is the approach presented here a complicated one to use. It may be summed up in three simple guidelines:

- *Forget about spelling while you are writing—turn your attention to it only after you have finished revising your rough drafts.* Looking up words while you are writing can interfere with the flow of thought and cause writer's block. In addition, since it is impossible to be sure during the writing stage which words will survive the revision stage, it is inefficient to look up words then.

- *Use your own personal spelling list and a spelling dictionary.* A speller's dictionary is more compact and easier to use than a regular dictionary because it contains no definitions. (There are a number of good spelling dictionaries on the market— ask your instructor or campus bookstore manager for help in choosing one.) Your personal spelling list should include any words your instructor indicates you have misspelled in your compositions. But you needn't wait to begin your list until you have received one or more corrected compositions. The rest of this section will help you begin creating your list immediately.

- *Learn the causes of spelling errors.* There are numerous causes of spelling errors. The five presented below are the most common. Read them carefully and circle all those words that have posed problems for you in the past. Then include them in your spelling list and use that list to edit your compositions.

1) Words That Are Often Mispronounced

Each of the following correctly spelled words is frequently misspelled because it is mispronounced.

apt
arctic
athlete
athletic
boundary
children
congratulate
drowned
February
generally
government
grievous

history
hundred
hungry
interest
kindergarten
laboratory
library
literature
memory
mischievous
nuclear
pertain

probably
recognize
relevant
represent
sophomore
strictly
surprise
temperament
temperature
veteran
Wednesday

2) Words That Are Similar in Sound

Each of the words in the following list is often confused with a word that sounds like it. The result is not only a spelling error but also an error in meaning. (Each pair listed here is also listed in the glossary of usage. Consult the glossary about any of these words you are unsure of.)

accept, except
affect, effect
allot, a lot
allude, elude
already, all ready
altogether, all together
always, all ways
anyway, any way
are, our
ascent, assent
beside, besides
board, bored
capital, capitol
censor, censer, censure
choose, chose
conscience, conscious
diner, dinner
forth, fourth
gorilla, guerrilla
hear, here
hole, whole
illusion, allusion
its, it's
lay, lie
lead, led
lightning, lightening
loose, lose

maybe, may be
moral, morale
passed, past
patience, patients
personal, personnel
petition, partition
phase, faze
presence, presents
principal, principle
propose, purpose
quite, quiet
rain, reign, rein
raise, raze
right, rite, write
rise, raise
road, rode
sent, cent, scent
sight, site, cite
since, sense
sit, set
so, sow, sew
stationary, stationery
straight, strait
then, than
there, their, they're
through, threw
to, too, two

tortuous, torturous
waist, waste
weak, week

were, where
whose, who's
your, you're

3) Related Words That Are Spelled Differently

Some words are spelled differently in their different forms. Spelling errors result from using the spelling of one form where it does not apply. Here are some examples of such words.

advice, advise
argue, argument
breath, breathe
comedy, comic
courtesy, courteous
descend, descent
describe, description
destroy, destruction
disaster, disastrous
enter, entrance
envy, enviable, envious
explain, explanation

generous, generosity
grief, grieve, grievance
high, height
hunger, hungry, hungrily
influence, influential
judge, judgment
marry, marriage
omit, omission
paralyze, paralysis
varied, various
vengeance, vengeful

4) Words with Prefixes, Suffixes, or Troublesome Internal Letter Combinations

The most common prefixes include *im-, a-, in-, un-, dis-, mis-, per-, pre-,* and *pro-.* Some spelling errors occur in words with prefixes because the writer is uncertain whether the root word stays the same or changes with the addition of the prefix. *Immoral* and *disappear,* for example, are commonly misspelled for this reason. Other errors occur because of confusion about the meaning of the prefix and thus about what prefix is appropriate to use in a particular situation. That is the case when a writer uses *per*scription to mean *prescription.* To gain more confidence in using prefixes correctly, use this approach—the next time you look up a word beginning with a particular prefix, look up several other common words beginning with that prefix and add to your list any that you are unsure of. Your investment in time will be minimal, and you will very soon have gained control over all your problem prefixes.

Suffixes cause even more spelling problems than prefixes. You will have to choose between *-able* and *-ible; -ant* and *-ent; -cede, -ceed,* and *-sede; -ery* and *-ary; -or, -er,* and *-ar;* and so on. Unfortunately, you can't put the alphabetical format of the dictionary to work for you with suffixes as you can with prefixes, so you must be prepared to look up each word with a problem suffix once. Nevertheless, by writing it down on your list when you look it up, you will at least ensure that you will not have to look it up more than once. Moreover, if you are alert to the correct spelling of words when you read, you can often save yourself even that first lookup.

Troublesome internal letter combinations are yet another cause of spelling errors. *Thief,* for example, may be incorrectly spelled *theif,* or *receive* incorrectly spelled *recieve* because the writer is not sure which vowel comes first. Or, to take a somewhat different problem, *existence* may be incorrectly spelled *existance* or *separate* incorrectly spelled *seperate* because the sound of the correct vowel is indistinguishable from the sound of the incorrect vowel. You need have no great difficulty overcoming these nagging problems if you write the troublesome word on your list correctly and consult the list when you write. (If any of the words used as examples in this paragraph are problem words for you, be sure you write down the correct spellings given here.)

5) Words with Unusual Plural Forms

Sometimes a writer spells a word correctly in the singular, but incorrectly in the plural. Not all English nouns form their plurals by adding a final *s.* Here are some of the other plural forms:

analysis, analyses   mother-in-law, mothers-in-law
body, bodies   phenomenon, phenomena
child, children   potato, potatoes
leaf, leaves

Whenever you look up a noun in the dictionary, note not only the singular form but the plural form as well, and write both on your spelling list. That will help you avoid errors caused by unusual plural forms.

EXERCISE

Check each of the following sentences for spelling errors. For every misspelling you find, write the correct spelling of the word.

1. Have you heard that old saying, "Absense makes the heart grow fonder"?
2. We tried to be sure Rebecca had enough cloths to last her for ten days of summer camp and to get her promise she would be conscientous about writing home.
3. If you can get him to except he must go slowly to loose weight, I think he will have more sucess this time.
4. What we wanted was a petition across this end of the room to give us more privecy.
5. Don't waist all that good juice; save it for you're breakfast.
6. Once Janice conceeded we could be right to, she went along with our suggestions.

7. That patient was refered to me by a former oponent of my procedures.

8. It's hard to relize Marcy is ten years old.

9. When the principle makes his announcements on the loud speaker, most students start talking or take an oportunity create a disturbance of some kind.

10. When I received my first paycheck, I took Jane and Judy to Juban's for lunch.

11. According to stereotype, mother-in-laws always make life difficult for their daughter-in-laws.

12. This is strickly confidential—those ackes and pains Agnes is always complaning about are more imaginary then real.

13. The way that doctor harrasses his patients, it's a wonder anyone goes to him.

14. Alcohol has been known to indeuce a certain paralasis of the tongue.

15. More and more people today seem to be demonstrating a complete lack of morale principal.

16. So far the attempts to inforce quiet hours in the dormatories have been disasterous.

17. Maude has an ingenius way of injecting her narrow little opinions into every discussion.

18. Separate checks please, waiter—I don't want my freind here to develope a dependancy on my generosity.

19. The personel policy of this company is to hire people on their merits, and not on the bases of age, color, or sex.

20. Talk about clumsiness—that's the forth time in recent weeks I've seen him brake a dish.

21. Allow me to purpose a toast—to loyalty, the hallmark of freindship.

22. The present administration is similiar to the previus one in at least one respect—its contempt for the common worker.

23. Any act that excedes the boundries of good taste is in my view a grievious offense.

24. The dean is accessable, all right, but there's little benefit in that because you can't recieve a strait anser from her.

6   PUNCTUATION (PUNCT)

Half the battle of solving punctuation problems is understanding that you are dealing with a limited number of punctuation marks to use and a limited number of ways to use them. Some students fail to understand this fact and panic before what seems to them an infinite array of marks and uses. If you are one of these writers, be assured that you can master this very important aspect of clear, effective writing.

Mastering the craft of punctuation is important because punctuation marks serve a very practical purpose—to enable readers to follow the writer's thinking and grasp his or her message not vaguely, but precisely. The contribution of punctuation to the overall effectiveness of a composition is much greater than is commonly realized. To appreciate this fact more fully, try to unravel the meaning of the following passage from the writing of T. S. Eliot, a master of English prose and poetry, with all his punctuation removed.

> For literary judgment we need to be acutely aware of two things at once of what we like and what we ought to like few people are honest enough to know either the first means knowing what we really feel very few know that the second involves understanding our shortcomings for we do not really know what we ought to like unless we also know why we ought to like it which involves knowing why we don't yet like it it is not enough to understand what we ought to be unless we know what we are and we do not understand what we are unless we know what we ought to be the two forms of self-consciousness knowing what we are and what we ought to be must go together.

If you were able to understand the passage, it wasn't without difficulty. Reading it undoubtedly took you much longer than was necessary. You may even have had the feeling you were working your way through a maze or piecing together a puzzle. To read that way is hardly an efficient or pleasurable activity. Now take another look at the same passage, this time as it was originally written by the author.

> For literary judgment, we need to be acutely aware of two things at once: of "what we like," and "what we *ought* to like." Few people are honest enough to know either. The first means knowing what we really feel: very few know that. The second involves understanding our shortcomings; for we do not really know what we ought to like unless we also know why we ought to like it, which involves knowing why we don't yet like it. It is not enough to understand what we ought to be, unless we know what we are; and we do not understand what we are, unless we know what we ought to be. The two forms of self-consciousness, knowing what we are and what we ought to be, must go together (T. S. Eliot, 1936, p. 83).

Your second reading was surely faster and easier, for the punctuation significantly aids your understanding of the rather complex idea that T. S. Eliot is communicating. This example should make abundantly clear that the words and sentence structure writers use are not enough to convey meaning. *The way they mark the spaces between words is as important as the words themselves.* Those marks are the reader's signposts along the path of meaning.

Let's examine punctuation by breaking down the marks of punctuation into four broad areas—end punctuation, internal punctuation, the punctuation of words, and the punctuation of quoted material. Then let's take each one and examine the limited number of marks in each.

End Punctuation

End punctuation marks are the period, the question mark, and the exclamation point.

6 a PERIOD (.)

1) Use a period to signal the end of a statement or command.

We all did well on the examination.
Try to keep your room neater.

2) Use a period after abbreviations.

Dr.   Mrs.   Ms.   B.A.   D.D.S.

6 b THE QUESTION MARK (?)

Use a question mark after a direct question.

Did that movie really receive rave reviews?

6 c THE EXCLAMATION POINT (!)

Use the exclamation point after an interjection or exclamatory statement. Do not overuse it, or you will reduce its effectiveness.

Help! Police!
The building is on fire!

Internal Punctuation

Internal punctuation is used within sentences to separate words, phrases, and clauses. There are five internal punctuation marks: the comma, the semicolon, the colon, the dash, and parentheses.

6 d THE COMMA (,)

1) Use a comma to link main clauses joined by a coordinating conjunction *(and, but, or, nor, for, so, yet)*.

Many farmers were financially harmed by the government's embargo on the sale of grain to the Soviet Union, and they instructed their representatives to oppose any similar action in the future.

They may decide to stay in the dormitory and study despite the noise, or they may work in the library instead.

My brother didn't get his application in on time to take the civil service examination, so he'll have to wait until they offer the examination again.

2) Use a comma to separate introductory phrases and clauses from a main clause and to separate an opening quotation from the rest of the sentence.

Phrases	As far as I know, you may take all the samples on the table.
	Happy at receiving the promotion, Ethel took her husband and children out to dinner at an expensive restaurant.
	According to the director of admissions, this college's enrollment has dropped four percent a year for the past three years.
Clauses	After the fight was over, Jerry walked home to tell his side of the story.
	If you plan to go to that game, you'd better get your ticket early.
	When you start your diet, you should join a support group.
	When my child is sick, I find it difficult to go to class.
Opening Quotation	"You mind your business and I'll mind mine," he said brusquely.

3) Use commas to separate items in a series and to separate coordinate adjectives (those that modify a noun separately).

Words	Their team was faster, taller, and more aggressive than ours.
	David, Robin, and Ed attended the seminar last night.
Phrases	Be sure to bring a tent, a sleeping bag, food for four days, and an extra pair of boots.
	My duties at home kept me busy—helping my mother with the cooking and cleaning, taking care of my younger sister, and washing and ironing clothes for the whole family.

Clauses	I really don't care about what you wear, how you comb your hair, or when you bathe.
	In case you haven't heard, John teaches in Norway, Alice practices medicine in Texas, and Mary keeps house at home.
Coordinate Adjectives	She is a determined, popular, able candidate.
	It was a dark, rainy, lonesome night.

4) Use commas to set off parenthetical elements—phrases and clauses that do not restrict the meaning of the sentence, contrasted elements, words that interrupt a quotation to provide information, transitional words and phrases, nouns of address, mild interjections, and absolute phrases.

Phrases	Stan, the leader of the protest, rose to speak.
Clauses	My father, who never slept late, was up at the crack of dawn to see us off.
Contrasted Elements	Our Tigers won the championship, not that team from Denham Springs.
Words Interrupting Quotation	"If I never see him again," she sobbed, "it'll be too soon."
Transitional Words and Phrases	However, the time is not right to quit.
	In fact, I don't care which you choose.
Interjections	I'll stick with this to the end, by George.
	Ah, I don't know when I've heard better music.
Absolute Phrases	The clock having stopped at 12 o'clock, we had to guess about when to start dinner.
	His health being what it is, Jimmy needs to lose some weight.

5) Use commas to separate items in geographical names, dates, addresses, and professional titles.

Geographical Names	New Orleans, Louisiana, is the home of the Sugar Bowl.
	Our family will have a reunion next year in Palestine, Texas.

Dates	Monday, March 10, is the deadline for all entries in the marathon.
	John wants your reply by December, 1992, but I happen to know he will give you until January 1, 1993, if you can't reach decision by then.
	or
	John wants your reply by December 1992, but I happen to know he will give you until 15 January 1993 if you can't reach a decision by then. (You may omit commas if you omit the day of the month or if you preceed the month with the day.)
	Our first child was born November 15, 1980, in Louisville.
Addresses	Just mail this to Sarah Burns, 908 University Drive, Vienna, VA 22180. (Note that no comma is used between state and zip code in addresses.)
Professional Titles	The name on the card is James Babin, Ph.D.
	Make your check out to Linda Steward, M.D., not to Linda Steward, M. A.
	Mercer C. Irwin, Chief Executive Officer, will address our annual meeting.

Exercise

In each of the following sentences add one or more commas, following the rules for the comma explained in the preceding pages.

1. Although Sara has called him repeatedly he refuses to have anything to do with her.
2. His face red with anger his voice loud and quivering the coach tried to rally the team to victory.
3. Maggie who often teases her little brother doesn't want to be teased herself.
4. What I want is a sunny warm quiet day on the beach.
5. My feet hurt my back is sore and I'm tired of hiking.
6. In my opinion students should go to school as a full-time job.
7. Go to bed right after supper buy three alarm clocks hire two strong men to shake you awake and do whatever else is necessary to get to class on time.

8. Unlike the student living in a dormitory the student living off campus faces few distractions.
9. My professor expects students to do their work neatly thoroughly and on time.
10. I found an old letter dated September 19 1895 written to my mother by the principal of her school.
11. My address will be 725 Bourbon Street Baton Rouge LA 70808 but if you forget just write me at my old address and my mother will forward your letter.
12. I found the music difficult the director unsympathetic and the choir dispirited.
13. If you ask me a little positive good natured criticism is in order.
14. Moreover the regulation about freshman parking is discriminatory.
15. They may decide to stay in the dormitory and study despite the noise or they may work in the library instead.
16. According to the director of admissions this college's enrollment has dropped four percent a year for the past three years.
17. Stan the leader of the protest rose to speak.
18. Her voice trailing off she finished quickly and sat down feeling she had failed miserably.
19. Their team was faster taller and more aggressive than ours.
20. My view in short is that the sex education in some form should begin in the first grade.

6 e   THE SEMICOLON (;)

Limit the use the semicolon to joining grammatically equal sentence elements.

1) Use the semicolon to join two main clauses not joined by a comma and coordinating conjunction.

Nothing could be further from the truth; I love to go to any old movie.

When I looked around the clerk had gone; evidently, he had a better customer.

I have kept quiet; however, I can't keep from protesting this affair much longer.

2) Use a semicolon to separate coordinate items containing commas.

The three speakers on our panel were Dorothy Malin, head of the English Department; Alice Walsh, director of the writing program; and Mark Andrews, a freshman, majoring in engineering.

Note: Do not use a semicolon to join sentence parts which are unequal grammatically.

Faulty	Although I need aerobics desperately; I am not yet willing to give the time required. (Adverb clause joined to a main clause)
Correct	Although I need aerobics desperately, I am not yet willing to give the time required.
Faulty	I started out with three goals in mind; to increase endurance, to become more flexible, and to lose weight. (Main clause joined to a list)
Correct	I started out with three goals in mind: to increase endurance, to become more flexible, and to lose weight.

EXERCISE

In each of the following sentences, add commas and semicolons wherever they are needed according to the preceding rules.

1. The road to excellence is long and hard only those who are dedicated can survive its rigors.
2. There are three kinds of people that I find insufferable: those who value money and position above friendship those who derive enjoyment from mockery and ridicule and those who lacking a particular virtue themselves find ways to harm those who possess it.
3. When you are in town and ready call me for a game of tennis I'd like nothing better than to beat you.
4. Henry has half a dozen women wild about him Bart can't even get a date.
5. I've used every dollar I had to get my car fixed therefore I can't even think about going to Florida for spring vacation.
6. When I inventoried my attic I was amazed to find such things as bits and pieces of cedar tattered faded clothes three tents some cracked dishes and a torn worn-out yellow rain slicker.
7. He attacked the problem with real style unfortunately more than style was needed to solve it.
8. Sally and Betty thought their losing streak would never end however they practiced for two weeks and found they were stronger than ever.
9. Whenever a new diet is called for Sam will supply it unfortunately no diet seems to work for him.
10. My wife expects me to do well in school however she has no idea how hard it is to work 40 hours a week and take 15 hours of classes.

6 f THE COLON (:)

Use the colon to separate, set off, or introduce certain sentence elements.

1) Use a colon to separate from the main clause any material that explains, illustrates, or amplifies it.

> There is one thing that no teacher need tolerate in class: loud snoring.
>
> Daydreamers seldom accomplish much: they exhaust themselves in imagining.

2) Use a colon to separate titles and subtitles, between time figures, and between chapter and verse in Biblical references.

> Someday I'm going to write a book. It will be titled *The Art of Procrastination: A Guide to Goofing Off.*
>
> My mother often quoted Galatians 6:7 to her children when they were growing up: "Be not deceived; God is not mocked: for whatsoever a man soweth, that shall he also reap."
>
> The meeting will start promptly at 10:30 A.M.

3) Use a colon to set off a list or series.

> Only three people are graduating with distinction: Bertha, Henry, and Clyde.
>
> My reasons for remaining here are the following: the trip is too costly, I can't take the time from my studies, and my part-time employer needs me to work this weekend.

4) Use a colon to introduce a formal quotation.

> G. K. Chesterton once offered this wry definition of journalism: "Journalism largely consists of saying 'Lord Jones Is Dead' to people who never knew Lord Jones was alive."

EXERCISE

In each of the following sentences add one or more semicolons or colons, following the rules explained on the preceding pages.

1. My landlord must be getting rich he has two large houses, each with twelve students, and charges an outrageously high rent.
2. If Anna thinks she can get away with browbeating me, she'd better think again I've had more than enough of her nonsense.
3. Few people in her class ever got to know her well she kept to herself during school hours and never attended after-school functions.

4. I can give you four reasons for staying here for graduate school you already know the professors well you can get a teaching assistantship with no problem and you are near several major companies where you can do consulting.
5. In some states the legal driving age is 16 in others, 18 in still others, 15.
6. Most everybody knows Psalm 23 1 from memory.
7. Hypocrisy is a kind of willful schizophrenia the hypocrite has two personalities, one of which he or she keeps hidden from public view.
8. I'm not going to give up on the problem however, I am going to put it aside until my frustration subsides.
9. I'm going to title my paper "Marriage A Risky Enterprise."
10. Of all the proverbs I've read, this one is my favorite "The person who can't dance says the band can't play."

Exercise

Following is a letter written by a student for his business writing class. Revise the punctuation by adding commas and semicolons where they are needed and deleting them where inappropriate.

Dear Dr. Taylor:

After watching your documentary last week on the five o'clock news I realized how much you care about cancer patients. Because of your deep concern, and willingness to help the sick; I am requesting permission to conduct research on the imagined interactions of cancer patients, with their doctors, at the research center. I feel this research will be extremely beneficial to patients, and doctors alike.

Imagined interaction research involves surveying, and interviewing patients on a voluntary basis. The primary focus is to ascertain how the patient envisions conversations with his or her doctor. In other areas of imagined interaction research such as debaters envisioning how different judges respond to their arguments; correlation was found between positive and negative imagined interaction and the degree of success, which actually occurred in real debates. I am hopeful some correlation can be found between cancer patients, who imagine positive conversations with their doctor concerning their cancer and the manner in which these patients handle their treatment, and cancer in general. My research to this point indicates that some correlation will be found, given a large enough sample, the research will also take into account different types of cancer treatment techniques and stages of cancer infection.

I would like to begin preliminary research in April, please inform me of your decision as soon as possible. My address and telephone number as well as references, and information concerning my qualifications are enclosed.

I hope to hear from you soon. You are on your way to curing cancer perhaps the research will help you meet the patients' needs until you get there.

Yours truly,

Darrell Porter

6 g THE DASH (—)

In recent years the distinction between the dash* and the colon has all but disappeared. Today many respected writers use them almost interchangeably—many even prefer the dash. (Two uses have resisted this change—the introduction of formal quotations and the separation of titles and subtitles. The colon alone is acceptable there.) Unless you are writing for an audience you have reason to believe will prefer the more traditional colon (for example, the readers of a scholarly journal), follow these guidelines:

Limit the use of a dash to separate from the main clause any material that explains, illustrates, or amplifies it, to set off a list, or to emphasize some parenthetical element.

There is one thing that no teacher need tolerate in class—loud snoring.

Daydreamers seldom accomplish much—they exhaust themselves in imagining.

*Note: Most typewriters do not have a dash key. To make a dash in typing, use two hyphens with no spacing before, after, or between them.

Only three people are graduating with distinction—Bertha, Henry, and Clyde.

His table manners—specifically, the way he chomps his food, wields his knife and fork like primitive weapons, and drools all over himself—leave something to be desired.

In addition, you may use the dash to set off a parenthetical element that occurs within a sentence and that you want to emphasize. Use one dash before the element and another after it, unless it occurs at the end of the sentence, in which case omit the second dash. Here are some examples of this use:

His table manners—specifically, the way he chomps his food, wields his knife and fork like primitive weapons, and drools all over himself—leave something to be desired.

Many a time she sat at home until the early hours of the morning—worried and angry and at a loss to understand— while her husband drank himself blotto at some bar.

He dug the well by hand—an exhausting procedure that left him lame for a week.

6 h PARENTHESES ( )

Parentheses may be used to de-emphasize certain elements in a sentence; specifically, elements that do not restrict the meaning of the sentence. For example, in the sentence "Only one boy, Tom, was late for class," "Tom" is a nonrestrictive element. It adds a specific detail, but the meaning of the sentence would not be changed if that detail were omitted. So we could place it in parentheses instead of commas if we wanted to de-emphasize it. (However, if the sentence were changed to "Only Tom was late for class," then we could not place "Tom" in parentheses, because the sentence depends on that word for its meaning.) In addition, parentheses are used for "asides," elements that interrupt the thought of the sentence. Careful writers avoid using parentheses too frequently, for frequent interruption of the flow of thought can be distracting to the reader.

Bill Johnson (whose father graduated from this college in 1950) earned the highest grade point average in this year's graduating class.

The men on this campus (excluding, of course, my boyfriend and yours) are incredibly ugly.

Mr. Norton holds (Can you believe it?) a *distinguished* teaching professorship at this college.

My roommate was arrested last night for littering (a charge that anyone who has seen his side of our room would find eminently believable).

Note that in the third example the question mark is placed inside the parentheses. This is the case whenever the words within the parentheses express a question. When the words outside the parentheses express a question, then the question mark is placed outside. Note too that in the last example the period is placed outside the parentheses. That is usually where it is placed. (The only exception to that rule is in cases where the parenthetical element comprises the entire sentence, as it does in this sentence.)

EXERCISE

Each of the following sentences contains a parenthetical element set off by commas (or one comma if it occurs at the end of the sentence). Decide whether the sense of the sentence suggests it should be left as it is, emphasized, or de-emphasized. If a change is desirable, rewrite the sentence providing the appropriate punctuation.

1. The widely supported tax measure was today vetoed by the governor, an action that dramatically demonstrates her "tax- payers-be-damned" attitude.

2. The two best players on the team, Ace and Brian, have had offers from several professional organizations.

3. My dormitory, affectionately known as "The Pit," is an experience in less-than-elegant living.

4. She worked hard to attain her lifelong dream, the presidency of a large corporation.

5. The know-it-all tone, which implies that the writer thinks he has all the answers and is unwilling to consider the views of others, makes readers resentful and uncooperative.

Punctuation of Words

The three punctuation conventions we will now consider are associated with the smallest unit of written expression—the individual word. These conventions are the apostrophe, the hyphen, the slash.

6 i THE APOSTROPHE (')

1) Use the apostrophe to show possession or ownership. (If the noun in question ends in **s,** add only an apostrophe. If it does not end in **s,** add an apostrophe and an **s.**)

John's anger

the dog's bone

the child's game

the children's game

Agnes' car

Lois' dress

the princess' carriage

the boy's shoes (one boy)

the boys' shoe (more than one boy)

the dinosaur's habitat

the dinosaurs' habitat

Bob and Bill's room (one room, joint possession)

Bob's and Bill's books (more than one book, individual possession)

the mother-in-law's kindness

the mothers-in-law's kindness

2) Use the apostrophe to form contractions.

can't

won't

there's

shouldn't

it's (Do not confuse with the possessive pronoun *its.*)

3) Use the apostrophe to form the plurals of numbers, letters, and
words used as words. (It is also acceptable to form such plurals
without an apostrophe.)

Mind your p's and q's. (or ps and qs)

His u's and n's are indistinguishable.

He makes his 4's strangely, too. (or 4s)

We are nearly into the 1990's (or 1990s)

There'll be no if's, and's, or but's about it. (or ifs, ands, or buts)

6 j THE HYPHEN (-)

1) Use a hyphen to divide a word when it will not fit at the end
of a written or typed line. Convention requires that the break
occur between syllables. For example, the word *experimentation*
could be broken as follows: *ex-peri-men-ta-tion.* (Notice that
where a syllable consists of a single letter, *i* in this case, that
syllable is usually not carried over to the next line.) A good dictionary is your best guide in questions of syllabication.

2) Use a hyphen to form compound numbers up to ninety-nine; to
express fractions *(two-thirds, one-fifth);* to join two or more words
used as a single adjective *(a fur-lined jacket);* and to separate some
prefixes, notably *self-, all-,* and *ex-,* from the words they modify *(a
self-made man, all-embracing policies,* and *ex-champion).*

3) Use a hyphen to form compound words. Since such words in
time become a single unhyphenated word *(wallboard, baseball,*

handyman), no list of compounds will remain accurate for very long. A current dictionary is your best guide here.

EXERCISE

Each of the following sentences contains one or more omissions or misuses of apostrophes or hyphens. Rewrite each sentence, making the necessary corrections. Be prepared to explain your changes.

1. He said he wouldn't be able to afford the tuition next year.
2. Freds sister is a lawyer in Philadelphia.
3. When it came to drooling, Pavlovs dog had no peer.
4. There are eighty six students in my biology lecture section.
5. She spends three quarters of her allowance on junk food.
6. No one would guess that Gerry is an ex convict.
7. I know she's a successful author, but buying a gold plated typewriter is a bit extravagant.
8. If you lack self esteem you cant really be happy.
9. My cars exhaust system has to be replaced.
10. Proficiency in writing doesnt depend so much on talent as on willingness to refine your first efforts.

6 k THE SLASH (/)

1) Use the slash between two terms to show they are related in some way.

Douglas decided to take his math course pass/fail.

Charlie's arguments nearly always take an either/or position. (Note: There is no space separating the slash from the words it connects.)

2) Use the slash to separate lines of poetry run into the text.

When Dewayne read "my father moved through dooms of love / through sames of am / through haves of give," he just gave up trying to understand poetry.

(Note: A space precedes and follows the slash in this usage.)

3) Use the slash to separate the numerator from the denominator in fractions.

7/8   5 1/3

EXERCISE

Each of the following sentences contains one or more omissions or misuses of apostrophes, hyphens, and slashes. Rewrite each sentence, making the necessary corrections. Be prepared to explain your changes.

1. Its too bad you couldnt find out what time the train arrives.
2. This is childs play, and I dont like being drawn into it.
3. There are eighty six students in my biology lecture section.
4. He learned late in his teens that his mothers family had been extremely wealthy in the 20s and 30s.
5. If youre going to keep a pet, you must be responsible for all its needs.
6. Margaret and Annies apartment is nicer than ours.
7. No one would ever guess that Chuck is an ex Marine.
8. The girls dresses need ironing before they go to school this morning.
9. Advance standing examinations are graded pass fail.
10. I know shes a successful author, but buying a gold plated typewriter is a bit extravagant.
11. We bought all our antiques at my sister in laws shop.
12. Here we have the engineers offices; in the next block you will find the studio of the designer / architect.
13. Since this is Al and Marys car I hate to keep it too long because theyll be needing it to haul their sons luggage to college.
14. Proficiency in writing doesnt depend so much on talent as on the willingness to refine your first efforts.
15. The recipe called for 2 and three fourths cups of flour.

61 QUOTATION MARKS (" ")

1) Use double quotation marks for direct quotations and words used in a special or ironic sense. For indirect quotations, use no quotation marks at all.

Correct   "Keep your eye on the ball," my tennis coach yelled.

Correct   My tennis coach yelled at me to keep my eye on the ball.

Correct   My girlfriend is truly, in Wordsworth's words, "Fair as a star, when only one / Is shining in the sky." (Note the slash between lines.)

Correct   His little "beauty" turned out to be a vicious shrew.

2) Omit quotation marks for prose quotation of more than four lines and poetry quotations of more than three lines. Instead, separate the quotation from the text of your paper by triple-spacing after your last line, then typing the quotation double-spaced, with every line indented ten spaces. Present more than three lines of poetry exactly as they appear in the original.

Sample prose quotation:

I frequently tell my students that writing must be concrete if it is to be memorable. And to show them what I mean, I treat them to a passage like this one from Russell Baker's book *Growing Up*. Baker makes his readers feel and see the work housewives did in another generation.

> They scrubbed floors on hands and knees, thrashed rugs with carpet beaters, killed and plucked their own chickens, baked bread and pastries, grew and canned their own vegetables, patched the family's clothing on treadle-operated sewing machines, deloused the chicken coops, preserved fruits, picked potato bugs and tomato worms to protect their garden crop, darned stockings, made jelly and relishes, rose before dawn to start the stove for breakfast and packed lunch pails, polished the chimneys of kerosene lamps, and even found time to tend the geraniums, hollyhocks, nasturtiums, dahlias, and peonies that grew around every house. By the end of a summer day a Morrisonville woman had toiled like a serf (Baker, 43).

Sample poetry quotation:

What human characteristic can most effectively corrupt judgment? Alexander Pope believed it to be pride:

> Of all the Causes which conspire to blind
>
> Man's erring judgment, and misguide the mind,
>
> What the weak head with strongest bias rules,
>
> Is Pride, the never-failing vice of fools.

3) Use single quotation marks for a quotation within a quotation.

He paused for a moment and then said, "What is the basic rule of philosophy? D. E. Trueblood's answer is best: 'It is not intellectually honest to hold a position after it is known that the position leads inevitably to other positions which are recognized as false.'"

4) Use quotation marks for the titles of songs, short stories, and newspaper and magazine articles. However, do not use them for the names of newspapers, the titles of magazines, or the titles of books. Those names and titles should be italicized (underlined).

"The Love Song of J. Alfred Prufrock" is a famous poem by T. S. Eliot.

My favorite Elvis Presley song is "You Ain't Nothin' but a Hound Dog."

The assignment in *Fictions* is "That Evening Sun" by William Faulkner.

The editorial in today's *Morning Advocate,* "Why Kids Do Dope," should make us all more alert to children's problems and their ways of coping with stress.

5) Always place commas and periods inside quotation marks, even when the marks set off only a word or phrase and not the entire sentence. However, always place semicolons and colons outside.

> Correct: His reaction to failing was philosophical. "I gave it my best shot," he said, "but that just wasn't good enough—I have no regrets."
>
> Correct   To be creative, we must be "alive to the moment"; in other words, we must be ready to seize the hints of meaning and challenges to problem solving that present themselves.

6) Put the question mark, the exclamation point, and the dash within the quotation marks when they apply only to the quoted matter. Put them outside when they do not.

> Correct   The professor asked plaintively, "Doesn't anyone know the answer to the question?"
>
> Correct   Frances yelled, "Not yet!"
>
> Correct   Did Charles say "I hate Lola"?

6 m   BRACKETS ([ ])

Use brackets to set off editorial comments from the quotations in which they are inserted for clarification or comment.

> Elbert Hubbard's tongue-in-cheek definition of an editor is often quoted: "[An editor is] a person employed on a newspaper, whose business it is to separate the wheat from the chaff, and to see that the chaff is printed."

The brackets in the above sentence make clear that the words "An editor is" were not in the original material but were added by the author to fit the quotation into her sentence structure.

6 n ELLIPSIS MARKS (. . .)

Use ellipsis marks (three spaced periods) to indicate an omission from quoted material. When the omission occurs at the end of the sentence, use an additional period.

Example without Ellipsis	Example without Ellipsis
Contemporary feminism inaugurated its existence as a movement with an attack on the teachings and principles of Sigmund Freud. Those women	"Contemporary feminism inaugurated its existence as a movement with an attack on the teachings and principles of Sigmund Freud. Those women

who have come to represent the movement to the news media have insisted that if any one man promoted the oppression of women it was he. Freud—that slave driver of the unconscious—chased women from the consulting room to the nursery and kitchen, they say, and generations of analysts and psychiatrists who came after him kept them bound to pots and pans, diapers and baby carriages. The liberation of women, feminists claimed, depended on exposing the errors of these theories which have chained women to traditional stereotypes and prevented them from taking charge of their lives and their worlds (Gordon, New York Times Magazine, 30 Jul. 1978.)

who have come to represent the movement to the news media have insisted that if any one man promoted the oppression of women it was he. Freud . . . chased women from the consulting room to the nursery and kitchen, they say, and generations of analysts and psychiatrists who came after him kept them bound to pots and pans, diapers and baby carriages. The liberation of women, feminists claimed, depended on exposing the errors of these theories. . . ."

As this example demonstrates, ellipses can save space, an important consideration in articles and essays with a word limit. But it is important to preserve the grammatical structure of the original sentences. Careless omission of words can turn a meaningful sentence into gibberish.

EXERCISE

Each of the following sentences contains one or more violations of the rules for using quotation marks. Rewrite each sentence, making the necessary corrections. Be prepared to explain your changes.

1. My instructor assigned three stories from "Fictions" and two poems from "The Norton Anthology of Poetry".
2. Our afternoon paper is called "The State Times" and our morning paper, "The Morning Advocate".
3. If I could sing, I would learn *Memories* from the Broadway musical "Cats".
4. His 'success' story turned out to be a lesson from that old adage, "Pride goeth before a fall".

5. When we have family gatherings, we all ask my grandmother to sing "I'm Only a Bird in a Gilded Cage;" we'll miss that performance when she dies.
6. My philosophy teacher is fond of beginning class with "What is truth"?
7. Professor Monahan announced, "Tomorrow's exam will be no more rigorous than usual:" in other words, the highest mark in the class will be a D.
8. "Please come as soon as you can", he said. "I need your help."
9. Who was the person who said "I'll take a second helping of steak?"
10. Agnes told me "to stop making eyes at her boyfriend or I'd be sorry."
11. "Moby Dick" is a long novel, but it's well worth reading.
12. "Most of the things we do", Oliver Wendell Holmes, Jr., wrote, "we do for no better reason than that our fathers have done them or that our neighbors do them. . ."

7   MECHANICS

Let us now examine the mechanics of italics, capitalization, abbreviations, and numbers.

7 a ITALICS

1) Use italics for the title of any separately published work. (In typing, the equivalent of italics is underlining.)

The New York Times   Newsweek   Roots   The Scarsdale Diet

2) Use italics for the names of ships, aircraft, works of art, movies, phonograph albums, and television shows.

H.M.S. *Queen Mary*   *The Spirit of St. Louis*   *The Mona Lisa*
Gone with the Wind   Michael Jackson's album *Thriller*
Sixty Minutes

3) Use italics for letters, words, and numbers used as words.

If you want to speak Italian like a native, learn to roll your *r's*.
The word *can't* is not in his vocabulary.
When you write a *7*, make it look like a *7* and not a *1*.

4) Use italics for foreign expressions.

In logic a conclusion that does not follow from its premises is called a *non sequitur*.
She graduated *cum laude*.

5) Use italics to emphasize a word, phrase, or clause. (Effective writers exercise restraint in this use of italics, confining it to those occasions where special emphasis is needed.)

Did you say you earned *forty thousand dollars* last year?

7 b CAPITALIZATION

Modern usage demands that capitalization be used in the following situations.

1) Capitalize proper names.

Names and places and any specific titles if they precede the name:

Robert A. Jones, Sam, Nicky, Professor Schwartz (but Dr. Schwartz, a professor I know)

Judge Paul Wilmarth (but not Paul Wilmarth, a Judge from New Orleans)

the Lincoln Memorial

Buick Century

Houston

219 Second Street

Names of the deity:
God, Creator, Emmanuel, Allah

Specific races, religions, nationalities:
African-American, Jew, Italian, Protestant

Days of the week and months of the year (Note that the names of seasons are not capitalized.):
Monday, March, spring, winter

Specific events, documents, and courses or programs:
the War of 1812, the Gettysburg Address, Psychology 102

Institutions and organizations:
The Urban League, Siena College, Ford Motor Company

The first and last words of titles and subtitles and all other words except articles *(a, the)*, conjunctions *(and, but, or)*, and prepositions of fewer than five letters *(for, to, from, near):*
"Sweet Georgia Brown"

"Why Women Went to Work"

"Ode to a Nightingale"

Reader's Digest

Family Circle

Nouns indicating family relationships when they are used in conjunction with proper names or are used as names themselves:
my aunt, Aunt Ruth, my father, Father

Specific regions of the country (Note that the words *east, south, north,* and *west* are not capitalized when they refer to simple direction.):

the South

the Midwest

Drive north for ten miles before you turn.

Peoples and their languages:
English

Russian

Europeans

Alaskan

Alabamians

2) Capitalize the first word of every sentence, of intentional fragments, and of directly quoted speech.

Alice turned and said, "Don't bother to call me."

How did you manage to calm that big dog? Very carefully.

E X E R C I S E

Each of the following sentences contains one or more omissions or misuses of italics or capitalization. Rewrite each sentence, making the necessary corrections. Be prepared to explain your changes.

1. The word tantalize has an interesting etymology.
2. My Father's family provided me with three Aunts and four Uncles.
3. I plan to visit the united nations building when I visit New York city next month.
4. Sometimes I read Prevention for articles on nutrition; for example; this month's issue had an article entitled DIETING ALONE WON'T DO IT.
5. My uncle lives twenty miles West of Cooperstown, New York, the Home of the Baseball Hall of Fame.
6. My brother has always had trouble pronouncing the word *salmon*.
7. We lost all the money we took to the Race Track, but as the french say, "c'est la vie."
8. My Professor said that I should drop economics 437 until I was ready to buckle down.
9. For her birthday, I am going to buy my mother a copy of the book "Mind over back pain" written by a doctor by the name of John Sarno.
10. The drought has just about devastated agriculture in the midwest this Summer.
11. One of my students had her poem *Walking on Thin Ice* published in the Delta Review, our school's literary magazine.
12. When you get in town, turn Left on Duplantier boulevard and then Right on Third avenue.

13. The name hiroshima will always be a reminder of the horror of nuclear war.
14. My instructor says I committed the logical fallacy of post hoc ergo propter hoc in my last paper.
15. In comparative religion 103 we're now studying buddhism.

7 c ABBREVIATIONS

Although abbreviations are used frequently in technical and scientific writing, they are usually avoided in other types of formal writing. There are, however, several exceptions to this practice.

1) Use standard abbreviations for personal titles or designations before and after names.

> Before names: Mr., Ms., Mrs., St. (Saint), Dr., Messrs.
> After Names: Jr., St., M.D., Ph.D., M.A.

2) Use standard abbreviations for time designations when they accompany numbers.

> 10:00 A.M., 7:00 P.M., 40 mph, A.D . 199, 400 B.C. (Note the number follows A.D., but precedes B.C.)

3) Use standard abbreviations of widely known organizations and acronyms (initials pronounced as words).

(Note: The most widely known are often written without periods.)

> CIA, FBI, ZIP, ROTC, NATO

(Note: Consult a style sheet for abbreviations used in documenting research papers.)

7 d NUMBERS

Numbers are used frequently in scientific and technical writing. However they are used sparingly in all other formal writing.

1) Use numerals for numbers if they require more than two words to spell out. Simply write out all others. Hyphenated words count as one word.

> 944 students, 1057 miles, 1532 acres

2) In a sentence containing more than one number, either spell out all of the numbers or use numerals for all.

> Harry had 10 sheep, 150 chickens, and 3 horses on his little farm.

3) Spell out a number used at the beginning of a sentence.

> Ten years is too long to wait.

4) Use numerals in expressions of time, dates, addresses, exact amounts of money, measurements, and sections of books.

> 4:30 P.M., May 15, 709 Carriage Way, $9.56, 5 feet 8 inches, 8-ounce cup, Chapter 19, pages 5–26.

Exercise

Correct the misuse of abbreviations and numbers wherever they occur in the following sentences.

1. I want support three hundred sixty-five days a year.
2. Jeffrey will try to be present for the ceremony on July twenty-six.
3. What I ordered was twenty bottles of Perrier, 5 bags of chips, and ten assorted dips.
4. Please read Chapter twenty-one for your lesson tomorrow.
5. Margaret wrote about an event that occured 500 years before Christ.
6. Just address your card to Horace White, Senior.
7. If you want to know a st. number, just will have to wait until I can find my address book.
8. The Federal Bureau of Investigation is frequently investigated itself.
9. I never get up before 7 in the A.M.
10. Zachary was five feet 4 inches tall when I last saw him.

8   SEXIST LANGUAGE

Careful writers avoid sexist language. Such language, although often used unintentionally, has the effect of excluding women or stereotyping them in certain sex roles. Use the following suggestions to become more aware of this problem and to learn alternative ways of expressing your ideas.

8 a AVOID THE GENERIC USE OF THE WORD *MAN* AND COMPOUND WORDS CONTAINING *MAN*

For some compounds, the word *woman* can be an alternative suffix, as in *congresswoman* or *businesswoman,* but note other alternatives below.

Problems	*Alternatives*
mankind	all people, humanity, human beings
the best man for the job	the best person for the job
fireman	firefighter
policeman	police officer
congressman	congressional representative
businessman	business executive, manager
the common man	ordinary people

8 b AVOID THE GENERIC USE OF *HE* OR *HIS*.

1) Drop the possessive form *his* altogether or substitute an article.

Problem   The professional singer is concerned about his critics.

Alternative	The professional singer is concerned about the critics.
Problem	When a customer complains about his bill, pay attention.
Alternative	When a customer complains about the bill, pay attention.

2) Use plurals followed by *their* as an alternative.

Problem	A customer should check his bill for errors.
Alternative	Customers should check their bills for errors.

3) When the subject is the indefinite pronoun, use either the terms *he* or *she* and *his* or *her* (best used sparingly when the terms are not repeated in the text) or recast the sentence.

Problem	If everyone will do his part, then we can finish the job quickly.
Alternatives	If everyone will do his or her part, then we can finish the job quickly.
	If all the members will do their part, then we can finish the job quickly.

8 c AVOID SEX-ROLE STEREOTYPING

Identify men and women in the same way, treat men and women in similar ways, and use alternatives to words and phrases that trivialize women.

Problems	*Alternatives*
stewardess	flight attendant
poetess	poet
coed	student
lady doctor	doctor . . . she
male nurse	nurse . . . he
men and ladies	men and women
Faulkner and Eudora Welty	William Faulkner and Eudora Welty or Faulkner and Welty
Don't be an old maid about this.	Don't be fussy about this.

E X E R C I S E

Rewrite the following sentences to avoid sexist language.

1. Janice was elected chairman for the sorority fund raiser.
2. Every public school teacher should be actively involved in policy making that affects his career.

3. Each student will make progress when he is motivated and takes his education seriously.
4. Do you know any lady lawyers?
5. We were privileged to have Chief Justice Warren Burger and Mrs. O'Connor on campus last year.
6. The ladies on the committee made the food, and the men served drinks.
7. We will read stories by Hemingway, Joyce, and Katherine Mansfield this semester.
8. Putting this office back together will be a man-sized job.
9. Rhonda went back to visit the girls at the office.
10. Ever since man has been on this earth, he has craved companionship.

A Glossary of Usage

Accept, Except

Accept is a verb meaning "to take willingly." *Except* is a preposition meaning "but."

> *Correct*   John can't *accept* the invitation.
> *Correct*   Everyone was on time *except* Tim.

Affect, Effect

Affect is a verb meaning "to influence." *Effect* can be either a verb or a noun. As a verb it means "to cause"; as a noun, its more common use, it means "a result."

> *Correct*   Don't let her nagging *affect* your disposition.
> *Correct*   Researchers have been unable to *effect* a cure.
> *Correct*   The *effect* of his drinking has been tragic.

Allot, A Lot

Allot is a verb meaning "to distribute or apportion." *A lot,* which is always written as two words, means "much."

All Right, Alright

All right is the preferred form. *Alright* is generally avoided by educated people.

Allude, Elude

Allude is a verb meaning "to refer to indirectly." *Elude* is a verb meaning "to avoid."

> *Correct*   Did he *allude* to her recent accident?
> *Correct*   They were trying to *elude* their creditors.

Allusion, Illusion

See Illusion, Allusion

Already, All Ready

Already means "before that time." But *all ready* means "completely prepared" (in colloquial usage, "all set").

> *Correct*   He was *already* at the party when she arrived.
> *Correct*   She was *all ready* to leave for the play when the phone rang.

Altogether, All Together

Altogether means "entirely" or "completely." *All together* means "everyone at the same time" or "with one another" and is usually separated by other words.

    Correct   It was an ***altogether*** useless experience.

    Correct   They ***all*** banded ***together*** against the common foe.

Always, All Ways

Always means "all the time, forever." ***All ways*** means "every method" and is often separated by another word or words.

    Correct   Must you ***always*** criticize my mother?

    Correct   They tried ***all*** honest ***ways*** to obtain the tickets.

Am Not, Ain't

Ain't is never an acceptable substitute for ***am not*** or related forms (***are not, is not***)

    Correct   I ***am not*** going to the party.

    Correct   You ***are not*** going to the party.

    Correct   Pam ***is not*** going to the party.

Among, Between

See Between, Among

Amount, Number

See Number, Amount

Anyway, Any Way, Anyways

Anyway means "nevertheless" or "in any case." ***Any way*** means "any manner" or "any method" or "any direction." ***Anyways*** is a nonstandard form.

    Correct   I didn't want to be Prom Queen ***anyway.***

    Correct   *Any way* we travel to Syracuse will take us at least two hours.

Are, Our

Are is part of the verb "to be." ***Our*** is a possessive pronoun.

    Correct   My brothers' names ***are*** Bill and Ted.

    Correct   It's ***our*** turn to do the dishes.

As, Like

See Like, As

Ascent, Assent

Ascent is a noun meaning "a rise." ***Assent*** is a verb meaning "to agree."

    Correct   The ***ascent*** of the mountain was risky.

    Correct   I'll never ***assent*** to her plan to cheat.

Awful, Awfully, Very

See Very, Awfully, Awful

Beside, Besides

Beside means "next to." ***Besides*** means "anyway" or "moreover."

    Correct   Why does she always have to sit ***beside*** me?

Correct   I haven't any money to lend you; ***besides,*** you didn't pay me back the ten dollars you borrowed.

Between, Among

Between is used when two persons, places, or things are involved; ***among,*** when more than two are involved.

Correct   There has never been any hostility ***between*** Tim and me.

Correct   There has never been any hostility ***among*** Tim, Ed, and me.

Board, Bored

Board is a noun meaning "a wooden plank." ***Bored*** means "uninterested."

Correct   I'll use that ***board*** for my bookcase.

Correct   Going to class leaves him ***bored.***

Can, May

Can means "able to do something." ***May*** means "having permission to do something." (There is one exception to this difference — a question in which the negative form of the expression is used. Thus "Why can't I go to the movies tonight?" is preferable to "Why may I not go to the movies tonight?" because it is less awkward.)

Correct   I know I ***can*** do better than D work in that course.

Correct   ***May*** I have an extension of the deadline for the assignment?

Can Hardly, Can't Hardly

Hardly in such expressions is synonymous with ***barely.*** The sense intended is therefore "I ***am*** able to, but just barely so." ***Can hardly*** conveys that intention. But ***can't hardly*** does not — it suggests inability rather than ability. For this reason, ***can't hardly*** is never acceptable.

Correct   I ***can hardly*** wait for the tournament to begin.

Capital, Capitol

Capital has a number of meanings. Two of the most common are the town or city that is the seat of government in a country, state, or nation; and money. ***Capitol*** refers to the building in which government business is conducted. (When capitalized, it refers to the building where the U.S. Congress conducts its business.)

Censor, Censer, Censure

Censor is both a verb and a noun. As a verb it means "to examine that which may be objectionable and, if it is, to suppress it." As a noun it means "the official who examines and decides whether to suppress." ***Censer*** is a noun meaning "a vessel containing incense, usually used in worship." ***Censure*** is both a verb and a noun: as a verb it means "to disapprove, blame, or condemn"; as a noun, "the expression of disapproval, blame, or condemnation."

Correct   They've decided to ***censor*** the book.

Correct   The ***censors*** seem to have missed that scene in the film.

Correct   The altar boy carried the ***censer*** in the procession.

> *Correct*   He's more to be pitied than ***censured.***
> *Correct*   If ever there was a congressman deserving of ***censure,*** it's ours.

Cent, Sent, Scent

See Sent, Cent, Scent

Choose, Chose

Both words are parts of the same verb—***to choose.*** But ***choose*** is a present tense form and ***chose,*** the past tense form. (***Choose*** rhymes with ***news, chose*** with ***those.***)

> *Correct*   Help me ***choose*** between these two dresses.
> *Correct*   He's not sorry he ***chose*** to study instead of party.

Cite, Sight, Site

See Sight, Site, Cite

Conscience, Conscious

Conscience is a noun meaning "inner moral guide, sense of right and wrong in ethical matters." ***Conscious*** is an adjective meaning "mentally awake, aware."

> *Correct*   Let your ***conscience*** be your guide.
> *Correct*   He was the only one ***conscious*** after the accident.
> *Correct*   Public servants must be ***conscious*** of their obligation to constituents.

Consensus, Consensus of Opinion

Consensus means "the opinion of a group of people." Therefore, the expression ***consensus of opinion*** is redundant.

Could Have, Could've, Could Of

Could have is standard English. ***Could've*** is an acceptable contraction of ***could have*** that is commonly used in speaking, but seldom in writing. ***Could of*** is never correct and probably results from hearing the contraction spoken but not recognizing it as such. (Note: The same rule applies to ***would have*** and ***should have.***)

Couldn't Care Less, Could Care Less

Couldn't care less is an expression of total lack of concern. It means one cares so little that it would be impossible to care less. ***Could care less*** is not a logical substitute because it violates the sense of the expression. (If one could care less than he does, then he does care somewhat).

> *Correct*   I ***couldn't care less*** whether he has a date for the prom.

Different From, Different Than

Different from refers to a difference between two or more people, places, or things. ***Different than*** refers to a difference in the ***same*** person, place, or thing over a period of time.

> *Correct*   Your idea of an interesting course is ***different from*** mine.

> *Correct*   My idea of an interesting course is **different** now **than** it was in high school.

Diner, Dinner

Diner means "an informal restaurant" or "a person who dines." *Dinner* means "the main meal of the day." (*Diner* rhymes with *miner; dinner,* with *thinner*)

Disinterested, Uninterested

Despite their similarity, these words have very different meanings. *Disinterested* means "free of bias, impartial." *Uninterested* means "not interested, indifferent."

> *Correct*   What we need here is a **disinterested** opinion.
> *Correct*   She was **uninterested** in him as a suitor.

Each Other, One Another

Each other is used in references to two people: *one another,* in references to more than two people.

> *Correct*   John and Agnes can't stand the sight of **each other.**
> *Correct*   The students in my division seem to like **one another.**

Effect, Affect

See Affect, Effect

Elude, Allude

See Allude, Elude

Enthusiastic, Enthused

Enthusiastic means "eager" or "intensely interested." *Enthused* is a substitute form that is considered acceptable in informal writing but not in formal writing.

Etc., &

Etc. is an abbreviation of the Latin *et cetera,* which means "and others" or "and so forth." The symbol *&* is used in place of *and.* Although both are widely used in informal writing, many authorities still consider them (especially &) unacceptable in formal writing.

Except, Accept

See Accept, Except

Explicit, Implicit

Explicit is an adjective meaning "expressed directly." *Implicit* is an adjective meaning "expressed indirectly."

> *Correct*   The manager gave explicit instructions for this operation.
> *Correct*   The implicit message behind that smile is "go ahead."

Farther, Further

Farther refers to distance; *further,* to degree.

> *Correct*   I live ***farther*** from college than you do.
> *Correct*   Each week I get ***further*** into debt.

Faze, Phase

See Phase, Faze

Fewer, Less

Fewer is used when speaking of things usually considered as individual units; ***less,*** when speaking of things not usually considered as individual units.

> *Correct*   fewer people, fewer potatoes, fewer towns, fewer paper clips
> *Correct*   less mashed potatoes, less hostility, less sugar

Flaunt, Flout

Flaunt means "to show off." ***Flout*** means "to show disrespect for, to scorn."

> *Correct*   At every opportunity she ***flaunted*** her knowledge of French.
> *Correct*   Must you ***flout*** every rule of etiquette?

Forth, Fourth

Forth means "forward." ***Fourth*** is the numerical reference between third and fifth.

> *Correct*   They went ***forth*** like the victors they were.
> *Correct*   This aspirin is the ***fourth*** I've taken today.

Fun is a noun meaning "to have a good time" when it is used formally. It is used as an adjective only informally.

> *Correct*   Having fun is a necessary part of childhood. (Formal)
> *Correct*   For a fun time, come to my house tomorrow night. (Informal)

Gorilla, Guerrilla

A ***gorilla*** is a primate. A ***guerrilla*** is a soldier in an unconventional war.

> *Correct*   If it weren't for the hair all over his body, that ***gorilla*** could be mistaken for my roommate.
> *Correct*   A ***guerrilla*** is often more dedicated to his cause than a conventional soldier is.

Healthy, Healthful

Healthy means "in good health" or "conducive to health in an indirect or figurative sense." ***Healthful*** means "nutritious," or "health-producing in a direct, literal sense."

> *Correct*   He is an unusually ***healthy*** old man.
> *Correct*   This climate is not too ***healthy.***
> *Correct*   The food served in my dining hall may be ***healthful,*** but it is rather unappealing.

Hear, Here

Though these words sound alike, their meanings are quite different. ***Hear*** is a verb, and ***here*** is an adjective indicating place.

> *Correct*   Please play your stereo quietly, so I don't have to ***hear*** it.
> *Correct*   ***Here*** I am — let the party begin.

Himself, Hisself

Himself is the correct form. *Hisself* is unacceptable.
>*Correct*   He decided to do his taxes *himself.*

Hole, Whole

A *hole* is an opening. *Whole* means "complete."
>*Correct*   The draft is coming through that *hole.*
>*Correct*   I can't believe you ate the *whole* pizza.

Hopefully

Many educated people object to the use of this word in constructions that express some particular person's hoping. For example, they would object to the sentence "*Hopefully,* this lecture will be more interesting than the one last week." They would prefer "I hope this lecture . . ." or "Let us hope this lecture. . . ." Nevertheless, its use is widespread and there is at least one accepted precedent for such an adverbial construction—the use of *admittedly,* as in "Admittedly, the error was mine." Therefore, it may be considered an acceptable form in many situations, but one that should be avoided when writing for a fastidious audience.

I, Me

See Me, I

Ignorant, Stupid

Ignorant means "lacking knowledge or education." *Stupid* means "unintelligent."

Illusion, Allusion

Illusion means "a false idea or impression or that which creates such an impression." *Allusion* means "a casual reference to a person, place, or thing."
>*Correct*   She is obsessed with the *illusion* that I love her.
>*Correct*   His writing is filled with biblical *allusions.*

Immoral, Amoral

Immoral means "not conforming to a moral code one endorses in theory." *Amoral* means "not having a moral code."

Implicit, Explicit

See Explicit, Implicit

Imply, Infer

Imply means "to suggest indirectly, to hint at." *Infer* means "to judge or conclude."
>*Correct*   You seem to be *implying* that I got this job by dishonest means. I resent that *implication.*
>*Correct*   The essay *infers* that nuclear war is unavoidable. I reject that *inference.*

In, In To, Into

These words have different uses. *In,* as a preposition, is used mainly to indicate position, location, or condition. *In to* (two words) is used when *in* is an adverb. And *into* indicates direction or movement or, in a figurative sense, a change of condition.

Correct The key is not lost. It's *in* your hand.

Correct My uncle is in the county jail, but no one is allowed *in to* see him.

Correct The hero and heroine rode off *into* the sunset.

In Regard To, In Regards To

In regard to is the accepted form of this expression; *in regards to* is a nonstandard form.

Irregardless, Regardless

See Regardless, Irregardless

Its, It's

Its is a possessive pronoun. *It's* is the contraction of *it is.*

Correct A dog will give *its* affection more quickly than a cat will.

Correct Hurry, please—*it's* closing time.

Kind Of, Sort Of

In informal writing, as in conversation, both *kind of* and *sort of* are commonly used instead of *somewhat* or *rather.* But in formal writing the latter expressions are preferred.

Lay, Lie

These words are both verbs. They are confused because one of the principal parts of each is the same. Remembering those principal parts is the key to overcoming confusion.

Lay means "to place or put." Its principal parts are lay/laid/laid.

Present tense—lay	I *lay* [am *laying*] my pencil on the desk.
Past tense—laid	Yesterday I *laid* my pencil on the desk.
Present perfect—have laid	I *have laid* my pencil on the desk.

Lie means "to rest or recline." Its principal parts are lie/lay/lain.

Present tense—lie	I *lie* down for a nap each day at noon.
Past tense—lay	I *lay* down yesterday at noon.
Present perfect—have lain	I *have lain* down regularly because the doctor ordered me to.

Lead, Led

Lead has two uses—as a present tense form of the verb *to lead* (rhymes with *seed*); as a noun meaning a type of metal (rhymes with *dead*). However, *led* (which also rhymes with *dead*) is the past tense of the verb *to lead.*

Correct Agnes is the best one to *lead* the group.

Correct The *lead* in your pencil is really graphite.

Correct Bill *led* his team to the championship.

Leave, Let

Leave means "to depart or to cause to remain." *Let* means "to permit."

    Correct   Please don't *leave* me — we've been through too much together.

    Correct   You can't *leave* all that junk in my closet.

    Correct   He'll join us if his mother will *let* him.

Less, Fewer

See Fewer, Less

Lightning, Lightening

Lightning accompanies thunder. *Lightening* means "making lighter."

    Correct   A flash of *lightning* lit up the sky.

    Correct   He removed the bundle, *lightening* the camel's load.

Like, As

Contemporary usage, particularly in the field of advertising, has blurred the traditional distinction between these words in some constructions. Nevertheless, most educated people avoid substituting *like* for *as* when the meaning intended is "in the same manner or way that." For example, "Wowies taste good *like* dog yummies should" would be unacceptable in formal writing.

Loose, Lose

Loose means "unattached" or "free from restraint." *Lose* means "to misplace or be deprived of." (*Loose* rhymes with *moose, lose* with *blues.*)

    Correct   His tie was *loose,* his jacket unbuttoned.

    Correct   Whatever you do, don't *lose* the tickets to the game.

Many, Much

Many means "a large number of individual units." *Much* means "a large quantity of something not usually considered in individual units."

    Correct   many horses, many nations, many postage stamps, many grapes

    Correct   much sand, much affection, much stupidity, much corn, much coffee

May, Can

See Can, May

Maybe, May Be

These expressions have essentially the same meaning. However, *maybe* is an adverb and *may be* is a verb form (the verb *to be* plus its auxiliary *may*). Which you use depends on the part of speech your sentence calls for.

    Correct   **Maybe** I'll order a pizza.

    Correct   I *may be* fat but she's fatter.

Me, I

Me and *I* are both personal pronouns. But *me* is in the objective case; and *I*, in the nominative. The most common error with these words is using *I* instead of *me* as the object of a preposition.

Correct   Bill went to the movies with Tom and **me.** (The word used here is the object of the preposition **with,** so **me** is correct.)

Correct   Bill, Tom, and **I** went to the movies. (The word used here is a subject of the sentence, not an object, so **I** is correct.)

Moral, Morale

Moral, as an adjective, refers to right conduct, knowing the difference between right and wrong. As a noun, it refers to a lesson. **Morale** refers to a person's mental state, his degree of confidence, cheerfulness, enthusiasm.

Correct   Agnes is a very **moral** person.

Correct   The **moral** of the story is don't hitchhike.

Correct   The players' **morale** was high.

Most, Almost

Most means "the highest degree." **Almost** means "nearly."

Correct   This is the **most** unusual course I've ever taken.

Correct   It is **almost** time to leave.

Much, Many

See Many, Much

Nauseated, Nauseous

Although the use of **nauseous** has become widespread, particularly in speaking and informal writing, the word continues to be considered nonstandard. Careful writers use **nauseated** instead.

Number, Amount

Use **number** when referring to persons, places, or things usually considered as individual units. Use **amount** when referring to things not usually considered as individual units.

Correct   a number of dogs, a number of seashells, a large number of cars, a small number of oilwells

Correct   an amount of oil, a large amount of corn, a small amount of paint

Numbers

In formal writing, all numbers that can be expressed in one or two words are written out. All others are expressed in figures. However, when several numbers are being mentioned in close proximity, at least one of which is expressed in figures, for the sake of consistency they all may be expressed in figures.

Correct   one hundred women, three billion dollars, thirty-eight elephants

Correct   73,300 paid attendance, $250,000, $14.75

OK, O.K., Okay

All three forms are acceptable in informal writing, but not in formal writing. (In formal writing choose a more exact word.)

One Another, Each Other

See Each Other, One Another

Passed, Past

Passed is a past tense form of the verb *to pass. Past* as an adjective means "gone by, ended"; as a noun, "that time which no longer is present."

    Correct I *passed* all my midterm examinations.

    Correct The *past* month has been my busiest this year.

    Correct It's foolish to try to live in the *past.*

Patience, Patients

Patience means "forbearance." *Patients* are a doctor's clients.

    Correct **Patience,** she reminded him, is a virtue.

    Correct With all his *patients,* no wonder he drives a Mercedes.

Percent, Percentage, Part

Percent is used in references to "rate per hundred" when numbers are also used. *Percentage* is used in such references when numbers are *not* used. *Part* is used in references to divisions of things that do not concern rate per hundred.

    Correct I spend more than thirty *percent* of my salary on food.

    Correct A large *percentage* of the national budget is allocated to defense spending.

    Correct He gave *part* of his wardrobe to his roommate.

Personal, Personnel

Personal (pronounced *per´-son-al*) is an adjective meaning "private." *Personnel* (pronounced *per-son-nel´*) is a noun meaning "employees."

    Correct This is a *personal* matter that doesn't concern anyone but Jan and me.

    Correct All college *personnel* are expected to attend the meeting.

Petition, Partition

A *petition* is a formal request or the document that expresses such a request. A *partition* is something that divides two or more things; for example, a wall.

    Correct They are circulating a *petition* to fire Dean Borden.

    Correct I wish I could build a *partition* in my room so I wouldn't have to see my roommate.

Phase, Faze

Phase is usually used as a noun meaning "one of a series of forms or stages." *Faze* is a verb meaning "to disturb."

    Correct I'm afraid I'm in the most boring *phase* of adolescence.

    Correct His threats didn't *faze* me a bit.

Principal, Principle

Principal as a noun means "the chief administrative officer of a school"; as an adjective, "main or primary." *Principle* is a noun meaning a "rule."

Correct   The ***principal*** called Arthur into her office.

Correct   The ***principal*** reason he left college was the poor quality of his work.

Correct   The law of supply and demand is one of the most important ***principles*** of economics.

Propose, Purpose

Propose is a verb meaning "to offer or suggest." ***Purpose*** is a noun meaning "reason or intention."

Correct   I ***propose*** we use the money for a concert.

Correct   A student's chief ***purpose*** in college should be to develop his mind.

Provided, Providing

Provided means "cared for" or "with the provision that." Providing means "furnishing."

Correct   She ***provided*** well for her family.

Correct   You may have the night off ***provided*** you get someone to work in your place.

Correct   He was responsible for ***providing*** refreshments.

Quite, Quiet

Quite is a one-syllable word that rhymes with ***bite***. ***Quiet*** is a two-syllable word that rhymes with ***diet***. ***Quite*** means "rather"; ***quiet*** means "silent."

Correct   His parents are ***quite*** concerned about his partying.

Correct   Sam has difficulty being ***quiet*** when someone else is talking.

Rain, Reign, Rein

Rain, like snow, is a form of precipitation. ***Reign*** is a verb meaning "to rule." A ***rein*** is a strap for controlling a horse, and is usually used in the plural.

Correct   We haven't had as much ***rain*** as usual this year.

Correct   Long may the queen ***reign.***

Correct   He held the ***reins*** loosely in his hand.

Raise, Raze

Raise is a verb meaning "to build up" (or "to lift up"). ***Raze*** is a verb with the exactly opposite meaning—"to tear down."

Correct   Let's ***raise*** our glasses in honor of Sharon.

Correct   The building where I was born was ***razed.***

Reasoning, Rationalizing

Reasoning means "the process of thought that leads to judgment." ***Rationalizing*** can have the same meaning, but since it also has the meaning of "defective reasoning, reasoning that aims at self-satisfaction rather than truth," it can confuse the reader as to your intended meaning. Careful writers, therefore, never use these words interchangeably.

Reason Is That, Reason Is Because

The accepted expression is ***reason is that.*** Since both the word "reason" and the word "because" refer to cause, the expression ***reason is because*** is redundant.

    Correct The ***reason*** I am in college ***is that*** I want to learn.

Regardless, Irregardless

The prefix ***ir-*** and the suffix ***less*** both mean "without." Therefore, ***regardless*** means "without regard" and ***irregardless,*** "without without regard." Because of its redundancy, ***irregardless*** is not accepted in modern usage.

Respectfully, Respectively

Respectfully means "with respect." ***Respectively*** means "pertaining to what has preceded, and in the same order."

    Correct Bill treats everyone ***respectfully.***

    Correct Bill, Bob, and Alice go to Georgia Tech, Indiana University, and Colgate, ***respectively.***

Right, Rite, Write

Right means "correct." A ***rite*** is a religious ceremony. ***Write*** is a verb meaning "to form letters."

    Correct He gave the teacher the ***right*** answer.

    Correct That ceremony is part of the pagan fertility ***rite.***

    Correct ***Write*** more legibly next time.

Rise, Raise

Rise means "to get up or go up." ***Raise*** means "to cause to rise, to lift."

    Correct I ***rise*** early in the summer.

    Correct My spirits ***rise*** when summer approaches.

    Correct He tried his best to ***raise*** the sunken treasure ship.

Road, Rode

A ***road*** is a surface on the ground. ***Rode*** is the past tense of the verb "to ride."

    Correct The ***road*** is long and lonely.

    Correct He ***rode*** a wild horse on his uncle's ranch.

Sent, Cent, Scent

Sent is a form of the verb ***to send. Cent*** means "penny." And ***scent*** means "odor."

Should Have, Should've, Should Of

See Could Have, Could've, Could Of

Sight, Site, Cite

Sight refers to vision, viewing, or that which is viewed. ***Site*** means "a location, often a building location." And ***cite*** means "to make reference to" or "to credit."

    Correct The mountains near my home are a majestic ***sight.***

    Correct He has a serious ***sight*** problem.

    Correct We've finally picked out a ***site*** for our new home.

    Correct The professor said to ***cite*** all our sources for the term paper.

Since, Sense, Sence

Since means "from a former time until now." *Sense* as a verb means "to perceive or feel intuitively"; as a noun, "the relative quality of one's judgment" or "one of the means of sensory perception." *Sence* is an incorrect form sometimes substituted for *since* or *sense.*

> *Correct* I haven't had a good night's sleep *since* I left home.
> *Correct* He seemed to *sense* what was about to happen.
> *Correct* I hope you'll have the good *sense* to drive safely.
> *Correct* His *sense* of smell was blocked by a powerful perfume.

Sit, Set

Both words are verbs. But *sit* means "to rest or recline" and *set* means "to place or put."

> *Present tense — sit* — Please *sit* down.
> *Past tense — sat* — Everyone but Tom *sat* quietly.
> *Present perfect — have sat* — I *have sat* in this seat every day this term.
>
> *Present tense — set* — **Set** the books on the table.
> *Past tense — set* — Yesterday you *set* them on the bookcase.
> *Present perfect — have set* — After you *have set* them down, you may go to lunch.

So, Sow, Sew

So has a variety of meanings. The most common ones are "in the way indicated," "in order," "in that degree," "very." *Sow* means "to scatter seed on the ground." And *sew* means "to stitch material."

> *Correct* I arrived early *so* I could avoid the crowd.
> *Correct* A man will reap only what he *sows.*
> *Correct* I hope you'll be able to *sew* this shirt before tonight.

So Do I, So Don't I

In some parts of the country, the expression *so don't I* is used in place of *so do I.* But *so don't I* makes no sense—it says the exact opposite of what is meant. Avoid this and related errors (for example, *so can't I, so won't I, so wouldn't I, so couldn't I*).

Stationary, Stationery

Stationary is an adjective meaning "fixed, not moving." *Stationery* is a noun meaning "writing materials" (Paper and envelopes).

Straight, Strait

Straight is the opposite of crooked. A *strait* is a water passageway.

> *Correct* He's headed *straight* for success.
> *Correct* Steer the boat gently through that *strait.*

Stupid, Ignorant

See Ignorant, Stupid

Than, Then

See Then, Than

Them, Those

Never use **them** as an adjective—that is, to modify a noun. Only **those** can be used that way.

Correct   He served **them** with an eviction notice.
Correct   **Those** shirts are the ones on sale.

Themselves, Themself, Theirselves

Only the first form—**themselves**—is standard English. The others are never acceptable.

Then, Than

Then indicates time. **Than** introduces the second part of a comparison.

Correct   First we visited my aunt; **then** we went shopping.
Correct   There is no more dedicated athlete **than** my brother.

There, Their, They're

These words are pronounced the same. But **there** is an adverb indicating place, **their** is a pronoun showing possession, and **they're** is a contraction of **they are.**

Correct   **There** she is—Miss Commercialism.
Correct   The students placed **their** library books in the book depository.
Correct   Al and Chris called to say **they're** going to be late.

Through, Thru, Threw

Through means "between" or "in one side and out the other." **Thru** is an abbreviated form of **through** that is unacceptable in formal (and most informal) writing. **Threw** is a past tense form of a verb meaning "projected or propelled."

Correct   The stake was driven **through** the werewolf's heart.
Correct   Our pitcher **threw** just nine pitches that inning.

Thus, Thusly

Thus means "accordingly." **Thusly** is an unacceptable substitute for **thus.**

To, Too, Two

To has many meanings, most of which you are familiar with. But it cannot be used as a substitute for **too,** which means "more than enough" or "also." Nor should either word be confused with **two,** which is the number between one and three.

Correct   Give the pencil **to** me.
Correct   When are you going **to** wash your clothes?
Correct   Henry says he is **too** tired to go to class.
Correct   Are you going **too?**

Tortuous, Torturous

Tortuous means "twisting, turning, winding, crooked." **Torturous** means "very painful."

Correct   The river winds its **tortuous** way to the sea.
Correct   English class is a **torturous** experience for some people.

Try to, Try and

Try to means "make an attempt." Never use *try and* as a substitute for *try to* because it wrongly suggests that *two* actions are taking place. (In "try and learn grammar," the suggestion is that there is trying *and* there is learning, when that is not the sense of the sentence.)

Correct   If you *try to* learn grammar, you will learn it.

Uninterested, Disinterested

See Disinterested, Uninterested

Unique

Unique means "without parallel, one of a kind." Therefore, the words *more, most,* and *very* shouldn't be used with it. (To say something is "more unique" than something else is a contradiction—if it is unique, then no comparison can properly be made. To say something is "very unique" is redundant.)

Use, Usage

Use may be either a verb or a noun. As a verb it rhymes with *news* and means "to employ or put into service." As a noun it rhymes with *loose* and means "the employment or application of something." *Usage* is a more specialized noun whose most common use concerns language.

Correct   Be sure to *use* the correct tool for the job.

Correct   Contemporary English *usage* frowns on slang in formal writing.

Used To, Use To

The correct expression is *used to,* never *use to.* The error of using *use to* undoubtedly arises from the fact that the *d* and *t* sounds blend together when the expression is spoken.

Correct   I *used to* be a careless driver, but I've reformed.

Very, Awfully, Awful

Very means "in high degree, extremely." *Awfully* means "extremely badly, terribly." Thus, *awfully* is really not a synonym for *very.* Still, it is an acceptable substitute in *informal* writing (and speaking). *Awful* is an adjective and should never be substituted for either *very* or *awfully.*

Always correct   Tim is a *very good* tennis player.
Always correct   Joe is an *awful* tennis player.
Correct informally Tim is an *awfully good* tennis player.
Never correct   Tim is an *awful good* tennis player.

Waist, Waste

The *waist* is the middle of the body. *Waste* is misused or discarded material.

Correct   My *waist* is a bit larger than it used to be.

Correct   I've decided that dieting is a *waste* of time.

Weak, Week

Weak means not strong. A *week* is seven days long.

Correct   I'd rather be mentally strong and physically **weak** than the reverse.

Correct   Only one more **week** until semester break!

Were, Where

Were is a form of the verb **to be; where,** an adverb denoting place.

Correct   We **were** the last ones to leave the library.

Correct   I want to go **where** you go, do what you do.

Which, That

Which refers to places and things, never to people. **That,** however, though it usually refers to places and things, can also refer to people.

Correct   The farm **which** my family used to own is just around the bend.

Correct   The dog **that** I'll always remember was a Saint Bernard named Agatha.

Correct   The man **that** steals my purse won't get much for his efforts.

Who, Whom

Who and **whom** are pronouns referring to people. When the word used will be the subject of a verb, use **who.** When the verb already has a subject, use **whom.**

Correct   The man **who** runs the restaurant is sitting in the next booth. (**Who** is the subject of **runs. Man** is the subject of **is sitting.**)

Correct   The man **whom** I introduced Sally to last night just came in the door. (The verbs in this sentence—**introduced** and **came in**—already have subjects, so **whom** is the correct form to use.)

Whoever, Whomever

The distinction between these two words is the same as that between **who** and **whom.**

Correct   I'll sell my car to **whoever** gives me a reasonable offer. (**Whoever** is the subject of **gives.**)

Correct   It is my right to sell it to **whomever** I wish. (**Is** and **wish** already have subjects.)

Whole, Hole

See Hole, Whole

Whose, Who's

In modern usage, **whose** is the possessive form of both **who** and **which. Who's,** though it is pronounced the same, is an entirely different word. It is the contraction of **who is.**

Correct   The man **whose** wife just left is a well-known actor.

Correct   The car **whose** engine caught on fire belonged to Ed.

Correct   Can you tell me **who's** in charge here?

Word Endings

Learning to *hear* your writing as you proofread it will help you to avoid omitting word endings.

Ending omitted	I have **listen** to him long enough.
Corrected	I have **listened** to him long enough.
Ending omitted	He was very jealous of what **belong** to him.
Corrected	He was very jealous of what **belonged** to him.
Ending omitted	I can't believe this is **happen** to me.
Corrected	I can't believe this is **happening** to me.

Would Have, Would've, Would Of

See Could Have, Could've, Could Of

Write, Right, Rite

See Right, Rite, Write

You, One, A Person, We

Traditionally, *you* has been frowned upon in most formal writing. *One* has been preferred. For example, unless the sentence "You should never waste your breath arguing with a bigot" were addressed to a specific person, it would have been considered appropriate only in speech or informal writing. It would have been written, "One should never waste his breath arguing with a bigot." Today many writers consider *one* too stilted for most writing situations. They prefer *a person* (or a more specific term, such as *a man* or *a woman*). *You* is also considered acceptable as long as it is not obtrusive or too personal in the particular context. In many writing situations, *we* offers a desirable balance between formality and casualness. There is no clear-cut rule, however, in this matter. To decide what is appropriate in a given situation, you should consider the occasion, the audience, and your purpose in writing.

Your, You're

Your is a possessive pronoun. *You're* is a contraction of *you are.*

Correct	**Your** coat is in the hall closet.
Correct	**You're** the only one I really care for.

Notes and Copyright Acknowledgments

Chapter 1 p3 Brenda Ueland, *If You Want to Write*, 2nd. ed. (St. Paul: Gray Wolf Press, 1987) 9. **p7** Brenda Ueland, *If You Want to Write*. **p14** Eudora Welty, *One Writer's Beginnings* (New York: Warner Books, 1984). **Chapter 2 p41** Ansen Dibell, "In Praise of 9 to 5," *WordPerfect Magazine*, May 1989. Reprinted by permission of WordPerfect Magazine. **Chapter 3 p56** Randy Fitzgerald, "America's Amazing Treasure Chest," *Reader's Digest*, June 1989. Copyright © 1989 by The Reader's Digest Assn., Inc. Reprinted by permission of *Reader's Digest*. **p60** Ardis Whitman, "Strangers Can Enrich Your Life," *Reader's Digest*, June 1989. Copyright © by The Reader's Digest Assn., Inc. Reprinted by permission of McIntose and Otis, Inc. **p64** Letitia Baldrige, "A Letter is Better," *Woman's Day Magazine*, May 1984. Reprinted by permission of the author. **p69** Michael Himowitz, "Kids' Program a Delight to Use," *Baltimore Evening Sun*. Copyright © 1989 by Michael Himowitz. Reprinted by permission of Los Angeles Times-Washington Post News Service. **p71** Fred Bayles, "Cities Find Pit Bull Laws Hard to Enact, Enforce." Reprinted by permission of the Associated Press. **Chapter 4 p105** Gary T. Marx, "New Phone Service Threatens Privacy," *Los Angeles Times*. Reprinted by permission of Gary T. Marx. **p107** Bernard R. Goldberg, "Television Insults Men, Too," *New York Times*, March 14, 1989 (op-ed). Reprinted by permission of the *New York Times*. **p109** Caryl Rivers, "The Luck Illusion," *Woman's Day Magazine*, June 1988. Reprinted by permission of the author. **p112** Allen L. Sack, "Looking Behind the Proposition 48 Image," *New York Times*, November 9, 1986. Reprinted by permission of the New York Times. **p115** Gary Roberts, "Can Big Times Athletes and Education Co-exist?" *New York Times*, October 4, 1986. Reprinted by permission of the *New York Times*. **p118** Letter courtesy of Amnesty International, "We Are God in Here." **Chapter 5 p143** Anna Quindlen, and the *New York Times*. "The Making of a Father." Reprinted with permission of the author. **p146** E.B. White, "Once More to the Lake," from *Essays of E.B. White*. Copyright 1941 by E.B. White. Reprinted by permission of Harper & Row, Publishers, Inc. **p152** Beverly Lowry, "Blackballed," Copyright © 1988 by Beverly Lowry. Reprinted by permission of the author. **p158** Ellen Goodman, "When Only the Phantom's Left," *Boston Globe* Newspaper. Copyright © 1989 by The Boston Globe Newspaper Company/Washington Post Writer's Group. Reprinted by permission of The *Boston Globe* Newspaper. **p161** Renee Hawkley, "Graduation Day," *Mountain Home News*, May 21, 1988. Reprinted by permission of the author. **p163** Linda Rivers, excerpt from *Through Her Eyes: A True Story of Love, Miracles and Realities*. Copyright © 1989 by Linda Rivers. Reprinted by permission of the author. **Chapter 9 p239** Mortimer J. Adler, "How to Make a Book," *Saturday Review*, July 6, 1940; 11. **p257** Letty Cottin Pogrebin, "Feeling Out 50," *Ms.* Magazine, June 1989. Copyright © 1989 by Letty Cottin Pogrebin. Reprinted by permission of *Ms.* Magazine. **p259** Suzanne Britt, "That Lean and Hungry Look," *Newsweek*, October 9, 1978. Reprinted by permission of the author. **p261** Jane Bryant Quinn, "Phone Fraud's Top Ten Can Rob Unwary," *Sunday Advocate*, April 16, 1989. Reprinted by permission of the Washington Post Writer's Group. **Chapter 10 p280** *U.S. News*, "Should Women Fight in War?" *U.S. News* (Pro and Con), February 13, 1978. Copyright © February 13, 1978 by U.S. News and World Report. Reprinted by permission of U.S. News. **Chapter 11 p286** Bob Beecroft, "The Winning of the West," *New York Sunday News Magazine*, August 28, 1977: 4. **p287** S.I. Hayakawa, *Language in Thought and Action*, 4th ed. (New York: Harcourt, 1978). **p288** John Rosemond, "Undisciplined Kids Much Like Gamblers," The *Charlotte Observer*. Reprinted by permission of the author. **p290** Molly Ivins, "Grin and Sell It," *Ms.* Magazine, June 1989. Reprinted by permission of *Ms.* Magazine. **p294** "The ABCs of School Violence," *Time*, January 23, 1978: 73–74. Copyright 1978 Time Inc. Reprinted by permission. **p297** Edmund S. Morgan, *The Puritan Family* (New York: Harper, 1966) 42, 100–1. **p298** Susan McHenry and Linda Lee Small, "Does Part-Time Pay Off?" *Ms.* March 1989: 88–89. **Chapter 12 p319** George Orwell, "Politics and the English Language" from *Shooting an Elephant and Other Essays*. Copyright © 1946 by Sonia Brownell Orwell. Renewed 1974 by Sonia Orwell. Reprinted by permission of Harcourt Brace Jovanovich, Inc. **p332** Martin Luther King, "Letter from a Birmingham Jail" from *Why We Can't Wait*. Copyright © 1963, 1964 by Martin Luther King. Reprinted by permission of Harper & Row, Publishers, Inc. **Chapter 13 p354** Iron Eyes Cody, "But You Promised," *Guideposts*, July 1988. Reprinted by permission of Guideposts Associates, Inc. **p355** Rawlings Sporting Goods, Company. Baseball ad copy. Reprinted with permission. **Chapter 15 p387** Anne Hollander, excerpts from "When Fat Was in Fashion," *New York Times*, 1977. Copyright 1977 by The New York Times Company. Reprinted by permission. **p388** James Stewart Gordon, excerpted from "The Mystery of the Missing Bones," *Reader's Digest* September 1976. Copyright 1976 by The Reader's Digest Assn., Inc. **p388** Michael Halbertsam, "Hey, You Ought to Sue the Doctor," *American Educator* Summer 1977: 7–8. **Chapter 16 p392** Anthony Lewis, *Gideon's Trumpet* (New York: Vintage Books, 1964) 214–5. **p392** Carl T. Rowan and David Mazio, Excerpted from "Our Immigration Nightmare," *Reader's Digest*, January 1983: 89–90. Copyright © 1982 by The Reader's Digest Assn. Inc. Reprinted by permission. **p393** Lance Morrow, "A World of Exaggeration," *Time* December 14, 1981. Copyright 1981 Time Inc. Reprinted by permission. **p393** George F. Kennan, *Democracy and the Student Left* (Boston: Little, Brown, 1988). **p395** John Knox Jessup, introd. to Russell W. Davenport, *Dignity of Man* (New York: Harper, 1955) 1–2. **p396** Grant H. Hendrick, "When Television is a School for Criminals," *TV Guide Magazine*, January 29, 1977. Reprinted with permission from *TV Guide Magazine*. Copyright 1977 by News America Publications Inc. **p398** Vincent Ryan Ruggiero, Adapted from a passage in *Beyond Feelings* (Port Washington: Alfred, 1975) 9–10. **p398** Elisabeth Kubler-Ross, adapted from a passage in *Death: The Final Stage of Growth*, Copyright 1975 by Elisabeth Kubler-Ross. Reprinted with permission. **p401** Theodore C. Sorensen, *Kennedy* (New York: Harper, 1985) 13. **p401** Thomas Ellis Katen, Excerpt from *Doing Philosophy*. Reprinted with permission. **p402** T.S. Eliot, *On Poetry and Poets* (New York: Farrar, 1957) 24. **p402** Jacques Barzun, *The Teacher in America* (New York: Little, Brown, 1945) 49. **p402** George Orwell, "Politics and the English Language." **p404** George Bernard Shaw, in *Shaw on Religion*, ed. Warren Sylvester Smith (New York: Dodd, 1967) 162. **p404** Joseph Wood Krutch, *The Twelve Seasons* (New York: Sloane, 1949) 109. **p404** Robert Penn Warren, *Who Speaks for the Negro?* (New York: Random, 1965) 432. **p404** Lewis Mumford, *The Myth of the Machine: The Pentagon of Power* (New York: Harcourt, 1970) 215. **p406** Sir James Jeans, *The Mysterious Universe* (London: Cambridge UP, 1948) 2–3. **p407** Hilton Kramer, "Michelangelo and Connoisseurship," *New York Times*, May 6, 1979: sec. 2, 1+. Copyright Time Inc. Reprinted with permission. **p407** George Orwell, Excerpts from "Homage to Catalina." Copyright 1952 and renewed 1980 by Sonia Brownell Orwell. Reprinted by permission of Harcourt Brace Jovanovich, Inc. **Chapter 17 p409** Gilbert Highet, Excerpt from "Man's Unconquerable Mind," *Reader's Digest*, August 1954. Reprinted with permission. **p417** John F. Kennedy, Inaugural Address, rptd. in Theodore C. Sorensen, *Kennedy* (New York: Harper, 1965) 245. **p418** Norman Cousins, "What Matters about Schweitzer," *Saturday Review*, September 25, 1965: 30–31. **p424** Martin Luther King, "I Have a Dream." Copyright © 1963 by Martin Luther King. Reprinted by permission of Joan Daves. **Chapter 18 p437** Quoted in Leon A. Harris, *The Fine Art of Political Wit* (New York: Dutton, 1964) 167. **p443** Douglas MacArthur, *Reminiscences* (New York: McGraw Hill, 1964) 426. **p443** Rex Reed, "Five Chums and a Doobie-Doobie," *New York Daily News*, March 19, 1978: 11c. **p446** Eldridge Cleaver, *Soul on Ice* (New York: McGraw Hill, 1966) 20. **p446** Jack London, "The Story of an Eyewitness: An Account of the San Francisco Earthquake," *Collier's Weekly* 1906. **p447** S. I. Hayakawa, "Red-Eye and the Woman Problem: A Semantic Parable," from *Language in Thought and Action*, 4th ed. Copyright © 1978 by Harcourt Brace Jovanovich, Inc. Reprinted with permission. **p453** Felicia Halpert, "You Call This Adorable," *Ms.* Magazine, October 1988. Reprinted with permission of *Ms.* Magazine. **Chapter 20 p453** Ray Blount, Jr., "Rita Mae Brown's Battle Hymn of the Ridiculous." Reprinted with permission. **p528** Shirley Jackson, "The Lottery," from *The Lottery*. Copyright © 1948, 1949 by Shirley Jackson. Copyright © 1976, 1977 by Lawrence Hyman, Barry Hyman, Mrs. Sarah Webster and Mrs. Joanne Schnurer. Reprinted by permission of Farrar, Straus and Giroux, Inc. **p547** William Faulkner, "A Rose for Emily" from *Collected Stories of William Faulkner*. Copyright © 1930, 1958 by William Faulkner. Reprinted by permission of Random House, Inc. **p561** Elizabeth Bowen, "My Demon Lover." Copyright © 1946, 1974 by Elizabeth Bowen. Reprinted from *The Collected Stories of Elizabeth Bowen*, by permission of Alfred A. Knopf. **p576** Kristine Batey, "Lot's Wife." Copyright © 1978 by JAM TO-DAY. Reprinted by permission of JAM TO-DAY. **p582** John Collier, "The Chaser." Copyright 1940, Renewed 1967 by John Collier. Reprinted with permission of the Harold Matsen Company, Inc. **p585** Margaret Atwood, "Siren's Song." Reprinted from *The Circle Game* by permission of Stoddart Publishing Co. Limited, 34 Lesmill Rd., Don Mills, Ontario, Canada.

Handbook

p649 T. S. Eliot, "Religion and Literature," *Essays Ancient and Modern* (New York: Harcourt, 1936) 83. **p664** Russell Baker, *Growing Up* (New York: Congdon & Weed, distr. by St. Martin's Press, 1982) 43. **p665** Suzanne Gordon, "Helene Deutsch and the Legacy of Freud," *New York Times Magazine*, July 30, 1978: 23.

Index